PACIFIC MEXICO HANDBOOK

ACAPULCO • PUERTO VALLARTA
OAXACA • GUADALAJARA • MAZATLÁN

SECOND EDITION

BRUCE WHIPPERMAN

MOON
PUBLICATIONS INC.

PACIFIC MEXICO HANDBOOK
SECOND EDITION

Published by
Moon Publications, Inc.
P.O. Box 3040
Chico, California 95927-3040, USA

Printed by
Colorcraft Ltd., Hong Kong

ISBN: 1-56691-032-3
ISSN: 1082-488x

Editor: Pauli Galin
Copy Editors: Nicole Revere and Deana Corbitt Shields
Production & Design: Karen McKinley
Cartographers: Bob Race and Brian Bardwell
Index: Nicole Revere

Front cover photo: Santa Prisca Church, Taxco, Mexico,
by Dwight B. Miller
All photos by Bruce Whipperman unless otherwise noted.

Distributed in the U.S.A. by Publishers Group West
Printed in Hong Kong

Please send all comments,
corrections, additions,
amendments, and critiques to:

**PACIFIC MEXICO HANDBOOK
MOON PUBLICATIONS, INC.
P.O. BOX 3040
CHICO, CA 95927-3040, USA
e-mail: travel@moon.com**

Printing History
1st edition — 1993
2nd edition — December 1995

To Mom, Dad, and Hilda,
Peter, Sara and Kent, and Linda.

ACKNOWLEDGMENTS

Kindness, in major part, was responsible for this book. I gratefully thank the host of Mexican people—at roadside, at their front doors, and behind store, hotel, and *turismo* counters—who patiently answered my requests for information and directions. At times, their help was vital—such as when two young men extracted my car from a creek, or when a pair of road workers helped me dig it out of a sandy embankment.

To others I owe a unique debt for their continuous generosity. In Puerto Vallarta, thanks to Nancy Adams, who made my work so much more pleasant by gracefully allowing me to set up shop in a corner of her lovely Cafe Sierra. I also owe much to Gary Thompson, of Galería Pacífico, who introduced me to both Puerto Vallarta art and his many gracious friends and associates. For their helpful kindness, I also specially thank John and Nancy Erickson, Kathy von Rohr, Diana Turn, and María Elena Zermeño.

Outside of Puerto Vallarta, on the Nayarit coast, I owe a debt for the kind help and hospitality of Mina and Carlos González in Bucerías; Professor and Mrs. Charles Sacamano, and Adrienne Adams, in Sayulita; Laura del Valle at Mar de Jade; and Mariano and Susana Valadez at the Huichol Center in Santiago Ixcuintla. This book is much richer because of them.

Likewise, in Puerto Vallarta's mountain country, thanks to Bud Acord at Hacienda Jalisco for his warm hospitality and for sharing his reminiscences of old times in Puerto Vallarta with me. Similar thanks are also due to Cuca Díaz at Posada Corona in Mascota, and to Guy Lawlor and Bill Worth at Hacienda Jacarandas in Talpa.

Back in California, thanks to Moon publisher Bill Newlin and his acquisitions committee for their vote of confidence in this project. Thanks, furthermore, to everyone else at Moon for their super-fine editing, graphics, and layout work.

I owe a special debt to Richard Paoli, former editor of the San Francisco *Examiner* travel section, who, in 1983, selected my story of the Raffles Hotel in Singapore, which became my first published work. Thanks also to the others who have encouraged me since then, especially Patricia Lee, president of the Bay Area Travel Writers, and many of my fellow members. Singular among them was the late Rebecca Bruns, whose excellent guidebook, *Hidden Mexico,* was a major inspiration for my present work.

Back home in Berkeley, thanks for the sympathetic cooperation of the friendly staff at my office-away-from home, Cafe Espresso Roma. Special acknowledgment is due to espresso maestro Miguel, whose delicious, individually decorated, early-morning lattes made this book possible.

Thanks also to my friend and business partner, Halcea Valdes, who generously managed without me while I was away in Mexico.

I owe a debt beyond counting to my mother Joan Casebier, my father and stepmother Bob and Hilda Whipperman, and my sister Doris Davis, for their help in making me who I am.

Finally, I owe a load of thanks to my wife Linda, who cheerfully kept our home together during my absence and lovingly welcomed me back when I returned.

CONTENTS

MAPS

MAP SYMBOLS

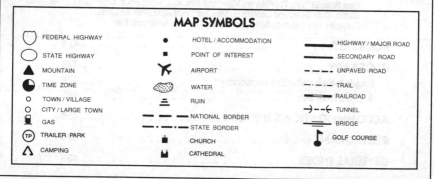

CHARTS

SPECIAL TOPICS

ABBREVIATIONS

a/c—air-conditioned
Av.—Avenida
C—Celsius
Calz.—Calzado (boulevard)
d—double occupancy
Fracc.—Fraccionamiento
    (subdivision)
km—kilometer
Km—Kilometer marker

kph—kilometers per hour
Nte.—Norte (north)
Ote.—Oriente (east)
Pte.—Poniente (west)
s—single occupancy
s/n—sin número (no street
    number)
t—triple occupancy
tel.—telephone number

PREFACE

Scarcely a generation ago, Mexico's tropical Pacific coast was dotted with a few sleepy, isolated towns and fishing villages, reachable only by sea or tortuous mountain roads from the interior. That gradually began to change, until, in 1984, the last link of Mexico's Pacific coast Highway 200 was completed, creating Pacific Mexico, an entire touristic region and palmy thousand-mile path for exploring Mexico.

The choices seem endless. You can choose among resorts, some glittering and luxurious and others quiet and homey. In between the resorts stretch jungle-clad headlands, interspersed with palm-shaded, pearly strands where the fishing is good and the living easy.

When weary of lazing in the sun, visitors can enjoy a trove of ocean sports. Pacific Mexico's water is always balmy and fine to fish, swim, surf, windsurf, kayak, water-ski, snorkel, and scuba dive. For nature enthusiasts, dozens of lush jungle-fringed coastal lagoons are ripe for wildlife viewing and photography.

The coastal strip would be enough but Pacific Mexico offers more: Within a hour's flight or a day's drive of the tropical shore rise the cool oak- and pine-studded highland valleys. Here, colonial cities—Guadalajara, Colima, Pátzcuaro, Taxco, Oaxaca—offer fine crafts, colorful festivals, baroque monuments, traditional peoples, and the barely explored ruins of long-forgotten kingdoms.

In short, Pacific Mexico is an exotic, tropical land, easy to visit, enjoy, and appreciate, whether you prefer glamourous luxury, back-country adventure, or a little bit of both. This book will show you the way.

IS THIS BOOK OUT OF DATE?

We're especially interested in hearing from female travelers, handicapped travelers, people who've traveled with children, RVers, hikers, campers, and residents, both foreign and Mexican. We welcome the comments of business and professional people—hotel and restaurant owners, travel agents, government tourism staff—who serve Pacific Mexico travelers.

We welcome submissions of unusually good photos and drawings for possible use in future editions. If photos, send duplicate slides or slides-from-negatives; if drawings, send clear photocopies. Please include a self-addressed stamped envelope if you'd like your material returned. If we use it, we'll cite your contribution and give you a free new edition. Please address your responses to:

Pacific Mexico Handbook
c/o Moon Publications, Inc.
P.O. Box 3040
Chico, CA 95927-3040, USA

BOB RACE

INTRODUCTION
LAND AND SEA

On the map of North America, Mexico appears as a grand horn of plenty, spreading and spilling to its northern border with the United States. Mexico encompasses a vast landscape, sprawling over an area as large as France, Germany, England, and Italy combined. Besides its size, Mexico is high country, where most people live in mountain valleys within sight of towering, snowcapped peaks.

Travelers heading south of the Río Grande do not realize the rise in elevation, however. Instead, brushy, cactus-pocked plains spread to mountain ranges on the far blue horizon. Northern Mexico is nevertheless a tableland—the *altiplano*—that rises gradually from the Río Grande to its climax at the very heart of the country: the mile-high Bajío (ba-HEE-oh) Valley around Guadalajara and the even loftier Valley of Mexico.

Here, in these fertile vales, untold generations of Mexicans have gazed southward at an awesome rampart of smoking mountains, a grand volcanic seam stretching westward from the Gulf of Mexico to the Pacific. In a continuous line along the 19th parallel, more than a dozen volcanoes have puffed sulfurous gas and spewed red-hot rock for an eon, building themselves into some of the mightiest peaks in the Americas. Most easterly and grandest of them all is Orizaba (Citlaltépetl, the "Mountain of the Star"), rising 18,860 feet (5,735 meters) directly above the Gulf. Then, in proud succession, the giants march westward: Malinche, 14,640 feet (4,450 meters); Popocatépetl, 17,930 feet (5,450 meters); Nevado de Toluca, 15,390 feet (4,680 meters); until finally the most active of all—snowcapped Nevado de Colima—smokes 14,220 feet (4,325 meters) over the long, plumy shoreline of Pacific Mexico.

PACIFIC MEXICO

This sun-drenched western coastland stretches along a thousand miles of sandy beaches, palm strewn headlands, and blue lagoons, from

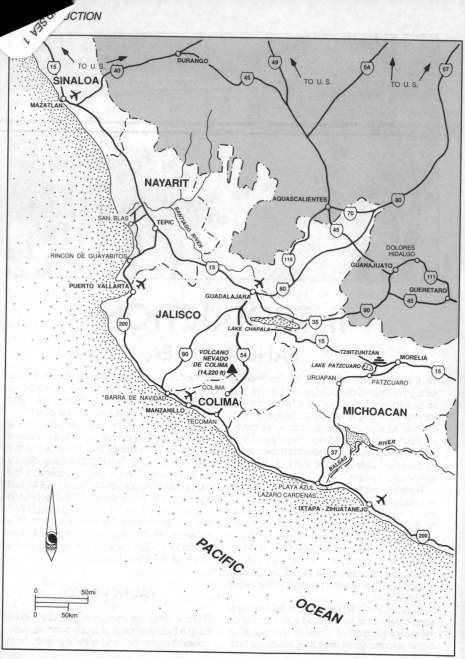

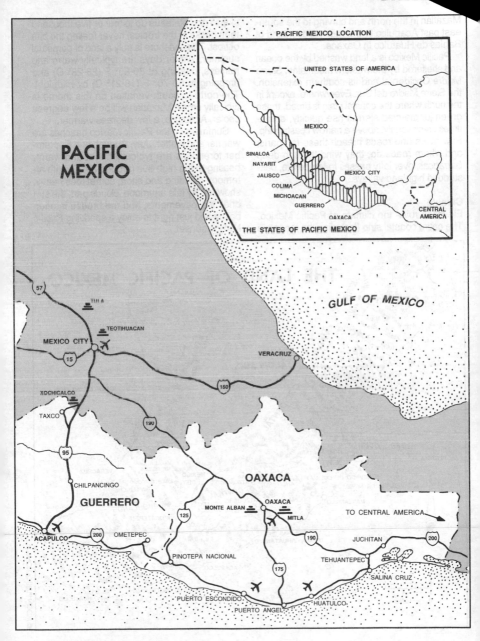

...n the north and curving to the south-...st Acapulco to the new vacationland of ...arras de Huatulco in Oaxaca.

Pacific Mexico is a land washed by the ocean and sheltered by the western mountains: Sierra Madre Occidental and its southern extension, the Sierra Madre del Sur. Everywhere, except in the north where the coastal plain is broad, these green jungle-clad sierras rise quickly, sometimes precipitously, above a narrow coastal strip. Few rivers and roads breach these ramparts, and where roads do, they wind through deep *barrancas*, over lofty passes to temperate, oak-studded highland valleys.

Climate

Elevation rules the climate of Pacific Mexico. The entire coastal strip (including the mountain slopes and plateaus up to four or five thousand feet) basks in the tropics, never feeling the bite of frost. The seashore is truly a land of perpetual summer. Winter days are typically warm and rainless, peaking at 80-85° F (26-28° C) and dropping to 60-70° F (16-21° C) by midnight. The north-to-south variation on this theme is typically small: Mazatlán will be a few degrees cooler, Acapulco, a few degrees warmer.

Summers on the Pacific Mexico beaches are warmer and wetter. July, August, and September forenoons are typically bright and warm, heating to the high 80s (around 30° C) with afternoon clouding and short, sometimes heavy, showers. By late afternoon, clouds part, the sun dries the pavements, and the breeze is often balmy and just right to enjoy a sparkling Pacific Mexico sunset.

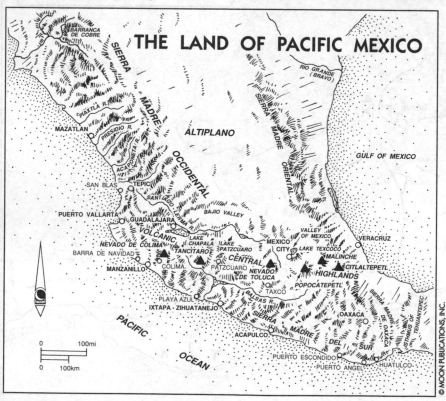

THE LAND OF PACIFIC MEXICO

© MOON PUBLICATIONS, INC.

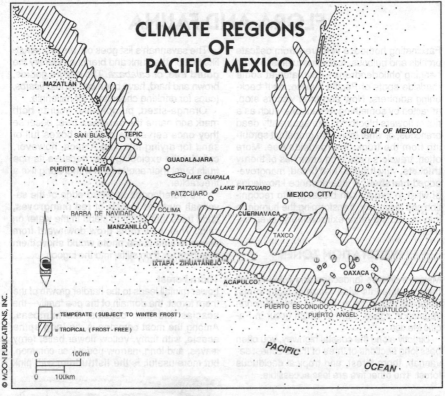

CLIMATE REGIONS
OF
PACIFIC MEXICO

MAZATLÁN

SAN BLAS   TEPIC

PUERTO VALLARTA   GUADALAJARA
LAKE CHAPALA
PATZCUARO   LAKE PATZCUARO
BARRA DE NAVIDAD   COLIMA   MEXICO CITY
MANZANILLO   CUERNAVACA
TAXCO
IXTAPA - ZIHUATANEJO   OAXACA
ACAPULCO
PUERTO ESCONDIDO   HUATULCO
PUERTO ANGEL

GULF OF MEXICO

PACIFIC

OCEAN

☐ = TEMPERATE (SUBJECT TO WINTER FROST)
▨ = TROPICAL (FROST - FREE)

0   100mi
0   100km

© MOON PUBLICATIONS, INC.

The highlands around Guadalajara, Pátzcuaro, Taxco, and Oaxaca experience similar, but more temperate seasons. Midwinter days are mild, typically peaking around 70° F (21° C). Expect cool, but frost-free, winter nights between 40 and 50° F (9-14° C). Highland summers are delightful, with afternoons in the 80s (27-32° C) and pleasant evenings in the mid-70s to 80s (21-26° C), perfect for strolling. May, before the rains, is often the warmest, with June, July, and August highs being moderated by afternoon showers. Many Guadalajara, Pátzcuaro, Taxco, and Oaxaca residents enjoy the best of all possible worlds: balmy summers at home and similarly balmy winters in vacation homes along the Pacific Mexico coast.

FLORA AND FAUNA

Fascinating hothouse verdure—from delicate orchids and bulbous, fuzzy succulents to giant hanging philodendrons—luxuriates at some roadside spots of Pacific Mexico, as if beckoning admirers. Now and then visitors stop, attracted by something remarkable, such as a riot of flowers blooming from apparently dead branches, or what looks like grapefruit sprouting from the trunk of a roadside tree. More often, travelers pass long stretches of thorny **thickets**, viny **jungles** and broad, mangrove-edged **marshes**. A little advance knowledge of what to expect can blossom into recognition and discovery, transforming the humdrum into something quite extraordinary, even exotic.

VEGETATION ZONES

Mexico's diverse landscape and fickle rainfall have sculpted its wide range of plant forms. Botanists recognize at least 14 major Mexican vegetation zones, eight of which occur in Pacific Mexico.

Directly along the coastal highway, you often pass long sections of three of these zones: savannah, thorn forest, and tropical deciduous forest. The other five are less accessible.

Savannah
Great swaths of pasturelike savannah stretch along the roadside south of Mazatlán to Tepic. In its natural state, savannah often appears as a palm-dotted sea of grass—green and marshy during the rainy summer, dry and brown by late winter.

Although grass rules the savannah, palms give it character. Most familiar is the **coconut**—the *cocotero*—used for everything from lumber to candy. Coconut palms line the beaches and climb the hillsides—drooping, slanting, rustling, and swaying in the breeze like troupes of hula dancers. Less familiar, but with as much personality, is the Mexican **fan palm**, the *palma real*, festooned with black fruit and its fronds spread flat like a señorita's fan.

The savannah's list goes on: the grapefruit-like fruit on the trunk and branches identify the **gourd tree**, or *calabaza*. The mature gourds, brown and hard, have been carved into *jícaros*, (cups for drinking chocolate) for millennia.

Orange-sized, pumpkinlike gourds both mark and name the **sandbox tree**, because they once served as desktop boxes full of sand for drying ink. The Aztecs, however, called it the exploding tree, because its ripe fruits burst their seeds forth with a bang like a firecracker.

The waterlogged seaward edge of the savannah nurtures forests of **red mangroves**, short trees that seem to stand in the water on stilts. Their new roots grow downward from above; a time-lapse photo would show them marching, as if on stilts, into the lagoon.

Thorn Forest
Lower rainfall leads to the hardier growth of the thorn forest, the domain of the pea family—the **acacias** and their cousins, the **mimosas**. Among the most common is the **long spine acacia**, with fluffy, yellow flower balls, ferny leaves, and long, narrow pods; less common, but more useful, is the **fishfuddle**, with pink

Lotus blossoms frequently decorate pond and lagoon edges of Pacific Mexico savannahs.

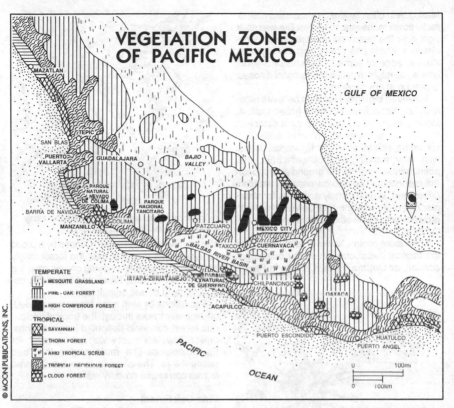

VEGETATION ZONES OF PACIFIC MEXICO

GULF OF MEXICO

MAZATLAN

SAN BLAS

TEPIC

PUERTO VALLARTA

GUADALAJARA

BAJIO VALLEY

PARQUE NATURAL NEVADO DE COLIMA

PARQUE NACIONAL TANCITARO

BARRA DE NAVIDAD

MANZANILLO

COLIMA

PATZCUARO

MEXICO CITY

BALSAS RIVER BASIN

TAXCO

CUERNAVACA

TEMPERATE

| | = MESQUITE GRASSLAND

||| = PINE - OAK FOREST

■ = HIGH CONIFEROUS FOREST

IXTAPA-ZIHUATANEJO

PARQUE NATURAL DE GUERRERO

CHILPANCINGO

OAXACA

ACAPULCO

TROPICAL

= SAVANNAH

= THORN FOREST

= AHID TROPICAL SCRUB

= TROPICAL DECIDUOUS FOREST

= CLOUD FOREST

PACIFIC

PUERTO ESCONDIDO

HUATULCO

PUERTO ANGEL

OCEAN

0   100mi

0   100km

© MOON PUBLICATIONS, INC.

pea-flowers and long pods, a source of fish-stunning poison. Take care around the acacias; some of the long-thorned varieties harbor nectar-feeding, biting ants.

Perhaps the most spectacular and famous member of the thorn forest community is the **morning glory tree,** which announces the winter dry season's end by blooming a festoon of white trumpets atop its crown of seemingly dead branches. Its gruesome Mexican name, *palo del muerto* (tree of the dead), is exceeded only around Taxco, where folks call it *palo bobo* (fool tree) because they believe if you take a drink from a stream near its foot, you will go crazy.

The cactuses are among the thorn forest's sturdiest and most spectacular inhabitants. In the dry Río Balsas basin (along Hwy. 95 inland from Acapulco) the spectacular **candelabra cactus** *(cordón espinosa)* spreads as much as 60 feet tall and wide.

Tropical Deciduous Forest
In rainier areas, the thorn forest grades into the tropical deciduous forest. This is the "friendly" or "short-tree" forest, blanketed by a tangle of summer-green verdure whose leaves fall in the dry winter, revealing thickets of dry branches. Some trees show bright fall reds and yellows, later blossoming with brilliant flowers—spider lily, cardinal sage, pink trumpet, poppylike yellowsilk *(pomposhutl),* and mouse-killer *(mala ratón),* which swirl in the spring wind like cherry-blossom blizzards.

The tropical deciduous forest is the lush jungle coat that swathes much of coastal Pacific

Mexico. And often, where the mountains rush directly down to the sea, the forest likewise spills right over the headland into the ocean. Vine-strewn thickets often overhang the highway, like the edge of some lost prehistoric world, where you might expect a last remnant dinosaur to rear up at any moment.

However, biological realities here are nearly as exotic: a four-foot-long green iguana, looking every bit as primitive as a dinosaur, slithers across the pavement; or at roadside, a spreading, solitary **strangler fig** stands, draped with hairy, hanging air roots (which, in time, plant themselves into the ground and support the branches). The Mexican name, *matapalo* (killer tree), is gruesomely accurate, for strangler figs often entwine themselves in a death embrace with some other, less aggressive, victim tree.

Much more benign, however, is my favorite of the tropical deciduous forest: the *guaycoyul, cohune,* or **Colima palm.** *Cohune* in Pacific

Spider monkeys, once common, are now rarely seen in the wild in Pacific Mexico.

Mexico means "magnificent." Capped by a proud cock-plume, it presides over the forest singly or in great, gracefully swaying groves atop the headlands. Its nuts, harvested like small coconuts, yield oil and animal fodder.

Excursions by jeep or on foot along shaded, off-highway tracks through the tropical deciduous forest can yield delightful jungle scenes; unwary travelers must watch out, however, for the poison-oak-like **mala mujer,** the "bad woman" tree. The oil on its large five-fingered leaves can cause an itchy rash.

Pine-Oak Forest

A couple of hours drive inland (especially on the mountain roads from the coast to Pátzcuaro, Taxco, and Oaxaca), the tropics give way to the temperate pine-oak forest, Pacific Mexico's most extensive vegetation zone. Here, most of Mexico's 112 oak and 39 pine species thrive. At the lower elevations, bushy, nut-yielding piñon pines sometimes cover the slope; then come the tall pines, often Chihuahua pine and Montezuma pine, both yellow varieties, similar to the ponderosa pine of the western United States.

Interspersed with them are oaks, in two broad classifications—*encino* (evergreen, small-leafed) and *roble* (deciduous, large-leafed)—both much like the oaks that dot California hills and valleys. Clustered in their branches and scattered in the shade are the *bellota* (acorns), which irrevocably mark them as oaks.

Yellow blooms of the rosa amarilla (yellow rose) *sometimes adorn forest roadsides during the winter dry season. Despite its name, its brown pods mark it as a member of the* cochlospermum (shell seed) *family.*

Arid Tropical Scrub and Cloud Forest

Pacific Mexico's two rarest and exotic vegetation zones are far from the coastal tourist centers. You can conveniently see the great cactus forests of the arid tropical scrub habitat (which occupies the wild, dry canyonland of the Río Balsas intermountain basin) either along Hwy. 95 inland from Acapulco, or along Hwy. 37 between Playa Azul and Pátzcuaro. Finally, travelers who drive to high, dewy mountainsides, beginning around 7,000 feet, can explore the plant and wildlife community of the cloud forest. The Parque Natural de Guerrero (around Corral Bravo, 50 miles west of Chilpancingo, Guerrero) preserves such a habitat, where abundant cool fog nourishes forests of tree ferns, lichen-draped pines, and oaks above a mossy carpet of orchids, bromeliads, and begonias. M. Walter Pesman's delightful *Meet Flora Mexicana* unfortunately is out of print, but libraries often have a copy. Also informative is the popular paperback *Handbook of Mexican Roadside Flora*, by Charles T. Mason, Jr. and Patricia B. Mason. (See the Booklist.)

WILDLIFE

Despite continued habitat destruction—logging of forests, filling wetlands, and plowing savannahs—Pacific Mexico still abounds with wildlife. In the temperate pine-oak forest zone of Pacific Mexico live most of the familiar birds and mammals—mountain lion, coyote, jackrabbit, dove, quail—of the American Southwest.

The tropical coastal forests and savannahs, however, are home to species seen only in zoos north of the border. The reality of this often first dawns on travelers when they glimpse something exotic, such as rau-

cous, screeching swarms of small green parrots rising from the roadside, or an armadillo or coati nosing in the sand just a few feet away at the forested edge of some isolated Pacific Mexico beach.

Armadillos, Coatis, Spider Monkeys, and Tapirs

Armadillos are cat-sized mammals that act and look like opossums, but carry reptilianlike shells. If you see one, remain still, and it may walk right up and sniff your foot before it recognizes you and scuttles back into the woods.

A common inhabitant of the tropics is the raccoonlike coati *(tejon, pisote)*. In the wild, coatis like shady stream banks, often congregating in large troops. They are identified by their short brown or tan fur, small round ears, long nose, and straight, vertically held tail. They make endearing pets; the first coati you see may be one on a string offered for sale at a local market.

If you are lucky, you may glimpse a band of now-rare reddish brown spider monkeys *(monos)* raiding a forest-edge orchard. And deep in the mountain fastness of Guerrero or Oaxaca, you may find a tracker who can lead you to a view of the endangered tapir. On such an excursion, if you are really fortunate, you may even hear the ghostly cry of or even see a jaguar, the fabled *tigre*.

El Tigre

"Each hill has its own *tigre*," a Mexican proverb says. With black spots spread over a tan coat, stretching five feet (1.5 meters) and weighing about 200 pounds (90 kilograms), the typical jaguar resembles a muscular spotted leopard. Although hunted since prehistory, and now endangered, the jaguar still lives throughout Pacific Mexico, where it hunts along thickly forested stream bottoms and foothills. Unlike the mountain lion *(puma)*,

KAREN McKINLEY

Jaguars still hunt in remote mangrove wetlands and mountain jungles of Pacific Mexico.

the jaguar will eat any game. They have even been known to wait patiently for fish in rivers and stalk beaches for turtle and egg dinners. If they have a favorite food, it is probably the piglike wild peccary. Experienced hunters agree that no two jaguars will, when examined, have the same prey in their stomachs.

Although humans have died of wounds inflicted by cornered jaguars, there is little or no hard evidence they are man-eaters, despite legends to the contrary.

BIRDS

The coastal lagoons of Pacific Mexico lie astride the Pacific Flyway, one of the Americas' major north-south paths for migrating waterfowl. Many of the familiar American and Canadian species, including pintail, gadwall, baldpate, shoveler, redhead, and scaup, arrive from October until January, when their numbers will swell into the millions. They settle near food and cover—sometimes, to the frustration of farmers—even at the borders of cornfields. Among the best places to see their spectacle is the **Marismas Nacionales** marsh complex around the Sinaloa-Nayarit border, west of coast Hwy. 15 between Mazatlán and Santiago Ixcuintla.

Besides the migrants, swarms of resident species—herons, egrets, cormorants, anhingas, lily-walkers, and hundreds more—stalk, nest, and preen in the same lagoons.

Few spots are better for observing **seabirds** than the beaches of Pacific Mexico. Brown pelicans and huge black-and-white frigate birds are among the prime actors. When a flock of pelicans spots a school of their favorite fish, they go about their routine deliberately: singly or in pairs they circle and plummet into the waves and come up, more often than not, with fish in their gullets. They bob and float over the swells for a minute or two, seemingly waiting for their dozen or so fellow pelicans to take their turns. This goes on until they've bagged a big dinner of 10-15 fish apiece.

Frigate birds, the scavengers par excellence of Pacific Mexico, often profit by the labor of the teams of fisherfolk who haul in fish right on village beaches by the netful. After the fishermen auction off the choice morsels—perch, tuna, red snapper, octopus, shrimp—to merchants, and the villagers have scavenged everything else edible, the motley residue of small fish, sea snakes, skates, squids, slugs, and sharks is often thrown to a screeching flock of frigate birds.

For more details of Mexico's mammals and birds in general, check out A. Starker Leopold's very readable classic, *Wildlife of Mexico*, and other works in the Booklist.

REPTILES AND AMPHIBIANS

Snakes and Gila Monsters

Mexico has 460-odd snake species, the vast majority shy and nonpoisonous. In Mexico, as everywhere, poisonous snakes have been largely eradicated in city and tourist areas. Even poisonous snakes such as *culebras* and *víboras* are generally shy and nonaggressive; they will generally get out of your way if you give plenty of warning. In brush or jungle areas, carry a stick or a machete and beat the bushes ahead of you, while watching where you put your feet. When hiking or rock-climbing in the country don't put your hand in niches you can't see.

You might even see a snake underwater while swimming offshore at an isolated Bay of Banderas beach: the **yellow-bellied sea snake,** *pelamis platurus* (to about two feet), although shy, can inflict fatal bites. If you see a yellow and black snake underwater, get away pronto.

Some eels, which resemble snakes but have gills like fish and inhabit rocky crevices, can inflict nonpoisonous bites and should also be avoided.

The Mexican land counterpart of the *pelamis platurus* is the coral snake *(coralillo)*, which occurs as about two dozen species, all with multicolored bright bands that always include red. Although relatively rare, small, and shy, coral snakes occasionally inflict serious, sometimes fatal bites.

More aggressive and generally more dangerous is the Mexican **rattlesnake** *(cascabel)* and its viper-relative, the **fer-de-lance** *(bothrops atrox)*. About the same size (to six feet) and general appearance of the rattlesnake, the fer-de-lance is known by various local names, such as *nauyaca, cuatro narices, palanca,* and *barba amarilla.* It is potentially more hazardous than the rattlesnake because it lacks a rattle to give warning.

The **Gila monster** (confined in Mexico to northern Sonora) and its southern tropical relative, black-with-yellow-spots *escorpión (heloderma horridum),* are the world's only poisonous lizards. Despite its beaded skin and menacing, fleshy appearance, the *escorpión* only bites when severely provoked; even then, its venom is rarely, if ever, fatal.

Crocodiles

The crocodile, *cocodrilo* or *caimán,* once prized for its meat and hide, came close to vanishing in Mexican Pacific lagoons until the government took steps to ensure its survival. Now officially protected, a few isolated breeding populations live in the wild, while government and private hatcheries are breeding more for the eventual repopulation of lagoons where they once were common. Hatcheries open for touring are located in San Blas and Lagunas de Chacagua.

Two crocodile species occur in the region. True crocodile *crocodilus acutus* has a narrower snout than its local cousin, *caiman crocodilus fuscus,* a type of alligator. Although past individuals have been recorded up to 15 feet long (see the stuffed specimen upstairs at the Tepic anthropology and history museum), living native crocodiles are usually young and two feet or less in length.

Turtles

The story of Mexican **sea turtles** is similar: they once swarmed ashore on Pacific Mexico beaches to lay their eggs. Prized for their meat, eggs, hide, and shell, they were severely decimated. Now officially protected, sea turtles come ashore in numbers at a few isolated locations. Of the three locally occurring species, the **green turtle,** *tortuga verde,* is by far the most common. From tour boats, it can often be seen grazing on sea grass offshore in the Bay of Banderas. For more sea turtle details, see the special topic "Saving Turtles," in the "Along the Road to Barra de Navidad" section in the South to Manzanillo chapter.

FISH AND MARINE MAMMALS

Shoals of fish abound in Pacific Mexico waters. Four **billfish** species are found in deep-sea grounds several miles offshore: **swordfish, sailfish,** and **blue** and **black marlin.** All are spirited fighters, though the sailfish and marlin are generally the toughest to bring in. The blue marlin is the biggest of the four; in the past, 10-foot specimens, weighing more than a thousand pounds, were brought in at Pacific coast marinas. Lately, four feet, 200 pounds for a marlin, and 100 pounds for a sailfish is more typical. Progressive captains are now encouraging victorious anglers to return these magnificent "tigers of the sea" (especially the sinewy, poor-eating sailfish and blue marlin) to the deep after they've won the battle.

Billfish are not the only prizes of the sea. Serious fish lovers also seek varieties of tuna-like **jack, such as yollowtail, Pacific amberjack, pompano, jack crevalle,** and the tenacious **roosterfish,** named for the "comb" atop its head. These, and the **yellowfin tuna, mackerel,** and **dorado,** which Hawaiians call mahimahi, are among the delicacies sought in Pacific Mexican waters.

Accessible from small boats offshore and by casting from shoreline rocks, are varieties of **snapper** *(huachinango, pargo),* and **sea bass** *(cabrilla).* Closer to shore, **croaker, mullet,** and **jewfish** often can be found foraging along sandy bottoms and in rocky crevices.

Sharks and **rays** seem to inhabit nearly all depths, with smaller fry venturing into beach shallows and lagoons. Huge **Pacific manta rays** often appear to be frolicking, their great wings flapping like birds, not far off Pacific Mexico shores. Just beyond the waves, local fisherfolk often bring in **hammerhead, thresher,** and **leopard sharks.**

Also common is the **stingray,** which can inflict a painful wound with its barbed tail. Experienced swimmers and waders avoid injury by both shuffling (rather than stepping) and watching their feet in shallow, sandy bottoms. (For more fish talk and a chart of species often encountered in Pacific Mexico waters, turn ahead to "Sports and Recreation" in the On the Road chapter.)

Seals, Sea Lions, Porpoises, and Whales
Although seen in much greater numbers in Baja California's colder waters, fur bearing species, such as seals and sea lions, do occasionally hunt in the tropical waters and bask on the sands of island beaches off the Pacific Mexico coast. With the rigid government protections that have been in force for a generation, their numbers appear to be increasing.

The **California Gulf porpoise**—*delfín,* or *vaquita* (little cow)—is much more numerous. The smallest member of the whale family, it rarely exceeds five feet. Their playful diving and jumping antics can occasionally be observed from Puerto Vallarta-based tour and fishing boats, and even sometimes right from Bay of Banderas beaches.

Although the **California gray whales'** migration extends only to the southern tip of Baja California, occasional pods stray farther south, where deep-sea fishermen and cruise and tour boat passengers occasionally see them in deep waters offshore.

Larger whale *(ballena)* species, such as **humpback** and **blue whales,** appear to enjoy tropical waters even more, ranging the north Pacific tropics, from Puerto Vallarta west to Hawaii and beyond.

Offshore islands, such as the nearby Marietas and Isla Isabel (accessible from San Blas), and the Revillagigedo (ray-vee-yah-hee-HAY-thoh) Islands, 300 miles due west of Puerto Vallarta, offer prime viewing grounds for Mexico's aquatic fauna. For access to the Marietas, see "Sports" in the "Puerto Vallarta" section of the Puerto Vallarta and the Bay of Banderas chapter; for Isabel, see "Sights" under "San Blas and Vicinity" in the South to Puerto Vallarta and Inland to Guadalajara chapter; and for the Revillagigedos, turn ahead to "By Tour, Cruise, and Sailboat" in the "Getting There" section of the On the Road chapter.

HISTORY

Once upon a time, maybe 50,000 years ago, the first bands of hunters, perhaps following great game herds, crossed from Siberia to the American continent. For thousands of years they drifted southward, eventually settling in the rich valleys and plains of North and South America.

Many thousands of years later, around 10,000 B.C., and in what would later be called Mexico, people began gathering and grinding the seeds of a hardy grass that required only the summer rains to thrive. By selecting and planting the larger seeds, their grain eventually yielded tall plants with long ears and many large kernels. This grain, which they eventually called *teocentli,* the "sacred seed" (maize or corn), led to prosperity.

EARLY CIVILIZATIONS

Plentiful food gave rise to leisure classes—artists, architects, warriors, and ruler-priests—

Mexican mothers still teach their daughters to weave with the backstrap loom exactly as did countless generations of their pre-Columbian forebears.

CODEX MENDOZA, M.N.A.H. LIBRARY

who had time to think and create. With a calendar, they harnessed the constant wheel of the firmament to life on earth, defining the days to plant, to harvest, to feast, to travel, and to trade. Eventually, grand cities arose.

Teotihuacán

Teotihuacán, with a population of perhaps 250,000 around the time of Christ, was one of the world's great metropolises, on a par with Rome, Babylon, and Chang'an. Its epic monuments still stand not far north of Mexico City: the towering Pyramid of the Sun at the terminal of a grand 150-foot-wide ceremonial avenue faces a great Pyramid of the Moon. Along the avenue sprawls a monumental temple-court surrounded by scowling, ruby-eyed effigies of Quetzalcoatl, the feathered serpent god of gods.

Teotihuacán crumbled mysteriously around A.D. 650, leaving a host of former vassal states from what would be the Yucatán to Pacific Mexico free to tussle among themselves. These included **Xochicalco**, not far from present-day Taxco, and the great Zapotec center of **Monte Albán** farther southwest in Oaxaca. From its regal hilltop complex of stone pyramids, palaces, and ceremonial ball courts, Monte Albán reigned all-powerful until it, too, was abandoned around A.D. 1000.

Quetzalcoatl

Xochicalco, however, was flourishing; its wise men tutored a young noble who was to become a living legend: In A.D. 947, Topiltzín (literally, "Our Prince") was born. Records recite Topiltzín's achievements. He advanced astronomy, agriculture, and architecture, and founded the city-state of Tula in A.D. 968, north of old Teotihuacán.

Contrary to the times, Topiltzín opposed human sacrifice; he taught that tortillas and butterflies, not human hearts, were the food of Quetzalcoatl. After ruling benignly for a generation, Topiltzín's name became so revered that the people began to know him as the living Quetzalcoatl, the plumed serpent-god incarnate.

Quetzalcoatl was not universally loved, however. Bloodthirsty local priests, desperate for human victims, tricked him with alcohol; he awoke, groggily, one morning in bed with his sister. Devastated by shame, Quetzalcoatl banished himself from Tula with a band of retainers. In A.D. 987, they headed east, toward Yucatán, leaving arrows shot through saplings, appearing like crosses, along their trail.

Although Quetzalcoatl sent word he would reclaim his kingdom during the 52-year cyclical calendar year of his birth, Ce Acatl, he never returned. Legends say that he sailed east and rose to heaven as the morning star.

Legends also say Quetzalcoatl was bearded and fair-skinned. It was a remarkable coincidence, therefore, that on 22 April 1519, during the eleventh 52-year anniversary of Ce Acatl, Quetzalcoatl's birth year, that bearded, fair-skinned Castilian Hernán Cortés landed on Mexico's eastern coast.

THE CONQUEST

Although a generation had elapsed since Columbus founded Spain's West Indian colonies, returns had been meager. Scarcity of gold and native workers, most of whom had fallen victim to European diseases, turned adventurous Spanish eyes westward once again, toward rumored riches beyond the setting sun. Cortés, then only 34, had left Cuba in February with an expedition of 11 small ships, 550 men, 16 horses, and a few small cannon. By the time he landed in Mexico, he was burdened by a mutinous crew. His men, mostly soldiers of fortune hearing stories of the great Aztec empire west beyond the mountains, realized the impossible odds they faced and became restive.

Cortés, however, cut short any thoughts of mutiny by burning his ships. As he led his grumbling but resigned band of adventurers toward the Aztec capital of Tenochtitlán, Cortés played Quetzalcoatl to the hilt, awing local chiefs. Coaxed by Doña Marina, Cortés's wily native translator-mistress-confidante, local chiefs began to add their armies to Cortés's march against their Aztec overlords.

Moctezuma

While Cortés looked down upon the shimmering Valley of Mexico from the great divide between the volcanoes, Moctezuma, the emperor of the Aztecs, fretted about the returned

"Quetzalcoatl." It is no wonder that the Spanish, approaching on horseback in their glittering, clanking armor, seemed divine to people who had never known steel, draft animals, or the wheel.

Inside the gates of the Venice-like island-city it was the Spaniards' turn to be dazzled: by gardens full of animals, gold and palaces, and a great pyramid-enclosed square where tens of thousands of people bartered goods gathered from all over the empire. Tenochtitlán, with perhaps a quarter of a million people, was the great capital of an empire larger and richer than any in Europe.

Moctezuma, the lord of that empire, was frozen by fear and foreboding, however. He quickly surrendered himself to Cortés's custody. After a few months his subjects, enraged by Spanish brutality and Moctezuma's timidity, rioted and mortally wounded the emperor with a stone. With Moctezuma dead, the riot turned into a counterattack against the Spanish. On 1 July 1520, Cortés and his men, forced by

MALINCHE

If it hadn't been for Doña Marina (whom he received as a gift from a local chief), Cortés may have become a mere historical footnote. Clever and opportunistic, Doña Marina was a crucial strategist in Cortés's deadly game of divide and conquer. She eventually bore Cortés a son and lived in honor and riches for many years, profiting greatly from the Spaniards' exploitation of the Mexicans.

Latter-day Mexicans do not honor her by the gentle title of Doña Marina. They call her Malinche, after the volcano—the ugly, treacherous scar on the Mexican landscape—and curse her as the female Judas who betrayed her country to the Spanish. *Malinchismo* has become known as the tendency to love things foreign and hate things Mexican.

the sheer numbers of rebellious Aztecs, retreated along a lake causeway from Tenochtitlán while carrying Moctezuma's treasure with them. Many of them drowned beneath their burdens of stolen Aztec gold, while others hacked a bloody path through thousands of screaming Aztec warriors to safety on the lakeshore.

That infamous night is now known as Noche Triste ("Sad Night"). Cortés, with half of his men dead, collapsed and wept beneath a great *ahuehuete* cypress tree (which still stands) in Mexico City.

A year later, reinforced by fresh soldiers, horses, a small fleet of armed sailboats, and 100,000 Indian allies, Cortés retook Tenochtitlán. The stubborn defenders, led by Cuauhtémoc, Moctezuma's nephew, fell by the tens of thousands beneath a smoking hail of Spanish grapeshot. The Aztecs, although weakened by smallpox, refused to surrender. Cortés found, to his dismay, that he had to destroy the city to take it.

The triumphant conquistador soon rebuilt it in the Spanish image: Cortés's cathedral and main public buildings—the present *zócalo*, central square of Mexico City—still rest upon the foundations of Moctezuma's pyramids.

Guerrero wooden mask of Malinche

BOB RACE

NEW SPAIN

With the Valley of Mexico firmly in his grip, Cortés sent his lieutenants south, north, and west to extend the limits of a domain that eventually expanded to more than a dozenfold the size of old Spain. He wrote his king, Charles V, "... the most suitable name for it would be New Spain of the Ocean Sea, and thus in the name of your Majesty I have christened it."

The Missionaries

While the conquistadores subjugated the local people, missionaries began arriving to teach, heal, and baptize them. A dozen Franciscan brothers impressed Indians and conquistadores alike by trekking the entire 300-mile stony path from Veracruz to Mexico City in 1523. Cortés knelt and kissed their robes as they arrived.

The missionaries, in contrast, were a slightly more humane counterbalance to the brutal conquistadores. Missionary authorities generally enjoyed a sympathetic ear from Charles V and his successors, who earnestly pursued Spain's Christian mission, especially when it dovetailed with their political and economic goals.

The King Takes Control

After 1525, the crown, through the Council of the Indies, began to wrest power away from Cortés and his conquistador lieutenants. Many of them had been granted rights of *encomienda:* taxes and labor of an Indian district. In exchange, the *encomendero,* who often enjoyed the status of feudal lord, pledged to look after the welfare and souls of his Indian charges.

From the king's point of view, though, tribute pesos collected by *encomenderos* translated into losses to the crown. Moreover, many *encomenderos* callously exploited their Indian wards for quick profit, sometimes selling them as slave labor in mines and on plantations. Such abuses, coupled with European-introduced diseases, began to reduce the Indian population at an alarming rate.

After 1530, the king and his councillors began to realize that the Indians were in peril, and without their labor, New Spain would vanish. They

acted decisively: new laws would be instituted by a powerful new viceroy.

Don Antonio de Mendoza, the Count of Tendilla, arrived in 1535. He set the precedent for an unbroken line of more than 60 viceroys who, with few exceptions, served with distinction until independence in 1821. Village after village along Mendoza's winding route to Mexico City tried to outdo each other with flowers, music, bullfights, and feasts in his honor.

Mendoza wasted no time. He first got rid of the renegade opportunist (and Cortés's enemy) Nuño de Guzmán, whose private army, under the banner of conquest, had been laying waste to a broad western belt of Pacific Mexico, now Jalisco, Michoacán, Nayarit, and Sinaloa. (Guzmán, during his rapacious five years in Pacific Mexico, did, however, manage to found several towns: Guadalajara, Tepic, and Culiacán being among them.)

Cortés, the Marqués del Valle Oaxaca

Cortés, meanwhile, had done very well for himself. He was one of Spain's richest men, with the title of Marqués del Valle Oaxaca. He received 80,000 gold pesos a year from hundreds of thousands of Indian subjects on 25,000 square miles from the Valley of Mexico through the present states of Morelos, Guerrero, and Oaxaca.

Cortés continued on a dozen projects: an expedition to Honduras, a young wife whom he brought back from Spain, a palace (which still stands) in Cuernavaca, sugar mills, and dozens of churches, city halls, and presidios. He supervised the exploits of his lieutenants in Pacific Mexico: Francisco Orozco subdued the Zapotecs in Oaxaca, while Pedro de Alvarado accomplished the same with the Mixtecs, then continued south to conquer Guatemala. Meanwhile, Cristóbal de Olid subjugated the Tarascans in Michoacán, then moved down the Pacific coast to Zacatula on the mouth of the Río Balsas. There (and at Acapulco and Tehuantepec), Cortés built ships to explore the Pacific. In 1535, he led an expedition to the Gulf of California (hence the Sea of Cortez) in a dreary six-month search for treasure around La Paz.

Cortés's Monument

Disgusted with Mendoza's meddling and discouraged by his failures, Cortés returned to Spain, where he got mired in lawsuits, a minor war, and his daughter's marital troubles, all of which led to his illness and death in 1547. Cortés's remains, according to his will, were eventually laid to rest in a vault at Hospital de Jesús, which he founded in Mexico City.

Since latter-day Mexican politics preclude memorials to the Spanish Conquest, no monument nor statue marks his achievements. Cortés's monument, historians note, is Mexico itself.

COLONIAL MEXICO

In 1542, the Council of the Indies, through Viceroy Mendoza, promulgated its liberal New Laws of the Indies. The New Laws rested on high moral ground: the only Christian justification for New Spain was the souls and welfare of the Indians. Colonists had no right to exploit the Indians. Slavery, therefore, was outlawed and *encomienda* rights were to revert to the crown at the death of the original grantees.

Despite uproar and near-rebellion by the colonists, Mendoza (and his successor in 1550, Don Luis Velasco) kept the lid on New Spain. Although some *encomenderos* held on to their rights into the 18th century, chattel slavery was abolished in Mexico—300 years before Lincoln's Emancipation Proclamation.

Peace reigned in Mexico for ten generations. Viceroys came and conscientiously served, new settlers arrived and put down roots, friars preached and built country churches, and the conquistadores' rich sons and daughters played while the Indians worked.

The Role of the Church

The church somewhat moderated the Indians' toil. Feast days came when they would dress up and parade their patron saint through the streets and later eat their fill, get tipsy on *pulque,* and ooh and aah at the fireworks.

The church profited from the status quo, however. The biblical tithe—one-tenth of everything, from crops and livestock to rents and mining profits—filled church coffers. By 1800, the church owned half of Mexico. Moreover, the clergy (including lay church officers) and the military were doubly privileged. They enjoyed right of *fuero* (exemption from civil law) and could be prosecuted by ecclesiastical or military courts only.

Trade and Commerce

In trade and commerce, New Spain existed for the benefit of the mother country. Spaniards enjoyed absolute monopolies by virtue of the complete prohibition of foreign traders and goods. Colonists, as a result, paid dearly for oft-shoddy Spanish manufactures. The Casa de Contratación, the royal trade regulators, always ensured the colony's yearly balance of payments would result in deficit, which would be made up by bullion shipments from New Spain mines (from which the crown raked 10% off the top).

Despite its faults, New Spain lasted three times longer than the Aztec empire. By most contemporary measures, New Spain was prospering in 1800. The Indian labor force was completely subjugated and increasing, and the galleon fleets were carrying home increasing tonnages of silver and gold worth millions. New Spain, however, had changed in 300 years.

Criollos, the New Mexicans

Nearly three centuries of colonial rule had given rise to a burgeoning population of more than a million criollos—Mexican-born white descendants of Spanish colonists, many of them rich and educated—to whom power was denied.

POPULATION CHANGES IN NEW SPAIN

	EARLY COLONIAL (1570)	LATE COLONIAL (1810)
peninsulares	6,600	15,000
criollos	11,000	1,100,000
mestizos	2,400	704,000
indígenas	3,340,000	3,700,000
negros	22,000	630,000

High government, church, and military office had always been the preserve of a tiny but powerful minority of *peninsulares*—whites born in Spain. All but three of the 61 viceroys and all of the bishops and archbishops were *peninsulares,* although their class comprised a tiny one-half percent of New Spain's population. Criollos could only watch in disgust as unlettered, unskilled *peninsulares* (derisively called *gachupines*—"wearers of spurs") were boosted to authority over them.

Second-class citizens in their own country, criollos had to be content with minor offices or modest careers in law, teaching, parish priesthood, or business but mostly consoled themselves with luxury. Many sank into idleness and cynicism masked by the artificial gaiety of a busy social carousel of operas, balls, and fancy picnics in the country.

Although the criollos stood high above the *mestizo,* Indian, and *negro* underclasses, that ooomed little compensation for the false smiles, the deep bows, and the costly bribes that *gachupines* demanded.

Mestizo, Indian, and *Negro* Classes

Upper-class luxury existed by virtue of the sweat of Mexico's mestizo, Indian, and *negro* laborers and servants. African slaves were imported in large numbers during the 17th century after typhus, smallpox, and measles epidemics had wiped out most of the Indian population. Although the Afro-Mexicans contributed significantly (crafts, healing arts, dance, music, drums and marimba), they had arrived last and experienced discrimination from everyone.

INDEPENDENCE

The chance for change came during the aftermath of the French invasion of Spain in 1808. As Napoleon Bonaparte displaced King Ferdinand VII with his brother Joseph on the Spanish throne, Mexico buzzed with excitement. People took sides. Most Mexican *peninsulares* backed the king, while most criollos, inspired by the example of the recent American and French revolutions, talked and dreamed of independence. One such group, urged on by a firebrand parish priest, acted.

El Grito de Dolores
Viva México! Death to the *Gachupines!*

Father Miguel Hidalgo's impassioned *grito* from the church balcony in the Guanajuato town of Dolores on 16 September 1810 ignited action. A mostly Indian, machete-wielding army of 20,000 coalesced around Hidalgo and his compatriots, Ignacio Allende and Juan Aldama. They had difficulty, however, controlling their mob, which raged through the Bajío, massacring hated *gachupines* and pillaging their homes.

Hidalgo advanced on Mexico City but, unnerved by stiff royalist resistance, retreated and regrouped around Guadalajara. His rebels, whose numbers had swollen to 80,000 criollo-officered Indians and mestizos, were no match for professionals, however. On 17 January 1811, Hidalgo (now "Generalisimo") was defeated and fled before a disciplined, 6,000-strong royalist force.

Hidalgo headed north for the U.S. but was soon apprehended, defrocked, and executed. His head and those of his comrades—Aldama, Allende, and Mariano Jiménez—were hung from the walls of the Guanajuato granary (site of the slaughter of 138 *gachupines* by Hidalgo's army) for 10 years as grim reminders of the consequences of rebellion.

The 10-Year Struggle

Others carried on, however. A former mestizo student of Hidalgo, José María Morelos, trained and led guerrilla bands, declared independence, and wrote a model constitution. Morelos led a revolutionary shadow government in the present states of Guerrero and Oaxaca for four years until apprehended and executed in December 1815.

Morelos's heroism, however, had saved his movement. Compatriot Vicente Guerrero carried the struggle to a climax, joining forces with criollo royalist Brigadier Agustín de Iturbide. Their **Plan de Iguala** promised "Three Guarantees"—the renowned **Trigarantes**—Independence, Catholicism, and Equality, which the army (commanded by Iturbide, of course) would enforce. On 21 September 1821, Iturbide rode triumphantly into Mexico City at the head of his army of *trigarantes*. Mexico was independent at last.

Independence, however, solved little except to expel the *peninsulares,* whom the criollo elite could no longer blame for Mexico's ills. With an illiterate populace and no experience in self-government, Mexicans began a tragic 40-year love affair with a fantasy: the general on the white horse, the gold-braided hero who could save them from themselves.

The Rise and Fall of Agustín I
Iturbide became Agustín I, the first emperor of independent Mexico—crowned by the bishop of Guadalajara on 21 June 1822. But Agustín's charisma soon faded. In a pattern that became sadly predictable for generations of topsy-turvy Mexican politics, an ambitious garrison commander somewhere gave a *pronunciamiento,* a declaration against the government. Supporting *pronunciamientos* followed, and old revolutionary heroes Guerrero, Guadalupe Victoria, and Nicolás Bravo endorsed a "plan"—the Plan of Casa Mata (not unlike Iturbide's previous Plan de Iguala)—dethroning Iturbide in favor of a republic. Iturbide, his braid tattered and brass tarnished, abdicated in March 1822.

Antonio López de Santa Anna, the eager 28-year-old military commander of Veracruz, whose *pronunciamiento* had pushed Iturbide from his white horse, maneuvered to gradually replace him on Mexico's shaky political stage. After Guadalupe Victoria had miraculously managed to remain Mexico's first president for four years, the presidency bounced between liberal and conservative hands six times in three years. Meanwhile, Santa Anna had jumped to prominence by defeating a half-starved Spanish regiment that had landed abortively at Tampico in 1829. "The Victor of Tampico," people called Santa Anna.

The Disastrous Era of Santa Anna
In 1833, the government was bankrupt; mobs demanded the ouster of conservative President Bustamante, who had executed the rebellious old revolutionary hero, Vicente Guerrero. Santa Anna gave *pronunciamiento* against Busta-mante; Congress obliged, elevating Santa Anna to "Liberator of the Republic" and "Conqueror of the Spaniards," and named him president in March 1833.

Santa Anna would pop in and out the presidency like a jack-in-the-box 10 more times before 1855. Texas, Mexico's northeast frontier province, was the first of several Santa Anna disasters. Inflated by his initial success against rebellious Anglo settlers at the battle of the Alamo in February 1836, Santa Anna foolishly lost both his army and Texas two months later. He later lost his leg (which was buried with full military honors) fighting the emperor of France.

Santa Anna's greatest debacle, however, was to declare war on the United States with just 1,839 pesos in the treasury. With Mexican forces poised to defend Mexico City against a relatively small 10,000-man American invasion force, Santa Anna inexplicably withdrew his intact division. United States Marines surged into the "Halls of Montezuma" (Chapultepec Castle, where Mexico's six beloved Niños Héroes cadets fell in the losing cause) on 13 September 1847.

In the subsequent treaty of Guadalupe Hidalgo, Mexico lost two-fifths of its territory—the present states of New Mexico, Arizona, California, Nevada, Utah, and Colorado—to the United States. Mexicans have never forgotten; they have looked upon *gringos* with a combination of awe, envy, admiration, and disgust ever since.

For Santa Anna, however, enough was not enough. Called back as president for the last time in 1853, Santa Anna, now "His Most Serene Highness," financed his extravagances by selling off a part of southern Arizona, known as the Gadsden Purchase, for $10 million.

The Reforms
Mexican leaders finally saw the light and exiled Santa Anna forever. While conservatives searched for a king to replace Santa Anna, liberals (whom Santa Anna had kept in jail) plunged ahead with three controversial reform laws: the Ley Juárez, Ley Lerdo, and Ley Iglesias. These *reformas,* augmented by a new Constitution of 1857, directly attacked the privilege and power of Mexico's landlords, clergy, and generals: Ley Juárez abolished *fueros,* the separate military and church courts; Ley Lerdo forbade excess corporate (read: church) landholdings, and Ley Iglesias reduced or transferred most church power to the state.

BOB RACE

President Benito Juárez, like his contemporary Abraham Lincoln, was a lawyer of humble origin who kept his country united through years of civil war.

Conservative generals, priests, and *hacendados* and their mestizo and Indian followers revolted. The resulting War of the Reform (not unlike the U.S. Civil War) ravaged the countryside for three long years until the victorious liberal army paraded triumphantly in Mexico City on New Year's Day, 1861.

Juárez and Maximilian

Benito Juárez, the leading *reformista,* had won the day. Juárez's similarity to his contemporary, Abraham Lincoln, is legend: Juárez had risen from humble Zapotec Indian origins to become a lawyer, a champion of justice, and the president who held his country together during a terrible civil war. Like Lincoln, Juárez's triumph didn't last long.

Imperial France invaded Mexico in January 1862. After two costly years, the French pushed Juárez's liberal army into the hills and gave Mexican conservatives the king they had been looking for. Austrian Archduke Maximilian and his wife Carlota, the very models of modern Catholic monarchs, landed at Veracruz on 28 May 1864.

The naive archduke, crowned Emperor Maximilian I of Mexico, was surprised some of his subjects resented his presence. Meanwhile, Juárez refused to yield, stubbornly performing his constitutional duties in a somber black carriage one jump ahead of the French occupying army. The climax came in June 1867, as Maximilian, deserted by the French, took the field himself. He watched in horror as Juárez's troops cut his army to pieces. Juárez gave no quarter. On 17 June, Juárez ordered Maximilian's execution.

Juárez worked day and night at the double task of reconstruction and reform. He won reelection, but died, exhausted, in 1871. The death of Juárez, the stoic partisan of reform, signaled hope to Mexico's conservatives. They soon got their wish: General Don Porfirio Díaz, the "Coming Man," was elected president in 1876.

Pax Porfiriana

Don Porfirio is often remembered wistfully, as old Italians remember Mussolini: "He was a bit rough, but, dammit, at least he made the trains run on time."

Although Porfirio Díaz's humble Oaxaca mestizo origins were not unlike Juárez's, the resemblance stopped there. Díaz was not a democrat; as a general, his officers often took no captives; as president, his country police, the *rurales,* often shot prisoners in the act of "trying to escape."

Order and progress, in that sequence, ruled Mexico for 34 years. Foreign investment flowed into the country, new railroads brought the products of shiny factories, mines, and farms to modernized Gulf and Pacific ports. Pesos flowed into government coffers; Mexico balanced its budget, repaid foreign debts, and became a respected member of the family of nations.

The price was high, however. Don Porfirio gave away more than a hundred million acres—one-fifth of Mexico's land area (including most of the arable land)—to friends and foreigners. Poor Mexicans, Indians especially, suffered. By 1910, 90% of the Indians had lost their *ejidos* (traditional communal land). In the spring of 1910, a smug, now-cultured and elderly Don Porfirio anticipated with relish the centennial of Hidalgo's Grito de Dolores.

THE REVOLUTION OF 1910

¡No Reelección!

Porfirio Díaz himself had first campaigned on the slogan. It was the idea that the president should step down after one term. Díaz had even stepped down (in favor of a puppet) once in 1880. But after that, he had gotten himself elected for 26 consecutive years. In 1910, Francisco I. Madero, a short, squeaky-voiced son of rich landowners, opposed Díaz under the same banner.

Díaz had jailed Madero before the election. Madero, however, refused to quit campaigning. Fleeing to the U.S., he declared the election of 1910 null and void and called for a revolution to begin on 20 November.

Not much happened. ¡No Reelección!, after all, is not much of a platform. But millions of poor Mexicans were going to bed hungry, and Díaz hadn't listened to them for years.

Villa and Zapata

The people began to stir. In Chihuahua, followers of Francisco (Pancho) Villa, an erstwhile ranch hand, miner, peddler, and cattle rustler, began attacking the *rurales,* dynamiting railroads, and raiding towns. Meanwhile, in the south, horse trader, farmer, minor official Emiliano Zapata's Indian guerrillas were terrorizing rich *hacendados* and forcibly recovering stolen ancestral village lands. Zapata's movement gained steam, and by May had taken the Morelos state capital, Cuernavaca. Meanwhile, Madero crossed the Río Grande and joined with Villa's forces, who took Ciudad Juárez.

The *federales,* the government army troops, began deserting in droves, and on 25 May 1911, Díaz submitted his resignation. As Madero's deputy, General Victoriano Huerta, put Díaz on his ship of exile in Veracruz, Díaz confided: "Madero has unleashed a tiger. Now let's see if he can control it."

Emiliano Zapata, it turned out, was the very tiger whom Madero had unleashed. Meeting with Madero in Mexico City, Zapata fumed over Madero's go-slow approach to the "agrarian problem," as Madero termed it. By November, Zapata had denounced Madero. "¡Tierra y Libertad!" the Zapatistas cried: "The lands, woods and water that the landlords ... have usurped will be immediately restored to the villages or citizens who hold the corresponding titles to them. ..."

The Fighting Continues

Madero's support soon faded. The army in Mexico City rebelled; Huerta forced Madero to resign on 18 February 1913, then murdered him four days later. The rum-swilling Huerta, however, ruled like a Chicago mobster; general rebellion, led by the "Big Four"—Villa, Álvaro Obregón, and Venustiano Carranza in the north, and Zapata in the south—soon broke out. Pressed by the rebels and refused U.S. recognition, Huerta fled into exile in July 1914.

The Constitution of 1917

Control seesawed for three years between Villa and Zapata on one hand and Obregón and Carranza on the other. Finally Carranza, who controlled most of the country by 1917, got a convention together in Querétaro to formulate political and social goals. The resulting Constitution of 1917, while restating most ideas of the Reformistas' 1857 Constitution, additionally prescribed a single four-year presidential term, labor reform, and subordinated private ownership to public interest. Every village had a right to communal *ejido* land, and subsoil wealth could never be sold away to the highest bidder.

The Constitution of 1917 was a revolutionary expression of national aspirations, and, in retrospect, represented a social and political agenda for the entire 20th century. In modified form, it has lasted to the present day.

Obregón Stabilizes Mexico

On 1 December 1920, General Álvaro Obregón legally assumed the presidency of a Mexico still bleeding from 10 years of civil war. Although a seasoned revolutionary, Obregón was also a negotiator who recognized peace was necessary to implement the goals of the revolution. In four years, his government pacified local uprisings, disarmed a swarm of warlords, executed hundreds of *bandidos,* obtained U.S. diplomatic recognition, assuaged the worst fears of the clergy and landowners, and began land reform.

All this set the stage for the work of Plutarco Elías Calles, Obregón's Minister of Gobernación

(Interior) and handpicked successor, who won the 1924 election. Aided by peace, Mexico returned to a semblance of prosperity. Calles brought the army under civilian control, balanced the budget, and shifted Mexico's revolution into high gear. New clinics vaccinated millions against smallpox, new dams irrigated thousands of previously dry acres, and *campesinos* received millions of acres of redistributed land.

By single-mindedly enforcing the proagrarian, prolabor, and anticlerical articles of the 1917 constitution, Calles made many influential enemies, however. Infuriated by the government's confiscation of church property, closing of monasteries, and deportation of hundreds of foreign priests and nuns, the clergy refused to perform marriages, baptisms, and last rites. Militant Catholics, as members of the Cristero movement, crying *"¡Viva Christo Rey!,"* armed themselves, torching public schools and government property and murdering hundreds of innocent bystanders.

Simultaneously, Calles threatened foreign oil companies, demanding they exchange their titles for fifty-year leases. A moderate Mexican supreme court decision over the oil issue and the skillful arbitration of U.S. Ambassador Dwight Morrow smoothed over both the oil and church troubles by the end of Calles's term.

Calles, who started out brimming with revolutionary fervor and populist zeal, became increasingly conservative and dictatorial. Although he bowed out peaceably in favor of Obregón (the constitution had been amended to allow one six-year nonsuccessive term), Obregón was assassinated two weeks after his election in 1928. Calles continued to rule for six more years through three puppet-presidents: Emilio Portes Gil (1928-30), Pascual Ortiz Rubio (1930-32), and Abelardo Rodríguez (1932-34).

For the 14 years since 1920, the revolution had waxed and waned. Although Calles had been the first president in 40 years to succeed without violence, the presidency had changed hands six times since then. Calles and his cronies had lined their pockets while Mexico, with a cash surplus in 1930, skidded into debt as the Great Depression deepened. By slowing the Revolution to a crawl, Calles had mollified the church, landowners, and foreign corporations. In blessing his Minister of War, General Lázaro Cárdenas for the 1934 presidential election, Calles expected more of the same.

Cárdenas Expropriates Foreign Oil

The 40-year-old former governor of Michoacán immediately set his own agenda, however. For six years, Cárdenas worked tirelessly to fulfill the social prescriptions of the revolution. While morning-coated diplomats and cabinet ministers waited, fretting in his outer office, Cárdenas ushered past delegations of *campesinos* and factory workers and sympathetically listened to their problems.

In his six years, Cárdenas moved public education and health forward on a broad front, supported strong, independent labor unions, and redistributed 49 million acres of farmland, more than any president before or since.

Cárdenas's resolute enforcement of constitution Articulo 123 brought him the most renown. Under this prolabor law, the government turned over a host of private companies to employee ownership and, on 18 March 1938, expropriated all foreign oil corporations.

In retrospect, the oil corporations (most of which were British) deserved what they got. They had sorely neglected the wages, health, and welfare of their workers while taking the law into their own hands with ruthless private police forces. Although U.S. President Franklin Roosevelt disagreed, and Standard Oil of New Jersey cried foul, the United States government did not intervene. Through negotiation and due process, the U.S. companies eventually received $24 million plus three percent interest in compensation. In the wake of the expropriation, President Cárdenas created Petróleos Mexicanos (Pemex), the national oil corporation, which has run all Mexican petroleum and gas operations to the present day.

Manuel Avila Camacho, elected in 1940, was the last general to be president of Mexico. His administration ushered in a gradual shift of Mexican politics, government, and foreign policy. Tourism, initially promoted by the Cárdenas administration, ballooned as Mexico allied itself with the U.S. cause during WW II. Good feeling surged as Franklin Roosevelt became the first U.S. president to officially cross the Río Grande when he met with Camacho in Monterrey in April 1943.

In both word and deed, moderation and evolution guided President Camacho's policies. *"Soy creente"* ("I am a believer"), he declared to the Catholics of Mexico as he worked earnestly to bridge Mexico's serious church-state schism. Land policy emphasis shifted from redistribution to utilization as new dams and canals irrigated hundreds of thousands of previously arid acres. On one hand, Camacho established IMSS (Instituto Mexicano de Seguro Social), and on the other, trimmed the power of labor unions.

As WW II moved toward its 1945 conclusion, both the U.S. and Mexico were enjoying the benefits of four years of governmental and military cooperation and mutual trade in the form of a mountain of strategic minerals, which had moved north in exchange for a similar mountain of U.S. manufactures south.

The Mature Revolution

During the decades after WW II, beginning with moderate President Miguel Alemán (1946-52), Mexican politicians gradually honed their skills of consensus and compromise as their middle-aged revolution bubbled along under liberal presidents and sputtered haltingly under conservatives. Doctrine required of all politicians, regardless of stripe, that they be "revolutionary" enough to be included beneath the banner of the PRI (Partido Revolucionario Institucional—the Institutional Revolutionary Party), Mexico's dominant political party.

Mexico's Revolution hasn't been very revolutionary about women's rights, however. The PRI didn't get around to giving Mexican women (millions of whom fought and died alongside their men during the revolution) the right to vote until 1953.

Adolfo Ruíz Cortínes, Alemán's secretary of the interior, was elected overwhelmingly in 1952. He fought the corruption that had crept into government under his predecessor, continued land reform, increased agricultural production, built new ports, eradicated malaria, and opened a dozen automobile assembly plants.

Women, voting for the first time in a national election, kept the PRI in power by helping to elect liberal Adolfo López Mateos in 1958. Resembling Lázaro Cárdenas in social policy, López Mateos redistributed 40 million acres of farmland, forced automakers to use 60% domestic components, built thousands of new schools, and distributed hundreds of millions of new textbooks. *"La electricidad es nuestra"* ("Electricity is ours"), Mateos declared as he nationalized foreign power companies in 1962.

Despite his left-leaning social agenda, unions were restive under López Mateos. Protesting inflation, workers struck; the government retaliated, arresting Demetrios Vallejo, the railway union head, and renowned muralist David Siqueiros, former communist party secretary.

Despite the troubles, López Mateos climaxed his presidency gracefully in 1964 as he opened the celebrated National Museum of Anthropolgy, appropriately located in Chapultepec Park, where the Aztecs had first settled 20 generations earlier.

In 1964, as several times before, the outgoing president's interior secretary succeeded his former chief. Dour and conservative, Gustavo Díaz Ordaz immediately clashed with liberals in his own party, labor, and students. The pot boiled over just before the 1968 Mexico City Olympics. Reacting to a student rebellion, the army occupied the National University; shortly afterwards, on 2 October government forces opened fire with machine guns on a downtown protest, killing and wounding hundreds of demonstrators.

Despite its serious internal troubles, Mexico's relations with the U.S. were cordial. President Lyndon Johnson visited and unveiled a statue of Abraham Lincoln in Mexico City. Later, Díaz Ordaz met with President Richard Nixon in Puerto Vallarta.

Meanwhile, bilateral negotiations produced the Border Industrialization Program. Within a 12-mile strip south of the border, foreign companies could assemble duty-free parts into finished goods and export them without any duties on either side. Within a dozen years, a swarm of such plants, called *maquiladoras,* were humming with hundreds of thousands of Mexican workers assembling and exporting billions in shiny consumer goods—electronics, clothes, furniture, pharmaceuticals, and toys—worldwide.

Concurrently, in Mexico's interior, Díaz Ordaz pushed Mexico's industrialization ahead full steam. Heavy foreign borrowing financed hundreds of new plants and factories. Primary among these was the giant Las Truchas steel plant at the new industrial port and town of Lázaro Cárdenas at the Pacific mouth of the Río Balsas.

Burgeoning prosperity and social programs boosted Mexico past most of the Third World in health, education, and income standards during the post-WW II decades. In terms of calories, 1970-generation Mexicans were eating twice as well as their grandparents. During the same time, life expectancy had doubled to nearly developed-world standards while infant mortality had dropped from a whopping 36% to five percent. Illiteracy had likewise plummeted to below 10%, and millions of Mexican families had joined the middle class, with cars, TVs, refrigerators, and children in high school and college.

ECONOMY AND GOVERNMENT

Despite huge gains, Mexico's 20th-century revolution remains incomplete. The land reform program, once thought to be a Mexican cure-all, is stalled. The *ejidos* of which Emiliano Zapata dreamed have become mostly symbolic. The communal fields are typically small; capital for machines and fertilizers and the expertise to use them are lacking. Farms are consequently inefficient. In corn, for example, the average Mexican field produces one-fifth as much per acre as a U.S. farm. Mexico must consequently use its precious oil dollar surplus to import millions of tons of food annually.

Economic Trouble of the 1980s

To make matters worse, Mexico's oil boom dollars of the 1970s aren't as plentiful as they used to be. President Luis Echeverría Alvarez (1970-76), diverted by his interest in international affairs, passed on a huge foreign debt to his successor, José López Portillo. The gigantic oil discoveries and burgeoning production only temporarily relieved Mexico's financial problems.

However, the world petroleum glut during the early 1980s finally burst the bubble and plunged Mexico into financial crisis. When the 1982 interest came due on its foreign debt, Mexico's largest holding company couldn't pay the $2.3 billion owed. The peso humiliatingly plummeted more than fivefold, to 150 per U.S. dollar. At the same time, prices were doubling every year.

But by the mid-1980s, President Miguel de la Madrid (1982-88) was straining to get Mexico's economic house in order. He sliced government and raised taxes, asking rich and poor alike to tighten their belts. Despite getting foreign bankers to reschedule Mexico's debt, de la Madrid couldn't stop inflation. Prices were skyrocketing as the peso deflated to 2,500 per U.S. dollar, becoming one of the world's most devalued currencies by 1988.

All this has made life rocky for Mexican wage-earning families. With inflation rapidly eroding their income (around $2000 per capita), the average family has to scratch hard to make ends meet.

But in Mexico averages mean little. A primary socio-economic reality of Mexican history remains: a few Mexicans are very rich; most are very poor. Despite recent gains, the typical Mexican family owns neither car nor refrigerator. The children do not finish elementary school, nor do their parents practice birth control.

Goverment and the Economy

On paper, Mexico's government appears much like its U.S. model: a federal presidency, a two-house congress, and a supreme court, with their counterparts in each of the 32 states. Political parties field candidates, and citizens vote by secret ballot.

Appearances, however, are sometimes deceiving. Although minority parties, such as the pro-Catholic PAN (Partido Acción Nacional or National Action Party) and the PRD (Partido Revolucionario Democratico), mount periodic gadfly challenges, presidents and governors have been traditionally hand-picked by the PRI. Political bosses and police have run roughshod over political opponents. Elections lost at the polling place have been won by faked recounts, threats, mayhem, and even murder.

Public disgust led to significant opposition during the 1988 presidential election. Billionaire PAN candidate Michael Clothier and liberal National Democratic Front candidate Cuauhtémoc Cárdenas ran against the PRI's Harvard-educated technocrat Carlos Salinas de Gortari. The vote was split so evenly that all three candidates claimed victory. Although Salinas eventually won the election, his showing, barely half of the vote, was the worst ever for a PRI president.

Salinas, however, became Mexico's "Coming Man" of the '90s. He was serious about democracy, sympathetic to the *indígenas* and the poor, and sensitive to women's issues. His major achievement, despite significant national opposition, was the North American Free Trade Agreement (NAFTA), which he, U.S. President George Bush, and Canadian Prime Minister Brian Mulroney negotiated in 1992.

Incoming U.S. President Bill Clinton continued the drama by pushing NAFTA through the U.S. Congress in November, 1993, and the Mexican legislature followed suit two weeks later. However, on the very day in January 1994 that NAFTA took effect, rebellion broke out in the poor, remote state of Chiapas. A small but well-disciplined *campesino* force, calling itself the Zapatista Liberation Front, captured a number of provincial towns and held the former governor of Chiapas hostage. Although PRI officials minimized the uprising and President Clinton expressed confidence in the Mexican government, many thoughtful observers wondered if Mexico was ready for NAFTA.

To further complicate matters, Mexico's already tense drama veered toward tragedy. While Salinas de Gortari's chief negotiator, Manuel Camacho Solis, was attempting to iron out a settlement with the Zapatista rebels, Luis Donaldo Colosio, Salinas's handpicked successor, was gunned down, just months before the August balloting. The nation, however, instead of disintegrating, united in grief; opposition candidates eulogized their fallen former opponent, and later earnestly engaged his replacement, stolid technocrat Ernesto Zedillo, in Mexico's first presidential election debate.

In a closely watched election marred by relatively few irregularities, Zedillo piled up a solid plurality against his PAN and PRD opponents. By perpetuating the PRI's 65-year hold on the presidency, the electorate had again opted for the PRI's familiar although imperfect middle-aged revolution.

Zedillo, however, had little time to savor his victory. The peso, long propped up by his predecessor's fiscal policies, lost one-third of its value in the few days before Christmas, 1994. After the dust settled a month later, the peso was trading at about six per dollar, and Mexican financial institutions, their dollar debt having nearly doubled in a month, were in danger of defaulting on their obligations to international investors. To stave off a worldwide financial panic, U.S. President Clinton, in February 1995, secured an unprecedented multibillion dollar loan package for Mexico, guaranteed by U.S. and international institutions.

Although disaster was temporarily averted and Mexico became an overnight bargain for dollar-spending travelers, the cure to Mexico's ills now necessitates another painful round of inflation and belt-tightening for poor Mexicans.

Strength, nevertheless, can spring from adversity. If President Zedillo can keep a lid on inflation, press legal reforms, and continue building bridges with his political opposition, he may be able to lead Mexico to a renewed basis of economic strength and political maturity so firm that his party could even afford, someday, to lose the presidential election.

But, whatever future candidates—liberal PRD, conservative PAN, or PRI—are chosen to lead the country into the 21st century, they will inherit both Mexico's problems and promise. The fact that the major parties now partly agree on the problems may be the beginning of a solution— a new Mexican revolution, this time economic—in which millions of jobs in new industries and enterprises will help Mexicans finally achieve their enormous but as yet untapped human potential.

NATIVE PEOPLES OF MEXICO

AM = Amuzgo	MA = Mazatec
CHC = Chocho	MI = Mixe
CHT = Chatino	MX = Mixtec
CHI = Chinantec	NA = Nahua
CHN = Chontal	TA = Tarascan
CO = Cora	(Purépecha)
CUI = Cuicatec	TE = Tepehuan
HUA = Huave	TP = Tlapanec
HUI = Huichol	TR = Trique
IX = Ixcatec	ZP = Zapotec

PEOPLE

Let a broad wooden chopping block represent the high plain, the *altiplano* of Mexico; imagine taking a sharp cleaver and hacking at one side of it until it is cut by a dozen grooves and pocked with voids. That fractured half resembles Mexico's central highlands, where most Mexicans, divided from each other by high mountains and yawning *barrancas,* have lived for millennia.

The Mexicans' deep divisions, in large measure, led to their downfall at the hands of the Spanish conquistadores. The Aztec empire Cortés conquered was a vast but fragmented collection of tribes. Speaking more than a hundred mutually alien languages, those original Mexicans viewed each other suspiciously, as barely human barbarians from strange lands beyond the mountains. And even today the lines that Mexicans still draw between themselves—of caste, class, race, and wealth—result, to a significant degree, from the realities of their mutual isolation.

POPULATION

The Spanish colonial government and the Roman Catholic religion provided the glue that

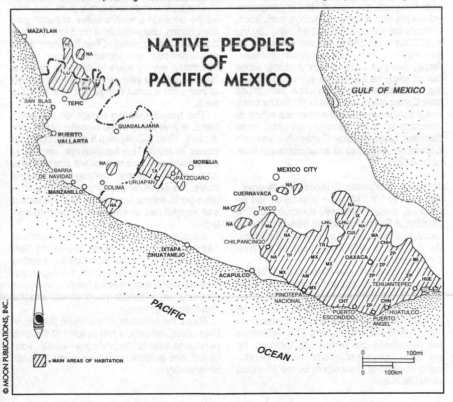

NATIVE PEOPLES OF PACIFIC MEXICO

MAZATLAN

SAN BLAS · TEPIC

PUERTO VALLARTA

GUADALAJARA

BARRA DE NAVIDAD

MANZANILLO · COLIMA · URUAPAN · PATZCUARO

MORELIA

MEXICO CITY

CUERNAVACA

TAXCO

CHILPANCINGO

IXTAPA ZIHUATANEJO

ACAPULCO

PINOTEPA NACIONAL

PUERTO ESCONDIDO · PUERTO ANGEL

OAXACA

TEHUANTEPEC

HUATULCO

GULF OF MEXICO

PACIFIC OCEAN

= MAIN AREAS OF HABITATION

0   100mi
0   100km

© MOON PUBLICATIONS, INC.

Rich colors, graceful designs, and fine quality draw streams of visitors to Teotitlán del Valle weaving village near Oaxaca.

over 400 years has welded Mexico's fragmented people into a nation. Mexico's population, officially estimated at around 90 million by the mid-1990s, is exploding. This was not always so. Historians estimate that European diseases, largely measles and smallpox, probably wiped out as many as 20 million—perhaps 95%—of the native population within a few generations after Cortés stepped ashore in 1519. The Mexican population dwindled to a mere one million inhabitants by 1600. It wasn't until 1950, more than four centuries after Cortés, that Mexico's population recovered to its preconquest level of 25 million.

Mestizos, *Indígenas,* Criollos, and *Negros*
Although by 1950 Mexico's population had recovered, it was completely transformed. The *mestizo,* a Spanish-speaking person of mixed blood, had replaced the pure Native American, the *indígena* (een-DEE-hay-nah), as the typical Mexican.

The trend continues. Perhaps three of four Mexicans would identify themselves as mestizo, that class whose part-European blood elevates them, in Mexican mind, to the level of *gente de razón*—people of "reason" or "right." And there's the rub. The *indígenas* (or, mistakenly but commonly, Indians), by the usual measure of income, health, or education, squat at the bottom of the Mexican social ladder.

The typical *indígena* family lives in a little adobe house in a remote valley, subsisting on corn, beans, and vegetables from its small unirrigated *milpa* (cornfield). Often there are chickens, a few pigs, and sometimes a cow, but no electricity; even if there is, however, the few hundred dollars a year cash income isn't enough to buy even a small refrigerator, much less a truck.

The typical mestizo family, on the other hand, enjoys many of the benefits of the 20th century. They usually own a modest concrete house in town. The furnishings, simple by developed-world standards, will often include an electric refrigerator, washing machine, gas stove, television, and a car or truck. The children go to school every day, and the eldest son sometimes even looks forward to college.

Sizable *negro* communities, descendants of 18th-century African slaves, live in the Gulf states and along the Guerrero-Oaxaca coastline of Pacific Mexico. Last to arrive, the *negros* experience discrimination at the hands of everyone else and are integrating very slowly into the mestizo mainstream.

Above the mestizos, a tiny criollo (Mexican-born white) minority, a few percent of the total population, inherits the privileges—wealth, education, and political power—of colonial Spanish ancestry.

THE INDÍGENAS

Although anthropologists and census takers classify them according to language groups (such as Nahuatl, Mixtec, and Zapotec), indígenas typically identify themselves as residents of a particular locality rather than by language or ethnic grouping. And although as a group they are referred to as indígenas (native, or aboriginal), individuals are generally made uncomfortable (or may even feel insulted) by being labeled as such.

While the mestizos are the emergent self-conscious majority class, the indígenas, as during colonial times, remain the invisible people of Mexico. They are politically conservative, socially traditional, and tied to the land. On market day, the typical indígena family might make the trip into town. They bag up some tomatoes, squash, or peppers, and tie up a few chickens or a pig. The rickety country bus will often be full, and the mestizo driver may wave them away, giving preference to his friends, leaving them to trudge stoically along the road.

INDIGENOUS POPULATIONS OF PACIFIC MEXICO

STATE	INDIGENOUS POPULATION (over five years of age)	TOTAL POPULATION (over five years of age)	PERCENT OF TOTAL
Oaxaoa	1,018,000	2,603,000	39.1%
Guerrero	299,000	2,228,000	13.4%
Michoacán	106,000	3,037,000	3.4%
Sinaloa	31,000	1,924,000	1.6%
Jalisco	25,000	4,585,000	0.5%
Nayarit	24,000	712,000	3.4%
Colima	1,500	372,000	0.4%

POPULATION		IMPORTANT CENTERS
By Language Grouping:		
Zapotec	402,000	Central, East, and South Oaxaca (Tlacolula)
Mixtec	387,000	West, Central, and Coastal Oaxaca (Santiago Jamiltepec)
Mazatec	168,000	North Oaxaca
Chinantec	104,000	Guerrero-Oaxaca (Ometepec)
Nahua	100,000	Guerrero (Taxco and Chilpancingo)
Mixe	95,000	East Oaxaca
Tarasco	95,000	Michoacán (Pátzcuaro)
Tlapanec	69,000	East Guerrero (Tlapa de Comonfort)
Chatino	29,000	South Oaxaca (Miahuatlán)
Amusgo	28,000	Oaxaca-Guerrero (Xochistlahuaca)
Chontal	24,000	Southeast Oaxaca (Tequisistlán)
Huichol	20,000	Nayarit-Jalisco (San Andrés)
Trique	15,000	North Oaxaca
Chocho	13,000	North Oaxaca (Telixtlahuaca)
Cuicatec	13,000	North Oaxaca
Cora	12,000	Nayarit (Acaponeta)
Huave	12,000	Southeast Oaxaca (Rincón Juárez)
Nahua	5,000	Jalisco and Colima (Ciudad Guzmán and Maruata)
Tepuan	5,000	Sinaloa

Note: All figures (probably low) are taken from the 1990 census.

Their situation has been slowly improving. *Indígena* families often now have access to a local school and a clinic. Improved health has led to a large increase in their population. Official census figures, however, are probably low. *Indígenas* are traditionally suspicious of government people, and census takers, however conscientious, seldom speak the local language.

Recent figures nevertheless indicate that about eight percent of Mexicans are *indígenas*—that is, they speak one of Mexico's 50-odd native languages. Of those, about a quarter speak no Spanish at all. These fractions, moreover, are changing slowly. Many *indígenas* prefer the old ways. If present trends continue, 500 years after the conquest, about the year 2019 will mark the return of the Mexican indigenous population to the preconquest level of roughly 25 million.

Indian Language Groups

The Maya speakers of Yucatán and the aggregate of the Nahuatl (Aztec language) speakers of the central plateau are Mexico's most numerous *indígena* groups, totaling roughly three million (one million Maya, two million Nahuatl).

Indigenous population centers, relatively scattered in the north of Pacific Mexico, concentrate in the southern states of Guerrero and Oaxaca. The groups are not evenly spread, however. The language map of Oaxaca, for example, looks like a crazy quilt, with important Zapotec, Mixtec, and other centers scattered along the coast and through the mountains surrounding Oaxaca city.

Dress

Maps and figures, however, cannot describe the color of a fiesta or market day. Many country people, especially in Oaxaca, still wear the traditional cottons, which blend the Spanish and native styles. Men usually wear the Spanish-origin straw sombrero (literally, "shade-maker") on their heads, baggy white cotton shirt and pants and leather *huaraches* on their feet. Women's dress is often more colorful. This can include a *huipil* (long, sleeveless dress), often embroidered in bright floral and animal motifs, and a handwoven *enredo* (wrap-around skirt that identifies the wearer with a particular local-

ity). A *faja* (waist sash) and, in the winter, a *quechquémitl* (shoulder cape) complete the costume.

RELIGION

"God and Gold" was the two-pronged mission of the conquistadores. Most of them concentrated on gold, while missionaries tried to shift the emphasis to God. They were famously successful: more than 90% of Mexicans profess to be Catholics.

Catholicism, spreading its doctrine of equality of all persons before God and incorporating native gods into the church rituals, eventually brought the Indians into the fold. Within a hundred years, nearly all Mexican Indians accepted the new religion, which raised the universal God of all humankind over local tribal deities.

The Virgin of Guadalupe

Conversion of the native Mexicans was sparked by the vision of Juan Diego, a simple farmer. On the hill of Tepeyac north of Mexico City in 1531, Juan Diego saw a brown-skinned Virgin Mary enclosed in a dazzling aura of light. She told him to build a shrine in her memory on that spot, where the Aztecs had long worshipped their "earth mother," Tonantzín. Juan Diego's brown Virgin told him to go to the cathedral and relay her instruction to Archbishop Zumárraga.

The archbishop, as expected, turned his nose up at Juan Diego's story. The vision returned, however, and this time Juan Diego's brown Virgin realized that a miracle was necessary. She ordered some roses to be grown (a true miracle, since roses had been previously unknown in the vicinity) and taken to the archbishop. Juan Diego wrapped the roses in his rude fiber cape, returned to the cathedral, and placed the wrapped roses at the archbishop's feet. When he opened the offering, Zumárraga gasped: imprinted on the cape was an image of the Virgin herself—proof positive of a genuine miracle.

In the centuries since Juan Diego, the brown Virgin—La Virgen Morena, or Nuestra Señora La Virgen de Guadalupe—has blended native and Catholic elements into something uniquely Mexican. In doing so, she has become the virtual patroness of Mexico, the beloved symbol of Mexico for *indígenas,* mestizos, *negros,* and criollos alike.

Every Mexican city, town, and village celebrates the cherished memory of their Virgin of Guadalupe on 12 December. This celebration, however joyful, is but one of the many fiestas Mexicans, especially the *indígenas,* live for.

Each village holds its local fiesta in honor of their patron saint, who is often a thinly veiled sit-in for some local preconquest deity. Themes often appear Spanish—Christians vs. Moors, devils vs. priests—but the native element is strong, sometimes dominant. During Semana Santa (Holy Week) at Pinotepa Nacional in coastal Oaxaca, for example, Mixtec people, costumed as Jews, shoot arrows skyward, simultaneously reciting traditional Mixtec prayers.

Jaguar God, Monte Albán

BOB RACE

ON THE ROAD

SPORTS AND RECREATION

BEACHES

It's easy to understand why many vacationers stay right at the beach. And not just at the famous crystalline stretches of Mazatlán, Puerto Vallarta, Manzanillo, Ixtapa, Acapulco, and Puerto Escondido. Many flee the big resorts and spread out along the whole coast—gathering at small beach resorts such as San Blas, Rincón de Guayabitos, Playa Azul, and Puerto Ángel—while others set up camp and enjoy the solitude and rich wildlife of hundreds of miles of even more pristine strands. Shorelines vary from mangrove-edged lagoons and algae-decorated tidepools to shoals of pebbles and sand of dozens of colors and consistencies.

Sand makes the beach, and Pacific Mexico has plenty, from warm, black mica dust to cool, velvety, white coral. Some beaches drop steeply to turbulent, close-in surf, fine for fishing. Others are level, with gentle, rolling breakers, made for surfing and swimming.

Beaches are fascinating for the surprises they yield. Pacific Mexico's beaches, especially the hidden strands near resorts and the hundreds of miles of wilderness beaches and tidepools, yield troves of shells and treasures of flotsam and jetsam for those who enjoy looking for them. **Beachcombing** is more rewarding during the summer storm season, when big waves deposit acres of fresh shells—among them conch, scallop, clams, combs of Venus, whelks, limpets, olives, cowries, starfish, and sand dollars.

Beaches near rivermouths during the summer-fall rainy season are often fantastic outdoor galleries of wind- and water-sculpted snags and giant logs deposited by the downstream flood.

Viewing Wildlife
Wildlife watchers should keep quiet and always be on the alert. Animal survival depends on them seeing you first. Occasional spectacular offshore sights, such as whales, porpoises, and manta rays, or an on-shore giant constrictor, beached

squid or octopus, crocodile, or even a jaguar looking for turtle eggs are the reward of those prepared to recognize them. Don't forget your binoculars and your *Field Guide to Mexican Birds*.

For extensive notes on good hiking, tide-pooling, wildlife-viewing, and shell-browsing spots, see each chapter's "Sights" section.

WATER SPORTS

Swimming, surfing, windsurfing, snorkeling, scuba diving, kayaking, sailing, and jet-skiing are Pacific Mexico's water sports of choice. For details on local favorite spots, conditions, rental shops, equipment, see "Sports and Recreation" in each travel chapter.

Safety First
As viewed from Pacific Mexico beaches, the Pacific Ocean usually lives up to its name. Many protected inlets, safe for child's play, dot the coastline. Unsheltered shorelines, on the other hand, can be deceiving. Smooth water in the calm forenoon often changes to choppy in the afternoon; calm ripples lapping the shore in March can grow to hurricane-driven walls of water in November. Such storms can wash away sand, changing a wide, gently sloping beach into a steep one, plagued by turbulent waves and treacherous currents.

Undertow, whirlpools, crosscurrents, and occasional oversized waves can make ocean swimming a fast-lane adventure. Getting unexpectedly swept out to sea or hammered onto the beach bottom by a surprise breaker are major hazards.

Never attempt serious swimming when tipsy or full of food; never swim alone where someone can't see you. Always swim beyond the breakers (which come in sets of several, climaxed by a big one, which breaks highest and farthest from the beach). If you happen to get caught in the the path of such a breaker, avoid it by diving under and letting it roll harmlessly over you. If you do get caught by a serious breaker, try to roll and tumble with it (as football players tumble) to avoid injury.

Now and then swimmers get a nettlelike jellyfish sting. Be careful around coral reefs and beds of sea urchins; corals can sting (like jellyfish) and you can get infections from coral cuts and sea-urchin spines. Shuffle along sandy bottoms to scare away stingrays before stepping on one. If you're unlucky, its venomous tail-spines may inflict a painful wound. (See "Staying Healthy" under "Other Practicalities" for first-aid measures.)

Snorkeling and Scuba Diving
Many exciting clear-water sites, such as Puerto Vallarta's Los Arcos, Zihuatanejo's Playa Las Gatas, Isla Roqueta at Acapulco, and Playa Estacahuite at Puerto Ángel await both beginner and expert skin divers. Veteran Pacific Mexico divers usually arrive during the dry winter and

Balmy water and gentle conditions make afternoon sailing a breeze in many of Pacific Mexico's protected coves and bays.

BRUCE WHIPPERMAN

FISH

A bounty of fish darts, swarms, jumps, and wriggles in Pacific Mexico's surf, reefs, lagoons, and off-shore depths. While many make delicious dinners (albacore, red snapper, pompano), others are tough (sailfish), bony (bonefish), and even poisonous (puffers). Some grow to half-ton giants (marlin, jewfish), while others are diminutive reef-grazers (parrot fish, damselfish, angelfish) whose bright colors are a delight to snorkelers and divers.

ENGLISH NAME	SPANISH NAME	AVERAGE SIZE	COLORS	EDIBILITY	OCCURRENCE
albacore	albacora atún	two to four feet	blue	excellent	deep
angelfish	ángel	one foot	yellow, orange, blue	*	reef
barracuda	barracuda, picuda	two feet	brown	good	deep
black marlin	marlin negro	six feet	blue-black	good	deep
blue marlin	marlin azul	eight feet	blue	poor	deep
bobo	barbudo	one foot	blue, yellow	fair	surf
bonefish	macabi	one foot	blue or silver	poor	inshore
bonito	bonito	two feet	black	good	deep
butterfly fish	muñeca	six inches	black, yellow	*	reef
chub	chopa	one foot	gray	good	reef
croaker	corvina	two feet	brownish	rare and protected	inshore bottoms
damselfish	castañeta	four inches	brown, blue, orange	*	reef
dolphinfish, mahimahi	dorado	three feet	green, gold	good	deep
grouper	garropa	three feet	brown, rust	good	offshore reefs
grunt	burro	eight inches	black, gray	*	rocks, reefs
jack	toro	one to two feet	bluish-gray	good	offshore
jewfish	mero	three feet	brown	good	rocky reef bottoms

barracuda

bonito

ENGLISH NAME	SPANISH NAME	AVERAGE SIZE	COLORS	EDIBILITY	OCCURRENCE
mackerel	*sierra*	two feet	gray with gold spots	good	offshore
mullet	*lisa*	two feet	gray	good	sandy bays
needlefish	*agujón*	three feet	blue-black	good	deep
Pacific porgy	*pez de pluma*	one to two feet	tan	good	sandy shores
parrot fish	*perico, pez loro*	one foot	green, pink, blue, orange	*	reef
pompano	*pómpano*	one foot	gray	excellent	inshore bottoms
puffer	*botete*	eight inches	brown	poisonous	inshore
red snapper	*huachinango, pargo*	one to two feet	reddish pink	excellent	deep
roosterfish	*pez gallo*	three feet	black, blue	excellent	deep
sailfish	*pez vela*	five feet	blue-black	poor	deep
sardine	*sardina*	eight inches	blue-black	good	offshore
seabass	*cabrilla*	one to two feet	brown, ruddy	good	reef and rock crevices
shark	*tiburón*	2-10 feet	black to blue	good	in- and offshore
snook	*róbalo*	two to three feet	black-brown	excellent	brackish lagoons
spadefish	*chambo*	one foot	black-silver	*	reef, sandy bottoms
swordfish	*pez espada*	five feet	black to blue	excellent	deep
triggerfish	*pez puerco*	one to two feet	blue, rust, brown, black	*	reef
wahoo	*peto, guahu*	two to five feet	green to blue	excellent	deep
yellowfin tuna	*atún amarilla*	two to five feet	blue, yellow	excellent	deep
yellowtail	*jurel*	two to four feet	blue, yellow	excellent	offshore

* reef fish are generally too small to be considered edible

damselfish

sailfish

early spring when river outflows are mere trickles, leaving offshore waters clear. In the major tourist centers, professional dive shops rent equipment, provide lessons and guides, and transport divers to choice sites.

While convenient, rented equipment is often less than satisfactory. To be sure, serious divers bring their own gear. This should probably include wetsuits in the winter, when many swimmers begin to feel cold after an unprotected half-hour in the water.

Boarding and Boating
In addition to several well-known surfing beaches, such as Matanchén at San Blas, Puerto Vallarta's Punta Mita, and Boca de Apiza south of Manzanillo, Pacific Mexico has the country's acknowledged best surfing beach at Puerto Escondido.

The surf everywhere is highest and best during the July-November hurricane season, when big swells from storms far out at sea attract platoons of surfers to favored beaches (except at crowded Acapulco Bay, where surfing is off-limits).

Windsurfers, sailboaters, and kayakers—who, by contrast, require more waters—do best in the Pacific Mexico winter or early spring. Then they gather to enjoy the near-ideal conditions at many coves and inlets near the big resorts.

While beginners can have fun with the equipment available from rental shops, serious surfers, windsurfers, sailboaters, and kayakers should pack their own gear.

POWER SPORTS

Acapulco and other big resorts have long been centers for water-skiing, parasailing, and jet-skiing. In parasailing, a motorboat pulls, while a parachute lifts you, like a soaring gull, high over the ocean. After ten minutes they deposit you gently back on the sand. Jet-ski boats are like snowmobiles except they operate on water, where, with a little practice, even beginners can quickly learn to whiz over the waves.

Although the luxury resorts generally provide experienced crews and equipment, crowded conditions increase the hazard to both participants and swimmers. You, as the paying patron, have a right to expect your providers and crew are well-equipped, sober, and cautious.

Beach Buggies and ATVs
Some visitors enjoy racing along the beach and rolling over dunes with beach buggies and ATVs (All-Terrain Vehicles—*motos* in Mexico), balloon-tired, three-wheeled motor scooters. While certain resort rental agencies cater to the growing use of such vehicles, limits are in order. Of all the proliferating high-horsepower beach pastimes, these are the most intrusive. Noise, exhaust and gasoline pollution, injuries to operators and bystanders, scattering of wildlife and destruction of their habitats has led (and I hope will continue to lead) to the restriction of dune buggies and ATVs on beaches.

TENNIS AND GOLF

Most Mexicans are working too hard to be playing much tennis and golf. Although there are almost no public courses or courts, Pacific Mexico's resort centers enjoy excellent private facilities. If you are planning on a lot of golf and tennis, check into one of the many hotels with these facilities. See the destination chapters' "Sports and Recreation" and "Accommodations" headings for plenty of golf and tennis listings.

FISHING AND HUNTING

Experts agree Pacific Mexico is a world-class deep-sea and surf fishing ground. Sportspersons routinely bring in dozens of species from among the more than 600 which have been hooked in Pacific Mexico waters.

Surf Fishing
Most good fishing beaches away from the immediate resort areas will typically have only a few locals (mostly with nets) and fewer visitors. Mexicans typically do little sportfishing. They either make their life from fishing, or they do none at all. Consequently, few shops sell sport-

fishing equipment in Mexico, so you should bring your own surf-fishing equipment, including hooks, lures, line, and weights.

Your best general information source before you leave for Mexico is a good shop around home. Tell them where you're going, and they'll often know the best lures and bait to use and what fish you can expect to catch with them.

In any case, the cleaner the water, the more interesting will be your catch. On a good day, your reward might be *sierras, cabrillas,* porgies, or *pómpanos* pulled from the Pacific Mexico surf.

You can't have everything, however. Foreigners cannot legally take Mexican abalone, coral, lobster, pismo clams, rock bass, sea fans, shrimp, turtles, or seashells. Neither are they supposed to buy them directly from fishermen.

Deep-Sea Fishing
Mazatlán and Manzanillo are renowned spots for the big prize marlin and sailfish, while Zihuatanejo, Puerto Vallarta, and Acapulco run close behind.

A deep-sea boat charter generally includes the boat and crew for a full or half day, plus equipment and bait for two to six persons, not including food or drinks. The full-day price depends upon the season. Around Christmas and New Year and before Easter (when advance reservations will be mandatory) a boat can run $400 at Mazatlán or Manzanillo. At lesser-known resorts, or even at the big resorts during low season, you might be able to bargain a captain down to as low as $200.

Renting an entire big boat is not the only choice. Winter business is sometimes so brisk at resorts that agencies can make reservations for individuals for about $60 per person per day.

Pangas, outboard launches seating two to six passengers, are available for as little $50, depending on the season. Once in Barra de Navidad six of my friends hired a *panga* for $50, had a great time, and came back with a boatload of big tuna, jack, and mackerel. A restaurant cooked them up as a banquet for a dozen of us in exchange for the extra fish and I discovered for the first time how heavenly fresh *sierra veracruzana* can taste.

Bringing Your Own Boat
If you're going to be doing lots of fishing, your own boat may be your most flexible and economical option. One big advantage is you can go to the many excellent fishing grounds the charter boats do not frequent. Keep your equipment simple, scout around, and keep your eyes peeled and ears open for local regulations and customs, plus tide, wind, and fish-edibility information.

Fishing Licenses
Anyone 16 or older who is either fishing or riding in a fishing boat in Mexico is required to have a fishing license. Although Mexican fishing licenses are obtainable from certain travel and insurance agents or at government fishing offices in coastal resorts, save yourself time and trouble by getting your fishing licenses ahead of time by mail from the Mexican Department of Fisheries. Call them first (tel. 619-233-6956, fax 233-0334), at least a month before departure and ask for an application and the license fee (which runs a minimum of about $20, depending upon the period of validity and the fluctuating exchange rate). On the application, fill in the names exactly as they appear on the passports of the persons requesting licenses. Include a cashier's check or a money order for the exact amount, along with a stamped, self-addressed envelope, with your application. Address it to the Mexican Department of Fisheries, 2550 Fifth Ave., Suite 101, San Diego, CA 92103-6223.

Hunting and Freshwater Fishing
Much game, especially winter-season waterfowl and doves, is customarily hunted in freshwater reservoirs and coastal brackish marshes in Sinaloa, Pacific Mexico's northernmost state. Some of the most popular hunting and fishing reservoirs are **Dominguez** and **Hidalgo,** near colonial El Fuerte town (an hour northeast of Los Mochis). Farther south, just north of Culiacán, is reservoir **López Mateos,** while farther south, is lake **Comedero** about two hours by car north of Mazatlán, or six hours north of Tepic.

Bag limits and seasons for game are carefully controlled by the government Secretary of Social Development (Secretaría de Desarrollo Social), SEDESOL. They and the Mexican consular service jointly issue the various required permits through a time-consuming and costly procedure, which, at minimum, runs months and hundreds of dollars. For more details on Mexican hunting regulations and permits, consult the AAA (American Automobile Association) *Mexico Travelbook* (see the Booklist).

Private fee agencies are a must to complete the mountain of required paperwork. Among the most experienced are the **Mexican Hunting Association**, 3302 Josie Ave., Long Beach, CA 90808 (tel. 310-421-1619) and **Wildlife Advisory Service**, P.O. Box 76132, Los Angeles, CA 90076 (tel. 213-398-5797, fax 385-0782). Both of these agencies also arrange guides and accommodations. For many useful hunting and fishing details, including many sites and lodges throughout Northern Mexico, get a copy of Sanborn's *Mexican Hunting and Fishing Guide,* published by Sanborn's insurance agency. Send a check for $7.95 to Sanborn's, P.O. Box 310, McAllen, Texas 78502, or order with credit card by calling (800) 222-0158.

FIESTAS

Here's a list of of national and notable region holidays and festivals. If you happen to be where one of these is going on, get out of your car or bus and join in!

1 Jan: ¡**Feliz Año Nuevo!** Happy New Year! (national holiday)

1-5 Jan.: **Inauguration of the Cora governor** in Jesús María, Nayarit (Cora indigenous dances and ceremonies)

6 Jan.: **Día de los Reyes** ("Day of the Kings"; traditional gift exchange)

17 Jan.: **Día de San Antonio Abad** (decorating and blessing animals)

20 Jan.-2 Feb.: **Fiesta of the Virgin of Candlemas**, in San Juan de los Lagos, Jalisco (Millions, from all over Mexico, honor the Virgin with parades, dances depicting Christians vs. Moors, rodeos, cockfights, fireworks, and much more.)

2 Feb.: **Día de Candelaria** (plants, seeds, and candles blessed; procession, and bullfights)

1-3 Feb.: **Festival of the Sea in San Blas**, Nayarit (dancing, horse races, and competitions)

5 Feb.: **Constitution Day** (national holiday; commemorates the constitutions of 1857 and 1917)

24 Feb.: **Flag Day** (national holiday)

February: The week before Ash Wednesday, usually in late February, many towns stage **Carnaval**—Mardi Gras—extravaganzas.

11-19 March: week before the Day of St. Joseph, in Talpa, Jalisco (food, edible crafts made of colored *chicle* (chewing gum), dancing, bands, and mariachi serenades to the Virgin)

18 March-4 April: **Ceramics and handicrafts fair,** in Tonalá (Guadalajara), Jalisco

19 March: **Día de San José** (Day of St. Joseph)

21 March: **Birthday of Benito Juárez**, the "Lincoln of Mexico" (national holiday)

1-19 April: **Fiesta de Ramos,** in Sayula, Jalisco (on Hwy. 54 south of Guadalajara; local area crafts fair, food, dancing, mariachis)

18-30 April: Big **country fair,** in Tepatitlán, Jalisco (on Hwy. 80 east of Guadalajara; many livestock and agricultural displays and competitions; regional food, rodeos, and traditional dances)

April: **Semana Santa** (pre-Easter Holy Week, culminating in Domingo Santa, Easter national holiday)

1 May: **Labor Day** (national holiday)

May (first and third Wednesday): **Fiesta of the Virgin of Ocotlán,** in Ocotlán, Jalisco (on Lake Chapala, religious processions, dancing, fireworks, regional food)

3 May: **Día de la Santa Cruz** ("Day of the Holy Cross")

3-15 May: **Fiesta of St. Isador the Farmer,** in Tepic, Nayarit (blessing of seeds, animals, and water; agricultural displays, competitions, and dancing)

5 May: **Cinco de Mayo** (defeat of the French at Puebla in 1862; national holiday)

BULLFIGHTING

It is said there are two occasions for which Mexicans arrive on time: funerals and bullfights.

Bullfighting is a recreation, not a sport. The bull is outnumbered seven to one and the outcome is never in doubt. Even if the matador (literally, "killer") fails in his duty, his assistants will entice the bull away and slaughter him in private beneath the stands.

La Corrida de Toros

Mexicans don't call it a "bullfight"; it's the *corrida de toros*, during which six bulls are customarily slaughtered, beginning at 1700 (1600 in the winter). After the beginning parade, the first bull rushes into the ring in a cloud of dust. Three clockwork *tercios* (thirds) define the ritual: the first, the *puyazos*, or "stabs," requires two *picadores* on horseback thrust lances into the bull's shoulders, weakening him. During the second *tercio*, the *bandilleras* dodge the bull's horns to stick three long, streamered darts into his shoulders.

10 May: **Mothers' Day** (national holiday)

10-12 May: **Fiesta of the Coronation of the Virgin of the Rosary,** in Talpa, Jalisco (processions, fireworks, regional food, crafts, and dances)

10-24 May: **Book fair** in Guadalajara (readings, concerts, and international book exposition)

24 June: **Día de San Juan Bautista** ("Day of St. John the Baptist," fairs and religious festivals, playful dunking of people in water)

15 June-2 July: **National Ceramics Fair** in the Tlaquepaque district, Guadalajara (huge crafts fair; exhibits, competitions, and market of crafts from all over the country)

28-29 June: **Regatta** in Mexcaltitán, Nayarit (friendly rivalry between boats carrying images of St. Peter and St. Paul to celebrate opening of the shrimp season)

29 June: **Día de San Pablo y San Pedro** ("Day of St. Peter and St. Paul")

14 Sept.: **Charro Day** ("Cowboy Day" all over Mexico; rodeos)

16 Sept.: **Independence Day** (national holiday; mayors everywhere reenact Father Hidalgo's 1810 **Grito de Dolores** from city hall balconies on the night of 15 September)

4 Oct.: **Día de San Francisco** ("Day of St. Francis")

12 Oct.: **Día de la Raza** (Columbus Day, national holiday that commemorates the union of the races)

12 Oct.: **Fiesta of the Virgin of Zapopan,** in Guadalajara (procession carries the Virgin home to Guadalajara cathedral; regional food, crafts fair, mariachis, and dancing)

October (last Sunday): **Día de Cristo Rey** in Ixtlán del Río, Nayarit ("Day of Christ the King," with "Quetzal y Azteca" and "La Pluma" *indígena* dances, horse races, processions, and food)

1 Nov.: **Día de Todos Santos** ("All Souls' Day," in honor of the souls of children. The departed descend from heaven to eat sugar skeletons, skulls, and treats on family altars.)

2 Nov.: **Día de los Muertos** ("Day of the Dead"; in honor of ancestors. Families visit cemeteries and decorate graves with flowers and favorite food of the deceased.)

20 Nov.: **Revolution Day** (anniversary of the revolution of 1910-17; national holiday)

1 Dec.: **Inauguration Day** (National government changes hands every six years: 1994, 2000, 2006 . . .)

8 Dec.: **Día de la Purísima Concepción** ("Day of the Immaculate Conception)

12 Dec.: **Día de Nuestra Señora de Guadalupe** (Festival of the Virgin of Guadalupe, patroness of Mexico; processions, music, and dancing nationwide, especially celebrated around the church in downtown Puerto Vallarta)

16-24 Dec.: **Christmas Week** (week of *posadas* and piñatas; midnight mass on Christmas Eve)

25 Dec.: **Christmas Day** (*¡Feliz Navidad!;* Christmas trees and gift exchange; national holiday)

31 Dec.: **New Year's Eve**

Bullfights, more correctly corridas de toros, are highly stylized rituals whose outcome is never in doubt.

BOB RACE

Trumpets announce the third *tercio* and the appearance of the matador. The bull—weak, confused, and angry—is ready for the finish. The matador struts, holding the red cape, daring the bull to charge. Form now becomes everything. The expert matador takes complete control of the bull, who rushes at the cape, past his ramrod-erect opponent. For charge after charge, the matador works the bull to exactly the right spot in the ring—in front of the judges, a lovely señorita, or perhaps the governor—where the matador mercifully delivers the precision *estocada* (killing sword thrust) deep into the drooping neck of the defeated bull.

Benito Juárez, as governor during the 1850s, outlawed bullfights in Oaxaca. In his honor, they remain so, making Oaxaca unique among Mexican states.

FESTIVALS AND EVENTS

Mexicans love a party. Middle- and upper-class families watch the calendar for midweek national holidays that create a *puente,* or "bridge" to the weekend and allow them to squeeze in a 3-5 day minivacation. Visitors should likewise watch the calendar. Such holidays (especially Christmas and Semana Santa pre-Easter week) often mean packed buses, roads, and hotels, especially in Pacific Mexico's beach resorts.

Country people, on the other hand, await their local saint's day for an excuse to dress up in their traditional best, sell their wares, join a procession, get tipsy, and do a little dancing in the plaza.

ACCOMMODATIONS

Pacific Mexico has thousands of lodgings to suit every style and pocketbook: world-class resorts, small beachside hotels, homey *casas de huéspedes* (guesthouses), palm-shaded trailer parks, and hundreds of miles of pristine camping beaches. The high seasons, when reservations are generally recommended, are mid-December through March, during pre-Easter week, and the month of August.

The hundreds of accommodations described in this book are positive recommendations—checked out in detail—good choices, from which you can pick, according to your own taste and purse.

Guesthouses and Local Hotels

Most coastal resorts began with an old town, which expanded to a new Zona Hotelera hotel strip, where big hostelries rise along a golden strand. In the old town, near the piquant smells, sights and sounds of traditional Mexico, are the *casas de huéspedes,* where families rent out rooms around their plant-decorated patio.

Guesthouses vary, from scruffy to spic-and-span, and from humble to luxurious. Typically, you can expect a plain room, a shared toilet and hot-water shower, and plenty of atmosphere for your money. Rates average around $10, depending upon amenities. Discounts are often available for long-term stays. *Casas de huéspedes* will rarely be near the beach, unlike many local hotels.

Locally owned and operated hotels make up the most of the recommendations of this book. Many veteran travelers find it hard to understand why people come to Mexico and spend

$200 a day for a hotel room when good alternatives run as little as $20. Most local hotels are dialable (dial 011, the international access code, then 52, the country code, then the local area code and number) directly for information and reservations; and, like the big resorts, many even have U.S. and Canada toll-free 800 information numbers. Always ask about money-saving packages and promotions when reserving.

Many locally run hostelries are right on the beach, sharing the same velvety sand and golden sunsets as their much more expensive international-class neighbors. Local hotels, which depend as much on Mexican tourists as foreigners, generally have clean, large rooms, often with private view balconies, ceiling fans, and toilet and hot water bath or shower. What they often lack are the plush extras—air-conditioning, cable TV, phones, tennis courts, exercise gyms, and golf courses—of the luxury resort hotels.

Luxury Resorts

Pacific Mexico has many beautiful, well-managed international-class resorts. They spread along the pearly strands of Mazatlán, Puerto Vallarta, Manzanillo, Ixtapa, Acapulco, and Bahías de Huatulco. Their super-deluxe amenities, moreover, need not be overly expensive. During the right time of year you can vacation at many of the big-name spots—Sheraton, Westin, Radisson, Hyatt, Holiday Inn—for surprisingly little. While high-season room tariffs ordinarily

run $100-200, low-season (May-Nov., and to a lesser degree, Jan.-Feb.) packages and promotions can cut these prices significantly. Shop around for savings via your Sunday newspaper travel section, travel agents, and by calling the hotels directly through their toll-free 800 numbers.

You will often save additional money if you deal in pesos only. Insist on both booking your lodging for an agreed price in pesos and paying the resulting hotel bill in the same pesos, rather than dollars. The reason is that dollar rates quoted by big resorts are often based on the hotel desk exchange rate, which is customarily about 10%, or even as much as 25%, less than bank rates. For example, if the clerk tells you your hotel bill is $1000, instead of handing over the dollars, or having him mark $1000 on your credit card slip, ask him how much it is in pesos. Using the desk conversion rate, he might say something like 4,000 pesos (considerably less than the 5,000 pesos that the bank might give for your $1000.) Pay the 4,000 pesos or have the clerk mark 4,000 pesos on your credit card slip, and save yourself $200.

Apartments, Condominiums, and Villas

For longer stays, many visitors prefer the convenience and economy of an apartment or condominium or the luxurious comfort of a villa vacation rental. Choices vary, from Spartan studios to deluxe beachfront suites and rambling, view homes big enough for entire extended families.

Guests commonly enjoy swimming pools, even in modest Pacific Mexico lodgings.

BRUCE WHIPPERMAN

RESORT TOLL-FREE NUMBERS

These hotel chains have branches (** = outstanding, * = recommended) at Mazatlán (MZ), Guadalajara (GD), Puerto Vallarta (PV), Manzanillo (MN), Ixtapa (IX), Acapulco (AC), Bahías de Huatulco (BH), and other Pacific Mexico locations.

RESORT	PHONE NUMBER	LOCATION
Camino Real	(800) 7-CAMINO	MZ, GD**, PV**, AC, Oaxaca**
Club Med	(800) CLUBMED	Playa Blanca*, IX, BH*
Club Maeva	(800) GOMAEVA	PV, MN*, BH**
Fiesta Americana	(800) FIESTA-1	GD*, PV**, AC*
Holiday Inn	(800) 465-4329	MZ, GD, IX, BH*
Hyatt	(800) 233-1234	GD*, AC*
Krystal	(800) 231-9860	PV**, IX*
Presidente	(800) 472-2427	IX
Radisson	(800) 333-3333	Nuevo Vallarta*, MN**
Sheraton	(800) 325-3535	PV, IX*, AC, BH*
Westin	(800) 228-3000	PV, IX**

Prices depend strongly upon season and amenities, from $400 per month for the cheapest, to at least 10 times that for the most luxurious.

At the low end, you can expect a clean, furnished apartment within a block or two of the beach, with kitchen and regular maid service. More luxurious condos (which usually rent for $1000 per month and up) are typically high-rise oceanview suites with hotel-style desk services and resort amenities, such as a pool, jacuzzi, sundeck, and beach-level restaurant.

Higher up the scale, villas vary from moderately luxurious homes to sky's-the-limit beach view mansions, blooming with built-in designer luxuries, private pools and beaches, tennis courts, and gardeners, cooks, and maids.

Shopping Around: You'll generally find the best rental deals through on-the-spot local contacts, such as the tourist newspaper want ad section, neighborhood "for rent" signs, or local listing agents.

If you prefer making rental arrangements prior to arrival, some agents (see the Puerto Vallarta, Bucerías, Manzanillo, and Ixtapa-Zihuatanejo "Accommodations" sections) will make long-distance rental agreements.

Additionally, a number of U.S.- and Canada-based agencies list some of the more expensive Pacific Mexico vacation rentals. You can often find their toll-free 800 information and reservations numbers in the want ads or Sunday travel section of a metropolitan daily newspaper, such as the Los Angeles *Times*. Also, local real estate agents, such as Century 21, who specialize in nationwide and foreign contacts, sometimes list (or know someone who does) Pacific Mexico vacation rentals.

Camping

Beach camping is popular among middle-class Mexican families, especially during the Christmas-New Year week and during Semana Santa, the week before Easter.

Other times, tenters and RV campers usually find beaches uncrowded. The best spots (see the destination chapter maps and text for details) typically have a shady palm grove for camping and a *palapa* (palm-thatched) restaurant that serves drinks and fresh seafood. (Heads up for falling coconuts, especially in the wind.) Cost for parking and tenting is often minimal; typically only the price of food at the restaurant.

Days are often perfect for swimming, strolling, and fishing; nights are usually balmy—too warm for a sleeping bag, but fine for a hammock (which allows more air circulation than a tent). Good tents, however, keep out mosquitoes and other pesties, which may be further discouraged with good bug repellent. Tents are generally warm inside, requiring only a sheet or very light blanket for cover.

As for camping on isolated beaches, opinions vary, from dire warnings of *"bandidos"* to

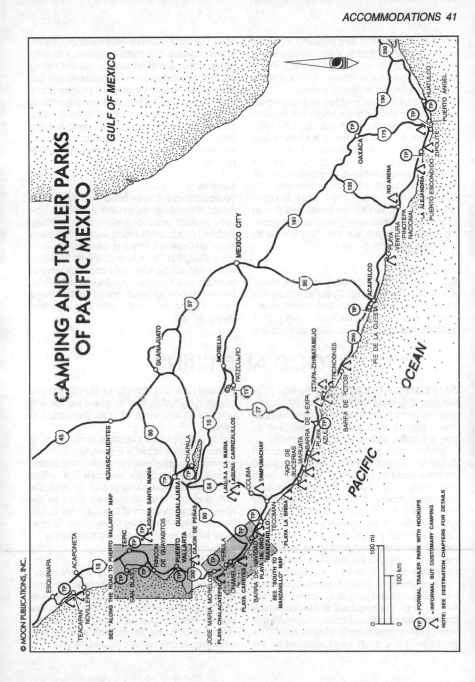

CAMPING AND TRAILER PARKS OF PACIFIC MEXICO

GULF OF MEXICO

PACIFIC OCEAN

TP = FORMAL TRAILER PARK WITH HOOKUPS

= INFORMAL BUT CUSTOMARY CAMPING

NOTE: SEE DESTINATION CHAPTERS FOR DETAILS

© MOON PUBLICATIONS, INC.

SEE "ALONG THE ROAD TO PUERTO VALLARTA" MAP

SEE "SOUTH TO MANZANILLO" MAP

ESQUINAPA
ACAPONETA
TEACAPAN
NOVILLERO
TECUALA
SAN BLAS
TEPIC
RINCON DE GUAYABITOS
PUERTO VALLARTA
LAGUNA SANTA MARIA
CAJON DE PEÑAS
PERULA
CHAMELA
PLAYA CAREYES
JOSE MARIA MORELOS
PLAYA CHALACATEPEC
BARRA DE NAVIDAD
PLAYA DE ORO
MANZANILLO
TECOMAN
AGUASCALIENTES
GUADALAJARA
CHAPALA
LAGUNA LA MARIA
LAGUNA CARRIZALILLOS
COLIMA
TAMPUMACHAY
FARO DE BUCERIAS
PLAYA LA BRISA
PLAYA DE BUCERIAS
MARUATA
BARRA DE NEXPA
PLAYA AZUL
BARRA DE POTOSI
TRONCONES
IXTAPA-ZIHUATANEJO
PIE DE LA CUESTA
ACAPULCO
GUANAJUATO
MORELIA
PATZCUARO
MEXICO CITY
OAXACA
RIO ARENA
PLAYA VENTURA
PINOTEPA NACIONAL
LA ALEJANDRIA
PUERTO ESCONDIDO
ZIPOLITE
PUERTO ANGEL
HUATULCO

100 mi
100 km

45
80
15
54
57
95
125
131
175
190
200
37
200

bland assurances that all is peaceful along the coast. The truth is probably somewhere in between. Trouble is most likely to occur in the vicinity of resort towns, where a few local thugs sometimes harass isolated campers.

When scouting out a campsite, a good general rule is to arrive early enough in the day to get a feel for the place. Buy a soda at the *palapa* or store and take a stroll up the beach. Say "buenos dias," to the people along the way; ask if the fishing is good: *"¿Pesca buena?"* Use your common sense. If the people seem friendly, ask if it's *seguro* (safe). If so, ask permission: *"¿Es bueno acampar aca?"* ("Is it okay to camp around here?"). You'll rarely be refused. For an informative and entertaining discussion of camping in Mexico, check out *The People's Guide to Mexico*. (See the Booklist.)

Trailer Parks
Campers who prefer company to isolation usually stay in trailer parks. Dozens of them dot Pacific Mexico's beaches and inland cities, towns, and scenic mountain spots. (For specifics, see the destination chapter maps and text.) The most luxurious have electricity, water, sewer hookups, and many amenities, including restaurants, recreation rooms, and swimming pools; the humblest are simple palm-edged lots beside the beach. Virtually all of them have good swimming, fishing, and beachcombing. Prices run from a maximum of $14 per night, including air-conditioning power, down to a few dollars for tent space only. Significant discounts are generally available for weekly and monthly rentals.

Palapas
Some *palapas* (thatched beach houses) are still rented in small coastal resorts. Amenities typically include beds or hammocks, a shady thatched porch, cold running water, a kerosene stove, and shared toilets and showers. You usually walk right out your front door onto the sand, where surf, shells, and seabirds will be there to entertain you. Rentals are available in Barra de Nexpa (Michoacán coast, not far north of Playa Azul), Puerto Escondido, and Zipolite (near Puerto Ángel).

FOOD AND DRINK

Some travel to Pacific Mexico for the food. True Mexican food is old-fashioned, home-style fare requiring many hours of loving preparation. Such food is short on meat and long on corn, beans, rice, tomatoes, onions, eggs, and cheese.

Mexican food is the unique end-product of thousands of years of native tradition. It is based on corn—*teocentli,* the Aztec "holy food"—called *maíz* (mah-EES) by present-day Mexicans. In the past, a Mexican woman spent much of her time grinding and preparing corn: soaking the grain in limewater (which swells the kernels and removes the tough seed-coat) and grinding the bloated seeds into meal on a stone *metate.* Finally, she would pat the meal into tortillas and cook them on a hot, baked mud griddle.

Sages (men, no doubt) have wistfully imagined the gentle pat-pat-pat of women all over Mexico to be the heartbeat of Mexico, which they feared would someday cease. Fewer women these days make tortillas by hand. The gentle pat-pat-pat has been replaced by the whir and rattle of automatic tortilla-making machines in myriad *tortillerías,* where women and girls line up for their family's daily kilo-stack of tortillas.

Tortillas are to the Mexicans as rice is to the Chinese and bread to the French. Mexican food is invariably some mixture of sauce, meat, beans, cheese, and vegetables wrapped in a tortilla, which becomes the culinary be-all: the food, the dish, and the utensil all wrapped into one. If a Mexican man has nothing to wrap in his tortilla, he will content himself by rolling a thin filling of *salsa* (chile sauce) into his lunchtime tortilla.

Hot or Not?
Much food served in Mexico is not "Mexican." Eating habits, as most other Mexican customs, depend upon social class. Upwardly mobile Mexicans typically shun the corn-based Indian fare in favor of the European-style food of the Spanish colonial elite: chops, steaks, cutlets, fish, clams, omelettes, soups, pasta, rice, and potatoes.

MEXICAN FOOD

Tortillas y frijoles refritos: cooked brown or black beans, mashed and fried in pork fat, and rolled into tortillas with a dash of vitamin-C-rich salsa to form a near-complete combination of carbohydrate, fat, and balanced protein

Tacos or **taquitos:** tortillas served open or wrapped around any ingredient

Enchiladas and **tostadas:** variations on the filled-tortilla theme. Enchiladas are stuffed with meat, cheese, olives, or beans and covered with sauce and baked, while tostadas consist of toppings served on crisp, open-faced tortillas.

Quesadillas: resemble tostadas, except they're made from soft flour tortillas, rather than corn, and always contain melted cheese

Tamales: as Mexican as apple pie is American. This savory mixture of meat and sauce imbedded in a shell of corn dough and baked in a wrapping of corn husks is rarely known by the singular, however. They're so yummy one tamal invariably leads to more tamales.

Chiles rellenos: fresh roasted green chiles, stuffed usually with cheese but sometimes with fish or meat, coated with batter, and fried. They provide a piquant, tantalizing contrast to tortillas.

Moles (MOH-lays): uniquely Mexican specialties. Mole poblano, a spicy-sweet mixture of chocolate, chiles, and a dozen other ingredients, is cooked to a smooth sauce, then baked with chicken (or turkey, a combination called mole de pavo). So típica it's widely regarded as the national dish.

Guacamole: This luscious avocado, onion, tomato, lime, and salsa mixture remains the delight it must have seemed to its Aztec inventors centuries ago. In Mexico, it's served sparingly as a garnish, rather than in appetizer bowls as is common in the U.S. Southwest.

Sopas: Soups consist of vegetables in a savory chicken broth, and are an important part of both comida (afternoon) and cena (evening) Mexican meals. Pozole, a rich steaming stew of hominy, vegetables, and pork or chicken, often constitutes the prime evening offering of small side street shops. Sopa de taco, an ever-popular country favorite, is a medium-spicy cheese-topped thick chile broth served with crisp corn tortillas.

Tortas: the Mexican sandwich, usually hot meat with fresh tomato and avocado, stuffed between two halves of a crisp bolillo (boh-LEE-yoh) or Mexican bun

Such fare is often as bland as Des Moines on a summer Sunday afternoon. "No picante"—not spicy—is how the Mexicans describe bland food. Caliente, the Spanish adjective for "hot" weather or water, does not, in contrast to English usage, also imply spicy, or picante.

Vegetarian Food
Strictly vegetarian cooking is rare in Mexico, as are macrobiotic restaurants, health-food stores, and organic produce. Meat is such a delicacy for most Mexicans they can't understand why people would give it up voluntarily. If vegetable-lovers can manage with corn, beans, cheese, eggs, legumbres (vegetables), and fruit and not be bothered by a bit of pork fat (manteca de cerdo), Mexican cooking will suit them fine.

Seafood
Early chroniclers wrote that Moctezuma employed a platoon of runners to bring fresh fish 300 miles every day to his court from the sea. In Pacific Mexico, fresh seafood is fortunately much more available from thousands of shoreline establishments, ranging from thatched beach palapas to five-star hotel restaurants.

Pacific Mexico seafood is literally there for the taking. When strolling on the beach, I have often seen well-fed, middle-class local vacationers breaking and eating oysters and mussels right off the rocks. In the summer on the beach at Puerto Vallarta, fish and squid sometimes swarm so thickly in the surf tourists can pull them out by hand. Villagers up and down the coast use small nets (or bare hands) to retrieve a few fish for supper, while communal teams

CATCH OF THE DAY

Ceviche (say-VEE-chay): a chopped raw fish appetizer as popular on Pacific Mexico beaches as sushi is on Tokyo side streets. Although it can contain anything from conch to octopus, the best ceviche consists of diced young shark *(tiburón)* or mackerel *(sierra)* fillet, plenty of fresh tomatoes, onions, garlic, and chiles, all doused with lime juice.

Pescado frito (pays-KAH-doh FREE-toh): Fish, pan-fried whole; if you don't specify that it be cooked lightly *(a medio)*, the fish will arrive well done, like a big, crunchy french fry.

Filete de pescado: fish fillet sautéed *al mojo* (ahl-MOH-hoh)—with butter and garlic.

Pescado veracruzana: a favorite everywhere. Best with red snapper *(huachinango)*, smothered in a savory tomato, onion, chile, and garlic sauce. *Pargo* (snapper), *mero* (grouper), and *cabrilla* (seabass) are also popularly used in this and other specialties.

Shellfish abound: *ostiones* (oysters) and *almejas* (clams) by the dozen; *langosta* (lobster) and *langostina* (crayfish) *asado* (broiled), *al vapor* (steamed), or fried. Pots of fresh-boiled *camarones* (shrimp) are sold on the street by the kilo; cafes will make them into *cóctel,* or prepare them *en gabardinas* (breaded) at your request.

haul in big netfuls of silvery, wriggling fish for sale right on the beach.

Despite the plenty, Pacific Mexico seafood prices reflect high worldwide demand, even at the humblest seaside *palapa*. The freshness and variety, however, make even the typical dishes seem bargains at any price.

Fruits and Juices

Squeezed vegetable and fruit juices *(jugos,* HOO-gohs) and fresh peanut and pecan butter are among the widely available delights of Pacific Mexico. Among the many establishments—restaurants, cafes, and *loncherías*—willing to supply you with your favorite *jugo,* the juice bars *(jugerías)* are often the most fun. Colorful fruit piles usually mark *jugerías;* if you don't immediately spot your favorite fruit, ask anyway; it might be hidden in the refrigerator.

Besides your choice of pure juice, a *jugería* will often serve *liquados*. Into the juice, they whip powdered milk, your favorite flavoring, and sugar to taste for a creamy afternoon pick-me-up or evening dessert. One big favorite is a cool banana-chocolate *liquado,* which comes out tasting like a milk shake minus the calories.

Alcoholic Drinks

The Aztecs usually sacrificed anyone caught drinking alcohol without permission. The later, more lenient, Spanish attitude toward getting *borracho* (soused) has led to a thriving Mexican renaissance of native alcoholic beverages: tequila, *mescal,* Kahlúa, pulque, and *aguardiente.* Tequila and mescal, distilled from the fermented juice of the maguey (century) plant, originated in Oaxaca, where the best are still made. Quality tequila and mescal come 76 proof (38% alcohol) and up. A small white worm, endemic to the maguey plant, is added to each bottle of factory mescal for authenticity.

Pulque, although also made from the sap of the maguey, is locally brewed to a small alcohol content, between beer and wine. The brewing houses are sacrosanct preserves, circumscribed by traditions that exclude both women and outsiders. The brew, said to be full of nutrients, is sold to local *pulquerías* and drunk immediately. If you are ever invited into a *pulquería,* it will be an honor you cannot refuse.

cherimoya

BOB RACE

Aguardiente, by contrast, is the notorious fiery Mexican "white lightning," a locally distilled, dirt-cheap ticket to oblivion for poor Mexican men.

While pulque comes from an age-old Indian tradition, beer is the beverage of modern mestizo Mexico. Full bodied and tastier than "light" U.S. counterparts, Mexican beer enjoys an enviable reputation.

Those visitors who indulge usually know their favorite among the many brands, from light to dark: Superior, Corona, Pacífico, Tecate (served with lime), Carta Blanca, Modelo, Dos Equis, Bohemia, Tres Equis, and Negra Modelo. Nochebuena, a flavorful dark brew, becomes available only around Christmas.

Mexicans have yet to develop much of a taste for *vino* (wine), although some domestic wines, such as the Baja California labels Cetto and Domecq, are quite drinkable.

Bread and Pastries

Excellent locally baked bread is a delightful surprise to many first-time visitors to Pacific Mexico. Small bakeries everywhere put out trays of hot, crispy-crusted *bolillos* (rolls) and sweet *pans dulce* (pastries). They range from simple cakes, muffins, cookies, and doughnuts to fancy fruit-filled turnovers and puffs. Half the fun occurs before the eating: grab a tray and tongs, peruse the goodies, and pick out the most scrumptious. With your favorite dozen finally selected, you take your tray to the cashier, who deftly bags everything up and collects a few pesos (a dollar or two) for your whole mouth-watering selection.

A TROVE OF FRUITS AND NUTS

Besides carrying the usual temperate fruits, *jugerías*, and especially markets, are seasonal sources of a number of exotic (*) varieties:

anona*—*anona:* greenish-pink and creamy, like a Southeast Asian custard apple

avocado—*aguacate* (ah-wah-KAH-tay): Aztec aphrodisiac

banana—*plátano:* many kinds—big and small, red and yellow

chirimoya*—*chirimoya:* green scales, white pulp

coconut—*coco:* coconut "milk" is *agua coco*

grapes—*uvas:* Aug.-Nov. season

guanábana*—*guanábana:* looks (but doesn't taste) like a green mango

guava—*guava:* delicious juice; widely available canned

lemon—*lima* (LEE-mah): uncommon and expensive, use lime instead

lime—*limón* (lee-MOHN): douse salads with it

mamey*—*mamey:* brown skin, red, puckery fruit, like persimmon

mango—*mango:* king of fruit, in a hundred varieties June-Nov.

orange—*naranja* (nah-RAHN-ha): greenish skin, but sweet and juicy

papaya—*papaya:* said to aid digestion and healing

peanuts—*cacahuates* (kah-kah-WAH-tays): home roasted and cheap

pear—*pera:* fall season

peach—*durazno* (doo-RAHS-noh): delicious and widely available as canned juice

pecan—*nuez:* for a treat, try freshly ground pecan butter

pineapple—*piña:* huge, luscious, and cheap

strawberry—*fresa* (FRAY-sah): local favorite

tangerine—*mandarina:* common around Christmas

watermelon—*sandía* (sahn-DEE-ah): perfect on a hot day

zapote*—*zapote* (sah-POH-tay): said to induce sleep

GETTING THERE

BY AIR

From the U.S. and Canada

The vast majority of travelers reach Pacific Mexico by air. Flights are frequent and reasonably priced. Competition sometimes shaves prices down as low as $250 or less for a Mazatlán or Puerto Vallarta roundtrip from Los Angeles, Denver, or Dallas.

Travelers can save even more money by shopping around. Don't be bashful about trying for the best price. Make it clear to the airline or travel agent you're interested in a bargain. Ask the right questions: Are there special incentive, advance-payment, night, midweek, tour-package, or charter fares? Peruse the ads in your Sunday newspaper travel section for bargain-oriented travel agencies. An agent costs you no money, although some don't like discounted tickets because their fee depends on a percentage of ticket price. Nevertheless, many agents will work to get you a bargain.

Although few airlines fly directly to Pacific Mexico from the northern U.S. and Canada, many **charters** do. In locales near Vancouver, Calgary, Ottawa, Toronto, Montreal, and Minneapolis, Chicago, and Cleveland, consult a travel agent. Northern folks can also fly to San Francisco, Los Angeles, Denver, Dallas, or Houston and connect with a direct flight to Pacific Mexico.

From Europe, Australasia, and Latin America

Few, if any, airlines fly across the Atlantic or Pacific directly to Mexico. Travelers from Australasia and Europe generally transfer at New York, Chicago, Dallas, San Francisco, or Los Angeles for Pacific Mexico destinations.

A number of Latin American flag carriers fly directly to Mexico City. From there, easy connections are available via Mexicana or Aeroméxico Airlines to Pacific Mexico destinations.

Baggage, Insurance, "Bumping," and In-Flight Meals

Tropical and temperate Pacific Mexico makes it easy to pack light. See the "Packing Checklist"

AIRLINES TO PACIFIC MEXICO FROM NORTH AMERICA

The busiest scheduled air carriers are Mexicana, Aeroméxico, Delta, Aero California, Alaska, American, Continental, and Canadian airlines.

Destination key: MZ: Mazatlán, PV: Puerto Vallarta, MN: Manzanillo, Guadalajara: GD, Ixtapa-Zihuatanejo: IX, Acapulco: AC, Mexico City: MX

Mexicana (tel. 800-531-7921)
Los Angeles: MZ, PV, GD, IX, MX
San Francisco: GD, MX
San Jose: GD
Tijuana: GD
Denver: MZ, PV, GD, MX
Chicago: PV, GD, AC
Miami: MZ
San Antonio: GD

Aeroméxico (tel. 800-237-6639)
Los Angeles: PV, GD, MN
Tijuana: MZ, PV, GD
New York: GD, MX
Miami: GD, MX
Houston: IX, AC, MX
Tucson: MZ
San Diego: PV, GD

Delta (tel. 800-221-1212)
Los Angeles: MZ, PV, GD, IX, AC, MX
Dallas: AC, MX
Atlanta: MX

Alaska (tel. 800-426-0333)
Seattle: MZ, PV, GD
San Francisco: MZ, PV, GD
Los Angeles: MZ, PV, GD

American (tel. 800-433-7300)
Dallas: PV, GD, AC, MX

Continental (tel. 800-231-0856)
Houston: PV, GD, AC, MX

Canadian Holidays (charter) (tel. 800-426-7000)
Toronto: MZ, PV, AC
Vancouver: MZ, PV, AC
Calgary: MZ, PV, AC

Less-frequented Pacific Mexico destinations, such as Oaxaca, Puerto Escondido, Puerto Ángel, and Bahías de Huatulco are air-accessible by connection through Mexico City.

at the end of this chapter. Veteran tropical travelers often condense their luggage to carry-ons only. Airlines routinely allow a carry-on (not exceeding 45 inches in combined length, width, and girth) and a small book bag and purse. Thus relieved of heavy burdens, your trip will become much simpler. You'll avoid possible luggage loss and long baggage-check-in lines by being able to check in directly at the boarding gate.

Even if you can't avoid having to check luggage, loss of it needn't ruin your vacation. Always carry your **non-replacable items in the cabin with you.** These should include all money, credit cards, traveler's checks, keys, tickets, cameras, passport, prescription drugs, and eyeglasses.

At the X-ray security check, insist your film and cameras be hand-inspected. Regardless of what attendants claim, repeated X-ray scanning will fog any film, especially the sensitive ASA 100 and 1000 high-speed varieties.

Travelers packing lots of expensive baggage, or who (because of illness, for example) may have to cancel a nonrefundable flight or tour might consider buying **travel insurance.** Travel agents routinely sell packages that include baggage, trip cancellation, and default insurance. Baggage insurance covers you beyond the conventional $1250 domestic, $400 international baggage liability limits, but check with your carrier. Trip cancellation insurance pays if you must cancel your prepaid trip, while default insurance protects you if your carrier or tour agent does not perform as agreed. Travel insurance, however, can be expensive. Traveler's Insurance Company (P.O. Box 5040, Hartford, CT 06183) for example, offers $1000 of baggage insurance per person for two weeks for about $50. Carefully weigh both your options and cost against benefits before putting your money down.

It's wise to **reconfirm** both departure and return flight reservations, especially during the busy Christmas and Easter seasons. This is a useful strategy, as is prompt arrival at check-in, against getting "bumped" (losing your seat) because of the tendency of airlines to overbook the rush of high-season vacationers. For further protection, always get your **seat assignment and boarding pass included with your ticket.**

Airlines generally try hard to accommodate travelers with **dietary or other special needs.** When booking your flight, inform your travel agent or carrier of your necessity for either a low-sodium, low-cholesterol, vegetarian, lactose-reduced meal or other requirements. Seniors, handicapped persons, and parents traveling with children, see the "Specialty Travel" section near the end of this chapter for more information.

BY BUS

As air travel rules in the U.S., bus travel rules in Mexico. Hundreds of sleek, luxury- and first-class bus lines with names such as Elite, Three Stars of Gold (Tres Estrellas de Oro), and White Star (Estrella Blanco) roar out daily from the border, headed for Pacific Mexico.

Since none of the North American bus lines cross the border, you must disembark, collect your things, and after having filled out the necessary but very simple paperwork at the immigration booth, proceed on foot across the border to Mexico where you can bargain with one of the local taxis to drive you the few miles to the *camionera central* (bus station).

First-class bus service in Mexico is generally cheaper and is better than in the United States. Tickets for comparable trips in Mexico cost a small fraction (as little as $40 for a thousand-mile trip, compared to perhaps $150 in the U.S.).

In Mexico, as on U.S. buses, you often have to take it like you find it. *Asientos reservados* (seat reservations), *boletos* (tickets), and information must generally be obtained in person at the bus station, and credit cards and traveler's checks are not often accepted. Neither are reserved bus tickets typically refundable, so don't miss the bus. On the other hand, plenty of buses roll south almost continuously.

Bus Routes to Pacific Mexico

From California and the west, cross the border to **Tijuana, Mexicali,** or **Nogales,** where you can ride one of three bus lines along the Pacific coast route (National Hwy. 15) to points south: Tres Estrellas de Oro (or its subsidiary, Elite), Transportes Pacífico, or Transportes Norte de Sonora.

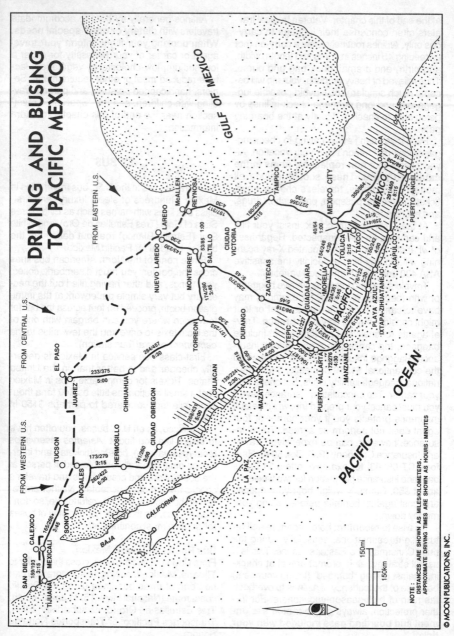

DRIVING AND BUSING TO PACIFIC MEXICO

GULF OF MEXICO

PACIFIC OCEAN

MEXICO

PACIFIC

BAJA CALIFORNIA

LA PAZ

FROM EASTERN U.S.

FROM CENTRAL U.S.

FROM WESTERN U.S.

SAN DIEGO

TIJUANA

CALEXICO
3:15
159/193

MEXICALI
3:45
165/266

SONOYTA

NOGALES
6:30
262/422

TUCSON

EL PASO
5:00
233/375

JUAREZ

HERMOSILLO
3:00
173/279

161/260

CIUDAD OBREGON
2:30
139/224

CHIHUAHUA
6:30
284/457

CULIACAN
288/463
6:00

MAZATLAN

TEPIC
4:00
182/293

DURANGO
3:30
157/253

TORREON

ZACATECAS
5:45
230/382

PUERTO VALLARTA
104/163
2:30
191/307

GUADALAJARA
198/318
5:45

TEPIC
141/227
3:00

MANZANILLO
193/311
4:30

PLAYA AZUL-IXTAPA-ZIHUATANEJO
72/116
2:30

MORELIA
224/361
5:45

TAXCO
74/119
2:15

TOLUCA
154/248
4:30

MEXICO CITY
227/366
7:30

ACAPULCO
130/242
4:00

OAXACA
148/238
8:15

PUERTO ANGEL
291/469
8:15

259/417
6:15

350/564
8:00

40/64
1:00

180/290
4:15

TAMPICO

CIUDAD VICTORIA
197/317
4:30

SALTILLO
53/85
1:00

MONTERREY
143/230
2:30

NUEVO LAREDO
174/280
3:45

LAREDO

McALLEN

REYNOSA

NOTE : DISTANCES ARE SHOWN AS MILES/KILOMETERS.
APPROXIMATE DRIVING TIMES ARE SHOWN AS HOURS : MINUTES

150 mi

150 km

© MOON PUBLICATIONS, INC.

At **Mazatlán** or **Tepic**, depending on the line, you transfer or continue on the same bus, south to Puerto Vallarta, and Manzanillo, or west to Guadalajara. Allow a full day and a bit more (about 30 hours), depending upon connections, for the trip. Carry liquids and food (which might only be minimally available en route) with you.

From the midwest, cross the border from El Paso to **Ciudad Juárez** and ride Estrella Blanca or Omnibus de Mexico via Chihuahua and Durango. At Durango, transfer to a Mazatlán-bound bus, and continue as above. Similarly, from the U.S. southeast and east, cross the border at Laredo to **Nuevo Laredo** and ride Transportes del Norte or Estrella Blanca via Monterrey to Durango. From Durango, transfer to a Mazatlán bus, where you can continue south, as described above.

Travelers heading directly to Acapulco and Pacific Mexico south should ride from the border directly to **Mexico City**. At the main southern Mexico City terminal (Terminal Central del Sur), you can continue south via Flecha Roja, Estrella de Oro or others to Acapulco, thence Ixtapa-Zihuatanejo or Puerto Escondido-Puerto Ángel. From the U.S. border, allow two days travel for Acapulco and Zihuatanejo, and half a day more for Puerto Escondido-Puerto Ángel. (See the chart "Bus Destinations" under "Getting Around" following for more details on Mexican bus travel.)

BY TRAIN

In contrast to airplanes and buses, the train is the leisurely, nostalgic route to Pacific Mexico. Trains roll into sleepy little stations and pass scenery far from the highway clutter and bustle. Instead of being wedged into a cramped seat, you can walk around, go to the restroom, or practice your Spanish with your aisle-mates.

The trains are not for people on a tight time budget. Delays are frequent; the train will sometimes stop and sit inexplicably for many minutes, then back up, and sit again before finally rolling ahead once more.

Mexican railroads are all government-subsidized, and tickets are consequently economical. A first-class coach seat runs less than $100 for a U.S. border-Mazatlán roundtrip. Second-class seating, service, and sanitation, although much cheaper, are poor and dirty. Better to go by bus if you're trying to save money.

Rail Routes to Pacific Mexico
The railroad of choice to Pacific Mexico is the Pacific route, which runs from Mexicali and Nogales, then south to Los Mochis, Mazatlán, Tepic, Guadalajara, and Mexico City. Passengers headed for Manzanillo by rail can continue at Guadalajara southward through Colima to the coast; rail connections are likewise available at Guadalajara for Morelia, Michoacán, where travelers can transfer to a train for Pátzcuaro, continuing south to Lázaro Cárdenas (near Playa Azul) on the coast. Oaxaca-bound rail passengers can similarly transfer at Mexico City and continue through Puebla to Oaxaca. For Pacific Mexico destinations not on rail lines, buses connect from the various railheads: at Tepic, connect to Puerto Vallarta; at Mexico City connect to Acapulco and Ixtapa-Zihuatanejo, and at Oaxaca connect to Puerto Ángel-Escondido. (See the map, "By Rail to Pacific Mexico.")

A popular alternative is to ride the train south from **Ciudad Juárez** and transfer at Chihuahua to the Chihuahua-Pacific Railway, which continues along the renowned **Barranca de Cobre** (Copper Canyon) route to Los Mochis, on the Pacific. Only finished during the early 1960s, this route traverses the spectacular canyon-land-home of the Tarahumara people. The winding, 406-mile (654-km) route parallels the labyrinthine Barranca del Cobre, a canyon so deep its climate varies from Canadian at the top to tropical jungle at the bottom. The railway-stop village of Creel, with a few stores and hotels and a Tarahumara mission, is the major jumping-off point for trips into the canyon. For a treat, reserve a stay en route to Puerto Vallarta at the **Copper Canyon Lodge** in Creel. From there, the canyon beckons: explore the village, enjoy panoramic views, observe mountain wildlife, and breathe pine-scented, mountain air. Farther afield, you can hike to a hot spring, or even spend a few days exploring the canyon bottom itself. For more information, call (800) 776-3942 or (810) 340-7320 or write Copper Canyon Lodges, 2741 Paldan St., Auburn Hills, MI 48326.

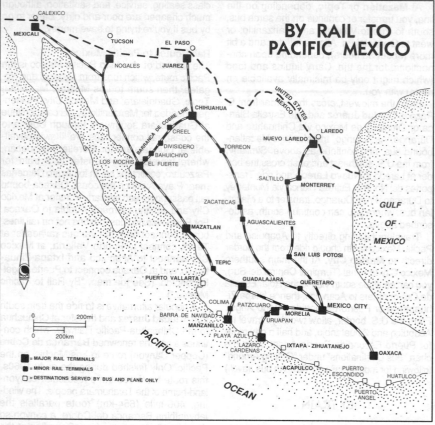

BY RAIL TO PACIFIC MEXICO

© MOON PUBLICATIONS, INC.

= MAJOR RAIL TERMINALS
= MINOR RAIL TERMINALS
= DESTINATIONS SERVED BY BUS AND PLANE ONLY

Some agencies arrange excellent Barranca del Cobre tours. See "Special Tours and Study Options" below for more details.

Train Departures and Tickets

North of the border, advance ticketing and reservations services for Mexican trains are not widely available. However, passenger trains (which depart in the midafternoon daily from Mexicali and Nogales) are almost never full. Most southbound travelers generally buy Mexican train tickets in person on their day of departure. At least one agency does, however, sell Mexican train tickets. Contact Mexico By Train, P.O. Box 2782, Laredo, TX 78044-2782, tel. (800) 321-1699 or tel./fax

(210) 725-3659, for more information, including their informative brochure. You may also call Mexican National Railways for more information, at their San Antonio office, tel. (210) 641-6169.

BY CAR OR RV

If you're adventurous, like going to out-of-the-way places, but still want to have all the comforts of home, you may enjoy driving your car or RV to Pacific Mexico. On the other hand, consideration of cost, risk, wear on both you and your vehicle, and the congestion hassles in towns may change your mind.

Mexican Car Insurance

Mexico does not recognize foreign insurance. When you drive into Mexico, Mexican auto insurance is at least as important as your passport. At the busier crossings, you can get it at insurance "drive-ins" just south of the border. The many Mexican auto insurance companies (AAA and National Automobile Club agents recommend La Provincial and Tepeyac insurance, respectively) are government-regulated; their numbers keep prices and services competitive.

Sanborn's Mexico insurance, one of the best known agents, certainly seems to be trying hard-

est. One of their spokespersons, "Mexico Mike" Nelson, drives 20,000-plus miles of Mexico highway for them each year, gathering information for their lively consumer-oriented newsletter, books, and services that include a guide to RV campgrounds, road map, *Travel With Health* book, "smile-by-mile" *Travelog* guide to "every highway in Mexico," hotel discounts, and a tripshare newsletter. All of the above is available to members of the "Sanborn's Mexico Club." You can buy insurance, sign up for membership, or order books through their toll-free number, (800) 222-0158. For other queries, call (512) 682-1354 or write Sanborn's Mexico, P.O. Box 310, McAllen, TX 78502.

Mexican car insurance runs from a barebones rate of about $2 a day to a more typical $8 a day for more complete coverage ($50,000/ $40,000/$80,000 public liability/property damage/medical payments) on a vehicle worth between $10,000-15,000. On the same scale, insurance for a $50,000 RV and equipment runs about $16 a day. These daily rates decrease sharply for one year policies, which run about $150 for the minimum to $400-800 for complete coverage.

If you get broken glass, personal effects, and legal expenses coverage with these rates, you're lucky. Mexican policies don't usually cover them. You should get something for your money. The deductibles should be no more than $200-400, the public liability/medical payments should be about double the ($25,000/ $25,000/ $50,000) legal minimum, and you should be able to get your car fixed in the U.S. and receive payment in U.S. dollars for losses. If not, shop around.

A Sinaloa Note of Caution

Although bandidos no longer menace Mexican roads, be cautious in the infamous drug-growing region of Sinaloa state north of Mazatlán. Do not stray from Hwy. 15 between Culiacán and Mazatlán and Hwy. 40 between Mazatlán and Durango. Curious tourists have been assaulted in the hinterlands adjacent to these roads.

The Green Angels

The Green Angels have answered many motoring tourists' prayers in Mexico. Bilingual teams of two, trained in auto repair and first

DISASTER AND RESCUE ON A MEXICAN HIGHWAY

My litany of Mexican driving experiences came to a climax one night when, heading north from Tepic, I hit a cow at 50 mph head on. The cow went flying about 150 feet down the road, while I and my two friends endured an impromptu rollercoaster ride.

All was well that ended well, however at least for we humans. Two buses stopped and about 40 men got out to move my severely wounded van to the shoulder. The cow's owner arrived to cart off the remains of his animal in a jeep. Then the police—a man and his wife in a VW bug—pulled up. *"Pobrecita camioneta,"* "Poor little van," the woman said, gazing at my vehicle, which now resembled an oversized, rumpled accordion. They gave us a ride to Mazatlán, found us a hotel room, and generally made sure we were okay.

If I hadn't had Mexican auto insurance I would have been in deep trouble. Mexican law—based on the Napoleonic Code—presumes guilt and does not bother with juries. It would have kept me in jail until all damages were settled. The insurance agent I saw in the morning took care of everything. He called the police station, where I was excused from paying damages when the cow owner failed to show. He had my car towed to a repair shop, where the mechanics banged it into good enough shape so I could drive it home a week later. Forced to stay in one place, I and my friends enjoyed the most relaxed time of our entire three months in Mexico. The *pobrecita camioneta,* all fixed up a few months later, lasted 14 more years.

SAFE RULES OF THE ROAD

Hundreds of thousands of visitors enjoy safe Mexican auto vacations every year. Their success is due in large part to their frame of mind: drive defensively, anticipate and adjust to danger before it happens, and watch everything—side roads, shoulders, the car in front, and cars far down the road.

Tips for motorists in Mexico include:

Don't drive at night. Animals, unmarked sand piles, pedestrians, one-lane bridges, cars without lights, and drunk drivers are doubly hazardous at night.

Although **speed limits** are rarely enforced, *don't break them.* Mexican roads are often narrow and shoulderless. Poor markings and macho drivers who pass on curves are best faced at a speed of 40 mph (64 kph) rather than 75 (120).

Even with four-wheel-drive, you'll eventually get stuck if you drive either often or casually on sand. When the tide comes in, who'll pull your car out?

Slow down at the *topes* (speed bumps) at the edges of towns and for *vados* (dips), which can be dangerously bumpy and full of water.

Yielding the **courtesy of the road** goes hand-in-hand with safe driving. Both courtesy and machismo are more infectious in Mexico; on the highway, it's much safer to spread the former than the latter.

aid, help distressed tourists along main highways. They patrol fixed stretches of road twice daily by truck. To make sure they stop to help, pull completely off the highway and raise your hood. You may want to hail a passing trucker to call them; dial toll-free 91-800-903-02 for the tourism hotline, which will alert the Green Angels for you.

If, for some reason, you have to leave your vehicle on the roadside, don't leave it unattended. Hire a local teenager or adult to watch it for you. Unattended vehicles on Mexican highways are quickly stricken by a mysterious disease, the symptoms of which are rapid loss of vital parts.

Mexican Gasoline

Pemex, short for Petróleos Mexicanos, the government oil monopoly, markets only two grades of gasoline: **Nova** (or "no va," which translates as "no go") regular leaded 82 octane, and 92 octane **Magna** "Sin" plomo ("Without" lead). Magna Sin is good gas, yielding performance similar to U.S.-style "super-unleaded" gasoline.

On main highways, Pemex makes sure major stations (typically spaced about 50 miles apart) stock Magna Sin. Since Mexicans typically use leaded gas, local stations, especially in outlying areas, do not customarily stock Magna Sin.

Gas Station Thievery

Kids who hang around gas stations to wash windows are notoriously light-fingered. When stopping at the *gasolinera,* make sure your cameras, purses, and other movable items are out of reach. Also, make sure your car has a **lockable gas cap.** If not, insist on pumping the gas yourself, or be super-watchful as you pull up to the gas pump. **Make certain the pump reads zero** before the attendant pumps the gas. Sad, but true, such overcharging for gas and oil is common, especially among teenage gas-station workers.

A Healthy Car

Preventative measures spell good health for both you and your car. Get that tune-up (or long-delayed overhaul) *before,* rather than after, you leave.

Carry a stock of spare parts, which will probably be both more difficult to get and more expensive in Mexico than at home. Carry an extra tire or two, a few cans of motor oil and octane enhancer, oil and gas filters, fan belts, spark plugs, tune-up kit, points, and fuses. Carry basic tools and supplies, such as screwdrivers, pliers (including Vise-Grip), lug wrench and jack, adjustable wrenches, tire pump and patches, pressure gauge, steel wire, and electrical tape. For breakdowns and emergencies, carry a folding shovel, a husky rope or chain, a gasoline can, and flares.

Car Repairs in Mexico

The American big three—General Motors, Ford, and Chrysler—and Nissan and Volkswagen are well represented by extensive dealer networks in Mexico. Getting your car or truck serviced at such agencies is usually straightforward. While parts will probably be higher, shop rates run about half U.S. prices, so repairs will generally come out cheaper than back home.

The same is not true for repairing other makes. Mexico has few, if any, Toyota or other Japanese car or truck dealers; other than Mercedes-Benz, which has some Mexican agencies, it is generally difficult to find officially certified mechanics for any British and European makes other than Volkswagen.

Many clever Mexican **independent mechanics,** however, can often fix any car that happens to come their way. Their humble *talleres mechánicos* (tah-YER-ays may-KAH-nee-kohs) (repair shops) dot the town and village roadsides everywhere.

Although most mechanics are honest, beware of unscrupulous operators who try to collect double or triple their original estimate. If you don't speak Spanish, find someone who can assist you in negotiations. **Always** get a cost estimate, including needed parts and labor, in writing, even if you have to write it yourself. Make sure the mechanic understands, then ask him to sign it before he starts work. Although this may be a hassle, it might save you a much nastier hassle later. Shop labor at small, independent, repair shops should typically run between $10 and $20 per hour. For much more information, and entertaining anecdotes of car and RV travel in Mexico, consult Carl Franz's *The People's Guide to Mexico.* (See the Booklist.)

Highway Routes from the U.S.

If you've decided to drive to Pacific Mexico, you have your choice of four general routes. At safe highway speeds, each of these routes require about 24 hours of driving time. For comfort and safety, most folks allow three full south-of-the-border driving days to Pacific Mexico.

From the U.S. Pacific coast and west, follow National Hwy. 15 from the border at **Nogales,** Sonora, an hour's drive south of Tucson, Arizona. Highway 15 continues southward smoothly, leading you through cactus-studded mountains and valleys, which green to lush farmland and tropical coastal plain by the time you arrive in Mazatlán. Peripheral bypasses *(periféricos)* route you past the congested downtowns of Hermosillo, Guaymas, Ciudad Obregón, and Culiacán. Between these centers, you speed along, via *cuota* (toll) expressways virtually all the way to Mazatlán. If you prefer not to pay the high tolls (around $50 total for a passenger car, much more for multiple-wheeled RVs) you should stick to the old *libre* (free) highway. Hazards, bumps, and slow going might force you to reconsider.

From Mazatlán, continue along the narrow two-lane route to Tepic, where Hwy. 15 heads east to Guadalajara and Hwy. 200 forks south to Puerto Vallarta. From there you can continue along Hwy. 200 southward along the entire plumy southern coast of Pacific Mexico.

If, however, you're driving to Pacific Mexico from the **central U.S.,** cross the border at El Paso to **Ciudad Juárez,** Chihuahua. There, the mostly two-lane National Hwy. 45 leads you southward through high dry plains through the cities of Chihuahua, Jiménez, and Hidalgo del Parral, to **Durango.** At Durango, head west along the winding but spectacular trans-Sierra National Hwy. 40, which intersects National Hwy. 15 just south of Mazatlán. From there, continue south as described above.

Folks heading to Pacific Mexico from the **eastern and southeastern U.S.** should cross the border from Laredo, Texas, to **Nuevo Laredo.** From there, National Hwy. 85 heads southwest toward sprawling Monterrey. On the city outskirts, follow the west (Saltillo-direction) bypass, which soon connects with National Hwy. 40. Continue westward on the two-lane asphalt highway—through Saltillo, Torreón and Durango over the Pacific crest all the way to National Hwy. 15, just south of Mazatlán. Continue southward, as described above.

If you're heading from the midwest or eastern U.S. directly to Pacific Mexico's southern destinations of Acapulco, Ixtapa-Zihuatanejo, or Oaxaca you should cross the border from McAllen, Texas to Reynosa. From there, head southward to Mexico City (see the special topic "Mexico City Driving Restrictions" in the Acapulco chapter), where you continue south via toll expressway 95 to Acapulco.

For more Mexico travel information, including updates on tolls, new highways, and much more, call Mexican tourism's hotline, (800) 662-MEXI.

Bribes *(Mordidas)*

The usual meeting ground between visitors and Mexican police is in their car on the highway or downtown street. To tourists, such cases sometimes appear as mild harassment, accompanied by vague threats of having to go to the police station, or having their car impounded for such-and-such a violation. The tourists often go on to say that "It was all right, though. We paid him ten dollars and he went away. Mexican cops sure are crooked, aren't they?"

And I suppose, if people want to go bribing their way through Mexico, that's their business. But calling the Mexican cops crooked isn't exactly fair. Police, like most everyone else in Mexico, have to scratch for a living, and they have found many tourists are willing to slip them a ten-dollar bill for nothing. Rather than crooked, I would call them hungry and opportunistic.

BY FERRY

The ferry from La Paz at the tip of Baja California across to Los Mochis or Mazatlán is a tempting route option, especially for travelers without cars. If you try to take your car or RV, you may get "bumped" by the large volume of commercial traffic (regardless of your reservation). You may end up stuck in La Paz with no way to get to the mainland except by a thousand-mile detour up the Baja Peninsula. The vehicle fares, moreover, are very high to Mazatlán: at least $100 for cars and much more for large RVs. Fares to Los Mochis are more reasonable.

What's more, the ferry situation often changes. For numbers to call for updated information and for addresses and numbers to contact for ferry reservations, try calling Mexican Tourism's information number (800) 662-MEXI. Better still, write or call "Mexico Mike" Nelson at Sanborn's Mexico Insurance, P.O. Box 310 McAllen, TX 78502, tel. (512) 682-1354, who makes it his business to know about volatile ferry schedules.

BY TOUR, CRUISE, AND SAILBOAT

For travelers on a tight time budget, prearranged tour packages can provide a hassle-free route for sampling the attractions of Pacific Mexico. If, however, you prefer a self-paced vacation, or desire thrift over convenience, you should probably defer tour arrangements until after arrival. Many Pacific Mexico resort agen-

cies, which are as close as your hotel telephone or lobby-front tour desk, can customize a tour for you. Options range from city highlight tours and bay snorkeling adventures to inland colonial cities shopping and sightseeing overnights and boat adventures through wildlife-rich mangrove jungle hinterlands. For locally arranged tours and guides, see the "Information" and "Sights" sections in destination chapters.

By Cruise or Sailboat

Travel agents will typically have a stack of cruise brochures that include Pacific Mexico ports such as Puerto Vallarta and Acapulco on their intineraries. People who enjoy being pampered with lots of food and ready-made entertainment (and don't mind paying for it) generally have great fun on cruises. Accommodations on a typical 10-day winter cruise can run as as little as $100 per day, per person, double occupancy to as much as $1000 or more.

If, however, you want to get to know Mexico and the local people, a cruise is not for you. On-board, food and entertainment is the main event of a cruise; shore sightseeing excursions, which generally cost extra, are a sideshow.

Sailboats, on the other hand, offer an entirely different kind of sea route to Pacific Mexico. Ocean Voyages, a California-based agency, arranges passage on a number of sail and motor vessels that regularly depart to Pacific Mexico from west coast ports, such as San Diego, Los Angeles, San Francisco, and Vancouver, British Columbia. They offer customized itineraries and flexible arrangements that vary from complete roundtrip voyages to weeklong coastal idylls between palmy Pacific Mexico ports of call. Some captains allow passengers to save money by signing on as crew. For more information, contact Ocean Voyages, 1709 Bridgeway, Sausalito, CA 94965, tel. (415) 332-4681, fax 332-7460.

Special Tours and Study Options

Some tours and work-study programs include in-depth activities centered around language and culture, wildlife-viewing, ecology, or off-the-beaten-track adventuring.

A number of agencies arrange interesting Copper Canyon tours (see "By Train" above). Outstanding among them are programs by Elderhostel, AAAS (American Association for the Advancement of Science), and Mexi-Maya Academic Travel, Inc. The Elderhostel tour, designed for seniors, is arranged with Cochise Community College. For details, write or call for their international catalog Elderhostel, 75 Federal St., Boston, MA 02110-1941, tel. (617) 426-0856. The naturalist-guided AAAS Copper Canyon tour is arranged by Betchart Expeditions, Inc., 21601 Stevens Creek Blvd., Cupertino, CA 95014. Call their toll-free number, (800) 252-4910 for information and a brochure. The nine-day Mexi-Maya trip includes visits to Chihuahua Mennonite colonies, the Tarahumara Indian mission in Creel, and climaxes with a Mayo Indian fiesta (or an Easter pageant) near Los Mochis. For details, contact Mexi-Maya Academic Travel, Inc., at 2216 W. 112th St., Chicago, IL 60643, tel. (312) 233-1711, fax 239-1208.

Mar de Jade, a holistic-style living center at Playa Chacala, about fifty miles (80 km) north of Puerto Vallarta, offers unique people-to-people work-study opportunities. These include Spanish language study at Mar de Jade's rustic beach study-center and/or assisting at their health clinic in Las Varas town nearby. They also offer accommodations and macrobiotic meals for travelers who would want to do nothing more than stay a few days and enjoy Mar de Jade's lovely tropical ambience.

For more details of the Mar de Jade area and accommodations, see "Mar de Jade" under "Along the Road to Puerto Vallarta." For more information about their course schedule and fees, write Mar de Jade, Apdo. Postal 81, Las Varas C.P. 63715, Nayarit, Mexico, or dial the clinic officially, the Casa Clínica de la Mujer Campesina, in Las Varas Monday, Wednesday, or Friday 1000-1300 directly at 011-52-327-200-42, or telex FEDEME 065552, Puerto Vallarta.

Adventurous, physically fit travelers might enjoy the off-the-beaten-path biking, snorkeling, fishing, kayaking, hiking, and sightseeing tours of Seattle-based **Outland Adventures.** Their itineraries (typically about $100 per day) run three to 10 days and include lots of local color and food, accommodations in small hotels, and sightseeing in the Puerto Vallarta region of beaches, forest trails, mangrove lagoons, and country roads. Itineraries, besides Puerto Vallarta itself, include villages of Rincón de Guayabitos, San Francisco and the Costa Azul Adventure Resort (see "South of Guayabitos" under "Rincón de Guayabitos and Vicinity"),

Mismaloya, Chamela, Tenacatita, La Manzanilla, and Barra de Navidad. For more information, contact Outland Adventures, P.O. Box 16343, Seattle, WA 98116, tel. and fax (206) 932-7012.

A Puerto Vallarta ranch, Rancho El Charro, Francisco Villa 895, Fracc. Las Gaviotas, Puerto Vallarta, Jalisco 48300, tel. (322) 401-14, organizes naturalist-led horseback treks in the mountains near Puerto Vallarta. Tours run a minimum of one week, which includes two or three days of guided backcountry horsebacking, exploring idyllic colonial villages, camping out on the trail, swimming and hot-tubbing, and hearty dinners and cozy evenings at luxurious haciendas. Tariffs begin at $900 per person, complete.

The remote **Revillagigedos Islands** (ray-vee-yah-hee-HAY-dohs), about 300 miles (500 km) due west of Puerto Vallarta, are a de facto treasury of marine and onshore wildlife. A number of high islands, among them Bagerón, Mexico's youngest (1952) volcano, have recently been the destination of winter **Oceanic Society** expedition-tours from La Paz, Baja California. The deluxe tour (about eight days, $4000 per person) usually covers seven islands and includes marine mammal watching, snorkeling, birding and eco-exploring, both on- and offshore. For details, contact the Oceanic Society, Fort Mason Center, Building E, San Francisco, CA 94123, tel. (800) 326-7491 or (415) 441-1106, fax 474-3395.

This trip might make an exciting overture or finale to your Mexico vacation. You can ride either Mexicana from Los Cabos or Aeroméxico from La Paz via Guadalajara if you are going directly between Puerto Vallarta and the expedition's point of departure.

Tours by Train

Some private agencies arrange rail tours and packages. Among them are Mexico Air and Rail Vacations, 8607 Wurzbach Rd., Suite V-100, San Antonio, TX 78240, which arranges rail-hotel tourist packages south from the Mexicali, Nogales, Juárez, and Nuevo Laredo border railheads. For more information, call them toll-free at (800) 228-3225, or local tel. (210) 727-3814, Mon.-Fri. 0900-1700. Another similar service is Mexico By Train, P.O. Box 2782, Laredo, TX 78044-2782, toll-free tel. (800) 321-1699, local tel./fax (210) 725-3659.

GETTING AROUND

BY AIR

Mexicana and Aeroméxico, and some smaller carriers, such as Aero California, Aeromorelos, Aviacsa, and Taesa, connect many of the main destinations of Pacific Mexico. In the north, a scheduled network connects Mazatlán, Puerto Vallarta, Guadalajara, Manzanillo-Barra de Navidad and other Mexican destinations. In the south, the same is true of Ixtapa-Zihuatanejo, Acapulco, Puerto Escondido, Puerto Ángel-Huatulco, and Oaxaca. Although much pricier than first-class bus tickets, domestic air fares are on a par with U.S. prices.

Travelers may book tickets by contacting agencies in the destination cities. (See destination chapters for airlines' local agency phone numbers.)

Local Flying Tips

If you're planning on lots of in-Mexico flying, get the airlines' handy, although rapidly changeable, *itinerarios de vuelo* (flight schedules) booklets at the airport.

Mexican airlines have operating peculiarities that result from their tight budgets: don't miss a flight; you will likely lose half the ticket price. Adjusting your flight date may cost 25% of the ticket price. Get to the airport an hour ahead of time. Last-minute passengers are often "bumped" in favor of earlybird waitees. Conversely, go to the airport and get in line if you must catch a flight that the airlines have claimed to be full. You might get on anyway. Keep your luggage small so you can carry it on. Lost luggage victims receive scant compensation in Mexico.

BY BUS

The bus is the king of the Mexican road. Dozens of lines connect virtually every town in Pacific Mexico. Three distinct levels of service—luxury or super first-class, first-class, and second-class—are generally available. **Super first-class** (usually called something like "Primera Plus," depending upon the line) luxury express coaches speed between major towns, seldom stopping en route. In exchange for relatively high fares (about $50 Puerto Vallarta-Guadalajara, for example) passengers enjoy rapid passage and airline-style amenities: plush reclining seats, air-conditioning, and on-board toilet, video, and aisle attendant.

Although much less luxurious, **first-class** service costs two-thirds less, is frequent, and always includes reserved seating. Additionally, passengers usually enjoy soft reclining seats and air-conditioning (if it is working). Besides their regular stops at or near most towns and villages en route, first-class bus drivers, if requested, will usually stop and let you off anywhere along the road.

Second-class bus seating is unreserved. In outlying parts of Pacific Mexico, there is a class of buses even beneath second-class, but given the condition of many second-class buses, it usually seems as if third-class buses wouldn't run at all. Second-class buses are the stuff of travelers' legends: the recycled old GMC, Ford and Dodge schoolbuses that stop everywhere and carry everyone and everything to the smallest villages tucked away in the far mountains. As long as there is any kind of a road to it, such a bus will most likely go there.

Now and then you'll read a newspaper story of a country bus that went over a cliff somewhere in Mexico, killing the driver and a dozen unfortunate souls. The same newspapers never bother to mention the half-million safe trips the same bus provided during its 15 years of service prior to the accident.

Second-class buses are not for travelers with weak knees or stomachs. You will often initially have to stand, cramped in the aisle, among a crowd of *campesinos*. They are warm-hearted, but poor people, so don't tempt them with open, dangling purses or wallets bulging in back pockets. Stow your money safely away. After a while, you will probably be able to sit down. Such privilege, however, comes with obligation, such as holding an old lady's bulging bag of carrots or a toddler on your lap. But if you accept your burden with humor and equanimity, who knows what favors and blessings may flow to you in return.

Tickets, Seating, and Baggage

Mexican bus lines do not usually publish schedules or fares. You have ask someone (such as your hotel desk clerk) who knows, or call (or have someone call) the bus station. Few travel agents handle bus tickets. If you don't want to spend the time to get a reserved ticket yourself, hire someone trustworthy to do it for you. Another way of doing it all is to get to the bus sta-

tion early enough on your traveling day to assure you'll get a bus to your destination.

Although some lines accept credit cards and issue computer-printed tickets at their major stations, most reserved bus tickets are sold for cash and handwritten, with a specific seat number *(número de asiento)* on the back. If you miss the bus, you lose your money. Furthermore, airlines-style automated reservations systems have not yet arrived at many Mexican bus stations. Consequently, you can generally buy reserved tickets only at the local departure *(salida local)* station. (An agent in Manzanillo, for ex-

BUS DESTINATIONS

DESTINATIONS	BUS LINES
Acapulco (Guerrero)	EB, EO, FR
Barra de Navidad (Jalisco)	AP, TCL, TEO
Colima (Colima)	AO, OM, TEO
Guadalajara (Jalisco)	AP, EB, EL, OM, TEO, TNS, TP
Lázaro Cárdenas (Michoacán)	EB, GA, RP, TEO
Manzanillo (Colima)	AO, ASJ, EL, GA, TCL, TEO, TNS
Mazatlán (Sinaloa)	EB, EL, TC, TEO, TNS, TP
Oaxaca (Oaxaca)	ADO, CC
Pátzcuaro (Michoacán)	AO, GA, RP, TEO
Pinotepa Nacional (Oaxaca)	EB, FR
Puerto Ángel (Oaxaca)	CC, EB
Puerto Escondido (Oaxaca)	CC, EB
Puerto Vallarta (Jalisco)	EL, TCL, TEO, TNS, TP
Rincón de Guayabitos (Nayarit)	EL, TEO, TNS, TP
San Blas (Nayarit)	TNS
Bahías de Huatulco (Oaxaca)	EB, CC
Taxco (Guerrero)	EO, FR
Tepic (Nayarit)	EL, TEO, TNS, TP
Zihuatanejo (Guerrero)	EB, EO, FR

Bus Key

ADO—Autobuses del Oriente
AO—Autobuses del Occidente
AP—Autocamiones del Pacífico
ASJ—Autotransportes Sur de Jalisco
CC—Cristóbal Colón
EB—Estrella Blanca
EL—Elite
EO—Estrella de Oro
FA—Flecha Amarilla
FR—Flecha Roja
GA—Galeana
OM—Ómnibus de Mexico
RP—Ruta de Paraíso
TC—Transportes Chihuahuenses
TCL—Transportes Cihuatlán
TEO—Tres Estrellas de Oro
TNS—Transportes Norte de Sonora
TP—Transportes del Pacifico

See "Getting There and Away" in travel chapters for more detailed bus information. See also "Second-Class Buses" in this same section.

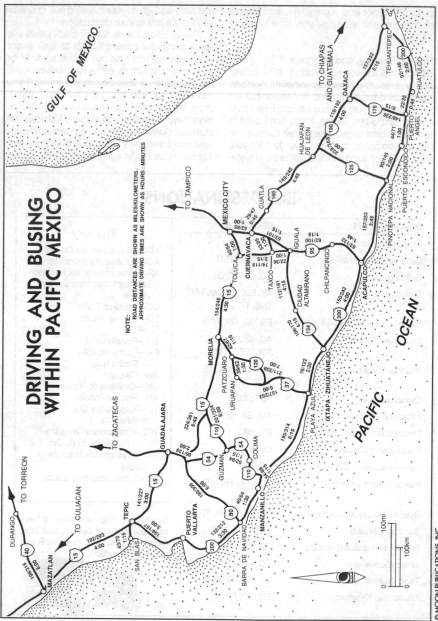

DRIVING AND BUSING WITHIN PACIFIC MEXICO

GULF OF MEXICO

PACIFIC OCEAN

NOTE:
ROAD DISTANCES ARE SHOWN AS MILES/KILOMETERS.
APPROXIMATE DRIVING TIMES ARE SHOWN AS HOURS : MINUTES

TO TORREON

TO CULIACAN

TO ZACATECAS

TO TAMPICO

TO CHIAPAS AND GUATEMALA

DURANGO

MAZATLAN

TEPIC

SAN BLAS

PUERTO VALLARTA

BARRA DE NAVIDAD

MANZANILLO

COLIMA

GUZMAN

GUADALAJARA

URUAPAN

PATZCUARO

MORELIA

PLAYA AZUL

IXTAPA · ZIHUATANEJO

ACAPULCO

CHILPANCINGO

CIUDAD ALTAMIRANO

TAXCO

TOLUCA

CUERNAVACA

MEXICO CITY

CUATLA

IGUALA

HUAJAPAN DE LEON

OAXACA

TEHUANTEPEC

PUERTO ANGEL

HUATULCO

PUERTO ESCONDIDO

PINOTEPA NACIONAL

188/318
6:00

40
15
15

182/293
4:00

141/227
3:00

43/70
1:15

104/167
3:00

132/212
3:30

200

190/306
6:30

40/64
1:30

110

52/84
1:15

54
54

110
120

224/361
5:45

20/32
6:30

15

39/62
1:30

15

86/139
2:00

7:00

211/339
5:15

157/253
5:00

37

195/314
6:15

76/122
2:30

200

134

159/242
4:00

50/96
1:30

63/101
1:15

112/181
4:15

74/119
2:15

40/64
1:00

154/248
4:30

95

157/253
3:45

83/133
3:45

SP-1

53/85
1:00

29/47
1:00

160

149/240
4:45

125

90/145
2:00

44/71
1:00

118/182
4:00

175

190

226/368
6:00

157/252
5:15

148/238
6:15

22/35
0:45

92/148
2:00

21/33
2:00

200

0   100mi

0   100km

© MOON PUBLICATIONS, INC.

ample, cannot ordinarily reserve you a ticket on a bus that originates in Zihuatanejo, a day's travel down the road.)

Request a reserved seat number, if possible, from numbers 1 to 25 in the front *(delante)* to middle *(medio)* of the bus. The rear seats are often occupied by smokers, drunks, and general rowdies. At night, you will sleep better on the right side *(lado derecho)* away from the glare of oncoming traffic lights.

Baggage is generally secure on Mexican buses. Label it, however. Overhead racks are often too cramped to accommodate airline-size carry-ons. Carry a small bag of your crucial

items on your person; pack clothes and less essentials in your checked luggage. For peace of mind, watch the handler put your checked baggage on the bus and watch to make sure it is not mistakenly taken off the bus at intermediate stops.

If, somehow, your baggage gets misplaced, remain calm. Bus employees are generally competent and conscientious; if you are patient, recovering your luggage will become a matter of honor for many of them. Baggage handlers are at the bottom of the pay scale; a tip for their mostly thankless job would be very much appreciated.

ROAD SIGNS

STOP

RAILROAD CROSSING

YIELD RIGHT OF WAY

SPEED BUMPS

ONE WAY

TWO WAY

PARKING

NO PARKING

DIP (across arroyo)

DIP (across arroyo)

BUS STOP

KEEP TO THE RIGHT

On long trips, carry food, drinks, and toilet paper. Station food may be dubious and the sanitary facilities ill-maintained.

If you are waiting for a first-class bus at an intermediate *salida de paso* (passing station), you often have to trust to luck there will be an empty seat. If not, your best option may be to ride a usually much more frequent second-class bus.

BY TRAIN OR CAR

Although trains connect several points in Pacific Mexico, they are slow and the routes circuitous. And even if you decide on a train option, you often will have to take long bus rides to make connections to get to the places where the train doesn't go. Better to take the bus in the first place.

Driving your car in Mexico may or may not be for you. (See "By Car or RV" in the preceding "Getting There" section.)

BY RENTAL CAR, TAXI, TOUR, AND HITCHHIKING

Car and jeep rentals are an increasingly popular transportation option for Pacific Mexico travelers. They offer mobility and independence for local sightseeing and beach excursions. In the resorts, the gang's all there: Hertz, National, Avis, Budget, and a host of local outfits. They generally require drivers to have a valid driver's license, passport, a major credit card, and may require a minimum age of 25. Some local companies do not accept credit cards, but offer lower rates in return.

Base prices of international agencies, such as Hertz, National, and Avis are not cheap. They run more than in the U.S., with a 10% "value added" tax tacked on. The cheapest possible rental car, usually a stick-shift VW Beetle, runs between $40-60 per day or $250-450 per week, depending on location and season. Prices are steepest during high Christmas and pre-Easter weeks. Before departure, use the international agencies' free 800 numbers to shop around for availability, prices, and reservations (see the chart). During non-peak seasons, you may save lots of pesos by waiting till arrival and renting a car through a local agency. Shop around, starting with the agent in your hotel lobby, or the local *Yellow Pages* (under "Automoviles, renta de").

Car insurance, which covers property damage, public liability, and medical payments, is a must with your rental car. If you get into an accident without insurance, you will be in deep trouble, probably jail. Driving in Mexico is more hazardous than back home. For important car safety and insurance information, see "By Car or RV" in the preceding "Getting There."

Taxis

The high prices of rental cars make taxis a viable option for local excursions. Cars are luxuries, not necessities, for most Mexican families. Travelers might profit from the Mexican money-saving practice of piling everyone in a taxi for Sunday park, beach, and fishing outings. You may find that an all-day taxi and driver (who, besides relieving you of driving, will become your impromptu guide) will cost less than a rental car.

The magic Mexican word for saving money by taxi is *colectivo:* a taxi that you share jointly with other travelers. Your first place to practice getting a taxi will be at the airport, where *colectivo* tickets are routinely sold from booths at the terminal door.

If, however, you want want your own private taxi, ask for a *taxi especial,* which will probably run about three or four times the individual tariff for a *colectivo.*

Your airport experience will prepare you for in-town taxis, which rarely have meters. You must establish the price before getting in. Bargaining comes with the territory in Mexico, so don't

CAR RENTAL TOLL-FREE NUMBERS

COMPANY	TEL. IN U.S.	TEL. IN CANADA
Avis	(800) 331-1084	(800) 879-2847
Budget	(800) 527-0700	(800) 527-0700
Dollar	(800) 800-6000	(800) 800-4000
Hertz	(800) 654-3001	(800) 654-3131
National	(800) 227-3876	(800) 227-7368

shrink from it, even though it seems a hassle. If you get into a taxi without an agreed-upon price, you are letting yourself in for a more serious, potentially nasty hassle later. If your driver's price is too high, he'll probably come to his senses as soon as you hail another taxi.

After a few days, getting taxis around town will be a cinch. You'll find you don't have to take the high-ticket taxis lined up in your hotel driveway. If the price isn't right, walk toward the street and hail a regular taxi.

In town, if you can't seem to find a taxi, it may be because they are all hanging around waiting for riders at the local stand, called a taxi *sitio*. Ask someone to direct you to it: Say *"Excúseme. ¿Donde está el sitio taxi, por favor?"* ("Excuse me. Where is the taxi stand, please?")

Tours and Guides

For many Pacific Mexico visitors, locally arranged tours offer a hassle-free alternative to rental car or taxi sightseeing. Hotels and travel agencies, many of whom maintain front-lobby travel and tour desks, offer a bounty of sight-seeing, water sports, bay cruise, fishing, and wildlife-viewing tour opportunities. For details, see both the "Sights" and "Information" sections in each destination chapter.

Hitchhiking

Most everyone agrees hitchhiking is not the safest mode of transport. If you're unsure, don't do it. Hitchhiking doesn't make a healthy steady travel diet, nor should you hitchhike at night.

The recipe for trouble-free hitchhiking requires equal measures of luck, savvy, and technique. The best places to catch rides are where people are arriving and leaving anyway, such as bus stops, highway intersections, gas stations, RV parks, and on the highway out of town.

Male-female hitchhiking partnerships seem to not the most rides (although it is technically illegal for women to ride in commercial trucks). The more gear you and your partner have, the fewer rides you will get. Pickup and flatbed truck owners often pick up passengers for pay. Before hopping onto the truck bed, ask how much the ride will cost.

OTHER PRACTICALITIES

TOURIST CARDS AND VISAS

For U.S. and Canadian citizens, entry by air into Mexico for a few weeks could hardly be easier. Airline attendants hand out tourist cards *(tarjetas turísticas)* en route, and officers make them official by glancing at passports and stamping the cards at the immigration gate. Business travel permits for 30 days or less are handled by the same simple procedures.

Otherwise, Mexican consulates, Mexican government tourist offices, offices of airlines serving Mexico, border immigration authorities, auto clubs (AAA and National Auto Club), and certain travel agencies issue free tourist cards to all travelers 15 years old or over who present proper identification. Rules state U.S. citizens must show either birth certificate, valid U.S. passport, or military I.D., while naturalized citizens must show naturalization papers or valid U.S. passport.

Canadian citizens must show a valid passport or birth certificate. Nationals of other countries (especially those, such as Hong Kong, which issue more than one type of passport) may be subject to additional entry regulations. For advice, consult your closest Mexican tourist information office or consulate. See chart "Mexican Information Offices and Consulates" below.

More Options

For more complicated cases, get your tourist card early enough to allow you to consider the options: tourist cards can be issued for multiple entries and a maximum validity of 180 days; photos are often required. If you don't request multiple entry or the maximum time, your card will probably be stamped single entry, valid for some shorter period, such as 90 days. If you are not sure how long you'll stay in Mexico, request the maximum and bring passport photos. One hundred eighty days is the absolute maximum for a tourist card; long-term foreign residents routinely make semiannual "border runs" for new tourist cards.

Student and Extended Business Visas

A visa is a notation stamped and signed into your passport showing the number of days and entries allowable for your trip. Apply for visas at the consulate nearest your home well in advance of your departure. One-year renewable student visas and business visas longer than the routine 30 days are available, though often with considerable red tape. Check with your local Mexican consulate for details; an ordinary 180-day tourist card may be the easist option, if you can manage it.

Your Passport

Your passport (or birth or naturalization certificate) is your positive proof of national identity; without it, your status in any foreign country is in doubt. Don't leave home without one. United States citizens may obtain passports at local post offices.

Don't Lose Your Tourist Card

If you do, present your passport at the police station and get an official police report detailing your loss. Take the report to the nearest federal *oficina de turismo* (in most major Pacific Mexico vacation centers) and ask for a duplicate tourist card. Savvy travelers carry a copy of their tourist card with them, while leaving the original safe in their hotel room.

Car Permits

If you drive to Mexico, you need to buy a permit for your car. Upon entry into Mexico, be ready with originals and copies of your proof-of-ownership papers (state title certificate and registration, or a notarized bill of sale), current license plates, and a current driver's license. The fee is about $12, payable only by non-Mexican bank MasterCard, Visa, or American Express credit cards. The credit-card-only requirement discourages those who sell or abandon U.S.-registered cars in Mexico without paying customs duties. Credit cards must bear the same name as the vehicle proof-of-ownership papers.

The resulting car permit becomes part of the owner's tourist card and receives the same

length of validity. Cars being purchased under finance contracts must be accompanied by a notarized written permission from the finance company. Vehicles registered in the name of an organization or other person must be accompanied by a notarized affidavit authorizing the driver to use the car in Mexico for a specific time.

Border officials generally allow you to carry or tow additional motorized vehicles (motorcycle, another car, a large boat) into Mexico, but will probably require separate documentation and fee for each vehicle. If a border official desires to inspect your trailer or RV, go though it with him.

Accessories, such as a small trailer, boat less than six feet, CB radio, and outboard motor may be noted on the car permit and must leave Mexico with the car.

For updates and details on documentation required for taking your car into Mexico, call the toll-free Mexican government number, tel. (800) 446-8277 in the United States. For many more details on motor vehicle entry and what you may bring in your baggage to Mexico, consult the AAA (American Automobile Association) *Mexico Travelbook* (see the Booklist).

Since *Mexico does not recognize foreign automobile insurance,* you must purchase Mexican automobile insurance. For more information on this and other details of driving in Mexico, see "By Car or RV" in the "Getting There" section. Also see "Sports and Recreation" for information about Mexican fishing and hunting licenses.

Entry for Children

Children under 15 can be included on their parents' tourist card, but complications occur if the children (by reason of illness, for example) cannot leave Mexico with both parents. Parents can avoid such possible red tape by getting a passport and a Mexican tourist card for each of their children.

In addition to a passport or birth certificate, minors (under age 18) entering Mexico without parents or legal guardians must present a notarized letter of permission signed by both parents or legal guardians. Even if accompanied by one parent, a notarized letter from the other must be presented. Divorce or death certificates must also be presented, when applicable.

MEXICAN TOURIST INFORMATION OFFICES AND CONSULATES

The U.S. has dozens of Mexican government tourist information offices and consulates. Consulates generally handle questions of Mexican nationals in the U.S., while tourist information offices service travelers heading for Mexico. To find the consulate office nearest you call the Mexican consulate office in Washington, D.C., (202) 728-1750. For very simple questions and Mexico regional information brochures, call the Mexican Government Tourism Office at (800) 446-3942 from the U.S., or (800) 2-MEXICO from Canada.

Otherwise, contact one of several regional or foreign Mexican government tourist information offices for guidance:

IN NORTH AMERICA

From Arizona, California, Colorado, Hawaii, Nevada, New Mexico, and Utah, contact **Los Angeles:** 10100 Santa Monica Blvd., Suite 224, Los Angeles, CA 90067, tel. (310) 203-8191, fax 203-8316

From Alaska, Washington, Oregon, Idaho, Montana, Wyoming, and from the Canadian provinces of Alberta, Saskatchewan, British Columbia, Yukon, and Northwest Territories, contact **Vancouver:** 999 W. Hastings St., Suite 1610, Vancouver, B.C. V6C 2W2, tel. (604) 669-2845, fax 669-3498

From Texas, Oklahoma, and Louisiana, contact **Houston:** 2707 N. Loop West, Suite 450, Houston, TX 77008, tel. (713) 880-5153, fax 880-1833

From Florida, Alabama, Arkansas, Mississippi, Georgia, Tennessee, South Carolina, and North Carolina, contact **Miami:** 128 Aragon Ave., Coral Gables, FL 33134, tel. (305) 443-9160, fax 443-1186

From Illinois, Indiana, Iowa, Kansas, Michigan, Minnesota, Missouri, Nebraska, Ohio, North Dakota, South Dakota, and Wisconsin, contact **Chicago:** 70 E. Lake St., Suite 1413, Chicago, IL 60601, tel. (312) 606-9015, fax 606-9012

From Pennsylvania, Delaware, Maryland, Virginia, West Virginia, Kentucky, and the District of Columbia, contact **Washington, D.C.:** 1911 Pennsylvania Ave. NW, Washington, D.C. 20006, tel. (202) 728-1750, fax 728-1758

From Maine, Massachusetts, New Hampshire, New Jersey, New York, Rhode Island, and Vermont, contact **New York:** 405 Park Ave., Suite 1401, New York, NY 10022, tel. (212) 755-7261, fax 753-2874

From Ontario and Manitoba, contact **Toronto:** 2 Bloor St. West, Suite 1801, Toronto, Ontario M4W 3E2, tel. (416) 925-0704, fax 925-6061

From Quebec and the Maritime Provinces of Canada, contact **Montreal:** 1 Place Ville Marie, Suite 1526, Montreal, Quebec H3B 2B5, tel. (514) 871-1052, fax 871-3825

IN EUROPE AND JAPAN

Mexico also maintains tourist information offices in Europe:

London: 60-61 Trafalgar Square, London, England WO2N 5DO, tel. (071) 734-1058, fax 930-9202

Frankfurt: Wiesenhüttenplatz 26, 6000 Frankfurt-am-Main 1, Germany, tel. (6) 925-3413, fax 925-3755

Paris: 4, rue Notre Dame des Victoires, 75002 Paris, France, tel. (1) 402-00734, 426-15180, fax 428-60580

Madrid: Calle Velásquez 126, Madrid 6, Spain, tel. (1) 261-1827, fax 411-0759

Rome: Via Barberini 3, 00187 Rome, Italy, tel. (6) 482-7160, fax 482-3630

Mexico's Japan tourist information office is in:

Tokyo: 2-15-2 Nagata-cho, Chiyoda-ku, Tokyo 100, tel. (3) 580-2962, fax 531-5539

Pacific Mexico travelers should navigate all such possible delays far ahead of time in the cool calm of their local Mexican consulate rather than the hot, hurried atmosphere of a border or airport immigration station.

Pets

A pile of red tape stalls the entry of many dogs, cats, and other pets into Mexico. Veterinary health and rabies certificates are required to be stamped by a Mexican consul responsible for a specific foreign zone (such as Texas, or Southern California). Contact your closest Mexican Tourist Information Office for assistance. (See the chart "Mexican Information Offices and Consulates.")

Returning Home

All returning United States citizens are subject to U.S. customs inspection. Rules allow $400 worth of duty-free goods per returnee. This may include no more than 1 liter of alcoholic spirits, 200 cigarettes, and 100 cigars. A flat 10% duty will be applied to the first $1000 (fair retail value, save your receipts) in excess of your $400 exemption.

You may, however, mail packages (up to $50 value each) of **gifts** duty-free to friends and relatives in the United States. Make sure to clearly write "unsolicited gift" and a list of the value and contents on the outside of the package. Perfumes (over $5), alcoholic beverages, and tobacco may not be included in such packages.

Improve the security of such mailed packages by sending them via special **Mexpost** class, similar to U.S. Express Mail service. Even better, send them by **DHL** international courier, which maintains offices in all major Pacific Mexico resort centers. (Consult the local *Yellow Pages* for phone numbers.)

For more information on customs regulations important to travelers abroad, write for a copy of the useful pamphlet, *Know Before You Go,* from the U.S. Customs Service, P.O. Box 7047, Washington, D.C. 20044.

Additional U.S. rules prohibit importation of certain fruits, vegetables, and domestic animal and endangered wildlife products. Certain live animal species, such as parrots, may be brought into the U.S., subject to 30-day agricultural quarantine upon arrival, at the owner's expense. For more details on agricultural product and live animal importation, write for the free booklet, *Travelers' Tips,* by the U.S. Department of Agriculture, Washington, D.C. 20250. For more information on the importation of endangered wildlife products, write the Wildlife Permit Office, U.S. Department of the Interior, Washington, D.C. 20240.

MONEY

Traveler's checks, besides being refundable, are widely accepted in Pacific Mexico. Before you leave, purchase enough of a well-known brand, such as American Express or Visa, of U.S. dollar traveler's checks to cover your Mexico expenses. Canadian traveler's checks and currency are not widely accepted; European and Asian even less so. Unless you like signing your name or paying lots of per-check commissions, buy denominations of US$50 or more.

Pottery making is a time-honored Pacific Mexico pastime. Here a potter of Comalá, near Mazatlán, works in his family shop.

The Peso: Down and Up

Overnight in early 1993, the Mexican government shifted its monetary decimal point three places and created the "new" peso worth about three per U.S. dollar. New pesos, in coins of denominations one, two, and five, and bills of 10, 20, and 100 pesos are common. Banks like to exchange your traveler's checks for a few crisp large bills, rather than the often-tattered smaller denominations, which are much more useful for everyday purchases. (A 100-peso note, while common at the bank, looks awfully big to a small shopkeeper, who might be hard-pressed to change it.) Ask the bank teller who changes your traveler's checks to break some of those big peso bills into a handful of 10- and 20-peso notes. **Note:** Because of the recent rapid inflation of the peso, all prices in this book are given in U.S. dollars.

Since the new peso has acquired respectable value, the centavo (one-hundredth new peso), now appears in coins of five, 10, 20, and 50 centavos. (Incidentally, in Mexico the dollar sign, "$," also marks Mexican pesos.)

Banks and Money Exchange Offices

Mexican banks are traditionally open Mon.-Fri. 0900-1330, although money exchange services may be shorter than this. Some banks, notably the Banco Nacional de Mexico (Banamex), are opening longer hours and staffing special after-hours money exhange windows in resort centers. Banamex traditionally posts the dollar exchange rate in the lobby like this: *Tipo de cambio: venta 6.413, compra 6.502,* which means that they will sell pesos to you at the rate of 6.413 per dollar, and inversely buy them back from anyone else for 6.502 per dollar. All of which means you get 641.30 pesos for each of your $100 traveler's checks.

You don't necessarily have to go to the trouble of changing your money at a bank. Merchants, hotels, and restaurants also change money, but usually at much less favorable rates. Consequently, money-exchange lines (on Monday mornings especially) at Banamex are often long. In such cases, look for a less-crowded (such as Bancomer, Banco Serfín, and Banco Confia) bank around the corner. Small money-exchange offices *(casas de cambio)* are the most convenient, sometimes offering long hours

and faster service for a pittance more than the banks (sometimes as little as 25 pennies on $100).

Credit Cards

Credit cards, such as Visa, MasterCard, and to a lesser extent, American Express, are widely honored in the hotels, restaurants, craft shops, and boutiques that cater to foreign tourists. You will generally get better bargains, however, in shops that depend on local trade and do not so readily accept credit cards. Such shops sometimes offer discounts for cash sales.

Whatever the circumstance, your travel money will usually go much farther in Pacific Mexico than back home. Despite the national 10% ("value added" IVA) sales tax, local lodging, food, and transportation prices will often seem like bargains compared to the developed world. Outside of the pricey high-rise beachfront strips, pleasant, palmy hotels often run $30 or less.

Keeping Your Money Safe

In Pacific Mexico, as everywhere, thieves circulate among the tourists. Keep valuables in your hotel *caja de seguridad* (security box). If you don't particularly like the desk clerk, carry what you cannot afford to lose in a money belt.

Pickpockets love crowded markets, buses, terminals, and airports, where they can slip a wallet out of a back pocket or dangling purse in a wink. Guard against this by carrying your wallet in your front pocket, and your purse, waist pouch, or daypack (which thieves can go so far as to slit open) on your front side.

Don't attract crooks; don't display wads of money or flashy jewelry. Don't get drunk; if so, you may become a pushover for a determined thief.

Don't leave valuables untended on the beach; share security duties with some of your trustworthy-looking neighbors, or leave a bag with a shopkeeper nearby.

Tipping

Without their droves of foreign visitors, Mexican people would be even poorer. Devaluation of the peso, while it makes prices low for visitors, makes it rough for Mexican families to get by. The help at your hotel typically get paid only a few dollars a day. They depend on tips to make

SHOPPING AROUND

The following towns or regions are sources for the finest examples of local crafts.

BASKETS AND WOVEN STRAW GOODS

baskets, figurines, Christmas ornaments, and small utensils: Lake Pátzcuaro and Michoacán

sombreros: Sahuayo, Michoacán

"Panama" hats: Campeche

CLOTHING AND EMBROIDERY

cotton "wedding" dresses: Valley of Oaxaca

native women's *huipiles:* San Pedro Amusgos, Oaxaca

men's *guayabera* pleated dress shirts: Yucatán

designer-label clothes and cotton resort wear: Guadalajara

hammocks: Yucatán

FURNITURE

colonial wooden chests, tables: Pátzcuaro and Guadalajara

equipal leather chairs and tables: Jalisco

GLASS

burbuja (boor-BOO-hah) bubbled glass tumblers and goblets: Puebla

blown and red glass: Guadalajara

MUSICAL INSTRUMENTS

guitars, violins, and mandolins: Paracho, Michoacán

harps: Veracruz

JEWELRY

silver and gold earrings, necklaces, pendants, bracelets: Taxco

silver and gold filigree: Pátzcuaro and Oaxaca

LEATHER

coats, jackets, purses, belts, wallets: Guadalajara

shoes and boots: León

MASKS AND WOODCARVING

animals, insects, and humans—jaguars, grasshoppers, saints, devils, villains, and heroes—in wood, coconut shell, paper, and stone: Michoacán, Guerrero, and Oaxaca

Huichol beaded masks of the spirit Tatei Nakawe (Grandmother Earth): Tepic and Santiago Ixcuintla, Nayarit

lacquerware: Olinalá, Guerrero, and Pátzcuaro

whimsical painted wooden animals: Arrazola, Oaxaca

painted wooden fish: Guerrero

ironwood animals: Sonora

METALWORK

copperware: Santa Clara del Cobre, Michoacán

ironwork: Puebla, Oaxaca, Guerrero

machetes and knives: Guerrero and Oaxaca

brass: Tonalá

tinware—mirror frames, masks, and Christmas ornaments: Oaxaca

PAPER

papier-mâché birds and animals: Tonalá

amate (bark paper) paintings: Guerrero

piñatas, decorative cutouts: San Salvador Huixcolotla, Puebla

POTTERY AND CERAMICS

stoneware dishes: Tonalá and Tlaquepaque

barra (black unglazed pottery): San Bartolo Colotepec, Oaxaca

green-glazed pottery: Atzompa, Oaxaca

painted and high-glazed animals and stoneware: Tonalá

"Talavera" multicolored, high-glazed tile, vases, and dishes: Puebla

Trees of Life: Metepec, state of México

painted, unglazed pottery animals: Guerrero

pre-Columbian pottery reproductions: Colima

TOYS

dollhouse furniture: Pátzcuaro

rattles, flutes, painted gourds; tin and wooden cars, airplanes, and trains; candy skulls and skeletons: from everywhere

WOOL

fine-weave rugs, blankets, and serapes: Teotitlán del Valle, Oaxaca

loose-weave serapes, rugs, and sweaters: Michoacán

Huichol *cuadras* yarn paintings: Tepic and Santiago Ixcuintla, Nayarit the difference between dire and bearable poverty. For good service, tip 15%. Give your chambermaid *(camarista)* and floor attendant a couple of new pesos every day or two. And whenever uncertain of what to tip, it will probably mean a lot to someone, maybe a whole family, if you err on the generous side.

In restaurants and bars, Mexican tipping customs are similar to U.S., Canada, and Europe: tip waiters, waitresses, and bartenders about 15% for satisfactory service.

SHOPPING

What to Buy

Although bargains abound in Mexico, savvy shoppers are selective. Steep import and luxury taxes drive up the prices of foreign-made goods, such as cameras, computers, sports equipment, and English-language books. Instead, concentrate your shopping on locally-made items: leather, jewelry, cotton resort wear, Mexican-made designer clothes, and the galaxy of handicrafts for which Mexico is renowned.

Handicrafts

A number of Puerto Vallarta regional centers are havens for crafts shoppers. Guadalajara, including its suburban villages of Tlaquepaque and Tonalá, and Tepic nurture vibrant traditions with roots in the pre-Columbian past. This rich cornucopia spills over to Puerto Vallarta, where shoppers enjoy a rich selection from both regional and national Mexican sources. These, along with a kaleidoscope of offerings from the local art colony, fill sidewalks, stalls, and shops all over town.

How to Buy

Bargaining will stretch your money even farther. It comes with the territory in Mexico and needn't be a hassle. On the contrary, if done with humor and moderation, bargaining can be an enjoyable path to encountering Mexican people and gaining their respect, and even friendship.

The local crafts market is where bargaining is most intense. For starters, try offering half the asking price. From there on, it's all psychology: you have to content yourself with not having to have the item. Otherwise, you're sunk; the vendor will probably sense your need and stand fast. After a few minutes of good-humored bantering, ask for *el último precio* (the "final price"), which, if it's close, you may have a bargain.

Buying Silver and Gold Jewelry

Silver and gold jewelry, the finest of which is crafted in Taxco, Guerrero, and Guanajuato, fills a number of Puerto Vallarta shops. One hundred percent pure silver is rarely sold because it's too soft. Silver (sent from mines all over Mexico to be worked in Taxco shops), is nearly always alloyed with 7.5% copper to increase its durability. Such pieces, identical in composition to sterling silver, should have ".925," together with the initials of the manufacturer, stamped on their back sides. Other, less common grades, such as "000 fine" (80% silver), should also be stamped.

If silver is not stamped with the degree of purity, it probably contains no silver at all and is an alloy of copper, zinc, and nickel, known by the generic label "alpaca," or "Mexican," or "German" silver. Once, after haggling over the purity and prices of his offerings, a street vendor handed me a shiny handful and said, "Go to a jeweler and have them tested. If they're not real, keep them." Calling his bluff, I took them to a jeweler, who applied a dab of hydrochloric acid to each piece. Tiny, tell-tale bubbles revealed the cheapness of the merchandise, which I returned the next day to the vendor.

Some shops price sterling silver jewelry simply by weighing, which typically translates to about $1 per gram. If you want to find out if the price is fair, ask the shopkeeper to weigh it for you.

People prize pure gold partly because, unlike silver, it does not tarnish. Gold, nevertheless, is rarely sold pure (24-karat); for durability, it is alloyed with copper. Typical purities, such as 18-karat (75%) or 14-karat (58%) should be stamped on the pieces. If not, chances are they contain no gold at all.

COMMUNICATIONS

Using Mexican Telephones

Although Mexican phone service is improving, it still can be hit-or-miss. If a number doesn't get through, you may have to redial it more than once. When someone answers (usually *"bueno"*) be especially courteous. If your Spanish is rusty, say *"¿Por favor, habla usted inglés?"* (POR fah-VOR AH-vlah oos-TAYD een-GLAYS). If you want to speak to a particular person (such as María), ask *"¿María se encuentra?"* (mah-REEAH SAY ayn-koo-AYN-trah).

In resort cities and larger towns, direct long-distance dialing is the rule—from hotels, public phone booths, and efficient private Computel telephone offices. Since the Mexican government imposes heavy taxes on international calls, the cheapest way to call home is usually **collect.** You can generally do this one of three ways: Simply dial 09 for the local English-speaking international operator; or alternatively, dial the U.S. long-distance operator by dialing 95-800-462-4240 for AT&T, 95-800-674-6000 for MCI, or 95-800-877-8000 for Sprint.

For **station-to-station** calls to the U.S. and Canada, dial 95 plus the area code and the local number. For other international calls, see the easy-to-follow directions in the local Mexican telephone directory.

To call all long-distance numbers within Mexico dial 91, followed by the Mexican area code *(lada)* and the local number.

In smaller towns, long-distance phoning is done in the *larga distancia* (long-distance) telephone office. Typically staffed by a young woman and often connected to a cafe or bus station, the *larga distancia* frequently becomes an informal community social center as people pass the time waiting for their telephone call connection to be made.

Calling Mexico

To call Mexico direct from the U.S., first dial 011 (the international access code), then 52 (the country code), followed by the Mexican area code and local number. Consult your local telephone directory or operator for more details.

Post and Telegraph

Mexican *correos* (post offices) operate similarly to their counterparts all over the world. Mail services include *lista de correo* (general delivery; address letters "a/c lista de correo") *servicios filatélicos* (philatelic services), *por avión* (airmail), *giros* (money orders), and Mexpost fast delivery service.

Telégrafos (telegraph offices), usually near the post office, send and receive *telegramas* (telegrams) and *giros* (money orders). *Telecommunicaciones,* the shiny high-tech telegraph offices, have added telephone and public fax to the available services.

Electricity and Time

Mexican electric power is supplied at U.S.-standard 110-volts, 60-cycles. Plugs and sockets are generally two-pronged, non-polar, like the old pre-1970s U.S. plugs and sockets. Bring adaptors for your appliances with two-pronged polar or three-pronged plugs. (Hint: A two-pronged "polar" plug has different prongs, one of which is generally too large to plug into an old-fashioned non-polar socket.)

Pacific Mexico operates on **central time** except for the states of Sinaloa and Nayarit, which operate on **mountain time.**

STAYING HEALTHY

In Pacific Mexico, as everywhere, prevention is the best remedy for illness. For those visitors who confine their travel to the beaten path, a few basic common sense precautions will ensure vacation enjoyment.

Resist the temptation to dive headlong into Mexico. It's no wonder that some people get sick—broiling in the sun, gobbling peppery food, downing beer and margaritas, then discoing half the night—all in their first 24 hours. Instead, they should give their bodies time to adjust.

Travelers often arrive tired and dehydrated from travel and heat. During the first few days, they should drink plenty of bottled water and juice and take siestas.

Traveler's Diarrhea

Traveler's diarrhea (known in Southeast Asia as "Bali Belly" and in Mexico as "Turista," or "Moctezuma's Revenge") persists even among prudent vacationers. You can even suffer *turista* for a week after simply traveling from California to New York. Doctors say the familiar symptoms of runny bowels, nausea, and sour stomach result from normal local bacterial strains to which newcomers' systems need time to adjust. Unfortunately, the dehydration and fatigue from heat and travel reduce your body's natural defenses and sometimes lead to a persistent cycle of sickness at a time when you least want it.

Time-tested protective measures can help your body either prevent or break this cycle. Many doctors and veteran travelers swear by Pepto-Bismol for soothing sore stomachs and stopping diarrhea. Acidophilus (yogurt bacteria), widely available in the U.S. in tablets, aids digestion. Warm chamomile *manzanilla* tea, used widely in Mexico (and by Peter Rabbit's mother), provides liquid and calms upset stomachs. Temporarily avoid coffee and alchohol, drink plenty of *manzanilla* tea, and eat bananas and rice for a few meals until your tummy can take regular food.

Although powerful antibiotics and antidiarrhea medications such as Lomotil and Imodium are readily available over *farmacia* counters, they may involve serious side effects and should not be taken in the absence of solid medical advice. If in doubt, see a doctor.

Sunburn

For sunburn protection, use a good sunscreen with a sun protection factor (SPF) of 10 or 15 or more, which will reduce burning rays to one-tonth or one-fifteenth or less of direct sun. Better still, take a shady siesta-break from the sun during the most hazardous three or four midday hours. If you do get burned, use a moisturizing lotion (or one of the "-caine" creams for numbing the pain) for healing.

Safe Water and Food

Although municipalities have made great strides in sanitation, food and water are still major potential sources of germs in Pacific Mexico. Do not drink Mexican tap water. Drink bottled water only. Hotels, whose success depends vitally on their customers' health, generally provide purified bottled water *(agua purificada)*. If, for any reason, water is doubtful, add a few drops of household chlorine bleach *(blanqueador)* or iodine *(yodo* from the *farmacia)* per quart. Iodine crystals or tablets are also readily available in the U.S. from pharmacies or outdoor recreation stores. Polarpure and Aquatabs are two popular brands.

Pure bottled water, soft drinks, beer, and pure fruit juices are so widely available that it is easy

---

MEDICAL TAGS AND AIR EVACUATION

Travelers with special medical problems might consider wearing a medical identification tag. For a reasonable fee, Medic Alert (P.O. Box 1009, Turlock, CA 95381, tel. 800-344-3226) provides such tags, coupled with an information hotline that will provide doctors with your vital medical background information.

For life-threatening emergencies, Critical Air Medicine (Montgomery Field, 4141 Kearny Villa Rd., San Diego, CA 92123, tel. 619-571-0482; toll-free from the U.S. 800-247-8326, toll-free from Mexico 24 hours 95-800-010-0268) furnishes high-tech jet ambulance service from any Mexican locale to the United States. For a fee running typically around $20,000, they promise to fly you to the right U.S. hospital in a hurry.

---

to avoid tap water, especially in restaurants. Ice and *paletas* (iced juice-on-a-stick) can be risky, especially in small towns.

Washing hands before eating in a restaurant is a time-honored Mexican ritual, which visitors should religiously follow. The humblest Mexican eatery will generally provide a basin and soap for washing hands *(lavar los manos)*. If it doesn't, don't eat there.

Hot, cooked food is generally safe, as are peeled fruits and vegetables. Milk and cheese these days in Mexico are generally processed under sanitary conditions and sold pasteurized (ask: *"¿pasteurizado?"*) and are typically safe. Mexican ice cream used to be both bad tasting and of dubious safety, but national brands available in supermarkets are so much improved that it's no longer necessary to resist ice cream in resort towns.

If you are a salad lover, eat with caution. In restaurants, you'd best avoid lettuce and cabbage unless you're sure they've been washed with purified water. If you must have a fresh salad, tomatoes, carrots, cucumbers, onions, and green peppers doused in vinegar or lime juice are generally safe.

Medications and Immunizations

A good physician can recommend the proper preventatives for your Pacific Mexico trip. If you are going to stay pretty much in town, your doctor will probably suggest little more than updating your basic typhoid, diptheria-tetanus, and polio shots.

For camping or trekking in remote tropical areas—below 4,000 feet or 1,200 meters—doctors often recommend a gamma-globulin shot against hepatitis-A and a schedule of chloroquine pills against malaria. While in backcountry areas, you should probably use other measures to discourage mosquitoes—and fleas, flies, ticks, no-see-ums, "kissing bugs" (see below)—and other tropical pesties from biting you in the first place. Common precautions include sleeping under mosquito netting, burning mosquito (espirales mosquito) coils, and rubbing on plenty of pure DEET (n,n dimethyl-meta-toluamide) "jungle juice," mixed 1:1 with rubbing (70% isopropyl) alcohol. (100% DEET, although super-effective, dries and irritates skin.)

Chagas' Disease, Scorpions, and Snakes

Chagas' disease, spread by the "kissing" (or, more appropriately "assassin") bug, is a potential but infrequent hazard in the rural Mexican tropics. Known locally as a vinchuca, the triangular-headed three-quarter inch (two centimeter) brown insect, identifiable by its yellow-striped abdomen, often drops upon its sleeping victims from the thatched ceiling of a rural house at night. It bites the victim, while frequently depositing its fecal matter. This may be followed by swelling, fever, and weakness, sometimes leading to heart failure if left untreated. Application of drugs at an early stage, however, can clear the patient of the trypanosome-parasites, which infect victims' bloodstreams and vital organs. See a doctor immediately if you believe you're infected.

Also while camping or staying in a palapa or other rustic accommodation, watch for scorpions, especially in your shoes (whose contents you should dump out every morning). Scorpion stings and snakebites are rarely fatal to an adult but are potentially very serious to a child. Get the victim to a doctor calmly but quickly. For precautions against **snakes and other venomous reptiles,** see "Reptiles and Amphibians" in the "Flora and Fauna" section.

Injuries from Sea Creatures

While snorkeling or surfing, you may suffer a coral scratch or jellyfish sting. Experts advise you should wash the afflicted area with ocean (not fresh) water and pour alcohol (rubbing alcohol or tequila), if available, over the wound, then apply hydrocortisone cream from your first-aid kit or the farmacia.

Injuries from sea urchin spines and sting-ray barbs are both painful and sometimes serious. Physicians recommend similar first aid for both: first remove the spines or barbs by hand or with tweezers, then soak the injury in hot-as-possible fresh water to weaken the toxins and provide relief. Another method is to rinse the area with an antibacterial solution—either rubbing alcohol, vinegar, wine, or ammonia diluted with water. If none are available, the same effect may be achieved by rinsing with urine, either your own or someone else's in your party. Get medical help immediately.

Poisonous sea snakes, although rare and shy, do inhabit Pacific Mexico waters. Much more common, especially around submerged rocks, is the moray eel. Don't stick your fingers or toes in any concealed cracks.

First-Aid Kit

In the tropics, ordinary cuts and insect bites are much more prone to infection and should receive immediate first aid. A first-aid kit (with a minimum of: aspirin, rubbing alcohol, hydrogen peroxide, Halazone tablets or bleach for water purification, swabs, Band-Aids, gauze, adhesive tape, an Ace bandage, chamomile, Pepto-Bismol, acidophilus tablets, antibiotic ointment, hydrocortisone cream, mosquito repellent, a knife, and tweezers) is a good precaution for any traveler and a top priority for campers.

Medical Care

For medical advice and treatment, let your hotel (or if you're camping, the closest farmacia) refer you to a good doctor, clinic, or hospital. Mexican doctors, especially in medium-size and small towns, practice like private doctors in the U.S. and Canada once did before health insurance, liability, and group practice. They will come to you if you request it; they often keep their doors open even after regular hours, and charge reasonable fees.

You will receive generally good treatment at one of the many local hospitals in Pacific Mexico's tourist centers. See individual destination chapters for details. For more useful information on health and safety in Mexico, consult Dr. William Forgey's *Mexico, A Guide to Health and Safety* (Merrillville, Indiana: ICS Books, 1991), or Dr. Dirk Schroeder's *Staying Healthy in Asia, Africa, and Latin America* (Chico, California: Moon Publications, Inc., 1995).

CONDUCT AND CUSTOMS

Safe Conduct

Mexico is an old-fashioned country where people value traditional ideals of honesty, fidelity, and piety. Crime rates are low; visitors are often safer in Mexico than in their home cities.

Even though three generations have elapsed since Pancho Villa raided the U.S. border, the image of a Mexico bristling with *bandidos* persists. And similarly for Mexicans: despite the century and a half since the *yanquis* invaded Mexico City and took half their country, the communal Mexican psyche still views *gringos* (and, by association all white foreigners) with revulsion, jealousy, and wonder.

Fortunately, the Mexican love-hate affair with foreigners does not necessarily apply to individual visitors. Your friendly *"buenos dias"* or *"por favor,"* when appropriate, is always appreciated, whether in the market, the gas station, or the hotel. The shy smile you will most likely receive in return will be your small, but not insignificant, reward.

Women

Your own behavior, despite low crime statistics, largely determines your safety in Mexico. For women traveling solo, it is important to realize the double sexual standard is alive and well in Mexico. Dress and behave modestly and you will most likely avoid embarrassment. Whenever possible, stay in the company of friends or acquaintances; find companions for beach, sightseeing, and shopping excursions. Ignore strange men's solicitations and overtures. A Mexican man on the prowl will invent the sappiest romantic overtures to snare a *gringa*. He will often interpret anything except silence or a firm "no" as a "maybe," and a "maybe" as a "yes."

Men

For male visitors, on the other hand, alcohol often leads to trouble. Avoid bars and cantinas, and if (given Mexico's excellent beers) you can't abstain completely, at least maintain soft-spoken self-control in the face of challenges from macho drunks.

The Law and Police

While Mexican authorities are tolerant of alcohol, they are decidedly intolerant of other substances such as marijuana, psychedelics, cocaine, and heroin. Getting caught with such drugs in Mexico usually leads to swift and severe results.

Equally swift is the punishment for nude sunbathing, which is both illegal in public and offensive to Mexicans. Confine your nudist colony to very private locations.

Traffic police in Pacific Mexico's resorts watch foreign cars with eagle eyes. Officers seem to inhabit busy intersections and one-way streets, waiting for confused tourists to make a wrong move. If they whistle you over, stop immediately or you really will get into hot water. If guilty, say "lo siento" (I'm sorry), and be cooperativo. Although he probably won't mention it, the officer is usually hoping that you'll cough up a $20 *mordida* (bribe) for the privilege of driving away.

Don't do it. Although he may hint at confiscating your car, calmly ask for an official *boleto* (written traffic ticket, if you're guilty) in exchange for your driver's license (have a copy), which the officer will probably keep if he writes a ticket. If no money appears after a few minutes, the officer will most likely give you back your driver's license rather than go to the trouble of writing the ticket. If not, the worst that will usually happen is you will have to go to the *presidencia municipal* (city hall) the next morning and pay the $20 to a clerk in exchange for your driver's license.

Pedestrian Hazards

Although Pacific Mexico's many pavement and sidewalk holes won't land you in jail, one of them might send you to the hospital if you don't watch your step, especially at night. "Pedestrian beware" is doubly good advice on Mexican streets, where it is rumored that some drivers speed up rather than slow down when they spot a tourist stepping off the curb. Falling coconuts, especially frequent on windy days, constitutute additional hazards to unwary campers and beachgoers.

Cars can get you both in and out of trouble in Mexico. Driving Mexican roads, where slow carts block lanes, *campesinos* stroll the shoulders, and horses, burros, and cattle wander at will, is more hazardous than back home, and doubly so at night.

Socially Responsible Travel

Latter-day jet travel has brought droves of vacationing tourists to third world countries largely unprepared for the consequences. As the visitors' numbers swell, power grids black out, sewers overflow, and roads crack under the strain of accommodating more and larger hotels, restaurants, cars, buses, and airports.

Worse yet, armies of vacationers drive up local prices and local people begin to lose their long-held values and customs. While visions of tourists as sources of fast money replace traditions of hospitality, television wipes out folk entertaiments, Coke and Pepsi replace fruit drinks, and prostitution and drugs flourish.

Some travelers are saying enough is enough, and are forming organizations to encourage visitors to travel with increased sensitivity to native people and customs. They have developed traveler's codes of ethics and guidelines that encourage visitors to stay at local-style accommodations, use local transportation, and seek al-

MACHISMO

I once met a man in Acapulco who wore five gold wristwatches and became angry when I quietly refused his repeated insistence I get drunk with him. Another time, on the beach near San Blas, two drunk *campesinos* nearly attacked me because I was helping my girlfriend cook a picnic dinner. Outside Taxco I once spent an endless hour in the seat behind a bus driver who insisted on speeding down the middle of the two-laned highway, honking aside oncoming automobiles.

Despite their wide differences (the first was a rich criollo, the *campesinos* were *indígenas,* and the bus driver, mestizo), the common affliction shared by all four men was machismo, a disease that seems to possess many Mexican men. Machismo is a sometimes reckless obsession to prove one's masculinity, to show how macho you are. Men of many nationalities share the instinct to prove themselves. Japan's *bushido* samarai code is one example. Mexican men, however, often seem to try the hardest.

When confronted by a Mexican braggart, male visitors should remain careful and controlled. If your opponent is yelling, stay cool, speak softly, and try to withdraw as soon as possible. On the highway, be courteous and unprovocative; don't use your car to spar with a macho driver. Drinking often leads to problems. It's best to stay out of bars or cantinas unless you're prepared to deal with the macho consequences. Polite refusal of a drink may be taken as a challenge. If you visit a bar with Mexican friends or acquaintants, you may be heading for a no-win choice of a drunken all-night *borrachera* (binge) or an insult to the honor of your friends by refusing.

The flip side of machismo is the extreme femininity it requires of women. In Mexico, women's liberation is long in coming. Few women hold positions of power in business or politics. One woman, Rosa Luz Alegría, did attain the rank of minister of tourism during the former López Portillo administration; she was the president's mistress.

Machismo requires that female visitors obey the rules or suffer the consequences. Keep a low profile; wear bathing suits and brief shorts only at the beach. Follow the example of your Mexican sisters: make a habit of going out, especially at night, in the company of friends or acquaintances. Mexican men believe an unaccompanied woman wants to be picked up. Ignore such offers; any response, even refusal, might be taken as a "maybe." If, on the other hand, there is a Mexican man whom you'd genuinely like to meet, the traditional way is an arranged introduction through family or friends.

Mexican families, as a source of protection and friendship, should not be overlooked—especially on the beach or in the park, where, among the gaggle of kids, grandparents, aunts, and cousins, there's room for one more.

ternative vacations and tours, such as language and cultural programs and people-to-people work projects.

Prominent in such efforts is the **Center for Responsible Tourism,** which publishes a newsletter and maintains contacts with the growing national and global network of socially and ecologically aware travelers and travel organizations. For more information, contact them at P.O. Box 827, San Anselmo, CA 94979, tel. (415) 258-6594, fax 258-6594.

SPECIALTY TRAVEL

Bringing the Kids
Children are treasured like gifts from heaven in Mexico. Traveling with your kids (or your neighbors' if you don't have any to bring) will ensure your welcome most everywhere. On the beach make sure they are protected from the sun. Children often adjust slowly to Mexican food, regardless the familar eggs, cheese, *hamburguesas,* milk, oatmeal, corn flakes, bananas, cakes, and cookies are readily available.

A sick child is no fun for anyone. Fortunately, clinics and good doctors are available even in small towns. When in need, ask a storekeeper or a pharmacist, *"Dónde hay doctor, por favor?"* (DOHN-day eye doc-TOHR por fah-VOHR?). In most cases within five minutes you will be in the waiting room of the local physician or hospital.

Your children will be more fun if they are given a little previous knowledge of Mexico and a stake in the trip. For example, help them select some library picture books and magazines, so they'll know where they're going and what to expect; or give them responsibility for packing and carrying their own small travel bag.

Be sure to mention your children's ages when making air reservations; child discounts of one-half or more are often available. Also, if you can arrange to go on an uncrowded flight, both you and your kids might be able to stretch out and rest on the empty seats. For many more details of travel with children, check out the excellent *Adventuring With Children,* by Nan Jeffries (see the Booklist).

Travel for the Handicapped
Mexican airlines and hotels are becoming increasingly aware of the needs of handicapped travelers. Open, street-level lobbies and large, wheelchair-accessible elevators and rooms are available in many Puerto Vallarta resort hotels.

United States law forbids travel discrimination against otherwise qualified handicapped persons. As long as your handicap is stable and not liable to deteriorate during passage, you can expect to be treated as any passenger with special needs.

Make reservations far ahead of departure and ask your agent to inform your airline of what you will need, such as boarding wheelchair, or in-flight oxygen. Be early at the gate in order to take advantage of the pre-boarding call.

For many helpful details that might smooth your trip, get a copy of *Traveling Like Everyone Else: A Practical Guide for Disabled Travelers* by Jaqueline Freeman and Susan Gerstein. It's available at bookstores or from the publisher (Modan Publishing, P.O. Box 1202, Bellmore, NY 11710, tel. 516-679-1380) for $11.95, plus $3.50 postage and handling. Another useful publication is the IATA (International Air Travel Association) booklet, *Incapacitated Passengers Air Travel Guide,* obtainable from IATA-member airlines and travel agents.

Certain organizations both encourage and provide information about handicapped travel. One with many Mexican connections is **Mobility International USA,** P.O. Box 10767, Eugene, OR 97440, tel. (503) 343-1284, fax 343-6812. A $20 membership gets you their quarterly newsletter and referrals for international exchanges and homestays. Similarly, **Partners of the Americas,** with chapters in 45 U.S. states, works to improve handicapped understanding and facilities in Mexico and Latin America. They maintain lists of local organizations and individuals whom handicapped travelers may contact at their destinations. For more information, contact them at 1424 K St. NW, Suite 700, Washington, D.C. 20005, tel. (800) 322-7844 or (202) 628-3300.

Travel for Senior Citizens
Age, according to Mark Twain, is a question of mind over matter: If you don't mind, it doesn't matter. Mexico is a country where whole ex-

PACKING CHECKLIST

NECESSARY ITEMS

- ❑ camera, film (expensive in Mexico)
- ❑ clothes, hat
- ❑ comb
- ❑ guidebook, reading books
- ❑ inexpensive watch, clock
- ❑ keys, tickets
- ❑ mosquito repellent
- ❑ prescription eyeglasses
- ❑ prescription medicines and drugs
- ❑ purse, waist-belt carrying pouch
- ❑ sunglasses
- ❑ sunscreen
- ❑ swimsuit
- ❑ toothbrush, toothpaste
- ❑ tourist card, visa
- ❑ traveler's checks, money
- ❑ windbreaker

USEFUL ITEMS

- ❑ address book
- ❑ birth control

- ❑ checkbook, credit cards
- ❑ contact lenses
- ❑ dental floss
- ❑ earplugs
- ❑ first-aid kit
- ❑ flashlight, batteries
- ❑ immersion heater
- ❑ lightweight binoculars
- ❑ passport
- ❑ razor
- ❑ travel booklight
- ❑ vaccination certificate

NECESSARY ITEMS FOR CAMPERS

- ❑ collapsible gallon plastic bottle
- ❑ dish soap
- ❑ first-aid kit
- ❑ hammock (buy in Mexico)
- ❑ insect repellent
- ❑ lightweight hiking shoes
- ❑ lightweight tent
- ❑ matches in waterproof case
- ❑ nylon cord
- ❑ plastic bottle, quart

- ❑ potscrubber-sponge
- ❑ sheet or light blanket
- ❑ Sierra Club cup, fork, and spoon
- ❑ single-burner stove with fuel
- ❑ Swiss army knife
- ❑ tarp
- ❑ toilet paper
- ❑ towel, soap
- ❑ two nesting cooking pots
- ❑ water-purifying tablets or iodine
- ❑ wire grate for barbecuing fish

USEFUL ITEMS FOR CAMPERS

- ❑ compass
- ❑ dishcloths
- ❑ hot pad
- ❑ instant coffee, tea, sugar, powdered milk
- ❑ moleskin (Dr. Scholl's)
- ❑ plastic plate
- ❑ poncho
- ❑ short candles
- ❑ whistle

---

tended families, from babies to great-grandparents, still live together. Elderly travelers will generally benefit from the resulting respect and understanding that Mexicans accord to older people. Besides these encouragements, consider the large numbers of retirees already in Pacific Mexico havens, such as Mazatlán, Puerto Vallarta, Guadalajara, Lake Chapala, Manzanillo, and Acapulco.

Certain organizations, furthermore, support senior travel. Leading the field is **Elderhostel,** 75 Federal St., third floor, Boston, MA 02110-1941, tel. (617) 426-7788, which sponsors special study, homestay, and people-to-people travel programs in Mexico. For more details, ask them for their international catalog.

A very good newsletter, targeted toward lovers of Mexico, is *Adventures in Mexico,* published six times yearly, and filled with pithy hotel, restaurant, touring, and real estate information for independent travelers and retirees seeking the "real" Mexico. For information, address Adventures in Mexico, P.O Box 31-70, Guadalajara, Jalisco 45050, Mexico. Back issues are $2, one-year subscription, $16, Canadian $19.

Several other books and newsletters publicize senior travel opportunities. *Mature Traveler* is a lively professional-quality newsletter featuring moneysaving tips, discounts, and tours for over-50 active senior and handicapped travelers. Individual copies are $4, a one-year subscription, $24.50. Editor Gene Mallot has compiled years of past newsletters and experience into *Get Up and Go,* a 325-page travel tip and opportunity book, which sells for $10.50. Order through GEM Publishing Group, 250 E. Riverview Circle, P.O. Box 50820, Reno, NV 89509-9905. Another good buy is the *Complete Guide to Discounts for Travellers 50 And Beyond,* which lists a plethora of hotel, travel club, cruise, air, credit card, single, and off-season discounts. Order for $3.95 from Vacation Publications, Inc., 1502 Augusta, Suite 415, Houston, TX 77057, tel. (713) 974-6903.

WHAT TO TAKE

"Men wear pants, ladies be beautiful" was once the dress code of one of Pacific Mexico's region's classiest hotels. Men in casual Pacific Mexico can get by easily without a jacket, women with simple skirts and blouses.

Loose-fitting, hand-washable, easy-to-dry clothes make for troublefree tropical vacationing. Synthetic, or cotton-synthetic blend shirts, blouses, pants, socks, and underwear will fit the bill everywhere in the coastal resorts. For breezy nights, bring a lightweight windbreaker. If you're going to the highlands (Guadalajara, San Sebastián-Mascota-Talpa, or Tepic), add a medium-weight jacket.

In all cases, leave showy, expensive clothes and jewelry at home. Stow items you cannot lose in your hotel safe or carry them with you in a sturdy zipped purse or waist pouch on your front side.

Packing

What you pack depends on how mobile you want to be. If you're staying the whole time at a self-contained resort you can take the two suitcases and one carry-on airlines allow. If, on the other hand, you're going to be moving around a lot, best condense everything down to one easily carryable bag that doubles as luggage and a soft backpack. Experienced travelers routinely accomplish this by packing prudently and tightly, choosing items that will do double or triple duty (such as a Swiss army knife with scissors).

Campers will have to be super-careful to accomplish this. Fortunately, camping along the tropical coast requires no sleeping bag. Simply use a hammock (buy it in Mexico), or if sleeping on the ground, a sleeping pad and a sheet for cover. In the winter, at most, you may have to buy a light blanket. A compact tent you and your partner can share is a must against bugs, as is mosquito repellent. Additionally, a first-aid kit is absolutely necessary (see "Staying Healthy").

Michoacán ceramic, mother and child

BOB RACE

BOB RACE

MAZATLÁN

The Pearl of the Pacific

Mazatlán (pop. 500,000) spreads for 15 sun-splashed miles along a thumb of land that extends southward into the Pacific just below the Tropic of Cancer. Mazatlán thus marks the beginning of the Mexican tropics: a palmy land of perpetual summer and a refuge from winter cold for growing numbers of international vacationers.

Mazatlán's beauty is renowned. Its coast sprinkled with beckoning islands and miles of golden beaches and blue lagoons, it aptly deserves its title as "Pearl of the Pacific."

Despite its popularity as a tourist destination, Mazatlán owes its existence to local industry. As well as being a leading manufacturing center in the state of Sinaloa, Mazatlán is home port for a huge commercial and sportfishing fleet, whose annual catch of shrimp, tuna, and swordfish amounts to thousands of tons.

Mazatlán, consequently, lives independently of tourism. The vacationers come and frolic on the beach beside their "Golden Zone" hotels, while in the old town at the tip of the peninsula, life goes on in the old-Mexico style: in the markets, the churches, and the shady plazas scattered throughout the traditional neighborhoods.

HISTORY

Pre-Columbian

For Mexico, Mazatlán is not an old city. Most of its public buildings have stood for less than a hundred years. Evidence of local human settlement dates back before recorded history, however. Scientists reckon petroglyphs found on offshore islands may be as much as 10,000 years old.

During the 1930s archaeologists began uncovering exquisite polychrome pottery, with elaborate black and red designs, indicative of a high culture. Unlike their renowned Tarascan, Aztec, and Toltec highland neighbors, those ancient potters, known as the Totorames, built no pyramids and left no inscriptions. They had been gone a dozen generations before conquistador Nuño de Guzmán burned his way through Sinaloa in 1531.

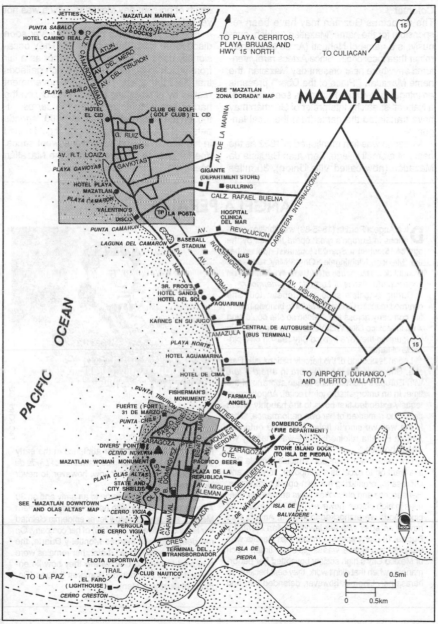

MAZATLAN

JETTIES
MAZATLAN MARINA
Punta Sabalo
HOTEL CAMINO REAL
CALZ. CAMARON SABALO
AV. ATUN
AV. DEL MERO
AV. DEL TIBURON
DOCKS
TO PLAYA CERRITOS, PLAYA BRUJAS, AND HWY 15 NORTH
15
TO CULIACAN
Playa Sabalo
HOTEL EL CID
CLUB DE GOLF (GOLF CLUB) EL CID
SEE "MAZATLAN ZONA DORADA" MAP
G. RUIZ
IBIS
AV. R.T. LOAIZA
GAVIOTAS
AV. DE LA MARINA
Playa Gaviotas
HOTEL PLAYA MAZATLAN
Playa Camaron
VALENTINO'S DISCO
GIGANTE (DEPARTMENT STORE)
BULLRING
CALZ. RAFAEL BUELNA
TP LA POSTA
HOSPITAL CLINICA DEL MAR
Punta Camahun
AV. REVOLUCION
Laguna del Camaron
BASEBALL STADIUM
AV. DEL MAR
AV. INDEPENDENCIA
AV. R. REFORMA
CARRETERA INTERNACIONAL
GAS
AV. INSURGENTES
SR. FROG'S
HOTEL SANDS
HOTEL DEL SOL
AQUARIUM
KARNES EN SU JUGO
CENTRAL DE AUTOBUSES (BUS TERMINAL)
TAMAZULA
15
Playa Norte
HOTEL AGUAMARINA
HOTEL DE CIMA
TO AIRPORT, DURANGO, AND PUERTO VALLARTA
Punta Tiburon
FISHERMAN'S MONUMENT
FUERTE (FORT) 31 DE MARZO
FARMACIA ANGEL
AV. GUTIERREZ NAJERA
Punta Chile
ZARAGOZA
CONSTITUCION
BENITO JUAREZ
AQUILES SERDAN
'DIVERS' POINT'
Cerro Nevaria
BOMBEROS (FIRE DEPARTMENT)
MAZATLAN WOMAN MONUMENT
PACIFICO BEER
STONE ISLAND DOCK (TO ISLA DE PIEDRA)
ZARAGOZA OTE.
Playa Olas Altas
PLAZA DE LA REPUBLICA
B. DOMINGUEZ
OLAS ALTAS
STATE AND CITY SHIELDS
AV. MIGUEL ALEMAN
SEE "MAZATLAN DOWNTOWN AND OLAS ALTAS" MAP
Cerro Vigia
AV. DEL PUERTO
Isla de Balvadere
PERGOLA DE CERRO VIGIA
CALZ. CARNAVAL
CRESTON AZADA
CANAL DE NAVEGACION
MOON
FLOTA DEPORTIVA
TERMINAL DEL TRANSBORDADOR
Isla de Piedra
TRAIL
TO LA PAZ
EL FARO (LIGHTHOUSE)
CLUB NAUTICO
Cerro Creston

PACIFIC OCEAN

0   0.5mi
0   0.5km

© MOON PUBLICATIONS, INC.

Colonial

The rapacious Guzmán may have been responsible for the name "Mazatlán," which, curiously, is a name of Nahuatl (Aztec language), rather than local origin. Since Aztecs rarely ventured anywhere near present-day Mazatlán, the name Mazatlán ("Place of the Deer") presents an intriguing mystery. Historians speculate that a Nahuatl-speaking interpreter of Guzmán may have translated the name from the local language.

Mazatlán was first mentioned in 1602 as the name of a small village, San Juan Bautista de Mazatlán (now called Villa Union), 30 miles south of present-day Mazatlán, which was not yet colonized.

English and French pirates however soon discovered Mazatlán's benefits. They occasionally used its hill-screened harbor as a lair from which to pounce upon the rich galleons that plied the coast. The colonial government replied by establishing a small *presidio* on the harbor and watchtowers atop the *cerros*. Although the pirates were gone by 1800, legends persist of troves of stolen silver and gold buried in hidden caves and under windswept sands, ripe for chance discovery along the Mazatlán coast.

ANGELA PERALTA

Diva Ángela Peralta (1845-83) was thrilling audiences in Europe's great opera houses by the age of 16, when a Spanish journalist dubbed her the "Mexican Nightingale." On 13 May 1863, she brought down the house at La Scala in Milan with an angelic performance of *Lucia de Lammermoor*.

During Ángela's second European tour she charmed maestro Guiseppi Verdi into bringing his entire company across the Atlantic so she could sing *Aida* in Mexico City. With Verdi conducting, Angela inaugurated the 1873 Mexico City season on a pinnacle of fame.

Legends abound of the fiercely nationalistic Peralta. She once got the last word in a *tête à tête* with Europe's most famous Italian soprano of the time. In an unforgettable joint recital, Ángela courteously extended first bows to the haughty Italian diva, who remarked of her own performance, "That is the way we sing in Italy." Not to be outdone, Ángela Peralta rejoined: "Mine was the way we sing in heaven."

Not content with mere performance, Ángela Peralta went on to excel as a composer, librettist, and impresario, organizing her own opera companies. Her success and outspoken ways earned her enemies in high places, however. In 1873, Mexico City bluebloods were shocked to find out Ángela was having an affair with her lawyer, Julian Montiel y Duarte. (It didn't seem to matter that Peralta was widowed and Montiel was single at the time.) Much of Mexico City's high society boycotted her performances; when that didn't work, they sent hecklers to harass her. Liberals, however, defended her, and

ERIC SCHNITTGER

Peralta finally regained her audience in the early 1880s with a heartrending performance of *Linda de Chamounix*. She kept her vow, however, to never sing again in Mexico City.

Her star-crossed life came to an early end on 30 August 1883. Touring with her company in western Mexico, a Mazatlán yellow fever epidemic claimed her life and the lives of 76 (of 80) of her company. On her deathbed, she married Montiel y Duarte, the only man she ever loved. Later, her remains were removed to Mexico City, where they now lie enshrined at the Rotunda de Hombres Ilustres (Rotunda of Illustrious Men).

hieroglyph of Mazatlán ("Place of the Deer")

Independence

Lifting of foreign trade restrictions in 1820 and Independence in 1821 seemed to bode well for the port of Mazatlán. However, cholera, yellow fever, and plague epidemics and repeated foreign occupations (the U.S. Navy in 1847, the French in 1864, and the British in 1871) slowed the growth of Mazatlán during the 19th century. It nevertheless served as the capital of Sinaloa from 1859 to 1873, with a population of several thousand.

The "Order and Progress" of dictator-President Porfirio Díaz (1876-1910) gave Mazatlán citizens a much-needed spell of prosperity. The railroad arrived, the port and lighthouse were modernized, and the cathedral was finished. Education, journalism, and the arts blossomed. The Teatro Rubio, completed in the early 1890s, was the grandest opera house between Baja California and Tepic.

The opera company of the renowned diva, Ángela Peralta, the "Mexican Nightingale," arrived and gave a number of enthusiastically received recitals in Mazatlán in August 1883. Tragically, Peralta and most of her company fell victim to a disastrous yellow fever epidemic, which claimed more than 2,500 Mazatlán lives.

The revolution of 1910-17 literally rained destruction on Mazatlán. In 1914, the city gained the dubious distinction of being the second city in the world to suffer aerial bombardment. (Tripoli, Libya, was the first.) General (later President) Venustiano Carranza, intent upon taking the city, ordered a biplane to bomb the ammunition magazine atop Nevería Hill, adjacent to downtown Mazatlán. But the pilot missed the target and dropped the crude leather-wrapped package of dynamite and nails onto the city streets instead. Two citizens were killed and several wounded.

Modern Mazatlán

After order was restored in the 1920s, Mazatlán soared to a decade of prosperity, followed by the deflation and depression of the 1930s. Recovery after WW II led to port improvements and new highways, setting the stage for the tourist "discovery" of Mazatlán during the 1960s and '70s. The city limits expanded to include the strand of white sand (Playa Norte) north of the original old port town. High-rise hotels sprouted in a new "Golden Zone" tourist area, which, coupled with Mazatlán's traditional fishing industry, provided thousands of new jobs for an increasingly affluent population, which, by the early '90s, was climbing past half a million.

BRUCE WHIPPERMAN

Children play beneath the Monument to the Mazatlán Woman.

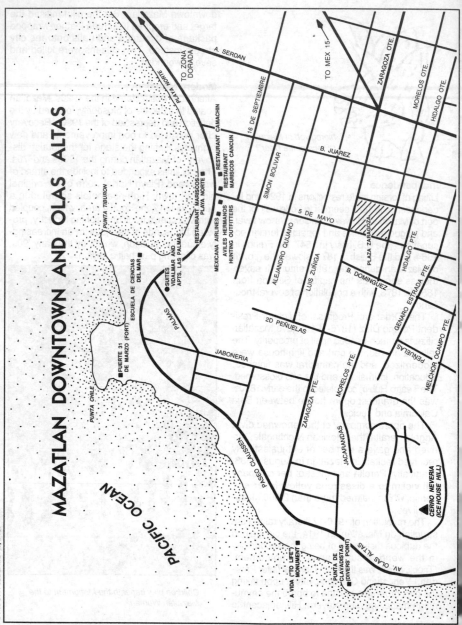

MAZATLAN DOWNTOWN AND OLAS ALTAS

PACIFIC OCEAN

TO ZONA DORADA

PLAYA NORTE

A. SERDAN

TO MEX 15

ZARAGOZA OTE.

MORELOS OTE.

HIDALGO OTE.

16 DE SEPTIEMBRE

B. JUAREZ

5 DE MAYO

SIMON BOLIVAR

ALEJANDRO QUIJANO

LUIS ZUÑIGA

B. DOMINGUEZ

GENARO ESTRADA PTE.

HIDALGO PTE.

PLAZA ZARAGOZA

2D PEÑUELAS

PEÑUELAS

MELCHOR OCAMPO PTE.

JABONERIA

MORELOS PTE.

ZARAGOZA PTE.

PASEO CLAUSSEN

JACARANDAS

AV. OLAS ALTAS

RESTAURANT CAMACHIN

RESTAURANT MARISCOS CANCUN

RESTAURANT MARISCOS PLAYA NORTE

MEXICANA AIRLINES

AVILES HERMANOS HUNTING OUTFITTERS

SUITES VIDALMAR AND APTS. LAS PALMAS

ESCUELA DE CIENCIAS DEL MAR

PALMAS

PUNTA TIBURON

PUNTA CHILE

FUERTE 31 DE MARZO (FORT)

CERRO NEVERIA (ICE HOUSE HILL)

A VIDA ("TO LIFE") MONUMENT

PUNTA DE CLAVADISTAS (DIVERS' POINT)

© MOON PUBLICATIONS, INC.

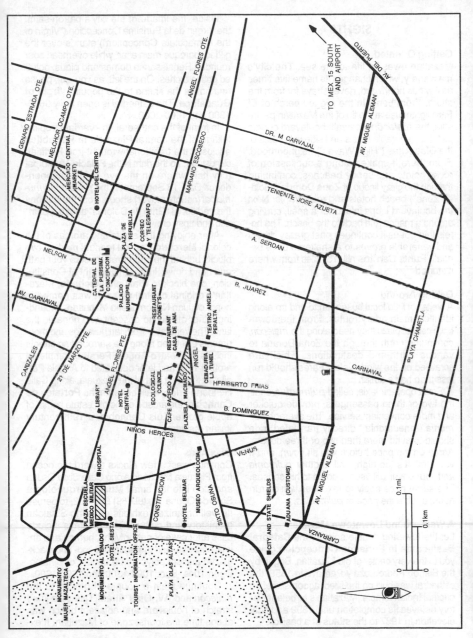

SIGHTS

Getting Oriented

Mazatlán owes its life to the sea. The city's main artery, which changes its name five times as it winds northward, never strays far from the shore. From beneath the rugged perch of **El Faro** lighthouse at the tip of the Mazatlán peninsula, the *malecón* (seawall) boulevard curves past the venerable hotels and sidewalk cafes of the **Olas Altas** ("High Waves") neighborhood. From there it snakes along a succession of rocky points and sandy beaches, continuing through the glitzy lineup of **Zona Dorada** ("Golden Zone") beach hotels and restaurants. Next the boulevard loops inland for a spell, curving around a marina and back to the beach. The hotels thin out as it continues past grassy dunes and venerable groves to a sheltered cove beneath **Punta Cerritos** hill, 15 miles from where it started.

Getting Around

A welter of little local buses run to and fro along identical main-artery routes. From the downtown central plaza they head along the *malecón,* continuing north through the Zona Dorada to various north-end destinations, which are scrawled on the windshields. Fares should run less than half a dollar.

Small open-air taxis, called *pulmonías,* seating two or three passengers, provide quicker and more convenient service. The average *pulmonía* ("pneumonia," directly translated) ride should total no more than two or three dollars. Agree on the price before you sit down, and if you think it's too high, hail another *pulmonía* and your driver will usually come to his senses. The same rules apply to taxi rides, which run about double the price of *pulmonías.*

A Walk around Downtown Mazatlán

Let the towering double spire of the **Catedral Basílica de la Purísima Concepción** guide you to the very center of old Mazatlán. Begun by the Bishop Pedro Loza y Pardave in 1856, the cathedral was built on the filled lagoon-site of an original Indian temple. Mazatlán's turbulent history delayed its completion until 1899 and final elevation in 1937 to the status of a basilica.

Inside, the image of the city's patron-saint, the Virgen de la Purísima Concepción ("Virgin of the Immaculate Conception") stands over the gilded, baroque main altar, while overhead soar rounded Renaissance domes and pious, pointed gothic arches. On the left, as you exit, pause and notice the shrine to the popular **Virgin of Guadalupe.** The cathedral is open daily 0600-1300 and 1600-2000.

In front of the cathedral, the verdant tropical foliage of the central **Plaza de la Republica** encloses the traditional wrought-iron Porfirian bandstand. To the right is the **Palacio Municipal** (city hall) where on the eve before Independence Day, 16 September, the *presidente municipal* (county mayor) shouts from the balcony the traditional "Grito de Dolores" above a patriotic and tipsy crowd.

After enjoying the sights and aromas of the colorful **Mercado Central** (central market) two blocks behind the cathedral, reverse your path and head down Juárez. Turn right at Constitución, one block to **Plazuela Machado,** Mazatlán's original central plaza. It was named in honor of Juan Nepomuceno Machado, a founding father of Filipino descent who donated the land. The venerable Porfirian buildings and monuments clustered along the surrounding streets include the **Teatro Ángela Peralta,** completed around 1890 and later dedicated to Ángela Peralta. At the west end of the Plazuela, along Calle Heriberto Frías, walk beneath the **Portales de Cannobio,** the arcade of the old estate house of apple grower Luis Cannobio, a 19th-century Italian resident.

Olas Altas

Continue west a few blocks toward the ocean from Plazuela Machado along Calle Sixto Osuna and step into the small **Museo Arqueología** Sixto de Osuna 76, tel. (69) 853-502, to peruse its well-organized exhibits outlining Sinaloan prehistory and culture. The displays include case after case of petroglyphs, human and animal figurines, and the distinctive red- and black-glazed ancient polychrome pottery of Sinaloa. Open Tues.-Sun. 1000-1300 and 1600-1800.

Continue west a couple of blocks to the *malecón* and **Av. Olas Altas.** This cafe-lined stretch of boulevard and adjacent beach was at one time *the* tourist zone of Mazatlán. It extends several shorefront blocks from the **Monumento al Venado** ("Monument to the Deer") north end, past Hotel Siesta to the **Escudos de Sinaloa y Mazatlán** ("City and State Shields of Sinaloa and Mazatlán) to the south in front of the distinguished 1889 school building at the foot of Cerro Vigia, the steep hill.

Cerro Vigía

Now, unless, you're in the mood for a hike, bargain for a *pulmonía* to take you up **Paseo Centenario,** the southern extension of Av. Olas Altas, to the **Pergola de Cerro Vigía** viewpoint at the top of the hill. There, next to the old cannon (stamped by its proud London maker, "Vavaseur no. 830, 1875"), you get the sweep of the whole city.

To the south rises Mazatlán's tallest hill, **Cerro Creston,** topped by the **El Faro** lighthouse, whose 515-foot (157-meter) elevation qualifies it as the world's highest natural lighthouse. Along the jetty-landfill that connects Cerro Creston to the mainland lie the docks and anchored boats of the several *flotas deportivas* (sport fleets). Every morning they take loads of tourists out in search of big fighting marlin and sailfish.

Across the deep-water harbor entrance looms the bulk of **Isla de la Piedra** ("Stone Island"), actually a peninsula. Its southern beach stretches to the horizon in a narrowing white thread, beneath the dark green plumes of Mexico's third largest coconut grove.

Cerro Vigía is the spot where, according to tradition, the colonial soldiers of the old Mazatlán presidio maintained their 200-year vigil, scanning the horizon for pirates. Step across the little hilltop plaza and down to the **Cafe El Mirador** and enjoy lunch, a drink, and the view; open daily 1200-2100.

Turning north, you'll see the rounded profile of **Cerro Nevería** ("Icehouse Hill") rising above the patchwork of city streets. Its unique label originated during the mid-1800s, when the tunnels that pock the hill served for storage of ice imported from San Francisco. Now the hilltop holds a number of radio and microwave beacons.

The curving white ribbon of sand north of the downtown area traces the *malecón* northward to **Punta Camarón** and the Golden Zone, marked by the cluster of shoreline high-rise hotels.

From Cerro Vigía, the three islands—**Chivos** ("Rams") and **Venados** ("Deer"), appearing together, and **Pájaros** ("Birds") near the horizon— seem to float offshore, like a trio of sleeping whales.

Along Paseo Claussen

Back downhill on Av. Olas Altas, pass the Statue of the Deer in the middle of the intersection where the *malecón* becomes Paseo Claussen. Named for the rich German immigrant who financed the blasting of the scenic drive, Paseo Claussen continues around the wave-tossed foot of Cerro Nevería. First, you will pass a striking bronze sculpture, the **Monumento Mujer Mazalteca,** nearly erotic in its intensity. Nearby, a yawning cave (plugged by heavy bars), pierces the hill. Known by local people as the **Caverna del Diablo** ("Devil's Cave"), it served as an escape route for soldiers guarding the ammunition stored in caves farther up the hill.

Not far ahead, a four-story platform at the **Punta de Clavadistas** ("Divers' Point") towers above the wave-swept tidepools. The divers— professionals, who take their work very seriously, especially at low tide, when their dives must coincide with the arrival of a big swell—perform a number of times daily, more frequently on Sundays and holidays.

Continue on past the 1892 fort turned maritime office, **Fuerte 31 de Marzo,** named in honor of the heroic stand of the local garrison, which repelled a French invasion on 31 March 1864.

BEACHES

Olas Altas to Punta Camarón

Exploration of Mazatlán's beaches can start at Av. Olas Altas, where narrow **Playa Olas Altas** offers some water sports opportunities. The strip is wide and clean enough for wading, sunning, bodysurfing, and boogie-boarding. Swimmers take care: the waves often break suddenly and recede strongly. Locally popular intermediate surfing breaks angle shoreward along the north end. Bring your own equipment, since there's rarely any for rent on this largely locals-only beach.

For fly- and bait-casting—although the beach surf is too murky to catch much of interest—

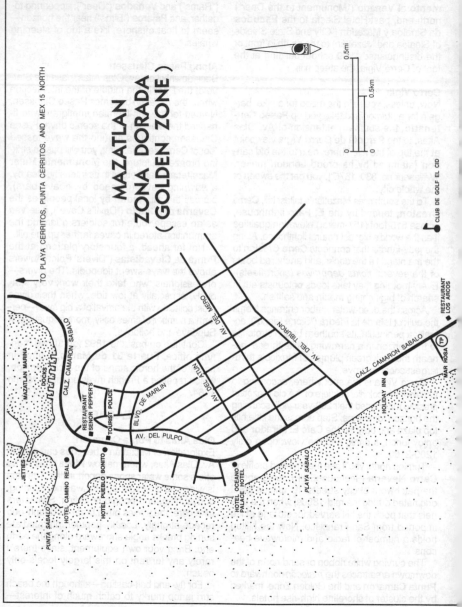

MAZATLAN
ZONA DORADA
(GOLDEN ZONE)

TO PLAYA CERRITOS, PUNTA CERRITOS, AND MEX 15 NORTH

MAZATLAN MARINA

DOCKS

JETTIES

PUNTA SABALO

CALZ. CAMARON SABALO

HOTEL CAMINO REAL

RESTAURANT
SEÑOR PEPPER'S

TOURIST POLICE

HOTEL PUEBLO BONITO

AV. DEL PULPO

BLVD. DE MARLIN

AV. DEL MERO

AV. DEL ATUN

AV. DEL TIBURON

HOTEL OCEANO
PALACE HOTEL

CALZ. CAMARON SABALO

PLAYA SABALO

HOLIDAY INN

MAR ROSA TP

RESTAURANT
LOS ARCOS

CLUB DE GOLF EL CID

0   0.5km

0   0.5mi

© MOON PUBLICATIONS, INC.

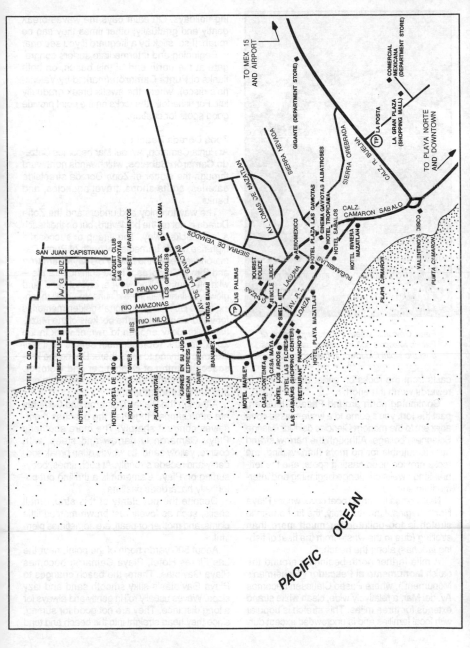

BRUCE WHIPPERMAN

Playa Gaviotas, where visitors enjoy some of Pacific Mexico's softest, silkiest sand, curves past the Hotel Cid tower in the background.

casts from the rocks on either end may yield rewards worth the effort.

Continuing north around Paseo Claussen, past the fort, you'll come to a wave-tossed cove adjacent to the modern Ciencias del Mar (Marine Sciences) college. Although the narrow strand here is suitable for no more than wading, the rocks provide good casting spots, and the left-breaking swells challenge beginning and intermediate surfers.

Next comes the small boat cove, where **Playa Norte** begins. Unfortunately, the first one-mile stretch is too polluted for much more than strolling (due to the waste from the fleet of fishing *lanchas*) along the beach.

A mile farther north beginning around the oafish **Monumento al Pescador** ("Fisherman's Monument"), where Paseo Claussen becomes Av. del Mar, a relatively wide, clean white strand extends for three miles. This stretch is popular with local families and is uncrowded except dur-

ing holidays. On calm days the waves break gently and gradually; other times they can be rough. If so, stick by a lifeguard if you see one.

Beginning and intermediate surfers congregate at the north end of this beach, on both flanks of **Punta Camarón** (marked by Valentino's disco), where the swells break gradually left. For fisherfolk, the rocks on the point provide good spots for casting.

Zona Dorada Beaches

At Punta Camarón, Av. del Mar becomes **Calzado Camarón Sábalos,** which winds northward through the clutter of Zona Dorada streetside eateries, crafts shops, travel agencies, and banks.

The way to enjoy and understand the Zona Dorada is not on the boulevard, but on the beach a few blocks away. The lineup of successful high-rise hotels immediately north of Punta Camarón testifies to the beauty of **Playa Camaròn** and **Playa Gaviotas.** These shining strands—with oft-gentle rolling waves, crystal sand, and glowing, island-silhouetted sunsets—give meaning to the label "Golden Zone": golden memories for visitors and gold in the pockets of the Mazatlán folks lucky enough to own or work in the Zona Dorada. (Sometimes it seems as if half the town *is* trying to work there. During the low-season months of September and October, beach-front crafts and food vendors often outnumber the sunbathers.)

Although the Playas Camarón and Gaviotas are often lumped together, the beaches themselves contrast sharply. The more southerly Playa Camarón is narrow and steep, with coarse, yellow sand. Its waves often break suddenly and recede strongly. At such times, body-surfing on Playa Camarón is a thrilling but potentially hazardous pastime.

Despite the popularity of this strip, small shells, such as lovely rust-brown-mottled little clams, and mother-of-pearl, are sometimes plentiful.

About 500 yards north of the point, near the Las Flores Hotel, Playa Camarón becomes Playa Gaviotas. There, the beach changes to Playa Gaviotas's silky smooth sand and lazy slope. Waves usually roll in gently and always for a long distance. They are not good for surfing, since they head straight into the beach and tend to break all at once along a long front, rather than angling left or right.

Another quarter mile north around Hotel El Cid, Playa Gaviotas becomes its identically lovely northward extension, **Playa Sábalo,** which stretches another mile to Punta Sábalo at the Hotel Camino Real.

Past the rocks of Punta Sábalo, the waters of the **Estero Sábalo** tidal lagoon (now the Marina Mazatlán's outer harbor) ebb through a boat channel. The beach boulevard loops a mile inland, past the Marina Mazatlán, curving north, back to the beach, where it becomes Calz. Sábalo Cerritos.

Northern Beaches

The strand north of Punta Sábalo, called **Playa Cerritos,** begins to look like a wild beach along its largely undeveloped northern stretch. Grass sways atop the dunes, flocks of sandpipers probe the wave-washed sand, pelicans and frigate birds glide overhead, and shells and driftwood accumulate.

At the northern end of Playa Cerritos, just south of the hill that marks Punta Cerritos, the beach becomes **Playa Brujas,** named for the *brujas,* female witch doctors, who used to perform their rituals there. If you're thirsty or hungry by that time, a seafood restaurant at the end of the beach will gladly accommodate you.

On the other side of Punta Cerritos, two more seafood restaurants perch at the very end of the beach boulevard. On the left, a rocky, tidepool-shelf juts out into the waves, forming a protected cove. This, some say, is the best **fishing** spot in Mazatlán. It appears so; half a dozen *lanchas* are usually pulled up on the rocky beach, while offshore, one or two divers hunt for oysters in the clear, calm waters.

Hikes

The best hike in Mazatlán leads right along the beach. Just walk any of your favorite stretches. You could do the whole thing (or just part of it) starting anywhere—Olas Altas, Playa Norte, Playa Gaviotas—and walking as far north (to avoid having the sun in your eyes) as you want. Other than a hat and sunscreen, you won't have to carry anything along; beach restaurants and stores along the way will provide the goodies. Neither will you have to walk back; just grab the bus or a *pulmonía* back to town whenever you decide you've walked enough.

Another good hike leads to the summit of **Cerro Creston** and provides a close, interesting look at **El Faro** lighthouse. The trail begins at the foot of the hill, at the end of the pavement past the *flotas deportivas* (sport fishing fleet) docks. Wear a hat, and take some insect repellent, water, and maybe food for a breezy summit picnic.

Follow the initially wide track as it zigzags up the hill. Sometimes overhung by vines, leafy trees, and gnarled cacti, the trail narrows to a rocky path about halfway to the summit. Nearing the top, you wind your way beside rocky outcroppings until you come to the fence around the lighthouse. If your group is small, the keeper may let you in for a look around and to sign his book. He claims the lighthouse is 400 years old.

If you arrive around dusk (bring a flashlight), you will see the beacon in action. The dazzling 1.5-million-watt beacon rotates gradually, like the spokes of a heavenly chariot, with several brilliant wheeling pencils of light focused by the great antique Fresnel lens atop the tower.

ACCOMMODATIONS

You can nearly predict the room price of a hotel by its position on a Mazatlán map. The farther north, away from the old downtown, the newer and more expensive it's likely to be.

Downtown Hotels

At one time, all Mazatlán hotels were downtown. The plush new hotels and condos on the Playa Norte-Zona Dorada luxury beach strip have drawn away practically all the high-ticket vacationers, leaving the old Olas Altas tourist zone to a few old-timers, a handful of budget travelers seeking the charms of traditional Mexico, and Mexican families on holiday outings. The exception to this is the week after Christmas, the week before Easter, and, most of all, Carnaval (Mardi Gras, in late February or March), when Olas Altas is awash with merrymakers.

The popular **Hotel Siesta** is tops for enjoying the flavor of the Olas Altas neighborhood. For balcony views of Carnaval, or lovely sunsets

MAZATLÁN HOTELS

Mazatlán (area code 69, postal code 82000 unless otherwise noted) hotels, in order of increasing approximate high-season double-room price:

HOTEL	ADDRESS	TELEPHONE	RATES
DOWNTOWN			
Hotel del Centro	Canizales 18	tel. 812-673	$18
Hotel Belmar	Av. Olas Altas 166	tel. 851-111	$20
Hotel Central	Belisario Dominguez 2 Sur	tel. 821-888	$24
Hotel Siesta	Av. Olas Altas 11	tel. 812-640 or 812-334	$25
Suites Vidalmar and Apts. Las Palmas	Calle Las Palmas 15	tel. 812-190 or 812-197	$35
PLAYA NORTE			
Hotel Sands	Av. del Mar 1910 (P.O. Box 309)	tel. 820-000	$25
Hotel del Sol	Av. del Mar s/n (P.O. Box 400)	tel. 851-103	$33
Hotel de Cima	Av. del Mar s/n (P.O. Box 350)	tel. 827-300 or 827-400	$45
Hotel Aguamarino	Av. del Mar 110 (P.O. Box 301)	tel. 817-080, 816-909, or (800) 528-1234 from the U.S. and Canada, fax 824-624	$50
ZONA DORADA			
Fiesta Apartmentos	Ibis 502, postal code 82110	tel. 135-355	$20
Hotel Tropicana	R.T. Loaiza 27 (P.O. Box 501), postal code 82110	tel. 838-000	$25
Las Gaviotas Racquet Club	Ibis at Bravo (P.O. Box 173)	tel. 135-939	$30
Playa Escondida Bungalows	Calz. Sábalo Cerritos 999 (P.O. Boxes 682 and 202), postal code 82110	tel. 880-077, fax 820-285	$30
Las Gaviotas Hotel Plaza	Bugambilias 100 (P.O. Box 970), postal code 82110	tel. 134-496, fax 136-685	$32
Apts. Girasoles	Av. Gaviotas 709, postal code 82110	tel. 135-288 or 113-835	$40
Hotel Riviera Mazatlán	Camarón Sábalo 51 (P.O. Box 795)	tel. 834-611, fax 844-532	$40
Motel Los Arcos	R.T. Loaiza 214 (P.O. Box 132)	tel. 135-066, fax 813-389	$50
Casa Contenta	R.T. Loaiza s/n	tel. 134-976	$50
Motel Marley	R.T. Loaiza 226 (P.O. Box 214)	tel./fax 135-533	$50
Hotel Las Flores	R.T. Loaiza 212 (P.O. Box 583), postal code 82110	tel. 135-011 or 835-100, fax 143-422	$60
Hotel Playa Mazatlán	Av. R.T. Loaiza 202 (P.O. Box 207), postal code 82110	tel. 134-444 or 134-455, fax 140-366	$64
Hotel Inn at Mazatlán	Camarón Sábalo 6291 (P.O. Box 1292), postal code 82110	tel. 135-500, fax 134-782	$80
Hotel El Cid	Camarón Sábalo s/n (P.O. Box 813)	tel. 833-333, fax 141-311	$100

any time of the year, reserve one of the several oceanfront rooms. Another extra is the charming old inner patio, decorated by the colorful umbrellas of the El Shrimp Bucket restaurant and shaded by towering, leafy trees festooned with hanging air-roots. A combo plays traditional Latin melodies on the patio (weather permitting) most nights till around 2200. Located at Av. Olas Altas 11, Mazatlán, Sinaloa 82000, tel. (69) 812-640, 812-334; the 57 rooms have TV, a/c, and phones. From about $25 d, somewhat higher during holidays, credit cards accepted.

A few blocks away stands the venerable six-story oceanfront **Hotel Belmar,** faded but still welcoming the longtimers who remember when it was *the* hotel in Mazatlán. Although now a bit tattered, its old amenities remain: pool, sidewalk restaurant, and many ocean-view rooms, some carpeted and modern and some so old and makeshift that they're quaint. Found on Av. Olas Altas 166, Mazatlán, Sinaloa 82000, tel. (69) 851-111; 200 rooms, with a/c, phones, and parking, from about $20 d, credit cards accepted.

About a half mile north, where Paseo Claussen bends around Cerro Nevería, a big sign on the hill above the Ciencias del Mar (Marine Sciences) college marks **Suites Vidalmar.** The modern stucco apartment complex clusters artfully above a blue designer swimming pool with a sweeping view of the nearby rocky bay and northward-curving shoreline. Ten one-bedroom suites—all spacious, tastefully furnished, with kitchenettes—can accommodate four in two double beds. One airy, two-story suite accommodates five. This is a place for those who want a restful vacation while enjoying quiet pursuits: cooking, basking in the sun, reading, and watching sunsets from the comfort of their own home in Mazatlán. For the high winter season, be sure to reserve early: Calle Las Palmas 15, Mazatlán, Sinaloa 82000, tel. (69) 812-190 or 812-197, a/c, phones, parking, pool, kitchenette; rates are about $35 for two, $45 for four, and $60 for the big five-person suite, credit cards accepted.

The same management operates **Apartmentos las Palmas,** a stack of apartments and a penthouse, across the street. Although not nearly as luxurious as Suites Vidalmar, the apartments are large, modern, and Spartan but thoughtfully furnished, and sleep up to four. Residents have access to the pool across the street. Same address and phone as Suites Vidalmar; the 11 one-bedroom apartments rent from about $32 d; the penthouse about $50, all with a/c, no parking, credit cards accepted. Bargain for lower low-season rates.

If you want to be near the center of colorful downtown bustle, try the no-frills **Hotel del Centro,** within sight of the cathedral, right around the corner from the market. (The hotel's streetfront, although busy, is too narrow for buses, and is consequently not very noisy.) Here you pay only for what you want: a/c $2, TV another $2. There's not much in the clean rooms but the basics. No matter; the attraction of this part of town is what's outside the door. Their 24 rooms rent for about $15 d low season, $18 high; Canizales 18, Mazatlán, Sinaloa 82000, tel. (69) 812-673.

For a little more luxury in the downtown district, walk about four blocks to the opposite and quieter west side of the cathedral to the **Hotel Central.** Past the upstairs lobby you'll find a small restaurant, a friendly place for meeting other travelers, and three floors of cool, clean, modern-style rooms. On Calle Belisario Domínguez 2 Sur at Calle Ángel Flores, Mazatlán, Sinaloa 82000, tel. (69) 821-888. The rates for their 40 rooms, with a/c, TV, and phones, are from about $24 d low season, higher during holidays.

Playa Norte Hotels

During the 1960s Mazatlán burst its old city limits at the end of Paseo Claussen and spilled northward along the long sand crescent called Playa Norte. Now, a three-mile string of '60s-style hotels and motels lines the breezy beachfront of Av. del Mar, an extension of Paseo Claussen. Unfortunately, however, the wide, busy thoroughfare intervenes between the hotels (save one, below) and the beach.

The one exception is the dignified **Hotel de Cima,** a few blocks north of the Fisherman's Monument. Its tunnel beneath Av. del Mar leads directly to the hotel's beachfront seafood *palapa* restaurant. Back inside, the staff try hard to live up to the hotel's "We Only Look Expensive" motto, maintaining a cool, relaxed restaurant, pool, nightclub, and bars all while keeping the spacious, comfortable ocean view rooms spotless. Reserve at Av. del Mar s/n, P.O. Box 350, Mazatlán, Sinaloa 82000, tel. (69) 827-300 or 827-400. Their 150 rooms, all with two double beds, are from about $45 d low season, with a/c, cable TV, phones, parking, tennis, and limited wheelchair access; credit cards accepted.

About two blocks farther north stands **Hotel Aguamarina,** Best Western's very worthy representative in Mazatlán. With a low-rise stucco motel facade, built around a pool-patio, its rooms (either ocean or garden view) are large and gracefully decorated with native-style handmade wood furniture. The wall art hangs tastefully on colonial-style textured white interiors. Contact them at Av. del Mar 110, P.O. Box 301, Mazatlán, Sinaloa 82000, tel. (69) 817-080 or 816-909, fax 824-624. The 101 rooms rent for about $50 d standard, $66 d deluxe, with a/c, cable TV, phones, parking, an airy, high-ceilinged restaurant, and pool; credit cards accepted. From the U.S. and Canada, reserve through the Best Western toll-free number, (800) 528-1234.

Farther north a few blocks (just past the Pizza Hut) appears the smallish facade of the motel-style **Hotel del Sol.** A few steps from the street-front reception, you will find that the Motel del Sol is larger than it looks. Its rooms cluster around an inviting pool-patio where, on one corner, a plaster Donald Duck squirts water from his mouth. Inside, tasteful wood furniture, white walls, and spotless tile floors decorate the spacious rooms. Thirteen of the 21 rooms are equipped with modern kitchenettes. Contact them at Av. del Mar s/n, P.O. Box 400, Mazatlán, Sinaloa 82000, tel. (69) 851-103. Rooms run about $33 d with kitchenette, $25 without, with a/c, phones, some TV, and parking.

Finally, next to the popular Restaurant Señor Frog's, comes the best-buy **Hotel Sands.** It's clean, and if you don't mind a bit of traffic noise from the avenue, has the ingredients for a pleasant beach vacation: sea-view rooms with balconies overlooking an inviting pool-patio, a/c, phones, and TV. Located at Av. del Mar 1910, P.O. Box 309, Mazatlán, Sinaloa 82000, tel. (69) 820-000. Their 50 rooms usually rent for about $25 d, a bit higher during holidays.

Zona Dorada
Budget-to-Moderate Lodgings

Along a six-mile strip of golden sand rise Mazatlán's newest, plushest hotels. But unlike some other world-class resorts, the Zona Dorada is not wall-to-wall high-rises. In the breezy, palm-fringed spaces between the big hotels, there are many excellent moderately priced hotels and apartment complexes.

For one of the most charming budget accommodations in Mazatlán, try **Fiesta Apartmentos,** a complex of studios and one-bedroom apartments within a jungle-garden blooming with bushy guavas, hanging vines, squawking parrots, and slinking iguanas. Hardworking owner-manager Yolanda Olivera and her carpenter spouse built the place from the ground up while raising a family during the '60s and '70s. Their units are each uniquely furnished with husband-made wooden chairs and tables, toilet, hot shower, and a double bed. Larger units have an additional bed, a sofa or two, and a kitchenette. While you may have to do some initial cleaning up, the price and ambience are certainly right. They're three blocks directly inland from beachside landmark Balboa Tower, at Calle Ibis 502, Fracc. Gaviotas, Mazatlán, Sinaloa 82110, tel. (69) 135-355. Their 11 studios and one-bedroom apartments rent from about $12/day ($250/month), while larger units with kitchenettes go for about $20/day ($450/month). All apartments come with fans and parking; reservations are mandatory during the winter.

Right next door is the less personal, but equally unique, **Racquet Club Las Gaviotas,** a complex of bungalow-apartments and condominiums spread around a spacious palm-shaded swimming-pool garden. While a good, moderately priced vacation lodging for anyone, this is a paradise for tennis buffs on a budget, with its row of seven well-maintained (three clay and four hard) courts. The bungalows themselves are spacious, one- and two-bedroom units with a living room/dining room furnished in Spanish-style tile and wood and equipped with modern kitchenettes. Reservations are mandatory year-round. On Calle Ibis at Bravo, P.O. Box 173, Mazatlán, Sinaloa 82000, tel. (69) 135-939. The 20 units rent from about $450/month for a one-bedroom bungalow and $650 for two bedrooms (with higher daily and weekly rates, fans and daily cleaning service included). Lower units are wheelchair-accessible.

Even lovelier (but minus the tennis courts) is the nearby **Los Girasoles**, a stucco apartment complex built around an inviting pool-patio and spacious garden. When ripe, the fruit of the banana trees which fringe the garden becomes available to guests. Inside, the airy Mexican-style wood and tile kitchenette apartments are comfortably furnished and spotless. They're at Av. Gaviotas 709, Mazatlán, Sinaloa 82110, tel. (69) 135-288 or 113-835, five blocks from the beach at the end of Gaviotas, next to Restaurant Casa Loma. The 22 units (both one- and two-bedroom) rent for about $40/day or $850/month. Low-season discounts may be available. Rental includes fans, parking, and daily cleaning service; credit cards are accepted.

On Mazatlán's most beautiful beach stand a number of small, moderately priced lodgings along Av. R.T. Loaiza, which, about a block north of Valentino's, loops left, one way, away from noisy Calz. Camarón Sábalo. Among the best is **Casa Contenta**, a comfortable two-story complex that lives up to its name. Step past the off-street parking and you will find seven roomy, tastefully furnished kitchenette apartments tucked behind a luxurious family house, all within a manicured garden. Besides the beach and a small pool in their backyard, Casa Contenta residents can enjoy good restaurants and the entertainment of plush hotels within a few minutes' walk. Reserve early: Playa Las Gaviotas, Calz. R.T. Loaiza s/n, tel. (69) 134-976, from about $50/day for an apartment, $150 for the house, with 10% discounts for one-month rentals. Rental includes daily cleaning service, a/c, and parking. Credit cards are accepted, and lower-level units have limited wheelchair access.

If Casa Contenta is full, you can try its plainer (but nevertheless beautifully located) neighbors, Motel Marley and Motel Los Arcos. Guests at the two story **Motel Marley** can choose between upper- or ground-level one- or two-bedroom units, all with living rooms and fully furnished kitchenettes, with daily maid service and air-conditioned bedrooms. Extras include parking and attractive garden grounds that spread from an inviting pool-patio. The majority of the apart-

ments are right on the beach. For the most privacy and best of best views, reserve one of their beachfront upper units early. Write or call them at R. T. Loaiza 226, P.O. Box 214, Mazatlán, Sinaloa 82000, tel./fax (69) 135-533. Rates run about $50 d for one bedroom (with two double beds), $70 for two bedrooms (four double beds) for four people. Add about $8 per additional person. Credit cards are accepted.

Accommodations at **Motel Los Arcos**, a block south, next to Hotel Las Flores, at R.T. Loaiza 214, P.O. Box 132, tel. (69) 135-066, fax 813-389, are similar to the Motel Marley. The scruffiness of the grounds and the lack of a pool don't seem to deter the many guests who return yearly to enjoy the sparkling sun, sea, and sand, right from their front doorsteps. The approximately 20 clean, brightly furnished kitchenette view apartments rent for about the same as the Motel Marley, above—$50 d for one bedroom, $70 for two bedrooms for four people. Add about $8 per additional person, credit cards accepted.

On the beachfront next door towers the **Hotel Las Flores**, R.T. Loaiza 212, P.O. Box 583, Mazatlán, Sinaloa 82110, tel. (69) 135-011 or 835-100, fax 143-422, very popular with North American winter package vacationers. In the standard-grade (but less than spotless) rooms, bright orange-red bedspreads blend with ruddy brick wall highlights. The deluxe rooms, in contrast, feature soothing blue and white decor and kitchenettes. All units enjoy expansive ocean views. Downstairs, the lobby spreads to an attractive restaurant, pool-bar, and tables beneath thatched-roof beachside *palapas*. During high season, their 119 rooms rent for about $60 d standard, $70 w/kitchenette, $80 deluxe w/kitchenette. You should never have to pay this, however. A few months before departure, shop around among agents for an air-hotel promotional package; also, monthly and weekly rates are often much cheaper. Rentals include a/c, TV, phones, and parking; credit cards are accepted.

Although only half a block from the beach, the low-rise **Hotel Plaza Las Gaviotas** Bugambilias 100, P.O. Box 970, Mazatlán, Sinaloa 82110, tel. (69) 134-496, fax 136-685, is easy to miss. It nevertheless offers plenty—good management, spacious, tastefully decorated rooms, peace and quiet—for surprisingly little. The petite, attractive lobby leads to a leafy, intimate inner patio with a small pool and restaurant on one side. The surrounding rooms are clean and tiled and decorated in light pastels. They rent for about $30 d, $36 for four, low season. With cable TV, a/c, and lower-floor wheelchair access; credit cards are accepted.

The **Hotel Tropicana**, R.T. Loaiza 27, P.O. Box 501, Mazatlán, Sinaloa 82110, tel. (69) 838-000, shares virtually everything—beach, shopping, restaurants, and nightlife—with Zona Dorada luxury hotels except prices. For many savvy vacationeers, the hotel's other big plusses—spacious rooms, private ocean-view balconies, big marble baths—far outweigh the sometimes worn furnishings and the half-block walk to the beach. To assure yourself of the best room (top floor, beach side) reserve early. Rooms go for about $27 s or d most times except 25 Dec.-1 Jan. and February and March, when prices are somewhat higher. Amenities include a/c, phones, a pool, beach club, restaurant-bar, and full wheelchair access; credit cards are accepted.

The mostly young guests at the **Hotel Riviera Mazatlán,** Camarón Sábalo 51, P.O. Box 795, Mazatlán, Sinaloa 82000, tel. (69) 834-611, fax 844-532, enjoy luxury beachfront amenities at moderate rates. The hotel's design makes the most of its already enviable location. The rooms, in a pair of sunny, breeze-swept tiers, enclose a spacious two-pool patio that looks out on a gorgeous beach, sea, and sunset vista. Upstairs, guest rooms have private balconies and are tiled, clean, and simply but thoughtfully decorated in blues and whites. Low-season rates run about $40 d with ocean view, $32 d without. Corresponding high-season rates are about $60 and $40. Amenities include nightly rock music in the patio, TV, a/c, parking, and full wheelchair access; credit cards are accepted.

Zona Dorada Luxury Hotels

A few blocks farther south along Loaiza stands the landmark of the Zona Dorada—the first hotel built (despite many doubters) on what was once an isolated sand-strip far from the city center. Even in the September and October low-occupancy months (when many Zona Dorada hotels and restaurants are virtually empty) everyone—Mexicans and foreigners alike—still flocks

to the **Hotel Playa Mazatlán.** The band plays every night, the Fiesta Mexicana buffet show goes on every Saturday, and the fireworks boom and flash above the beach every Sunday night. To enjoy the Playa Mazatlán, you don't have to stay there; just order something at the beachside *palapa*-terrace restaurant and enjoy the music, the breeze, and the same ocean view shared by its luxurious rooms. In the heart of the Zona Dorada at Av. R.T. Loaiza 202, P.O. Box 207, Mazatlán, Sinaloa 82110, tel. (69) 134-444 or 134-455, fax 140-366. The 425 rooms go for about $64 d standard low season, $73 deluxe one-bedroom suite—$90 and $100 high season, respectively; with a/c, TV, phones, pool, jacuzzi, tennis, parking, and full wheelchair access; credit cards accepted.

For the classiest tropical retreat in town, step northward to the **Hotel Inn at Mazatlán.** Although mostly a time-share (buy a room for a specified week or two each year), they do rent out their vacant units, hotel-style. All guests, furthermore, whether owners or one-time renters, receive the same tender loving service. Every lovely feature of the Inn at Mazatlán shines with care and planning, from the excellent inside-outside beachview restaurant and the artistically curved pool to the palms' sunset silhouettes and the spacious, luxuriously appointed sea-view rooms. Right on silky Playa Camarón at Camarón Sábalo 6291, P.O. Box 1292, Mazatlán, Sinaloa 82110, tel. (69) 135-500, fax 134-782; their 126 rooms rent from about $80 d low season, $100 high. For a bit more, you can have a one-bedroom suite sleeping six including kitchenette. All rentals enjoy a/c, phones, refrigerators, and parking. For recreation there is tennis but no TV. Reservations are generally necessary; credit cards are accepted.

No discussion of Mazatlán hotels would be complete without mention of the **Hotel El Cid** "mega resort," the hotel that tries to be everything. The huge complex, which sprawls over the north end of Av. Camarón Sábalo, claims to be the biggest in Mexico—with 1,000 rooms in three separate hotels, 15 separate bars and restaurants, a health club, a giant glittering disco, and a country club subdivision, a marina development, and a world-class 18-hole golf course and 17 tennis courts. Size, however, gives El Cid a definite institutional feeling—as if everyone, the

2,000 employees and 2,000 guests alike, were simply numbers. The El Cid's saving grace (besides its velvet-sand beachfront), however, may be its huge pool. It meanders among the three hotels, a palm-fringed blue lagoon complete with a fake (albeit very clever fake) rock waterslide, waterfall, and diving platform straight from an old Tarzan movie. This doesn't seem to matter, however to the poolside crowd of guests, from ages four to 90, who enjoy watching each other slipping, sliding, and jumping into the cool water. Located on Camarón Sábalo s/n, P.O. Box 813, Mazatlán, Sinaloa 82000, tel. (69) 833-333, fax 141-311. High-season room rates are from about $100 d with everything, including complete wheelchair access. They often offer cheaper low-season promotions, obtainable through travel agents or their reservations office.

Beyond the Zona Dorada

Vacationers who hanker for a more rustic beach atmosphere enjoy the **Bungalows Playa Escondida** on palmy Playa Cerritos, about five miles north of the Zona Dorada. Administered by the trailer park office across the boulevard, the 20 whitewashed bungalows laze beneath a swaying coconut palm grove. The clean, Spartan, tile kitchenette units, in parallel rows facing the ocean, sleep two to four. The more heavily used beachfront row enjoys sweeping ocean views, while the others lie sheltered beneath the palms behind the dune. During the winter season you can enjoy plenty of friendly company at the trailer park pool across the street. Stores and restaurants are within a short drive nearby. Reserve at Calz. Sábalo Cerritos 999, P.O. Boxes 682 and 202, Mazatlán, Sinaloa 82110, tel. (69) 880-077, fax 820-285. The bungalows rent for about $24/day d without a/c; add about $5 for a/c, and about $5 per additional person. A one-month rental gets a 10% discount.

Homestay Program

Besides offering Spanish classes, the privately owned **Centro de Idiomas** (Language Center) also runs a homestay program. Participants live with a Mexican family (about $150/week, including three meals). They also offer person-to-person contacts, in which such visiting professionals as teachers, nurses, and doctors meet with and learn from their local counterparts. Contact them in their downtown school on Belisario Domínguez 1908, upstairs, tel. (69) 822-053, fax 855-606, Compuserve 74174, 1340.

RV and Trailer Parks

Mazatlán beachfront trailer space is an increasingly scarce commodity, victim to rising land values. If you're planning on a Christmas stay, phone or mail in your reservation and deposit by September or you may be out of luck, especially for the choice spaces.

One trailer park owner who is determined never to sell out is Gabriela, of **Mar Rosa Trailer Park.** Besides being the on-the-spot manager, she's Mazatlán's informal one-woman welcoming committee and information source. "I will never sell. The people who come here are my friends . . . like my family." If you ask if she has a pool, she will probably point to the beach a few feet away, and say, "one big pool." She's just north of the Hotel Holiday Inn at Calz. Camarón Sábalo 702, P.O. Box 435, Mazatlán, Sinaloa 82000, tel. (69) 136-187 or 165-967; 55 mostly unshaded spaces, all hookups, from $13/day ($17-19 for the choice beachfront spaces). With toilets, hot showers, a/c power, cable TV; near markets and restaurants, and leashed dogs okay.

Another popular close-in (Zona Dorada, two blocks from the beach) trailer park is the **Las Palmas,** in a big, palm-shaded lot off Camarón Sábalo, about half a block south of the Dairy Queen. Address is Calz. Camarón Sábalo 333, tel. (69) 135-311. Spaces cost about $12/day, $270/month, with pool, all hookups, toilets, showers, leashed dogs okay, camping available, and it's near everything.

Nearby (on Calz. R. Buelna, two blocks inland from Valentino's Disco), the **Trailer Park La Posta** spreads beneath the shade of a banana, mango, and avocado grove (all-you-can-eat in season). Residents enjoy a plethora of facilities, including all hookups, showers and toilets, a big pool and sundeck, shaded picnic *palapas,* a small store, and the beach two blocks away. Their 180 spaces rent for about $10/day or $270/month; add $2 daily for a/c power. Early winter reservations are generally necessary:

P.O. Box 362, Mazatlán, Sinaloa 82000, tel. (69) 835-310.

In the quieter country a block off northside Playa Cerritos the **Playa Escondida Trailer Park,** Calz. Sábalo Cerritos 999, P.O. Box 682 or 202, Mazatlán, Sinaloa 82110, tel. (69) 880-077, fax 820-285, spreads for acres beneath a lazy old coconut grove. Residents enjoy direct access to the long, uncrowded beach across the road and to nearby supermarkets and restaurants. They can also stay in the trailer park's Bungalows Playa Escondida (see above) across the street. The 200 spaces are $11/day or $270/month, all hookups, big saltwater pool, rec room, hot showers, toilets, leashed dogs okay.

Camping

Although there is no established public campground in Mazatlán, camping is allowed for a fee in the **La Posta, Las Palmas,** and **Playa Escondida** trailer parks.

If, however, you prefer solitary beach camping, there are plenty of empty grassy dunes on the northerly end of **Playa Cerritos** that appear ripe for tenting. If you are uncertain about the safety or propriety of a likely looking spot, inquire locally.

Other, more isolated spots (be sure to bring water) lie along the long curve of sand on the south shore of **Stone Island;** catch a ride on the launch across from the Stone Island dock, at the foot of Av. Gutiérrez Najera on Playa Sur. To get to **Isla Venados,** a mile off Playa Sábalo, ride the boat from the El Cid beachfront. On Isla Venados, don't set up your tent on the narrow beach; it's under water at high tide.

For wilderness beach camping, try **Playa Delfín,** the pearly sand crescent north of Punta Cerritos. Get there by taking the right fork toward Hwy. 15 *cuota* about a mile before the northern end of Calz. Sábalo Cerritos. Pass Mazagua water park, continue about another mile and turn left at the gravel road just before the railroad track. This soon leads past the big white El Delfín condo complex, which marks the beginning of Playa Delfín, a 10-mile breezy strip of sand, unused except by occasional local fishermen. There's little of civilization here (not even any trees)—simply sand, surf (steep beach: careful for undertow), seabirds, and a seemingly endless carpet of shells.

FOOD

Mazatlán abounds in good food. The competition is so fierce that bad eateries don't survive. The best are easy to spot because they have customers even during the quiet Sept.-Nov. low season.

Snacks, Stalls, and Market

With care, you can do quite well right on the street downtown. An afternoon cluster of folks around a streetside cart piled with oyster shells and shrimp is your clue that their fare is fresh, tasty, and very reasonably priced. These carts usually occupy the same place every day and, for most of them, the quality of their food is a matter of honor. One of the best is **El Burro Feliz,** which occupies a spot at 61 Calle Sixto Osuna, outside of their family house across from the Archaeological Museum. Try their dozen-oyster cocktail, enough for two, $7.

For dessert, an elderly gentleman runs a shaved—literally, with a hand tool—ice stand across the street, from which he serves the best old-fashioned (safe ice) snowcones in Mazatlán.

If you're cooking your own meals, or simply hanker for some fresh fruit and vegetables, the best place to find the crispest of everything is the **Central Market** on the corner of Calles Benito Juárez and Melchor Ocampo, two short blocks behind the cathedral. Open daily 0600-1800.

After an hour of hard market bargaining, you may be in the mood for a cool, restful lunch. If so, step upstairs inside the market to the leafy balcony *fonda* over the the corner of Juárez and Valle and enjoy the scene. Alternatively, walk one block down Juárez and enter the air-conditioned interior of **Pastelería Panamá,** Av. Juárez, corner of Canizales, tel. (69) 851-853, and try one of their tasty lunch specials or treat yourself to their excellent *helado chocolate* (chocolate ice cream). Open daily 0800-2200.

Afterwards, just outside the door, you may see the *churro* cart that always seems to be parked at that corner. Try three of these uniquely Mexican, foot-long thin sugar doughnuts for $1.

Downtown and Olas Altas Restaurants
Complete meal price key: Budget: under $7; Moderate: $7-14; Expensive: over $14.

Restaurant Doney is located two blocks from the central plaza at Calle Mariano Escobedo 610, tel. (69) 812-651. One of Mazatlán's "must" eateries, Doney is a labor of love of the owners, Sr. and Sra. Alfonso T. Velarde (one or both of whom usually can be seen occupying one of the side tables an hour before closing). For a relatively new (started in 1980) location, the cool, airy ambience—towering arched brick ceiling, Victorian chandelier, old Mazatlán photos—is refreshingly traditional. The mostly local, upper-class patrons enjoy a broad menu of home-style Mexican food, such as chorizo (spiced sausage), various *antojitos* (small tacos, tostadas, tamales), Mazatlán's regional specialty, *asado* (spicy beef stew), and a scrumptious selection of homemade pies and cakes. Open daily 0800-2200; credit cards accepted. Moderate.

Although macrobiotic fare is a novelty in Mexico, downtown Mazatlán has **La Casa de Ana,** on Plazuela Machado, two minutes' walk south of the central plaza at Constitución 515. The friendly owner serves a delicious daily meat-free *comida* (set lunch) that's designed to please. The four courses usually begin with a crisp salad, continue with a savory soup and a hearty main dish, and often conclude with a tasty pudding for dessert. She's open 1200-1600 for lunch daily except Saturday. Budget.

For a special treat, you can return to the same neighborhood for supper and sample the homey fare of the **Cenaduréa El Tunel.** Tucked just off the southeast corner of Plazuela Machado at Carnaval 1207 and open 1800-2200 daily, El Tunel leads you to a narrow corridor where customers are enjoying the craft of a squad of grandmotherly chefs who carry out their mission at stoves in the interior dining room. Their delectable enchiladas, crunchy tacos, rich *pozole* (pork with hominy stew), and creamy refried beans are bound to please all devotees of true Mexican food. Budget.

If you're in a festive mood, **El Shrimp Bucket,** Av. Olas Altas 11, bottom floor of Hotel La Siesta, tel. (69) 816-350, is open daily 0600-2300, credit cards accepted. The restaurant, hung with a riot of taffeta flowers and balloons inside, with the marimba combo humming away by dinnertime in the tropical patio outside, is a party waiting to happen. This is especially true when you call for their bounteous bucket of shrimp ($16, enough for two or three), which they will fix exactly as you wish—breaded, grilled, steamed, or barbecued. Moderate.

Playa Norte Restaurants
It's hard to imagine a restaurant closer to the source than the rough and ready family-style **Restaurant El Camachín,** 97 Paseo Claussen and 5 de Mayo, tel. (69) 850-197, located where the boats bring the fish in every morning. In true Mexican tradition, they augment many of their dishes with a number of flavorful sauces, which range from a mild salsa Oriental (onions, celery, and a bit of soy) to a peppery salsa ranchero. Pick your favorite and have them serve it with their recommended catch of the day. Open daily 1000-2200. Moderate.

Heading north along the *malecón,* a bright sign marks one of the two branches of **Karnes en Su Jugo,** Av. del Mar 550, tel. (69) 821-322. If personable owner Jorge Pérez (who, with his red hair, looks more like a Swede than most Swedes do) is there, let him place your order: a bounteous table, likely set with a plate of savory roast beef in juice, hot melted Chihuahua white cheese, refried beans, and enough salsa and hot corn tortillas for a dozen yummy tacos or tostadas. Open daily 1300-0100; credit cards accepted. Moderate to expensive. The same description applies to the second Karnes en Su Jugo branch, in the Zona Dorada at Camarón Sábalo 1541, across from the Dairy Queen.

A stay in Mazatlán wouldn't be complete without a trip to **Señor Frog's,** Calz. Camarón Sábalo s/n, next to Frankie Oh's disco, tel. (69) 851-110, the second (El Shrimp Bucket was the first), and perhaps the best, creation of late owner Carlos Anderson's worldwide chain. Many extreme adjectives—brash, bold, loud, risqué, funny, far-out—have been used to describe the waiters, patrons, and the music at Señor Frog's. Most everyone agrees the ribs are the best and the margaritas the most potent in town. Open daily noon to midnight, credit cards accepted. Expensive.

Zona Dorada Restaurants

Despite their "Golden Zone" locations, Zona Dorada restaurant tariffs needn't be excessive. When you're in a sweat from shopping, sunburn, and street vendors, and you're ready to escape from Mexico, try Mexico's first **Dairy Queen** instead, Camarón Sábalo 500, corner of R.T. Loaiza, tel. (69) 161-522. The regular hamburgers and the associated soft-ice-cream goodies will taste better than home. When you emerge, you'll feel like staying another couple of months. Open daily 1000-2300. Budget.

For fast food, in contrasting Mexican style, step across the street to **Tortas Hawaii,** Camarón Sábalo s/n, at Gaviotas, tel. (69) 141-600. The name Hawaii, however, seems to have little relation to their food except for the pineapple in some of their huge sandwiches. These include your choice of ham, roast pork, or chicken, with Chihuahua or Oaxaca cheese on a big *bolillo* bun—enough for a light lunch for two—from $3. Open daily 0900-2200. Budget.

For a pleasant surprise, walk two blocks south from the Dairy Queen corner to the Zona Dorada branch of the **Pastelería Panamá,** tel. (69) 136-977. Here, a legion of local middle-to-upper class folks flock for everything from ham and eggs and hamburgers, to *enchiladas suizas* and chocolate malts. Open daily 0700-2300. Moderate.

For more serious eaters, the big beach-view **Terraza Playa** restaurant at Hotel Playa Mazatlán, R.T Loaiza 202, tel. (69) 134-455, is so popular, tables are sometimes hard to get. This is frequently true Sunday nights when families begin to arrive two hours early for the free eight o'clock fireworks show. The Terraza Playa offers excellent entrees, such as *pescado veracruzana* for $5-10. Open daily 0700-2300; credit cards accepted. Moderate.

A number of worthy open-air *palapa* restaurants cluster along Loaiza across from the Hotel Playa Mazatlán. Among the best in food, service, and friendly, airy ambience is **Tío Juan's.** Here, you can start the day with fruit, coffee, eggs, and toast ($3), return for a big *ensalada de atún* (tuna salad; $3) for lunch, and return at suppertime for a hearty Mexican plate ($7, enough for two). Open daily 0700-2300.

Nearby **Lario's,** on side-street Bugambilias, across Loaiza from the Hotel Playa Mazatlán, tel. (69) 141-767, is so popular that, when it moved in 1993, it survived by taking its brigade of loyal customers with it. Customers continue to enjoy gratis happy-hour margaritas, live music nightly, and bountiful, expertly prepared and served meat, fish, and Mexican plates at reasonable prices. Open daily 0800-2200. Moderate to expensive.

A spectacular beachfront view, cool breezes, snappy service, and fresh salads, sandwiches, and seafood at reasonable prices keep patrons coming to restaurant **Pancho's** year-round, located at the beach end of the small complex across from Shell City, tel. (69) 140-911. During the winter season, when vacationers crowd in, come early. The dozen tables can fill by noon. Open daily 0800-2300. Moderate.

For impeccable service and tranquil, palm-framed sunsets, **Papagayo** restaurant at the Hotel Inn at Mazatlán is hard to beat. Found on Camarón Sábalo 6291, a low-rise behind wall and trees between Hotels El Cid and Costa de Oro, tel. (69) 135-500, ext. 1235. Their menu caters to the tastes of their mostly North American clientele, with salad bar and reasonably priced complete dinner specials, notably, a mouth-watering chicken-rib combo. Open daily 0700-2200; credit cards accepted. Moderate.

Across the street, outside **Restaurant Los Arcos,** as at Señor Frog's, the patrons line up during the high season. Los Arcos is situated on Camarón Sábalo s/n (look for the big thatched *palapa* between Holiday Inn and El Cid), tel. (69) 139-577. Los Arcos claims to specialize in "the secret flavor which the sea has confided," meaning piquant sauces, many of them peppery hot. Specify *pica* (spicy) or *no pica* before you order your shrimp, oysters, smoked swordfish, snapper, or other seafood—they'll all be good. Open daily 1200-2200; credit cards accepted. Moderate.

One of the most successfully exclusive restaurants in town is **Casa Loma,** which, besides tucking itself behind a wall on a quiet dead-end street, manages to close July to October. Located at Gaviotas 104, at end of street, tel. (69) 135-398. The Casa Loma secret: a secluded location, subdued tropical atmosphere, excellent service, and a selection of tasty international specialties continue to attract a clubby list of affluent patrons. Open 1200-2200; credit cards accepted, reservations recommended. Expensive.

The low-key facade of **Señor Pepper's** Camarón Sábalo, north end, across from Hotel Camino Real, tel. (69) 131-111, gives little hint of what's inside: a flight of fancy away from Mexico to some Victorian polished brass, mirror, and wood-paneled miniplanet, more San Francisco than San Francisco ever was. When you sit down at a table and ask for a menu, the tuxedo-attired waiter will probably do a double take, scurry away, and return with a small tray of a few thick steaks, a pork chop huge enough for two, and a big lobster. You choose one of these as the basis for your dinner. The meal proceeds from there like a Mozart symphony, through each delectable course, until dessert served with coffee, which one of your three waiters will rush to your table in polished silver and pour with a determined flourish. You look up at him, convinced that he *believes* in his mission; by the time you exit the front door, comfortably satisfied, you will probably be convinced of his mission, also. Señor Pepper's is open daily 1800-2400, credit cards accepted, reservations recommended. Expensive.

ENTERTAINMENT AND EVENTS

Just Wandering Around

A good morning place to start is the little beach at the beginning of **Playa Norte,** at the north end of Av. 5 de Mayo, where the fishermen sell their daily catches. As the cluster of buyers busily bid for the choicest tuna, shrimp, mahimahi, and mackerel, a flock of pelicans and seagulls scurry after the leftovers.

Come back later, around supper time, to enjoy the end-product: fresh-cooked seafood (try Restaurant Camachin or Mariscos Cancún), accompanied by the tunes of one of many strolling mariachi bands—perhaps even one of the famous Sinaloan-style brass bands. If someone else is paying, just sit back and enjoy, especially the tuba solo. If you are paying, however, make sure that you agree upon the price, usually around $2 per selection, before the performance begins.

Around noon, the area around the central plaza downtown (Juárez and Ángel Flores) is equally entertaining. Take a seat beneath the shade of the big trees and have your shoes polished for about $1.50.

Shady Plazas

Downtown Mazatlán has a number of neighborhood squares within strolling distance of the central plaza. Five blocks north along Calle Guillermo Nelson lies **Plaza Zaragoza** and its colorful row of little flower shops.

West of the central plaza, two short blocks behind the Palacio Municipal, is the **Plazuela de Los Leones** (Calles Ángel Flores and Niños Héroes), marked by a pair of brass lions guarding the city library. Upstairs, you can peruse the venerable collection of the all-English **Benjamin Franklin Library.**

In a southerly direction from the cathedral, stroll along Juárez three blocks; at Constitución turn right one block to **Plazuela Machado,** the gem of old Mazatlán. Depending upon the time, you may want to stop for a light lunch in the charming Casa de Ana, 515 Constitución at the north side of plaza, or a drink and a round of pool at the friendly, elegantly Victorian (or, in Mexico, Porfirian, after former President Porfirio Díaz) Cafe Pacífico at the adjacent corner. Across the square, in the midafternoons on school days, you can take a park bench seat and listen to the sounds of violin lessons wafting down from the upstairs chambers of the **Academia Ángela Peralta.**

Sidewalk Cafes

A few blocks west, on beachfront **Av. Olas Altas,** watch the passing parade from a table at one of the shady sidewalk cafes clustered around the old **Hotel Belmar.** If it's summer and you're lucky, you may get a chance to enjoy a Pacific Mexico rainstorm. It usually starts with a few warm drops on the sidewalk. Then the wind starts the palms swaying. Pretty soon the lightning is crackling and the rain is pouring as if from a million celestial faucets. But no matter; you're comfortably seated, and even if you happen to get a little wet it's so warm you'll dry off right away.

Late afternoons on Olas Altas yield a feast of quiet people-watching delights. Perch yourself on the old *malecón* and watch the sunset, the surfers tackling the high waves (*olas altas*) offshore, and the kids, old folks, and loving couples strolling along the sidewalk.

Old-Fashioned Shops

During your wanderings around old Mazatlán be sure to step into some of the traditional *papelerías, dulcerías,* and *ferreterías* (stationery, candy, and hardware stores) that still sell the quaint dime-store style of goods that only grandparents back home remember. For starters, try the Dulcería La Fiesta, two blocks north of the cathedral at Melchor Ocampo 612, for enough candy to fill a truck, plus a delightful selection of huge Minnie Mouse, Donald Duck, and Snow White piñatas.

Special Cultural Events

Mazatlán's century-old **Carnaval** is among the world's renowned Mardi Gras. The merry-making begins the week before Ash Wednesday (usually late February or early March, when the faithful ceremoniously receive ash-marks on their foreheads), beginning the period of fasting called Lent. Mazatlán Carnaval anticipates all this with a vengeance in a week-long series of folk dances, balls, ballets, literature readings, beauty contests, and "flower" games. The celebration climaxes on Shrove Tuesday (the day before the beginning of Lent) with a parade of floats and riotous merrymakers, which by this time includes everyone in town, culminating along Av. Olas Altas. If you'd like to join in, reserve your hotel room (streetfront rooms at the Hotels Siesta and Belmar are best located for Carnaval) at least six months in advance.

Other unique local celebrations include the 8 Dec. **Feast of the Immaculate Conception** and the **Cultural Festival of Sinaloa,** a statewide (but centering in Mazatlán) month-long feast of concert, sports, and cultural events in November. Check with the tourist information office (see "Information" following) for details.

Bullfights, Rodeos, and Baseball

Every Sunday from mid-December through Easter, bullfights (not really "fights"), called *corridas de toros,* are held at the big bullring, Plaza Monumental (Av. R. Buelna at Av. de la Marina), about a mile from the beach. The ritual begins at 1600 sharp. Get your tickets through a travel agency or at the bullring.

Once or twice a year the Mazatlán professional association of *charros* (gentleman cowboys) holds a rodeo-like *charreada.* Some events (such as jumping from one racing, unbroken horse to another, or trying to flatten an angry steer by twisting its tail!) make the garden-variety North American rodeo appear tame.

Los Venados ("The Deers"), Mazatlán's entry in the Mexican Pacific Coast Baseball (Béisbol) League (AAA), begins its schedule in early October and continues into the spring. Get your tickets at the stadium (Estadio Teodoro Mariscal), whose night lights are so bright that when the team is home you can't help but see a quarter mile inland from Av. del Mar. Baseball fever locally heats up to epidemic proportions when Culiacán, Los Venados's arch-rival, is in town.

Tourist Shows

While a number of hotels present folkloric song and dance shows, the Hotel Playa Mazatlán's **Fiesta Mexicana** remains the hands-down favorite. The entire three-hour extravaganza, including a sumptuous buffet, begins at 1900 every Tuesday, Thursday, and Saturday during high season (Saturday only during low). Call the hotel (tel. 69-134-455) or a travel agent for tickets, which run about $25 per person. If you miss Fiesta Mexicana on Saturday, you can get in on the free beach fireworks show the next evening at 2000. It's popular, so arrive an hour early to ensure yourself a seat.

Others are trying harder. Wednesday nights, Hotel El Cid succeeds in capturing the spirit of Mazatlán's pre-Lenten Carnaval with a sumptuous buffet and a Mardi Gras-style song and dance extravaganza. Call the Hotel El Cid (tel. 69-1333-333) for information and tickets (about $26, half price for kids).

Movies

A number of Mazatlán cinemas screen first-run Hollywood movies. Try **Cinemas Gaviotas y Albatroses,** Camarón Sábalo 218, a few blocks north of Valentino's disco; call (69) 837-554 for programs. On the other hand, you can sample popular Mexican movies at the double cinema, **Cine Tauro and Scorpio** downtown, where in one afternoon you can enjoy such simmering potboiler epics as *Born to Die* or *Flight of the Intruder,* each accompanied by complimentary Disney cartoons. Located at Ángel Flores and Belisario Domínguez, four short blocks past the Palacio Municipal from the central plaza, $3 per movie, open daily 1600-2400.

Nightlife

It's difficult not to enjoy the sunset in Mazatlán, especially on the beach, where the sun ends most days with a spectacular show. And with your evening having been properly begun, you have your choice of entertainment in dozens of dances, discos, clubs, and bars.

Dance music is plentiful in Mazatlán. You can start out by enjoying drinks or dinner with the medium-volume, '50s- and '60s-style bands that play nightly around 2000 at the more popular hotels, especially the **Playa Mazatlán,** and others, such as **El Cid, Los Sábalos, Costa de Oro,** and **La Siesta.**

Then, around 2300 or 2400, while the Mazatlán night is still young, you can go out and jump at one of several local discos. **Valentino's** (tel. 69-841-666) jumble of white spires and turrets perched on Punta Camarón inspires intense curiosity, if not wonder, among newcomers. Its three separate dance floors have the requisite flashing lights and speakers varying from loud, louder, and the loudest (with a booming bass audible for a couple of miles up and down the beach).

On the other hand, what **El Caracol** (tel. 69-133-333, open Tues.-Sat.) at El Cid lacks on the outside, it makes up on the inside. There is one huge dance floor beneath two upper levels, which patrons can exit to the lower by sliding down a chute or slithering down a brass firehouse pole.

The discos, which charge a cover of about $10 and expect you to dress casually but decently (slacks and shirts, dresses or skirts and blouses, and shoes), open around 2200 and go on until 0400 or 0500 in the morning.

Bars and Hangouts

Mazatlán has a few romantic, softly lighted piano bars. Besides the suave **Mikonos** piano bar (right next to Valentino's at Camarón Sábalo and Rafael Buelna), you can sample the elegant sophistication of **Señor Pepper's** (tel. 131-111) piano bar across from the Hotel Camino Real at the north end of Camarón Sábalo.

For high-volume '70s rock and beer-and-popcorn camaraderie, **Jungle Juice** restaurant's upstairs bar on a side street off R.T Loaiza, one block from Hotel Playa Mazatlán, tel. (69) 133-315, is literally wall-to-wall customers during the high season. The same is true for the disco-style **Pepe Toro** (diagonally across the street) and the open-air cantina **Gringo Lingo,** around the corner, except that, at Gringo Lingo, there's more room and more air.

Child's Play

When your kids get tired of digging in the sand and playing in the pool, take them to the **Aquarium,** Mexico's largest, with many big, well-maintained fish tanks—of flinty-eyed sharks, comical wide-bodied box fish, and shoals of luminescent damselfish. Found on Av. de Los Deportes 111, just off Av. del Mar about a mile south of Valentino's; watch for the "Acuario" sign; tel. (69) 817-815, admission about $6 adults, $2.50 kids, open daily 1000-1800. Outside, don't miss the exotic tropical botanical garden, where you'll find a pair of monstrously large alligators. Time your arrival to take in one of the three daily sea lion shows around 1300, 1530, and 1730. For details of the Aquarium's very worthy ecological efforts, see the "Information" section of this chapter.

For a different type of frolic, take the kids to **Aquatico Mazagua** water park, where they'll be able to slip down the hundred-foot-long Kamikaze slide, swish along the toboggan, loll in the wave pool, or simply splash in the regular pool. Located at Playa Cerritos s/n, open daily 1000-1800, about $10 entry for everyone over three, restaurant, snack bar; follow the right fork toward Hwy. 15 near the north end of Calz. Camarón Sábalo and you'll immediately see the water park on the left.

During the adult fun and games of Carnaval, there's no reason your kids have to feel left out if you take them to the **"Carnival"** (as known in North America). You'll find it by looking for the Ferris wheel near the bus terminal on Calle Tamazula and the Hwy. 15 downtown boulevard.

SPORTS AND RECREATION

Walking and Jogging

The Mazatlán heat keeps walkers and joggers near the shoreline. On the beaches themselves, the long, flat strands of **Playa Norte** (along Av. del Mar), **Playa Gaviotas** (north from about the Hotel Los Flores), and the adjoining **Playa Sábalo** (north from about El Cid) provide firm stretches for walking and jogging. If you prefer an even firmer surface, the best uncluttered stretch of the *malecón* seaside sidewalk is along **Av. del Mar** from Valentino's disco south about three miles to the Fisherman's Monument.

Swimming, Boarding, and Sailing

During days of calm water, you can safely swim beyond the gentle breakers, about 50 yards off **Playa Gaviotas and Playa Sábalo.** Heed the

Tough-eating sailfish and black marlin (above) are often discarded after they are brought in. Progressive captains encourage anglers to turn them loose when caught.

BRUCE WHIPPERMAN

usual precautions. (See "Water Sports" in the On the Road chapter.)

On rough-water days you'll have to do your laps in a hotel pool, since there is no public pool in Mazatlán. If your hotel has no pool, some of the big hotels allow day-use by outside guests.

There are several challenging intermediate surfing spots along the Mazatlán shoreline, mostly adjacent to rocky points, such as **Pinos** (next to Ciencias del Mar off Paseo Claussen), **Punta Camarón** (at Valentino's disco), and **Punta Cerritos** at the far north end of the *malecón*. (For more details, see "Beaches" preceding.)

Bodysurfing and boogie-boarding are popular on calm days on Mazatlán's beaches. Boogie boards may be rented for about $3 an hour on the beachfronts of some Zona Dorada hotels, such as Los Sábalos, Playa Mazatlán, El Cid, and Camino Real.

Windsurfing is possible nearly anywhere along Mazatlán's beaches. An especially good, smooth spot is the protected inlet at the north end of Av. Sábalo Cerritos. Bring your own equipment, as there's little windsurfing rental gear available in Mazatlán.

Aqua Sports Center at El Cid and beach shops at other hotels (see above) rent Hobie Cats, small catamaran sailboats, for around $25 per hour (three-person limit) to sail from the beach.

Snorkeling and Scuba Diving

The water near Mazatlán's beaches is generally too churned up for good visibility. Serious snorkelers and divers head offshore to the outer shoals of **Isla Venados** and **Isla Chivos**. A number of shops along the Zona Dorada beaches arrange such trips. The best equipped is El Cid's Aqua Sports Center (tel. 133-333, ext. 341), marked by the clutter of equipment on the beach, on the south side of Hotel El Cid. A three-hour snorkeling or scuba excursion, including equipment and instructor, runs $50-70 per person, while snorkel, mask, and fins rent for about $7 per day.

Jet-Skiing And Parasailing

The highly maneuverable snowmobile-like jet-ski water beetles have completely replaced water-skiing at Mazatlán. Three or four of them can usually be seen tearing up the water, hotdogging over big waves, gyrating between the swells, and racing each other far offshore. For a not-so-cheap thrill, rent one of them at Aqua Sports Center at El Cid (tel. 133-333, ext. 341), which has the best and most equipment, for about $30 per half hour for one, $45 for two persons.

Parasailing chutes are continually ballooning along high over Zona Dorada beaches. For about $25 for a 10-minute ride, you can fly like a bird through arrangements made at any of the following hotels: El Cid, Playa Mazatlán, or Camino Real.

Tennis and Golf

If you're planning on playing lots of tennis in Mazatlán, best check into one of the several hotels, such as **Playa Mazatlán, Inn at Mazatlán,** or **El Cid** (which charges $10/hour even for guests), all of which have courts. If your lodging does not provide courts, you can rent one at **Gaviotas Racquet Club,** tel. (69) 135-939 (three clay, four hard courts, some lighted), for $10/hour. They're popular and likely to be crowded during the winter season, however. Otherwise, try **Club Deportiva Reforma,** Rafael Buelna s/n, with six lighted courts next to the bullring, about a mile from the beach.

Mazatlán golf is even more exclusive. The 18-hole course at **El Cid** is the only one within the city limits, and they allow only their (and Hotel Camino Real's) guests to play. On top of this, the greens and caddy fees total an additional $30. Double this if you're merely from the Camino Real.

There is a more egalitarian, although more pedestrian, nine-hole course at the **Club Campestre,** tel. (69) 800-202 or 801-570, next to the Coca-Cola factory on the airport highway just beyond the south edge of town.

Sportfishing

Competent captains and years of experience have placed Mazatlán among the world's leading billfish (marlin, swordfish, and sailfish) ports. The several licensed *flotas deportivas* (sports fleets) line up along the jetty road beneath the El Faro lighthouse point. They vary, mostly in size of fleet; some have two or three boats, others have a dozen. Boats generally return with about three big fish—one of them a whopping marlin or sailfish—per day.

The biggest is the **Bill Heimpel Star Fleet,** owned and operated by personable Bill Heimpel, a descendant of a German immigrant family. During the high season he sends out a hundred customers a day. He organizes the groups so you can fish without having to rent a whole boat. One day's fishing runs about $60 per person, complete. Entire boats for about eight passengers (six of whom can fish at a time) rent for around $300 per day, complete. May-Oct., reservations are not generally necessary; call them in Mazatlán, tel. (69) 823-878, for information. During the high season (Nov.-April) prepaid reservations at Star Fleet's Texas booking office are mandatory. For more details, contact Star Fleet, P.O. Box 290190, San Antonio, TX 78280, tel. (800) 426-6890, fax (512) 377-0454.

There are smaller fleets equally as competent, however. Heimpel's neighbor is **Mike Maxemin Sportfishing Marina,** whose office is invitingly plastered with yellowing "big catch" photos (Mazatlán's record fish was a half-ton, 13-foot black marlin) beneath huge stuffed marlin and sailfish trophies. Like Heimpel, Maxemin (who has 10 boats) accepts individual reservations. His prices are about $5 less per person for a completely supplied fishing outing. Be at the dock at 0600 sharp; expect to return before 1500. Call Mike Maxemin for information and reservations at (69) 812-824 or 824-977, or write him at P.O. Box 235, Mazatlán, Sinaloa 82000.

A bit farther down the scale, you can check out some of the more local boats, such as **Flota Neptuno,** owned and operated by captain Ricardo Salazar. He rents out a big 42-foot, six person boat with skipper, bait, and poles for billfish for about $160 low season, $200 high. Ask him and he might also be able to furnish a group of four with a launch and skipper, fully equipped for half a day to catch smaller fry, such as 30-pound tuna, or *sierra,* for around $100. Contact him at the dock, or call (69) 824-565.

You can also negotiate with one of the fishermen on **Playa Norte** (at the foot of 5 de Mayo at Paseo Claussen) to take you and a few friends out in his *panga* for half a day. He'll supply lines and bait enough to hook several big mahimahi and red snapper for a total price of about $60, depending on the season.

Boat Launching

If you have your own boat, there are a couple of official launching ramps in Mazatlán. One ramp is at the **Ciencias del Mar** college (on the point just past the boat cove on Paseo Claussen). The school office (tel. 69-828-656, ask for Gloria) inside sells tickets for about $20 to use the ramp for one day 0700-1800. The tariff for a one-month permit is only triple that. That would entitle you to anchor your boat, among a dozen neighbors, in the sheltered Playa Norte cove for a month. No facilities are available except the ramp, however.

The other boat ramp is at **Club Nautico**, Explanada del Faro s/n, Mazatlán, Sinaloa 82000, tel. (69) 815-195, at the far end of the line of sportfishing docks. A one-day launching permit runs about $20. They have a first-class yacht harbor with hoists, a repair shop, and gasoline, but unfortunately no room for outsiders to store boats, either in or out of the water. You may, however, be able to get permission to park your boat and trailer on the road outside the gate.

Hunting Outfitters and Guides

The best outfitters in town are the Aviles Hermanos (Aviles Brothers) at 5 de Mayo and Paseo Claussen. Their business peaks during the winter duck season, when they drive groups about 60 miles south to hunting grounds in the Marismas Nacionales near Esquinapa; their other options include an airplane, which will take you anywhere to legally hunt most anything else. Contact them at their office, 5 de Mayo y Paseo Claussen, P.O. Box 221, Mazatlán, Sinaloa 82000, tel. (69) 813-728, or 816-060, or 143-130, fax (69) 146-598, on Paseo Claussen next to Mexicana Airlines..

SHOPPING

Judging from the platoons of racks in the Zona Dorada and in the Central Market, T-shirts would seem to be the most popular sale item in Mazatlán. Behind the racks, however, Mazatlán's curio shops stock an amazing bounty of goods from all over the country. The best route to quality purchases at reasonable prices is first to look downtown for the lowest prices, next search the Zona Dorada for the best quality, and then make your choice.

Central Market Shopping

The market occupies one square block near the cathedral, between Calles Juárez, Ocampo, Serdan, and Valle. Here, bargaining is both expected and essential unless you don't mind paying $20 for a $5 item. See "Shopping" in the On the Road chapter.

Although the colorful mélange of meat and vegetable stalls occupies most of the floor space, dozens of small curio shops are tucked inside on the Juárez and Valle sides (west and south) and along all four outside sidewalks.

Perhaps the most unusual of the outside shops is **Artesanías Marina Mercante,** a dusty clutter of handmade accessories, including big Zapatista-style sombreros from Oaxaca, wallets and belts from Guadalajara, and locally made hammocks. Located on the market southeast corner, at Valle and Serdan.

Nothing more typifies Mexico than **huaraches.** One of Mazatlán's best selections is at **Huarachería Internacional** on the outside market sidewalk at Ocampo and Juárez. Their Michoacán goods are all authentic and, with bargaining, very reasonably priced.

For a big, air-conditioned selection of everything, from hardware and cosmetics to film and groceries, local people and tourists flock to Mexico's Kmart look-alikes, **Gigante,** on R. Buelna, about a mile from Valentino's disco, open daily 0900-2100, and **Comercial Mexicana** at the Gran Plaza mall. Follow R. Buelna inland from Valentino's, turn right just past the La Posta trailer park, and continue for a quarter mile to Comercial Mexicana's big orange pelican emblem-sign.

Zona Dorada Shopping

The Zona Dorada presents a bewildering variety of curio shops—in small shopping centers, hotel malls, and at streetside along Av. Camarón Sábalo. Nearly everything you're looking for, however, probably can be found in the concentration of many good and unusual shops along the side street R.T. Loaiza, which forks left, one-way, off of Av. Camarón Sábalo a block north of Valentino's disco. The following are a few highlights, moving north on Loaiza.

One of your first stops should be at a trio of shops in the Hotel Playa Mazatlán shopping center on the left. First, on the center's left corner, is **La Carreta,** open daily 0900-1800, an

BRUCE WHIPPERMAN

A worker crafts one of dozens of ornaments for sale at Shell City.

invitingly arranged museum of fine crafts, including bright Talavera pottery, whimsical Oaxaca wooden animals, bright paper flowers, and shining copper and brass chandeliers.

Next door, let the equally attractive selection of **Mexico, Mexico** lead you on, past its racks of colorful women's cotton resort wear, choice Oaxaca wool carpets, eerie Guerrero masks, and shining Tlaquepaque glassware. Open Mon.-Sat 0900-1800, closed Sunday.

Continue one door uphill to admire the glistening collection of the **Playa** silver store. Virtually all Mexican silver jewelry (see "Buying Silver and Gold Jewelry" under "Shopping" in the On the Road chapter) is crafted far away in Taxco, Guerrero. Without bargaining, Mazatlán silver prices may be a bit steep. You can compare prices against other shops (see "Pardo Jewelry" following) or ask them to weigh the piece. Many shops sell silver jewelry for one U.S. dollar per gram. If your choice is significantly greater than that, you'd better bargain. (See "Shopping" in the On the Road chapter.)

Back on the street, head north half a block to the big bargain-basement **Mercado Viejo,** R.T. Loaiza 315, tel. (69) 136-366, open daily 0900-2100, enclosing a small acre of all-Mexico crafts. If you can name it they probably have it: giant ceramic trees of life, a zoo of onyx animals, black Oaxaca pottery, carved and gilded wooden fish—the items so common in stores here they seem ordinary—until you take them back home, where, on your bookshelf they will become precious mementos.

Among the finest of Mazatlán's art galleries is **Sí Como No,** around the corner on Garzas, one short block off R.T. Loaiza, across from Jungle Juice restaurant. Specializing in prints and originals of famous Latin painters, a plethora of hard-to-find Orozcos, Dalís, Ertés, and Viejos decorates its walls and windows. Open 1000-1800, closed Sunday and the months of September and October.

Back on Loaiza a few steps farther, **Shell City,** Av. R.T. Loaiza 407, tel. (69) 131-301, is not only a store, it's a virtual museum of shells (and perhaps the reason they've become so scarce on Mazatlán's beaches). Constellations of pearly curios—swirling conches, iridescent abalones, bushy corals, and in one single deviation, whimsical coconut faces—fill Shell City's seeming acres of displays. Open daily 0900-2000; credit cards accepted.

After Shell City, cross the street and browse for a spell in some of the attractive shops of the intimate beachside **Cabañas** mall. Their varied assortments are so excellent and well-selected many folks could probably do all of their Mazatlán shopping right there.

Pardo Jewelry, 411 Loaiza, tel. (69) 143-354, back across the street adjacent to Shell City, specializes in unusually fine gems and jewelry. Their glittering silver- and gold-set diamonds, rubies, emeralds, lapis, opals, and amethysts are worth appreciating whether you're buying or not. Open Mon.-Sat. 0930-1730, closed Sunday; credit cards accepted.

The **Casa Maya** fine leather store is unmissable because of its replica Mayan pyramid looming above the street. Like Pardo Jewelry nearby, many of Casa Maya's one-of-a-kind leathercraft items—boots, coats, jackets, shoes, purses, stuffed animals, and Indian motifs—are interesting as works of art alone. The Casa is open 1000-1800, closed Sunday; no phone.

For a look at more of Mazatlán's finest, continue along Loaiza for three blocks, and bear left for a block (passing American Express) on Camarón Sábalo to the **Mazatlán Art Gallery,** tel. (69) 143-612 or 165-258. Their collection focuses on fine impressionist-style Mexican landscapes and folk scenes. Additionally, they carry the near-surrealistic paintings of artist Paul Modlin. Open Mon.-Sat. 0900-1900.

SERVICES

Money Exchange

Obtain the most pesos for cash and traveler's checks at **Banamex,** Camarón Sábalo 424, tel. (69) 138-101, in the Zona Dorada across the corner from Dairy Queen. They have a special longer-hours cashier outside and to the right of the regular bank, open Mon.-Fri. 0830-1600, closed weekends. The downtown main branch at the central plaza, corner of Juárez and Ángel Flores, tel. (69) 827-733, changes both Canadian and U.S. dollars and traveler's checks Mon.-Fri. 0830-1600, closed weekends.

After bank hours, change money at one of the many of *casas de cambio* along the Avs. del Mar and Camarón Sábalo (such as the counter at the north end of R.T. Loaiza, across from Dairy Queen, open daily 0900-1900, Sunday 1000-1600, tel. 69-139-209). The **Hotel Playa Mazatlán** reception money-exchange counter, R.T. Loaiza 202, tel. (69) 134-444, services both outside customers and guests daily 0600-2200.

American Express maintains a full-service money counter and travel agency on Camarón Sábalo, half a block from Dairy Queen, tel. (69) 130-600, open Mon.-Fri. 0900-1700, Saturday 0900-1200, which gives bank rates for American Express U.S. dollar traveler's checks. No others accepted, however.

Communications

Mazatlán area code is 69

For routine mailings, use one of the several **post boxes** *(buzones)* at the big hotels, such as Los Sábalos, Playa Mazatlán, El Cid, Camino Real, and others.

Otherwise, the **post office** *(correo)* is adjacent to the central plaza downtown, corner of Juárez and Ángel Flores, tel. (69) 812-121. Open Mon.-Fri. 0800-1800, Saturday 0900-1300, philatelic services in the morning only.

The **telegraph office** *(telégrafo),* tel. (69) 812-220, open Mon.-Fri. 0800-1730, Saturday 0800-2300, is also in the post office building; enter half a block along Ángel Flores from the corner at Juárez.

Operator-assisted **long-distance telephone** *(larga distancia)* service is generally available from telephones in Mazatlán. For calls within Mexico, dial 02; for international calls, dial 09. (For other hints on using telephones in Mexico, see "Communications" in the On the Road chapter.)

Mazatlán also has Computel, an efficient computer-assisted *larga distancia* and **fax** service: in the Zona Dorada (daily 0700-2000, tel. 69-140-034) on Camarón Sábalo a few doors from Dairy Queen; at the bus terminal (open 24 hours, tel. 69-853-930) at Calle Tamazula and National Hwy. 15; and downtown (tel. 69-853-912) at Aquiles Serdán 1512. A call to the U.S. runs about $2.50 per minute, although the bus station office sometimes offers discounts.

Immigration and Customs

For visa extensions up to 180 days total (or more, in cases of real emergency) or loss of tourist card (make a copy beforehand and get a loss report from the tourist police—see "Police and Fire Emergencies" below) go to **Migración** at Aquiles Serdán and Playas Gemelas, on the south side of downtown, near the ferry dock, tel. (69) 813-813. They are open Mon.-Fri. 0900-1500 for business, closed weekends. For general hints on Mexican immigration and customs procedures, see "Other Practicalities" in the On the Road chapter.

For customs matters, such as leaving your car behind in Mexico while you leave the country temporarily, contact the **Aduana** in the old historic building corner of Calle V. Carranza 107, corner of Cruz in the Olas Altas district, tel. (69) 816-109, open Mon.-Fri. 0800-1500.

Consulates

The **United States Consular Agent,** Geri Nelson de Gallardo, helps U.S. citizens with legal and other urgent matters in her office, tel./fax (69) 165-889, open Mon.-Fri. 0900-1300, on R.T. Loaiza, directly across from the Hotel Playa Mazatlán. In emergencies, call the nearest U.S. consulate, in Hermosillo, tel. 91-62-172-375.

The **Canadian Consular Office** on Av. R.T. Loaiza, just adjacent to the Hotel Playa Mazatlán, tel. (69) 137-320, is open Mon.-Fri. 0900-1300. In emergency, contact consul Fernando Romero through the Canadian Embassy, tel. 91-5-724-7900, in Mexico City.

Language Courses and Lessons

The downtown Centro de Idiomas ("Language Center"), owned and operated by friendly and very knowledgeable American resident Dixie Davis, offers good beginning and advanced Spanish courses. Tuition runs about $80/week for small, two-hour daily classes. They also sponsor homestay and person-to-person programs (see "Accommodations" above). Contact them in their downtown school on Belisario Domínguez 1908, upstairs, tel. (69) 822-053, fax 855-606, Compuserve 74174, 1340.

Arts and Music Classes

The **Centro Regional de Bellas Artes Ángela Peralta** periodically offers ballet, instrumental and choral music, painting, and other instruction for adults and children. Their sessions are conducted in the airy old-world buildings that cluster around the charming downtown Plazuela Machado. For more information, contact the director, Ricardo Urquijo, at Teatro Ángela Peralta, tel. (69) 826-853, at the Plazuela Machado.

Afternoons and evenings, the halls of the **Academia de Artes Centro Francisco Martines Cabrera** echo with the cheerful sounds of students and their violins, guitars, and dancing feet. They offer many semester

courses, beginning September and January, including instrumental music, dance, painting, and theater, for children and adults. For more information, drop in and talk to the friendly director, Prof. José Guadalupe L. Sánchez, 1600-2100 at the old landmark school building at the south end of Av. Olas Altas, adjacent to the streetside city and state shields monument.

Special Tours

Augustin Arellano Tirado, a very knowledgeable local college teacher and guide, leads special-interest individual and small-group ecological, archaeological, and sacred-sites tours. Contact him through the Francisco Iriarte Conde Tour Guides Association, P.O. Box 1144, Mazatlán, Sinaloa 82000, fax (69) 840-708, or homo tel. 839-438.

Massage

The Centro de Massage of Mazatlán, R.T. Loaiza 204, tel. (69) 137-666, provides massage therapy for around $10 per hour using a variety of techniques, such as Swedish, water, and sport massage, acupressure, and foot reflexology in their studio in the Coral shopping center by the Coral Reef Hotel. A sign in their window, announcing the "Land of the Deer Healing Center," quotes a Yaqui proverb: "In gentleness there is great strength." Local hotels refer many customers there.

Photography

Although many big hotel shops develop and sell film, their services are limited and expensive. Competition lowers the prices on "photo row," Calle Ángel Flores downtown, just west of the central plaza. For reasonable one-hour developing and jumbo printing, try **Photo Arauz,** Ángel Flores 607, tel. (69) 822-015, open Mon.-Sat. 0800-2000, Sunday 0900-1400. They do 35 mm rolls for about $12. Nearby **Photo de Llano,** Ángel Flores 820, tel. (69) 816-277, open Mon.-Sat. 0900-1330 and 1600-1900, develops, prints, and enlarges in color on site. They also stock some professional sheet and 120 film, in addition to cameras, photo equipment and supplies.

INFORMATION

Tourist Information Office

The Mazatlán information office of Sinaloa state tourism is in the big Banamex bank plaza, Av. Olas Altas 1300, corner of Mariano Escobedo, tel. (69) 851-220, fax 851-222, open Mon.-Fri. 0900-1700. A young enthusiastic staff answers questions and dispenses maps and brochures. If you have a difficult problem, or need more than the usual information, ask for Victor, Luis, or Lourdes.

Hospitals and Pharmacies

Its 24-hour duty staff of specialists earns the **Hospital Militar** high recommendations. Despite its exclusive-sounding title, anyone can receive treatment at the Hospital Militar, in the Olas Altas district at Malpica and Venus, tel. (69) 812-079, one block from the Hotel Siesta.

Another good place to be sick is the brand new, big **Hospital Sharp,** tel. (69) 865-676, at Rafael Buelna and Reforma, about a quarter-mile along Buelna from Valentino's disco. One of Mexico's newest and best, Sharp Hospital's cadre of highly trained specialists uses its mountain of high tech equipment to set new Mexican diagnostic and care standards. Prices, however, are generally higher than other Mexican hospitals.

The **Cruz Roja** (private Red Cross), tel. (69) 813-690 or 851-451, operates ambulances and is usually called to auto accidents when the victims are incapacitated. The Cruz Roja hospital is not highly recommended, however. Tell them to take you to Hospital Militar or Sharp, if you can manage it.

If you must have a bona fide American-trained doctor, try surgeon Dr. Gilberto Robles Guevara's **Clínica Mazatlán** (office tel. 69-812-917, home 851-923) at Zaragoza and 5 de Mayo, on the downtown "doctors' row."

Farmacias in Mexico are allowed wide latitude to diagnose illnesses and dispense medicines. For a physician and pharmacy all in one right on the *malecón,* try **Farmacia Ángel,** run by **Dr. Ángel Avila Tirado,** who examines, diagnoses, prescribes, and rings up the sale on the spot, Av. del Mar s/n, one block from the Fisherman's Monument, tel. (69) 824-746 or 816-831, open daily 0800-2400.

Another good pharmacy (with bookstore to boot) is in the shopping center in front of the Hotel Playa Mazatlán: Farmacia Playa, R.T. Loaiza 202, tel. (69) 134-016 (or the hotel, tel. 134-444), open daily 0800-2045.

Police and Fire Emergencies

For police emergencies in the Zona Dorada, the special **Policía Turística,** which patrols the Zona Dorada exclusively, can respond quickly. Call (69) 148-444 or go to their headquarters at the corner of Gabriel Ruiz and Santa Monica just off Camarón Sábalo, not far from the Hotel Costa de Oro.

For **downtown police emergencies,** contact the *preventiva* police, in the Palacio Municipal on the central plaza, tel. (69) 813-919.

In case of **fire,** call the *bomberos* ("pumpers"), tel. (69) 813-600 or 839-920.

Publications

Some of the most bountiful English-language bookracks in town are at the bookstore-pharmacy, the Farmacia Playa, tel. (69) 134-016, open daily 0800-2045, at the Hotel Playa Mazatlán. They stock a few hundred titles, mostly thick popular novels, a raft of U.S. popular magazines, and a small but solid collection of Mexico travel, folklore, art, history, and language books. They also sell the L.A. *Times* and *U.S.A. Today* (which arrive around 1600) and the daily English-language Mexico City *News.*

You will usually find the same three newspapers and many U.S. magazines at the **Librería Plus** bookstore, at 351 Camarón Sábalo, tel. (69) 144-867, open 0830-2030, right across from Banamex, not far from the Dairy Queen.

The unique new age **Evolución Bookstore** stocks many English-language occult/self-help/meditation/music/astrology titles, along with assorted used paperbacks, cards, Mexico state and city maps, crystals, incense, and oils.

They also rent their fax machine and allow local calls on their phone for 30 cents each. Evolución is open daily except Sunday about 1000-2100 and is located in the Coral shopping center, R.T. Loaiza 204, local 37, tel. (69) 160-839, behind Señor Frog's.

Public Library
Mazatlán's respectable public library is downtown, at **Plazuela de Los Leones,** two short blocks behind the Palacio Municipal. Of special interest is the upper-floor **Benjamin Franklin Library:** row upon row of venerable volumes of classic American literature. Open Mon.-Fri. 0800-2000, Saturday 0900-1200.

Ecology and Volunteer Work
Mazatlán has a small but growing ecological movement, which has coalesced under the acronym **CEMAZ** (Consejo Ecologico de Mazatlán). Their main focus has been on education by example—cleaning up and restoring Mazatlán's offshore islands and lagoons. Operating out of a small city-financed office on Plazuela Machado, Constitución 511, tel. (69) 852-552, they occasionally need volunteers for projects. Drop in and let them know you're around.

The Mazatlán **Acuario** (Aquarium), Av. de Los Deportes, one block off Av. del Mar about a mile south of Valentino's disco (watch for the signs), tel. (69) 817-815, 817-816, or 817-818, is another center of ecological activity. Mainly through school educational programs, they are trying to save the marine turtles that come ashore to lay eggs along local beaches during the summer and early fall. They may be able to use volunteers to help with such efforts. Check with their public-relations officer for more details; open daily 1000-1800.

GETTING THERE AND AWAY

By Air
A number of reliable U.S. and Mexican airlines connect Mazatlán with many destinations in Mexico and the United States.

Alaska Airlines flights connect daily with Los Angeles, San Francisco, and Seattle. Their local flight information office is at the airport, tel. (69) 852-7300 or 852-731. For reservations and tickets, call their centralized U.S. toll-free booking number, (95) 800-426-0333.

Mexicana Airlines flights connect daily with Los Angeles, Denver, Miami, Puerto Vallarta (high season), Mexico City, and Los Cabos. Their local reservations offices are on the malecón, at Paseo Claussen #101B, corner Belisario Domínguez, tel. (69) 827-722. For flight information, call them at the airport at (69) 827-292 or toll-free from the U.S. (800) 531-7921.

Aeroméxico flights connect daily with Tucson, Tijuana, Mexico City, Durango, Hermosillo, and Los Mochis. Their local reservations/information offices are in the Zona Dorada, at Calz. Camarón Sábalo 310, tel. (69) 141-111 or 141-609, and at the airport, tel. 823-444 or toll-free from the U.S. (800) 237-6639.

Delta Air Lines flights connect daily with Los Angeles. For reservations, call their toll-free booking number, (91) 800-902-21 in Mexico City. For flight information, call them at the airport, (69) 824-155, or toll-free from the U.S., (800) 221-1212.

Canadian Holiday Airlines charter flights connect with Toronto, Vancouver, and Calgary. For information, call their agent at the Hotel Playa Mazatlán, tel. 134-444, toll-free in the U.S. (800) 420-7000, or a travel agent in Canada.

Mazatlán Airport Arrival and Departure
For arrivees, the Mazatlán Airport (code-designated MZT, though officially the General Rafael Buelna Airport) unfortunately lacks many basic services. There are neither money exchange, tourist information, nor hotel-booking services. Car-rental (Budget, National, Hertz, and the local "AIAI" agency) clerks try to help, but independent travelers should have their first-night hotel reservations and guidebook in hand when they arrive. (Otherwise, they'll be at the mercy of their taxi driver, who will most likely collect a commission from the hotel where he deposits them.)

Taxi and *colectivo* transportation for the 15-mile (25-km) ride into town is, by contrast, well organized. Booths sell both kinds of tickets: *colectivo* about $5 per person, taxi about $14 per car. No public bus runs from town to the airport.

For departure, *colectivos* are harder to find around hotels than are departing tourists. Share a regular taxi and save on your return to the airport.

The **airport-departure tax** runs $12. If you've lost your tourist card and haven't had time to get a duplicate at the tourist information office (see above), you may be able to avoid the $20 departure fine by presenting a copy of your original tourist card and a police report of your loss. See the Zona Dorada Tourist Police, at the corner of Gabriel Ruiz and Santa Monica, not far from the Costa de Oro Hotel, tel. (69) 14-84-44, for such a report.

By Car or RV

There are three highway routes to and from Mazatlán: from the U.S. through Nogales and Culiacán; from the northeast, through Durango, and from the southeast, from Guadalajara or Puerto Vallarta through Tepic.

The quickest and safest way to drive to Mazatlán from the U.S. border is by **Mexico National Hwy. 15,** which connects with U.S. Interstate 19 from Tucson, at Nogales, Mexico. A four-lane superhighway for most of the 743-mile (1,195-km) route, Hwy. 15 allows a safe, steady 55 mph (90 kph) pace. Although the tolls total about $60 for a car (more for trailers and big RVs) the safety and decreased wear and tear are well worth it. Take it easy and allow yourself at least two full days travel to or from Nogales.

Heading to Mazatlán from the northeast, the winding (but spectacular) two-lane **National Hwy. 40** crosses the Sierra Madre Occidental from Durango. Steep grades over the 7,350-foot (2,235-meter) pass will stretch the trip into the better part of a day, even though it totals only 198 miles (318 km). During the winter, snow can temporarily block the route.

From the southeast, heavy traffic slows progress along the mostly two-lane narrow **National Hwy. 15,** which connects with Guadalajara (323 miles, 520 km) via Tepic. Allow at least a full day for this trip.

The same is true of the two-lane route from Puerto Vallarta. Each leg, first **National Hwy. 200** (104 miles, 167 km) to Tepic, thence **National Hwy. 15** (182 miles, 293 km), is sometimes slowed by heavy traffic and will require at least a full day.

By Bus

The **Central de Autobuses** (Central Bus Terminal) is at the corner of Hwy. 15 and Calle Tamazula, about two miles north of downtown and four blocks from Playa Norte behind the Sands Hotel.

The terminal, efficiently divided into *primera-* and *segunda-clase* (first- and second-class) sections, has big suitcase lockers (about $5/day) and a number of clean snack stands and stores where travelers can purchase food, pure water, and drinks. Stock up before you leave.

Several well-equipped bus lines provide frequent local departures. Go first class whenever possible. The service, speed, and reserved seats *(asientos reservados)* of first-class buses far outweigh their small additional cost. All connections listed below are first class and depart locally *(salidas locales)* unless otherwise noted.

Super-luxury **Elite** (EL) and its parent line, **Tres Estrellas de Oro** (TEO, Three Stars of Gold, tel. 69-813-680), connect with **southeast** destinations of Tepic, Guadalajara, and Mexico City and intermediate points. *Salidas de paso* (buses passing through) connect en route **south** to Tepic and Puerto Vallarta. Buses connect with **northwest** destinations of Culiacán and Los Mochis (hourly), Nogales (two per day), and Tijuana (three per day), including intermediate points.

Every two hours, **Transportes Norte de Sonora** (TNS, tel. 69-821-949) connects **northwest** with Culiacán and Tijuana and **southeast** with Tepic, Guadalajara, Mexico City, San Blas, Puerto Vallarta, and intermediate points.

Transportes Chihuahuenses (TC, tel. 69-812-335) buses connect twice a day with the **north** via Durango, Chihuahua, Juárez, and intermediate points. **Transportes del Norte** buses (TN, operating out of the same office) connect (nine per day) **northeast** with Durango, Torreón, Monterrey, and Nuevo Laredo.

Transportes del Pacífico (TP, tel. 69-820-577) *salidas de paso* connect hourly en route **northwest** to Tijuana and **southeast** to Tepic, Guadalajara, Mexico City and intermediate points. You can change buses at Tepic, however, and continue to Puerto Vallarta.

Estrella Blanca (EB, tel. 69-815-381) and its subsidiary carrier, **Rojo de los Altos,** connect with the **north** via Durango, Torreón, and Juárez. They also connect with the **east** via Fresnillo, Zacatecas, and San Luis Potosí. To the **southeast,** buses connect with Tepic (thence to Puerto Vallarta), Guadalajara, and Mexico City.

By Train

The first-class (coach only) accommodation is so cheap (the Mexicali-Mazatlán fare is around $50 for 1,100 miles) that it doesn't make sense to most folks to take any other class. The **Estrella** is the only train that runs the long Ferrocarriles del Pacífico (Pacific Railroad) line from Mexicali-Nogales to Guadalajara. Two trains run per day, one north, one south. The northbound train leaves Guadalajara around 0900, stops in Tepic, and arrives at Mazatlán around 1800. It chugs out of Mazatlán around 1900, heading for Culiacán, continuing overnight, rolling into Nogales next morning around 1100. It finally gets to Mexicali about 32 hours after it left Guadalajara, around 1700.

The next day, the Estrella turns around and moves out of Mexicali around 0900. En route, it hooks up with a similar southward-bound train from Nogales, and continues, rolling into Mazatlán about 22 hours later, around 0600. It departs Mazatlán around 0700, bound for Tepic and Guadalajara, where it arrives around 1800. If you think the Estrella is slow, reflect on this: the second-class train that used to make this same trip was called El Burro.

Make your reservations by phone (tel. 69-846-710) and verify times at the Mazatlán train station. You can buy tickets at the station booth an hour before departure. The station is called Colonia Esperanza, for the east-side district where it's located. Since you're saving so much on the train, invest in a *pulmonía* to the station.

By Ferry

The only ferry runs to and from **La Paz,** Baja California, leaving daily at 1500 sharp, from the terminal at the foot of Av. Carnaval. Passengers in cars should get there around 1330 to ensure adequate loading time. Vehicle tickets (cars from around $150, big RVs and trailers much more) are sold at the terminal ticket office, open daily 0800-1200. Save yourself *mucho* trouble, however, and reserve your ferry tickets through a travel agent, such as Marza Tours, in the Galería shopping center across from the Hotel Costa de Oro, tel. (69) 160-896.

You cannot remain in your vehicle during the 16-hour trip. There are four kinds of accommodations: salon (sitting room, $20/person), tourist (four-person cabin with beds, $38/person), cabin (for four with bath, $60/person), and special (suite, $90/person).

Feo (ugly) used to be the local description of the La Paz ferry. Service, however, has improved in recent months. Authorities, especially in La Paz, have reduced the practice of "bumping" private cars and RVs (even with confirmed reservations) in favor of trucks and buses during peak seasons. Hint: If the Mazatlán-La Paz ferry prices are too steep for you, consider crossing via **Topolobampo** (near Los Mochis, half a day north of Mazatlán) to or from La Paz. It takes only about 10 hours and costs about half as much.

Mixtec deer, motif from pictorial manuscript

BOB RACE

SOUTH TO PUERTO VALLARTA
AND INLAND TO GUADALAJARA

ALONG THE ROAD TO SAN BLAS

National Hwy. 15 winds southward from Maza tlán through a lush, palm-dotted patchwork of pasture, fields, and jungle-clad hills. To the east rise the sculpted domes of the Sierra Madre Occidental, while on the west, a grand, island-studded marshland stretches to a virtually un-broken barrier of ocean sand.

Although a few scattered fishing villages edge this 150-mile (250-km) coastline, it remains mostly wild, the domain of hosts of shorebirds and waterfowl, and, in the most remote man-grove reaches, jaguars and crocodiles. Its palmy, driftwood-strewn beaches invite adventurous trekkers, RV campers, and travelers who enjoy Pacific Mexico beaches at their untouristed best.

PLAYA CAIMANERO

A cluster of beachside *palapa* restaurants marks the southern end of Playa Caimanero, a 20-mile barrier dune that blocks Laguna Caimanero from the sea. (The salinity of Laguna Caimanero, however, is a mystery to local people, who spec-ulate that the salt water migrates under the dune.)

Besides most of the low-key beach pas-times, both Playa Caimanero and its lagoon are a birdwatcher's heaven (bring your bird book, binoculars, and repellent). The broad, shallow **Laguna Caimanero** is less than a mile from the beach along any one of a dozen little tracks through the grove. Local people could probably point you to a boatman who could take you on a birdwatching ex-cursion.

Besides birds, Playa Caimanero is a prime hatching ground for endangered species of sea turtles. They crawl ashore, especially during the later summer and fall, when volunteers patrol the sand, trying to protect the eggs from poach-ers and predators.

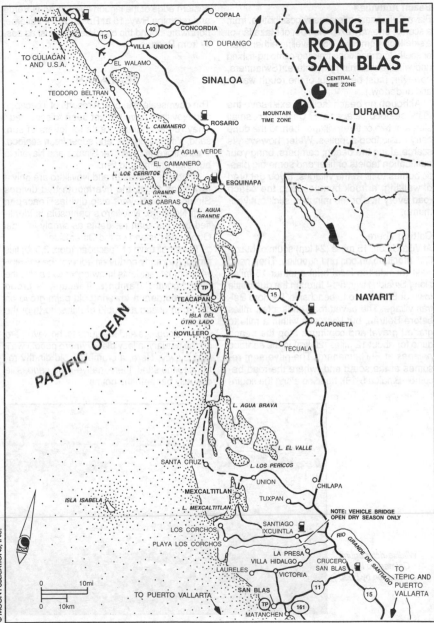

Beach Activities

Playa Caimanero offers many possibilities, from a scenic, one-day excursion out of Mazatlán or a side loop from Hwy. 15, traveling either north or south, to a weeklong trekking-camping-fishing and wildlife-watching adventure. (Swimmers, however, must be careful of the rough waves and undertow.)

Although no beach facilities exist save the rustic seafood *palapas* at El Caimanero, small stores at two or three villages behind the dune carry basic food supplies. Water, however, is scarce along the beach; campers, bring your purification tablets or filter and some big plastic bottles to fill at the villages. If you get tired of walking, a truck bumps along the beach road every five or ten minutes; stick out your thumb.

Getting There

At Villa Union, 15 miles (24 km) south of Mazatlán, stock up on gas and supplies. Then head west (or ride the local bus) another 15 miles along Sinaloa Hwy. 5-14 through the dusty little town of El Walamo to beachside Teodoro Beltrán village. The paved road ends a few miles before Beltrán, but improves within a mile to graded gravel and continues atop the beach dune for about 12 miles (20 km) to the seafood *palapas* at El Caimanero. The pavement resumes at the south end (where the road becomes Sinaloa 5-19), heading along the south-eastern edge of the lagoon through Agua Verde and rejoining Hwy. 15 at Rosario. The reverse, northward-bound trip could be done just as easily from Rosario.

TEACAPÁN

The downscale little beach resorts of Teacapán and Novillero have not yet been "discovered." They remain quiet retreats for lovers of sun, sand, simple lodgings, and super-fresh seafood. Trucks travel from all over Sinaloa and Nayarit to buy their shrimp and fish.

Although Teacapán and Novillero are only a few miles apart, the rivermouth that divides Sinaloa from Nayarit also divides Teacapán from Novillero. Novillero's peninsula is identified by Teacapán residents as simply Isla del Otro Lado ("Island on the Other Side").

The small town of Teacapán (pop. 3,000) lies along the sandy northeast edge of the estuary, which most residents know only as *la boca,* the river "mouth." Tambora, Teacapán's broad beach, borders a towering old palm grove on the open ocean a couple of miles north of town.

Most lodgings and restaurants, however, are on the estuary, a lazy place, where people walk very slowly. Here, a crumbling old dinghy returns to the sand; there, native-style *canoas* lie casually beneath the palms.

Wildlife-rich Laguna Caimanero invites exploration by boat.

BRUCE WHIPPERMAN

The shimmering expanse of the Marismas Nacionales ("National Marshes") wetlands spreads west from Hwy. 15 south of Mazatlán.

BRUCE WHIPPERMAN

Accommodations and Food

A few restaurants line the estuary beach; the best is seafood **Restaurant Mr. Wayne** (from the name of an American friend of the enterprising Mexican owner). He employs his own fisherman to bring the best *pargo, robalo,* and *mero* to the barbecue every afternoon.

The best of Teacapán's accommodations is **Hotel Denisse**, on the main plaza, diagonally adjacent to the church. Enterprising partners Jose Jesús "Pepe" Morales and Carol Snobel revitalized a former private home, and now they have six clean, attractively furnished rooms with bath, spread around an inviting inner patio. The rooms rent for about $25 d with a/c, and $22 with fan only. Although reservations aren't usually necessary, it is best to write the hotel in advance: Hotel Denisse, Calles R. Buelna y Morelos, Teacapán, Sinaloa 82560.

Beneath a palm grove on the town's outskirts is the **RV Park Las Lupitas,** owned and operated by a friendly refugee from L.A. smog, Hugh Thompson, and his Mexican wife. They, along with many other longtime Teacapán residents, lament the overfishing of the estuary. "When I arrived in the seventies," Hugh reports, "they were pulling big turtles out of the lagoon by the truckloads." There are now no turtles or oysters left from the many acres of original beds, and precious few fish, which the local fishermen must now dive for with spearguns.

Hugh and his wife have 20 shady spaces a quarter-mile from Tambora beach that rent for

$8.50/day, tents $4. Their address is simply Teacapán, Sinaloa 82560; no phone, all hookups, showers with hot water, a satellite dish available if you have your own lead-in and connectors, discounts available for monthly rentals and self-sufficient units, reservations generally not necessary.

Hugh also has a good motorboat, which he likes to use to take visitors on wildlife-viewing, photograpy, and fishing excursions in the nearby jungle estuaries.

Back in town, once-thriving **Motel-Trailer Park Oregon** has been hit hard by the decrease in RV visitors since 1992, and has only operated seasonally in recent years. The trailer section (right on the estuary) has about 15 shadeless pads with all hookups, which rent for about $9 per night or $200 per month. They also rent a pair of motel-style tiled rooms for $20 d per night with ceiling fans, and screened doors and windows against bugs. Best to write or call ahead if you're planning on staying: Calle Reforma 50, Teacapán, Sinaloa 82560, tel. (695) 310-76, ext. 166. Get there by turning right at the sign before the town plaza. Ask for owner Vicki Sambrano, or her brother Vicente.

Beach Activities

Fortunately, **ocean fishing** remains good off Tambora beach. Watch for the sign on the right about two miles before town. You can rent a *lancha* or launch your own boat right on the beach.

Tambora is a very broad silky sand beach where the waves normally roll in gently from about a hundred yards out, breaking gradually both left and right for **surfing. Windsurfing** would also be good here, although the water is too sandy for snorkeling. Various **clam, cowrie,** and **cockle shells** turn up at seasonal times. A permanent beachside *palapa* restaurant serves fresh seafood and drinks. Other food and supplies are available in stores back in town.

Camping is customary most anywhere, either on the sand or beneath the big palm grove that edges the shoreline, curving south back to the estuary. To the north, the beach stretches, wild and breeze-swept, for several miles.

Services
Along the main street back in town, residents enjoy the services of a doctor, a pharmacy, a fairly well-stocked grocery, and a long-distance telephone office.

Getting There
Teacapán is accessible from Hwy. 15 by Sinaloa Hwy. 5-23 from Esquinapa. Ride the local *urbano* or red Transportes Escuinapa buses from in front of the little park adjacent to the plaza cathedral.

Southbound drivers, just before you enter downtown Esquinapa, a diversion funnels through traffic one-way to the right, then left within a block or two. Instead of following left, continue straight ahead for several blocks until you arrive at the asphalt westbound highway out of town, where you should turn right for Teacapán. The all-paved 24 miles (38 km) passes quickly, through bushy thorn forest and past shallow lagoons dotted with waterbirds and rafts of wild lotus. Palm groves and broad fields of *chiles* (chile peppers, which make Sinaloa one of Mexico's top chili-producing states) line the roadside.

Esquinapa (pop. 40,000), a busy farm town, has a good overnight hotel, the IQ de Esquinapa (with restaurant), half a block from the downtown plaza at Gabriel Leyva 7 Sur, tel. (695) 304-71, (695) 307-82. The 30 luxurious rooms around an enclosed courtyard rent for about $30 d, with TV, a/c, phones, and parking; credit cards accepted.

NOVILLERO

Little Novillero (pop. about 1,000) enjoys one of the longest (55 miles, 90 km), smoothest stretches of sand in Mexico. The waves roll in gently from a hundred yards out and swish lazily along a velvety, nearly level beach. Here, all of the ingredients for a perfect beach stay come together: *palapa* seafood restaurants, hotels, a big palm grove for RV or tent camping, ocean fishing, and a broad creamy strand for beachcombers and wilderness campers stretching from both ends of town.

Moreover, Novillero's mangrove hinterland, about a mile or two inland from beach, is a yet-to-be-discovered wildlife-viewing wonderland. You might be able to enjoy such an opportunity by hiring a local boatman (expect to pay about $15 an hour after bargaining) to take your party on an excursion along pristine jungle waterways. Ask at the hotel, around town, or in the fishing village beneath the estuary bridge (about two miles before town).

Accommodations and Food
Foremost among the several lodgings is the aging, 40-room **Hotel Playa Novillero** beside the palm grove about two blocks from the beach (P.O. Box 56, Tequala, Nayarit 63440, no phone). The hotel encloses a bushy green garden and patio with a spacious, well-maintained pool. The tile-floored rooms are simple but comfortable. Carved dark hardwood doors and tight shutters add a homey touch of class and keep out bugs. A wide, screened-in porch furnished with plants, big wooden rockers, and rustic chairs and tables provides a shady setting for reading and relaxing. Rates run about $10 for one, $20 for two to four; with ceiling fans and restaurant in season. It's popular with North Americans and Europeans; best make winter reservations.

If you must stay right on the beach, however, the **Hotel Paraíso de Novillero** can accommodate you (same owner, address, and approximate prices as Hotel Playa Novillero, 24 rooms, a pool, parking, and a restaurant). This lodging's air-conditioned Motel 6-style ambience would appeal most to families busily heading for the pool or beach.

If both of these are full, you can try third-choice **Hotel Miramar** across the street, or fourth-choice **Bungalows** on the beach dirt road past the grove on the north edge of town.

For food, Novillero offers a number of choices: a well-stocked country grocery (here called the "mini-super") and half a dozen *palapa* restaurants accustomed to serving a generation of vacationers. Try the big beachside **Hotel Miramar** *palapa,* or look into Lola's **La Gaera,** on the town street two blocks south, where Lola has built a *palapa* furnished by a rainbow assortment of chairs and oilcloth-covered tables. Her son sometimes arrives about nine o'clock and belts out gratis serenades for customers on his guitar.

Getting There

Novillero is about halfway between Tepic and Mazatlán; a two hour drive for 22 miles (35 km) by paved side road from Hwy. 15. To get there southbound, turn right (west) only a few hundred yards after the Pemex station (at the junction to Acaponeta), at the unsigned paved side road. For northbound drivers, a "Novillero" sign marks the same turnoff. Continue about eight (13 km) miles and, as you're entering Tecuala, turn right just after the Pemex station. Continue another half mile and turn right at the paved highway, which continues west another 14 (22 km) miles west to Novillero.

MEXCALTITÁN

Mexcaltitán (pop. about 3,000), the "House of the Mexicans," represents much more than just a scenic little island town. Archaeological evidence indicates that Mexcaltitán may actually be the legendary Aztlán ("Place of the Herons") where, in 1091, the Aztecs (who called themselves the México—"MAY-shi-kuh") began their generations-long migration to the Valley of Mexico.

Each year on 28 and 29 June, the feast days of St. Peter and St. Paul, residents of Mexcaltitán and surrounding villages dress up in feathered headresses and jaguar robes and breathe life into their tradition. They celebrate the opening of the shrimp season by staging a grand regatta, driven by friendly competition between decorated boats carrying rival images of St. Peter and St. Paul.

Getting There

The southbound Hwy. 15 turnoff for Mexcaltitán is 136 miles (219 km) miles south of Mazatlán, four miles (six km) after the village of Chilapa. The 25-mile (40-km) southbound side trip passes its last half along a rough gravel road-dike through the marsh, edged by bushy mangroves and lotus ponds and inhabited by constellations of waterbirds and water-lily-munching cattle.

Northbound from Hwy. 15, follow the signed Santiago Ixcuintla turnoff, 38 miles (60 km) north

Mexcaltitán children pose before the town mural, which depicts the traditional story of the migration of their Aztec ancestors to the Valley of Mexico.

of Tepic; continue five miles past Santiago Ix-cuintla (see below) to the signed and paved Mexcaltitán side road, which continues another 15 miles (25 miles total from Hwy. 15) to the Mexcaltitán *embarcadero* (boat landing).

Sights

From either of the Mexcaltitán road's-end *embarcaderos*, boatmen ferry you across (from the south side, about $4 each way) to Mexcaltitán is-land-village, some of whose inhabitants have never crossed the channel to the mainland. The town itself is not unlike many Mexican small towns, except more tranquil, due to the absence of motor vehicles.

Mexcaltitán is prepared for visitors. The INAH (Instituto Nacional de Arqueología y Historia) has put together an excellent museum, with several rooms of artifacts, photos, paintings, and maps describing the cultural regions of pre-Columbian Mexico. The displays climax with the museum's centerpiece exhibit, which tells the story of the Aztecs' epic migration to the Valley of Mexico from legendary Aztlán, now believed by experts to be present-day Mexicaltitán.

Outside, the proud village **church** and city hall preside over the central plaza, from which the town streets radiate to the broad lagoon surrounding the town. In the late afternoons where the watery lagoon meets the end of the streets, village men set out in canoes and boats for the open-ocean fishing grounds, where, armed with kerosene lanterns, they attract shrimp into their nets. Occasionally during the rainy season, water floods the entire town, so that folks must then navigate in boats the streets that become Venice-style canals.

Food and Accommodations

On the town plaza, oppo-site the church, stands the airy **El Camarón** seafood res-taurant, and, at the view-edge of

the lagoon behind the museum is Mexcaltitán's first **hotel,** yet to be named. More like a guest-house than a hotel, its four clean, comfortable tiled rooms with bath, some with a/c, rent from $20 d. Write the manager, Juliana Piña at 7 Calle Venezia, Mexcaltitán, Nayarit 63560, or call prepared to speak in Spanish, tel. (323) 100-28, for reservations.

SANTIAGO IXCUINTLA

If you take the southern approach to Mexcaltitán, you get the added bonus of Santiago Ixcuintla (eeks-KOOEEN-tlah), on the north bank of the Río Grande de Santiago, Mexico's longest river. Get there via the signed turnoff from Hwy. 15, 38 miles (60 km) north of Tepic; continue five miles to the town.

Just past the solitary hill that marks the town, turn right at the first opportunity, on to the one-way main street 20 de Noviembre, which in a couple of blocks runs past the picturesque main plaza. Linger a bit to admire the voluptuous Por-firian nymphs who decorate the restored band-stand and the pretty old colonial church. Stroll beneath the shaded porticos and visit the colorful market two blocks north of the plaza.

Although its scenic appeal is considerable, the Huichol people are the best reason to come to Santiago Ixcuintla. Hundreds of Huichol fami-lies migrate seasonally (late winter and early spring, especially) from their Sierra Madre high-country homeland to work for a few dollars a day in the local to-bacco fields. For many Hui-chol, their migration in search of money includes a serious hidden cost. In the mountains, they have their homes, their friends and relatives around them, and the familiar rituals and ceremonies that they have tena-ciously preserved in their centuries-long struggle against Mexicanization. But when the Huichol come to lowland towns and cities, they often encounter the mocking laugh-

BOB RACE

THE HUICHOL

Because the Huichol have retained more of their traditional religion than perhaps any other group of indigenous Mexicans, they offer a glimpse into the lives and beliefs of dozens of now-vanished Mesoamerican peoples.

The Huichol's natural wariness, plus their isolation in rugged mountain canyons and valleys, has saved them from the ravages of modern Mexico. Despite increased tourist, government, and mestizo contact, prosperity and better health swelled the Huichol population to around 15,000 by the 1990s.

Although many have migrated to coastal farming towns and cities such as Tepic and Guadalajara, several thousand Huichol remain in their ancestral heartland—roughly 50 square miles (80 square km) centered about 50 miles (80 km) northeast of Tepic as the crow flies. They cultivate corn and raise cattle on 400 *rancherías* in five municipalities not far from the winding Altongo River valley: Guadalupe Ocotán in Nayarit, and Tuxpan de Bolanos, San Sebastián Teponahuaxtlán, Santa Catarina, and San Andrés Cohamiata in Jalisco.

Although studied by a procession of researchers since Carl Lumholtz's seminal work in the 1890s, the remote Huichol and their religion remain enigmatic. As Lumholtz said long ago, "Religion to them is a personal matter, not an institution and therefore their life is religion—from the cradle to the grave, wrapped up in symbolism."

Hints of what it means to be Huichol come from their art. Huichol art contains representations of the prototype deities—Grandfather Sun, Grandmother Earth, Brother Deer, Mother Maize—that once guided the destinies of many North American peoples. It blooms with tangible religious symbols, from green-faced Mother Earth (Tatei Urianaka) and the dripping Rain Goddess (Tatei Matiniera), to the ray-festooned Father Sun (Tayau) and the antlered folk hero Brother Kauyumari, forever battling the evil sorcerer Kieri.

The Huichol are famous for their use of the hallucinogen peyote, their bridge to the divine. Peyote (eaten in the gathered buds—buttons—of a humble cactus) contains mescaline and a score of other vision-inducing ingredients and grows in the Huichol's Elysian land of Wirikuta, in the San Luis Potosí desert 300 miles east of their homeland, near the town of Real de Catorce.

To the Huichol, a journey to Wirikuta is a dangerous trip to heaven. Preparations go on for weeks, and include innumerable prayers and ceremonies, as well as the crafting of feathered arrows, bowls, gourds, and paintings for the gods who live along the way. Only the chosen—village shamans, temple elders, those fulfilling vows or seeking visions—may make the journey. Each participant in effect becomes a god, whose identity and very life are divined and protected by the shaman en route to Wirikuta.

The fertility goddess symbolically gives birth in a Huichol yarn painting.

ter and hostile stares of townspeople, whose Spanish language they do not understand, and whose city ways seem alien. As strangers in a strange land, the pressure for the migrant Huichol to give up their old costumes, language, and ceremonies to become like everyone else is powerful indeed.

Centro Cultural Huichol

Be sure to reserve a portion of your time in Santiago Ixcuintla to stop by the Centro Cultural Huichol, 20 de Noviembre 452, Santiago Ixcuintla, Nayarit 63300, tel. (323) 511-71. The immediate mission of founders Mariano and Susana Valadez—he, a Huichol artist and community leader, and she, a U.S.-born anthropologist—is to assure the Huichol people enter the 21st century with their traditions intact and growing. Their instrument is the Centro Cultural Huichol—a clinic, dining hall, dormitory, library, craftsmaking shop, sale gallery, and interpretive center—which provides crucial focus and support for local migratory Huichol people.

As well as filling vital human needs, the Huichol Cultural Center is actively nurturing the vital elements of a nearly vanished heritage. The need to safeguard the traditional ways is exemplified by the Huichol, but is the same as the lost hopes of generations of indigenous peoples—Aleut, Yahi, Lacandones, and myriad others—who succumbed to European diseases and were massacred in countless fields, from Wounded Knee and the Valley of Mexico all the down way to Tierra del Fuego.

Although they concentrate on the immediate needs of the people, Mariano and Susan also reach out to local, national, and international communities. Their center's entry corridor, for example, is decorated with illustrated Huichol legends in Spanish, especially for Mexican visitors to understand. An adjacent gallery exhibits a treasury of Huichol art for sale—yarn paintings, masks, jewelry, gourds, God's eyes—adorned with the colorful deities and animated heavenly motifs of the Huichol pantheon. Copies of their luscious new coffee-table-sized book, *Huichol Indian Sacred Rituals* (published by Amber Lotus Press, 1241 21st Street, Oakland, CA 94607), are also on sale for about $35. Amber Lotus additionally publishes several gorgeous Huichol art calendars; contact them, tel. (510) 839-3931, for a catalog.

Get to the Centro Cultural Huichol by heading north, away from the river, along 20 de Noviembre, the main street that borders the central plaza. Within about a mile, you'll see the Centro Cultural Huichol, number 452, on the right.

Services, Accommodations, and Food

Santiago Ixcuintla (pop. 20,000), the commercial center of a rich farming region, has many services, including banks (Banamex on the plaza), post office (just off the plaza, facing the church), long-distance telephone (look for the phone-symbol sign), and many pharmacies and doctors. If you want to stay overnight, Susana recommends the Hotel Casino, corner of Ocampo and Rayon, Santiago Ixcuiltla, Nayarit 63300, tel. (323) 508-50 or 508-51, fax 508-52, adjacent to the market. They have a good restaurant and bar and about 35 comfortably furnished rooms for about $23 d, with a/c, parking, and wheelchair access to the lower level; credit cards are accepted.

SAN BLAS AND VICINITY

San Blas (pop. 6,000) is a little town slumbering beneath a big coconut grove. No one seems to care the clock on the crumbling plaza church remains stuck at 1352. Neither is there anyone who remembers San Blas's glory days, when it was Mexico's burgeoning Pacific military headquarters and port, with a population of 30,000. Ships from Spain's Pacific-rim colonies crowded its harbor, silks and gold filled its counting-houses, and noble Spanish officers and their mantilla-graced ladies strolled the plaza on Sunday afternoons.

Times change, however. Politics and San Blas's pesky *jejenes* (hey-HEY-nays, invisible "no-see-um" biting gnats) have always conspired to deflate any temporary fortunes of San Blas.

The *jojonoo'* brooding ground, a vast hinterland of mangrove marshes may, paradoxically, give rise to a new, prosperous San Blas. Those thousands of acres of waterlogged mangrove jungle and savannah are a nursery-home for dozens of Mexico's endangered species. This rich trove is now protected by ecologically aware governments and admired (not unlike the game parks of Africa) by increasing numbers of eco-tourists.

HISTORY

Conquest and Colonization
San Blas and the neighboring, southward-curving Bay of Matanchén were reconnoitered by gold-hungry conquistador Nuño de Guzmán in May of 1530. His expedition noted the protected anchorages in the Bay and the Estero El Pozo adjacent to the present town. Occasionally during the 16th and 17th centuries, Spanish explorers and galleons (and pirates lying in wait for them) would drop anchor in the Estero or the adjacent Bay of Matanchén for rendezvous, resupply, or cargo-transfer.

By the latter third of the 18th century, New Spain, reacting to the Russian and English threats in the North Pacific, launched plans for the colonization of California through a new port called San Blas. The town was officially founded atop the hill of San Basilio in 1768. Streets were surveyed; docks were built. Old documents record that more than a hundred pioneer families received a plot of land and "a pick, an adze, an axe, a machete, a plow . . . a pair of oxen, a cow, a mule, four she-goats and a billy, four sheep, a sow, four hens and a rooster."

They multiplied, and soon San Blas became the seat of Spain's eastern Pacific naval command. Meanwhile, simultaneously with the founding of the town, the celebrated Father Junípero Serra set out for California with 14 missionaries-brothers on the *La Concepción,* a sailboat built on Matanchén beach just south of San Blas.

Independence
New Spain's glory, however, crumbled in the bloody 1810-21 War of Independence, taking San Blas with it. In December 1810, the *insurgente* commander captured the Spanish fort atop San Basilio hill and sent 43 of its cannon to fellow rebel-priest Miguel Hidalgo to use against the loyalists around Guadalajara.

After independence, fewer and fewer ships called at San Blas; the docks fell into disrepair, and the town slipped into somnolence, then complete slumber when president Lerdo de Tejada closed San Blas to foreign commerce in 1872.

SIGHTS

Getting Oriented
The overlook atop the **Cerro de San Basilio** is the best spot to orient yourself to San Blas. From this breezy point, the palm-shaded grid of streets stretches to the sunset-side of **Los Pozos** estuary and the lighthouse-hill beyond it. Behind you, on the east, the mangrove-lined **San Cristobal** river-estuary meanders south to the **Bay of Matanchén.** Along the south shore, the crystalline white line of San Blas's main beach, **Playa el Borrego** ("Sheep Beach"), stretches between the two estuary-mouths.

THE BELLS OF SAN BLAS

Renowned Romantic poet Henry Wadsworth Longfellow (1807-82) visited San Blas during the early 1870s, just after the town's door was closed to foreign trade. With the ships gone, and not even the trickle of tourists it now enjoys, Longfellow's San Blas was perhaps then even dustier and quieter than it is today.

The visit must have meant quite a lot to him. Ten years later, ill and dying, Longfellow hastened to complete "The Bells of San Blas," which became his very last poem, finished nine days before he passed away on 24 March 1882. Longfellow wrote of the silent bells of the old Nuestro Señora del Rosario ("Our Lady of the Rosary") church, which still stands atop the Cerro San Basilio, little changed to this day.

THE BELLS OF SAN BLAS
by Henry Wadsworth Longfellow

What say the Bells of San Blas
To the ships that southward pass
From the harbor of Mazatlán?
To them it is nothing more
Than the sound of surf on the shore,——
Nothing more to master or man.

But to me, a dreamer of dreams,
To whom what is and what seems
Are often one and the same,——
The Bells of San Blas to me
Have a strange, wild melody,
And are something more than a name.

For bells are the voice of the church;
They have tones that touch and search
The hearts of young and old;
One sound to all, yet each
Lends a meaning to their speech,
And the meaning is manifold.

They are a voice of the Past,
Of an age that is fading fast,
Of a power austere and grand;
When the flag of Spain unfurled
Its folds o'er this western world,
And the Priest was lord of the land.

The chapel that once looked down
On the little seaport town
Has crumbled into the dust
And on oaken beams below
The bells swing to and fro,
And are green with mould and rust.

"Is then, the old faith dead,"
They say, "and in its stead
Is some new faith proclaimed,

That we are forced to remain
Naked to sun and rain,
Unsheltered and ashamed?

"Once in our tower aloof
We rang over wall and roof
Our warnings and our complaints;
And round about us there
The white doves filled the air,
Like the white souls of the saints.

"The saints! Ah, have they grown
Forgetful of their own?
Are they asleep, or dead,
That open to the sky
Their ruined Missions lie,
No longer tenanted?

"Oh, bring us back once more
The vanished days of yore,
When the world with faith was filled;
Bring back the fervid zeal,
The hearts of fire and steel,
The hands that believe and build.

"Then from our tower again
We will send over land and main
Our voices of command,
Like exiled kings who return
To their thrones, and the people learn
That the Priest is lord of the land!"

O Bells of San Blas, in vain
Ye call back the Past again!
The Past is deaf to your prayer;
Out of the shadows of night
The world rolls into light;
It is daybreak everywhere.

Around Town

While you're atop the hill, take a look around the old *contaduría* countinghouse and fort (built in 1770) where the riches were tallied and stored en route to Mexico City, the Philippines, or China. Several of the original great cannons still stand guard at the viewpoint, like aging sentinels waiting for long-dead adversaries.

Behind and a bit downhill from the weathered stone arches of the *contaduría* stand the gaping portals and towering, moss-stained belfry of the old church of **Nuestra Señora del Rosario,** built in 1769. Undamaged by war, it was still an active church in 1872, when visiting poet Henry W. Longfellow was captivated by the melancholy tolling of its aging bells.

Historic houses and ruins dot San Blas town downhill. The old hotels **Bucanero** and **Flamingos** on the main street, Juárez, leading past the central plaza, preserve some of their original charm (see "Hotels" below). Just across the street from the Hotel Flamingos you can admire the crumbling yet monumental brick colonnade of 19th-century **ex-Aduana,** now supplanted by a nondescript new customshouse at the foot of Av. Juárez.

At that shoreline spot, gaze across El Pozo estuary. This was both the jumping-off point for Father Junípero Serra's colonization of the Californias and the anchorage of the silk- and porcelain laden Manila Galleon and the bullion ships from the northern mines.

El Faro lighthouse across the estuary marks the top of **Cerro Vigía,** the southern hill-tip of Isla del Rey (actually a peninsula). There, the first beacon shone during the latter third of the 18th century.

Although only a few local folks ever bother to cross over to the island, it is nevertheless an important pilgrimage site for Huichol people from the remote Nayarit and Jalisco mountains. Huichols have been gathering on the Isla de Los Reyes for centuries to make offerings to Aramara, their goddess of the sea. (A not-so-coincidental shrine to a Catholic virgin-saint stands on an offshore sea rock, visible from the beach-endpoint of the Huichol pilgrimage a few hundred yards beyond the lighthouse.)

A large cave at the foot of Cerro Vigía, sacred to the Huichols, sadly was demolished by the government during the early 1970s for rock for a breakwater. Fortunately, however, President Salinas de Gortari partly compensated for the insult by deeding the sacred site to the Huichols during the early '90s.

Two weeks before Easter, they begin arriving by the hundreds, the men decked out in their flamboyant feathered hats. On the ocean beach, 10 minutes' walk straight across the island, anyone can respectfully watch them perform their rituals: elaborate marriages, feasts, and offerings of little boats laden with arrows and food, consecrated to the sea-goddess to assure good hunting, crops, and many healthy children.

Hotel Playa Hermosa

For a glimpse of a relic from San Blas's recent past, head across town to the crumbling Hotel Playa Hermosa. Here, one evening in 1951, President Miguel Alemán came to dedicate San Blas's first luxury hotel. As the story goes, the *jejenes* descended and bit the President so fiercely the entire entourage cleared out before he even finished his speech. Rumors have been going around town for years that someone's going to re-open the Playa Hermosa, but, judging from the vines creeping up the walls and the orchids blossoming on the balconies, they'd best hurry, or the jungle is going to get the old place first. To get there follow H. Batallón to-

The palapa *restaurant and spring (background) at* La Tovara *reward visitors with refreshment after the boat tour through the jungle from San Blas.*

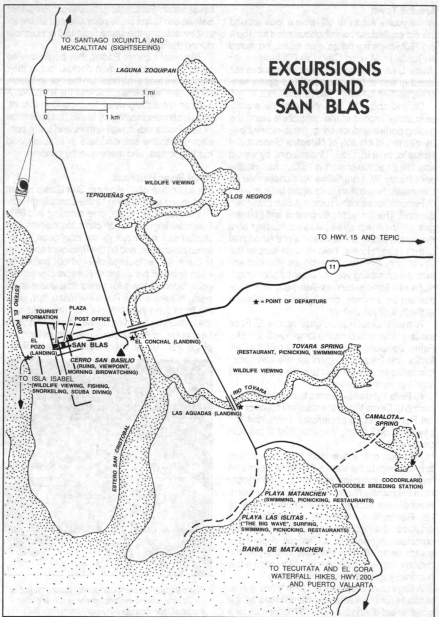

TO SANTIAGO IXCUINTLA AND
MEXCALTITAN (SIGHTSEEING)

LAGUNA ZOQUIPAN

EXCURSIONS
AROUND
SAN BLAS

0   1 mi

0   1 km

WILDLIFE VIEWING

TEPIQUEÑAS

LOS NEGROS

TO HWY. 15 AND TEPIC

11

★ = POINT OF DEPARTURE

TOURIST
INFORMATION   PLAZA

POST OFFICE

EL
POZO   SAN BLAS   EL CONCHAL (LANDING)
(LANDING)

ESTERO EL POZO

CERRO SAN BASILIO
(RUINS, VIEWPOINT,
MORNING BIRDWATCHING)

TO ISLA ISABEL
(WILDLIFE VIEWING, FISHING,
SNORKELING, SCUBA DIVING)

ESTERO SAN CRISTOBAL

TOVARA SPRING
(RESTAURANT, PICNICKING, SWIMMING)

WILDLIFE VIEWING

RIO TOVARA

LAS AGUADAS (LANDING)

CAMALOTA
SPRING

COCODRILARIO
(CROCODILE BREEDING STATION)

PLAYA MATANCHEN
(SWIMMING, PICNICKING, RESTAURANTS)

PLAYA LAS ISLITAS
("THE BIG WAVE", SURFING,
SWIMMING, PICNICKING, RESTAURANTS)

BAHIA DE MATANCHEN

TO TECUITATA AND EL CORA
WATERFALL HIKES, HWY. 200,
AND PUERTO VALLARTA

© MOON PUBLICATIONS, INC.

ward the beach and turn left just after the Los Cocos Trailer Park and continue along the jungle road for about half a mile.

La Tovara Jungle River Trip

On the downstream side of the bridge over Estero San Cristobal, launches-for-hire will take you up the Tovara River, a side channel that winds into the jungle about a mile downstream.

The channel quickly narrows into a dark tree-tunnel, edged by great curtainlike swaths of mangrove roots. Big snowy egrets *(garza)* peer out from leafy branches; startled turtles slip off their soggy perches into the river, while big submerged roots, like gigantic pythons, bulge out of the Inky water. Riots of luxuriant plants—white lilies, green ferns, red *romelia* orchids—hang from the trees and line the banks.

Finally you reach Tovara Springs, which wells up from the base of a verdant cliffside. On one side, a bamboo-sheltered *palapa* restaurant serves refreshments, while on the other, families picnic in a hillside pavilion. In the middle, everyone jumps in and paddles in the clear, cool water.

You can enjoy this trip either of two ways: the longer, three-hour excursion as described (for about $40/boatload of six to eight) from Conchal landing on the estuary, or the shorter version (two hours, about $30/boatload) beginning upriver at road-accessible Aguada landing (near Matanchén village—take the hourly Matanchén bus from the San Blas central plaza).

The more leisurely three-hour trip allows more chances, especially in early morning, to spot a jaguar or crocodile, or a giant boa constrictor hanging from a limb (no kidding). Many of the boatmen are very professional; if you want to view wildlife, tell them, and they'll go slower and keep a sharp lookout. For one of the better boatmen, ask for Elias Partida.

More Options: Some boatmen offer more extensive trips to less-disturbed sites deeper in the jungle. These include the *Camalota* spring, a side-branch of the Tovara River (where you can see a crocodile breeding farm) and the even more remote and pristine Tepiqueñas, Los Negros, and Zoquipan lagoons in the San Cristobal Estero's upper reaches.

Compared to the wildlife-viewing rewards, trip prices are very reasonable. For example, the very knowledgable bird specialist Oscar Partida Hernandez, Comonfort 134 Pte., San Blas, Nayarit 63740, tel. (321) 504-14, will guide a four-person boatload to La Tovara for about $40 total. More extensive options include a combined Camalota-La Tovara trip (allow four to five hours) for approximately $70, or Tepiqueñas and Los Negros (about six hours) for about $90. For each extra person, add about $8, $12, and $16, respectively, to the price of each of these options.

Isla Isabel

Isla Isabel is a two-square-mile offshore bird and wildlife study area 40 miles (65 km), three hours north by boat. The cone of an extinct volcano, Isla Isabel is now home for a small government station of eco-scientists and a host of nesting boobies, frigate birds, and white-tailed tropic birds. Fish and sea mammals, especially dolphins, and sometimes whales, abound in the surrounding clear waters. Although not a recreational area, local authorities allow serious visitors—accompanied by authorized guides—entrance for a few days of camping, snorkeling, scuba diving, and wildlife-viewing. A primitive dormitory can accommodate several persons. Bring everything, including food and bedding. Contact English-speaking **Tony Aguayo, Armando Navarrete,** or **Abraham "Pipila" Murillo** for arrangements and prices, which typically run $200 per day for parties of up to four persons. Their "office" is the little *palapa* to the left of the small floating boat dock at the El Pozo estuary end of Juárez.

Birdwatching

Although San Blas's extensive mangrove and mountain jungle hinterlands are renowned for their birds and wildlife, rewarding birdwatching can start in the early morning right at the edge of town. From Motel-Suites San Blas, walk one block to Calle Conchal. Turn left and continue a few blocks to a small pond on the left. With binoculars, you will have good views of local species of cormorants, flycatchers, grebes, herons, jacanas, and motmots. A handy copy of Peterson's *Field Guide to Mexican Birds* will assist in further identification.

Profitable birdwatching is also possible on the **Isla del Rey.** Bargain for a launch (from the foot of Juárez, about $2 roundtrip) across to the opposite shore. (Watch for wood, clapper, and Virginia rails, and boat-billed herons near the estuary shore.) Then follow the track across the island (look for warblers and a number of species of sparrows) to the beach where you might enjoy good views of plovers, terns, Heerman's gulls, and rafts of pelicans. In early morning, look around the hillside cemetery and the ruins atop **Cerro San Basilio** for good views of hummingbirds, falcons, owls, and American redstarts.

You can include serious birdwatching with your boat trip through the mangrove channels branching from the **Estero San Cristobal** and **La Tovara River.**

For many more details on birdwatching and hiking around San Blas, get a copy of the booklet *Where to Find Birds in San Blas, Nayarit* by Rosalind Novick and Lan Sing Wu, at the shop at the Las Brisas Hotel for around $4; or order from them directly at 178 Myrtle Court, Arcata, CA 95521. If they're on a birding trip, the American Birding Association Bookstore, P.O. Box 6599, Colorado Springs, CO 80934, and the Los Angeles and Tucson Audubon Society bookstores stock it.

Waterfall Hikes

A number of waterfalls decorate the lush jungle foothills above the Bay of Matanchén. Two of these, near Tecuitata and El Cora villages, respectively, are accessible from Hwy. 28 about 10 miles (16 km) south of San Blas. The local white bus *(autobús blanca)* will take you most of the way. It runs south to Santa Cruz del Miramar every two hours, 0830-1630, from the downtown corner of Sinaloa and Paredes, by the market, a block west of the church. See the access details under "Waterfall Hikes" in the "Around the Bay of Matanchén" section below.

While rugged adventurers may guide themselves to the waterfalls, others rely upon guide Lucio Liñan, who contacts travelers at the Botica Mexicana pharmacy (on Juárez at the plaza). His full-day guided hikes, which cost about $20 per person, go at 0830 or 1030, by either your car or public bus.

Beaches and Activities

San Blas's most convenient beach is **Playa el Borrego,** at the south end of Calle Cuauhtémoc

about a mile south of town. With a lineup of *palapas* for food and drinks, the mile-long, broad, fine-sand beach is ripe for all beach activities except snorkeling (due to the murky water). The gradual-breaking waves provide **boogie-boarding** and intermediate **surfing** challenges, however. Bring your own equipment, because no one rents any on the beach (although the Pato Loco beachware shop on Juárez across the street from Restaurant McDonald in town rents surfboards and boogie boards for $9 a day).

Shoals of shells—clams, cockles, mother-of-pearl—wash up on Borrego Beach during storms. **Fishing** is often good, especially by casting from the jetty and rocks at the north and south ends.

ACCOMMODATIONS

Hotels

San Blas has several hotels, none of them huge, but all with personality. They are not likely to be full even during the high winter season (unless, however, the surf off Mantanchén Beach runs high for an unusually long spell).

At the low end, the family-run *casa de huéspedes* (guesthouse) **Casa María** makes a reality of the old Spanish saying, *"Mi casa es tu casa."* located at Heroico Batallón 108, San Blas, Nayarit 63740, at Michoacán, two blocks from the plaza. With 10 rooms around homey, cluttered patios on opposite sides of the street, they offer to do everything for the guests except give them baths (which they would probably do if someone got sick). Not too clean, but very friendly and with kitchen privileges. Rooms rent for about $12 s or d with bath; $9 without; ceiling fans, hot water, dinner for $3.

The **Hotel Flamingos** seems like a vision of old San Blas. Located on Juárez 105, San Blas, Nayarit 63740, no phone, three blocks down Juárez from the plaza. Once the German consulate, it looks scarcely changed since the day it opened in 1863. A leafy jungle blooms in the patio, enfolded by shaded porticoes. The best rooms are airy, high ceilinged, and graceful; others are smaller. Look before you put your money down. Rates for the 20 recently renovated rooms, with hot water and ceiling fans,

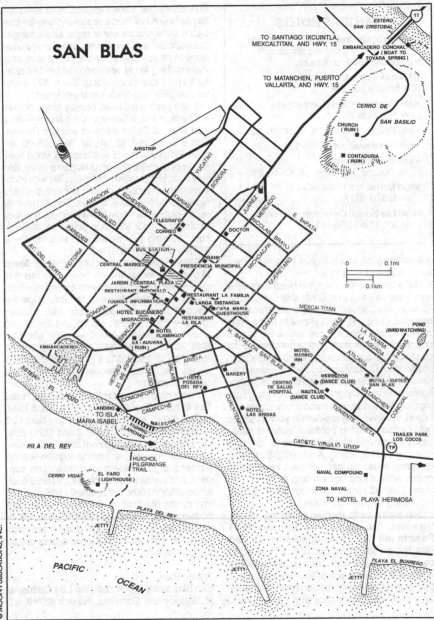

SAN BLAS

TO SANTIAGO IXCUINTLA,
MEXCALTITAN, AND HWY. 15

TO MATANCHEN, PUERTO
VALLARTA, AND HWY. 15

ESTERO
SAN CRISTOBAL

EMBARCADERO CONCHAL
(BOAT TO TOVARA SPRING)

CERRO DE
SAN BASILIO

CHURCH
(RUIN)

CONTADURIA
(RUIN)

AIRSTRIP

YUCATAN

SONORA

JUAREZ

AVIACION

ECHEVERRIA

J. FARIAS

NICOLAS BRAVO

E. ZAPATA

CANALIZO

TELEGRAFO

MERCADO

PAREDES

CORREO

DOCTOR

MICHOACAN

QUERETARO

VICTORIA

BUS STATION

BANK

AL. DEL PUERTO

CENTRAL MARKET

PRESIDENCIA MUNICIPAL

SONORA

JARDIN (CENTRAL PLAZA)

RESTAURANT McDONALD

TOURIST INFORMATION

RESTAURANT LA FAMILIA

LARGA DISTANCIA

MEXCALTITAN

HOTEL BUCANERO

CASA MARIA
GUESTHOUSE

LAS ISLITAS

LA TOVARA

POND
(BIRDWATCHING)

MIGRACION

RESTAURANT
LA ISLA

HOTEL
FLAMINGOS

OAXACA

LA AGUADA

ATOKAMA

LAS PALMAS

EMBARCADERO

EX-ADUANA
(RUIN)

H. BATALLON SAN BLAS

MOTEL
MARINO
INN

SINALOA

HEROES
21 DE ABRIL

ARISTA

MOTEL-SUITES
SAN BLAS

MATANCHEN

ESTERO EL POZO

HIDALGO

SALAS

HOTEL
POSADA
DEL REY

BAKERY

MERREDOR
(DANCE CLUB)

CENTRO
DE SALUD
HOSPITAL

CONCHAL

COMONFORT

CAMPECHE

NAUTILUS
(DANCE CLUB)

TENIENTE AZUETA

ISLA DEL REY

LANDING
TO ISLA
MARIA ISABEL

MALECON

FISHING
LANCHAS

CUAUHTEMOC

HOTEL
LAS BRISAS

TRAILER PARK
LOS COCOS

TP

CADETE VIRGILIO URIBE

CERRO VIGIA

EL FARO
(LIGHTHOUSE)

HUICHOL
PILGRIMAGE
TRAIL

NAVAL COMPOUND

ZONA NAVAL

TO HOTEL PLAYA HERMOSA

PLAYA DEL REY

JETTY

JETTY

JETTY

PACIFIC OCEAN

PLAYA EL BORREGO

0   0.1mi

0   0.1km

© MOON PUBLICATIONS, INC.

11

SAN BLAS HOTELS

San Blas hotels (area code 321, postal code 63740) in order of increasing approximate high-season double-room price:

Casa de Huéspedes Casa María,
H. Batallón 108, $12

Hotel Posada del Rey, Campeche 10, tel. 501-23, $27

Hotel Bucanero, Juárez 75, tel. 501-01, $27

Hotel Flamingos, Juárez 105, $30

Motel-Suites San Blas,
Aticama and Las Palmas, tel. 505-05, $33

Motel Marino Inn, H. Batallón s/n, tel. 503-03, $33

Hotel Las Brisas, Cuauhtémoc 106 Sur, tel. 501-12 or 504-80, $70

will certainly be much higher than they once were. Figure around $30 d.

Half a block along Juárez, the **Hotel Bucanero** appears to be living up to its name at Calle Juárez 75, San Blas, Nayarit 63740, a block from the plaza, tel. (321) 501-01. A stanza from the *Song of the Pirate* emblazons one wall, a big stuffed crocodile bares its teeth beside the other, and a crusty sunken anchor and cannons decorate the shady patio. Despite peeling paint the rooms retain a bit of spacious, old-world charm, with high-beamed ceilings under the ruddy roof tile. (High, circular vent windows in some rooms cannot be closed, however. Use repellent or your mosquito net.) Outside, the big pool and leafy old patio-courtyard provide plenty of nooks for daytime snoozing and socializing. A noisy nighttime (winter-spring seasonal) bar, however, keeps most guests without earplugs jumping till about midnight. Their 32 rooms run about $22 s, $27 d, with ceiling fans and hot water.

San Blas's more modern hotels are nearer the water. The lively, family-operated **Hotel Posada del Rey,** Calle Campeche 10, San Blas, Nayarit 63740, tel. (321) 501-23, seems to be trying hardest. It encloses a small but inviting pool-patio beneath a top-floor viewpoint bar (and high-season-only restaurant) that bubbles with continuous soft rock and salsa tunes.

Friendly owner Mike Vasquez, who splits his day between his Pato Loco everything-for-the-beach store and his bar at night, also arranges tours and fishing, snorkeling, and diving excursions to nearby coastal spots. His hotel rooms, while nothing fancy, are comfortable. The rates for their 12 rooms are about $23 s, $27 d with fan; a/c $9 extra, credit cards accepted.

In the palm-shadowed, country fringe of town not far from Playa Borrego is the **Motel-Suites San Blas,** at Calles Aticama and Las Palmas, San Blas, Nayarit 63740, tel. 321-505-05, left off H. Batallón a few blocks after the Motel Marino. Its pool-patio, playground, game room, and spacious, but somewhat worn, suites with kitchenettes (dishes and utensils *not* included) are nicely suited for active families. The 23 fan-only suites include 16 singles for two adults and kids renting for about $33, and seven doubles accommodating four adults with kids for about $47; credit cards accepted.

Although the facilities list of the four-star **Motel Marino Inn** looks fine on paper, the place is generally unkempt. Its tattered amenities—from the bare-bulb reception and cavernous upstairs disco to the mossy pool-patio and mildewy rooms—sorely need scrubbing and a modicum of care. Located at Av. H. Batallón s/n, San Blas, Nayarit 63740, tel. (321) 503-03. The 60 rooms go for about $33 s or d, all with a/c and private balconies; seasonal restaurant, credit cards accepted.

In fortunate contrast is San Blas's best, **Hotel Las Brisas,** Cuauhtémoc 106 Sur, San Blas, Nayarit 63740, south end of town, two blocks off H. Batallón, tel. (321) 501-12 and (321) 504-80. The careful management of its family-owners shows everywhere: manicured palm-shaded gardens, crystal-blue pool, immaculate sundeck, and centerpiece restaurant. The 60 cool, air-conditioned (and consequently slightly clammy) rooms are tiled, tastefully furnished, and squeaky clean. Rates run about $60 s, $70 d, with a hearty breakfast included and credit cards accepted; a gift shop and a travel agency are on the premises.

Trailer Park

San Blas's only trailer park, the **Los Cocos,** at H. Batallón s/n, San Blas, Nayarit 63740, tel.

(321) 500-55, is a two-minute walk from the wide, yellow sands of Playa Borregos. Friendly management, spacious, palm-shaded grassy grounds, pull-throughs, unusually clean showers and toilet facilities, a laundry next door, fishing, and a good, air-conditioned bar with satellite TV all make this place a magnet for RVers and tenters from Mazatlán to Puerto Vallarta. The biting *jejenes* require the use of strong repellent for residents to enjoy the balmy evenings. The 100 spaces rent for about $8/day for two persons, $1 for each additional, with all hookups. Monthly rates run $130 low season, $190 high; pets okay.

Camping

The *jejenes* and occasional local toughs and Peeping Toms make camping on close-in Borrego Beach a marginal possibility only. On the other side of town, however, **Isla del Rey** (accessible by *lancha* from the foot of Calle Juárez) presents possibilities for prepared trekker-tenters. The same is true for eco-sanctuary **Isla Isabel**, two hours by hired boat from San Blas. For those less equipped, the palm-lined strands of **Playa Islitas, Playa Matanchén,** and **Playa Cocos** on the Bay of Matanchén are ripe for camping. (For details on all these, see "Beaches and Activities" above, and "Around the Bay of Matanchén" below.)

FOOD

Snacks, Stalls, and Market

During the mornings and early afternoons try the fruit stands, groceries, *fondas,* and *jugerías* in and around the **Central Market** (behind the plaza church). Late afternoons and evenings, many semipermanent streetside stands around the plaza, such as the **Taquería Las Cuatas** on the corner of Canalizo and Juárez, offer tasty *antojitos* and drinks.

For sit-down snacks every day till midnight, drop in to the **Lonchería Ledmar** (also at the Canalizo-Juárez corner) for a hot *torta,* hamburger, quesadilla, tostada, or fresh-squeezed *jugo* (juice).

Get your fresh cupcakes, cookies, and crispy *bolillos* at the **bakery** at Comonfort and Cuauh-

témoc, around the uptown corner from Hotel Posada del Rey, closed Sunday. You can get the same (but not quite so fresh) at the small bakery outlet across from the plaza, corner of Juárez and Canalizo.

Restaurants

Complete dinner price key: Budget: under $7; Moderate: $7-14; Expensive: more than $14.

Family-managed **Restaurant McDonald,** 36 Juárez, tel. 504-32, half a block from the plaza, is one of the gathering places of San Blas. Their bit-of-everything menu features soups (cream of asparagus $2), meat (pork chops $5), and seafood (shrimp $7, fish filet $5), besides a hamburger that beats no-relation U.S. McDonald's by a mile. Open daily 0700-2200. Budget to moderate.

For TV with dinner, the **Restaurant La Familia** is just the place at H. Batallón between Juárez and Mercado. American movies, sarape-draped walls, and colorful Mexican tile supply the ambience, while a reasonably priced seafood and meat menu furnishes the food. For dessert, step into their luminescent-decor bar next door for giant-screen American baseball or football. Open for lunch and dinner daily except Sunday. Moderate.

For subdued marine atmosphere and good fish and shrimp, both local folks and visitors choose **Restaurant La Isla,** at Mercado and Paredes, tel. (321) 504-07. As ceiling fans whir overhead and a guitar strums softly in the background, the net-draped walls display a museum-load of marine curiosities, from antique Japanese floats and Tahitian shells to New England ship models. Open Tues.-Sun. 1400-2100. Moderate.

San Blas's class-act restaurant is the **El Delfín** at the Hotel Las Brisas, Cuauhtémoc 106, tel. (321) 501-12. Potted palms and leafy planter-dividers enhance the refined tropical atmosphere of this air-conditioned dining room-in-the-round. Meticulous preparation and service, bountiful breakfasts, savory dinner soups, and fresh salad, seafood, and meat entrees keep customers returning year after year. Open daily 0800-1200 and 1600-2100, credit cards accepted. Moderate to expensive.

ENTERTAINMENT

Sleepy San Blas's entertainment is mostly of the local, informal variety. Visitors usually content themselves with strolling the beach or riding the waves by day, and reading, watching TV, listening to mariachis, or dancing at a handful of clubs by night.

Nightlife
Owner-manager Mike McDonald works hard to keep **Mike's Place,** Juárez 36, tel. (321) 504-32 (on the second floor, above his family's restaurant), the classiest club in town. Ordinarily, he runs it as a sing-along "karaoke" bar. Sometimes, however, he heats things up with his own combo. Lights flash, and dancers whirl on the small dance floor to blues, Latin, and '60s-style rock tunes from his own guitar, accompanied by his equally excellent drum and electronic keyboard partners. Live music seasonally Friday, Saturday, and Sunday nights 2100-2400, small cover, reasonable drinks.

Another spot featuring an upstairs view for sunsets and offering satellite TV and an occasional live combo is the **El Mirador** bar above the Hotel Posada del Rey, at Campeche 10, tel. (321) 501-23.

A few other places require nothing more than your ears to find. During high season music booms out of **Nautilus** dance hall and its neighbor, **Herredor,** down H. Batallón, a block past the Marino Inn. The same is true seasonally of the bar at the **Hotel Bucanero,** Calle Juárez 75, tel. (321) 501-01.

SPORTS

Walking and Jogging
The cooling sea breeze and the soft but firm sand of **Playa el Borrego** at the south end of H. Batallón make it the best place around town for a walk or jog. Arm yourself against *jejenes* with repellent and long pants, especially around sunset.

Water Sports
Although some intermediate- and beginner-level surfing breaks roll in at Borrego Beach, nearly all of San Blas's action goes on at world-class surfing mecca Matanchén Beach. See "Around the Bay of Matanchen" below, for details.

The mild offshore currents and gentle, undertow-free slope of Borrego Beach are nearly always safe for good swimming, bodysurfing, and boogie-boarding. Wind and water are often right for good **windsurfing.** Bring your own equipment, however; no rentals are available, except a few surfboards and one windsurfing outfit at the Pato Loco beach shop on Juárez, across from Restaurant McDonald.

Sediment-fogged onshore water limits snorkel and scuba possibilities around San Blas to offshore eco-preserve **Isla Isabel.** See "Sights" above, for details.

Sportfishing
Tony Aguayo and **Abraham "Pipila" Murillo** are highly recommended to lead fishing excursions. Tony's "office" is the *palapa*-shelter to the left of the little dock at the foot of Calle Juárez. You can reach Abraham (distinguished winner of six international tournament grand prizes) at his home, Comonfort 248, tel. (321) 507-19. Expect to pay about $80 for a complete six-hour outboard *lancha* outing, which can accommodate three to four passengers, for "chico" fish—snapper, mackerel, tuna, yellowtail. Longer "grande" excursions—for big-game dorado and sailfish—run about $120 for seven hours.

Otherwise, you can simply bargain with any one of the owners of the many craft docked at the foot of Juárez or on the nearby estuary shoreline.

During the latter few days in May, San Blas hosts its long-running (30-plus years) **International Fishing Tournament.** The entrance fee runs around $250; prizes range from automobiles to Mercury outboards and Penn International fishing rods. For more information, contact the local tourist information office, downtown, on Juárez, across from McDonald's Restaurant.

SHOPPING

San Blas visitors ordinarily spend little of their time shopping. For basics, however, the stalls at the **Central Market** offer lots of good tropical fruits, meats, and staples; open daily 6 a.m.-2 p.m. For used clothes and a little bit of everything else a **flea market** operates on Calle Canalizo a block past the bus station (away from the *jardín*) each Saturday morning and early afternoon.

One of the most distinguished for-sale handicrafts collections in Nayarit state is at the **Las Brisas Hotel** shop. Lovingly selected pieces from the famous Pacific Mexico crafts centers—Guadalajara, Tlaquepaque, Tonalá, Pátzcuaro, Olinalá, Taxco, Oaxaca, and more—decorate the shop's cabinets, counters, and shelves.

One or two permanent *artesanías* (handicrafts) shops and a *huarachería* are behind the church on the block of Calle Sinaloa between Paredes and H. Batallón San Blas.

The plaza-corner store, **Comercial de San Blas**, corner of Juárez and H. Batallón, offers a unique mix of everything from film developing and Hohner harmonicas to fishing poles and hooks, sinkers and line. Open 0900-1400 and 1700-2100, except Sunday.

SERVICES

Bank and Moneychanger
Banamex, one block east of the plaza at Juárez 36 Ote, tel. (321) 500-30, 500-31, exchanges U.S. traveler's checks and cash weekday mornings 0800-1100 only. After hours, try your hotel desk or the Pato Loco beach shop across from McDonald's restaurant.

Post Office, Telegraph, and Telephone
The *correo* and *telégrafo* stand side by side at Sonora and Echeverría (one block behind, one block east of the plaza church). The *correo*, tel. (321) 502-95, is open Mon.-Fri. 0900-1300 and 1500-1700, Saturday 0900-1300; *telégrafo*, tel. 501-15, is open Mon.-Fri. 0800-1400.

San Blas area code is 321

Be sure to do your long-distance phoning before 2100, as San Blas long distance lines are dead after that. A few *larga distancia* offices sprinkle the town; try the Liquor Store San Blas, one block off the plaza, at H. Batallón and Mercado.

Immigration and Customs
Migración, at Juárez 150, across from Hotel Bucaneros, tel. 501-78, will help you if you lose your tourist card. Open weekdays 0900-1400 and 1700-1900. The federal *hacienda* (treasury) on the plaza performs port customs duties and will assist you with the paperwork necessary to temporarily leave Mexico without your car.

INFORMATION

Tourist Information Office
The local tourist office, supervised by officer-in-charge Manuela de Cordoba, is downtown, on Juárez, across from restaurant McDonald. Open Mon.-Fri. 0900-1400 and 1800-2200, Sat. 1000-1400. If Manuela is out of the office on business in the morning, you can often catch either her or a volunteer there in the evening.

Health and Police
One of San Blas's most highly recommended physicians is **Dr. Alejandro Davalos,** three blocks east of the plaza at Juárez 202 Ote. (corner of Gómez Farías), tel. (321) 503-31.

Alternatively, you can go to San Blas's respectable local hospital, the government **Centro de Salud,** at Yucatán and H. Batallón (across the street from the Motel Marino Inn), tel. (321) 503-32. For routine advice and medications, the **Botica Mexicana** pharmacy, on the plaza opposite the church, tel. (321) 501-22, stocks a large variety of medicines, along with a bit of everything, including film. Open daily 0830-1330 and 1700-2100.

For **police** emergencies, contact the headquarters in the Presidencia Municipal (City Hall), on Canalizo, east side of the central plaza, tel. (321) 500-28.

Publications
English-language reading material in San Blas is as scarce as tortillas in Nome. The **newsstand,** on the Juárez side of the plaza, sometimes has *Time, Newsweek,* and *People* magazines. The **Hotel Las Brisas** shop stocks a few books, and the **tourist information office** across from Restaurant McDonald has a shelf of used English and American paperbacks.

GETTING THERE AND AWAY

By Car or RV

To and from the north and east, paved roads connect San Blas to main-route National Hwy. 15. From the northeast, National Hwy. 11 winds 19 miles (31 km) downhill from its junction 161 miles (260 km) south of Mazatlán and 22 miles (35 km) north of Tepic. From the turnoff, marked by a Pemex gas station, the road winds through a forest of vine-draped trees and tall palms. Drive slowly; the road lacks a shoulder, and cattle or people may appear unexpectedly around any blind, grass-shrouded bend.

From the east, Nayarit Hwy. 28 leaves Hwy. 15 at its signed "Miramar" turnoff at the northern edge of Tepic. The road winds downhill about 3,000 feet (1,000 meters) through a jungly mountain forest to **Santa Cruz del Miramar.** It continues along the **Bahía de Matanchén** shoreline to San Blas, a total of 34 miles (76 km) from Tepic. Although this route generally has more shoulder than Hwy. 11, frequent pedestrians and occasional unexpected cattle nevertheless necessitate caution.

To and from southern Nayarit coastal points and Puerto Vallarta, the new Hwy. 161 cutoff from Hwy. 200 at Las Varas bypasses the slow climb to Tepic, shortening the San Blas-Puerto Vallarta connection to 94 miles (151 km), or about two and a half hours.

If your vehicle requires **unleaded gas** fill up with Magna Sin in Las Varas, Tepic, or the Hwy. 11 junction station. Magna may not be available at the San Blas gas station.

By Bus

The San Blas bus terminal stands adjacent to the plaza church, at Calles Sinaloa and Canalizo. First-class **Transportes Norte de Sonora** (TNS) buses connect several times a day with Tepic, one continuing to Guadalajara. Additionally, two daily departures connect north with Mazatlán and south with Puerto Vallarta.

Three daily regional second-class black-and-white **Transportes Noroeste de Nayarit** departures connect with Santiago Ixcuintla in the north and Las Varas in the south, including all in-between destinations, such as (from south to north) Santa Cruz de Miramar, Los Cocos, Matanchén, Villa Hidalgo, and La Presa.

Local white *(autobús blanco)* buses connect San Blas with the Bay of Matanchén points of Las Aguadas, Matanchén, Aticama, Los Cocos, and Santa Cruz del Miramar. They depart from the downtown corner of Paredes and Sinaloa (a block west of the church) about every hour, 0830-1630 daily.

AROUND THE BAY OF MATANCHÉN

The shoreline of the Bahía de Matanchén sweeps southward from San Blas, lined with an easily accessible, pearly crescent of sand, ripe for beachcombers and tenters. In the luxuriant foothill forest above the bay, trails lead to bubbling waterfalls and idyllic jungle pools, fine for picknicking or wilderness camping. The villages of Matanchén, Aticama, Los Cocos, and Santa Cruz del Miramar dot this strand with *palapa* restaurants and stores offering food and basic supplies. A pair of trailer parks and two good small hotels provide accommodations.

Beaches, Activities, Food, And Accommodations

The beaches of **Matanchén** and **Las Islitas** make an inseparable pair. Las Islitas (if heading south, turn right at the Matanchén village junction) is dotted by little outcroppings topped by miniature jungles of swaying palms and spreading trees. One of these is home for a colony of surfers waiting for the Big Wave, the Holy Grail of surfing. The Big Wave is one of the occasional gigantic 20-foot breakers that rise off Playa Las Islitas and carry surfers as much as a mile and a quarter—an official Guinness world record—to the soft sand of Playa Matanchén.

For camping, the scenic, intimate protected curves of sand around Playa Islitas are ideal. Although few facilities exist (save for a few winter-season food *palapas*), the beachcombing, swimming, fishing from the rocks, shell-collecting, and surfing are usually good even without the Big Wave. The water, however, isn't clear enough for good snorkeling. Campers, be prepared with plenty of good insect repellent.

In season (around Nov.-March) the Team Banana and other *palapa*-shops open up at Matanchén and Las Islitas to rent surfboards and sell what each of them claims to be the "world's original banana bread."

Getting There

Drive or ride either the local *autobús blanco* Santa Cruz del Miramar-bound bus, which departs several times a day from the corner of Paredes and Sinaloa, a block west of the San Blas church. Also, you can ride the second-class black-and-white Noroeste de Nayarit bus, which leaves from the San Blas bus station three times daily.

South from Matanchén

Bending south from Playa Islitas past a lineup of beachfront *palapa* restaurants, the super-wide and shallow (like a giant kiddie-pool) Playa Matanchén stretches to a palm-fringed, sand-ribbon washed by gentle rollers and frequented only by occasional fisherfolk.

About two miles south of Matanchén, a sign marks a side road to a *cocodrilario* (crocodile farm). At the end of the two-mile track (truck okay, car-negotiable with caution when dry), you'll arrive at "El Tanque." a spring-fed pond, home of the **Ejido de la Palma** crocodile farm. About 50 toothy crocs, large and small, snooze in the sun within several enclosures. Half the fun is the adjacent spring-fed freshwater lagoon, so crystal clear you can see half a dozen big fish wriggling beneath the surface. Nearby, ancient trees swathed in vines and orchids tower overhead, butterflies flutter past, and turtles sun themselves on mossy logs. Bring a picnic lunch, your binoculars, bird book, insect repellent, and bathing suit.

Continuing down the road a mile farther, past a marine sciences school, the beach sand gives way to rocky shoals beneath a jungle headland. The road climbs and curves to choroline **Aticama** village (small stores and restaurants) and continues along a beachside coconut grove, name-source of the bordering Playa Los Cocos. Unfortunately, the ocean is eroding the beach, leaving a crumbling, ten-foot embankment along a mostly rocky shore.

The place is, nevertheless, balmy and beautiful enough to attract a winter RV colony to **Trailer Park Playa Amor**, overlooking the waves, right in the middle of Playa Los Cocos. Besides excellent fishing, boating, boogie-boarding, swimming, and windsurfing prospects, the park offers about 30 grassy spaces for very reasonable prices. Rentals run $7, $8, and $9 for small, medium, and large RVs, respectively,

roadside sign at Matanchén, near San Blas

BRUCE WHIPPERMAN

with all hookups, showers, toilets, and pets okay. Write c/o Gerente Reynaldo, Playa Los Cocos, San Blas, Nayarit. Although you can expect plenty of friendly company during the winter months, reservations are not usually necessary.

Casa Mañana

A mile or two mile farther south, the diminutive shoreline retreat Casa Mañana perches at the south end of breezy Los Cocos beach. Owned and managed by an Austrian man, Reinhardt, and his Mexican wife Lourdes, Casa Mañana's double-storied tier of rooms rises over a homey, spic-and-span beach-view restaurant. Very popular with European and North Americans seeking south-seas tranquility on a budget, Casa Mañana offers fishing, beachcombing, hiking, swimming, volleyball right in the palm-adorned front yard, and self-contained RV parking and tent-camping in the lot next door. Their 20 rooms rent for about $25 d with kitchenette, $18 without, longer-stay discounts negotiable, winter reservations strongly recommended. For reservations, write P.O. Box 49, San Blas, Nayarit at 63740; or fax their Tepic office (321) 304-60; or call their local phone, tel. (324) 806-10.

A couple of miles farther south, above rocky **Playa La Manzanilla,** a mile north of Santa Cruz del Miramar village, follow the roadside sign to the big garden-*palapa* **Restaurant La Playa Manzanilla.** From there, atop the Manzanilla headland, you can feast on seafood and the cloud-tipped vista of the broad blue bay, enfolded by a green mountain hinterland. Open Mon.-Fri. 0800-1700, Saturday and Sunday 0800-1900.

Paraíso Miramar

Continue south another half mile and you will pass through rustic Manzanilla village, where a small right-side sign marks the driveway to Paraíso Miramar. The spacious, green bayview park is bedecked by palms and sheltered by what appears to be the grandmother of all banyan trees. Beneath the great tree on a cliff-bottom beach the surf rolls in gently, while the blue bay, crowned by jungle covered ridges, curves gracefully northward toward San Blas.

Paraíso Miramar's owner, who lives in Tepic, and his personable, hardworking manager Porfirio Hernández, offer a little bit for everyone: six simple but clean and comfortable rooms with bath facing the bay; behind that, 12 grassy RV spaces with concrete pads and all hookups, and three kitchenette bungalows sleeping six. A small view restaurant and blue pools—swimming, kiddie, and jacuzzi—complete the lovely picture.

Rooms rent for about $17 s, $20 d; bungalows, about $70. For a week's stay, you get one day free. RV spaces go for about $9/day. If, on the other hand, you'd like to set up a tent, the shady hillside palm grove on the property's south side appears just right. Make reservations by writing Paraíso Miramar directly at Km 1.2 Carretera a San Blas, Playa La Manzanilla, Santa Cruz de Miramar, Nayarit, or calling Tepic (in Spanish), tel. (321) 222-09, or Guadalajara, tel. (36) 414-675.

Waterfall Hikes

A number of pristine creeks tumble down boulder-strewn beds and foam over cliffs as waterfalls *(cataratas)* in the jungle above the Bay of Matanchén. Some of these are easily accessible and perfect for a day of hiking, picnicking, and swimming. Don't hesitate to ask local directions: say *"¿Dónde está la senda a* (path to) *la catarata, por favor?"* If you would like a guide, ask *"¿Hay guia, por favor?"* One (or all) of the local crowd of kids may immediately volunteer.

You can get to within walking distance of the waterfall near **Tecuitata** village either by car or the Tepic-bound bus a few miles out of Santa Cruz del Miramar along Nayarit Hwy. 28. Half a mile uphill past the village, a sign "Balneario Nuevo Chapultepec" marks a dirt road heading downhill half a mile to a creek and a bridge. Cross over to the other side ($3 entrance), where you'll find a *palapa* restaurant and a hillside waterslide and small swimming pool.

Continue upstream along the right-hand bank of the creek for a much rarer treat, however. Half the fun are the sylvan jungle delights—flashing butterflies, pendulous leafy vines, gurgling little cascades—along the meandering path. The other half is at the end, where the creek spurts through a verdure-framed fissure and splashes into a cool, broad pool, festooned with green, giant-leafed *chalata* (taro in Hawaii, tapioca in Africa) plants. Both the pool area (known locally as Arroyo Campiste, popular with kids and women who bring their washing) and the trail have several possible campsites. Bring everything, especially your water purification kit and insect repellent.

Another waterfall, the highest in the area, near the village of **El Cora,** is harder to get to but the reward is even more spectacular. Again, on the west-east Santa Cruz de Miramar-Tepic Hwy. 28, a negotiable dirt road to El Cora branches south just before Tecuitata. At road's end, after about five miles, you can park by a banana loading platform. From there, the walk (less than an hour) climaxes with a steep, rugged descent to the rippling, crystal pool at the bottom of the waterfall. Best ask for a local guide, or contact Lucio Liñan at Botica Mexicana, the plaza-front pharmacy in San Blas. His tours begin around 0830, go by local bus or your car, and cost about $20 per person for the whole day.

Shortcut South to Puerto Vallarta

Newly paved Nayarit Hwy. 161 allows Puerto Vallarta-bound drivers to bypass the old route—the slow, roundabout climb and descent—via Tepic. Instead, Hwy. 161 forks south from Tepic-bound Hwy. 28 (about 11 miles, 18 km, south of San Blas), just south of Santa Cruz de Miramar village. It continues through lush foothill farms and tropical forest, joining Hwy. 200 at Las Varas, about 53 miles (85 km) north of Puerto Vallarta.

Travelers who wish to explore Tepic, Nayarit's colonial state capital and its lush, volcano-rimmed valley, should continue uphill along Hwy. 28.

TEPIC

Tepic (elev. 3001 feet, 915 meters) basks in a lush highland valley beneath a trio of giant, slumbering volcanoes: 7,600-foot Sanganguey and 6,630-foot Tepetiltic in the east and south, and the brooding Volcán San Juan (7,350 feet, 2,240 meters) in the west. The waters that trickle from their cool green slopes have nurtured verdant valley fields and gardens for millennia. The city's name itself reflects its fertile surroundings: from the Nahuatl *tepictli*, meaning "land of corn."

Resembling a prosperous U.S. county seat, Tepic (pop. 200,000) is the Nayarit state capital—the service, manufacturing, and government center for the entire state. Local people flock to deposit in its banks, shop in its stores, and visit its diminutive main-street state legislature.

The **Huichol** Indians are among the many who come to trade in Tepic. The Huichol fly in from their remote mountain villages, loaded with crafts—yarn paintings, beaded masks, ceremonial gourds, God's Eyes—which they sell at local handicrafts stores. Tepic has thus accumulated a few troves of their intriguing ceremonial art, whose hallucinogenic animal and human forms symbolize the Huichol's animistic world view. (See special topic "The Huichol" in the "Along the Road to San Blas" section above.)

Beyond the city limits, the Tepic valley also offers an unusual bonus for lovers of the outdoors. About 45 minutes from town by car, sylvan mountain-rimmed lake Santa María brims with opportunity for a relaxing day or week of camping, hiking, and wildlife viewing.

HISTORY

Scholars believe that around A.D. 1160 the valley of Tepic may have been a stopping place for a generation of the Méxica (Aztecs) on their way to the Valley of Mexico. By the eve of the conquest, however, Tepic was ruled by the kingdom of Xalisco, whose capital occupied the same ground as the present-day city of Jalisco, a few miles south of Tepic.

In 1524, the expedition headed by the Cortés's nephew, Francisco Cortés de Buenaventura, explored the valley in peaceful contrast to those who followed. The renegade-conquistador Nuño de Guzmán, bent on accumulating gold and *indígena* slaves, arrived in May 1530 and seized the valley in the name of King Charles V. After building a lodging-house for future immigrants, Guzmán hurried north, burning a pathway to Sinaloa. He returned a year later and founded a settlement near Tepic, which he named Espíritu Santo de la Mayor España.

Guzmán's excesses soon caused him serious trouble. The king ordered his settlement's name changed to Santiago de Compostela in 1532. Today it is Nayarit's oldest municipality, located 36.8 kilometers south of present-day Tepic. Soon, immigrants began colonizing the countryside of the sprawling new province of Nueva Galicia, which today includes the modern states of Jalisco, Nayarit, and Sinaloa. Guzmán managed to remain as governor until 1536, when the viceroy finally had him arrested and sent back to Spain in chains.

With Guzmán gone, Nueva Galicia began to thrive. The colonists settled down to raising

JUNÍPERO SERRA: APOSTLE OF CALIFORNIA

His untiring, single-minded drive to found a string of missions and save the souls of native Californians has lifted Junípero Serra to prominence and proposed sainthood. Not long after he was born, on 24 November 1713, to illiterate parents, on the Spanish island of Mallorca, he showed a fascination for books and learning. After taking his vows at the Convent of St. Francis in Palma on 15 September 1531, he changed his name to Junípero, after the beloved friend and "merry jester of God" of St. Francis Assisi.

Ordained in 1738 into the Franciscan order, Junípero was soon appointed professor of theology at the age of 30. He made up for his slightness—in height he was only 5' 2"—by a penetrating intelligence, engaging wit, and cheery disposition. Serra was popular with students, and, in 1748, when he received the missionary call, two of them—Francisco Palóu and Juan Bautista Crespi—accompanied Serra to Mexico, beginning their lifelong sojourn with him.

Serra inspired his followers by example, sometimes to the extreme. On arrival at Veracruz in December 1749, he insisted on walking the rough road all the way to Mexico City. The injuries he suffered led to a serious infection that plagued him for the rest of his life. During his association with the Mexico City College of San Fernando (1750-1767), which included an extensive mission among the Pames Indians around Jalpan, in Querétaro state, he practiced self-flagellation and wore an undercoat woven with sharp bits of wire. Often he would inspire his indigenous flock during Holy Week, as he played the role of Jesus, lugging a ponderous wooden cross through the stations. Afterwards, he would humbly wash his converts' feet.

Serra's mission to the Californias was triggered by the 24 June 1767, royal decree of King Carlos III, which expelled the Jesuit missionaries from the New World. The king's inspector general of the Indies, José de Galvez, ordered Serra, at age 55, to fulfill a double agenda: organize a Franciscan mission to staff the former Jesuits' several Baja California missions, then push north and found several more in Alta California.

From the summer of 1767 to the spring of 1768, Serra paused in Guadalajara, Tepic, and San Blas with his fellow missionaries en route to the Californias. They sailed north from San Blas in March 1768.

They found the Baja California missions in disarray. The soldiers, having been left in custody of the missions, were running amok—raping native women, murdering their husbands, and squandering supplies. With the cooperation of military commander and governor Gaspar de Portolá, Serra managed to set things straight within a year and continue northward. On 25 March 1769, Serra, weak with fever, had two men lift him onto his mule, beginning the thousand-mile desert trek from Loreto to San Diego. On 17 May Serra's leg became so infected that Portolá insisted he return to Loreto. Serra refused. ". . . I shall not turn back. . . . I would gladly be left among the pagans if such be the will of God."

Serra, however, was always practical. He asked the mule driver's advice. "Imagine I am one of your mules with a sore on his leg. Give me the same treatment." The mule driver applied the ordinary remedy, a soothing ointment of herbs mixed with lard, to Serra's leg. Serra resumed the trip and reached San Diego where, on 16 July 1769, he founded San Diego Mission.

The following years would see Serra laboring on, trekking by muleback up and down California, founding eight more missions, encouraging the padres whom he assigned, and teaching and caring for the welfare of the Indians in his charge. Given the few padres (only two per mission) and the few stores brought by the occasional supply ship from San Blas, it was a monumental, backbreaking task.

In the end, Serra's sacrifices probably shortened his life. On 18 August 1784, at his beloved headquarters mission in Carmel, Serra spent his last days with Palóu, his companion of 40 years. Palóu gave the last sacrament, and two days afterward, Serra, in pain, re-traced the stations of the cross with his congregation for the last time. He died peacefully in his cell eight days later.

Regardless of whatever one believes about Spain's colonial role, the fate of the indigenous inhabitants, and sainthood, it is hard not to be awed by this compassionate, gritty little man who would not turn back.

cattle, wheat, and fruit; the padres founded churches, schools, and hospitals. Explorers set out for new lands: Coronado to New Mexico in 1539, Legazpi and Urdaneta across the Pacific in 1563, Vizcaíno to California and Oregon in 1602, and Father Kino to Arizona 1687. Father Junípero Serra stayed in Tepic for several months en route to the Californias in 1767. Excitement rose in Tepic when a troop of 200 Spanish dragoons stopped by on their way to establishing the new port of San Blas in 1768.

San Blas's glory days, as Spain's, were numbered, however. Insurgents captured its fort cannons and sent them to defend Guadalajara in 1810, and finally the president closed the port to foreign commerce in 1872.

Now, however, trains, jet airplanes, and a seemingly interminable flow of giant diesel trucks carry mountains of produce and manufactures through Tepic to the Mexican Pacific and the United States. Commerce hums in suburban factories and banks, stores, and shops around the plaza, where the aging colonial cathedral rises, a brooding reminder of the old days, which few have time remember.

SIGHTS

Getting Oriented

Tepic has two main plazas and two main highways. If you're only passing through, stay on the *libramiento* Hwy. 15 throughway, which efficiently conducts traffic around the city-center congestion. Near the mid-point of the *libramiento*, a Hwy. 15-Hwy. 200 interchange distributes southbound traffic three ways: either east by *libramiento* Hwy. 15 toward Guadalajara; or south via Hwy. 200 toward Puerto Vallarta; or north, to downtown Tepic, along Blvd. Xalisco.

Av. México, Tepic's main north-south downtown street, angles from Blvd. Xalisco just south of big **Parque La Loma.** A few blocks farther north, Av. México crosses main east-west boulevard **Av. Insurgentes** and continues downtown, past the two main plazas: first Plaza Constituyentes, and then Plaza Principal, about half a mile farther north.

A Walk around Downtown

The **cathedral,** adjacent to Av. México, at the east side of the Plaza Principal, marks the center of town. Dating from 1750, the cathedral was dedicated to the Purísima Concepción (Immaculate Conception). Its twin neo-Gothic bell towers rise somberly over everything else in town, while inside, contrasting cheerier white walls and neo-classic gilded arches lead toward the main altar. There, the pious, all-forgiving Virgen de la Asunción appears to soar to heaven, borne by a choir of adoring cherubs.

The workaday **Palacio Municipal** (City-County Hall) stands on the plaza opposite the cathedral, while behind it and half a block to the north at 284 Zacatecas Nte. the **Museo Amado Nervo** occupies the house where the renowned poet was born on 27 August 1870. The four-room permanent exhibition displays photos, original works, a bust of Nervo, and paintings donated by artists J.L. Soto, Sofía Bassi, and Erlinda T. Fuentes. The Museo is open Mon.-Fri. 0900-1300 and 1500-1900, Saturday until 1300.

Return back to the plaza and join the shoppers beneath the arches in front of the Hotel Fray Junípero Serra on the plaza's south side, where a platoon of shoeshiners ply their trade.

Head around the corner, south, along Av. México. After two blocks you will reach the the venerable 18th-century Casa de los Condes de Miravalle, which houses the Regional Anthropology and History Museum, Av. México 91 Nte., tel. (321) 219-00. The palatial residence was built with profits from silver and gold mined at great human cost by the rich merchant-family of Don Carlos Rivas. Its downstairs rooms now house a host of charming, earthy, pre-Columbian pottery artifacts, including dancing dogs, a man scaling a fish, a boy riding a turtle, a dog with a corncob in its mouth, and a very unusual explicitly amorous couple. In another room, displays illustrate the Huichol symbolism hidden in the Cicuri (Eye of God) yarn sculptures, yarn paintings, ceremonial arrows, hats, musical instruments, and other tokens. Open Mon.-Sat. 0900-1800.

Continue south along Av. México; pass the state legislature across the street on the left and the **federal-state tourist information office** on the right just before **Plaza Constituyentes.**

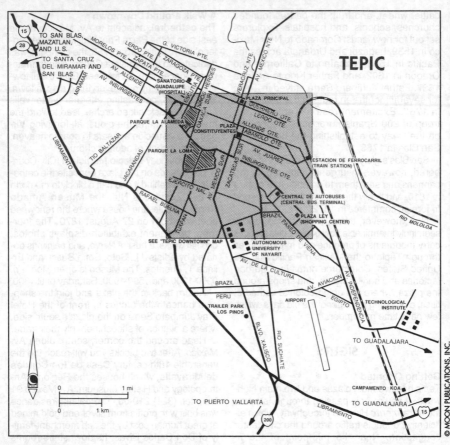

On your right, along the west side of the plaza, spreads the straightlaced Spanish classical facade of the State of Nayarit **Palacio de Gobierno**. Inside, in the center, rises a cupola with a 1975 collection of paintings by artist José Luis Soto. In a second, rear building, a mural by the same artist portrays the struggles of the Independence and the 1910-17 Revolution.

Continuing about a mile south of Plaza Constituyentes past Insurgentes, where Av. México crosses Ejercito Nacional, you will find the **Templo y Ex-convento de la Cruz de Zacate,** the "Church and Ex-convent of the Cross of Grass." This venerable but lately restored monument has two claims to fame: the rooms where Father

Junípero Serra stayed for several months in 1767 en route to California, and the miraculous cross, which you can see in the open-air enclosure adjacent to the sanctuary. According to chroniclers, the cross-shaped patch of grass has grown for centuries (from either 1540 or 1619, depending upon the account), needing neither water nor cultivation.

Out-of-Town Sights: Crater Lake Santa María
Easily accessible by car and about 45 minutes south of town, Laguna Santa María, tucked into an ancient volcanic caldera, offers near-perfect opportunities for outdoor relaxation. The lake itself, accessible by a good paved road, is big,

blue, and rimmed by forested, wildlife-rich hills. You can hike trails through shady woods to ridgetop panoramic viewpoints. Afterwards, cool off with a swim in the lake. On another day, row a rental boat across the lake and explore hidden, forested inlets and sunny, secluded beaches. Afterward, sit out in a palm-fringed grassy park and enjoy the lake view and the orange blossom-scented evening air.

The driving force behind this seemingly too-good-to-be-true scene is Chris French, the personable owner-operator of lakeshore Koala

Bungalows and Trailer Park. He's dedicated to preserving the beauty of the lake and its surroundings. It seems a miracle that, lacking any visible government protection, the lake and its forest hinterland remain lovely and pristine. The answer may lie partly in its isolation, the relatively sparse local population, and the enlightened conservation efforts of Chris and his neighbors. For accommodations and access details, see "Motel, Trailer Parks, and Camping" following.

ACCOMMODATIONS

Downtown Hotels

Tepic has a pair of good deluxe and several acceptable moderate downtown hotels. Starting in the north, near the Plaza Principal, the **Hotel Cibrian** is located on Amado Nervo, a block and a half behind the Presidencia Municipal, Amado Nervo 163 Pte. Tepic, Nayarit 63000, tel. (321) 286-98, and offers clean, no-frills rooms with bath, ceiling fans, telephones, parking, and a pretty fair local restaurant. The Cibrian's only apparent drawback is the noise that might filter into your room through louvered windows facing the tile (and therefore sound-reflective) hallways. The 46 rooms go for about $23 s, $27 d; credit cards are accepted.

Right on the Plaza Principal stands the five-story tower of Tepic's **Hotel Fray Junípero Serra**, Lerdo 23 Pte., Tepic, Nayarit 63000, tel. (321) 225-25. It offers spacious, tastefully furnished view rooms with deluxe amenities, efficient service, convenient parking, and a cool plaza-front restaurant. The 90 rooms run $52 s and $58 d, and have satellite TV, a/c, and phones; no pool, limited wheelchair access, credit cards accepted.

On Av. México, half a block to the right (south) of the Cathedral, the **Hotel Sierra de Alica**, Av. México 180 Nte., Tepic, Nayarit 63000, tel. (321) 203-25, fax 220-51, remains a longtime favorite of Tepic business travelers. Polished wood paneling downstairs and its plain but comfortable rooms upstairs reflect the Sierra de Alica's solid unpretention. The 60 rooms rent for $27 s, $33 d with fan and a/c, satellite TV, phones, parking, and credit cards accepted.

The newly refurbished **Hotel Real de Don Juan**, Av. México 105 Sur, Tepic, Nayarit 63000, tel. (321) 618-20 or 618-80, fax 618-28, on Plaza Constituyentes is trying hard to become Tepic's class-act hotel A plush, gleaming lobby and adjoining restaurant-bar matches the luxury of the king-size beds, thick carpets, marble baths, and soft pastels of the rooms. Rates for the 48 rooms are $65 s or d, with a/c, TV, parking, and limited wheelchair access; credit cards are accepted.

Nearby on Mina, half a block from the Av. México plaza corner, the **Hotel Altamirano**, Mina 19 Pte., Tepic, Nayarit 63000, tel. (321) 271-31, offers basic bare-bulb rooms with bath at moderate rates. The hotel, although clean, is nondescript to the point of shabbiness. The 31 rooms rent for $17 s, $20 d; fans and parking.

Motel, Trailer Parks, and Camping

If you prefer to stay out of the busy city center, try the motel-style **Hotel Las Palomas**, Av. Insurgentes 2100 Ote., Tepic, Nayarit 63000, tel. (321) 402-39 or 409-48, fax 409-53, about two miles southeast of downtown. Its two stories of double rooms and suites surround a colonial-chic pool and parking patio. The reception opens into an airy solarium-restaurant, which is especially inviting for breakfast. The 67 clean and comfortable Spanish-style tile-floored rooms rent for $51 s or d, with a/c, satellite TV, and phones; credit cards are accepted.

Farther south, on Blvd. Xalisco about a mile before the Puerto Vallarta (Hwy. 200) interchange, the **Trailer Park Los Pinos** offers, besides trailer and camping spaces, six large kitchenette rooms and plenty of homey atmosphere, contributed by the grandmotherly on-site owner. The 25 pine-shaded concrete trailer pads, with all hookups and good drinkable well water, spread in two rows up a gradual, hillside slope. Los Pinos's mailing address is P.O. Box 329, Tepic, Nayarit 63000, or contact them at (321) 312-32. The rooms rent for $20 low season, trailer spaces go for $10/night, camping is $5, with discounts for weekly and monthly rentals; includes showers and toilets.

Farther out of town still, RVers and campers can try **Campamento KOA,** Mexico's first KOA campground, at Carretera México-Nogales Km 899, tel. (321) 404-86, fax 326-99. Their spacious, grassy park offers 65 trailer spaces for $17 with sewer hookup, $12 without. At these rates, they're empty most of the time, so try bargaining for a better deal. Amenities include two pools (one for adults, the other for kids), showers, toilets, and a rec room; pets okay. Directions: They're located by the railroad track, off the *libramiento,* Guadalajara-direction, about two miles east of the Hwy. 200 interchange. Get there by turning north on the first paved street, Calle Las Sauces, just east of the *libramiento* railway overpass; after about 200 yards, turn left at Jacarandas, then, at the railroad track, turn right one block. Alternatively, you can get there via Insurgentes by heading southeast out of town; turn right (south) just past the railroad track, and continue along the trackside road a mile to the park.

RV and tent camping and comfortable rooms are also available at the **Koala Bungalows and Trailer Park** at the gorgeous semi-tropical mountain lake Santa María (see "Sights" preceding), about 45 minutes away via Hwy. 15 southeast of Tepic. Owner Chris French maintains a tranquil, palm-studded lakeside park, with bungalow-style rooms, RV and tenting sites, a snack bar, kiddie pool, and rowboat rentals. Koala's mailing address is P.O. Box 493, Tepic, Nayarit 63000, or reach them at (321) 237-72. The three or four Spartan but clean and comfortable garden rooms with bath rent for $20 daily, $120 weekly, and $250 monthly for one or two persons. A bungalow with kitchenette rents for $35 daily, $200 weekly, and $400 monthly. A small house and a larger two-bedroom house are also available for $25 and $50 per day, respectively. About 20 well-maintained leafy RV sites rent for $10 daily, $60 weekly, and $190 monthly, with all hookups, and toilets and showers. Add $1 per day for a/c power. Campsites go for $3 per night, add $2 for kids.

Find it by heading along Hwy. 15 southeast toward Guadalajara. About 16 miles (26 km) east of Tepic, between roadside kilometer markers 194 and 195, follow the signed turnoff south toward Santa María del Oro. Keep on four more miles (6.4 km) to the town (pop. 3,000). Continue another five miles (eight km), winding downhill to the lake. For a breathtaking lake view, stop at the roadside viewpoint about a mile past the town. At the lakeshore, head left a few hundred yards to Koala Bungalows and Trailer Park.

FOOD

Complete dinner price key: Budget: under $7; Moderate: $7-14; Expensive: more than $14.

Traffic noise and exhaust smoke sometimes spoil the atmosphere in downtown restaurants. The **Hotel Fray Junípero Serra** restaurant does not suffer such a drawback, however, located in air-conditioned serenity behind its plate glass, plaza-front windows at Lerdo 23 Pte., tel. (231) 225-25. Open daily 0700-2100, credit cards accepted. Moderate to expensive.

A much humbler but colorful and relatively quiet lunch or supper spot is the downtown favorite **Lonchería Flamingos,** on Puebla Nte., behind the Presidencia Municipal, where a cadre of spirited female chefs puts out a continuous supply of steaming *tortas,* tostadas, tacos, *liquados,* and *hamburguesas.* The Torta Ahogado, however, is their supreme specialty. Here, the question is: "Are you big enough for the Torta Ahogado?" Open daily except Wednesday, 1000-2230. Inexpensive.

On Av. México, a block south of the Plaza Principal at Av. México 139 Nte. (near the corner of Hidalgo), the **Restaurant Candiles** offers a bit of atmosphere with your *huevos mexicanos, ensalada de vegetales,* or chiles rellenos. Open daily 0700-2200. Moderate.

Farther down Av. México, just past the Plaza Constituyentes, the very popular evening spot **Restaurant Los Molcajetes** names itself after the *molcajete,* the big stone bowl in which native Mexican delicacies are often served (and in which they offer *queso fundido,* cheese fondue). Located at Mexico 133 Sur, tel. (321) 364-59. Open daily 1000-2400. Moderate.

Chic's, a big Mexican version of Denny's by the big Ley shopping center, on Av. Insurgentes about a mile and a half southeast of downtown, offers a bit of everything for the travel-weary: tasty American-style specialties, air-conditioned ambience, and a mini-playground for kids around back. Open daily 0630-2400 Moderate.

If Chic's is not to your liking, go into Plaza Ley nearby for about half a dozen more alternative pizzerias, *jugerías, taquerías,* and *loncherías.*

SHOPPING

Its for-sale collections of Huichol art provide an excellent reason for stopping in Tepic. At least four downtown shops specialize in Huichol goods, acting as agents for for more than just the commissions they receive. They have been involved with the Huichol for years, helping them preserve their religion and traditional skills in the face of expanding tourism and development. See the special topic "The Huichol" in the "Santiago Ixcuintla" section above.

Starting near the Plaza Principal, the **Casa Arguet,** 132 Amado Nervo, tel. (321) 241-30 (on

Nervo, a block behind the Presidencia Municipal), has an upstairs attic-museum of Huichol art. Open Mon.-Sat. 0900-1400 and 1600-2000, Sunday 0900-1400. The founder's son, personable Miguel Arguet, knows the Huichol well. His copy of *Art of the Huichol Indians* furnishes authoritative explanations of the intriguing animal and human painting motifs.

The government handicrafts store, **Tienda de Artesanías Wereme,** corner Nervo and Mérida, next to the Presidencia Municipal, stocks some Huichol and other handicrafts. The staff, however, does not appear to be as knowledgeable as the private merchants. Open Mon.-Fri. 0900-1400 and 1600-1900, Saturday until 1400.

Several blocks south on Av. México, just past Plaza Constituyentes, **Artesanías Cicuri,** Av. México 110 Sur, tel. (321) 237-14 or 214-16, names itself after the renowned Cicuri, the "Eye of God" of the Huichol. Their collection, although not as extensive as some others, is particularly fine, especially the eerie beaded masks. Open Mon.-Sat. 0900-1400 and 1600-2000.

A few doors farther south, the **Galerías Xiecá,** Av. México 39 Sur, tel. (321) 227-76, displays a galaxy of museum-quality Huichol *cuadra* yarn paintings, masks, gourds, shamanistic tokens, and much more Open Mon.-Sat. 0900-1400 and 1600-2100. The owner, José Ramon Mercado Acuña, a local Huichol authority, gives frequent lectures and leads discussions of Huichol crafts, religion, and folkways. His shop also operates a coffeehouse; a pleasant place for a bit of cake or a sandwich to go with your conversation and cappuccino.

SERVICES

For best **money exchange** rates, go to a bank, such as the main Banamex branch on Av. México at Zapata, which is open 0900-1100 for U.S. dollar cash and traveler's check exchange only. If the lines at Banamex are too long, go to the Banco Promex across the street, or Banco Serfin on the main square next to the Presidencia Municipal at Mérida 184 Nte., open for U.S. dollar money exchange Mon.-Fri. 0830-1030.

After hours, try one of the *casas de cambio* (money exchange counters) nearby, such as the Cerdana at Av. México 139 Nte. (near the corner of Hidalgo), open Mon.-Fri. 0800-2000, or Lidor, just north of Plaza Constituyentes at Av. México Sur 44 , tel. 233-84, open Mon.-Sat. 0830-1400 and 1600-2000.

Tepic has two **post offices.** The main branch is downtown at Durango Nte. 27, corner of Morelos Pte., about two blocks west and three blocks south of the Plaza Principal; the other is at the Central de Autobuses (Central Bus Terminal) on Av. Insurgentes about a mile east (Guadalajara direction) from downtown.

Telecomunicaciones, which provides telegraph, telephone, and public fax, likewise has both a downtown branch on Av. México, corner of Morelos, open Mon.-Fri. 0900-1800, and a Central de Autobuses branch, tel. (321) 323-27.

> **Tepic area code is 321**

INFORMATION

Tepic's **tourist information office** is near the north corner of Av. México and the Plaza Constituyentes on Av. México 34 Sur, tel. (321) 295-4.

English books and magazines are scarce in Tepic. Newsstands beneath the plaza portals (just west of the Hotel Fray Junípero Serra) and the bookstore Publicaciones Azteca on Av. México, corner Morelos (open daily 0800-2400), usually have the *News* from Mexico City. Also, the Restaurant Terraza, on Insurgentes, across from Parque La Loma, between Querétaro and Oaxaca, stocks a number of popular American magazines.

If you need a **doctor,** contact the Sanitorio Guadalupe, on Juan Escuita 68 Nte., tel. (321) 294-01 or 227-13, seven blocks west of the Plaza Principal. They have a 24-hour emergency room and a group of specialists on call.

Common charms that Huichol pilgrims carry with them include a rattle and a small gourd for collecting peyote.

ERIN DWYER

A fire-department paramedic squad is also available by calling tel. (321) 318-09.

For **police** emergencies, call the municipal police station, tel. (321) 201-63. For **fire** emergencies, call the *bomberos* (firemen), tel. (321) 316-07.

GETTING THERE AND AWAY

By Car or RV

Main highways connect Tepic with Puerto Vallarta in the south, San Blas In the west, Guadalajara in the east, and Mazatlán in the north.

To and from **Mazatlán**, traffic, towns, and rough spots slow progress along the 182-mile (293-km) two-lane stretch of National Hwy. 15. Expect four or five hours of driving time under good conditions.

Two-lane Hwy. 200 from Puerto Vallarta is in good condition for ito 104 milo (167 km) length. Curves, traffic, and the 3,000-foot Tepic grade, however, usually slow the northbound trip to about three hours, a bit less southbound.

A pair of routes, both about 43 miles (70 km), connect Tepic with San Blas. The most scenic of the two takes about an hour and a half, heading south from San Blas along the Bay of Matanchén to Santa Cruz del Miramar, then climbing 3,000 feet west to Tepic via Nayarit Hwy. 28. The quicker route leads west from San Blas along National Hwy. 11, climbing through the tropical forest to Hwy. 15, where four lanes guide traffic rapidly to Tepic.

To and from Guadalajara, the new Hwy. 15 *cuota* (superhighway) allows motorists to safely complete the 141-mile (227-km) cross-Sierra trip in about two and a half hours, two hours less than the congested and much more hazardous old *libre* road. Toll cost is about $20 per car.

By Bus

The shiny, modern *central de autobuses* on Insurgentes Sur about a mile southeast of downtown has many services, including left-luggage lockers, a cafeteria, a post office, and long-distance telephone, public fax, and telegraph services. First-class ticket windows occupy the left side of the terminal as you enter, second-class the left.

Both **Transportes del Pacífico,** tel. (321) 323-20, and **Transportes Norte de Sonora,** tel. (321) 323-15 have many local departures, connecting with Puerto Vallarta, San Blas, Guadalajara, Mazatlán, and the U.S. border at Tijuana and Nogales.

Super-luxury **Elite** and its parent, **Tres Estrellas de Oro,** tel. (321) 323-26, in addition to connecting with Mazatlán, the U.S. border, Guadalajara and Puerto Vallarta, also connect southward to Barra de Navidad and Manzanillo.

By Train

The *estación de ferrocarril* (railway station) is also on the south side of town (prolongation of Av. Allende Ote.). Call (321) 348-61 for tickets and schedule confirmation. Two first-class coach trains, Estrella, headed in opposite directions, depart daily: at around 4 p.m. for Guadalajara, and around 2 p.m. for Mazatlán and the U.S. border (both Mexicali and Nogales). At Guadalajara, connections are available for Mexico City and Pacific destinations of Colima, Manzanillo, Pátzcuaro, and Playa Azul (Lázaro Cárdenas), and Oaxaca.

crouching man motif (from impression of clay seal, Guerrero)

BOB RACE

GUADALAJARA

Puerto Vallarta people often go to Guadalajara (pop. 3,000,000, elev. 5,214 feet, 1,589 meters), the capital of Jalisco, for the same reason Californians frequently go to Los Angeles: to shop and choose from big selections at correspondingly small prices.

But that's only part of the fascination. Although Guadalajarans like to think of themselves as different (calling themselves, uniquely, "Tapatíos") their city is renowned as the "most Mexican" of cities. Crowds flock to Guadalajara to bask in its mild, spring-like sunshine, savor its music, and admire its grand monuments.

HISTORY

Before Columbus
The broad Atemajac Valley, where the Guadalajara metropolis now spreads, has nurtured humans for hundreds of generations. Discovered remains date back at least 10,000 years. The Río Lerma—Mexico's longest river, which meanders across six states—has nourished Atemajac Valley cornfields for at least three millenia.

Although they built no pyramids, high cultures were occupying western Mexico by A.D. 300. They left sophisticated animal- and human-motif pottery in myriad bottle-shaped underground tombs of a style found only in Jalisco, Nayarit, and Colima. Intriguingly, they are found in Colombia and Ecuador.

During the next thousand years, waves of migrants swept across the Valley of Atemajac: Toltecs from the northeast; the Aztecs much later from the west. As Toltec power declined during the 13th century, the Tarascan civilization took root in Michoacán to the south and filled the power vacuum left by the Toltecs. On the eve of the Spanish conquest, semi-autonomous local chiefdoms, tributaries of the Tarascan Emperor, shared the Atemajac valley.

Conquest and Colonization
The fall of the Aztecs in 1520 and the Tarascans a few years later made the Valley of Atemajac a plum ripe for the picking. In the late 1520s, while Cortés was absent in Spain, the opportunistic Nuño de Guzmán vaulted himself to power in Mexico City on the backs of the native peoples and at the expense of Cortés's friends and relatives. Suspecting correctly that his glory days in Mexico City were numbered, Guzmán cleared out three days before Christmas, 1529, at the head of a small army of adventurers seeking new conquests in western Mexico. They raped, ravaged, and burned for half a dozen years, inciting dozens of previously pacified tribes to rebellion.

Hostile Mexican attacks repeatedly foiled Guzmán's attempts to establish his western Mexico capital, which he wanted to name after his Spanish hometown, Guadalajara (from the Arabic wad al hadjarah, "River of Stones"). Ironically, it wasn't until the year of Guzmán's death in Spain in 1542, six years after his arrest by royal authorities, that the present Guadalajara was founded. At the downtown Plaza de Los Fundadores, a panoramic bronze frieze (see "Sights" following) shows cofounders Doña Beátriz de Hernández and governor Cristóbal de Oñate christening the soon-to-become capital of the "Kingdom of Nueva Galicia."

The city grew; its now-venerable public buildings rose at the edges of sweeping plazas, from which expeditions set out to explore other lands. In 1563, Legazpi and Urdaneta sailed west to conquer the Philippines; 1602 saw Vizcaíno sail for the Californias and the Pacific Northwest. In 1687 Father Kino left for 27 years of mission-building in Sonora, and what would be Arizona and New Mexico; finally, during the 1760s, Father Junípero Serra and Captain Gaspar de Portola began their arduous trek to discover San Francisco Bay and found a string of California missions.

During Spain's Mexican twilight, Guadalajara was a virtual imperial city, ruling all of northwest Mexico, plus what would become California, Arizona, New Mexico, and Texas—an empire twice the size of Britain's 13 colonies.

Independence

The cry, "Death to the *gachupines,* Viva México" by insurgent priest Miguel Hidalgo ignited rebellion on 16 September 1810. Buoyed by a series of quick victories, Hidalgo advanced on Mexico City in command of a huge ragtag army. But, facing the punishing fusillades of a small but disciplined Spanish force, Hidalgo lost his nerve and decided to occupy Guadalajara instead. Loyalist General Felix Calleja pursued and routed Hidalgo's forces on the bank of the Lerma, not far east of Guadalajara. Although Hidalgo and Allende escaped, they were captured in the north a few months later. It wasn't for another dozen bloody years that others—Iturbide, Guerrero, Morelos—from other parts of Mexico realized Hidalgo's dream of independence.

Guadalajara, its domain reduced by the new republican government to the new state of Jalisco, settled down to the production of corn, cattle, and tequila. The railroad came, branched north to the United States and south to the Pacific, and by 1900, Guadalajara's place as a commercial hub and Mexico's second city was secure.

Modern Guadalajara

After the bloodbath of the 1910-17 revolution, Guadalajara's growth far outpaced the country in general. From a population of around 100,000, Guadalajara ballooned to nearly 3,000,000 by the 1990s. People were drawn from the countryside by jobs in a thousand new factories, making everything from textiles and shoes to chemicals and soda pop.

Handicraft manufacture, always important in Guadalajara, zoomed during the 1960s when waves of jet-riding tourists came, saw, and bought mountains of blown glass, leather, pottery, and metal finery.

During the 1980s, Guadalajara put on a new face while at the same time preserving the best part of its old downtown. An urban-renewal plan of visionary proportions created Plaza Tapatía—acres of shops, stores, and offices beside fountain-studded malls—incorporating Guadalajara's venerable theaters, churches, museums, and government buildings into a single grand open space.

SIGHTS

Getting Oriented

Although Guadalajara sprawls over a hundred square miles, the treasured mile-square heart of the city is easily explorable on foot. The cathedral corner of north-south **Av. 16 de Septiembre** and **Av. Morelos** marks the center of town. A few blocks south, another important artery, east-west **Av. Juárez,** runs above the new metro subway line through the main business district, while a few blocks east, **Av. Independencia** runs beneath Plaza Tapatía and past the main market to the railway station a couple of miles south.

A Walk around Old Guadalajara

The twin steeples of the **cathedral** serve as an excellent starting point to explore the city-center

BRUCE WHIPPERMAN

An arch on Plaza Laureles frames the glistening yellow tile spires of Guadalajara's downtown cathedral.

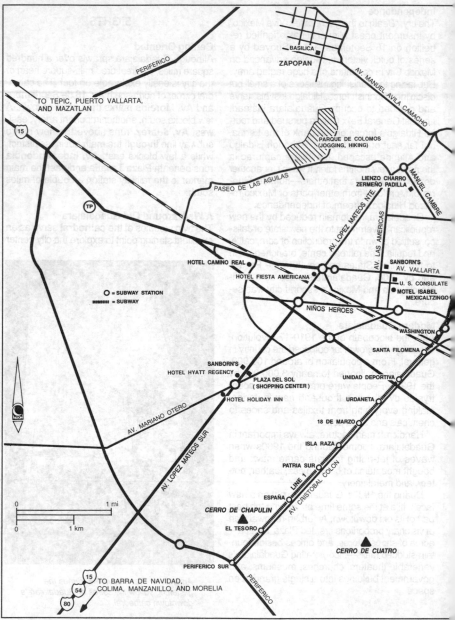

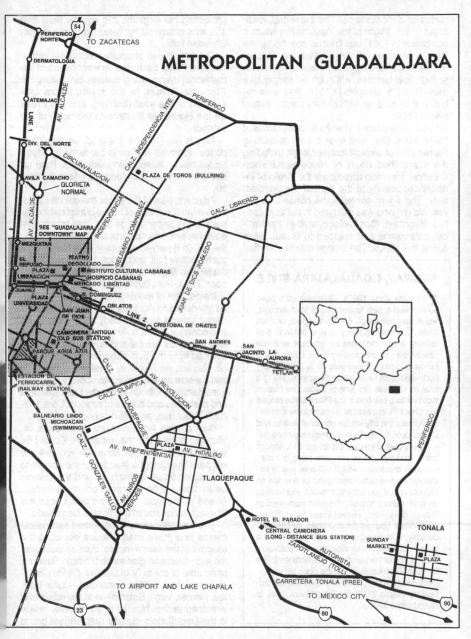

METROPOLITAN GUADALAJARA

TO ZACATECAS

PERIFERICO NORTE

54

DERMATOLOGIA

ATEMAJAC

AV. ALCALDE

LINE 1

PERIFERICO

PERIFERICO NTE.

DIV. DEL NORTE

CIRCUNVALACION

CALZ. INDEPENDENCIA NTE.

AVILA CAMACHO

GLORIETA NORMAL

AV. ALCALDE

INDEPENDENCIA

PLAZA DE TOROS (BULLRING)

BELISARIO DOMINGUEZ

CALZ. OBREROS

MEZQUITAN

EL REFUGIO

TEATRO DEGOLLADO

INSTITUTO CULTURAL CABAÑAS (HOSPICIO CABAÑAS)

PLAZA LIBERACION

MERCADO LIBERTAD

JUANEZ

B. DOMINGUEZ

PLAZA UNIVERSIDAD

SAN JUAN DE DIOS

OBLATOS

LINE 2

JUAN DE DIOS ROSEDO

CRISTOBAL DE OÑATES

CAMIONERA ANTIGUA (OLD BUS STATION)

SAN ANDRES

PARQUE AGUA AZUL

CALZ.

SAN JACINTO

LA AURORA

SAN JACINTO

TETLAN

ESTACION DE FERROCARRIL (RAILWAY STATION)

CALZ. OLIMPICA

AV. REVOLUCION

PERIFERICO

BALNEARIO LINDO MICHOACAN (SWIMMING)

CALZ. TLAQUEPAQUE

CALZ. J. GONZALES GALLO

AV. INDEPENDENCIA

PLAZA

AV. HIDALGO

AV. NIÑOS HEROES

TLAQUEPAQUE

HOTEL EL PARADOR

CENTRAL CAMIONERA (LONG-DISTANCE BUS STATION)

TONALA

SUNDAY MARKET

PLAZA

ZAPOTLANEJO

AUTOPISTA (TOLL)

CARRETERA TONALA (FREE)

TO AIRPORT AND LAKE CHAPALA

23

TO MEXICO CITY

80

90

plazas and monuments. The cathedral, dedicated to the Virgin of the Assumption when it was begun in 1561, was finished about 30 years later. A potpourri of styles—Moorish, Gothic, Renaissance, and Classic—make up its spires, arches, and facades. Although an earthquake demolished its steeples in 1818, they were rebuilt and resurfaced with cheery canary yellow tiles in 1854.

Inside, side altars and white facades climax at the principal altar, built over a tomb containing the remains of several former clergy, including the mummified heart of renowned Bishop Cabañas. The main attraction is the **Virgin of Innocence,** usually to the right of the principal altar. The figure contains the bones of a 12-year-old girl who was martyred in the third century, forgotten, then rediscovered in the Vatican catacombs and shipped to Guadalajara during the 1800s. The legend claims she died

---

SUBWAY, GUADALAJARA STYLE

Since the early 1990s, Guadalajarans have enjoyed a new underground train system, which they call simply the **Tren Ligera,** or "Fast Train." It's nothing fancy, a kind of Motel 6 of subway lines—inexpensive, efficient, and reliable. A pair of intersecting lines, Línea 1 and Línea 2, carry passengers in approximately north-south and east-west directions, along a total of 15 miles (25 km) of track. The station most visitors see first is the **Plaza Universidad** (on Línea 2), accessible by staircases that descend near the city-center corner of Juárez and Colón. Look for the Denny's restaurant nearby.

Downstairs, if you want to take a ride, deposit coins totaling 1.50 pesos (one peso, 50 centavos) in machines, which will give you in exchange a brass *ficha* token, good for one ride on a single line. If you want to transfer, you have to do it at **Juárez** station, the next stop west of Plaza Universidad, where Líneas 1 and 2 intersect. When you get off at Juárez (which, incidentally, is the end of Línea 2), you'll need a transfer token; get it by slipping another 50 *centavos* in one of the transfer token machines *inside* the gate. Then simply follow the signs to Línea 1. (Hint: Best begin your Guadalajara subway adventure before 2100; the Tren Ligera goes to sleep before 2300.)

---

protecting her virginity; it is equally likely that she was martyred for refusing to recant her Christian faith.

Outside, broad plazas surround the cathedral: the **Plaza Laureles,** in front (west) of the cathedral, then moving counter-clockwise, the **Plaza de Armas** to the south, **Plaza Liberación** to the east (behind), and the **Plaza de los Hombres Ilustres** to the north of the cathedral.

Across Av. Morelos, the block-square Plaza de los Hombres Ilustres is bordered by fifteen sculptures of Jalisco's eminent sons. Their remains lie beneath the stone rotunda in the center.

Adjacent, east of the plaza, the colonial building behind the lineup of horse-drawn *calandrias* housed the Seminario de San José for six generations, since its construction in 1696. During the 1800s it served variously as a barracks, a public lecture hall, and, since 1918, has housed the **Museo Regional de Guadalajara,** 60 Liceo; open Tues.-Sun. 0900-1545.

Inside, tiers of rooms surrounding a tree-shaded interior patio illustrate local history. Exhibits depict scenes from as early as the Big Bang and continue with a hulking mastodon skeleton and whimsical animal and human figurines recovered from the bottle-shaped tombs of Jalisco, Nayarit, and Colima. Upstairs rooms contain life-size displays of contemporary but traditional fishing methods at nearby Lake Chapala and costumes and culture of regional Cora, Huichol, Tepehuan, and Méxica peoples.

Back outside, head east two blocks down Av. Hidalgo, paralleling the expansive Plaza Liberación behind the cathedral. On your left you will pass the baroque facades of the *congreso del estado* (state legislature) and the *palacio de justicia* (state supreme court) buildings. Ahead at the east end of the plaza rises the timeless silhouette of the **Teatro Degollado.**

The theater's classic, columned facade climaxes in a grand marble frieze depicting the allegory of the seven muses. Just up the steps, the arch overhead glows with Gerardo Suárez's panorama of canto IV of Dante's *Divine Comedy,* complete with its immortal cast—Julius Caesar, Homer, Virgil, Saladin—and the robed and wreathed author himself in the middle. Inside is the Degollado's equally resplendent grand salon, said to rival the gilded refinement of Milan's renowned La Scala. Named for the millionaire who financed its construction, the Degollado opened with appropriate fanfare on 13 September 1866, with a production of *Lucia de Lammermoor*, starring Ángela Peralta, the "Mexican Nightingale." An ever-changing menu of artists still graces the Delgollado's stage. These include an excellent local folkloric ballet troupe every Sunday morning (see "Entertainment and Events" following).

Walk behind the Degollado, where a modern bronze frieze, the **Frisa de Los Fundadores,** decorates its back side. Appropriately, a mere two blocks from the spot where the city was founded, the 68-foot sculpture shows Guadalajara's cofounders facing each other on opposite sides of a big tree. Governor Cristóbal de Oñate strikes the tree with his sword, while Doña Beátriz de Hernández holds a fighting cock, symbolizing her gritty determination (and that of dozens of fellow settlers) that Guadalajara's location should remain put.

Plaza Tapatía

Turn around and face east. The 17 acres of the Plaza Tapatía complex extend ahead for several blocks across sub-plazas, fountains, and malls. Initially wide in the foreground of Plaza de Los Fundadores, the Tapatía narrows between a double row of shiny shops and offices, then widens into a broad esplanade and continues beside a long pool-fountain that leads to the monumental, domed Hospicio Cabañas a third of a mile away. Along the Tapatía's lateral flanks, a pair of long malls—continuations of Avs. Hidalgo and Morelos—parallel the central Paseo Degollado mall for two blocks.

The eastern end of the Morelos mall climaxes with the striking bronze **Escudo** ("Coat of Arms") of Guadalajara. Embodying the essence of the original 16th-century coat of arms authorized by Emperor Charles V, the Escudo shows a pair of lions protecting a pine tree. The lions represent the warrior's determination and discipline, and the solitary pine symbolizes noble ideals.

Continue east, to where the Plaza Tapatía widens, giving berth for the sculpture-fountain **Imolación de Quetzalcoatl,** designed and executed by Víctor Manuel Contreras in 1982.

MARIACHIS

Mariachis, those thoroughly Mexican troubador bands, have spread from their birthplace in Jalisco throughout Mexico and into much of the United States. The name itself reveals their origin. "Mariachi" originated with the French *mariage,* or marriage. When French influence peaked during the 1864-67 reign of Maximilian, Jaliscans transposed *mariage* to "mariachi," a label they began to identify with the five-piece folk bands that played for weddings.

The original ensembles, consisting of a pair of violins, *vihuela* (large eight-stringed guitar), *jarana* (small guitar), and harp, played exclusively traditional melodies. The song titles, such as "Las Moscas" ("The Flies"), "El Venado" ("The Stag"), and "La Papaya," thinly disguised their universal themes, mostly concerning love.

Although such all-string folk bands still play in Jalisco, notably in Tecalitlán and other rural areas, they've largely been replaced by droves of trumpet-driven commercial mariachis. The man who sparked the shift was probably Emilio Azcárraga Vidaurreta, the director of radio station XEW, which began broadcasting in Mexico City in 1930. In those low-fidelity days, the subdued sound of the harp didn't broadcast well, so Azcárraga suggested the trumpet as a replacement. It was so successful the trumpet has become the signature sound of present-day mariachis.

Still, mariachis mostly do what they've always done—serenade sweethearts, play for weddings and parties, even accompany church masses. They seem to be forever strolling around town plazas on Saturday nights and Sunday afternoons, looking for jobs. Their fees, which should be agreed upon before they start, often depend on union scale per song, per serenade, or per hour.

Sometimes mariachis seem to serve as a kind of live jukebox, which, for a coin, will play your old favorite. And even if it's a slightly tired but sentimental "Mañanitas" or "Cielito Lindo," you can't help but be moved by the singing violins, bright trumpets, and soothing guitars.

Four bronze serpent-birds, representing knowledge and the spirit of humankind, stretch toward heaven at the ends of a giant cross. In the center, a towering bronze spiral represents the unquenchable flame of Quetzalcoatl, trans-

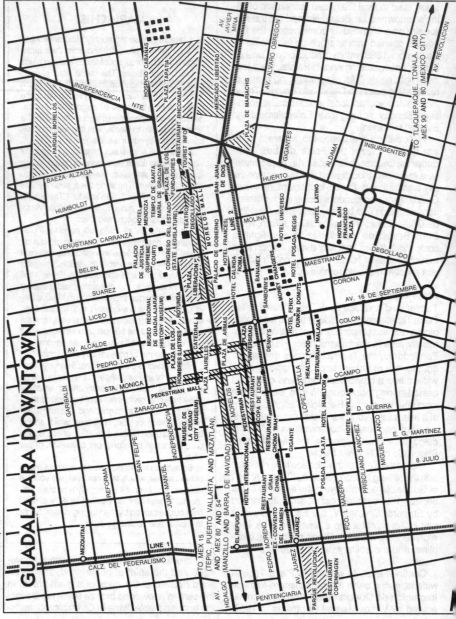

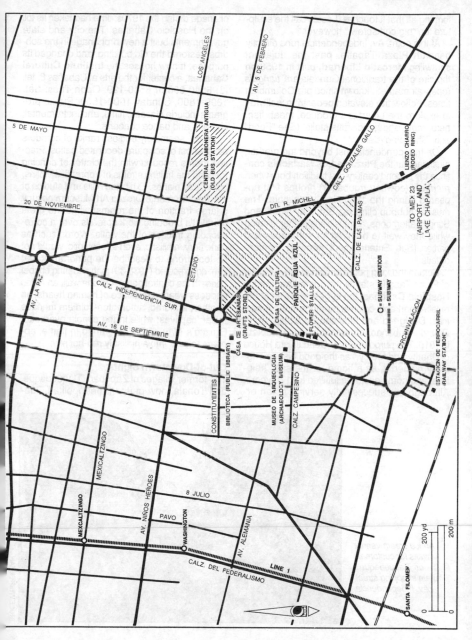

forming all that it touches. Locals call the sculpture the "big corkscrew," however.

At this point, Av. Independencia runs directly beneath Plaza Tapatía, past the adjacent sprawling **Mercado Libertad,** built in 1958 on the site of the traditional Guadalajara *tianguis* (open-air market), known since pre-Columbian times. Follow the elevated pedestrian walkway to explore the Libertad's produce, meat, fish, herb, food, and handicrafts stalls. (See "Food" and "Shopping" below.)

On Independencia, just beyond the market, musicians at the **Plaza de Los Mariachis** continue the second century of a tradition born when *mariachi* (cowboy troubador) groups first appeared during the 1860s in Guadalajara. The musical hubbub climaxes Saturday nights and Sunday afternoons, as musicians gather, singing while they wait to be hired for serenades and parties. (See "Entertainment" following, for more details.)

Behind the long pool-fountain at the east end of Plaza Tapatía stands the domed neoclassic **Hospicio Cabañas,** the largest and one of the most remarkable colonial buildings in the Americas. Designed and financed by Bishop Juan Ruiz de Cabañas, construction was complete in 1810. The purpose of the "Guadalajara House of Charity and Mercy," as the good bishop originally named it, as a home for the sick, helpless, and homeless, was fulfilled for 170 years. Although still successfully serving as an or-

phanage during the 1970s, time had taken its toll on the Hospicio Cabañas. The city and state governments built a new orphanage in the suburbs, restored the old building, and changed its purpose. It now houses the **Instituto Cultural Cabañas,** a center for the arts at Cabañas 8, tel. (3) 6540-008 or 6540-129. Open Tues.-Sat. 1000-1800, Sunday 1000-1500. Public programs include classes, films, and instrumental, chorale, and dance concerts.

Inside, seemingly endless ranks of corridors pass a host of sculpture-decorated patios. Practice rooms resound with the clatter of dancing feet and the halting strains of apprentice violins, horns, and pianos. Exhibition halls and studios of the José Clemente Orozco Art Museum occupy a large fraction of the rooms, while the great muralist's brooding work spreads over a corresponding fraction of the walls. Words such as dark, fiery, nihilistic, even apocalyptic, would not be too strong to describe the panoramas that Orozco executed (1938-39) in the soaring chapel beneath the central dome. On one wall, an Aztec goddess wears a necklace of human hearts; on another, armored, automaton-soldiers menace Indian captives; while in the cupola overhead, Orozco's *Man of Fire,* wreathed in flame, appears to soar into a hellishly red-hot sky.

Out-of-Downtown Sights
The former villages of Zapopan, Tlaquepaque, and Tonalá, now parts of metropolitan Gua-

An ice cream vendor waits for customers on Tlaquepaque's main shopping street, Av. Independencia.

BRUCE WHIPPERMAN

dalajara, make interesting day-trip destinations from the city center. Although local buses or your own wheels can get you there, crowds of bus commuters and congested city streets increase the desirability of the local tour option. Contact your hotel travel desk, a travel agent, or call a well-equipped agency—such as Panoramex, at Federalismo Sur 944, tel. (3) 610-5057 or 610-5005—which conducts reasonably priced bilingual tours daily from the city center.

Zapopan, about six miles northwest of downtown, is famous for its soaring baroque (1730) basilica, home of the renowned Virgin of Zapopan. The legendary image, one of the beloved "three sisters" virgins of Mexico, has enjoyed generations of popularity so enormous that it must be seen to be believed. Local folks, whenever they happen by, often stop to say a prayer (or at least make the sign of the cross as they pass) in front of the cathedral gate. Inside, the faithful crawl the length of the sanctuary to pay their respects to the diminutive blue and white figure. The adoration climaxes on 12 October when a rollicking crowd of hundreds of thousands accompanies the Virgin of Zapopan from the downtown Guadalajara cathedral home to Zapopan, where she stays from 13 October until June.

Afterward, look over the displays of Huichol Indian handicrafts in the adjacent museum-shop **Artesanías Huichola.** Located on your left as you exit the basilica; open Mon.-Sat. 1000-1400 and 1600-1900, Sunday 1000-1300. Sale items include eerie beaded masks, intriguing yarn paintings, and Ojos de Dios (God's Eyes) yarn sculptures. Later, browse for bargains among the handicrafts stalls in front of the basilica and in the municipal market in the adjacent plaza on the corner of Av. Hidalgo and Calle Eva Briseño.

Getting There: From downtown Guadalajara, local Zapopan buses depart from the southside Camionera Antigua ("Old Bus Station") end of Av. Estadio, just north of Parque Agua Azul) and continue through the downtown, stopping at the corner of López Cotilla and 16 de Septiembre. By car, follow Av. Manuel Avila Camacho, which diagonals northwest for about four miles from the city center to Zapopan, marked by the old Baroque arch on the left. After one block,

THE THREE SISTERS OF MEXICO

In all of Mexico, only the Virgin of Guadalupe exceeds in adoration the all-Jalisco trio—the "Three Sister" Virgins of Talpa, Zapopan, and San Juan de los Lagos. Yearly they draw millions of humble Mexican pilgrims who bus, walk, hitchhike, or, in some cases crawl, to festivals in their honor. Each virgin's popularity springs from some persistent, endearing legend. The Virgin of Talpa defied a haughty bishop's efforts to cage her; the Virgin of Zapopan rescued Guadalajara from war and disaster; the Virgin of San Juan de los Lagos restored a dead child to life.

Talpa, Zapopan, and San Juan de los Lagos townsfolk have built towering basilicas to shelter and honor each virgin. Each small and fragile figurine is draped in fine silk and jewels and worshipped by a continuous stream of penitents. During a virgin festival the image is lifted aloft by a platoon of richly costumed bearers and paraded to the clamor, tumult, and cheers of a million or more of the faithful.

Even if you choose to avoid the crowds and visit Talpa, Zapopan, or San Juan de los Lagos on a nonfestival day, you'll soon see the hubbub continues. Pilgrims come and go, bands and mariachis play, and curio stands stuffed with gilded devotional goods crowd the basilica square.

If you choose, you can join the other sojourners and pay your own respects to the diminutive figures who've touched the hearts of so many.

turn left onto Av. Hidalgo, the double main street of Zapopan. Within four blocks you'll see the plaza and the basilica on the left.

Zapopan town is the *cabecera* (headquarters) of the sprawling *municipio* of Zapopan, farm and mountain hinterland, famous for **La Barranca,** the 2,000-foot deep canyon of the Río Grande de Santiago. At the viewpoint past San Isidro, around Km 15, Saltillo Hwy. 54 north of Guadalajara, motorists stop at the viewpoint, **Mirador Dr. Atl,** to admire the canyon vista and the waterfall **Cola del Caballo** ("Horse's Tail") as it plummets hundreds of feet to the river below.

Past that, a small paradise of springs decorates the lush canyonland. First, at Km 17, comes **Los Camachos,** a forest and mountain-framed *balneario* (bathing park) with pools and restaurants; a few miles farther along, is the hot spring bathing complex, **Balneario Nuevo Paraíso,** at Km 24. A kilometer farther (follow the left side road from the highway about a half kilometer) you can view the **Geiseres de Ixcatan** (Ixcatan Geysers) near the village. Get there by car via Hwy. 54, the Saltillo-Zacatecas highway, which heads northward along Av. Alcalde from the city-center cathedral. Bus riders can board the "Los Camachos" bus, which leaves the Glorietta Normal (on Av. Alcalde about a mile north of the downtown cathedral) about every 45 minutes. For more information about Zapopan sights, drop by the Zapopan tourist information office at Vicente Guerrero 11, two blocks behind the basilica, or call (3) 633-0571.

Tlaquepaque and **Tonalá,** in the southeast suburbs, are among Mexico's renowned handicrafts villages. Tlaquepaque (tlah-kay-PAH-kay) (now touristy, but still interesting), about five miles from the city center, is famous for fine stoneware and blown glass; Tonalá, another five miles farther, retains plenty of sleepy, colorful country ambience. Shops abound in celebrated ceramic, brass, and papier mâché animal figurines. The most exciting, but crowded, time to visit is during the Sunday market. (For more Tlaquepaque and Tonalá details, see "Shopping" following.)

ACCOMMODATIONS

Downtown Hotels
Several good hotels, ranging from budget to plush, dot the center of Guadalajara, mostly in the Av. Juárez business district, a few blocks from the cathedral and plazas. Many have parking garages; a desirable downtown option for auto travelers. Hotels farthest from the cathedral plazas are generally the most economical.

The **Posada Tapatía,** López Cotilla 619, Guadalajara, Jalisco 44100, tel. (3) 691-49146, one block off Juárez, near the corner of Calle 8 Julio, is about 10 blocks from the cathedral. Its plain but clean rooms with bath are spread around a light, cheerily restored central patio. Tightly managed by the on-site owner, the Tapatía's prices are certainly right. Try for a room away from the noisy street. The 12 rooms rent $10 s, $13 d, with fans.

Three blocks closer in, on Prisciliano Sánchez between Ocampo and D. Guerra, the old standby **Hotel Sevilla,** Prisciliano Sánchez 413, Guadalajara, Jalisco 44100, tel. (3) 614-9172, 614-9354, or 614-9037, offers basic accommodation at budget prices. Its 80 rooms, furnished in dark brown wood and rugs to match, are plain but comfortable. For more light and quiet, get an upper-story room. Amenities include a lobby with TV, parking, a hotel safe for storing valuables, and a restaurant open daily except Sunday. Rates run $15 s, $22 d, $25 t; fans and telephones included.

One block away, on Madero, the even plainer **Hotel Hamilton,** Madero 381, Guadalajara, Jalisco 44100, tel. (3) 614-6726, offers a rock-bottom alternative. The 32 bare-bulb, not-so-clean rooms border on the dingy; their steel doors seem to enhance the drabness more than increasing security. Store your valuables in the hotel safe. For less noise and more light, get a room in back, away from the street. Rooms rent $12 s, $15 d, and $17 t, with fans but no parking.

Cheerier and closer in, where the pedestrian strolling mall begins on Moreno, stands the big, 110-room **Hotel Internacional,** Pedro Moreno 570, Guadalajara, Jalisco 44100, tel. (3) 613-0330 or 613-0420. Downstairs, a small lobby with chairs and soft couches adjoins the reception. In the tower upstairs, the 60s-modern rooms, most with city views, are plain but clean and comfortable. Rates have doubled lately, although it remains to be seen whether the management can make them stick. Try for a discount below the asking prices of $30 s, $37 d (with 20% discount for a one-week rental). Amenities include fans, phones, and TV, but no parking.

Equally well-located but more upscale, **Best Western Hotel Fénix,** Corona 160, Guadalajara, Jalisco 44100, tel. (3) 614-5714, or (800) 528-1234 from the U.S. and Canada, fax 613-4005, lies on Corona, smack in the downtown business center, a short walk from everything. The owners have managed to upgrade this rather basic small-lobby hotel into something more elaborate. The somewhat cramped result, while not unattractive, is sometimes noisy and crowded. During the day, tour groups traipse in and out past the reception desk, while at night guests crowd the adjacent lobby bar for drinks

GUADALAJARA HOTELS

Guadalajara hotels, grouped by location, in order of increasing approximate high-season double-room price. (The postal code is 44100 unless otherwise noted, the area code is 3, and all toll-free numbers are reached from the U.S. and Canada only.)

DOWNTOWN HOTELS

Posada Tapatía, L. Cotilla 619, tel. 614-9146, $13

Hotel Hamilton, F. Madero 381, tel. 614-6726, $15

Hotel Latino Plaza, P. Sánchez 74, tel. 614-4484 or 614-6214, $17

Hotel Sevilla, P. Sánchez 413, tel. 614-9172, 614-9037, or 614-9354, $22

Hotel Posada Regis, Corona 171, tel. 613-3026 or 614-8633, $33

Hotel San Francisco Plaza, Degollado 267, tel. 613-8954, fax 613-3257, $35

Hotel Universo, L. Cotilla 161, tel. 613-2815, $33

Hotel International, P. Moreno 570, tel. 613-0330 or 613-0420, $37

Hotel Calinda Roma, Juárez 170, tel. 614-8650 or (800) 221-2222, fax 613-0557, $50

Hotel Frances, Maestranza 35, tel. 613-1190 or 613-0936, fax 658-2831, $55

Best Western Hotel Fénix, Corona 160, tel. 614-5714 or (800) 528-1234, fax 613-4005, $66

Hotel Mendoza, V. Carranza 16, tel. 613-4646, fax 613-7310, $80

HOTELS OUT OF DOWNTOWN

Hotel El Parador, Carretera Zapotlanejo 1500, postal code 45625, tel. 600-0910, $40

Motel Isabel, J. Guadalupe Montenegro 1572, tel. 626-2630, $44

Hotel Hyatt Regency, L. Mateos and Moctezuma, postal code 45050, tel. 622-7778 or 678-1234, (800) 233-1234, fax 678-1222, $100

Holiday Inn, L. Mateos Sur 2500, postal code 45050, tel. 634-0650 or (800) 465-4329, fax 631-9393, $140

Hotel Camino Real, Av. Vallarta 5005, postal code 45040, tel. 647-8000 or (800) 7-CAMINO, fax 647 4781, $150

Hotel Fiesta Americana, Aurelio Aceves 225, tel. 625-3434 or (800) FIESTA-1, fax 630-3725, $160

---

and live combo music. Upstairs the 200 air-conditioned rooms are spacious and comfortably furnished with American-standard motel amenities. Walk-in rates, which run $70 s or d, are high for a hotel with neither pool nor parking. You might get a better deal in advance by booking a package through a travel agent or by calling the Best Western toll-free number above.

With the same prime location right across the street, the second-floor **Hotel Posada Regis** offers both economy and a bit of old-world charm, Corona 171, Guadalajara, Jalisco 44100, tel. (3) 613-3026 or 614-8633. Its very clean and comfortable high-ceilinged rooms enclose a gracious Porfirian-era indoor lobby-atrium. Evening videos, friendly atmosphere, and a good breakfast-lunch cafe provide opportunities for relaxed exchanges with other travelers. The 19 rooms cost $27 s, $33 d, with phones, fans, optional TV, but no parking; credit cards are accepted.

Central location, near-deluxe rooms, and moderate prices explain the popularity of the nearby **Hotel Universo,** López Cotilla 161, Guadalajara, Jalisco 44100, tel. (3) 613-2815, corner of Cotilla and Degollado, just three blocks from the the Teatro Degollado. Guests enjoy very clean, carpeted, and draped air-conditioned rooms with wood furniture and ceiling-to-floor tiled bathrooms. The 137 rooms and suites are $30 s, $33 d, suites from about $36, with TV, phones, and parking; credit cards are accepted.

The Universo's competent owner-managers also run a pair of good-value hotels two blocks away. Their graceful, authentically colonial **Hotel San Francisco Plaza,** Degollado 267, Guadalajara, Jalisco 44100, tel. (3) 613-8954, fax 613-3257, is replete with traditional charm. The reception area opens to an airy and tranquil inner patio, where big soft chairs invite you to relax amid a leafy garden of potted plants. The venerable stone walls are decorated with a gallery of intriguing etchings depicting Don Quixote's celebrated adventures. Upstairs, the rooms are no less than you would expect: high-ceilinged, with plenty of polished brown wood, traditional handmade furniture, rustic brass lamps by the bed, and sentimental old-Mexico paintings on the walls. Each room has a phone, TV, fan, and a large, modern-standard bathroom with marble sink. You'll find a homey restaurant downstairs in front and plenty of parking. All this for $30 s, $35 d; credit cards are accepted.

The same owners run the **Hotel Latino Plaza,** one of Guadalajara's better cheap hotels, just around the corner at Prisciliano Sánchez 74, Guadalajara, Jalisco 44100, tel. (3) 614-4484 or 614-6214. It's a simple, plain, small-lobby hotel, but nevertheless enjoys a modicum of care. The 57 rooms in four stories (no elevator) are clean, carpeted, and thoughtfully furnished, albeit a bit worn around the edges. Baths are modern-standard, with shiny-tile showers and marble sinks. Rates run about $15 s, $17 d, including fans, TV, parking, and phones; credit cards are accepted.

Guests of the nearby **Hotel Calinda Roma,** Av. Juárez 170, Guadalajara, Jalisco 44100, tel. (3) 614-8650, (800) 221-2222 from the U.S. and Canada, fax 613-0557, enjoy luxurious amenities—plush lobby, shiny restaurant-bar, rooftop rose garden and pool—usually available only at much pricier hostelries. The 150 rooms cost $50 s or d; suites from about $95; TV, phones, a/c, parking, credit cards, limited wheelchair access. Some rooms, although clean and comfortable, are small. Look before moving in.

The three-story baroque **Hotel Frances,** Maestranza 35, Guadalajara, Jalisco 44100, tel. (3) 613-1190 or 613-0936, fax 658-2831, rises among its fellow monuments on a quiet side street within sight of the Teatro Degollado. Guadalajara's first hotel, built in 1610, has been restored to its original splendor. The 40-odd rooms, all with bath, glow with polished wood, bright tile, and frosted cut glass windows. Downstairs, an elegant chandelier illuminates the dignified, plant-decorated interior patio and adjacent restaurant. Rates run $48 s, $55 d, and $64 t, credit cards accepted, discounts sometimes available, fans only, no parking.

The big colonial-facade **Hotel Mendoza,** V. Carranza 16, Guadalajara, Jalisco 44100, tel. (3) 613-4646, fax 613-7310, on the north side of the Teatro Degollado, is a longtime favorite of Guadalajara repeat visitors. Refined traditional embellishments—neo-Renaissance murals and wall portraits, rich dark paneling, glittering candelabras—grace the lobby, while upstairs, carpeted halls lead to spacious, comfortable rooms furnished with tasteful dark decor, including large baths, thick towels, and many other extras. The 100 rooms and suites rent from $73 s, $80 d, with American cable TV, phones, a/c, a small pool, pricey restaurant, parking, credit cards accepted, and limited wheelchair access.

Although not in the immediate downtown area, the **Motel Isabel,** J. Guadalupe Montenegro 1572, Guadalajara, Jalisco 44100, tel. (3) 626-2630, in the affluent west-side embassy neighborhood, offers a flowery garden setting at moderate prices. The Isabel's 60s-modern amenities—comfortably but not luxuriously furnished rooms with phone, small blue pool, dining room, and parking—have long attracted a loyal following of Guadalajara returnees. Buses (10 minutes to the city center) run nearby. Their 50 rooms rent $35 s, $44 d, with ceiling fans and limited wheelchair access.

West Side Luxury Hotels

During the 1980s the Plaza del Sol, a large American-style hotel, shopping and entertainment complex, mushroomed on west-side Av. Adolfo López Mateos. The Hyatt Regency and the Holiday Inn, the pair of plush hostelries that anchor the development, have drawn many of the high-ticket visitors away from the old city center to the Plaza del Sol's shiny shops, restaurants, and clubs.

The **Hyatt Regency,** Av. López Mateos and Moctezuma, Guadalajara, Jalisco 45050, tel. (3) 678-1234 or 622-7778, (800) 233-1234 from the U.S. and Canada, fax 678-1222, occupies the giant glass tower right across the boulevard from the Plaza Del Sol. Inside, life fills the plush, cool lobby. Vacationers, convention-goers, and tour groups stroll to and fro; conversation overflows from the bar, where the band plays every evening. Outside, during the days, people sun themselves by the pool; at night they dance in the disco till three. The 346 rooms include all amenities and rent for $80-120 s or d; with health spa, gym, no tennis courts, complete wheelchair access.

The **Holiday Inn**, Av. López Mateos Sur 2500, Guadalajara, Jalisco 45050, tel. (3) 634-0650, (800) 465-4329 from the U.S. and Canada, fax 631-9393, a quarter mile south on López Mateos (past the traffic circle), offers much of the same, but in a more relaxed resort setting. The rooms, most with private view balconies, rise in a 10-story tower above the pool and garden. Their luxurious furnishings, in soothing earthtones, include spacious, marble-accented baths. The 285 rooms start at $140 s or d, with everything; spa, sauna, gym, children's area, miniature golf, tennis courts, and wheelchair access.

About a mile north of Plaza del Sol, the **Hotel Fiesta Americana**, Aurelio Aceves 225, Guadalajara, Jalisco 44100, tel. (3) 625-3434, (800) FIESTA-1 from the U.S. and Canada, fax 630-3725, towering above Av. Vallarta, the Hwy. 15 Blvd. Ingrosso, offers another luxury hotel option. From the reception area, a serene, carpeted lobby spreads beneath a lofty, light atrium. The 396 plush view rooms are furnished in pastel tones with soft couches, huge beds, and a host of luxury amenities. Rooms rent from $160, with tennis courts, spa, restaurants, pool, and sundeck.

Along the same boulevard, about a mile farther west. is the **Hotel Camino Real**, Av. Vallarta 5005, Guadalajara, Jalisco 45040, tel. (3) 647-8000, (800) 7-CAMINO from the U.S. and Canada, fax 647-4781, the graceful queen of Guadalajara luxury hotels. In contrast to its high-rise local competitors, the Camino Real spreads through a luxurious park of lawns, pools, and shady tropical verdure. Guests enjoy tastefully appointed bungalow-style units opening onto semi-private pool-patios. Rates run from $150 s or d, and include cable TV, phone, four pools, tennis courts, and a nearby golf course.

Hotel El Parador

The big long-distance Central Camionera bus station is at Guadalajara's far southeast edge, at least 20 minutes by taxi from the center. Some bus travelers find it convenient to stay at the huge, two-pool, moderately priced modern Hotel El Parador and restaurant, Carretera Zapotlanejo 1500, Guadalajara, Jalisco 45625, tel.

(3) 600-0910. It's adjacent to the sprawling terminal and has a restaurant. Bus and truck noise, however, may be a problem. Ask for a quiet *(tranquilo)* room. The place is impersonal, so be prepared to show your receipts. The 600 tidy and comfortable rooms, all with bath, rent for about $33 s, $40 d.

FOOD

Breakfast and Snacks

Local folks flock to the acres of *fondas* (permanent foodstalls) on the second floor of the **Mercado Libertad.** Located at the east end of Plaza Tapatía; open daily about 0700-1800. Hearty homestyle fare, including Guadalajara's specialty, *birria*—pork, goat, or lamb in savory, spiced tomato-chicken broth—is at its safest best here. It's hard to go wrong if you make sure your choices are hot and steaming. Market stalls, furthermore, depend on repeat customers and are generally very careful their offerings are wholesome. Though be sure to douse fresh vegetables with plenty of lime *(limón)* juice.

Downtown Guadalajara is not overloaded with restaurants, and many of them close early. For round-the-clock breakfast or supper, however, you can always rely on **Denny's,** on the corner of Juárez and 16 de September, which has the same food, prices, and 1950s vinyl-stainless ambience as Denny's restaurants everywhere.

For a local variation, head upstairs to **Restaurant Esquina** on the same corner as Denny's, open 0700-2230, or **Sanborn's** across the street, open daily 0730-2300. Besides a fair-to-middling North American-style coffee shop, Sanborn's has a big gift shop, offering maps, guidebooks, and magazines.

For a light breakfast or snack, try the Guadalajara branch of **Dunkin Donuts** nearby at the southeast corner of Corona and Madero; open Mon.-Sat. 0700-2100, Sunday 0800-1400.

Downtown Restaurants

Complete dinner price key: Budget: under $7; Moderate: $7-14; Expensive: more than $14.

Moving west across downtown, from the Plaza Tapatía, first comes the airy, restored Victorian **Restaurant Rinconada,** 86 Morelos, across the plaza behind the Teatro Degollado, tel. (3) 613-9914. The mostly tourist and upper-class local customers enjoy Rinconada for its good meat-fish-fowl entrees plus the mariachis who wander in from the Plaza Mariachi near-by. By 1600 many afternoons, two or three groups are filling the place with their melodies. Moderate to expensive. Open Mon.-Sat. 0800-2100, Sunday 1300-1800.

A few blocks west and south, near the business center, is the plain but worthy **Restaurant Málaga**, 16 de Septiembre 210, whose hard-working owner really does come from Malaga, Spain. The food shows it: an eclectic feast of hearty breakfasts (which include a fruit plate and good french bread), a bountiful four-course *comida corrida* for around $6, many salads, sandwiches and desserts, and savory expresso coffee. Open Mon.-Sat. 0700-2100, Sunday 0800-2100. Budget.

Customers at the **Restaurant Copa de Leche**, one of Guadalajara's acknowledged best restaurants, enjoy an open-air view of the passing sidewalk scene at Juárez and Galeana, two blocks south and two blocks west of the cathedral. Cool salads and tasty regional en-trees, plus prompt service by dinner-jacketed waiters continues to satisfy a legion of repeat customers. Open daily 0730-2100. Moderate to expensive.

Continue west along Juárez to **Restaurant La Gran China**, Juárez 590, between Martinez and 8 Julio, where the Cantonese owner-chef puts out an authentic and tasty array of dish-es. Despite the reality of La Gran China's crisp bok choy, succulent spareribs, and smooth sa-vory noodles, they nevertheless seem a small miracle here, half a world away from Hong Kong. Open daily 1200-2130. Budget to moderate.

For a variation, try Gran China's plainer, but equally authentic neighboring **Restaurant Chong Wah**, Juárez 558, half a block east, at the corner of E.G. Martinez, open approximately the same hours.

Continue about a mile west of the cathedral to **Restaurant Copenhagen 77,** 140.2 Caste-llanos, tel. (3) 625-2803, one of Guadalajara's classiest institutions. Its brand of unpretentious elegance—polished 1940s decor, subdued live jazz, correct, attentive service, tasty entrees—will never go out of style. Moderate to expensive.

Follow Juárez nine blocks west of Av. 16 de Septiembre, to the west end of Parque Revolu-ción. Open Mon.-Sat. 0800-2400, Sunday 1200-1800, live jazz afternoons 1500-1630 and nights 2000-2400.

ENTERTAINMENT AND EVENTS

Just Wandering Around

Afternoons any day, and Sunday in particular, are good for people-watching around Guadala-jara's many downtown plazas. Favorite strolling grounds are the broad Plaza Tapatía west of the cathedral and, evenings especially, along the pedestrian mall-streets, such as Colón, Galeana, Morelos, and Moreno, which meander south and west from cathedral-front Plaza Lau-reles.

If you time it right you can enjoy the band concert in the Plaza de Armas adjacent to the cathedral (Sunday at 1900), or take in an art film at the Hospicio Cabañas (screenings Mon.-Sat. 1600, 1800, and 2000). If somehow you miss these, climb into a *calandria* (horse-drawn carriage) for a ride around town, available on Liceo, between the rotunda and the history mu-seum, just north of the cathedral, about $17/hour.

Parque Agua Azul

Some sunny afternoon, hire a taxi (about $2 from the city-center) and find out why Guadala-jara families love Parque Agua Azul. The en-trance is on Independencia, about a mile south of Plaza Tapatía. It's a green shaded place where you *can* walk, roll, sleep, or lie on the grass. When weary of that, head for the bird park, admire the banana-beaked toucans and squawking macaws and continue into the aviary where free-flying birds flutter overhead. Nearby, duck into the butterfly aviary and enjoy the flick-ering rainbow-hues of a host of *mariposas*. Con-tinue to the orchids in a towering hothouse, fes-tooned with growing blossoms and misted con-tinuously by a rainbow of spray from the center. Before other temptations draw you away, stop for a while at the open-air band or symphony concert in the amphitheater. Open Tues.-Sun. 1000-1800.

Music and Dance Performances

The **Teatro Degollado** hosts world-class opera, symphony, and ballet events. While you're in the Plaza Liberación, drop by the theater box office and ask for a *lista de eventos*. You can also call, or ask your hotel desk clerk to call, the theater box office at (3) 614-4773 (in Spanish only) for reservations and information. Pick up tickets 1600-1900 on the day of the performance. For a typically Mexican treat, attend one of the regular Sunday morning University of Guadalajara folkloric ballet performances. They're immensely popular; get tickets in advance.

You can also sample the offerings of the **Instituto Cultural Cabañas**, tel. 618-8135, housed in the Hospicio Cabañas at the western end of the Plaza Tapatía. They sponsor many events, both experimental and traditional, including frequent folkloric ballet performances. For more information, ask at the Hospicio Cabañas admission desk. Open Tues.-Sun. 1000-1700.

Local jazz mecca Restaurant Copenhagen 77, 140 Z. Castellanos, tel. (3) 625-2803, presents Maestro Carlos de la Torre and his group nightly Mon.-Sat. 0800-2400 and afternoons 1500-1630. At the west end of Parque Revolución, about a mile west of the cathedral.

Fiestas

Although Guadalajara people always seem to be celebrating, the town really heats up during its three major annual festivals. Starting the second week in June, the southeast neighborhood, formerly the separate village of Tlaquepaque, hosts the **National Ceramics Fair.** Besides its celebrated stoneware (See "Shopping" following), a riot of ceram-

ics and folkcrafts from all over Mexico stuff its shops and stalls, while cockfights, regional food, folkdances, fireworks, and mariachis fill its streets.

A few months later, the whole city, Mexican states, and foreign countries get into the **Festival of October.** For a month, everyone seems to contribute something, from ballet performances, plays, and soccer games to selling papier mâché parrots and sweet corn in the plazas. Concurrently, Guadalajarans celebrate the traditional **Festival of the Virgin of Zapopan.** Church plazas are awash with merrymakers enjoying food, mariachis, dances (don't miss the often performed Dance of the Conquest), and fireworks. The merrymaking peaks on 12 October, as a huge crowd conducts the Virgin from the downtown cathedral to Zapopan. The merrymakers' numbers often swell to a million faithful, who escort the Virgin, accompanied by ranks of costumed saints, devils, Spanish conquistadores, and Aztec chiefs.

Nightlife

The big west-side hotels are among the best spots in town for **dancing.** Moving west from the city center, first comes the **Hotel Fiesta Americana,** about four miles along Avs. Juárez and Vallarta, on the left side of the Minerva traffic circle. Patrons enjoy dancing both in the lobby-bar nightly from about 1900 and in the nightclub Caballo Negro from about 2130. Call (3) 625-3434 to doublecheck the times.

Another two miles southwest, on the right side of Av. López Mateos, rises the big glass tower of the **Hotel Hyatt Regency.** A group in the lobby bar plays for dancing nightly from

The strum of guitars is pleasantly common, especially weekend afternoons and evenings near the Plaza Tapatía.

MIKE WELLINS

CHARREADAS

The many Jalisco lovers of *charrera*, the sport of horsemanship, enjoy a long-venerated tradition. Boys and girls, coached by their parents, practice riding skills from the time they learn to mount a horse. Privileged young people become noble *charros* or *charras*—gentleman cowboys and cowgirls—whose equestrian habits follow old aristocratic Spanish fashion, complete with broad sombrero, brocaded suit or dress, and silver spurs.

The years of long preparation culminate in the *charreada*, which entire communities anticipate with relish. Although superficially similar to an Arizona rodeo, a Jalisco *charreada* differs substantially. The festivities take place in a *lienzo charro*, literally, the passageway through which the bulls, horses, and other animals run from the corral to the ring. First comes the *cala de caballo*, a test of the horse and rider. The *charros* or *charras* must gallop full speed across the ring and make the horse stop on a dime. Next is the *piales de lienzo*, a roping exhibition, during which an untamed horse must be halted and held by having its feet roped. Other bold performances include *jineteo de toro* (bull riding and throwing), and the super-hazardous *paso de la muerte*, in which a rider tries to

jump upon an untamed bronco from his or her own galloping mount. *Charreadas* often end in a flourish with the *escaramuza charra*, a spectacular show of riding skill by *charras* in full, colorful dress.

A charra

BOB RACE

about 2000 while the disco Iceberg fires up Tues.-Sun. from about 2100. For info, call (3) 678-1234.

The **Hotel Holiday Inn**, a quarter-mile farther, past the traffic circle, also has a live trio for dancing afternoons and evenings in the lobby-bar La Cantera (happy hour 1700-2000), and another trio (Thurs.-Sat. from about 2100) at the Bar La Fiesta. Additionally, their Da Vinci disco booms away, seasonally from about 2100. Call (3) 634-0650 for confirmation.

Bullfights and Rodeos

Winter is the main season for *corridas de toros,* or bullfights. The bulls charge and the crowds roar *"Olé"* (oh-LAY) Sunday afternoons at the Guadalajara Plaza de Toros (bullring), on Calz. Independencia about two miles north of the Mercado Libertad.

Local associations of *charros* (gentleman cowboys) stage rodeo-like Sunday *charreadas* at Guadalajara *lienzos charro* (rodeo rings).

Oft-used Guadalajara rodeo rings include Lienzo Charro de Jalisco, 477 Calz. Las Palmas, tel. (3) 619-3232, just beyond the southeast side of Parque Agua Azul and the Lienzo Charro Zermeño Padilla, on the northwest side at Manuel Cambre 1963, tel. (3) 626-5555, about a mile from the city center. Watch for posters, or ask at your hotel desk or the tourist information office, tel. 658-2222, for *corrida de toros* and *charreada* details and dates.

For many more entertainment ideas, see the "About Town" community calendar page of the weekly **Guadalajara *Reporter*** newspaper (Duque de Rivas 254, Guadalajara, tel. 6-152-177).

SPORTS

Walking, Jogging, and Exercise Gyms

Walkers and joggers enjoy several spots around Guadalajara. Close in, the **Plaza Liberación** behind the cathedral provides a traffic-free (although concrete) jogging and walking space. Avoid the crowds with morning workouts. If you prefer grass underfoot, try **Parque Agua Azul** (entrance $3) on Calz. Independencia about a mile south of the Libertad Market. An even better jogging-walking space is the **Parque de los Colomos**—hundreds of acres of greenery, laced by special jogging trails—four miles northwest from the center, before Zapopan; take a taxi or bus 51C from the old bus terminal, end of Av. Estadio, east of the traffic circle at north edge of Parque Agua Azul.

Guadalajara has a number of exercise gyms with the usual machines, plus jacuzzis and steam rooms. Try, for example, the Hotel Hyatt Regency (tel. 3-622-7778, open 0600-2100, $12 public use fee) and the Holiday Inn (tel. 3-634-0650, facilities for guests only).

Tennis, Golf, and Swimming

Although Guadalajara has no public tennis courts, the west side Hotel Camino Real, Av. Vallarta 5005, tel. (3)647-8000, rents its tennis courts to the public, by appointment, for about $8 per hour. Also, the Hotels Fiesta Americana, Aurello Aceves 225, Glorietta Minerva, tel. 625-3434, and the Holiday Inn, Av. López Mateos Sur 2500, tel. (3) 634-0650, have courts for guests.

The 18-hole **Club de Golf Atlas** welcomes nonmembers from dawn to dusk Tues.-Sunday. Greens fee runs $50 Tues.-Fri. and $60 Saturday and Sunday. Clubs and carts rent for about $14 and $23; a caddy will cost about $12. Get there via Chapala Hwy. 23, the south-of-town extension of Calz. J. Gonzales Gallo. The golf course is at Km 6.5, past the edge of town, near Parque Montenegro.

Nearly all the plush hotels have swimming pools. One of the prettiest pools, however, perches atop the moderately priced Hotel Calinda Roma in the heart of town (corner Juárez and Degollado, see "Downtown Hotels" preceding). If your hotel hasn't a pool, go to the very popular public pool and picnic ground at Balneario Lindo Michoacán, Rio Barco 1614, corner Calz. J. Gonzalez Gallo, tel. (3) 635-9399, about two miles along Gallo southeast of Parque Agua Azul. Open 0900-1800 daily. Farther out but even prettier are the canyon-country *balnearios* **Los Camachos** and **Nuevo**

Paraíso on Hwy. 54 north toward Saltillo. (For more details, see "Out-of-Downtown Sights" above.)

SHOPPING

Downtown

The sprawling **Mercado Libertad,** at the east end of Plaza Tapatía, has several specialty areas distributed through two main sections. Most of the handicrafts are in the eastern, upper half. While some stalls carry guitars and sombreros, leather predominates—in jackets, belts, saddles, and the most huaraches you'll ever see under one roof. Here, bargaining *es la costumbre*. Competition, furthermore, gives buyers the advantage. If the seller refuses your reasonable offer, simply turning in the direction of another stall will often bring him to his senses. The upper floor also houses an acre of food-stalls, many of them excellent. (See "Breakfast and Snacks" above.)

A central courtyard leads past a lineup of bird-sellers and their caged charges to the Mercado Libertad's lower half, where produce, meat, and spice stalls fill the floor. (Photographers, note the photogenic view of the produce floor from the balcony above.) Downstairs, don't miss browsing intriguing spice and *yerba* (herb) stalls, which feature mounds of curious dried plants, gathered from the wild, often by village *brujos* (shamans or witch-doctors). Before you leave, be sure to look over the piñatas, which make colorful, unusual gifts.

Outside of Mercado Libertad, a pair of downtown government stores have excellent, reasonably priced selections of both local and national folkcrafts. The closest, the **Casa de las Artesanías Normal,** is at Av. Alcalde 1211 (from the front of the cathedral take a taxi or walk 12 blocks north to traffic circle Glorietta Normal, named after the adjacent teacher's college). There, you can find everything—brilliant stoneware, endearing ceramic, brass, and papier mâché animals, and handsome gold and silver jewelry—short of actually going to Tonalá, Tlaquepaque, and Taxco. The very similar alternate store, the **Casa de Artesanías Agua Azul,** is at Calz. Gonzales Gallo 20, in Parque Agua Azul (off of Independencia, a mile south of the Libertad market). Both stores are open Mon.-Sat. 1000-1900, Sunday 1000-1400.

Tlaquepaque

Tlaquepaque was once a sleepy village of potters miles from Guadalajara. Attracted by the quiet of the country, rich families built palatial homes during the 19th century. Now, entrepreneurs have moved in and converted them into upscale restaurants, art galleries, and showrooms, stuffed with quality Tonalá and Tlaquepaque ceramics, glass, metalwork, and papier mâché.

In spite of having been swallowed by the city, Tlaquepaque still has the feel and look of a small colonial town, with its cathedral and central square leading westward onto the mansion-decorated main street, now mall, Av. Independencia.

Although generally pricier than Tonalá, Tlaquepaque still has bargains. Proceed by finding the base prices at the crafts stalls edging Independencia and Calles Madero and P. Sanchez, around the central plaza, then price out the tonier merchandise in the galleries along the next three blocks west along Independencia. For super-fine examples of Tlaquepaque and Tonalá crafts, be sure to stop by the **Museo Regional de Cerámica y Arte Popular** (237 Independencia, open Tues.-Sun. 1000-1500).

From the *museo,* cross the street to the **Sergio Bustamante** store, upscale outlet for the famous sculptor's arresting, whimsical studies in juxtaposition. Bustamante supervises an entire Guadalajara studio-factory of artists who put out hundreds of one-of-a-kind variations on a few human, animal, and vegetable themes. Prices seem to depend mainly on size; rings and bracelets may go for as little as $200, while a two-foot humanoid chicken may run $2000. Don't miss the restroom. Open daily 1000-1900.

Next to Bustamante, at 232 Independencia, **La Rosa Cristal,** tel. 639-7180, is one of the few spots where (until 1400 daily) visitors may see glassblowers practicing their time-honored Tlaquepaque craft. Samples of their work—clutches of big red, green, blue, and silver glass balls—decorate the room. Open Mon.-Sat. 1000-1900, Sunday 1000-1400.

Not far west, at the intersection of Independencia and Alfarareros ("Potters"), a pair of regally restored former mansions, now galleries, enjoy a dignified retirement facing each other on opposite sides of the street. **La Casa Canela,** Independencia 258, tel. (3) 657-1343, takes pride in its museum-quality lace, cloth, pottery, blown glass, and classic, blue-on-white Tlaquepaque stoneware. Open Mon.-Fri. 1000-1400 and 1500-1900, Saturday 1000-1800, Sunday 1100-1500. Across the street, **Antigua de Mexico,** Independencia 255, tel. (3) 635-3402, specializes in baroque gilt wood antiques and reproductions, being one of the few studios in Mexico to manufacture fine 17th century-style furniture. Open Mon.-Fri. 0900-1400 and 1500-1800, Saturday 0900-1400 and 1500-1700.

Getting to Tlaquepaque: Taxi (about $15 return) or ride the usually crowded city bus, 275A, from stops (such as at Madero) along downtown Av. 16 de Septiembre. By car, from the center of town, drive Av. Revolución southeast about four miles to the Niños Héroes traffic circle. From Av. Niños Héroes, the first right off the traffic circle, continue about a mile to the west end of Av. Independencia, on the left.

Tonalá

About five miles past Tlaquepaque, Tonalá perches at Guadalajara's country edge. When the Spanish arrived in the 1520s, Tonalá was dominant among the small kingdoms of the Atemajac Valley. Tonalá's widow-queen and her royal court were adorned by the glittering handiwork of an honored class of silver and gold crafters. Although the Spaniards carted off the valuables, the tradition of Tonalá craftsmanship remains today. To the visitor, everyone in Tonalá seems to making something. Whether it be pottery, stoneware, brass, or papier mâché, Tonalá family patios are piled with their specialties.

Right at the source, bargains couldn't be better. Dozens of shops dot the few blocks around Tonalá's central plaza corner at Av. Hidalgo (north-south) and Av. Juárez (east-west). For super-bargaining opportunities and *mucho* holiday excitement and color, visit the Sunday *tianguis* (market), which spreads along the tree-lined *periférico* highway about four blocks west of the Tonalá plaza.

Under any circumstances, make the **Museo de Cerámicas,** 104 Constitución, at Morelos, one of your first Tonalá stops. If you arrive before 1400, you may get to see someone turning out a classic vase or painting the smile on a Tonalá cat. Two blocks north, one block west of the plaza; open Tues.-Fri 1000-1700, Saturday 1000-1500, Sunday 1000-1400.

Several Tonalá shops stand out. Moving south along Hidalgo toward the town plaza from Constitución, **Artesanías Garay,** one of several *fíbrica* (factory) shops that retail directly, offers a host of Tonalá motifs. They're especially proud of their fine floral-design stoneware. Located at Hidalgo 86; open Mon.-Sat. 1000-1500 and 1600-1900, Sunday 1000-1500; credit cards accepted.

El Bazar de Sermel, Hidalgo 67, diagonally across the street, has stretched the Tonalá papier mâché tradition to the ultimate. Stop in and

Stalls and shops lining Tonalá's narrow village streets offer a galaxy of papier mâché and pottery handicrafts.

pick out the lifesize flamingo, pony, giraffe, or zebra you've always wanted for your living room. Open Mon.-Fri. 0900-1830, Saturday 0900-1400, Sunday 1000-1500.

La Hacienda, 13 Hidalgo, corner of the plaza, offers an interesting eclectic assortment, both from Tonalá and other parts of Mexico. These include Huichol Indian yarn paintings and God's Eyes, painted tin Christmas decorations from Oaxaca, and Guanajuato papier mâché clowns. Open Mon.-Sat. 1000-1800, Sunday 1200-1500.

Around the corner, a few steps west on Juárez, **Artesanías Nuño,** Juárez 59, displays a fetching menagerie, including parrots, monkeys, flamingos, and toucans, in papier mâché, brass, and ceramics. Open daily 1000-1900; bargain for very reasonable buys.

Continue south past the Juárez plaza corner (where Hidalgo becomes Madero) one block, to **La Antigua Tonalá,** Madero 50, tel. (3) 830-200. There you'll find a storeful of hand-hewn tables, chairs, and chests all complete with the Tonala stoneware place settings to go with them. Open Mon.-Sat. 1000-1400 and 1600-1900, Sunday 1000-1500; they ship.

Getting to Tonalá. Taxi (about $25 roundtrip) or ride the oft-crowded city bus 275B from the stops (such as the corner of Madero) on downtown Av. 16 de Septiembre. By car, drive Av. Revolución about six miles southeast of the city-center to the big Plaza Camichines interchange. Continue ahead along the Carretera Tonalá *libre* (free) branch; avoid forking onto the Hwy. 90 Carretera Zaplotanejo *cuota* toll road. The Carretera Tonalá continues due east for about three more miles, passing under the Carretera Zaplotanejo. Continue across the arterial *periférico* (peripheral highway); three blocks farther turn left and within a few blocks you'll be at the Tonalá central plaza.

Photo, Grocery, Department, And Health Food Stores

The several branches of the **Laboratorios Julio** chain offer quick photofinishing and a big stock of photo supplies and film, including professional 120 transparency and negative rolls. Their big downtown branch is at Colón 125 between Juárez and Cotilla, tel (3) 614-2850. Open Mon.-

Sat. 1000-1400 and 1600-2000, Sunday 1000-1500. Their Plaza del Sol store is in Zone F, local no. 9, tel. (3) 621-5359. Open Mon.-Sat. 1000-2030 and Sunday 1100-1900.

For convenient, all-in-one shopping, including groceries, try **Gigante**, downtown on Juárez, corner of Martinez, tel. 613-8638. Open daily 0800-2100. For even more under one air-conditioned roof, try the big **Comercial Mexicana** at Plaza del Sol, Av. López Mateos Sur 2077. Open daily 0900-2100.

Nectar, Guadalajara's downtown health food store, is open Mon.-Sat. 0900-2100, at the corner of Galeana and Madero.

SERVICES AND INFORMATION

Money Exchange

Change more types of money (U.S., Canadian, German, Japanese, French, Italian, and Swiss) for the best rates at the downtown streetfront Banamex office (Juárez, corner of Corona, open Mon.-Fri. 0900-1700).

The Guadalajara branch of **American Express**, at Plaza Los Arcos, Av. Vallarta 2440, tel. 630-0305 or 630-3821, about three miles west of the city center provides travel-agency and member financial services, including personal-check and traveler's-check cashing.

Consulates

The **U.S. Consulate** is at Progreso 175 (between Cotillo and Libertad) about a mile west of the town-center (open Mon.-Fri. 0800-1200, tel. 625-2700 and 625-2998). The **Canadian Consulate** is in the Hotel Fiesta Americana at Aurelio Aceves 225, near the intersection of Av. López Mateos and Av. Vallarta, tel. 625-3434, ext. 3005, open Mon.-Fri. 1000-1300.

Hospital, Police, and Emergencies

If you need a doctor, the **Hospital Mexico Americano,** Colomos 2110, tel. 641-3141, 642-4520, ambulance emergency 642-7152 has specialists on call. For **police** emergencies, call the radio patrol (dial 06) or the police headquarters at 617-6060 and 618-0260. In case of **fire,** call the *servicio bomberos* fire station at 619-5241 or 619-0794.

Tourist Information Office

The main Jalisco tourist information office is in the Plaza Tapatía, on Paseo Morelos, the mall-extension of Av. Morelos, behind the Teatro Degollado. At Morelos 102, tel. 658-2222, open Mon.-Fri. 0900-2100 and Sat. 0900-1300.

> **Guadalajara area code is 3**

Publications

Perhaps the best downtown source of English-language books, newspapers, and magazines is the **Hotel Fénix** shop, Av. Corona at Cotilla. They stock dozens of U.S. popular magazines, a rack of paperback bestsellers, and newspapers, such as *USA Today* and the Los Angeles *Times*. Open daily 0800-2130.

Sanborn's, a North American style coffee shop chain, also has a big selection of cultural books on Mexico, plus a load of American newspapers and popular magazines at its Guadalajara stores: downtown, corner Juárez and 16 de September, open 0730-2300; Plaza Vallarta, at Av. Vallarta 1600, open 0700-0100; and Plaza del Sol, 2718 López Mateos Sur, next to the Hyatt, open 0700-0100.

While you're at Sanborn's pick up a copy of the informative local weekly, the *Colony Reporter.* Its pages are stuffed with valuable items for visitors, including local events calendars, restaurant and performance reviews, meaty feature articles on local customs and excursions, and entertainment, restaurant, hotel, and rental listings.

Language and Cultural Courses

El Centro de Estudios Para Extranjeros (the University of Guadalajara Study Center for Foreigners), Guanajuato 1047, Guadalajara, Jalisco 44100, tel. (3) 653-2150, conducts an ongoing program of cultural studies for foreigners. Besides formal language, history, and art instruction, students may also opt for live-in arrangements with local families. Their campus office is on the west side of Glorietta Normal (traffic circle), a dozen blocks from the city-center cathedral north along Av. Alcalde. Open Mon.-Fri. 0830-1430.

GETTING THERE
AND AWAY

By Air

Several jet carriers connect the **Guadalajara airport** (officially, the Miguel Hidalgo International Airport, code-designated GDL) with many U.S. and Mexican destinations. All telephone numbers are for Guadalajara, unless designated otherwise.

Mexicana Airlines flights, tel. (3) 647-2222, connect frequently with U.S. destinations of Los Angeles, San Francisco, San Jose, San Antonio, Denver, and Chicago, and Mexican destinations of Puerto Vallarta, Mazatlán, Manzanillo, Tijuana, and Mexico City.

Aeroméxico, tel. (3) 669-0202, connects frequently with U.S. destinations of Los Angeles, Ontario, San Diego, Miami, New York, and Mexican destinations of Puerto Vallarta, Mazatlán, Manzanillo, Tijuana, and Mexico City.

Alaska Airlines, toll-free 95-800-426-0333, connects daily with Los Angeles, San Francisco, Seattle, and Ontario.

Other carriers include: **American Airlines**, toll-free 91-800-36270 or 91-800-90460, which connects daily with Dallas; **Delta Air Lines**, tel. (3) 630-3530, which connects twice daily with Los Angeles; and **Continental Airlines**, tel. (3) 647-6672 or 647-4446, which connects twice daily with Houston.

Airport arrival is simplified by a money exchange counter (daytime hours only) and major car rental (Avis, Hertz, and Optima) booths. Ground transportation is likewise well organized to shuttle arrivees the 12 miles (19 km) along Chapala Hwy. 23 into town. Tickets for *colectivos* (shared VW van taxis, about $12 for one or two persons) and *taxis especiales* (individual taxis, $18 for one to four persons) are sold at a booth just outside the terminal door. No public buses serve the Guadalajara airport.

Airport departure is equally simple, as long as you save enough for your international departure tax of $19 ($12 federal tax, $7 local) cash (no credit cards, no traveler's checks) per person. A post office (inside, right of the entrance), *telecomunicaciones* (telegraph, fax, long-distance phone), newsstand (lobby floor), bookstore (upstairs), and many crafts and gift shops are convenient for last minute business and purchases.

By Car or RV

Four major routes connect Guadalajara to the rest of Pacific Mexico. From **Tepic-Compostela-Puerto Vallarta** in the west, federal Hwy. 15 winds about 141 miles (227 km) over the Sierra Madre Occidental crest. The new *cuota* (toll) expressway, although expensive ($30 for a car, RVs more), greatly increases safety, decreases wear and tear, and cuts the Guadalajara-Tepic driving time to two hours. The *libre* (free) route, by contrast, has two oft-congested lanes that twist steeply up and down the high pass and bump through towns. For safety, allow around four hours to and from Tepic.

To and from Puerto Vallarta, bypass Tepic via the toll *corta* (cutoff) that connects Hwy. 15 (at Chapalilla) with Hwy. 200 (at Compostela). Figure on four hours total if you take the toll expressway, six hours if you don't.

From Barra de Navidad in the southwest, traffic curves and climbs smoothly along Hwy. 80 for the 190 miles (306 km) to Guadalajara. Allow around five hours.

An easier road connection from Barra de Navidad runs through Manzanillo along *autopistas* (superhighways) 200, 110, and 54. Easy grades allow a leisurely 55 mph (90 km/hour) most of the way for this 192-mile (311-km) trip. Allow about four hours from Manzanillo; add another hour for the additional smooth 38 miles (61 km) of Hwy. 200 from Barra de Navidad.

From **Lake Chapala** in the south, the four level, straight lanes of Hwy. 23 whisk traffic safely the 33 miles (53 Km) to Guadalajara in about 45 minutes.

By Bus

The long-distance Guadalajara *camionera central* (central bus terminal) is at least twenty minutes by taxi (about $10) from the city center. The huge, clean, and modern complex sprawls past the southeast-sector intersection of the old Tonalá Hwy. (Carretera Antigua Tonalá) and the new Zaplotanejo Autopista (Freeway) Hwy. 90. The *camionera central* is sandwiched between the two highways. Tell your taxi driver which bus line you want and he'll drop you at one of the terminal's seven *modulos* (sections).

To and from western and northwestern destinations, such as Puerto Vallarta, Tepic, Mazatlán and the U.S. western border, you can go by either Transportes del Norte (TN, tel. 3-600-0069 or 600-0042, *modulo* 3), Tres Estrellas de Oro (TEO, 3-600-0083 or 600-0333, *modulo* 3), Transportes del Pacífico (TP, tel. 3-600-0965 or *modulo* 4), or by super first-class Elite (EL, tel. 3-600-0587 or 600-0843, *modulo* 4).

To and from southern destinations, such as Barra de Navidad, Manzanillo, Colima, and Ixtapa-Zihuatanejo, ride either Tres Estrellas de Oro or Elite, Estrella Blanca (EB), or Autocamiones del Pacífico (AP), which goes to Barra and Manzanillo via Hwy. 80.

For many other subsidiary destinations, buses arrive and depart from the *camionera antigua* (old bus terminal), at the end of Estadio, off Calz. Independencia downtown. For Lake Chapala, ride one of several daily departures of the second-class red and white Autotransportes Guadalajara-Chapala buses. For Talpa, Mascota, and San Sebastián in the western mountains, go by the red second-class Transportes Guadalajara-Talpa-Mascota (tel. 3-619-0708). The same line also departs from the new *camionera central* (tel. 3-600-0588, *modulo* 4).

By Train

The rail terminal (for ticket and exact schedule details), tel. (3) 650-0826, fronts the end of Calz. Independencia, about a mile south of the city-center. The subsidized seat prices are extremely reasonable. Three major passenger lines branch out from Guadalajara: **northwest** to Tepic, Mazatlán, and the U.S. border, **south** to Colima and Manzanillo, and **east** to Morelia and Mexico City.

The first-class coach **Estrella** leaves Guadalajara around 0930, stopping en route at Tepic (around 1500) and Mazatlán (around 1900), arriving in Mexicali (or Nogales) on the U.S. border about 35 hours later. An Estrella train also departs Mexicali in the morning, arriving in Guadalajara the same time frame of 35 hours.

The southern-line pair of trains, known perfunctorily as "nos. 91 and 92," are lowly second-class diesels. Number 92 leaves Guadalajara at around 0900, rolling downhill to Colima by about 1600, and Manzanillo two hours later. Number 91 starts out earlier, at 0600 from Manzanillo, arriving in Colima about two hours later. It continues, chugging uphill to Guadalajara, arriving by the late afternoon.

The crack first-class sleeper-equipped **Tapatío** heads out from Guadalajara about 2100, stopping in Morelia, where connections to Pátzcuaro and Lázaro Cárdenas on the coast may be made. The Tapatío continues overnight, arriving in Mexico City the next day around 0830. A two-person sleeper on the Tapatío runs about $55 per person; coach seats, while less than half the cost, are correspondingly less comfortable.

The Mágica Sol, worshipped universally in preconquest Mexico, continues as a popular pottery and metal work motif.

ALONG THE ROAD TO PUERTO VALLARTA

The lush, hundred-mile stretch between Tepic and Puerto Vallarta is a Pacific Eden of flowery tropical forest and pearly palm-shaded beaches, largely unknown to the outside world. The gateway Mexican National Hwy. 200 is still relatively new; the traffic and development that will inevitably follow have barely begun. Only a few roadside villages, pastures, tobacco fields, and tropical fruit orchards encroach upon the vine-strewn jungle.

PLAYA CHACALA AND MAR DE JADE

Side roads off Hwy. 200 often provide exotic, close-up glimpses of Nayarit's tangled, tropical woodland, but rarely will they lead to such a delightful surprise as the green-tufted golden crescent of Playa Chacala and its diminutive neighbor, Playa Chacalilla.

Two miles south of Las Varas, 19 miles (31 km) north of Rincón de Guayabitos, follow the six-mile cobble and gravel road to the great old palm grove at Chacala. Beyond the line of rustic *palapa* seafood restaurants lies a heavenly curve of sand, enfolded on both sides by palm-tipped headlands.

A mile farther north, past Chacala village on the headland, the road ends at Chacalilla, Chacala's miniature twin, with its own sandy beach, grove, and *palapa*. There, on Sunday and holidays (unless access is restricted by a rumored development project), families crowd in, and someone sells drinks and stokes up a fire to barbecue fish for the picnickers.

Beach Activities

Chacala's oft-gentle surf is good for close-in bodysurfing and boogle-boarding, swimming, and beginning-to-intermediate surfing. Furthermore, the water is generally clear enough for snorkeling off the rocks on either side of the beach. If you bring your equipment, kayaking, windsurfing and sailing might be possible. Fishing is so good local people make their living at it. Chacala Bay is so rich and clean tourists eat oysters right off the rocks.

Food and Accommodations

Supplied by the beachside restaurants and the stores in the village, Playa Chacala is ideal for tent or small RV **camping**, though the sometimes rough, steep, and narrow entry road appears too difficult for most big trailers and motorhomes.

Roadside stalls at Las Varas offer a trove of local fruit. Sometimes more exotic varieties, such as guanábanas, *shown, are available.*

BRUCE WHIPPERMAN

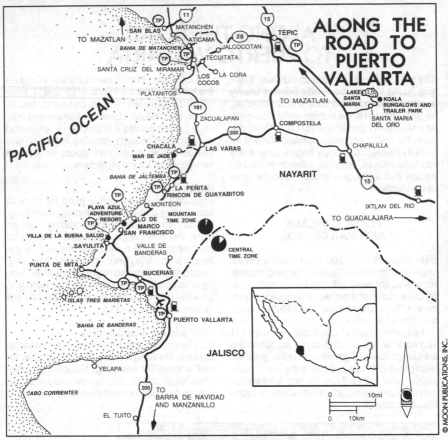

ALONG THE ROAD TO PUERTO VALLARTA

© MOON PUBLICATIONS, INC.

Mar de Jade

The Mar de Jade, a holistic-style living center at the south end of Playa Chacala, offers unique alternatives. Laura del Valle, Mar de Jade's personable and dynamic physician-founder, has worked hard since the early 1980s, building living facilities and a learning center, while simultaneously establishing a local health clinic. Now, Mar de Jade offers Spanish-language and work-study programs for people who enjoy the tropics but want to do more than laze in the sun. The main thrust is interaction with local people. Spanish, for example, is the preferred language at the dinner table.

Their thatched, cool, and clean adobe and brick cabins and adjacent two-story lodging complex (with concrete floors, showers, restrooms, and good water) nestle among a flowery, palm-shaded garden of fruit trees. Stone pathways lead to the beachside main center, which consists of a dining room, kitchen, offices, library, and classroom overlooking the sea.

While Mar de Jade's purpose is serious, they have nothing against visitors who *do* want to laze in the sun. Mar de Jade invites travelers to make reservations (or simply drop in) and stay as long as they like, for adults $40/day, children 6-18, $20/day, including three hearty meals.

Another possibility is a one-week vacation, combined with 15 hours of Spanish instruction ($330); another is a work-study program, including 15 hours of Spanish instruction and 18 hours of work per week (27-day minimum, $920). A third option is a work-vacation, including the 18 hours per week of work but no Spanish (27-day minimum, $750).

For more information on their program schedule and fees, write them (officially, the Casa Clínica de la Mujer Campesina) at P.O. Box 81, Las Varas, Nayarit 63715, or call (or preferably, fax) the clinic Monday, Wednesday, or Friday 1500-2000 (Pacific standard time) at (3) 272-0184.

RINCÓN DE GUAYABITOS AND VICINITY

Rincón de Guayabitos (pop. about 3,000 permanent, maybe 6,000 in the winter) lies halfway between Tepic and Puerto Vallarta, at the tiny south-end *rincón* (wrinkle) of the broad, mountain-rimmed Bay of Jaltemba. The full name of Rincón de Guayabitos's sister town, La Peñita (Little Rock) de Jaltemba, comes from its perch on the sandy edge of the bay.

Once upon a time, Rincón de Guayabitos (or simply, Guayabitos, meaning "Little Guavas") lived up to its diminutive name. During the 1970s, however, the government decided that Rincón de Guayabitos was to become both a resort and one of the three places in the Puerto Vallarta region (the other two were to be Bucerías and Nuevo Vallarta) where foreigners could own property outright. So now Rincón de Guayabitos is a summer, Christmas, and Easter haven for Mexicans and a winter haven for Canadians and Americans weary of big, pricey resorts.

SIGHTS

Getting Oriented

Guayabitos and La Peñita (pop. 8,000) comprise practically a single town. Guayabitos has the hotels and the sleepy scenic ambience, while, two miles north, La Peñita's main street, Emiliano Zapata, bustles with stores, restaurants, a bank, and a bus station.

Guayabitos's main street, **Avenida del Sol Nuevo,** curves lazily for about a mile parallel to the beach. From the Avenida, several short streets and *andandos* (walkways) lead to a line of *retornos* (cul-de-sacs). Nearly all of Guayabitos's community of small hotels, bungalow complexes, and trailer parks lie on these *retornos,* within a block of the beach.

Isla Islote

From every spot along the bay, the rock-studded humpback of Isla Islote beckons a few miles offshore. A flotilla of wooden glass-bottomed launches plies the Guayabitos shoreline, ready to whisk visitors across to the island. For about $30 an hour parties of up to six or eight can view the fish through the boat-bottom and see the colonies of nesting terns, frigate birds, and boobies on Islote's guano-plastered far side. Often dolphins will play in your boat's wake, and occasionally a pod of whales will spout and dive not far away.

Beaches and Activities

The main beach, Playa Guayabitos-La Peñita, curves two miles northerly from the rocky Guayabitos point, growing wider and steeper at La Peñita. The shallow Guayabitos cove, lined by *palapa* restaurants and dotted with boats, is a favorite of Mexican families on Sunday and holidays. They play in the one-foot surf, ride the boats, eat barbecued fish, and throw everything on the sand. During busy times, the place can get a bit polluted from the people, boats, and fishing.

Farther along toward La Peñita, however, the beach broadens and becomes much cleaner, with surf good for swimming, bodysurfing, and boogie-boarding. Afternoon winds are often brisk enough for sailing and windsurfing if you've brought your own equipment—none is available locally. Scuba and snorkeling are good near the offshore Isla Islote, accessible via rental boat from Guayabitos. Local stores sell inexpensive but serviceable masks, snorkels, and fins.

Just past the palm-studded headland a mile north of La Peñita (where another long, inviting

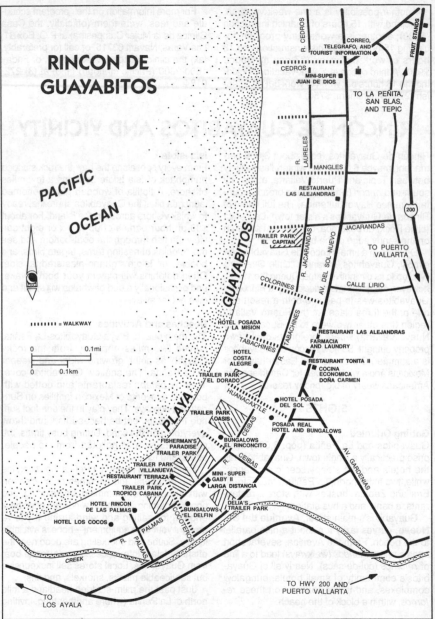

RINCON DE GUAYABITOS

PACIFIC OCEAN

R. CEDROS

FRUIT STANDS

CORREO, TELEGRAFO, AND TOURIST INFORMATION

CEDROS

MINI-SUPER JUAN DE DIOS

TO LA PEÑITA, SAN BLAS, AND TEPIC

R. LAURELES

MANGLES

RESTAURANT LAS ALEJANDRAS

200

GUAYABITOS

JACARANDAS

R. JACARANDAS

AV. DEL SOL NUEVO

TRAILER PARK EL CAPITAN

TO PUERTO VALLARTA

COLORINES

CALLE LIRIO

= WALKWAY

R. TABACHINES

RESTAURANT LAS ALEJANDRAS

HOTEL POSADA LA MISION

FARMACIA AND LAUNDRY

TABACHINES

0   0.1mi

RESTAURANT TONITA II

HOTEL COSTA ALEGRE

COCINA ECONOMICA DOÑA CARMEN

0   0.1km

TRAILER PARK EL DORADO

HUANACAXTLE

HOTEL POSADA DEL SOL

PLAYA

TRAILER PARK OASIS

R. CEIBAS

POSADA REAL HOTEL AND BUNGALOWS

FISHERMAN'S PARADISE TRAILER PARK

BUNGALOWS EL RINCONCITO

R. CEIBAS

AV. GARDENIAS

TRAILER PARK VILLANUEVA

RESTAURANT TERRAZA

MINI - SUPER GABY II

LARGA DISTANCIA

TRAILER PARK TROPICO CABANA

DELIA'S TRAILER PARK

HOTEL RINCON DE LAS PALMAS

BUNGALOWS EL DELFIN

COCOTEROS

HOTEL LOS COCOS

R. PALMAS

CREEK

© MOON PUBLICATIONS, INC.

TO LOS AYALA

TO HWY 200 AND PUERTO VALLARTA

beach begins) the waves angle in, offering good chances for beginning and intermediate surfing.

Playa Los Muertos and Playa Los Ayala

Follow the paved road to Los Ayala (over the headland adjacent to Guayabitos cove) and you will see a dirt road that forks right downhill through a cemetery (thus Los Muertos, "The Dead") to Playa Los Muertos, where the graves come right down to the beach.

Ghosts notwithstanding, this is a scenic little sandy cove, where on fair days you can get your fill of safe swimming, sunning on the beach, or tidepooling amongst the clustered oysters and mussels and the crabs that skitter on the rocks nearby. Recently the owners of houses above the beach have placed a gate across the private entrance road to discourage cars driving in. They cannot legally bar people from the beach, so, even if you have to hire a launch to drop you there, Playa Los Muertos is worth it.

Continue along the road about a mile farther, and you'll reach the tiny rustic settlement and half-mile yellow strand of Playa Los Ayala. With no facilities other than a dusty little store and a lineup of beachside *palapas,* Los Ayala retains its Sunday popularity among local families because of its long, lovely beach. All of the beach sports possible at Guayabitos are possible here, with the added advantage that, away from the fishing cove, the beach is much cleaner.

Like Guayabitos, Los Ayala also has its secluded south-end cove. Follow the path up the palmy, beach-end headland. Ten minutes' walk along a tropical forest trail leads you to the romantic little jungle-enfolded sand crescent called **Playa del Beso** ("Beach of the Kiss"). Except during holidays, few if any people come here for hours on end.

Playa Raza

The road to Playa Raza, while not long, requires a maneuverable high-clearance vehicle. The reward is a long wild beach, perfect for beachcombing and camping. Bring everything, including water.

Three miles south of Guayabitos along Hwy. 200, turn off at Monteon; pass through the village, turn right just before the pavement ends, and follow the rough road through the creek and over the ridge north of town. At the summit,

stop and feast your eyes on the valley view below, then continue down through the near-virgin jungle, barely scratched by a few poor cornfields. Halfway to the beach, stop to see if the seasonal hillside restaurant is open.

At the bottom of the steep grade, the track parallels the beach beneath big trees; sandy trails run through the brush to the beach—experienced sand drivers only; it's very easy to get stuck. You have two straight miles of pristine, jungle-backed sand virtually to yourself.

The beach itself slopes steeply, with the resulting close-in crashing waves and undertow. The water would be fine for splashing, but swimmers be careful. Because of jungle hinterland, birds and other wildlife are plentiful here. Bring your repellent, binoculars, and identification books.

Turtles also arrive periodically in late summer and fall to lay eggs here. Look for obvious tracks in the sand. The turtles attract predators—cats, iguanas, birds, and human poachers. If you find an egg nest, keep watch over it; your reward may be to witness the birth and return to the ocean of dozens of baby turtles.

ACCOMMODATIONS

Guayabitos Hotels

Guayabitos has more hotels than any other town in Nayarit, including the capital, Tepic. Competition keeps standards high and prices low. During the low season (Aug.-Nov.) most places are only half full and ready to bargain. The livelier part of town is at the south end, where most of the foreigners, mostly Canadians and Americans, congregate during the winter.

Guayabitos has many lodgings that call themselves "bungalows." This generally implies a motel-type kitchenette-suite with less service than a hotel.

Perhaps the cheapest good lodging in town is the friendly 32-room **Posada Real Hotel and Bungalows,** Retorno Ceibas and Andando Huanacaxtle, Rincón de Guayabitos, Nayarit 63726, tel. (327) 401-77, built around a cobbled parking courtyard-jungle of squawking parrots and shady palms, mangos, and bamboo. The bungalow units are on the ground floor in

RINCÓN DE GUAYABITOS HOTELS

Guayabitos (area code 327, postal code 63726) hotels, in order of increasing approximate high-season double-room price:

Posada Real Hotel and Bungalows, Posada Real Retorno Ceibas s/n, tel. 401-77, $25

Bungalows El Delfín, Retorno Ceibas s/n, tel. 403-85, $33

Hotel Posada del Sol, Retorno Tabachines s/n, tel. 401-52, $33

Hotel Posada La Misión, Retorno Tabachines 6, tel. 403-57, $34

Hotel Rincón de las Palmas, Retorno Palmas s/n, tel. 403-50, fax 401-74, $45

Bungalows El Rinconcito, Retorno Ceibas s/n (P.O. Box 19), tel. 402-29, $40

Hotel Costa Alegre, Retorno Tabachines s/n, tel. 402-41 or 402-42, fax 402-43, $60

the courtyard; the hotel rooms are stacked in three plant-decorated tiers above the lobby in front. Both the 26 four-person bungalows with kitchenette and the 20 two-person hotel rooms rent for about $18/day low season d, $25 high, with discounts possible for longer-term stays. Amenities include ceiling fans, a small pool and a kiddie pool, racquetball, and parking; credit cards accepted.

Immediately north, across Andando Huanacaxtle, **Hotel Posada del Sol** (managed by Trailer Park Posada del Sol, see below) offers 14 tastefully furnished bungalows around a palmy garden-patio, from about $33/day, $600/month.

One of the most charming off-beach Guayabitos lodgings is **Bungalows El Delfín,** Retorno Ceibas and Andando Cocoteros s/n, Rincón de Guayabitos, Nayarit 63726, tel. (327) 403-85, with its intimate banana- and palm-fringed pool-patio, including recliners and umbrellas for resting and reading. Chairs on the shaded porch-walkways in front of the three room-tiers invite quiet relaxation and conversation with neighbors. The pastel-walled four-person suites are large and plainly furnished, with basic stove, refrigerator, and utensils, rear laundry porches,

and big, tiled toilet-showers. The 15 bungalows with kitchenette sleep four and rent for about $25 low season, $33 high; with ceiling fans, pool, and parking; pets okay.

Right-on-the-beach **Bungalows El Rinconcito,** Retorno Ceibas s/n and Calle Ceibas, (P.O. Box 19), Rincón de Guayabitos, Nayarit 63726, tel. (327) 402-29, is one of the best buys in Guayabitos. The smallish whitewashed complex set back from the street offers large, tastefully furnished units with yellow and blue tile kitchens and solid, Spanish-style dark-wood chairs and beds. Its oceanside patio opens to a grassy garden overlooking the surf. They rent three two-bedroom bungalows for about $50, and seven one-bedroom bungalows for about $30 low season, $40 high, with fans and parking. Discounts are generally available for longer-term stays.

One of the fancier Guayabitos lodgings is the colonial-style **Hotel Posada La Misión,** Retorno Tabachines 6, Rincón de Guayabitos, Nayarit 63726, tel./fax (327) 403-57, whose centerpiece is a beachside restaurant-bar-patio, nestled beneath a spreading, big-leafed *hule* (rubber) tree. Extras include a luxurious shady garden-veranda and an inviting azure pool and patio, thoughtfully screened off from the parking. Their rooms are high-ceilinged and comfortable except for their unimaginative bare-bulb lighting; bring your favorite bulb-clip lampshades. Doubles rent for about $23 low-season, $34 high; quadruples, $30 low-season and $40 high; suites sleeping six, $40 and $65. Two kitchenette bungalows go for $45 low-season, $60 high. Amenities include a pool, good restaurant, ocean-view bar, ceiling fans, and parking; credit cards are accepted.

Travelers who play tennis and prefer an air-conditioned, modern-style lodging should pick the compact, pool-patio ambience of the **Hotel Rincón de Las Palmas,** Retorno Palmas s/n at Calle Palmas, Rincón de Guayabitos, Nayarit 63726, tel. 403-50, fax 327-401-74, near the south end. With airy beachview restaurant and bar for sitting and socializing, this is a lodging for those who want company. Guests may often have a hard time *not* getting acquainted. The smallish rooms are packed in two double parallel breezeway tiers around a pool-patio above the beach. Right outside your room during the high season you will probably have your pick of around 50 sunbathing bodies to gaze at and meet. This hotel is operated by its big neighbor Hotel Los Cocos, which handles reservations (tel. 327-401-90, 401-91, and 401-92), which are mandatory during the winter. The 40 rooms rent for about $45 d, with a/c, pool, TV, tennis court, breezy sea-view restaurant-bar, parking; credit cards accepted.

Just as modern but more spacious is the family-oriented **Hotel Costa Alegre,** Retorno Tabachines s/n at Calle Tabachines, Rincon de Guayabitos, Nayarit 63726, tel. (327) 402-41, 402-42, fax 402-43, where the Guayabitos beach widens out. Its plusses include a big, blue pool-patio on the street side and a broad, grassy, ocean-view garden on the beach side. Although the rooms are adequate, the kitchenette bungalows are set away from the beach with no view but the back of neighboring rooms. The best choices are the several upper-tier oceanfront rooms, all with sliding glass doors leading to private sea-view balconies. Rates for the 30 view rooms run about $50 d low-season, $60 high; the 43 kitchenette bungalows $65 d. With a/c, pool, parking, and restaurant-bar; credit cards accepted.

Guayabitos Trailer Parks

All but one of the several Guayabitos trailer parks are wall-to-wall RVs most of the winter. Some old-timers have painted and marked out their spaces for years of future occupancy. The best spaces of the bunch are all booked by mid-October. And although the longtime residents are polite enough, some of them are clannish and don't go out of their way to welcome new kids on the block.

This is fortunately not true at **Delia's,** Guayabitos's funkiest trailer park, Retorno Ceibas 4, Rincón de Guayabitos, Nayarit 63726, tel. (327) 403-98. Friendly realtor-owner Delia Priske has 15 spaces, a good number of which are unfilled even during the high season. Her place, alas, is not right on the beach, nor is it as tidy as some folks would like. On the other hand, Delia offers a little store, insurance, long-distance phone service, and a small cafe, Abel's Lonchería, with good breakfasts, right next to the premises. She also rents two bungalows for about $400 a month. Spaces run about

$8/night, $220/month with all hookups, room for big rigs, pets okay, showers, toilets.

The rest of Guayabitos's trailer parks line up right along the beachfront. Moving from the south end, first comes **Trailer Park Tropico Cabaña,** built with boats and anglers in mind. One old-timer, a woman, the manager says, has been coming for twenty years running. It must be for the avocados—bulging, delicious three-pounders, which hang from a big shady tree. Other extras are a boat launch and storage right on the beach, with an adjacent fish-cleaning sink and table. This is a prime, very popular spot; get your reservation in early to Retorno Las Palmas, P.O. Box 3, Rincón de Guayabitos, Nayarit 63726. The 28 cramped spaces, six 38-footers and 22 33-footers rent for about $12/day with all hookups, discounts for longer stays; includes showers, toilets, barbecue; pets okay.

The single Guayabitos trailer park that celebrates a traditional Christmas-eve *posada* procession is the family-run **Trailer Park Villanueva,** Retorno Ceibas s/n, P.O. Box 25, Rincón de Guayabitos, Nayarit 63726, tel. (327) 403-70. Allowing for 30 spaces, including three drive-throughs, they can still stuff in some big rigs, although room is at a premium. Shade, however, is not; lovely palms cover the entire lot. Moreover, their romantic *palapa* restaurant, Terraza, is very popular with Guayabitos long-timers. Spaces go for $11/daily (or $300 monthly), add $2/day for a/c power; with all hookups, restaurant, showers, toilets, boat ramp, pets okay. They also have four bungalows that rent for about $33 d.

Next door to the north comes **Fisherman's Paradise Trailer Park,** which is also popular as a mango-lover's paradise, Retorno Ceibas s/n, Rincón de Guayabitos, Nayarit 63726, tel. (327) 400-14. Several spreading mango trees shade the park's 33 concrete pads, and during the late spring and summer when the mangos ripen, you'll probably be able to park under your own tree. Spaces rent for $13.50/day, $11/day (four month rental), with all hookups, showers, toilets, pets okay.

Neighboring **Trailer Park Oasis** is among Guayabitos's newest and loveliest trailer parks, Retorno Ceibas s/n, Apdo. 42, Rincón de Guayabitos, Nayarit 63726. Its 19 all-concrete partly palm-shaded spaces are wide and long enough for 40-foot rigs. Plusses include green grassy grounds, beautiful blue pool, a designer restaurant, and a luxury ocean-view *palapa* above the beach. Spaces rent for about $25/day, $15/day (monthly), with all hookups; with showers, toilets, fish-cleaning facility, boat ramp, pets okay.

Residents of **Trailer Park El Dorado,** Retorno Tabachines s/n, Rincón de Guayabitos, Nayarit 63726, tel. (327) 401-52, enjoy shady, spacious, grass-carpeted spaces beneath a rustling old palm grove, all the result of the tender loving care of the friendly on-site owner-manager. Other extras include a pool and recreation *palapa* across the street in **Hotel Posada Del Sol,** which has 14 tastefully furnished bungalows around a palmy garden-patio, from about $33/day, $600/month. They are also managed by the Trailor Park El Dorado. The 21 trailer park spaces rent for about $12/day, with all hookups, add $2 for a/c; with pool, showers, toilets, pets okay. Very popular; get your winter reservations in early.

Three blocks farther north along the beach, friendly newcomer **Trailer Park El Capitán** seems to be trying harder, Retorno Jacarandas at Andando Jacarandas, Rincón de Guayabitos, Nayarit 63726, tel. (327) 403-04. They should have no trouble acquiring a following. Their majestic, rustling palm grove provides shade, their rustic *palapa* restaurant supplies food and drinks, while, a few steps nearby, the loveliest part of Playa Guayabitos brims with natural entertainments. Their 14 spaces rent for $12/day (one week free per month's stay), with all hookups, larger RVs cost more; with showers, toilets, and pets okay.

La Peñita Hotel and Trailer Park

It will be good news to many Pacific Mexico longtimers that **Hotel Russell** has re-opened and is ready for guests. The scene is vintage Pacific Mexico—peeling paint, snoozing cats, lazy palms, and a beautiful beach with boats casually pulled onto the sand a few steps from your door—all for rock-bottom prices. Come and populate the place before the octogenarian owner gives up the ghost. Reserve at Calle Ruben C. Jaramillo no. 24, La Peñita de Jaltemba, Nayarit, tel. (327) 402-02. There are about 15 clean,

Spartan, one-bedroom kitchenette bungalows with fans, $13 d low-season, $18 high. Great fishing and two blocks from everything in La Peñita. Get there by driving to the beach end of La Peñita's main street, Emiliano Zapata. Turn right and parallel the beach for about two blocks.

The big **Trailer Park Hotelera La Peñita,** P.O. Box 22, La Peñita, Nayarit 63726, enjoys a breezy ocean-view location one mile north of La Peñita; watch for the big highway sign. Their 128 grassy spaces cover a tree-dotted, breezy hillside park overlooking a golden beach and bay. Rates run $11/day, with all hookups. The many amenities include a pool, hilltop terrace club, restaurant, showers, and toilets; fine for tenting, surfing, and fishing.

FOOD

Fruit Stands and Mini-Supermarkets

The farm country along Hwy. 200 north of Puerto Vallarta offers a feast of tropical fruits. Roadside stands at Guayabitos, La Peñita, and at Las Varas, half an hour north, offer mounds of papayas, mangos, melons, and pineapples in season. Watch out also for more exotic species, such as the *guanabana,* which looks like a spiny mango, but whose pulpy interior looks and smells much like its Asian cousin, the jackfruit.

A number of small Guayabitos mini-supermarkets supply a little bit of everything. Try **Mini-Super Gaby II,** Retorno Ceibas across from Trailer Park Villanueva, on the south end, for vegetables, a small deli, and general groceries. Open daily 0700-1230 and 1600-1930. Competing next door is **Mini-Super Juan de Dios,** open daily 0700-2000. On the north end, another branch of Mini-Super Juan de Dios, Av. del Sol Nuevo and Laureles, stocks more, including fresh baked goods. Open daily 0800-2100.

For larger, fresher selections of everything, go to one of the big main-street *fruterías* or supermarkets in La Peñita, such as **Supermercado Lorena,** tel. (327)402-55; open daily 0800-2000.

Restaurants

Complete dinner price key: Budget: under $7; Moderate: $7-14; Expensive: more than $14.

Several Guayabitos restaurants offer good food and service during the busy winter, spring, and August seasons. Hours and menus are often restricted during the midsummer and October and November low seasons. La Peñita, on the other hand, has a number of dependable eateries that do not rely so heavily on the tourist trade and consequently offer steadier, year-round service.

By location, moving from the Guayabitos south end, first comes **Abel's Lonchería,** which serves a North American-style menu all day, including pancakes, french toast, eggs any style, and sandwiches. With a small, shady front patio between a minimarket and the long-distance telephone office, Abel's is a popular Guayabitos gathering and people-watching place. Located on Retorno Ceibas across from Trailer Park Villanueva; open daily 0700-2100 in season. Budget.

Right across the street, another "best" of Guayabitos is the restaurant **Terraza** at Trailer Park Villanueva. Within their ocean-view *palapa*-patio, they offer a menu specializing in caught-in-the-bay fresh seafood. You can find them at the south end of Retorno Ceibas, at Andando Cocoteros; open daily 0800-2100 in season. Moderate.

On Av. Sol Nuevo a few blocks north, the family-run **Cocina Económica Doña Carmen,** Av. del Sol Nuevo at Andando Tabachines, puts out hearty tacos, enchiladas, spicy *pozole* (shredded pork roast and hominy vegetable stew), and the catch of the day at budget prices. Open every day from early morning till about 2200 year-round. Its open-air rival, **Toñita II** accomplishes about the same right across the street.

Nearby, the very clean, airy **Restaurant Las Alejandras** offers good breakfasts and a general Mexican-style menu; Av. del Sol Nuevo, near the pharmacy; second location two blocks north, across from Hotel Peñamar. Open Mon.-Fri. 0730-1700, Saturday and Sunday until 2100; tel. (327) 404-88.

The restaurant **Piña Colada** in front of the **Hotel Posada la Misión,** Retorno Tabachines 6 at Calle Tabachines, tel. (327) 403-57, is a long-time favorite of the North American trailer colony. The menu features bountiful salad, fresh seafood, meat, and Mexican plates at reasonable prices. Open 0800-2100 in season; credit cards accepted. Moderate.

For a change of pace or if your preferred Guayabitos restaurants are seasonally closed, try **Chuy's,** La Peñita's local and tourist favorite. It offers a broad, reasonably priced menu within a *típica* Mexican patio setting. Located about five blocks from Hwy. 200, on Calle Bahía Punta Mita, half a block right, off Emiliano Zapata. Open daily till around 2100.

SPORTS AND ENTERTAINMENT

Nightlife

Although Guayabitos is a resort for those who mostly love peace and quiet, there is at least one nightspot. The liveliest place in town is **Hotel Los Cocos,** the high-rise at the very south end, Retorno Palmas, tel. (327) 401-90, where a mostly Canadian and American crowd gyrates to rock most winter nights till the wee hours.

Sports

Aquatic sports center around the south end of Guayabitos beach, where launches ply the waters, offering banana (towed-tube) rides and **snorkeling** at offshore Isla Islote. Rent **sportfishing** launches along the beach. If you want to launch your own boat, ask one of the trailer parks if you can use their ramp. For more beach sports details, see "Beaches and Activities" described above.

For **tennis,** check into the Hotel Rincón de Las Palmas or its oversize brother Hotel Los Cocos, which maintain a tennis court for guests only.

SERVICES AND INFORMATION

The well-informed, friendly local officer of Nayarit State Tourism, **Pedro Galaviz,** maintains an information office (no phone, open Mon.-Fri. approximately 0900-1100, 1300-1600) in the tree-shaded municipal plaza at the beginning of Av. del Sol Nuevo near the highway, behind the church.

> **Rincón de Guayabitos area code is 327**

The *correo* (open Mon.-Fri. 0900-1300 and 1500-1800) and *telégrafo* (open Mon.-Fri. 0800-1400) are next door. If, however, you just need stamps or a *buzón* (mailbox), they're available at the *farmacia* on Av. Sol Nuevo at Andando Tabachines.

Guayabitos has no money-exchange agency, although some of the Mini-Supers may exchange U.S. or Canadian dollars or traveler's checks. More pesos for your cash or traveler's checks are available at the **Bancomer** branch in La Peñita, E. Zapata 22, tel. (327) 402-37; open Mon.-Fri. 0830-1100.

Guayabitos has no hospital. For serious medical consultations and emergency treatment, drive or taxi 14 miles (22 km) south to the small general hospital in San Francisco (known locally as "San Pancho"). They offer X-ray, laboratory, gynecological, pediatric, and internal medicine consultations and services both during regular office hours, weekdays 1030-1200 and 1600-1800, and on call.

For less urgent medical matters, Jorge Castuera, the well-informed, veterinarian-owner of the *farmacia*, Av. del Sol Nuevo at Tabachines, tel. (327) 404-00, fax 404-46, can recommend medicines or put you in contact with a local doctor. Open 0800-1400 and 1600-2000. While Jorge fills the prescriptions his wife handles their *larga distancia* service, sells postage stamps, and does washing at their **laundry** on the same premises. They also stock a rack of popular **U.S. magazines.**

Another popular Guayabitos *larga distancia* telephone office is next to Abel's Lonchería on Retorno Ceibas. Open Mon.-Sat. approximately 0900-2000 winter season, but maintains shorter hours otherwise. They also offer a shelf of used mostly-English paperbacks for purchase or a two-for-one exchange.

Getting There and Away
Puerto Vallarta- and Tepic-bound Transportes Pacífico (TP) second-class buses routinely stop (about once every daylight hour, each direction) on the main highway entrance to Guayabitos Av. del Sol Nuevo. Additionally, several daily first-class buses pick up Puerto Vallarta- and Tepic-bound passengers at the Transportes Pacífico station, tel. (327) 400-25, at the main street highway corner in La Peñita.

Transportes Norte de Sonora (TNS), Tres Estrellas de Oro (TEO), and Elite (EL) buses routinely stop at their small La Peñita station, tel. (327) 405-08, main street highway corner, east side of the highway. Northern destinations include Tepic, Mazatlán; southern, Puerto Vallarta, Manzanillo, and Colima.

The Guayabitos coast is easily accessible by bus or taxi from the **Puerto Vallarta International Airport,** the busy terminal for flight connections with U.S. and Mexican destinations. Buses and taxis cover the 39-mile (62 km) distance to Guayabitos in less than an hour. For more details, see "Puerto Vallarta Airport Arrival and Departure" at the end of the Puerto Vallarta chapter.

SOUTH OF GUAYABITOS

Playa Lo de Marco
Follow the signed Lo de Marco ("That of Marco") turnoff eight miles, 13 km south of Rincón de Guayabitos (31 miles, 49 km, north of the Puerto Vallarta airport). Continue about a mile through the town to the beach lineup of *palapa* restaurants. Playa Lo de Marco is popular with Mexican families, when, mostly on Sunday and holidays, they dig in the fine golden sand and frolic in the gentle, rolling waves. The surf of the nearly level, very wide Playa Lo de Marco is good for most aquatic sports except surfing and snorkeling-diving. For those you can rent boats, however, to take you to the offshore Isla Islote. The south end has a rocky tidepool shelf, fine for bait-casting.

Lo de Marco has a superb trailer park-bungalows complex, **El Caracol,** owned and operated by German expatriate Gunter Maasan and his wife. Their nine luxuriously large, "little bit of Europe in the tropics" motel-bungalows-beneath-the-palms sleep four to six persons with all the comforts of Hamburg. With a/c, fans, and complete kitchenettes, they rent for $30 d low season, $55 d high, depending on size and amenities. Add about $8 per extra person.

Their trailer park is correspondingly luxurious, with concrete-pad spaces (up to 40 feet) in a palm- and banana-shaded grassy park right on the beach. With a pool, all hookups, and immaculate hot showers and toilet facilities, the

15 spaces rent for about $12/day, or $11/day (two-month rental), pets okay. Add $4 per extra person. It's popular, so get your winter reservations in by September. Write P.O. Box 89, La Peñita de Jaltemba, Nayarit 63726, tel. (327) 500-50, or Guadalajara tel. (3) 684-3301.

If El Caracol is full, a possible alternative is the more rustic, but palm-shaded and right on the beach trailer park and campground **Pequeño Paraíso** ("Little Paradise"), located beside the jungly headland at the south end of the beach. Their couple of grassy acres have about 20 concrete pads with hookups, toilets and showers, adjacent to a spacious camping area beneath a tufted grove. Stores in town can furnish basic supplies.

Continuing south along the Lo de Marco beach road, you will soon come to two neighboring miniature pearly sand paradises, **Playa las Minitas** and **Playa El Venado**. Bring your swimsuit, picnic lunch, and, if you crave isolation, your camping gear.

Playa San Francisco
And the Costa Azul Adventure Resort

The idyllic beach and hotel at the little mango-processing town of San Francisco—"San Pancho," as locals say—offers yet another bundle of pleasant surprises. Exit Hwy. 200 at the road sign 14 miles (22 km) south of Rincón de Guayabitos (or 25 miles, 40 km, north of the Puerto Vallarta airport) and continue straight through the town to the beach.

The broad, golden-white strand, enclosed by palm-tipped green headlands, extends for half a mile on both sides of the town. Big open-ocean waves (take care—undertow) pound the beach for nearly its entire length. Offshore, flocks of pelicans dive for fish while frigate birds sail overhead. At night during the rainy months, sea turtles come ashore to lay their egg clutches, which a determined group of nearby volunteers is trying to protect from poachers.

A sign on the right a couple of blocks before the beach marks the bumpy dirt road to the **Costa Azul Adventure Resort.** In-hotel activity centers around the beach and palm-shaded pool-bar-restaurant patio. Farther afield, owner-manager John Cooper and his assistants guide guests on kayaking, biking, surfing, snorkeling, and naturalist-guided horseback adventures in

nearby coves, beaches, and jungle trails. The hotel itself, located on a hillside beneath a magnificent Colima palm grove, has 20 large, comfortable room-suites, six one-bedroom villas, and a pair of two-bedroom villas (all with fans only), which rent for about $57, $72, and $87 double, respectively. Make reservations (mandatory in winter) through their U.S. booking agent, tel. (800) 365-7613.

Sayulita

Little Sayulita, 17 miles (27 km) south of Rincón de Guayabitos (or 22 miles, 35 km north of the Puerto Vallarta airport), is the kind of spot that romantics always seem to hanker for: a drowsy village on a palmy arc of sand—an untouristed retreat for those who enjoy the quiet pleasures and local color of Mexico. Sayulita's clean waters are fine for swimming, bodysurfing, and fishing, while stores, a homey restaurant, a palm-shadowed bungalows-trailer park-campground, and a lovely bed-and-breakfast provide food and lodging.

Accommodations and Food: Adrienne Adams, owner-manager of the bed-and-breakfast **Villa de la Buena Salud** rents six luxurious rooms with bath (about $35 d, including breakfast for two, minimum three days, adults only) in her airy, art-draped, three-story house, a few steps from the Sayulita beach. Families with children are welcome in a downstairs apartment sleeping five, with kitchen, VCR, and TV, for about $75 per night. Get your winter reservations in early; Adrienne enjoys dozens of repeat customers. Adrienne's daughter Lynn, at 1754 Caliban Dr., Encinitas, CA 92024, tel. (619) 942-9640, handles reservations year-round. Adrienne also takes reservations Nov.-June in Sayulita; write P.O. Box 5, La Peñita de Jaltemba, Nayarit 63726. You can contact Adrienne quickly by calling the local operator, tel. (327) 405-65, and asking for Tía Adriana ("Auntie Adriana"), as she is known locally. The operator will summon Adrienne, who will be waiting for your second call ten minutes later.

RV and tent campers love the **Sayulita Trailer Park,** in a big shady sandy lot with about 36 hookups (some for rigs up to 40 feet) right on the beach. Guests enjoy just about everything—good clean showers and toilets, electricity, water, a bookshelf, concrete pads, dump station, pets okay—for about $11/day for two persons, discounts available for extended stays. Add $1.50 per extra person, and $1.50 for a/c power.

They also rent out six comfortable two-bedroom bungalows with kitchen, some of them right on the beach beneath the palms. Rates begin at $35 double, add about $7 per extra person. Discounts are available for weekly and monthly rentals. During the two weeks before Easter and 15-31 December, rates run about 20% higher and reservations must include a minimum seven-day stay and a 50% advance deposit. For reservations, contact the owners, Thies and Cristina Rohlfs, P.O. Box 5-585, Mexico, D.F. 06500, tel. (5) 572-1335, fax (5) 390-2750. You can also write the trailer park directly at P.O. Box 11, La Peñita de Jaltemba, Nayarit 63726.

Third choice in Sayulita goes to the very plain, oft-empty **Hotel Sayulita.** Although they ask about $25 double for 33 very basic rooms that surround a cavernous interior courtyard you might be able to bargain for a better price.

Vegetables, groceries, and baked goods are available at a pair of stores by the town plaza. Local cuisine is supplied by a good plaza taco stand weekend nights, a few *loncherías,* and best of all, **Amparo,** an elderly woman who cooks for a few dinner guests a day. Ask for directions (Amparo's house is only a couple of blocks from the plaza) and drop by a day ahead of time to tell her you're coming. The next day, don't eat much lunch. At dinnertime you will be ready for Amparo's bountiful table of homemade enchiladas, chiles rellenos, tacos, perhaps tamales, plus rice, beans, and all of the hot tortillas you can eat for about $12 per person.

Beach Hike: Adventurers enjoy the beach and jungle walk from Sayulita to San Francisco, four miles to the north. Besides the birds, flowers, and plants of the palmy forest wilderness and breezy beach in between, your reward at trail's end will be the pool and restaurant at the hotel Costa Azul Adventure Resort. Wear walking shoes and a hat for sun, and carry insect repellent and water. Allow a whole day for strolling both ways and lingering at the hotel.

Head out north along the beach at Sayulita. After about a mile the beach ends at some rocks, but you can continue along a dirt road above the beach to the right. After about a hundred yards, cut to the left, parallel to the beach, several steps across a small meadow (marshy in the wet season) to another dirt road, which dead-ends at a beachfront house on the left. Follow the palm-shaded jungle track about another mile, bearing left downhill to the beach. If you come to a house with a fence and barking dogs, you haven't gone far enough.

Continue north beneath the beachside grove of spreading *manzanilla* trees. Careful: Their bark and nuts, which look like little brown or green apples, secrete an irritating sap. Ahead, you'll soon be walking along a driftwood-strewn wild beach beneath a towering jungle headland. Here, pelicans, boobies, and cormorants fish just beyond the surf, and occasional manta rays, porpoises, and even whales might surface offshore. Swim with much caution, however. The oft-rough waves recede with strong undertow.

Past a cliffside spring (good water during the rainy season), you will soon see a big *palapa*-roofed house on the rocky point ahead. This is the former home of President Luis Echeverría (1970-76). At the end of the beach, continue up the stone stairs and straight ahead to San Francisco beach on the other side. In another mile, past the lagoon and *palapa* restaurants, you will arrive at the hotel. If you prefer not to walk back to Sayulita, hire a taxi in San Francisco.

PUERTO VALLARTA AND THE BAY OF BANDERAS

PUERTO VALLARTA

The city of Puerto Vallarta (pop. 300,000) perches at the most tranquil recess of one of the Pacific Ocean's largest, deepest bays, the Bay of Banderas. The city owes its prosperity, in good measure, to this most fortunate location. The sun, the golden sand, the bay's rich blue waters and the seafood they nurture are magnets for a million seasonal visitors. On the map of Pacific Mexico, the Bay of Banderas looks as if it were gouged from the coast by some vengeful Aztec god (perhaps in retribution for the conquest) with a single 20-mile-wide swipe of his giant hand, just sparing the city of Puerto Vallarta.

Time, however, has healed the great cataclysm. The jagged mountains, Sierra Vallejo on the north and Sierra Cuale on the south, have acquired a green coat of jungle on their slopes, and a broad river, the Ameca, winds serenely through its fertile vale to the bay.

Sand has accumulated on the great arc of the Bay of Banderas, where fisherfolk have built little settlements: Punta Mita, Cruz de Huanacaxtle, and Bucerías north of Puerto Vallarta; and Mismaloya, Boca de Tomatlán, and Yelapa to the south.

Taking a look at the city proper, visitors find that Puerto Vallarta is really two cities in one—a new town strung along the hotel strip on its northern beaches, and an old town nestled beneath jungle hills on both sides of a small river, the Río Cuale, which rushes from a deep gap in the hills.

Travelers arriving from the north, whether by plane, bus, or car, see the new Puerto Vallarta first—a parade of luxury hotels, condominiums, apartments, and shopping centers. Such visitors could stay for a month in a slick new Vallarta hotel, sun on the beach every day, disco half of every night, and return home, never having experienced the old Puerto Vallarta, which lives beside the Río Cuale.

HISTORY

Before Columbus

For centuries prior to the arrival of the Spanish, the coastal region that includes present-day Puerto Vallarta was subject to the Indian kingdom of Xalisco, centered at the modern Nayarit city of Jalisco (founded around A.D. 600 by the Toltecs), near Tepic. The Xalisco civilization was ruled by chiefs who worshipped a trinity of gods: foremost, Naye, a legendary former chief elevated to a fierce god of war, followed by the more benign Teopiltzin, god of rain and fertility, and finally by wise Heri, the god of knowledge.

Recent archaeological evidence indicates another influence: the Aztecs, who probably left Nahuatl-speaking colonies along the southern Nayarit coastal valleys during their centuries-long migration to the Valley of Mexico.

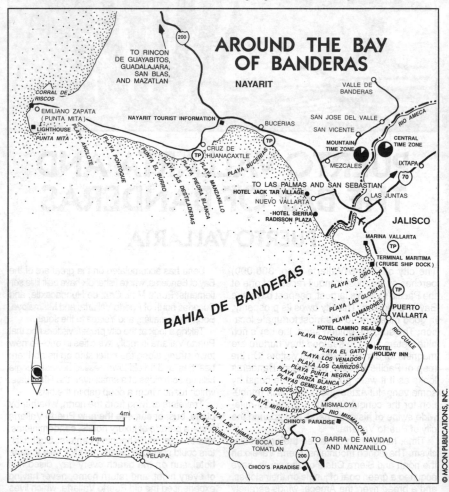

NIGHT OF THE IGUANA:
THE MAKING OF PUERTO VALLARTA

The idea to film Tennessee Williams's play *Night of the Iguana* in Puerto Vallarta was born in the bar of the Beverly Hills Hotel. In mid-1963, director John Huston (whose movies had earned a raft of Academy Awards) met with Guillermo Wulff, a Mexican architect and engineer. For the film's location Wulff proposed Mismaloya, an isolated cove south of Puerto Vallarta. On leased land, Wulff would build the movie set and cottages for staff housing, which he and Huston would later sell for a profit as tourist accommodations. Most directors would have been scared away by the (no road, no phones, no electricity) Mismaloya jungle. But, according to Alex Masden, his biographer, Huston loved Mismaloya: "To me, *Night of the Iguana* was a picnic, a gathering of friends, a real vacation."

A "gathering of friends," indeed. The script required most of the cast to be dissolute, mentally ill, or both: a blonde nymphet tries to seduce an alcoholic defrocked minister while his voluptuous, hard-drinking former lover keeps a clutch of vulturous biddies from destroying his last bit of self-respect—all while an iguana chained to a jungle tree screams pathetically for its freedom.

Huston's casting was perfect. The actors simply played themselves. Richard Burton (the minister) came supplied with plenty of booze. Burton's lover, Elizabeth Taylor (who was not part of the cast but still married to singer Eddie Fisher) accompanied him.

Sue Lyon (the nymphet) came with her lover, whose wife was rooming with Sue's mother; Ava Gardner (the voluptuous former lover) became the toast of Puerto Vallarta while romping with her local beach boyfriend; Tennessee Williams (advising the director) came with his lover Freddy; while Deborah Kerr (who acted the only prim lead role) jokingly complained that she was the only one not having an affair.

With so many temperamental characters isolated together in Mismaloya, the international press flew to Puerto Vallarta in droves to record the expected fireworks. Huston gave each of the six stars a velvet-lined case containing a gold derringer with five bullets, each engraved with the names of the others. Unexpectedly (and partly due to Huston's considerable charm), none of the bullets were used. Bored by the lack of major explosions, the press corps discovered Puerto Vallarta instead.

As Huston explained later to writer Lawrence Grobel: "That was the beginning of its popularity, which was a mixed blessing." Huston nevertheless stayed on until his death in 1987; Burton and Taylor bought Puerto Vallarta houses, got married, and also stayed for years. Although his Mismaloya tourist accommodations scheme never panned out, Guillermo Wulff became wealthy building for the rich and famous many of the houses and condominiums that now dot Puerto Vallarta's jungly hillsides and golden beaches.

Conquest and Colonization

Some of those villages still remained when the Spanish conquistador Francisco Cortés de Buenaventura, nephew of Hernán Cortés, arrived on the Jalisco-Nayarit coast in 1524.

In a broad mountain-rimmed green valley, an army of 20,000 warriors, their bows decorated by myriad colored cotton banners, temporarily blocked the conquistador's path. So impressive was the assemblage that Cortés called the fertile vale of the Ameca River north of present Puerto Vallarta the Valle de las Banderas ("Valley of the Banners"), and thus the great bay later became known as the Bahía de Banderas.

The first certain record of the Bay of Banderas itself came from the log of conquistador

Don Pedro de Alvarado, who sailed into the bay in 1541 and disembarked (probably at Mismaloya) near some massive sea rocks. He named these Las Peñas, undoubtedly the same as the present "Los Arcos" rocks that draw daily boatloads of snorkelers and divers.

For 300 years the Bay of Banderas slept under the sun. Galleons occasionally watered there; a few pirates hid in wait for them in its jungle-fringed coves.

Independence

The rebellion of 1810-21 freed Mexico, and finally, a generation later, the lure of gold and silver led, as with many of Mexico's cities, to the settlement of Puerto Vallarta. Enterprising

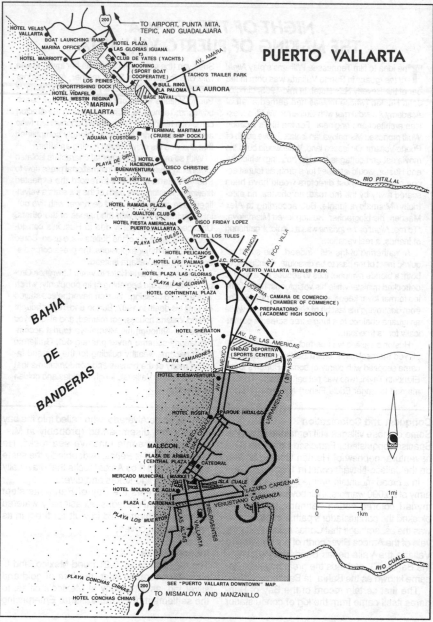

PUERTO VALLARTA

HOTEL VELAS VALLARTA
BOAT LAUNCHING RAMP
MARINA OFFICE
HOTEL MARRIOTT
LOS PEINES (SPORTFISHING DOCK)
HOTEL VIDAFEL
HOTEL WESTIN REGINA
MARINA VALLARTA

TO AIRPORT, PUNTA MITA, TEPIC, AND GUADALAJARA

HOTEL PLAZA LAS GLORIAS IGUANA
CLUB DE YATES (YACHTS)
MOORING (SPORT BOAT COOPERATIVE)
BULL RING LA PALOMA
BASE NAVAL

AV. AMARA
Tacho's Trailer Park
LA AURORA

ADUANA (CUSTOMS)
TERMINAL MARITIMA (CRUISE SHIP DOCK)

PLAYA DE ORO
HOTEL HACIENDA BUENAVENTURA
HOTEL KRYSTAL
DISCO CHRISTINE

RIO PITILLAL

HOTEL RAMADA PLAZA
QUALTON CLUB
HOTEL FIESTA AMERICANA PUERTO VALLARTA
DISCO FRIDAY LOPEZ
PLAYA LOS TULES
HOTEL LOS TULES
HOTEL PELICANOS
HOTEL LAS PALMAS
J.C. ROCK
PUERTO VALLARTA TRAILER PARK
HOTEL PLAZA LAS GLORIAS
PLAYA LAS GLORIAS
HOTEL CONTINENTAL PLAZA

AV. DE INGRESO
AV. FCO. VILLA
FRANCIA
LUCERNA

CAMARA DE COMERCIO (CHAMBER OF COMMERCE)
PREPARATORIO (ACADEMIC HIGH SCHOOL)

HOTEL SHERATON

BAHIA DE BANDERAS

AV. DE LAS AMERICAS
UNIDAD DEPORTIVA (SPORTS CENTER)

PLAYA CAMARONES

HOTEL BUENAVENTURA

AV. MEXICO
LIBRAMIENTO (BYPASS)

HOTEL ROSITA
PARQUE HIDALGO

MALECON
PLAZA DE ARMAS (CENTRAL PLAZA)
CATEDRAL

PASEO DIAZ ORDAZ

MERCADO MUNICIPAL (MARKET)
HOTEL MOLINO DE AGUA
PLAZA L. CARDENAS
PLAYA LOS MUERTOS

ISLA CUALE
LAZARO CARDENAS
VENUSTIANO CARRANZA

INSURGENTES
CONSTITUCION
VALLARTA
OLAS ALTAS

0   1mi
0   1km

RIO CUALE

SEE "PUERTO VALLARTA DOWNTOWN" MAP
TO MISMALOYA AND MANZANILLO

PLAYA CONCHAS CHINAS
HOTEL CONCHAS CHINAS

© MOON PUBLICATIONS, INC.

(previous page) Guadalajara's main market, Mercado Libertad; (this page, top) dyeing and drying, Teotitlán del Va
Oaxaca; (bottom) pre-Columbian-motif onyx masks, Taxco, Guerrero (photos by Bruce Whipperman)

merchant Don Guadalupe Sanchez made a fortune (paradoxically, not from gold, but from salt, for ore processing), which he hauled from the beach to the mines above the headwaters of the Río Cuale. Don Guadalupe and his wife soon built a hut and brought their family. Their tiny trading station grew into a little town, Puerto de Las Peñas, at the mouth of the river.

Later, the local government founded the present municipality, which, on 31 May 1918, officially became Puerto Vallarta, in honor of the former governor of Michoacán, Ignacio L. Vallarta. The mines, however, had gradually petered out, and Puerto Vallarta, isolated, with no road to the outside world, slumbered again.

Modern Puerto Vallarta

But not for long. Passenger planes began arriving sporadically from Tepic and Guadalajara in the 1950s; a gravel road was pushed through from Tepic in the 1960s. The International Airport was built, the highway was paved, and tourist hotels sprouted on the beaches. Meanwhile, in 1963, director John Huston, at the peak of his creative genius, arrived with Richard Burton, Elizabeth Taylor, Ava Gardner, and Deborah Kerr to film *Night of the Iguana*. Huston, Burton, and Taylor stayed on for years, waking Puerto Vallarta from its long slumber. It hasn't slept since.

SIGHTS

Getting Oriented

Puerto Vallarta is a long beach town, stretching about five miles from the Riviera-like Conchas Chinas condo headland at the south end. Next, heading north, comes the popular Playa Los Muertos beach and the intimate old Río Cuale neighborhood, which join, across the river, with the busy central *malecón* (seawall) shopping and restaurant (but beachless) bayfront. North of there, the beaches resume again at Playa Camarones and continue past the Zona Hotelera string of big resorts to the Marina complex, where tour boats and cruise liners depart from the Terminal Maritima dock. In the Marina's northern basin lie the Peines (pay-EE-nays) sportfishing and Club de Yates docks. A mile farther north, the city ends at the bustling International Airport.

One basic thoroughfare serves the entire beachfront. Called **Avenida de Ingreso** as it conducts express traffic south past the Zona Hotelera, it changes names three times. Narrowing, it becomes the cobbled **Av. México,** then **Paseo Díaz Ordaz** along the seafront *malecón* with tourist restaurants, clubs, and shops, changing finally to **Av. Morelos** before it passes the Presidencia Municipal (city hall) and central plaza.

The Chino's Paradise restaurant palapa perches on the jungle canyon above the clear, rushing Mismaloya River.

BRUCE WHIPPERMAN

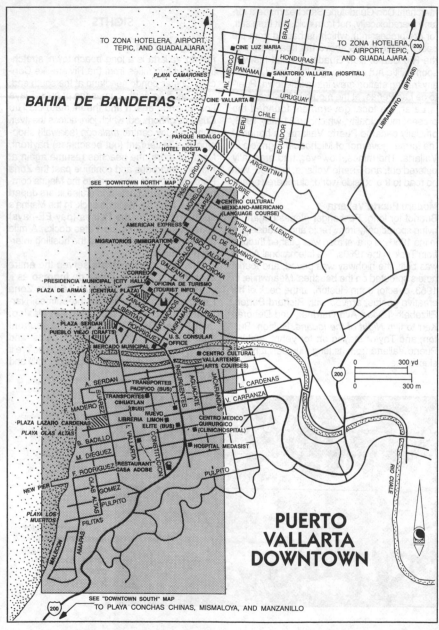

BAHIA DE BANDERAS

TO ZONA HOTELERA, AIRPORT, TEPIC, AND GUADALAJARA

TO ZONA HOTELERA, AIRPORT, TEPIC, AND GUADALAJARA

CINE LUZ MARIA

PLAYA CAMARONES

SANATORIO VALLARTA (HOSPITAL)

CINE VALLARTA

PARQUE HIDALGO
HOTEL ROSITA

SEE "DOWNTOWN NORTH" MAP

CENTRO CULTURAL MEXICANO-AMERICANO (LANGUAGE COURSE)

AMERICAN EXPRESS

MIGRATORIOS (IMMIGRATION)

CORREO

PRESIDENCIA MUNICIPAL (CITY HALL)
PLAZA DE ARMAS (CENTRAL PLAZA)

OFICINA DE TURISMO (TOURIST INFO)

PLAZA SERDAN
PUEBLO VIEJO (CRAFTS)

MERCADO MUNICIPAL

U.S. CONSULAR OFFICE

CENTRO CULTURAL VALLARTENSE (ARTS COURSES)

TRANSPORTES PACIFICO (BUS)

TRANSPORTES CIHUATLAN (BUS)

NUEVO
LIBRERIA LIMON
ELITE (BUS)

CENTRO MEDICO QUIRURGICO (CLINIC/HOSPITAL)

HOSPITAL MEDASIST

PLAZA LAZARO CARDENAS
PLAYA OLAS ALTAS

RESTAURANT CASA ADOBE

NEW PIER

PLAYA LOS MUERTOS

PULPITO

0   300 yd

0   300 m

PUERTO VALLARTA DOWNTOWN

RIO CUALE

© MOON PUBLICATIONS, INC.

Streets: BRAZIL, HONDURAS, PANAMA, AV. MEXICO, URUGUAY, CHILE, PERU, ECUADOR, ARGENTINA, LIBRAMIENTO (BYPASS), PASEO ORDAZ, 31 DE OCTUBRE, MORELOS, JUAREZ, PIPILA, L. VICARIO, ALLENDE, O. DE DOMINGUEZ, HIDALGO, ALDAMA, GALEANA, CORONA, ZARAGOZA, LIBERTAD, RODRIGUEZ, MATAMOROS, MINA, ITURBIDE, MIRAMAR, A. SERDAN, AGUACATE, INSURGENTES, JACARANDAS, L. CARDENAS, V. CARRANZA, SUAREZ, F. MADERO, VALLARTA, CONSTITUCION, B. BADILLO, M. DIEGUEZ, F. RODRIGUEZ, GOMEZ, PULPITO, PILITAS, ANAPAS, MALECON

SEE "DOWNTOWN SOUTH" MAP
TO PLAYA CONCHAS CHINAS, MISMALOYA, AND MANZANILLO

When southbound traffic reaches Isla Río Cuale, the tree-shaded, midstream island where the city's pioneers built their huts, traffic slows to a crawl and finally dissipates in the colorful old neighborhood on the south side of the river.

There being little traffic south of the Cuale, people walk everywhere, and slowly, because of the heat. Every morning men in sombreros lead burros down to the mouth of the river to gather sand. Little *papelerías, miscelaneas,* and streetside *taquerías* serve the local folks while small restaurants, hotels, and clubs serve the visitors.

Getting Around

Since nearly all through traffic flows along one thoroughfare, Puerto Vallarta transportation is a snap. Simply hop on one of the frequent (but usually crowded) city buses (fare 15-30 cents), virtually all of which end up at Plaza Lázaro Cárdenas on Av. Olas Altas a few blocks south of the river. Northbound, the same buses retrace the route through the Zona Hotelera to one of several destinations scrawled across their windows. Taxis, while much more convenient, are all individual and rather expensive (about $3-4 per trip within the city limits; don't get in until the price is settled).

Drivers who want to quickly travel between the north and the south ends of town often take the *libramiento* bypass (see the map "Puerto Vallarta Downtown") and avoid the crowded downtown traffic.

A Walk around Isla Cuale

Start at the **Museo Río Cuale,** a joint government-volunteer effort near the very downstream tip of Isla Río Cuale. Inside is a small but fine collection of paintings by local artists as well as locally excavated pre-Columbian artifacts (open Mon.-Sat. when volunteers are available, no phone).

Head upstream beneath the bridge and enjoy the shady *paseo* of shops and restaurants. For fun, stroll out on one of the two quaint **suspension bridges** over the river. Evenings, these are the coolest spots in Puerto Vallarta. A river of cool night air often funnels down the Cuale valley, creating a refreshing breeze along the length of the clear, tree-draped stream.

The Río Cuale was not always so clean. Once upon a time, a few dozen foreign resi-

dents, tired of looking down upon the littered riverbank, came out one Sunday and began hauling trash from the riverbed. Embarrassed by the example, a neighborhood crowd pitched in. The river has been clean ever since.

Farther upstream, on the adjacent riverbank, stands the **Mercado Municipal Río Cuale,** a honeycomb of stalls stuffed with crafts from all over Mexico. Continue past the upriver (Av. Insurgentes) bridge to **Plaza John Huston,** marked by a smiling bronze likeness of the renowned Hollywood director who helped put Puerto Vallarta on the map with his filming of Tennessee Williams's *Night of the Iguana* in 1963.

About 50 yards farther on, stop in at the small gallery of the **Centro Cultural Vallartense,** a volunteer organization that conducts art classes, sponsors shows of promising artists, and sometimes invites local artists to meet the public and interested amateurs for informal instruction and idea exchange. Ask the volunteer on duty for more information or see the community events listings in *Vallarta Today,* the local English-language community newspaper.

A few more steps upstream you will pass the round stucco headquarters and practice room of the **Escuela Municipal de Musica.** They, along with the Centro Cultural Vallartense, offer courses to the general public. See "Language, Arts, and Music Courses" below.

At the boulder-strewn upstream point of the island, a cadre of women wash clothes. Many of them are professionals who practice their craft on special rocks, perfectly positioned for a day of productive washing. Their clean handiwork stretches out to dry—on rocks, on grass, on bushes—in rainbow arrays beneath the sun.

Gringo Gulch

The steep, villa-dotted hillside above the island's upper end is called Gringo Gulch, for the colony of rich *norteamericanos* who own big homes there. It's an interesting place for a stroll.

Back at the Insurgentes bridge, head right, toward the center of town, bear right to the end of one-block Calle Emilio Carranza, and continue up a steep, bougainvillea-festooned staircase to Calle Zaragoza one block above.

At Zaragoza and the upper level of Emilio Carranza, you are at the gateway to Gringo

Gulch. Wander through the winding, hillside lanes and enjoy the picturesque scenes that seem to appear around each rickety-chic corner. For example, note the luxurious *palapas* perched atop the tall villa on Carranza, half a block above Zaragoza.

During your meanderings, don't miss the Gringo Gulch centerpiece mansion at Zaragoza 446, once owned by Elizabeth Taylor. (You'll scarcely be able to miss it, for it has a pink passageway arching over the street.) The house was a gift to Taylor from Richard Burton. After they were married, they also bought the house on the other side of Zaragoza, renovated it, and built a pool; thus the passageway became necessary. It is now a private residence.

The **Club Internacional de la Amistad** (Friendship Club) on weekends conducts seasonal tours through some of Puerto Vallarta's showplace homes, beginning at the central plaza around 1100. Look for announcement posters, or community events listings in *Vallarta Today* (see "Volunteer Work" under "Information" below).

On the *Malecón*
Head back down Zaragoza, and let the church belfry be your guide. Named **La Parroquia de Nuestra Señora de Guadalupe,** for the city's patron saint, the church is relatively new (1951) and undistinguished except for the very unusual huge crown atop the tower. Curiously, it was modeled after the crown of the tragic 19th-century Empress Carlota, who went insane after her husband was executed. On the church steps, an Indian woman frequently sells textiles, which she weaves on the spot with a traditional backstrap loom (in Spanish, *tela de otate,* loom of bamboo, from the Nahuatl *otlatl,* bamboo).

Continue down Zaragoza past the Palacio Municipal at one side of the central Plaza de Armas, straight toward the Los Arcos ("The Arches"), right at the water's edge. They form a backdrop for frequent free weekend evening music and dance performances. From there, the *malecón* seawall-walkway stretches north toward the Zona Hotelera hotels, which you can see along the curving northern beachfront.

The *malecón* marks the bay's innermost point. From there the shoreline stretches and curves westerly many miles on both sides, adorned by dozens of sandy beaches until it reaches its wave-washed extremities at Punta Mita (on the distant horizon, at the bay's northwest extremity) and Punta La Iglesia to the far southwest.

BEACHES

Playa Los Muertos
Generations ago, when Puerto Vallarta was a small, isolated town, there was only one beach, Playa Los Muertos, the strand of yellow sand that stretches for a mile south of the Cuale River. Old-timers still remember the Sundays and holidays when it seemed as if half the families in Puerto Vallarta had come south of the Río Cuale, to Los Muertos Beach especially, to play in the surf and sand.

This is still largely true, although now droves of winter-season North American vacationers and residents have joined them. Fortunately, Playa Los Muertos is much cleaner than during the polluted 1980s. The fish are coming back, as evidenced by the flocks of diving pelicans and the crowd of folks who drop lines every day from the **New Pier** (foot of Francisca Rodriguez).

Fishing is even better off the rocks on the south end of the beach. *Lisa* (mullet), *sierra* (mackerel), *pargo* (snapper), and *torito* are commonly caught anywhere along close-in beaches. On certain unpredictable occasions, fish (and one memorable time even giant 30-pound squids) swarm offshore in such abundance that anyone can pick them out of the water barehanded.

Gentle waves and lack of undertow make Playa Los Muertos generally safe for wading and good for **swimming** beyond the close-in breakers. The same breakers, however, eliminate Los Muertos for bodysurfing, boogie-boarding, or surfing (except occasionally at the far south end).

Playas Conchas Chinas
Playa Conchas Chinas ("Chinese Shells Beach") is not one beach but a series of small sandy coves dotted by rocky outcroppings beneath the condo-clogged hillside that extends for about a mile south of Playa Los Muertos. A number of

streets and driveways lead to the beach from the Manzanillo Hwy. 200 (the extension of Insurgentes) south of town. Drive—or taxi, or ride one of the many the minibuses marked "Mismaloya" or "Boca," which leave the from Olas Altas's Plaza Lázaro Cárdenas, corner Carranza and Suárez—or hike along the tidepools from Los Muertos Beach.

Fishing off the rocks is good here; the water is even clear enough for some **snorkeling.** Bring your gear, however, as there's none for rent. The usually gentle waves, however, make any kind of surfing very doubtful.

Beach Exploring

Beach lovers can spend many enjoyable days poking around the many little beaches south of town. Drive, taxi, or take a Mismaloya- or Boca-marked minibus from Plaza Lázaro Cárdenas.

Just watch out the window, and when you see a likely spot, ask the driver to stop. Say *"Pare (PAH-ray) por favor."* The location will most likely be one of several lovely *playas:* **El Gato** ("Cat"), **Los Venados** ("Deers"), **Los Carrizos** ("Reeds"), **Punta Negra** ("Black Point"), **Garza Blanca** ("White Heron"), or **Gemelas** ("Twins").

Although many of these little sand crescents have big hotels, it doesn't matter, because beaches are public in Mexico up to the high-tide line. There is always some path to the beach used by local folks. Just ask *"¿Dónde está el camino* (road, path) *a la playa?"* and someone will probably point the way.

Mismaloya and Los Arcos

If you ride all the way to Playa Mismaloya, you will not be disappointed, despite the oversize Hotel Mismaloya crowding the beach. Follow the dirt road just past the hotel to the intimate little curve of sand and lagoon where the cool, clear Mismaloya stream meets the sea. A rainbow array of fishing *lanchas* lie beached around the lagoon's edges, in front of a line of beachside *palapa* restaurants.

Continue a few hundred yards past the *palapas* to the ruins of the movie set of the *Night of the Iguana.* Besides being built for the actual filming, the rooms behind those now-crumbling stucco walls served as lodging, dining, and working quarters for the hundreds of crew who camped here for those eight busy months in 1963.

North, offshore beyond the Mismaloya cove, rise the green-brushed **Los Arcos** sea rocks, a federal underwater park and eco-preserve. The name comes from the arching grottoes that channel completely through the bases of some of the rocks. Los Arcos is one of the best snorkeling grounds around Puerto Vallarta. Get there by hiring a glass-bottomed boat in the lagoon.

Snorkeling near the wave-washed Los Arcos is a Puerto Vallarta "must do." Swirling bunches of green algae and branching ruddy corals attract schools of grazing parrot, angel, butterfly, and goat fish. Curious pencil-thin cornet fish may sniff you out as they pass, while big croakers and sturgeon will slowly drift, scavenging along the coral-littered depths.

Fishing, especially casting from the rocks beneath the movie set, and every other kind of beach activity are good at Mismaloya, except surfing and boogie-boarding, for which the waves are generally too gentle.

Stop for food (big fish fillet plate, any style, with all the trimmings, $6, breakfast eggs from their own hens) or a drink at the **Restaurant Las Gaviotas** *palapas* behind the lagoon.

For still another treat, visit nearby **Chino's Paradise.** Follow the riverside, lower road that forks upstream at the north end of the bridge across the road from the hotel. Arrive in the late morning (around eleven, or around three in the late afternoon) to avoid the tour-bus rush. Chino's streamside *palapas* nestle like big mushrooms on a jungle hillside above a cool, cascading creek. Adventurous guests enjoy sliding down the cascades (be careful—some have injured themselves seriously), while others content themselves with lying in the sun or lolling in sandy-bottomed, clear pools. Beneath the *palapas,* they serve respectable but uninspired seafood and steak plates and Mexican *antijitos.* (Be wary of their very bold parrots, however.) Open daily 1100-1700.

Beaches Farther South

Three miles south of Mismaloya is the very tranquil, jungle-fringed beach and bay of **Boca de Tomatlán,** where you can rent boats and head out for the pristine paradises of **Las Animas, Quimixto,** and **Yelapa** farther south. Las Animas has seafood *palapas,* an idyllic beach, and snorkeling; the same is true for Quimixto, which also has a waterfall nearby for splashing.

Yelapa, a settlement nestled beneath verdant, palm-crowned hills beside an aquamarine cove, is home for perhaps a hundred local families and a small colony of foreign expatriates. For visitors, it offers a glimpse of south seas life as it was before the automobile. Accessible only by sea, Yelapa's residents get around on foot or horseback. A waterfall cascades through the tropical forest above the village, and a string of *palapa* restaurants lines the beach. Lodging is available in the *palapas*-roofed *cabañas* of the rustic **Hotel Lagunitas.** Rooms run about $25 d, and reservations are generally not necessary, but you can try writing the hotel (no phone in paradise, of course) at simply Hotel Lagunitas, Yelapa, Jalisco, Mexico.

Cruises to Las Animas, Quimixto, and Yelapa: Most Puerto Vallarta visitors reach these little southern beaches by a different route than by Boca Tomatlán. They usually go by one of several all-day tourist cruises, which leave (around 0900 and return by 1600) from the dock at the Puerto Vallarta Maritime terminal. During the high winter season, a number of these cruises pick up additional passengers at the New Pier on Playa Los Muertos downtown.

One of the most popular and least expensive of these excursions is aboard the big *Princess Yelapa,* a tripled-decked white steel tub with room for 400. The cruise follows the coastline past Los Arcos, Mismaloya, Las Animas, and Quimixto. Passengers disembark at Yelapa for two hours, just long enough for the short waterfall hike (or by horseback, if desired) and lunch at a beach *palapa.* This no-frills ($18) trip includes a no-host bar and restrooms.

The *Princess Vallarta,* a scaled-down version of the *Princess Yelapa,* offers a more luxurious, all-inclusive ($33/person) cruise, with on-board continental breakfast, live music for dancing, and open bar. They head out, enjoying views of the town, beaches, and hills, stopping at Los Arcos for snorkeling. Continuing past Mismaloya and Tomatlán, they arrive at Las Animas for lunch, relaxing on the beach, and snorkeling for a couple of hours before returning.

The *Vagabundo,* a smaller but comfortable 50-person sportfishing-type motor yacht, heads straight across the bay, as guests enjoy drinks

BRUCE WHIPPERMAN

A trove of sleepy tropical havens, such as Boca de Tomatlán, shown, dot the Bay of Banderas' jungly shore.

from the open bar. They anchor at Yelapa for two hours, enough time for the waterfall hike. On the way back, a modest buffet lunch is served as the cruise continues to Los Arcos for snorkeling. Then they return, enjoying views of intimate rocky beaches, green jungle-strewn hills, and a procession of palm-fringed shoreline hotels ($28/person, includes restrooms).

The *Buenaventura,* a 40-foot double-decker, offers a deluxe ($45 per person) cruise, which includes continental breakfast, a stop at Los Arcos for snorkeling, open bar all the way, and lunch at Las Animas Beach. From there they continue to the beach and waterfall at Quimixto, then return.

If you tend toward seasickness, fortify yourself with Dramamine before these cruises. Destination disembarkation is by motor launch and can be difficult for the physically handicapped.

You may buy tickets for any of these cruises from travel agents, such as your hotel travel desk, or Servicios Turisticos Miller, with headquarters (tel. 322-411-97, 412-97, and 413-97) in the Zona Hotelera near the Hotel Krystal, Paseo Las Garzas 10, and branches at hotels, such as the Playa Los Arcos, Vidafel, Melia, Plaza Las Glorias, and Sheraton.

North-End (Zona Hotelera) Beaches
These are Puerto Vallarta's cleanest, least crowded, in-town beaches, despite the many hotels that line them. Beginning at the Hotel Rosita at the north end of the *malecón,* **Playas Camarones, Las Glorias, Los Tules,** and **de Oro** form a continuous three-mile strand to the Marina. Stubby rock jetties about every quarter-mile have succeeded in retaining a 50-yard-wide strip of golden-cream sand most of the way.

The sand is midway between coarse and fine, the waves are gentle, breaking right at the water's edge, and the ocean past the breakers is relatively clear (10- or 20-feet visibility) and blue. Stormy weather occasionally dredges up clam, cockle, limpet, oyster, and other shells from the offshore depths.

Fishing by pole, net, or simply line is common along here. Surfing, bodysurfing, and boogie-boarding, however, are not. All other beach sports, especially the high-powered variety, are available at nearly every hotel along the strand (see "Sports" below).

Beach Hikes
A pair of good close-in hikes are possible. For either of them don't forget a sun hat, sunscreen, repellent, a shirt, and some light shoes. On the south side, walk from **Playa Los Muertos** about a mile and a half along the little beaches and tidepools to **Playa Conchas Chinas.** Start at either end and take half a day swimming, snorkeling, sunning, and poking among the rocks.

More ambitiously, you can hike the entire three-mile beach strip from the northern end of the *malecón* to the Marina. If you start by nine you'll enjoy the cool of the morning with the sun at your back. Stop along the way at the show-place pools and beach restaurants of hotels such as the Sheraton, the Plaza Las Glorias, the Fiesta Americana Vallarta, and Krystal. Walk back, or opt for a return by taxi or city bus.

ACCOMMODATIONS

In Puerto Vallarta you can get any type of lodging you want at nearly any price. The location sets the tone, however. The relaxed, relatively tranquil but interesting neighborhood south of the Río Cuale (especially around Av. Olas Altas) has many budget and moderately priced hotels, apartments, and condos within easy walking distance of restaurants, shopping, and services. Many of them are very close, if not right on, lively Los Muertos Beach. While no strict dividing line separates the types of available lodgings, hotels (listed first, below) generally offer rooms with maximum service (desk, daily cleaning, restaurant, pool) without kitchens for shorter-term guests, while apartments and condos virtually always offer multiple-room furnished kitchen units for greatly reduced per diem rates for longer term rentals. If you're staying more than two weeks, you'll save money and also enjoy more of the comforts of home in a good apartment or condo rental.

Hotels, Río Cuale and South
Although landmark **Hotel Molino de Agua** ("Water Mill"), located at the corner of Ignacio Vallarta and Aquiles Serdán, Puerto Vallarta 48380, tel. (322) 219-07 or 219-57, fax 260-56, occupies two riverfront blocks right on the beach, many visitors miss it completely. Its very tranquil colony of rustic-chic *cabañas* hide in a jungle-garden of cackling parrots, giant-leafed vines, and gigantic, spreading trees. Most of the *cabañas* are at ground level and unfortunately don't feel very private inside unless you close the shutters—which seems a shame in a tropical garden. The very popular beachside upstairs units remedy this dilemma. The hotel's 40 garden rooms rent $48 d low season, $55 high, while the upstairs beach-side rooms go for about $70 d low season, $80 high season; two pools, restaurant, a/c, credit cards accepted.

Adjacent to the Hotel Molino de Agua, as you head south, away from the river at the corner of I. Vallarta and A. Serdán, the diminutive **Hotel Posada Río Cuale** packs a lot of hotel into a small space at Av. Aquiles Serdán 224, P.O. Box 146, Puerto Vallarta 48300, tel. (322) 204-50

PUERTO VALLARTA DOWNTOWN NORTH

CARLOS O'BRIEN'S

CENTRO CULTURAL MEXICANO-AMERICANO (LANGUAGE COURSE)

PIPILA

LEONA VICARIO

PASEO D. ORDAZ

HARD ROCK CAFE

RITO'S BACI

RESTAURANT CAFE DES ARTISTES

PAPAYA 3

ORTIZ DE DOMINGUEZ

RESTAURANT LAS PALOMAS

MALECON

MORELOS

MIGRATORIOS (IMMIGRATION)

ABASOLO

ALDAMA

CAFE SAN CRISTOBAL

RESTAURANT BRAZZ

HOTEL LOS CUATROS VIENTOS

CORONA

BAHIA DE BANDERAS

JUAREZ

GALEANA

CORREO

MINA

PRESIDENCIA MUNICIPAL (CITY HALL)

OFICINA DE TURISMO (TOURIST OFFICE)

ITURBIDE

MIRAMAR

PLAZA DE ARMAS (CENTRAL PLAZA)

MATAMOROS

ZARAGOZA

HIDALGO

RODRIGUEZ

PLAZA A. SERDAN

PUEBLO VIEJO (CRAFTS)

LIBERTAD

RESTAURANT CHEF ROGER

ENCINO

HOTEL ENCINO

MUNICIPAL CRAFTS MARKET

CASA DEL PUENTE

RIO CUALE

RESTAURANT CUIZA

ISLA RIO CUALE

U.S. CONSULAR OFFICE

CENTRO CULTURAL VALLARTENSE (ARTS COURSES)

PLAZA JOHN HUSTON

RESTAURANT LE BISTRO

GALERIA PACIFICO

5 DE FEBRERO

HOTEL MOLINO DE AGUA

IGNACIO VALLARTA

SUPERMARKET GUTIERREZ RIZO

CONSTITUCION

INSURGENTES

CINE BAHIA

AGUACATE

HOTEL VILLA DEL MAR

JACARANDAS

AQUILES SERDAN

HOTEL POSADA RIO CUALE

FCO. MADERO

0 100 yd
0 100 m

© MOON PUBLICATIONS, INC.

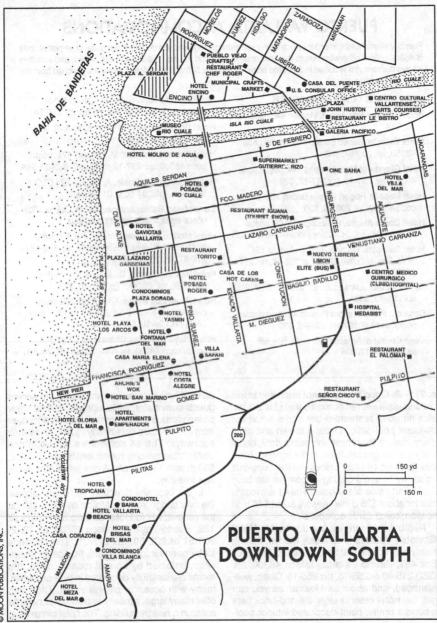

PUERTO VALLARTA
DOWNTOWN SOUTH

BAHIA DE BANDERAS

RODRIGUEZ
MORELOS
JUAREZ
HIDALGO
MATAMOROS
ZARAGOZA
MIRAMAR

LIBERTAD

PLAZA A. SERDAN

PUEBLO VIEJO (CRAFTS)/
RESTAURANT CHEF ROGER

HOTEL ENCINO

MUNICIPAL CRAFTS MARKET

ENCINO

CASA DEL PUENTE

U.S. CONSULAR OFFICE

RIO CUALE

CENTRO CULTURAL VALLARTENSE (ARTS COURSES)

PLAZA JOHN HUSTON

RESTAURANT LE BISTRO

MUSEO RIO CUALE

ISLA RIO CUALE

GALERIA PACIFICO

5 DE FEBRERO

HOTEL MOLINO DE AGUA

SUPERMARKET GUTIERREZ RIZO

CINE BAHIA

HOTEL VILLA DEL MAR

AQUILES SERDAN

HOTEL POSADA RIO CUALE

FCO. MADERO

JACARANDAS

INSURGENTES

AGUACATE

CLAS ALTAS

RESTAURANT IGUANA (TOURIST SHOW)

HOTEL GAVIOTAS VALLARTA

LAZARO CARDENAS

VENUSTIANO CARRANZA

PLAZA LAZARO CARDENAS

RESTAURANT TORITO

CASA DE LOS HOT CAKES

NUEVO LIBRERIA

ELITE (BUS)

CENTRO MEDICO QUIRURGICO (CLINIC/HOSPITAL)

CONSTITUCION

BASILIO BADILLO

PLAYA CLAS ALTAS

CONDOMINIOS PLAZA DORADA

HOTEL POSADA ROGER

HOTEL PLAYA LOS ARCOS

HOTEL YASMIN

HOSPITAL MEDASIST

HOTEL FONTANA DEL MAR

PINO SUAREZ

M. DIEGUEZ

IGNACIO VALLARTA

CASA MARIA ELENA

VILLA SAFARI

RESTAURANT EL PALOMAR

FRANCISCA RODRIGUEZ

HOTEL COSTA ALEGRE

PULPITO

NEW PIER

ARCHIE'S WOK

HOTEL SAN MARINO

RESTAURANT SEÑOR CHICO'S

GOMEZ

HOTEL APARTMENTS EMPERADOR

HOTEL GLORIA DEL MAR

PULPITO

200

PLAYA LOS MUERTOS

PILITAS

0   150 yd

0   150 m

MOON

HOTEL TROPICANA

CONDOHOTEL BAHIA

HOTEL VALLARTA BEACH

CASA CORAZON

HOTEL BRISAS DEL MAR

MALECON

CONDOMINIOS VILLA BLANCA

AMAPAS

HOTEL MEZA DEL MAR

© MOON PUBLICATIONS, INC.

PUERTO VALLARTA ACCOMMODATIONS

Puerto Vallarta hotels, in order of increasing approximate high-season double-room price. (The postal code is 48300 unless otherwise noted; the area code is 322; and "all inc." means all food, drinks, and activities for two persons are included in the listed price. All toll-free 800 numbers listed below are reached from the U.S. and Canada only.)

HOTELS: RÍO CUALE AND SOUTH

Hotel Villa del Mar, Fco. I. Madero 440, tel. 207-85, $14

Hotel Yasmin, Basilio Badillo 168, postal code 48380, tel. 200-87, $23

Hotel Gloria del Mar, Amapas 114, postal code 48380, tel. 251-43, fax 217-67, $29

Hotel Posada Roger, Basilio Badillo 237, postal code 48380, tel. 208-36, $30

Hotel Costa Alegre, F. Rodríguez 168, postal code 48380, tel. 247-93 or (800) 648-2403, $33

Hotel Gaviotas Vallarta, Fco. I. Madero 154 (P.O. Box 497), tel. 215-00 or 255-18, fax 255-16, $33

Hotel Encino, Juárez 122, tel. 200-51 or 202-80, fax 225-73, $33

Casa del Puente, sobre Puente Av. Insurgentes, postal code 48380, tel. 207-49, $33

Casa Corazón, Amapas 326 (P.O. Box 66), tel./fax 213-17, $35

Hotel Tropicana, Amapas 214, postal code 48380, tel. 209-12 or 209-52, fax 267-37, $41

Hotel Brisas del Mar, Privada Abedul 10, tel. 218-00 or 218-21, $44

Hotel Fontana del Mar, M. Dieguez 171, postal code 48380, tel. 207-12 or (800) 648-2403, $44

Hotel Posada Río Cuale, A. Serdán 224 (P.O. Box 146), tel. 204-50 or 211-48, $46

Condohotel Bahía, Amapas 299 (P.O. Box 150), postal code 48380, tel. 237-40, $50

Hotel Molino de Agua, I. Vallarta at A. Serdán (P.O. Box 54), postal code 48380, tel. 219-07 or 219-57, fax 260-56, $55

Hotel Vallarta Beach, Calle Malecón s/n (P.O. Box 329), tel. 250-40, fax 251-76, $55

Hotel Playa Los Arcos, Olas Altas 380, postal code 48380, tel. 205-83, 215-83, or (800) 648-2403, fax 224-18, $57

Hotel Playa Conchas Chinas, P.O. Box 346, postal code 48390, tel. 157-63, fax 157-70, $63

---

or 211-48. Good management is the key to this picturesque warren of rooms that clusters beside its good restaurant-bar and a small but pleasant pool-patio. Tasteful brown and brick decor makes the rooms somewhat dark, especially on the ground floor. Artful lighting, however, improves on this. Unless you like diesel-bus noise, try to avoid getting a room on the busy Av. Vallarta side of the hotel. The 41 a/c rooms rent for about $25 d low season, about $46 high season; credit cards accepted.

Nearby, the high-rise but downscale **Hotel Gaviotas Vallarta** is curiously hidden, though nearly on the beach at Fco. I. Madero 154, P.O. Box 497, Puerto Vallarta, Jalisco 48300, tel. (322) 215-00 or 255-18, fax 255-16. Clean, well-managed, and about as Mexican as you can get, the hotel rises in eight tile-and-brick tiers around a pretty, plant-decorated interior pool-

patio. A small restaurant and snack bar serves guests downstairs, while, upstairs, guests enjoy ocean vistas directly from their room windows, or from arch-framed breezeways just outside their doorways. The 84 non-deluxe but clean and comfortable fan-only rooms rent for about $30 s, $33 d; with TV and a/c. A one-week stay earns one free day.

In the opposite direction, north, just across the river bridge from the Molino de Agua, stands the renovated old **Hotel Encino** at Av. Juárez 122, Puerto Vallarta, Jalisco 48300, tel. (322) 200-51 or 202-80, fax 225-73. The entrance lobby opens into a pleasant, tropical fountain-patio, enfolded by tiers of rooms. Inside, the rooms are tastefully decorated in blue and white, many with ocean or city-hill views. They also offer many large, similarly-appointed kitchenette suites in a nearby building. The hotel climaxes at

Hotel San Marino, Rudolfo Gómez 111, postal code 48380, tel. 215-55, 230-50, or (800) 962-8920, fax 224-31, $70

Hotel Meza del Mar, Amapas 380, tel. 248-88, fax 223-08, $80 all inc.

Holiday Inn, Km 4, Carretera a Barra de Navidad, P.O. Box 385, tel. 155-15 or or (800) 465-4329, fax 151-05, $200 all inc.

Hotel Camino Real, P.O. Box 95, Playa de las Estacas, tel. 150-00 or (800) 7-CAMINO, fax 160-00, $200

HOTELS: NORTH OF THE RÍO CUALE

Hotel Rosita, Díaz Ordaz 901 (P.O. Box 32), tel. 221-71, fax 210-33, $27

Hotel Los Cuatro Vientos, Matamoros 520 (P.O. Box 520), tel. 201-61, fax 228-31, $39

Hotel Hacienda Buenaventura, Paseo de la Marina (P.O. Box 95B), postal code 48310, tel. 466-67 or (800) 223-6764, fax 464-00, $60

Hotel Buenaventura, México 1301 (P.O. Box 8B), postal code 48350, tel. 237-37, $78

Hotel Los Palmas, Km 2.5, Av. de Ingreso, tel. 406 50, 444-06, or (800) 995-0504, fax 405-43, $85

Hotel Plaza Las Glorias, Km 2.5, Plaza Las Glorias, tel. 444-44 or (800) 342-AMIGO, fax 564-59, $120

Hotel Continental Plaza, Km 2.5, Av. de Ingreso Plaza Las Glorias, tel. 401-23 or (800) 88-CONTI, fax 452-36, $135

Hotel Fiesta Americana Puerto Vallarta, P.O. Box 270, tel. 420-10, or (800) 223-2332, fax 421-08, $170

Hotel Krystal, Av. de las Garzas s/n, tel. 402-02 or (800) 231-9860, fax 401-11, $165

Hotel Qualton Club and Spa, Km 2.5, Av. de las Palmas s/n, tel. 444-46 or (800) 421-2134, fax 444-45, $100 all inc.

APARTMENTS AND CONDOMINIUMS

Prices listed are the approximate high-season monthly rental rate for a one-bedroom unit.

Emperador, Amapas 114, postal code 48380, tel. 251-43, fax 210-47, $600

Hotel Brisas del Mar, Privada Abedul 10, tel. 218-00 or 218-21, $670

Condohotel Bahía, Amapas 299 (P.O. Box 150), postal code 48380, tel. 237-40, $750

Villas Safari, F. Rodríguez 203 (P.O. Box 203), postal code 48380, tel./fax 210-47, $800

Hotel Gloria del Mar, Amapas 114, postal code 48380, tel. 251-43, fax 217-67, $900

Casa María Elena, F. Rodríguez 163, tel. 201-13, fax 210-47, $900

Condominios Villa Blanca, Amapas 349, tel./fax 261-90, $1375

Condominios Plaza Dorada, Olas Altas 246, tel. 306-53, $1500

the rooftop pool and sundeck, where guests enjoy a panoramic view of the surrounding green jungly hills above the white-stucco-and-tile old town, spreading to the blue, mountain-rimmed bay. The 75 rooms and suites rent for about $25 d low season, $33 high season; one- and two-bedroom kitchenette suites begin at about $50 low season, $70 high season; a/c, phones, security boxes, restaurant-bar.

Head directly upstream, to the upper (Av. Insurgentes) river bridge, and you'll find **Casa del Puente** tucked uphill behind the sidewalk cafe by the bridge. The elegant villa-home of Molly Stokes, grand-niece of celebrated naturalist John Muir, Casa del Puente is a lovely home-away-from-home. Antiques and art adorn the spacious, beamed-ceiling rooms, while outside its windows and around the decks great trees spread, tropical birds flit and chatter, jungle hills

rise, and the river gurgles, hidden from the city hubbub nearby. Molly offers three lodging options: an upstairs riverview room with big bath and double bed for around $33, and a pair of spacious apartments (a one-bedroom, one bath, and a two-bedroom, two bath) for around $70. Discounts may be negotiated, depending upon season and length of stay. Reserve early for the winter season. For more information contact Molly Stokes, Casa del Puente, sobre Puente Av. Insurgentes, Puerto Vallarta, Jalisco 48380, tel. (322) 207-49.

Nearby, across the river and two more blocks upstream, along Avs. Aquiles Serdán and Fco I. Madero, are a number of super-economy hotels. These bare-bulb lodgings, with rates averaging about $10 d, offer tiers of interior rooms with few amenities other than four walls, a bath (check for hot water), and a bed.

One notable exception is the **Hotel Villa del Mar,** whose longtime loyal patrons swear by it as the one remnant of Puerto Vallarta "like it used to be." Located at Fco. I. Madero 440, corner of Jacarandas, Puerto Vallarta, Jalisco 48300, tel. (322) 207-85. The rather austere dark-wood streetcorner lobby leads to a double warren of clean upstairs rooms, arranged in a pair of separate "A" and "B" wings. The "A" wing rooms are generally the best, with non-deluxe but comfortable amenities, including queen-size beds, traditional-style dark wood decor, and, in some cases even private street-view balconies. Section "A," with exterior-facing windows, has the triple advantage of more privacy, light, and quiet. "B" rooms, by contrast, have windows that line walkways around a sound-reflective, and therefore oft-noisy, interior tiled atrium, where guests must draw curtains for quiet and privacy. Low season rates for all 50 fan-only rooms run about $11 s, $14 d, and $17 t. During the high season, rates rise for the "A" rooms to $13 s, $17 d, and $20 t. Rooms vary, inspect a few before you decide. No TV, phones, or pool available, and credit cards are not accepted.

Head three blocks farther away from the river and back downstream to Av. I. Vallarta (corner Basilio Badillo) to the longtime favorite **Hotel Posada Roger,** Basilio Badillo 237, Puerto Vallarta, Jalisco 48380, tel. (322) 208-36. Although not the budget bargain it once was, the Hotel Posada Roger's three stories of rooms still enclose an inviting vine-decorated courtyard with plenty of quiet nooks for reading and relaxing. The Tucan, the hotel's breakfast cafe (open daily 0800-2000), provides yet another setting for relaxed exchanges with other travelers. A small pool-patio on the roof adds a bit of class to compensate for the increased price of the many drab, cramped, fan-only rooms that Roger offers. The 50 rooms run $22 d low season, $30 high season, three blocks from the beach, with TV and some rooms with a/c; credit cards accepted.

The **Hotel Yasmin,** nearby at Basilio Badillo 168, at Pino Suárez, Puerto Vallarta, Jalisco 48380, tel. (322) 200-87, offers a viable budget-lodging alternative. The Yasmin's main attractions are its two short blocks to the beach, its verdant, plant-festooned inner patio, and the La Olla, a good cafe next door. The three tiers of fan-only rooms are clean, but small and mostly dreary. Inspect before you pay. You can compensate by renting one of the lighter, more secluded sunnyside upper rooms. Rates for all 30 rooms run $17 d low season, $23 high.

Head downhill toward the beach and left around the Av. Olas Altas corner and you are in the popular Olas Altas neighborhood. At the hub of activity is the **Hotel Playa Los Arcos** (middle of the block between Calles Basilio Badillo and M. Dieguez), a best-buy favorite of a generation of savvy American and Canadian winter vacationers. The Playa Los Arcos is the flagship of a triad that includes the nearby **Hotel Fontana del Mar** and the **Hotel Costa Alegre,** whose guests are welcome to enjoy all of the Playa Los Arcos's attractive facilities in exchange for even more reasonable tariffs than the Playa Los Arcos itself.

All three of these hotels have swimming pools and comfortable, tastefully decorated, air-conditioned rooms with TV, phones, and even some mini-refrigerators in the Fontana and Alegre. The mecca, however, is the deluxe Playa Los Arcos, with its palm- and vine-decorated inner pool-patio sundeck, restaurant with salad bar, a live combo every night, and beach chairs in the sand beneath shady palms or golden sun. The Hotel Playa Los Arcos is at Olas Altas 380, Puerto Vallarta, Jalisco 48380, tel. (322) 205-83, 215-83, or from U.S. and Canada toll-free (800) 648-2403, fax 224-18. The 135 rooms rent from about $48 d low season, approximately $57 high season, for standard grade rooms. More spacious, some with ocean views, superior-grade rooms run about $55 d low season, $72 high season, with credit cards accepted.

The Hotel Fontana del Mar is around the corner at M. Dieguez 171, Puerto Vallarta, Jalisco 48380, tel. (322) 207-12, or (800) 648-2403. Its 42 rooms rent from about $32 d low season, about $44 high season; credit cards accepted. A block away is the modest tourist-class Hotel Costa Alegre at Francisco Rodríguez 168, Puerto Vallarta, Jalisco 48380, tel. (322) 247-93, or (800) 648-2403 from the U.S. and Canada. Tariffs for its 30 rooms run about $25 d low season, $33 high; credit cards accepted.

The Hotels Playa Los Arcos, Fontana, and Costa Alegre all accept bookings through travel agents. In all three, two kids under 12 are free when sharing with parents. They often offer long-term discounts, such as during April, May, and June, the fourth night of your stay is free, while during September and October, both the sixth and seventh nights are often free.

Vacationers who require a bit more luxury often pick the Playa Los Arcos's Swiss-managed beachside neighbor, the **Hotel San Marino** at Rudolfo Gómez 111, Puerto Vallarta, Jalisco 48380, tel. (322) 215-55, 230-50, (800) 962-8920 from the U.S. or Canada, fax 224-31. The San Marino's soaring *palapa*-restaurant patio opens to an ocean-view pool and courtyard with a sundeck. Occupants of all of the marble-floored, pastel- and white-decor rooms enjoy city, mountain, or ocean views. The 160 rooms and suites rent for about $55 d low season, about $70 high season; ocean-view suites $70 low season and $87 high season; a/c, radio, phones, and access to the bar and two restaurants.

Farther south on Playa Los Muertos, the Hotel Tropicana and its nearby brother, condo-style Hotel Gloria del Mar, offer ocean-view lodgings at moderate prices. Though the seven-story beachfront **Hotel Gloria del Mar** at Amapas 114, Puerto Vallarta, Jalisco 48380, tel. (322) 251-43, fax 217-67, has no pool or beach facilities, the guests are invited to enjoy all of the Tropicana's facilities. Additionally, Gloria del Mar adds the option of 50 bright kitchenette suites, many with ocean views. For a hill-view suite, expect to pay $24 low season, $29 high; for ocean view, $28 and $34, with a/c, phones, TV, and credit cards accepted. Monthly rates are only available at the brother lodging of the Emperador across the street. (See "Apartments and Condominiums, Río Cuale and South" following.)

The **Hotel Tropicana**, Amapas 214, Puerto Vallarta, Jalisco 48380, tel. (322) 209-12 or 209-52, fax 267-37, although large, is easy to miss, because the beach-level lobby is street-accessible only by an unobtrusive downward staircase. From there the hotel's popular beachfront amenities—pool, sundeck, restaurant, volleyball court, and shady *palapas*—spread all the way to the surf. Upstairs, nearly all of the comfortable rooms enjoy private balconies and ocean vistas. The 160 rooms run about $33 d low season, about $41 high; with a/c, security boxes, and credit cards accepted.

About a block south along Amapas, the breezy, plant-decorated room tiers of **Casa Corazón** spread down their beachfront hillside at Amapas 326, P.O. Box 66, Puerto Vallarta, Jalisco 48300, tel./fax (322) 213-17. Tucked on one of the middle levels, a homey open-air restaurant and adjacent soft-couch lobby with a shelf of used paperbacks invite relaxing, reading, and socializing with fellow guests. No TVs, no ringing phones, or buzzing air-conditioners disturb the tranquility; the people and the natural setting—the adjacent lush garden and the boom and swish of the beach waves—set the tone. The 14 rooms, while not deluxe, are varied and comfortably decorated with tile, brick, and colorful native arts and crafts. Guests in some of the most popular rooms enjoy spacious, sunny beach-view patios. For such amenities, the prices are certainly right: smaller rooms, during high season, run about $25 s, $35 d; larger run $40 and $45. During low season, tariffs drop by about one-third to one-half the high-season rates. You may book directly by contacting either the hotel above, or owner George Tune, P.O. Box 937, Las Cruces, NM 88004, tel. (505) 523-4666, fax 523-4684.

Nearby, on the short beachfront Calle Malecón, stands the neighboring condo-style **Hotel Vallarta Beach**, P.O. Box 329, Puerto Vallarta, Jalisco 48300, tel. (322) 250-40. Aptly named for its location right on popular Los Muertos Beach, the hotel's five stories of attractively furnished, tile and stucco kitchenette apartments offer all the ingredients for a restful beach vacation: queen-size bed, private sea-view balconies, restaurant, and rooftop pool-sundeck with panoramic beach and bay view. During high season, the spacious, one-bedroom apartments rent for $50 s, $55 d, and $65 t. Depending upon occupancy, longer term and low season discounts may be available; with cable TV and a/c, no phones.

The all-inclusive **Hotel Meza del Mar,** Amapas 380, Puerto Vallarta 48300, tel. (322) 248-88, fax 223-08, a block farther south, offers a contrasting alternative. A host of longtime returnees swear by the hotel's food, service, and friendly company of fellow guests, who, during the winter, seem to be divided equally between Americans, and English and French-speaking Canadians. The Meza del Mar's 127 rooms and suites are distributed among two adjacent buildings: the Main Tower, which is a view high-rise overlooking the pool deck, and the Ocean Building, a three-story tier with views right over the beach. Guests in the preferred rooms, most of which are in the Ocean Building, enjoy private balconies and the sound of the waves outside their window. Other guests are quite happy with the expansive ocean view from the top floors of the Main Tower. The hotel rooms, while not super-deluxe, are comfortably furnished in the Mexican style of handcrafted leather furniture. Although all rooms are clean, details, especially in the cheaper rooms, sometimes appear makeshift. If possible, ask for another room if your assignment isn't satisfactory. Rates vary sharply according to season and grade of room, and include all food (not gourmet, but good), drinks, and entertainment in the hotels' restaurants, bars, pools, and beachfront club. Rates, quoted per person double occupancy, for a minimum three-night stay, run from $35/night, low season, for a bare bones no view room to $80/night for a choice view suite. All rooms have a/c, no TV nor phones, and limited wheelchair access. Add $7 per person in lieu of tipping. Book through a travel agent, who in turn must work through the Denver-based wholesaler, Tour Express. From U.S. phones, agents should call (800) 525-1948, from Canada, (800) 338-4850, from Colorado, (800) 332-1197, or from the Denver metropolitan area, (303) 321-0382. The above-quoted rates depend on Tour Express issuing the air tickets. If not, add $18 per person to the minimum first three-night tariff.

Hotels South of Town

Follow the Manzanillo Hwy. 200 (the southward extension of Insurgentes) about a mile south of town and your reward will be the **Hotel Playa Conchas Chinas,** one of Puerto Vallarta's most charming hotels at any price, P.O. Box 346, Puerto Vallarta, Jalisco 48390, tel. (322) 157-63, fax 157-70. The stucco and brick complex rambles down a palm-shaded hillside several levels to an intimate cove on Conchas Chinas beach. Here, a series of intimate sandy crescents nestle between tidepool-dotted sandstone outcroppings. Standard-grade rooms are spacious, decorated in Mexican traditional tile-brick, and furnished in brown wood with kitchenette and tub

bath, most have an ocean view. Superior- and deluxe-grade rooms also include luxurious spas and ocean-view patio-balconies. Very popular, reserve early, especially during high season. Of their 39 rooms, the standard cost $28 d low season, $63 high, while superior and deluxe rooms begin at about $42 d low season, $76 high; with a/c, phones, and the romantic "El Set" sunset restaurant; no pool or elevator, credit cards accepted. They often offer discounts, such as one day free for a four-day stay or two days free for a one-week stay.

Another mile south, you can enjoy the extravagant isolation of the **Hotel Camino Real** (formerly Westin Camino Real), P.O. Box 95, Playa de las Estacas, Puerto Vallarta, Jalisco 48300, tel. (322) 150-00, (800) 7-CAMINO from the U.S. and Canada, fax 160-00, at correspondingly extravagant prices. Puerto Vallarta's first world-class hotel, the Camino Real has aged gracefully. Luxuriously set in a lush tropical valley, its polished wooden walkways still shine, and its walkways still wind along a beachside garden intermingled with blue swimming pools. A totally self-contained resort on a secluded, sometimes seasonally narrow, strip of golden-white sand, the twin-towered Camino Real offers everything—luxury view rooms, all water sports, restaurants, bars, and live music every night. The 250 rooms of the "Main" tower begin at about $150 d low season, $200 high, while the 150 jacuzzi-equipped rooms of the "Royal Beach Club" tower go for about $240 d high season, with everything, including wheelchair access.

On the other hand, folks who prefer activity over serenity, the all inclusive **Holiday Inn** another mile south may be the right choice for a hassle-free tropical vacation. Find it at Km 4, Carretera a Barra de Navidad, P.O. Box 385, Puerto Vallarta, Jalisco 48300, tel. (322) 155-15, (800) 465-4329 in the U.S. and Canada, fax 151-05. Although the hotel's tower rises like a giant space-age beehive sandwiched between the highway and the sea, the beach-level pool deck reveals an entirely different scene: Platoons of guests—reclining, socializing, snoozing, frolicking, and eating—enjoy at no extra charge the hotel's generous menu of activities. These vary from paddleboard, Ping-Pong, scuba lessons, and exercise machines for the athletic, to Spanish lessons, bingo, and pool-soaking in the airy solarium spa for the more sedentary. With so much going on, the hotel beach hardly seems necessary for an enjoyable week in the sun. A luxurious room with private sea-view balcony with cable TV, a/c, and phone, runs about $120 s and $150 d low season, $150 s, $200 d high, with all food, drinks, and activities included. Big discounts for kids 12 and under.

Hotels North of the Río Cuale

Hotels generally get more luxurious and expensive the farther north of the Río Cuale you look. Most of the central part of town, which stretches for a mile along the *malecón*, has no good beach and is too noisy and congested for comfortable lodgings.

A notable exception, however, is the **Hotel Los Cuatro Vientos,** Matamoros 520, P.O. Box 520, Puerto Vallarta, Jalisco 48300, tel. (322) 201-61, fax 228-31, perched in the quiet, picturesque hillside neighborhood above and behind the main town church. The 16 rooms and suites are tucked in tiers above a flowery, colonial-style patio and the restaurant Chez Elena (see "Food" below), beneath a rooftop panoramic view bar-sundeck. The fan-only units are simply but attractively decorated in colonial style, with tile, brick, and traditional furniture and crafts. High-season (excluding 15 Dec.-5 Jan.) room rates run about $39 d, suites for four about $61, continental breakfast included; a small pool is available, and credit cards are accepted.

Around the north end of the *malecón,* where the good beach resumes at Playa Camarones, so do the hotels. They continue, dotting the tranquil, golden strands of Playa Las Glorias, Playa Los Tules, and Playa de Oro. On these beaches are the plush hotels (actually, self-contained resorts) from which you must have wheels to escape to the shopping, restaurants, and the piquant sights and sounds of old Puerto Vallarta.

At the north end of the *malecón* (at 31 de Octubre) stands one of Puerto Vallarta's popular old mainstays, the friendly, beachfront **Hotel Rosita,** Díaz Ordaz 901, P.O. Box 32, Puerto Vallarta, Jalisco 48300, tel. (322) 210-33, fax 221-71. The Rosita centers on a grassy, palm-shadowed ocean-view pool-patio and restaurant, with plenty of space for relaxing and socializing. About half of the spacious rooms, of *típica* Mexican tile and white-stucco and wood,

look down upon the tranquil patio scene, while others, to be avoided if possible, border the noisy, smoggy main street. An unfortunate wire security fence mars the ocean view from the patio. Egress to the beach, **Playa Camarón,** is through a side door. The Rosita's 90 rooms range from about $23-31 d low season, $27-38 high season, including security boxes and a bar; credit cards accepted. Rooms are equipped with either fans or a/c.

The **Hotel Buenaventura,** Av. México 1301, P.O. Box 8B, Puerto Vallarta, Jalisco 48350, tel. (322) 237-37, on the beach several blocks farther north (between Calles San Salvador and Nicaragua, where the airport boulevard becomes cobblestone), is one of Puerto Vallarta's few close-in deluxe hotels. The lobby rises to an airy wood-beamed atrium then opens toward the beach through a jungle walkway festooned with giant hanging leafy philodendrons and exotic palms. At the beachfront Los Tucanes Beach Club, a wide, palm-silhouetted pool-patio borders a line of shade *palapas* along the whitish-yellow sand beach. Most of the small rooms, decorated in wood, tile, and earth-tone drapes and bedspreads, open to small, private ocean-facing balconies. The 206 rooms go for about $47 d low season, $78 high; with a/c, phones, restaurant, bar, live music nightly in season, and credit cards accepted.

Zona Hotelera Luxury Hotels

Puerto Vallarta's plush hostelries vary widely, and higher tariffs do not guarantee quality. Nevertheless, some of Pacific Mexico's best-buy luxury gems glitter among the twenty-odd hotels lining Puerto Vallarta's north-end Zona Hotelera beaches. The prices listed are "rack rates"—the highest prices paid by walk-in customers. Much cheaper—as much as 50% discount—airfare-lodging packages are often available, especially during low seasons, which are January, May-July, and Sept.-November. Get yourself a good buy by shopping around among travel agents several weeks before departure.

Heading north, the **Hotel Continental Plaza,** Av. de Ingreso Km 2.5, Zona Hotelera, Plaza Las Glorias, Puerto Vallarta, Jalisco 48300, tel. (322) 401-23, (800) 88-CONTI from the U.S. and Canada, fax 452-36, buzzes all day with activities: tennis in the eight-court John Newcombe Tennis Club, aerobics, water polo and volleyball in the big pool, and parasailing, jet-skiing, and windsurfing from the golden Playa Las Glorias beach. Happy hours brighten every afternoon, and live music fills every balmy evening. The luxurious but not large rooms, decorated in soothing pastels, open to balconies overlooking the broad, palmy patio. The Continental Plaza's 434 room tariffs run about $105 d low season, $135 high; with a/c, all sports, restaurants, bars, sauna, jacuzzi, exercise room, wheelchair access, and parking.

The **Hotel Plaza Las Glorias,** Plaza Las Glorias s/n, Puerto Vallarta, Jalisco 48300, tel. (322) 444-44 or (800) 342-AMIGO in the U.S. and Canada, fax 564-59, next door is as Mexican and relaxed as the Continental Plaza is *norteamericano* and busy. At Plaza Las Glorias, a blue swimming pool meanders beneath a manicured patio-grove of rustling palms. The rooms, behind the Spanish-style stucco, brick, and tile facade, overlook the patio and ocean from small view balconies. Inside, the luxurious rooms are tile-floored, in dark wood, white stucco, and blue and pastels. The 237 rooms rent for about $80 d low season, $120 high. The hotel's "villa" section is just as deluxe but has no ocean view and offers studios with kitchenette for about $100 d high season, with discounts for longer stays. All rooms have a/c, cable TV, phone, two pools, bars, restaurants, use of tennis courts next door at John Newcombe Tennis Club, access to beach sports, parking, and wheelchair access. Credit cards are accepted.

The Best Western affiliate, **Hotel Las Palmas,** Av. de Ingreso, Km 2.5, Puerto Vallarta, Jalisco 48300, tel. (322) 406-50, 444-06, or (800) 995-8584 in the U.S. and Canada, fax 405-43, a quarter-mile farther north, is an older, scaled-down, less luxurious version of the Plaza Las Glorias. An airy, rustic *palapa* shelters the lobby, which continues to a palm-adorned beachside pool-patio. Here, on the wide, sparkling Playa Las Glorias, opportunities for aquatic sports are at their best, with the Silent World Diving Center located right on the beachfront. The 114 rooms, most with private ocean-view balconies, are comfortable, but not deluxe. Rates run about $57 d low season, $85 high. Rooms have a/c, phones, TV, restaurant, snack bar, bars, pool, parking; credit cards are accepted.

The **Hotel Fiesta Americana Puerto Vallarta,** P.O. Box 270, Puerto Vallarto, Jalisco 48300, tel. (322) 420-10, or (800) 223-2332 from the U.S. and Canada, fax 421-08, another quarter-mile north, is, for many, the best hotel in town. The lobby-*palapa,* the world's largest, is an attraction unto itself. Its 10-story palm-thatch chimney draws air upward, creating a continuously cool breeze through the open-air reception. Outside, the high-rise rampart of ocean-view rooms overlooks a pool and garden of earthly delights, complete with a gushing pool fountain, water volleyball, swim-up bar, and in-pool recliners. Beyond spreads a 150-foot-wide strip of wave-washed yellow sand. The 291 super-deluxe view rooms sometimes go for as low as $90 d low season, rising to $170 during the high, with a/c, TV, phones, all sports, three restaurants, huge pool, three bars, disco, wheelchair access, and parking.

Next door, the **Hotel Qualton Club and Spa,** Km 2.5, Av. de las Palmas s/n, Puerto Vallarta, Jalisco 48300, tel. (322) 444-46, or (800) 421-2134 from the U.S. and Canada, fax 444-45, offers an attractive all-inclusive option for vacationers who enjoy lots of food, fun, and company. On a typical day, hundreds of fellow sunbathing guests line the rather cramped poolside, while, a few steps away, dozens more relax beneath shady beachfront *palapas.* Nights glow with beach buffet theme dinners—Italian, Mexican, Chinese, and more—for hundreds, followed by shows where guests often become part of the entertainment. The list goes on—continuous food, open bars, complete gym and spa, tennis by night or day, scuba lessons, volleyball, water sports, free discos, golf privileges, stress therapy, yoga, aerobics galore—all included at no extra charge. If you want relief from the hubbub, you can always escape to the greener, more spacious Fiesta Americana poolside next door. The Qualton Club's 320 rooms, all with private view balconies, are luxuriously decorated in pastels and include a/c, cable TV, and phone. All-inclusive low-season rates run around $73 per person, double occupancy, about $100 high season, with wheelchair access; credit cards accepted.

Another half-mile north, the **Hotel Krystal,** Av. de las Garzas s/n, Puerto Vallarta, Jalisco 48300, tel. (322) 402-02, or (800) 231-9860 from the U.S. or Canada, fax 401-11, is more than a hotel, it's a palm manicured resort-village, exactly what a Mexican Walt Disney would have built. The Krystal is one of the few Puerto Vallarta ultra-luxury resorts designed by and for Mexicans. Scores of deluxe garden bungalows, opening onto private pool-patios, are spread over its 34 beachside acres. A Porfirian bandstand stands proudly at the center, while nearby a colonial-style aqueduct gushes water into a pool at the edge of a serene spacious palm-shaded park. Guests who prefer a more lively environment can have it. Dancing goes on every night in the lobby or beside the huge, meandering beachside pool, where the music is anything but serene. The Krystal's 460 rooms and suites rent from about $100 d low season, $165 high; with a/c, phones, TV, 44 pools—no joke—six restaurants, all sports, including donkey polo.

Next door to the north, the colonial-style **Hotel Hacienda Buenaventura**, Paseo de la Marina, P.O. Box 05B, Puerto Vallarta, Jalisco 48310, tel. (322) 466-67, fax 464-00, offers a load of luxurious amenities at very reasonable rates (for reservations, call a travel agent or 800-223-6764 from the U.S. or Canada, or 800-663-3141 from Canada). Its 150 low-rise room tiers enfold a quiet patio-garden, graced by a blue free-form pool and a slender, rustic *palapa*. On one side, water spills from an antique aqueduct, while guests linger at the adjacent airy restaurant. The rooms are spacious, with high, hand-hewn beam ceilings, marble floors, and rustic-chic tile and brick baths. The only drawback to all this is guests must walk a couple of easy blocks to the beach, where their hotel pass entitles them to enjoy the luxurious beachside facilities of the Hotel Krystal. Rates run around $48 d low season, $60 d high, with a/c, phones, cable TV, some wheelchair access, and credit cards accepted.

Apartments and Condominiums, Río Cuale and South

Puerto Vallarta abounds with apartments and condominiums, mostly available for rentals of more than two weeks. Although a number of reliable stateside agencies (see "Apartments, Condominiums, and Villas" under "Accommodations" in the On the Road chapter) specialize in the more luxurious rentals scattered all over the city,

the best-buy Puerto Vallarta apartments and condos are concentrated in the colorful Olas Altas-Conchas Chinas southside district and are available only through local managers or owners. The following list, by location, moving south from the Río Cuale, includes some of the better Olas Altas apartments and condominiums.

The **Condominios Plaza Dorada**, Olas Altas 246, southwest corner of Basilio Badillo, at the corner of Plaza Lázaro Cárdenas, contains fifty spacious apartments in a six-story beachside complex on Playa Los Muertos. Although the furnished units vary, they're generally homey and very comfortable, many including elegant wall art, overstuffed couches, and luxurious king-size beds. All floors are of creamy-tinted handmade tiles, and bathrooms are embellished by handpainted highlights and hugo bathtubs. Services include hotel-like desk clerk, maid cleaning every other day, and a sunny beachfront pool patio adjacent to a good downstairs restaurant. While all of the units have private balconies, guests in the most desirable beachfront units enjoy lovely beach and ocean views. One- and two-bedroom units are available starting at $1000 per month low season, about $1500 high season. Reserve many months in advance for the best units in the winter season. Contact the administrators, José Carlos Tapia G., or Guillermo Villa at Condominios Plaza Dorada, Olas Altas 246, Puerto Vallarta, Jalisco 48300, tel. (322) 306-53.

Walk south three short blocks along Olas Altas and a few steps uphill along Francisca Rodríguez to the **Casa María Elena**, one of three complexes conscientiously managed by articulate, English-speaking María Elena Zermeño Santana. Located at Francisca Rodríguez 163, Puerto Vallarta, Jalisco 48380, tel. (322) 201-13, fax 210-47. The eight attractive fan-only brick-and-tile units stand in a four-story stack on a quiet, cobbled side street just a block and a half from the beach. The immaculate, light and spacious units have living room, bedroom, and modern kitchenettes and are all comfortably decorated with local crafts chosen by María Elena (who owns a nearby crafts store) herself. Daily cleaning service is included, although the units have neither swimming pool, TV, nor phones. High season rates per apartment run about $50/day, $45/day when rented by the week, and $30/day when rented by the month. Corresponding low-season (May-Nov.) rates are about $40, $35, and $25. An additional discount of up to 10% is sometimes negotiable for rentals of three or more months.

Guests in all three of María Elena's complexes (the others are Villas Safari and Condohotel Bahía, see below) enjoy the option of three weekly hours of free **Spanish lessons** taught by María Elena herself.

Uphill along Francisca Rodríguez it is one block to a gargantuan tree spreading over the entry driveway to **Villas Safari**, a 16-unit apartment-cottage complex that rambles over a secluded hilltop garden-park. Find it at Francisca Rodríguez 203, P.O. Box 203, Puerto Vallarta, Jalisco 48380, tel./fax (322) 210-47. The apartments, of stone, brick, and stucco, are clean and comfortably appointed with Mexican crafts and furniture and equipped with modern kitchenettes. The units, mostly one-bedroom, but with some two-bedrooms, are generally light and spacious. Most have living rooms opening to semi-private plant-decorated patios, ideal for reading and relaxing. The cottages surround a panoramic city view patio occupied by a large (but now defunct) restaurant *palapa* and swimming pool. Rates for all apartments run the same—either about $60 nightly, 10% discount for weekly, or around $800 per month for two persons, $900 for four. Although daily cleaning service is included, apartments have neither TV, phones, nor swimming pool. An added plus is free Spanish lessons by the general manager, María Elena Zermeño Santana at the Casa María Elena (see above). Since all units are at ground level, a number of them are wheelchair-accessible. Reserve either directly or through general manager María Elena.

Three blocks closer to the beach downhill and a block north on Amapas the **Emperador** offers monthly apartment rentals at very reasonable prices. The plainly furnished but clean and comfortable kitchenette studios and one bedrooms run about $450 low season, $600 high; with phones, a/c, and credit cards accepted. Emperador guests enjoy use of the extensive beach club and pool facilities of the Hotel Tropicana one block south on Amapas. Reserve through the Hotel Gloria del Mar located across the street at Amapas 114, Puer-to Vallarta, Jalisco 48380, tel. (322) 251-43, fax 217-47.

A block and a half farther south, on the uphill side of Amapas from the Hotel Tropicana, the **Condohotel Bahía** apartments stairstep upward through a shady banana, palm and fern garden at Amapas 299, P.O. Box 150, Puerto Vallarta, Jalisco 48380, tel. (322) 237-40. The 13 units are clean, bright, and equipped with modern kitchenettes and shower baths, and charmingly adorned by brick, tile, wood-beamed ceilings, and colored bottle-bottoms in the walls. Tiles, painted with names such as "Mi Castillo" and "Mi Rinconcito," decorate the door-fronts. While guests in nearly all the units enjoy ocean vistas, some have the added plus of spacious sundeck or balcony. Studios rent for $25-35 nightly, 10% discount for weekly, or $550-600 monthly. One bedrooms go for $50-60 nightly, 10% discount for weekly, and $700-800 monthly. Guests enjoy the option of free Spanish lessons by general manager María Elena Zermeño Santana. Reserve either directly or through her at the Casa María Elena (see above).

Just next door, the path to the 63-unit condo-style **Hotel Brisas del Mar** snakes uphill through its view restaurant, across its expansive pool-deck to the big white main building perched a short block below the highway. Located at Privada Abedul 10, Puerto Vallarta, Jalisco 48300, tel. (322) 218-00 or 218-21. If this place weren't such a climb (although aerobicists might consider it a plus) from the beach, the builders would have sold all the units long ago. Now, however, it's owned and operated by the downhill Hotel Tropicana, whose attractive beachside facilities Brisas del Mar guests are invited to enjoy. The Brisas del Mar itself is quite comfortable, with light, comfortable, kitchenette suites with private view balconies. Most units are one-bedroom, with either one king-size bed or a double and twin combination. Rates run from about $37/night or $550/month low season to $44 and $670 high season, with a/c, pool, desk service, restaurant, limited wheelchair access, and credit cards accepted. Book either directly or through a travel agent. Get there either by car or taxi from the highway, or by climbing from Amapas through the doorway at no. 307, labeled both "Casa del Tigre" and restaurant "Sevilla."

Back down on Amapas, a half-block farther south, the ten white designer units of the **Condominios Villa Blanca**, Amapas 349, Puerto Vallarta, Jalisco 48300, tel./fax (322) 261-90, stairstep artfully above the street. These are light, attractive luxury apartments, rented out for the owners by the friendly manager Jose Luis Alvarez, whose office is at the streetfront. While the apartments vary from studios to two bedrooms, they all have ocean views, modern kitchenettes, and rustic decorator vine-entwined palm trunks adorning the doors and walls. The best apartments occupy the upper levels; the least desirable are the pair of apartments at the bottom, where a pump buzzes continuously near the complex's small soaking pool. All rentals are by the month only. Studios rent for about $1100, one-bedrooms, $1375, and two-bedrooms, about $2000, all with a/c.

Trailer Parks and Camping
Puerto Vallarta visitors can enjoy two good trailer parks, both of them owned and managed by the same family. The small, palm-shaded **Puerto Vallarta Trailer Park**, Francia 143, Puerto Vallarta, Jalisco 48300, tel. (322) 428-28, is two blocks off the highway at Francia at Lucerna, a few blocks north of the *libramiento* downtown bypass fork. Their 65 spaces four blocks from beach rent for $10 per day, with one free day per week, one free week per month; with all hookups, including showers, toilets, long-distance phone access, laundromat, pets okay. Luxury hotel pools and restaurants are nearby.

Much more spacious **Tacho's Trailer Park** is half a mile from Hwy. 200 on Av. Aramara, the road that branches inland across the airport highway from the cruise ship dock, and offers a large grassy yard, with some palms, bananas, and other trees for shade. Reach them at P.O. Box 315, Puerto Vallarta, Jalisco 48300, tel. (322) 421-63. Tacho's 100 spaces run $11/day (one free week on a monthly rental), including all hookups and use of showers, toilets, laundry room, pool and *palapa*, and shuffleboard courts. Pads are paved and pets are okay.

Other than the trailer parks, Puerto Vallarta has precious few campsites within the city limits. Plenty of camping possibilities exist outside the city, however. Especially inviting are the pearly little beaches, such as Las Animas, Quimixto,

Caballo, and others that dot the verdant, wild coastline between Boca de Tomatlán and Yelapa. *Colectivo* water taxis regularly head for these beaches for about $3.50 per person from Boca de Tomatlán (see "Beaches" above). Local stores at Quimixto, Las Animas, and Boca de Tomatlán can provide water (bring water purification tablets or filter) and basic supplies. (For more camping possibilities, see "Around the Bay of Banderas" following.)

FOOD

Puerto Vallarta is brimming with good food. Dieters beware: "light" or "nouveau" cuisine, tasty vegetables, and bountiful salads are the exception, as in all Mexico. In the winter, when the sun-hungry vacationers crowd in, a table at even an average restaurant may require a reservation. During the low season, however, Puerto Vallarta's best eateries are easy to spot. They are the ones with the customers.

Stalls, Snacks, and Breakfast
Good Puerto Vallarta eating is not limited to sit-down restaurants. Many foodstalls offer wholesome, inexpensive snacks to hosts of loyal repeat customers. It's hard to go wrong with hot, prepared-on-the-spot food. Each stand specializes in one type of fare—seafood, *tortas*, tacos, hot dogs—and occupies the same location daily. For example, a number of them concentrate along **Avs. Consitución and Pino Suárez** just south of the River Cuale; several others cluster on the side-street corners of **Av. Olas Altas** a few blocks away.

A number of such foodstalls have graduated to storefronts. **Rickey's Tamales**, at 325 Basilio Badillo, capitalizes on the general Mexican belief that tamales (like Chinese food and pizza in the U.S.) are hard to make and must be bought, take-out style. Big rolls of husk-wrapped, lime-soaked cornmeal are stuffed with beef, chicken, or pork, and baked; three for $2. Open Mon.-Sat. 1800-2200.

If you're lusting for a late-night snack, walk a few doors west toward the beach to either **Cenaduría La Jolla**, open nightly 1800-2400, for great *pozole* or neighboring **Armando's**, open Mon.-Sat. 1900-0300, for a dozen styles of succulent tacos.

An exceptionally well located late-night taco stand is **El Gallo** at the night-club crossroads of Avs. I. Vallarta and Lázaro Cárdenas across from Mariachis Locos. Start with steaming *tacos al pastor* (bean, chicken, or beef, two for a dollar) and end with a fat enchilada or chile relleno, all of which you may smother in any of several delectable sauces. Open nightly to around 0200.

Other tasty late-night options are available at many of the eateries along main street Av. Insurgentes, just south of the upstream Río Cuale bridge. For example, drop into the no-name *jugería* a few doors from the Cine Bahía. Try one of their luscious *tortas de pierna,* roast leg of pork smothered in avocado on a bun, $1.75. Top it off with a banana *liquado,* with a touch of *(un poquito de)* chocolate. It's located at Insurgentes 153 and open daily 0700-2400.

Similar is **Tuti Fruti,** a good spot for a refreshing snack, especially while sightseeing or shopping around the *malecón.* Find it at the corner of Morelos and Corona, one block from the *malecón;* open Mon.-Sat. 0800-2300. You could even eat breakfast, lunch, and dinner there, starting with juice and granola or eggs in the morning, a *torta* and a *liquado* during the afternoon, and a *hamburguesa* for an evening snack.

Some of the most colorful, untouristed places to eat in town are, paradoxically, at the tourist-mecca **Mercado Municipal** on the Río Cuale, at the Av. Insurgentes (upstream) bridge. The *fondas* tucked on the upstairs floor (climb the streetside staircase) specialize in steaming, homestyle soups, fish, meat, tacos, *moles,* and chiles rellenos. Point out your order to the cook and take a seat at their cool, river-view seating area. Open daily 0700-1800.

For breakfast, **La Casa de Los Hot Cakes and Diner,** skillfully orchestrated by personable owner Memo Barroso, has become a Puerto Vallarta institution at Basilio Badillo 289, between I. Vallarta and Constitución, tel. 262-72. Breakfast served Tues.-Sun. 0800-1400. Besides bountiful Mexican and North American style breakfasts—orange juice or fruit, eggs, toast, and hash browns for about $4—Memo offers an indulgent list of pancakes. Try his nut-topped, peanut butter-filled "O. Henry" chocolate pancakes, for example. Add his bottomless cup of coffee and you'll be buzzing all day. For lighter eaters, vegetarian and less indulgent options are available.

Another good spot for breakfast served 0700-1130 is the sunny beachfront terrace of the **Hotel Playa Los Arcos** restaurant at 380 Olas Altas. Here the ambience—tour boats arriving and leaving, the passing sidewalk scene, the swishing waves, the swaying palms—is half the fun. The other half is the food, either a hearty $7 buffet, or a briskly served a la carte choice of your heart's desire, from fruit and oatmeal to eggs, bacon, and hash browns.

Coffeehouses

Good coffee has arrived at Puerto Vallarta, where some cafes now roast from their own private sources of beans. Just a block from Los Muertos Beach, coffee and book lovers get the best of both worlds at **Page In The Sun,** corner Olas Altas and M. Dieguez, diagonally across from Hotel Playa Olas Altas. There, longtimers sip coffee and play chess while others enjoy their pick of lattes, cappuccinos, ice cream, muffins, and walls of used paperbacks and magazines. Open daily 0800-2100.

If, on the other hand, you're on the other side of the river near the *malecón* shopping-entertainment district, it will be difficult *not* to miss the perfume of roasting coffee from **Cafe San Cristobal** at Corona 172, a block and a half uphill from the *malecón.* Friendly co-owner Diana Turn retired from her Dallas, Texas, travel agency to find that good coffee, despite excellent local sources, was hard to get in Puerto Vallarta. Now, she and her partners roast the best of Chiapas, Oaxaca, Veracruz, and Nayarit coffees, which they serve, along with juices, fruits, cheese, bread, quiche, and desserts. Open Mon.-Sat. 0800-2200.

Restaurants: Río Cuale and South

Complete dinner price key: Budget: under $7; Moderate: $7-14; Expensive: more than $14.

Archie's Wok, Francisca Rodríguez 130, between Av. Olas Altas and the beach, tel. (322) 204-11, is the founding member of a miniature "gourmet ghetto" that is flourishing in the Olas Altas neighborhood. The owner, now deceased, was John Huston's longtime friend and personal chef. However, Cindy his wife carries on the culinary mission. A large local following swears by Archie's menu of vegetables, fish, meat, and noodles. Favorites include Thai Coconut Fish,

Barbecued Ribs Hoi Sin, and Spicy Fried Thai Noodles. Make up a party of three or four, and each order your favorite. Arrive early; there's usually a line by 1930 for dinner. Open Mon.-Sat. 1400-2300; Visa accepted. Moderate to expensive.

Right next door to Archie's spread the inviting outdoor tables of **Restaurant Santos,** Francisca Rodríguez 136, tel. (322) 256-70. The all-fresh, carefully prepared salads and entrees, such as leg of pork, spaghetti al pesto, and whole broiled fish, together with a carefully chosen wine selection (try the excellent Baja California Cetto-label varietals) reflect Santos's graceful continental ambience. Open daily 1600-2400; credit cards accepted. Moderate to expensive.

Another of Olas Altas's low-profile gourmet gems, the **da Franco** Italian restaurant, Centro Comercial Costa Alegre 16, at Olas Altas and R. Gómez, next to the Hotel San Marino, tel. (322) 246-65, lies tucked away in the little shopping square behind Santos and Archie's. The Brindisi-born owner-chef personally directs preparation of every dish, old-country style. His favorites are Lobster Franco, Shrimp de Mancuso, and Filete Rossini. For an extra treat, leave room for his melt-in-your-mouth apple strudel. Open daily 1600-2300 except Sunday; credit cards accepted. Moderate to Expensive.

Just across the street, **Karpathos Taverna,** R. Gomez 110, has acquired a considerable local following by creating a little corner of Greece here in Puerto Vallarta. Although the ambience comes, in part, from very correct service and the Greek folk melodies emanating from the sound system, the food—genuine Greek olives, feta cheese, rolled grape leaves, savory moussaka, spicy layered eggplant, piquant roast lamb, garlic-rubbed fish with olive oil—seem a small miracle here, half a world from the source. Open daily 0900-2400. Moderate to expensive.

Mexican food is well represented by a trio of good south-of-Cuale restaurants. Restaurant **Tres Huastecas'** charming, pure-blooded Huastec owner calls himself "El Querreque," while others call him the "Troubador of Puerto Vallarta." His poetry, together with sentimental Mexican country scenes, covers the walls, while everything from soft-boiled eggs and toast to frog legs and enchiladas Huastecas fills the tables. Find it at Olas Altas, corner of F. Rodríguez, no phone; open daily 0800-2000. Moderate.

Nearby, the **Cafe de Olla,** B. Badillo 168, a few doors uphill from the Olas Altas corner, draws flocks of evening customers with its bountiful plates of scrumptious local delicacies. They serve Mexican food the way it's supposed to be, starting with enough salsa and *totopes* (chips) to make appetizers irrelevant. Your choice comes next—either chicken, ribs, and steaks from their streetfront grill—or the savory *antojitos* platters piled with either tacos, tostadas, chiles rellenos, or enchiladas by themselves, or all together in their unbeatable *plato Mexicano.* Prepare by skipping lunch and arriving for an early dinner to give your tummy time to digest it all before bed. Open daily 0800-2300. Budget to moderate.

Los Arbolitos, Camino Rivera 184, bear right at the upper end of Av. Lázaro Cárdenas, way upstream along the River Cuale, remains very popular, despite its untouristed location. Here, home-style Mexican specialties reign supreme. The house pride and joy is the Mexican plate, although they serve dozens of other Mexican and international favorites. Colorful decor, second-floor river-view location, and attentive service spell plenty of satisfied customers. Open daily 0800-2300. Moderate.

As Archie's Wok did in the Olas Altas neighborhood years ago, Memo Barroso's Casa de Hotcakes has sparked a small restaurant and cafe renaissance on upper Basilio Badillo (the block between I. Vallarta and Constitución), now so popular it's becoming known as the "Calle de Cafes." Memo responded to the trend he started by adding "Diner" to the name of his breakfast restaurant and opening for dinner with a reasonably priced, tempting menu of all-American specialties, such as meat loaf, baked fish, chicken, and pasta. Casa de Los Hot Cakes and Diner is located at Basilio Badillo 289, tel. (322) 262-72; open Tues.-Sun. 0800-1400 and 1800-2300.

Some evening when you're lusting for seafood, cross the street from Memo's place and visit **Restaurant Puerto Nuevo,** Basilio Badillo 284, tel. (322) 262-10, for an no-nonsense gourmet's gourmet seafood dinner. Completely without pretention, owner-chef Roberto Castellon brings in the customers with his ingeniously varied list of specialties. For a real party for four, try his guaranteed bottomless seafood special, served course by course, including clams, oysters, lobster, scallops, and red snapper-stuffed chiles rellenos thrown in for good measure. For dessert, he recommends either his Kahlúa cheesecake or fried ice cream. (What?) Open daily, 1200-2300, credit cards accepted. Moderate to expensive.

Two doors uphill, step into the **Cafe Adobe,** Basilio Badillo 300, corner of Constitución, tel. (322) 267-20, and escape from the colorful but insistent Puerto Vallarta street-bustle into the Adobe's cool, refined American Southwest ambience. You'll enjoy soft music, flowers, and white table linens while you make your choice from a short but tasty menu of soups, fettuccine, poultry, seafood, and meats. Open Wed.-Mon. 1700-2300; reservations recommended. Expensive.

Noisy, smoky bus traffic mars daytime dining at Av. Basilio Badillo sidewalk cafes. Fortunately, this is not true in the evening or any time at both Cafe Adobe and Casa de Los Hot Cakes and Diner as both have inside seating.

For ambience, the showplace **Le Bistro** is tops, at Isla Río Cuale 16A, just upstream from the Av. Insurgentes bridge, tel. (322) 202-83. The river gurgles past outdoor tables, plants festoon the greenhouse roof, a tree trunk twists upward into a leafy tree canopy, while jazz CDs play so realistically that you look in vain for the combo. All this creates the impression of life at the bottom of some fantastic, giant, show-biz terrarium. Dieters, furthermore, encounter serious dilemmas at Le Bistro. Many of this short menu of intriguingly labeled and skillfully served entrees, such as Steak Lena, Brubeck Brochette, and Mignon Ellington, come with gobs of cheese, butter, or cream. Open Mon.-Sat. 0900-2330; reservations recommended. Expensive.

Your stay in Puerto Vallarta would not be complete without sunset cocktails and dinner beneath the stars at one of the Puerto Vallarta's south-of-Cuale hillside view restaurants. Of these, **Señor Chico's,** Pulpito 377, tel. (322) 235-70, remains a longtime favorite, despite its so-so tasting, but nicely presented food. The atmosphere—soft guitar solos, flickering can-

dlelight, pastel-pink tableclothes, balmy night air, and the twinkling lights of the city below—is memorable. Open daily 1700-2300; reservations recommended. Expensive. For how to get there, see below.

Another equally romantic option is nearby **Restaurant El Palomar,** a luxurious family villa, which they operate as a restaurant by night at Aguacate 425, tel. (322) 207-95. Here, again, the atmosphere—a tranquil pool and garden above a panoramic city and sunset view—is the main course. Entrees, nevertheless, are served with delicious sauces, with plenty of good vegies and rice tucked around the edges. Service, which includes serapes draped over guests' shoulders during the cooler winter evenings, is crisp and friendly. Open 1800-2300 nightly; reservations recommended. Expensive.

Get to both Señor Chico's and El Palomar by turning left at Pulpito, the first left turn possible uphill past the gasoline station as you head south on Hwy. 200 out of town. After about two winding blocks, you'll see Sr. Chico's as the street climaxes atop a rise; continue down the other side a block, turn left at Aguacate and continue half a block to El Palomar on the right at the dead-end.

Restaurants North of Río Cuale

Chef Roger, arguably the best restaurant in Puerto Vallarta, is among the least visible at Av. Agustín Rodríguez, between Hidalgo and Juárez, one block downstream from the Río Cuale Market, tel. (322) 259-00. A legion of satisfied customers, however, is the Swiss owner-chef's best advertisement. Heated dinner plates, chilled beer and white wine glasses, candlelight, etchings hung on pastel stucco walls, guitars strumming softly, and an eclectic list of exquisitely executed continental dinner entrees keep the faithful coming year-round. Open Mon.-Sat. 1830-2300; reservations mandatory. Expensive.

With its air-conditioned restaurant section glass-partitioned from its airy concert-bar, **Restaurant Brazz,** Morelos 518, at the bend in the *malecón* at Galeana, tel. (322) 203-24, offers something for everyone. During the high winter season, they are usually open for lunch (good sandwich plates); during the low season it is dinner only, specializing in steaks and seafood. After dinner, guests often stay to enjoy the live mariachi concerts 2100-2300 nightly. Open daily. Moderate to expensive.

Within the bustle of the *malecón* restaurant row stands the longtime favorite **Las Palomas,** *malecón* at Aldama. Soothing suppertime live marimba music and graceful colonial decor, all beneath a towering big-beamed ceiling, affords a restful contrast from the sidewalk hubbub just outside the door. Both the breakfasts and the lunch and dinner entrees (nearly all Mexican style) are tasty and bountiful. Open daily 0800-2400. Moderate.

A couple of blocks away, **Papaya 3,** Abasolo 169, a block and a half uphill from the Hard Rock Cafe, tel. (322) 203-03, has achieved success with a dazzlingly varied repertoire for Puerto Vallarta's growing oodro of hoalth oonooioue visitors and locals. Their list begins with dozens of creamy tropical fruit *liquados*, which they call "shakes," but which contain no ice cream, and oontinuoo through a host of salads, pastas, omelettes, sandwiches, Mexican specialties, and chicken and fish plates. The atmoophoro, augmented with plants and soft music, is refined but relaxed. Moderate.

If, however, you hanker for home-cooked Italian food, stop by **Rito's Baci,** the labor of love of the sometimes taciturn, but warmhearted owner-chef, who stays open seven days a week because his "customers would be disappointed if I closed." His establishment, as plain as Kansas in July, requires no atmosphere other than Rito himself, a member of the Mexican football league hall of fame, to be successful. All of his hearty specialties, from the pestos through the pastas and the eggplant Parmesan, are handmade from traditional family recipes. Rito's Baci is located on the corner of Juárez and Ortíz de Dominguez. Open Mon.-Sat. 0800-2200. Moderate.

A choice pair of romantic hillside restaurants concludes the list of north-of-Cuale dining options. Highest on the hill is the longtime favorite **Restaurant Chez Elena,** Matamoros 520, tel. (322) 201-61, on a quiet side street a few blocks above and north of the downtown church. Soft live guitar music and flickering candlelight in a colonial garden terrace set the tone, while a brief but solid Mexican-international menu, augmented by an innovative list of daily specialties,

provides the food. On a typical evening, you might be able to choose between entrees such as *cochinita pibil* (Yucatecan-style shredded pork in sauce), banana leaf-wrapped Oaxacan tamales, or dorado fillet with cilantro in white sauce. Chez Elena guests often arrive early for sunset cocktails at the rooftop panoramic view bar, then continue with dinner downstairs. Open nightly 1800-2300; reservations are recommended. Moderate to expensive.

A few blocks downhill and north, the striking castle-tower of **Restaurant Cafe des Artistes** rises above the surrounding neighborhood at 740 Guadalupe Sanchez at Leona Vicario, tel. (322) 232-28. Romantics only need apply. Candlelit tables, tuxedoed servers, gently whirring ceiling fans, soothing live neoclassical melodies, and gourmet international cuisine all set a luxurious tone. You might start with your pick of soups, such as chilled cream of watercress or cream of prawn and pumpkin, continue with a salad, perhaps the smoked salmon in puff pastry with avocado pine nut dressing. For a finale, you might choose honey- and soy-glazed roast duck or shrimp sautéed with cheese tortellini and served with a carrot custard and a spinach-basil puree. Open Mon.-Sat. 1900-2400; reservations recommended. Expensive.

Supermarkets, Bakeries, and Health Food
The acknowledged best national supermarket chain is **Comercial Mexicana,** Mexico's Kmart with groceries. The quality is generally good to excellent, and the prices match those in the U.S. and Canada. Comercial Mexicana maintains two Puerto Vallarta branches, both in the north-side suburbs: at **Plaza Marina,** Km 6.5, Hwy. 200, just before the airport, beneath the McDonald's sign, tel. (322) 100-53; and three miles closer in, at **Plaza Genovese,** Km 2.5, Hwy. 200, near the John Newcombe Tennis Club, tel. (322) 440-09 or 466-95. Both are open daily, 0900-2100.

Much closer to downtown is the big, locally owned **Supermarket Gutiérrez Rizo,** a remarkably well-organized dynamo of a general store at Constitución and Vallarta, just south of the Río Cuale, tel. (322) 202-22. Besides vegetables, groceries, film, socks, spermicide, and sofas, they stock one of the largest racks of English-language magazines (some you'd be hard pressed to find back home) outside of Mexico City. Open 0630-2200, 365 days of the year.

Panadería Mungía is nearly worth the trip to Puerto Vallarta all by itself. The two branches are: downtown at Juárez and Mina; and south-of-Cuale, corner Insurgentes and A. Serdán. Big, crisp cookies, flaky fruit tarts, hot, fresh rolls, and cool cream-cakes tempt the palates of visitors, locals, and resident foreigners alike. Open Mon.-Sat. 0700-2100.

Rival **Panadería Los Chatos** offers an equally fine selection, also at two locations: downtown, at north-end Plaza Hidalgo, Av. México 995; and in the Hotel Zone, across from the Hotel Sheraton, Fco. Villa 359, tel. (322) 304-85. Both are open Mon.-Sat. 0700-2100.

If you've run out of *salvado* (oat bran), stock up at the **health food store** *(tienda naturista)* at Morelos 794 at Pipila. Their shelves are packed with hundreds of items, such as soya milk, vitamins, aloe vera cream, and tonics purported to cure everything from warts and gallstones to impotence. Open Mon.-Sat. 0900-1400 and 1600-2000.

A similar selection is available in the health food store in the Villas Vallarta Shopping center, Km. 2.5, across the interior street from the Hotel Continental Plaza. Open Mon.-Sat. 0900-1400 and 1600-2000.

ENTERTAINMENT AND EVENTS

Wandering Around

The *malecón,* where the sunsets seem the most beautiful in town, is a perfect place to begin the evening. Make sure you eventually make your way to the downtown central plaza by the Presidencia Municipal (city hall). On Friday and Saturday, the city often sponsors free music and dance concerts beginning around 2000 at the bayside **Los Arcos** amphitheater. Later, you can join the crowds who watch the **street artists** painting plates, watercolor country scenes, and fanciful, outer-galaxy spray-can spacescapes.

If you miss the weekend Los Arcos concert, you can usually console yourself with a balloon, *palomitas* (popcorn), and sometimes a band concert in the plaza. If you're inconsolable, buy some peanuts, a roasted ear of sweet corn, or a

Fireworks-stuffed papier-mâché bulls provide exciting finales to local fiestas.

hot dog from a vendor. After that, cool down with an *agua* or *jugo* fruit juice from the *juguería* across the bayside plaza corner, or a cone from Bing Ice Cream on the other.

A tranquil south-of-Cuale spot to cool off evenings is the **Muelle Nuevo** (New Pier) at the foot of Francisca Rodríguez (beach side of Hotel Playa Los Arcos). On a typical evening you'll find a couple dozen folks—men, women, and kids—enjoying the breeze, the swish of the surf, and, with nets or lines, trying to catch a few fish for sale or dinner.

Special Cultural Events

Puerto Vallarta residents enjoy their share of local fiestas.

One of the earliest fiestas marks a religious holiday. Preparations for **Semana Santa** (Easter week) begin in earnest, often with a modest **Carnaval** parade and dancing on Shrove Tuesday, and continue for the seven weeks before Easter. Each Friday until Easter, you might see processions of people bearing crosses filing through the downtown for special masses at neighborhood churches. This all culminates during Easter week, when Puerto Vallarta is awash with visitors, crowding the hotels, camping on the beaches, and filing in somber processions, which finally brighten to fireworks, dancing, and food on Domingo Santa (Easter Sunday).

The town quiets down briefly until the May **Fiesta de Mayo,** a countywide celebration of sports contests, music and dance performances, art shows, parades, and beauty pageants.

On the evening of 15 September, the Plaza de Armas (city hall plaza) fills with tipsy merrymakers, who gather to hear the mayor reaffirm Mexican independence by shouting the Grito de Dolores—Long Live Mexico! Death to the Gachupines!—under booming, brilliant cascades of fireworks.

Celebration again breaks out during the first twelve days of December, when city groups—businesses, families, neighborhoods—try to outdo each other with music, floats, costumes, and offerings all in honor of Mexico's patron, the Virgin of Guadalupe. The revelry climaxes on 12 December, when people, many in nativo garb to celebrate their indigenous origins, converge on the downtown church to receive the Virgin's blessing. If you miss the main 1-12 December fiesta, you can still enjoy a similar, but smaller-scale celebration in El Tuito (south of Puerto Vallarta, see the next chapter), a month later, 1-12 January.

Visitors who miss such real-life fiestas can still enjoy one of several local **Fiesta Mexicana** tourist shows, which are as popular with Mexican tourists as foreigners. The evening typically begins with a sumptuous buffet of salads, tacos, enchiladas, seafood, barbecued meats, and flan and pastries for dessert. Then begins a nonstop program of music and dance from all parts of Mexico: a chorus of revolutionary *soldaderas* and their *zapatista* male compatriots; raven-haired *señoritas* in flowing, flowered Tehuantepec silk dresses; rows of dashing Guadalajaran *charros* twirling their fast-stepping Chinas Poblanas sweethearts, climaxing with enough fireworks to swab the sky red, white, and green.

The south-of-Cuale **Restaurant Iguana,** Calle Lázaro Cárdenas 311, between Insurgentes and Constitución, tel. (322) 201-05, stages a very popular and *auténtico* such show Thursday and Sunday, Sunday only low season, around 1900. Another safe bet is the **Hotel Krystal** show, tel. (322) 402-02, Tuesday and Saturday, Saturday only low season, at 1900.

Other such shows are held seasonally at the **Playa Los Arcos** (Saturday), at Av. Olas Altas, tel. (322) 215-83, the **Sheraton** (Thursday), tel. (322) 304-04, and the **Costa Vida** (Saturday), south of town, tel. (322) 150-59.

The tariff for these shows typically runs $30 per person—except for the Playa Los Arcos show, which runs $16, drinks extra. During holidays and the high winter season reservations are generally necessary; best to book through a travel or tour desk agent.

Movies

Puerto Vallarta's former "art" movie house, the **Sala Elizabeth Taylor,** 5 de Febrero 19, just south of the River Cuale and a few doors upstream from Av. I. Vallarta, tel. (322) 206-67, has, sadly, gone nearly all hard core. The **Cine Bahía** nearby at Insurgentes 189, between Madero and Serdán, tel. (322) 217-17, however, remains a typical 50s-style small-town movie house, running a mixture of Mexican and American pop horror, comedy, and action, such as *Monkey Trouble* and *Robocop III*. Two similar movie houses on the north side of town are the **Cine Luz María,** at Av. México 227, across the street from the Pemex *gasolinera,* tel. (322) 207-05, and the nearby **Cine Vallarta** at the corner of Uruguay and Peru, tel. (322) 205-07.

Get into the Puerto Vallarta mood and make a night of it at **Hotel La Jolla de Mismaloya,** which shows a video of *Night of the Iguana* nightly at 1930 in the restaurant's bar, tel. (322) 306-60, ext. 3036; dinner reservations mandatory. The hotel is at Mismaloya Beach, seven miles (12 km) south of town; go by taxi, or the Mismaloya- or Boca-marked white minibus from south-of-Cuale Plaza Lázaro Cárdenas.

Music and Dancing

Cover charges are not required at the hotel lobby-bars, many of which offer nightly live music and dancing. For example, the **Hotel Krystal,** tel. (322) 402-02, band, plays Mexican-romantic-pop daily, 2000-2400, directly adjacent to the hotel reception desk.

The **Hotel Continental Plaza** tropical music group, tel. (322) 401-23, is practically guaranteed to brighten the spirits of any vacationer after a hard day on the beach.

The **Hotel Fiesta Americana,** tel. (322) 420-10, offers an entertaining mix of oldies-but-goodies, Latin, and soft rock nightly from around 1900. The **Hotel Playa Los Arcos,** tel. (322) 205-83, combo in the *palapa*-restaurant bar offers a little bit of everything nightly 2000-2200 from "Yellow Bird" and "Yesterday" to "La Bamba," with requests thrown in.

Other hotels with similar nightly offerings are the Sheraton, tel. (322) 304-04, the Plaza Las Glorias, tel. (322) 444-44, the Westin Regina, tel. (322) 111-00, and the Meliá, tel. (322) 102-00.

Discoing

Discos open quietly around 2200, begin revving up around midnight, and usually pound on till about 0500 in the morning. They have dress codes requiring shoes, shirts, and long pants for men, and blouses and skirts or pants, or modest shorts for women. Often they serve only (expensive) soft drinks. Discos that cater to tourists (all of the following) generally monitor their front doors very carefully; consequently they are pleasant and, with ordinary precautions, secure places to have a good time. If you use earplugs, even the high-decibel joints needn't keep you from enjoying yourself. Listings below are grouped by Zona Hotelera (northside), *malecón,* and south-of-Cuale locations, in approximate order of increasing volume:

Zona Hotelera: The mostly young, genteel customers at **J.C. Rock** on the airport boulevard in front of the Hotels Los Pelicanos and Las Palmas enjoy a repertoire of medium-volume mixed Latin and rock for a small cover charge of about $5.

The same is true less than a quarter mile north at **Friday Lopez,** on the airport boulevard in front of the Hotel Fiesta America Puerto Vallarta, tel. (322) 420-10, one of the most amicable (although a bit smoky) discos in Puerto Vallarta. The youngish crowd pays an approximate $10 entrance tariff for live, medium-volume, mostly Latin rock and rap (sometimes do-it-yourself-style karaoke) on a small, crowded dance floor. The room, however, is high ceilinged, well-lit, and the atmosphere is congenial.

Another half mile north stands **Christine,** the showplace of Puerto Vallarta discos, in front of Hotel Krystal, tel. (322) 402-02, ext. 878. They

entice customers to come and pay the $15 cover charge early (2300) to see their display of special fogs, spacy gyrating colored lights, and sophisticated woofers and tweeters, which, even when loud as usual, are supposed to leave you with minimum hearing impairment.

Malecón: Many popular *malecón* spots regularly pound out a continous no-cover repertoire of recorded rap and rock. One of the longtime standouts, popular with all generations, is **Carlos O'Brien's,** *malecón* at Pipila, tel. (322) 303-55. High-volume recorded rock, revolutionary wall-photos, zany mobiles, zingy margaritas, and "loco" waiters often lead patrons to dance on the tables by midnight. Folks who generally shy away from loud music can still have fun at Carlos O'Brian's, since the place is big and the high volume speakers are confined to one area.

Since most *malecón* discos are trying to imitate the **Hard Rock Cafe,** you might as well go right to the source at *malecón* at Abasolo, tel. (322) 255-32.

The **Zoo,** however, across Abasolo from the Hard Rock Cafe, tel. (322) 249-45, appears not to be imitating anyone. While animals—hippos, swooping birds, zebras, even a circulating gorilla—entertain the customers, reggae, rap, and rock thunder from overhead speakers.

South of Cuale: Longtime favorite **Cactus,** south end of I. Vallarta, tel. (322) 260-67, continues to attract youngish crowds with its super lights, sound, and whimsical Disneyland-like decor. Cover charge is 410.

Newcomer **Diva** one block north at I. Vallarta, between Badillo and Carranza, is trying harder to do the same thing by charging no cover.

Malecón Cafes, Bars, and Hangouts

One of the simplest Puerto Vallarta entertainment formulas is to walk along the *malecón* until you hear the kind of music at the volume you like.

Traditionalists like the big bar at **Brazz,** Morelos 518 at Galeana, tel. (322) 203-24, where a crowd of regulars fills the leather chairs around 2100 to enjoy the nightly mariachi concert. (See "Restaurants North of Río Cuale" above for more details.)

Four blocks north, the African safari-decorated **Mogambo,** *malecón* between Ortíz and

Abasolo, tel. (322) 234-76, restaurant-bar offers low-volume live music, often piano or jazz, nightly during high season.

The same is generally true a block south at Restaurants **Las Palomas** at the corner of Aldama, and **Mama Mía,** corner of Allende, a few blocks north. Las Palomas features a marimba duo 1900-2200 nightly, while a live reggae, flamenco, folk, and blues repertoire entertains dinner customers at Mama Mía 2100-2400 nightly in season, tel. (322) 235-44.

Those who desire a refined, romantic ambience go to **Restaurant Cafe des Artistes,** tel. (322) 232-28, and take a table for dinner or a seat at the bar, where they enjoy soothing neoclassical and jazz piano melodies nightly during high season, Friday and Saturday during low season. Find it by walking three blocks along Leona Vicario inland from the *malecón.* (See "Restaurants North of Cuale" for more details.)

South-of-Cuale Cafes, Bars, and Hangouts
The increasingly popular little entertainment district along I. Vallarta between V. Carranza and L. Cárdenas has acquired a number of lively spots, among them the **Mariachis Locos** bar-restaurant (corner of L. Cárdenas). Inside, a mostly local clientele enjoys a lively nonstop mariachi show nightly from about 2000 to the wee hours.

One block south (corner of V. Carranza), party animals crowd into the **King's Head Pub** for loud rhythm and blues, rock, jazz, and satellite TV sports, nightly from around 2200.

Across the street, the longtime favorite, friendly **Restaurant Torito,** tel. (322) 237-84, has good ribs, reasonable prices, and seasonal live music from around 2200-2400, bar open till around 0500.

Many folks' nights wouldn't be complete without stopping in at the **Andale** Mexican pub, tel. 210-54, Olas Altas 425, whose atmosphere is so amicable and lively that few even bother to watch the nonstop TV. So-so restaurant upstairs; open till around 0200.

Those who desire a more subdued atmosphere head two blocks farther south to **Sí Señor** bar, R. Gómez, corner of Olas Altas, tel. 264-50, for virtuoso jazz and rock until around 0100 nightly in season.

SPORTS

Jogging and Walking
Puerto Vallarta's cobbled streets, high curbs (towering sometimes to six feet!), and "holey" sidewalks make for tricky walking around town. The exception is the *malecón,* which can provide a good two-mile roundtrip jog when it is not crowded. Otherwise, try the beaches or the big public sports field, **Unidad Deportiva,** on the airport boulevard across from the Sheraton.

Swimming and Boarding
While Puerto Vallarta's calm waters are generally safe for swimming, they are often too tranquil for surfing, bodysurfing, and boogie boarding. Sometimes, strong, surfable waves rise along Playa Los Muertos. Another notable possibility is at the mouth of the **Ameca River** (north of the airport) where, during the rainy summer season, the large river flow helps create bigger than normal waves. Surfing is also common at **Bucerías** and **Punta Mita.** (For details, see under "Around the Bay of Banderas" below.)

Sailing and Windsurfing
Island Sailing International offers sailboat rentals and lessons from their Marina Vallarta dockside in front of the Hotel Plaza Las Glorias Iguana. Their boats, all with keel, range from Optimist dinghies for kids ($7/hour) to Impulse 21's for serious ocean sailing ($160/day). Their lessons vary from a six-hour ($120) half course to an entire 12-hour ($200) American Sailing Association certification course. Call them for more information at (322) 108-80, or drop by their hotel office, open Mon.-Fri. 0900-1300 and 1600-1800. Directions: One mile north of the Maritime Terminal cruise ship berth, a phony lighthouse at a gate marks the entrance to the Isla Iguana development. Ask the gatekeeper to direct you toward the Hotel Plaza Las Glorias Iguana.

A small but growing nucleus of local windsurfing enthusiasts practice their sport from Puerto Vallarta's beaches. They sometimes hold a **windsurfing tournament** during the citywide Fiesta de Mayo in the first week in May.

Silent World Diving water sports center, tel. (322) 406-50, ext. 626, headquartered on the Las Palmas Hotel beachfront, also offers windsurfing lessons and equipment rentals. Additionally, they rent simple-to-operate Hobie Cat sailboats (no lessons required) for $30/hour. Open daily 0900-1700.

Snorkel and Scuba

The biggest scuba instructor-outfitter in town is **Chico's Dive Shop,** on the *malecón* at Díaz Ordaz 770, between Pipila and Vicario, tel. (322) 218-95, fax (322) 254-39; open daily 0900-2200. They offer complete lessons, arrange and lead dive trips, and rent scuba equipment to qualified divers (bring your certificate). A beginning scuba lesson in the pool runs about $14, after which you'll be qualified to dive at **Los Arcos.** A day boat trip, including one 40-minute dive, costs $50 per person, gear included. Snorkelers on the same trip pay about $25. Chico's takes only certified divers to the **Marietas Islands,** the best site in the bay, for $85, including gear and two dives; snorkelers go for $40.

Other shops that offer similar services are **Silent World Diving Center** at the Hotel Las Palmas (see "Zona Hotelera Luxury Hotels" above), and **Paradise Divers** at Av. Olas Altas 443, between Dieguez and Rodríguez, tel. (322) 240-04; open daily 0900-2200.

Jet-Skiing, Water-Skiing, and Parasailing

These are available right on the beach at a number of the northside resort-hotels, such as the Sheraton, Fiesta Americana Plaza Vallarta, Hotel Las Palmas, Fiesta Americana Puerto Vallarta, and Krystal.

Parasailing and water-skiing are often available on Playa Los Muertos, in front of the Hotels Playa Los Arcos and Tropicana.

Expect to pay about $30 per half hour for a jet-ski boat, $70/hour for water-skiing, and $25 for a 10-minute parasailing ride.

Tennis and Golf

The eight—four outdoor clay, four indoor—courts at the friendly **John Newcombe Tennis Club,** Hotel Continental Plaza, tel. (322) 401-23, rent all day for about $12/hour. A sign-up board is available for players seeking partners. They also offer massage, steam baths, equipment

sales and rentals, and professional lessons ($30/hour).

The **Raquet Club Iguana,** adjacent to the airport Hwy. 200, Marina side about a block north of the Isla Iguana fake lighthouse, tel. (322) 106-03, rents its three lit astroturf courts for $7 per hour. Professional lessons run $17/hour, junior pro, $12/hour. Clients can also use their pool and locker rooms for small additional fees.

The several night-lit courts at the **Hotel Krystal,** tel. 402-02, rent for about $10/hour. They also offer equipment sales, rentals, and professional lessons. Other clubs, such as at the **Sheraton,** tel. (322) 304-04, **Los Tules,** tel. (322) 429-90, and the **Tennis Club Puesta del Sol,** tel. (322) 107-70, also rent their courts to the public.

The 18-hole, par-71 **Marina Vallarta Golf Course,** tel. (322) 101-71, designed by architect Joe Finger, is one of Mexico's best. It is only open, however, to club members and guests of some of the big hotels, such as Vela Vallarta, Quinta Real, Camino Real, Plaza Las Glorias, Sheraton, Westin Regina, Vidafel, Krystal, Isla Iguana, and Melia. The greens fee (about $75) includes caddy and cart. It's open daily 0730 to dusk.

The green, palm-shaded 18-hole **Los Flamingos Golf Course,** at Km 145 Hwy. 200, eight miles (13 km) north of the International Airport, tel. (329) 802-80, offers an attractive alternative, however. Open to the public daily 0700-1630, the Los Flamingos services include carts ($25), caddies ($14), club rentals ($15), a pro shop, restaurant, and locker rooms. The greens fee runs about $30. Their pink shuttle bus leaves daily from the Zona Hotelera (front of the Sheraton) at 0630, 0930, and 1130, returning at 1300, 1500, and 1700.

Bicycling

Bike Mex offers mountain bike adventures in surrounding scenic country locations. They tailor trips from beginning to advanced levels according to individual ability and interests. Rock Hopper mountain bikes (21-gear), helmets, gloves, purified water, and bilingual guides are included. Drop by or call their downtown office for information at 361 Guerrero, tel. (322) 316-80.

Horseback Riding

A pair of nearby ranches give visitors the opportunity to explore scenic tropical forest, river, and mountainside country. Options include either English or Western saddles, and rides ranging from two hours to a whole day. Call either Rancho Ojo de Agua, tel. (322) 482-40 or 406-07, or Rancho El Charro, tel. (322) 401-14, for information.

Gyms

Puerto Vallarta has a number of good exercise gyms. The **European Health Spa** (say "ays-PAH") at the Marina, Tennis Club Puesta del Sol, tel. (322) 107-70, offers 40 machines, complete weight sets, professional advice, aerobics workouts, and separate men's and women's facilities. Day use runs about $10.

Similar facilities and services are available at the **Hotel Qualton Club and Spa**, tel. (322) 444-45 or 444-46, next to the Hotel Fiesta Americana, and the **Hotel Continental Plaza** spa, tel. (322) 401-23, at Km 2.5, Plaza Las Glorias, in the central hotel zone.

Sportfishing

You can hire a *panga* (outboard launch) with skipper on the beach in front of several hotels, such as Los Arcos on Playa Los Muertos, the Buenaventura and Sheraton on Playa Los Camarones, the Plaza Las Glorias, Las Palmas, and Fiesta Americana Puerto Vallarta on Playa Las Glorias, and Krystal on Playa de Oro. Expect to pay $25/hour for a two- or three-hour trip that might net you and a few friends some five-pound jack, bonito, toro, or dorado for dinner. Ask your favorite restaurant to fix you a fish banquet with them.

Another good spot for *panga* rentals is near the **Peines** (pay-EE-nays) docks, where the fishermen keep their boats. You may be able to negotiate a good price, especially if you or a friend speaks Spanish. Access to the Peines is along the dirt road to the left of the Isla Iguana entrance (at the fake roadside lighthouse a mile north of the Marina cruise ship terminal). The fishermen, 16 members of the Cooperativa de Deportes Aquaticos Bahía de Banderas, have their boats lined up along the roadside channel to the left a few hundred yards from the highway.

At the end-of-road dock complex (the actual Peines) lie the big-game sportfishing boats that you can reserve only through agents back in town or at the hotels. For sailfish and marlin, call **Miller Travel Agency** for individual reservations on their 40-foot boats. They go out mornings at 0730 and return about eight hours later with an average of one big fish per boat. The tariff is $65 per person; food and drinks available but cost extra. Big boats generally have space for 10 passengers, about half of whom can fish at any one time. If not a big sailfish or marlin, most everyone usually gets something. Contact Miller's main office at 100 Paseo Las Garzas, behind the Hotel Hacienda Buenaventura, tel. (322) 411-97, 412-97, or 413-97, or one of their subsidiary branches at the Hotels Sheraton, Plaza Las Glorias, Melia, Vidafel, and Fiesta Americana.

Miller also rents entire 40-foot boats for $300 per day (50-foot, $350) for around eight passengers, food and drinks extra. Another agency that rents big sportfishing boats is the **Sociedad Cooperativa Progreso Turístico**, which has 10 boats, ranging from 32 to 40 feet. Rentals run $200-300 per day for a completely outfitted boat. For more information, drop by or call their office on the north end of the *malecón* at 31 de Octubre, across the street from the Hotel Rosita, tel. (322) 212-02. Best to talk to the manager, Hilarion Rodríguez, who is usually there Mon.-Sat. 0800-1200 and 1600-2000.

If you'd like to enter the Puerto Vallarta **Sailfish Tournament,** held annually in November (1995 marks the 40th), call the Club de Yates (YAH-tays), tel. (322) 107-40 or 108-40, or the Club de Pesca, tel. (322) 203-45 or 238-84, or write Puerto Vallarta Torneo de Pez Vela (Sailfish Tournament), P.O. Box 212, Puerto Vallarta, Jalisco 48300. The registration fee runs $400 per person, which includes the welcome dinner and the closing awards dinner. The five grand prizes include automobiles. The biggest sailfish caught was a 168-pounder in 1957.

At their present rates of attrition, sailfish and marlin will someday disappear from Puerto Vallarta waters. Some captains and participants have fortunately seen the light, and are releasing the fish after they're hooked in accordance with IFGA (International Fish and Game Association) guidelines.

Boating

The superb 350-berth **Marina Vallarta** has all possible hookups, including certified water, metered 110-220 volts, phone, fax, showers, toilets, laundry, dock lockers, trash collection, pump-out, and 24-hour security. With a yacht club and complete repair yard, it is surrounded by luxurious condominiums, tennis courts, a golf course, and dozens of shops and offices. Slip rates run around 60 cents per foot per day (minimum charge, around $20 per day) for up to six days. Prices are lower for longer stays and during the low season (June through November). For more information, write the Marina at P.O. Box 350-B, Puerto Vallarta, Jalisco 48300, or call (322) 102-62.

The Marina has a **public boat-launching ramp** where you can float your craft into the Marina's sheltered waters for about $5. If the guard isn't available to open the gate, call the Harbor Master, tel. (322) 102-75, for entry permission. To get there, follow the street marked "Proa," one block south of the main Marina Vallarta entrance, about a mile north of the cruise-ship terminal.

Sporting Goods Stores

Given the sparse and pricey local sporting goods selection, serious sports enthusiasts should pack their own equipment to Puerto Vallarta. A few stores carry some items. Among the best is **Deportes Gutiérrez Rizo**, corner of south-of-Cuale Avs. Insurgentes and A. Serdán, tel. (322) 225-95. Although fishing gear—rods, reels, line, sinkers—is their strong suit, they also stock a general selection including sleeping bags, inflatable boats, tarps, pack frames, wet suits, scuba tanks, and water skis. Open Mon.-Sat. 0900-1400 and 1700-2000.

Not far away, **Surfing and Hobbies**, at I. Vallarta 335B, tel. (322) 244-70, has a few surfboards, boogie boards, and some accessories. Surfboards rent $15-18/day; boogie boards, although not for rent, sell for around $200. Open Mon.-Sat. 1000-1400 and 1700-2030.

SHOPPING

Although Puerto Vallarta residents make very few folk crafts themselves, they import tons of good—and some very fine—pieces from the places where they *are* made. Furthermore, Puerto Vallarta's scenic beauty has become an inspiration for a growing community of artists and discerning collectors who have opened shops filled with locally crafted sculpture, painting, and museum-grade handicrafts gathered from all over Mexico. Furthermore, resort wear needn't cost a bundle in Puerto Vallarta, where a number of small boutiques offer racks of stylish, comfortable Mexican-made items for a fraction of stateside prices.

South-of-Cuale Shopping

The couple of blocks of Av. Olas Altas and side streets around the Hotel Playa Los Arcos are alive with a welter of T-shirt and *artesanías* (crafts) stores loaded with the more common items—silver, onyx, papier-mâché, pottery—gathered from all over Mexico.

A few shops stand out, however. **Teté**, owned by María Elena Zermeño and run by her daughters Olimpia and Ester, contains a treasury of unusual pre-Columbian reproductions and modern original masks, pottery, human figurines, and bark paintings. Besides such for-sale items, they also display (and if you ask, competently interpret) other pre-Columbian and modern pieces that are not for sale. Located half a block from the beach at 135 F. Rodríguez, across from Restaurant Santos, tel. (322) 247-97; open Mon.-Sat. 1000-1400 and 1600-2200.

A block up Olas Altas, near the corner of R. Gómez, the **Galería Museo Olas Altas,** R. Gómez 158, tel. (322) 323-53, offers an eclectic collection of arts and crafts. These range from wooden masks from Guerrero and local color paintings to Huichol bead masks and wooden sculptures from Michoacán. Open daily 1000-2200.

Back down Olas Altas, the **Boutique Con Juntos** in the Hotel Playa Los Arcos, Olas Altas 380, tel. (322) 215-83, offers a broad selection of reasonably priced women's resort wear. Many of their racks are filled with the popular style of Guadalajara-made, loose-fitting cotton gauze tops, skirts, and pants. Open Mon.-Fri. 0930-1400, 1630-2000, Saturday 0930-1800.

A number of other interesting shops and museum-galleries are sprinkled nearby, on the blocks uphill from Av. Olas Altas. For a treat, head up B. Badillo to **Galería Pyramid,** B. Badillo 272, near the corner of I. Vallarta, tel. (322) 231-61. There, amicable owner J. Jesus Avelar offers a large selection of ceramics, paintings, masks, and Huichol ceremonial objects. These include *cuadras* (yarn paintings), beaded masks, ritual gourds and animals all colorfully adorned with the spirits of the Huichol pantheon. Periodic public openings feature the works of promising local artists. Open Mon.-Sat. 1000-1400 and 1800-2200, Sunday 1000-1400.

Head north a block and a half along I. Vallarta to **Talavera, Etc.,** 266 I. Vallarta, tel. (322) 241-00, fax 224-13, for an elegant exposition of fine Talavera ceramics. As friendly owner Jackie Kilpatrick explains, the label "Talavera" comes from the town in Spain where the potters, who settled in Puebla in the 16th century, originated. They brought with them their pottery tradition, an ancient blend of Chinese, Moorish, and Mediterranean styles and methods. Jackie's wares all come from the source at Puebla, where she buys from families expert in the Talavera tradition. "They use no lead," she says, "Only cobalt for blue, copper for green, iron for red, manganese for yellow, and tin for white." Her prices, though not cheap, reflect the quality of her offerings. Open Mon.-Sat. 1000-1400 and 1700-2000. For a more economical but more ordinary selection, continue to **Artesanías San Miguel,** on the adjacent corner, at L. Cárdenas 236.

Head half a block up Lázaro Cárdenas for a look around **Olinala Gallery,** 274 Lázaro Cárdenas, tel. (322) 274-95, Nancy and John Erickson's mini-museum of intriguing masks and fine lacquerware. Although their "Olinala" name originates from the famed Mexican lacquerware village where they used to get most of their pieces, ceremonial and festival masks—devils, mermaids, goddesses, skulls, crocodiles, horses, and dozens more—crafts from all parts of Mexico now dominate their fascinating selection. Their offerings, moreover, are priced to sell; open Mon.-Sat. 1000-1400 and 1700-2100.

Farther uphill, at the south end of the Av. Insurgentes bridge, fine art blooms at Gary Thompson's **Galería Pacífico,** 109 Insurgentes, tel. (322) 219-82. The attractive upstairs showroom shines with the paintings, prints, and sculpture of Mexican artists, both renowned and up-and-coming. The mostly realistic works cover a gamut of styles and feelings, from colorful and sentimental to stark and satirical. Gary often hosts Friday-meet-the-artist openings, where visitors are invited to socialize with the local artistic community. Open Mon.-Sat. 1000-1400 and 1700-2100.

Shopping along the River: Mercado Municipal and Pueblo Viejo

For the more ordinary, yet attractive, Mexican handicrafts, head any day except Sunday (when most shops are closed) to the **Mercado Municipal** at the north end of the Av. Insurgentes bridge. Here, most shops begin with prices two to three times higher than the going rate. You should counter with a correspondingly low offer. If you don't get the price you want, always be prepared to find another seller. If your offer is fair, the shopkeeper will often give in as you begin to walk away. Theatrics, incidentally, are less than useful in bargaining, which should merely be a straightforward discussion of the merits, demerits, and price of the article in question.

The Mercado Municipal is a two-story warren of dozens upon dozens of shops filled with jewelry, leather, papier-mâché, T-shirts, and everything in between. The congestion can make the place hot; after a while, take a break at a cool river-view seat at one of the *fonda* restaurants on the second floor.

One of the most unusual Mercado Municipal stalls is **Cabaña del Tío Tom,** whose menagerie of colorful papier-mâché parrots are priced a peg or two cheaper than at the tonier downtown stores.

It's time to leave when you're too tired to distinguish silver from tin and Tonalá from Tlaquepaque. Head downstream to the **Pueblo Viejo** complex on Calle Augustín Rodríguez between Juárez and Morelos, near the Av. I. Vallarta lower bridge. This mall, with individual stores rather than stalls, is less crowded but pricier than the **Mercado Municipal.** Some shopkeepers will turn their noses up if you try to bargain. If they persist, take your business elsewhere.

Ric jewelry, Pueblo Viejo's most unique store, tel. (322) 301-43, has cases of original designs in sterling and gold by owner Erika Hult de Corral. Open daily 0900-2000. She also maintains another outlet in the Villas Vallarta Shopping

Center, Km 2.5, Hwy. 200, local C-8, tel. (322) 215-04, directly across the interior street from the Hotel Continental Plaza.

Downtown Shopping: Along Juárez and Morelos

A sizable fraction of Puerto Vallarta's best boutiques and arts and crafts stores lie along the six downtown blocks of Av. Juárez, beginning at the Río Cuale. The **Felix Boutique** heads the parade at Juárez 126, half a block north of the river. The friendly, outgoing owner offers reasonably priced women's resort wear of her own design. Open Mon.-Sat. 1100-1400 and 1600-1930.

Galería La Indígena, Juárez 168, tel. (322) 230-07, in the second block of Juárez, features a broad selection of indigenous artifacts. Their relatively high prices reflect the quality of their diverse treasury of fine Huichol yarn paintings and ceremonial paraphernalia and rare ritual masks and sculpture brought from all over Mexico. Open Mon.-Sat. 1100-1400 and 1700-2100.

Not so unusual—and consequently less pricey—is the merchandise at **Jaguar Galería 270,** Juárez 270, tel. (322) 249-66. They feature a galaxy of masks, some authentic, others made for tourist consumption, from Michoacán, Guerrero, and Oaxaca. Open Mon.-Fri. 0900-1400 and 1630-1830, Sat. 0900-1330.

For more reasonable mask prices you'll have to travel about 10 miles south of town, to Boca de Tomatlán. On the side of the highway a couple of hundred yards north of the village, a log-walled store contains a fascinating array of Mexican bric-a-brac—altar angels, antique clocks, pottery—and dozens of masks, many very strange, at rock-bottom prices if you bargain. If you're in the market, it might be worth a special trip; in any case, it's worth a stop if you're in the neighborhood.

Back in town along Juárez, arts and crafts lovers Barbara and Jean Peters collected so many Mexican handicrafts over the years they had to find a place to store their finds. **Galería Vallarta,** a small museum of singular paintings, ceremonial masks, lampshades, art-to-wear, and more, is the result. Find it at Juárez 263, across from Jaguar Galería, tel. (322) 202-90; open Mon.-Sat. 1000-2100.

A few doors away, the store of renowned **Sergio Bustamante** (who lives in Guadalajara) contains so many unique sculptures it's hard to believe how a single artist could be so prolific. (The answer: He has a factory-shop full of workers who execute his fanciful, sometimes unnerving, studies in juxtaposition.) Bustamante's more modest faces on eggs, anthropoid cats, and double-nosed clowns go for as little as $200; the largest, most flamboyant, $10,000 or more. Located at Juárez 275, tel. (322) 211-29; open Mon.-Sat. 0900-2100.

Back across the street, the government **Instituto de Arte Jaliscense** store displays ex-

The renowned black barra pottery from Colotepec village near Oaxaca is available in shops all over Pacific Mexico.

BRUCE WHIPPERMAN

(top) in the valley of the the River Purificación, Jalisco;
(bottom) guest palapas at Lo Cosmico Zipolite Beach, Puerto Ángel (photos by Bruce Whipperman)

(top left) comblike *peineta* blossom, Oaxaca coast; (top right) *flamboyán* (royal poinciana) tree decorates a village near San Blas; (bottom left) coffee berries, Colima; (bottom right) *ahuehuete* (Mexican cypress) (photos by Bruce Whipperman) amples of nearly every Jalisco folk craft, plus popular items, such as Oaxaca fanciful wooden animals, from other parts. Find it at Juárez 284, tel. (322) 213-01; open Mon.-Fri. 1000-1400 and 1600-2000, Saturday until 1800. Since they have a little bit of everything at relatively reasonable prices, this is a good spot for comparison-shopping.

A couple of blocks farther on, at the corner of Galeana, an adjacent pair of stores, the **Queribines** ("Cherubs") and **La Reja** ("Grillwork"), display their excellent traditional merchandise—riots of papier-mâché fruit, exquisite blue pottery vases, gleaming pewter, clay trees of life, rich Oaxaca and Chiapas textiles, shiny Tlaquepaque handpainted pottery—so artfully done they are simply fun to walk through. The stores are at Juárez 501A and 501B. Queribines, tel. (322) 229-88, is open Mon.-Sat. 0900-2100; La Reja, tel. (322) 222-72, is open Mon.-Sat. 0900-1400 and 1600-2000.

Across the street, the restaurant-courtyard **Bazar Las Margaritas** has a number of interesting galleries and shops. Prominent in the front is **La Bohemia**, Juárez 512, a boutique with a varied and thoughtfully selected collection of women's resort wear. Open Mon.-Sat. 1000-2100, Sunday 1100-1400.

Another block north on the short block of Corona (downhill between Juárez and Morelos) are a number of interesting fine crafts stores. First is the ceramics gallery **Majolica**, 183 Corona, which uses the older name (from the Mediterranean island of Majorca) of where the Talavera pottery style originated, before migrating to Spain and Mexico. The personable owner-manager hand-selects the pieces, all of which come from the Puebla family-workshops that carry on the Talavera tradition. Her prices reflect the high demand that the Talavera style of colorful classic elegance has commanded for generations. Open Mon.-Sat. 1000-1400 and 1700-2000.

Downhill a few doors, **Arte Mágico Huichol** displays an unusually fine collection of Huichol yarn paintings by renowned artists, such as Mariano Valadez, Hector Ortiz, and María Elena Acosta, at Corona 179, tel. (322) 230-77. Open Mon.-Sat. 1000-1400 and 1600-2000.

Continue downhill to **El Patio**, Corona 169, tel. (322) 226-26, the labor of love of Bonnie Miller,

Mexican maskmaking traditions live on, especially in rural areas of Michoacán, Guerrero, and Oaxaca.

ERIN DWYER

who has spent half a life accumulating a trove of antiques from Mexico's quiet corners. Although her shelves contain many newly made traditional craft items, such as nativity sets and Talavera pottery, her pride is in the hundreds of country relics—wooden saddles, huge keys, hand-wrought scissors—whose designs reach back to Roman times. Open Mon.-Sat. 0930-1400 and 1700-2000.

Next door, at the corner of Morelos, you'll find **El Baul**, Morelos 558, tel. (322) 301-69, whose best customers are interior designers. They get their pick from choirs of fine Talavera ceramics, Tlaquepaque colored crystal balls, hand-hewn Baroque furniture, sentimental Mexican paintings, and much more. Open Mon.-Sat. 1000-1400 and 1700-2000.

Step across Morelos to **Galería Uno**, one of Puerto Vallarta's longest-established fine art galleries, at Morelos 561, tel. (322) 209-08. Their collection—featuring internationally recognized artists with whom they often schedule exhibition openings for the public—tends toward the large, the abstract, and the primitive. Open Mon.-Sat 1000-2000.

Finally, head a few blocks back along Morelos to the **Onix and Silver Factory,** Morelos 434, on the *malecón* by the post office, tel. (322) 224-87, for just about the broadest selection and best prices in town. Charges for their seeming acres of gold, silver, and jeweled chains, bracelets, pendants, necklaces, and earrings are usually determined simply by weight; a dollar per gram for silver. Open Mon.-Sat. 1000-2200.

Department Stores

The best department stores in Puerto Vallarta are the two branches of the big **Comercial Mexicana** chain and the equally excellent local store, **Guitierrez Rizo.** For details, see the "Supermarkets" heading under "Food" listed above.

Photography

Although a number of downtown stores do one-hour developing and printing at U.S. prices, **Photo Rey,** Libertad 330, tel. (322)) 209-37, is one of the few in town that develops and prints black and whites. Open Mon.-Sat. 0900-2200, Sunday 0900-1500.

Right across the street, **Laboratorios Vallarta,** Libertad 335, tel. (322) 250-70, stocks the most cameras, accessories, and film of any Vallarta store: lots of Fuji and Kodak color negative (print) film in many speeds and sizes plus transparency, professional 120 rolls, and black and white. Open Mon.-Sat. 0900-2200, Sunday 1000-2000. If they don't have what you need, perhaps you'll find it at their second branch, around the corner at Morelos 101.

Cameras are an import item in Mexico and consequently very expensive. Even the simplest point-and-shoot cameras cost half again as much as in the U.S. or Canada. It is best to bring your own.

SERVICES

Money Exchange

The **National Bank of Mexico** (Banamex), corner of Juárez and Zaragoza, tel. (322) 219-98 or

Puerto Vallarta area code is 322

209-11, on the central plaza, changes U.S. and Canadian cash and traveler's checks at the best rates in town. Money exchange open Mon.-Fri. 0900-1300.

Huichol ritual yarn painting depicts a pilgrim praying to the sea gods.

ERIN DWYER

If the lines at Banamex are too long, try **Bancomer** two blocks north at Juárez and Mina, tel. (322) 208-78 or 250-50, money exchange hours Mon.-Fri. 0900-1200, or **Banco Serfin** across the street.

Scores of little *casas de cambio* (exchange booths) dot the old town streetsides, especially along the *malecón* downtown, and along Av. Olas Altas and Insurgentes south of the Río Cuale. Although they offer about $2 per $100 less than the banks, they compensate with long hours, often 0900-2100, daily. In the big hotels, cashiers will generally exchange your money at rates comparable to the downtown exchange booths.

The local **American Express** agency cashes American Express traveler's checks and offers full member travel services, such as personal-check cashing (up to $1000, every 21 days—bring your checkbook, your ID or passport, and your American Express card). The office is downtown at the corner of Abasolo and Morelos, one block inland from the Hard Rock Cafe. It's open Mon.-Fri. 0900-1800.

Communications

Puerto Vallarta has a number of branch post offices. The smallish main *correo,* on the *malecón,* Morelos 444, at Mina, tel. (322) 218-88, is open Mon.-Fri. 0800-1930, Saturday 0900-1300, and Sunday 0900-1200. The branch at the Edificio Maritima (Maritime Building) at the cruise liner dock is open Mon.-Fri. 0800-1500. The airport branch, on the ground level check-in floor, is open Mon.-Fri. 0900-1900, Saturday 0900-1300. (After hours they have a mailbox outside the door.)

Express mail, telegraph, fax, telex, and money order *(giros)* services are available at the **Mexpost** office, 584 Juárez, five blocks north of the central plaza, fax (322) 301-44; open Mon.-Fri. 0900-1730.

Nearly all Puerto Vallarta hotels have *larga distancia* telephone service. Lacking this (or if you don't like their extra charges), go to one of the many *casetas de larga distancia,* long-distance telephone offices, sprinkled all over town. For example, Computel, the efficient computer-assisted long-distance and public fax service maintains a number of Puerto Vallarta offices: south of Cuale, next to the Transportes Cihuatlán bus terminal at Madero 296, tel. (322) 318-50, (open daily 0700-2130); at Plaza Genovese, Km 2.5 airport highway, on the south side of Comercial Mexicana, tel. (322) 477-73 (open daily 0900-2200); and at the Marina inner harbor, *puerto interior,* yacht basin, tel. (322) 455-61.

A number of other offices offer *larga distancia* and public fax in the downtown area: south of the Río Cuale, on the north side of Plaza Lázaro Cáardenas, 181A L. Cárdenas, tel. (322) 308-50, fax 308-51 (open daily 0830-2200); or just north of the river, at Juárez 136, below the bridge, half a block from the Hotel Encino (open Mon.-Fri. 0900-1400 and 1600-1900, Saturday until 1330); or farther north by the *malecón* at Aldama 180, five blocks north of the central plaza, tel. (322) 301-99 (open Mon.-Sat. 0900-2100).

Immigration, Customs, and Consulates

If you need an extension to your tourist card, you can get a total of 180 days at the **Migratorios** at 600 Morelos, at Aldama, tel. (322) 214-78; open Mon.-Fri. 0900-1400. If you lose your tourist card, however, go first to the tourist information office (see "Information" below).

If you have to temporarily leave your car in Mexico check with either the tourist information office (see "Information" below) or take your tourist permit, car permit, your car ownership and registration documents (all with copies) to the **Aduana,** tel. (322) 406-60, in the Edificio Maritima, at the cruise liner dock. Open Mon.-Fri. 0900-1500. The Aduana presently hasn't room to store cars; until they do, you don't have to leave your car with them as is customary in many other Mexican localities.

The small local **United States Consular Office,** supervised by consular agent Alison Holmstrom, issues passports and does other essential legal work for U.S. citizens. Contact P.O. Box 462, Puerto Vallarta, Jalisco 48300, tel. (322) 200-69, fax 300-74; open Mon.-Fri. 0900-1300. Look for the little second-story office, marked by the U.S. flag, on the uphill side of the Av. Insurgentes Río Cuale bridge. In true emergencies, you may phone any time.

The Canadian consular agent, Nicolo Gorindo Vasquez, tel. (322) 253-98, provides similar services for Canadian citizens.

Language, Arts, and Music Courses

The private, volunteer **Centro Cultural Vallartense** periodically sponsors theater, modern dance, painting, sculpture, aerobics, martial arts, and other courses for adults and children. From time to time they stage exhibition openings for local artists, whose works they exhibit at their gallery-information center. For more information, drop by and talk to the volunteer in charge at the Plaza del Arte, at the upstream end of Río Cuale (see "Sights" preceding).

Sharing the Plaza de Arte is the round **Escuela Municipal de Música** building, where, late weekday afternoons, you may hear the strains of students practicing the violin, guitar, piano, flute, and pre-Columbian instruments. Such lessons are open to the general public; apply in person during the late afternoons or early evening.

The excellent language school, **Centro Cultural Mexicano Americano,** three blocks off the *malecón* at Av. Pipila 213, Puerto Vallarta, Jalisco 48300, tel. (322) 234-88 or 248-10, offers tutorial and small group instruction in Spanish for reasonable rates. Also, the University of Guadalajara operates a Puerto Vallarta language school at Jesús Langarica 200, tel. (322) 300-43, fax 244-19. Programs include small, individually tailored classes, live-in study programs, and university credits.

INFORMATION

Tourist Information Offices

The joint federal-state *oficina de turismo,* tel. (322) 202-42, is at the street-level (Juárez and central plaza) corner of the Presidencia Municipal. They provide assistance and information, and dispense whatever maps, pamphlets, and copies of *Vallarta Today* and *Puerto Vallarta Lifestyles* (see below) they happen to have. Open Mon.-Fri. 0900-2000, Saturday 0900-1300.

If you've lost your tourist card, tell them and they'll fill out a loss report, which you then take to Migratorios, 600 Morelos, tel. (322) 214-78, to get a duplicate; open Mon.-Fri. 0900-1400.

Luis Rodríguez, one of the tourist office's most friendly and knowledgeable staff, handles the front information desk after about 1500 most afternoons (after working mornings in the local U.S. consular office).

This *oficina de turismo* is also a good spot to contact members of the Puerto Vallarta **Asociación Cooperativo de Guías** (Guides Association Cooperative) who can arrange out-of-the-ordinary cultural, ecological, and historical tours. Carlos Patino, their personable, English-speaking executive officer, invites visitors to contact him at his office, Av. Niza 153, Colonia Díaz Ordaz, tel. (322) 455-35 or 449-39; open Mon.-Fri. 0900-1130.

Another good source of local information is the Puerto Vallarta branch of the **Cámara Nacional de Comercio** ("Chamber of Commerce"), which publishes an excellent *Directorio Comercial Turístico,* a directory to everything you might be likely to need in Puerto Vallarta. Find the chamber at Morelia 138, 2nd floor, tel. (322) 427-08, one block off the *libramiento* downtown bypass boulevard, four blocks from the airport highway. Open Mon.-Fri. 0900-1400 and 1700-2000, Saturday 0900-1300.

Health, Police, and Emergencies

If you need medical advice, ask your hotel desk for assistance, or go to one of Puerto Vallarta's several good hospitals. One of the most respected hospital-clinics in town is the **CMQ (Centro Médico Quirúrgico)** south of the Río Cuale at 305 Basilio Badillo, between Insurgentes and Aguacate, tel. (322) 308-78. The hospital section, tel. (322) 319-19, is at no. 364 on the same street.

Right around the corner on Insurgentes, across from the gas station, the bilingual-staffed Hospital Medasist, which advertises it accepts "all worldwide medical insurance for emergencies," with emergency room, lab, diagnostic equipment, and a staff of specialists, appears to be another good place to seek assistance when you're sick.

On the north side, closer to the Hotel Zone, stands the equally well-respected hospital-clinic of **Servicios Médico de la Bahía,** Km 1 on the airport boulevard across from the Sheraton, tel. (322) 226-27.

If you must have an English-speaking doctor, **IAMAT** (International Association for Medical Assistance to Travelers) has two associate U.S.-trained doctor-members in Puerto Vallarta. Contact either John H. Mabrey, M.D., at Miramar 356, Casa Las Campañas, tel. (322) 243-09, or António Sahagún Rodríguez, M.D., Corona 224, tel. (322) 213-05.

For round-the-clock prescription service, call one of the five branches of **Farmacia CMQ;** for example, in Olas Altas at Basilio Badillo 367, tel. (322) 229-41, or on the northside, at Peru 1146, tel. (322) 242-73.

A legion of loyal local customers swear by the diagnostic competence of the owner of **Farmacia Olas Altas,** Av. Olas Altas 365, two blocks south of Hotel Playa Los Arcos, tel. (322) 223-74, whom they simply know as "Freddy." Although a pharmacist and not a physician, they say he is a wizard at recommending remedies for their aches and pains.

For either **police or fire** emergencies, call the police headquarters, tel. 201-23, at the Presidencia Municipal at the central plaza.

Publications

New books in English are not particularly common in Puerto Vallarta. However, a number of small stores and stalls, such as the **Nuevo Librería Limón,** regularly sell newspapers, including Mexico City *News,* and sometimes *USA*

Today, and the Los Angeles *Times.* In addition, they have a collection of used English-language paperback novels and some local, state, and national maps. Find it at 310 Carranza, between Vallarta and Constitución, tel. (322) 224-52, open daily 0800-2100. English-language magazines and newspapers are also available at the no-name **newsstand** at 420 Olas Altas, across from Andale pub; open daily 0900-2200.

Supermercado Gutiérrez Rizo, corner Constitución and F. Madero, offers an excellent American magazine selection and some new paperback novels; open daily 0630-2200.

Comercial Mexicana (see "Supermarkets, Bakeries, and Health Food" above) and certain big hotels—Camino Real, Sheraton, Continental Plaza, Fiesta Americana, Melia, and Westin Regina—and *tabaquerías,* tobacco shops, also stock U.S. newspapers, magazines, and paperbacks.

Vallarta Today, an unusually informative tourist daily, is handed out free at the airport and hotels all over town. Besides detailed information on hotels, restaurants, and sports, they include a local events and meetings calendar and good historical, cultural, and personality feature articles. Call them if you can't find a copy, tel. (322) 429-28, Mérida 118, Colonia Versalles.

Equally excellent is *Puerto Vallarta Lifestyles,* tel. (322) 104-64, the quarterly English-language tourist magazine, which also features unusually detailed and accurate town maps. Pick up a free copy at the airport or your hotel.

The local **public library** has a small general collection, including Spanish-language reference books and a dozen shelves of English-language paperbacks, at Parque Hidalgo, one block north of the end of the *malecones,* in front of the church. Open Mon.-Fri. 0800-2000, Saturday 0900-1700.

Women's Organization

The **Asociación Femenil Vallartense,** an organization of mostly professional women, maintains active civic programs. One major project is fund-raising for construction of a new orphanage. They welcome exchanges with visitors. Check with tourist information or the chamber of commerce (see above) for contact persons.

Volunteer Work

A number of local volunteer clubs and groups invite visitors to their meetings and activities. Check with the tourist information office or see the "Community Corner" listing in *Vallarta Today* for current meeting and activity details:

The **Club Internacional de la Amistad** (International Friendship Club), an all-volunteer service club, sponsors a number of health, educational, and cultural projects. They welcome visitors to their (usually second Monday) monthly general membership meeting. Call Paul Bernholz at (322) 260-60 for more information. One of the best ways to find out about their work is on the popular tour of Puerto Vallarta homes, which begins at the central plaza, near the bandstand, Saturday and Thursday mornings (usually at 1100) during the Nov.-April high season. They ask a $17 donation per person to further their charitable programs.

The **Ecology Group of Vallarta,** a group of local citizens willing to work for a cleaner Puerto Vallarta, welcomes visitors to their activities and regular monthly meetings. Call Rosa Limon, tel. (322) 224-52, or Ron Walker, tel. 208-97, for more information.

GETTING THERE AND AWAY

By Air

Several major carriers connect Puerto Vallarta by direct flights with United States and Mexican destinations.

Mexicana Airlines flights connect daily with Los Angeles, Denver, Chicago, Mexico City, Los Cabos, and Guadalajara. In Puerto Vallarta, telephone (322) 112-66 for reservations and airport flight information.

Aeroméxico flights connect daily with Los Angeles, San Diego, Guadalajara, and Mexico City; for reservations, call tel. (322) 42-777.

Alaska Airlines flights connect daily with Los Angeles, San Francisco, and Seattle; for reservations, call a local travel agent or telephone their U.S. direct toll-free number, tel. 95-800-426-0333.

American Airlines flights connect daily with Dallas-Ft. Worth; call (322) 117-99 or 119-27 for reservations.

Delta Air Lines flights connect daily with Los Angeles; for reservations, call a local travel agent, or telephone their local toll-free reservations number, tel. 91-800-902-21.

Continental Airlines flights connect daily with Houston; call (322) 110-96 for reservations.

Canadian Holiday Airlines charter flights connect with Toronto, Vancouver, Calgary, and other Canadian gateways (mostly during the winter); for information, call their local agent at (322) 112-12 or 107-36.

Puerto Vallarta Airport
Arrival and Departure

Air arrival at Puerto Vallarta (code-designated PVR, officially the Gustavo Díaz Ordaz International) Airport is generally smooth and simple. After the cursory (if any) customs check, arrivees can avail themselves of: **money-exchange counters,** open daily 0900-2000, but offering relatively unfavorable rates, however; a lineup of **car rental booths,** e.g., Budget, National, Avis, Dollar, and Hertz; and the arrival desk of the **Mexican Association of Travel Agents,** whose main job is to meet tours, but who will call specific hotels for reservations if they have time.

Transportation to town is easiest by *colectivo* (VW van collective taxi) or *taxi especial* (individual taxi). Booths sell tickets at curbside. The *colectivo* fare runs about $4 per person to the northern hotel zone, $6 to the center of town, and $7 or more to Mismaloya and other beaches south of town. Individual taxis run about $9, $17, and $20 for the same rides. Taxis to more distant northern destinations, such as **Rincón de Guayabitos** (30 miles, 50 km) and San Blas or Tepic (100 miles, 160 km), run about $60 and $190, respectively. A much cheaper alternative is to ride one of the second-class "Tepic"-marked **Transportes del Pacífico** green-and-white northbound buses. Wave them down across the highway outside the airport gate. The Guayabitos fare should run around $3, Tepic, $7. They are often crowded; don't tempt people with a dangling open purse or a bulging wallet pocket.

Airport departure is as simple as arrival. Save by sharing a taxi with departing fellow hotel guests. Agree on the fare with the driver before you get in. If the driver seems too greedy (see inbound fares above) hail another taxi. Once at the

airport, you can do last-minute shopping at a number of airport shops, or mail a letter at the airport post office, which is open Mon.-Fri. 0900-1900, Saturday 0900-1300, or their *buzón* (mailbox) after hours.

If you've lost your tourist card, be prepared to pay a (roughly $20) fine unless you've gotten a duplicate through the tourist information office (see under "Information" above). In any case, be sure to save enough pesos or dollars to pay your **$12 departure tax.** They don't accept credit cards.

By Car or RV

There are three good road routes to Puerto Vallarta: from the north through Tepic or San Blas, from the east through Guadalajara, and from the south through Barra de Navidad and Manzanillo. They are all two-lane roads, requiring plenty of caution.

From Tepic, **Mexican National Hwy. 200** is all-asphalt and in good condition most of its 104 miles (167 km) to Puerto Vallarta. Heavy trucks and buses sometimes slow traffic around Tepic and over a few low passes, but traffic is ordinarily light to moderate, except for the 10 miles around Puerto Vallarta. Allow three hours for the southbound trip and half an hour longer in the reverse direction for the winding 3,000-foot climb to Tepic.

A recently completed shortcut connects **San Blas** directly with Puerto Vallarta, avoiding the oft-congested uphill route through Tepic. Heading north on Hwy. 200, at Las Varas turn off west on Nayarit Hwy. 161 to Zacualapan and Platanitos, where the road continues through the jungle to Santa Cruz de Miramar on the Bay of Matanchén. From there you can continue along the shoreline to San Blas. In the opposite direction, heading south from San Blas, follow the signed "Puerto Vallarta" turnoff to the right (south) a few hundred yards after the Santa Cruz de Miramar junction. Allow about three hours, either direction, for the entire San Blas-Puerto Vallarta trip.

The story is similar for Mexican National Hwy. 200 along the 172 miles (276 km) from Manzanillo via Barra de Navidad (134 miles, 214 km). It may be slow going while climbing the 2,400-foot Sierra Cuale summit south of Puerto Vallarta, but light traffic should prevail along the other stretches. Allow about four hours to Manzanillo, three from Barra de Navidad, and the same in the opposite direction. The Guadalajara route is a bit more more complicated. From Guadalajara, follow **Mexican National Hwy. 15** toll *autopista* to Chapalilla. Although expensive (about $30 per car, more for motorhomes) it's a breeze in two hours. At Chapalilla, fork onto the 22-mile (36-km) toll cutoff to Compostela. At Compostela, head left (south) on Hwy. 200 and sail the remaining 80 miles (129 km) in an hour and a half. Grand total to Puerto Vallarta, 214 miles (344 km), four hours, either way.

By Bus

Many bus lines run through Puerto Vallarta, and they each have their own small stations, many clustering south of the Río Cuale on or near Av. Insurgentes.

All departures listed are local *(salidas locales)* unless otherwise noted as *salidas de paso.*

The super first-class **Elite** line and its first-class parent, **Tres Estrellas de Oro** (TEO) operate from the new Elite terminal, corner of B. Badillo and Insurgentes, tel. (322) 311-17. Both Elite and TEO buses connect with Guadalajara and intermediate points a dozen times a day. A few daily *salidas de paso* connect en route with southern destinations of Manzanillo and Lázaro Cárdenas and northern destinations of Tepic, Mazatlán, Tijuana, and intermediate points. A pair of TEO *salidas de paso* connect daily via the entire Pacific coast route. One connects north (transfer at Tepic, to Mazatlán, Mexicali, and Tijuana) with the U.S. border; the other connects south (direct, no transfer, via Manzanillo, Zihuatanejo, Acapulco, and Puerto Escondido) with Salina Cruz, Oaxaca.

Second-class **Transportes del Pacífico,** TP, Insurgentes 260, tel. (322) 210-15, connect with Tepic every half hour during the day and early evening. Several first-class buses connect with Guadalajara via the "corta" (cutoff), stopping at La Peñita, Compostela, Ixtlán del Río, and intermediate points along the way.

Several first-class **Transportes Norte de Sonora** Buses V. Carranza 322, tel. (322) 266-66, buses connect daily with Tepic, where connections can be made with the U.S. border, Guadalajara, and Mexico City. Two other departures connect with Mazatlán via San Blas, bypassing Tepic.

Transportes Cihautlán, tel. (322) 234-36, corner Madero and Constitucíon, provides the most frequent connections with southern destinations of Barra de Navidad, Manzanillo, and intermediate points. Two Super-first-class "Primera Plus" buses per day connect with Manzanillo, while many second-class buses travel the same route, and are willing to stop along the way.

Jalisco ceramic, mother and child

AROUND THE BAY OF BANDERAS

Puerto Vallarta is a tourist city with all the convenient services, food, and good accommodations that a resort can supply. What Puerto Vallarta sometimes cannot supply, however, is peace and quiet.

An out exists, however. A diadem of rustic nearby retreats—fishing villages and sandy beaches—around the Bay of Banderas can provide a retreat for a day, a week, or a month from the tourist rush.

The Southern Arc: Mismaloya and Beyond

The southern-arc beach gems of **Mismaloya, Boca de Tomatlán, Las Animas, Quimixto,** and **Yelapa** are described under "Sights" above.

The Northern Arc: Nuevo Vallarta, Bucerías, and Punta Mita

The northern curve of the Bay of Banderas begins as Hiwy. 200 crosses the Ameca River and enters the state of Nayarit, where clocks shift from central to mountain time. (Heading north, set your watch back one hour.)

NUEVO VALLARTA

The Nuevo Vallarta development, just north of the river, is Nayarit's design for a grand resort, comparable to the Zona Hotelera 10 miles south. For years, however, miles of boulevard parkways dotted with streetlights and empty cul-de-sacs remained deserted, waiting for homes, condos, and hotels that were never built. A spurt of activity in the early '90s seemed to promise the potential of Nuevo Vallarta might someday be realized. The **Club de Playa Nuevo Vallarta,** the core of the original development, is indeed a pretty place—perfect for a relaxing beach afternoon. Get there by turning left at Av. Nuevo Vallarta about five miles (eight km) north of the airport at the Jack Tar Village sign (one mile past the north end of the Ameca bridge). At the end of the 1.4 mile driveway entrance you will come to the Club de Playa, with a parking lot, small regional art and artifacts museum, pool, snack bar, and seemingly endless beach.

The miles-long beach is the main attraction. The nearly level golden white sand is perfect for beachcombing, and the water is excellent for surf fishing, swimming, bodysurfing, and boogie-boarding. Beginning or intermediate surfing might be possible for those who bring their own board. Enjoy isolated beach camping during the temperate winter on the endless dune past the north end beach boulevard of Paseo Cocoteros. Bring everything, including water and a tarp for shade.

Accommodations

Adjacent to the Club de Playa is the big Club-Med-style **Jack Tar Village,** which often invites the public to drop in on its continuous party, which includes sports, crafts, games, and food and drink for about $40 per person, per day. If you take a room, the all-inclusive lodging and activities run about $160 per day for two. Reservations are available only through the hotel's Texas office at 5949 Sherry Lane, Suite 1800, Dallas 75225. Call (800) 999-9182 in the U.S. and (800) 952-2582 in Mexico; from Canada, call (214) 987-4909.

About three miles south of the Jack Tar Village a cluster of big new hotels woo vacationers with a plethora of facilities and long, velvety beaches. The 344-room **Hotel Sierra Radisson Plaza** seems to be the most successful, located at Paseo de Cocoteros 19, Nuevo Vallarta, Nayarit 63732, tel. (329) 713-00, fax 708-00. Arriving at the hotel feels like approaching a small, Elysian planet. You drive for miles past uninhabited verdure-lined boulevards, finally pulling up to a huge, apparently deserted structure, where, inside, to your surprise, droves of relaxed, well-fed tourists are socializing in half a dozen languages. Above the reception area rises a starkly angular atrium, hung with a squadron of big piñatas. Nearby, a garden of lovely ceramic fruits decorates whitewashed stairsteps leading downstairs. There, a buffet loaded with salads, fruit, poultry, fish, meats, and desserts is spread on one side of an airy, guest-filled dining area. Outside are pools beneath palm trees along the beach, where crowds enjoy nightly dancing and shows. By day, guests lounge, swim, and frolic amid a varied menu of activities, from water aerobics and yoga to beach volleyball, bicycling, and kayaking.

Rates include all food, drinks, activities, and a deluxe ocean-view room. They begin at about $120 s, $90 d per person. Children under seven stay free; there's a tariff of $15 for those from seven to 12, and children over 12 are considered adults. For information and reservations, call (800) 333-3333. If the season is right, a travel agent may be able to secure a reduced-rate package.

Next door the **Diamond Resort,** Paseo de los Cocoteros 18, Nuevo Vallarta, Nayarit 63732, tel. (329) 704-00, fax 700-82, offers a similar all-inclusive vacation package at somewhat lower rates. The hotel, while still deluxe, lacks the smooth management and super-luxurious feel of its bigger Radisson brother. For reservations, call a travel agent; bargain packages may be available during non-peak seasons.

BUCERÍAS

The scruffy roadside clutter of Bucerías ("Place of the Divers") is deceiving. Located 12 miles (19 km) north of the Puerto Vallarta airport, Bucerías (pop. 5,000) has the longest, creamiest beach on

the Bay of Banderas. Local people flock there on Sunday for beach play, as well as fresh seafood from one of a dozen seaside *palapa*-restaurants.

Bucerías offers many options. It is basically a country town of four long streets running for several miles parallel to the beach. The town features small businesses and grocery stores and at least a dozen local-style restaurants. Bucerías furthermore has lots of old-fashioned local color, especially in the evenings around the lively market at the south end of the business district.

The beach—seemingly endless and nearly flat, with slowly breaking waves and soft, golden-white sand—offers shells for the taking, swimming, bodysurfing, boogie-boarding, beginning and intermediate surfing, and surf fishing. Tent camping is customary beyond the edges of town, especially during the Christmas and Easter holidays.

Accommodations

At the town's serene north end is the Playas de Huanacaxtle subdivision, with big flower decorated homes owned by rich Mexicans and North Americans. Sprinkled among the intimate, palm-shaded *retornos* (cul-de-sacs) are a number of good bungalow-style beachside lodgings. Moving southward from the north edge of town, the top accommodations begin with the **Condo-Hotel Vista Vallarta,** Av. de los Picos s/n, Playas de Huanacaxtle, Bucerías, Nayarit 63732, tel. (329) 803-61, fax 803-60, three stories of stucco and tile apartments clustered inti-

at Bucerías on the Bay of Banderas

BRUCE WHIPPERMAN

mately around a palm-tufted beachside pool-patio. A loyal cadre of longtime guests—mostly U.S. and Canadian retiree-couples—return year after year to enjoy the big blue pool, the *palapa* restaurant, walks along the beach, and the company of fellow vacationers. All enjoy fully furnished suites with bedroom, dining room, kitchenette, living room, and private ocean-view balconies. Maids clean rooms daily, while downstairs, friendly, English-speaking clerks manage the desk and rent cars, boogie boards, and surfboards. High-season rates, for up to four persons per suite, run $65/night, $60/night weekly, $55/night monthly. Low-season or longer-term discounts may be negotiable.

A block south, the family-style **Bungalows Princess** looks out on the blue Bay of Banderas beneath the rustling fronds of lazy coco-palms. The two-story beachfront bungalows provide all the ingredients for a restful vacation for a family or group of friends. Behind the *cabañas,* past the swimming pools a stone's throw from the beach, a motel-style lineup of suites fills the economy needs of couples and small families. Contact Retorno Destiladeras, Playas Huanacaxtle, Bucerías, Nayarit 63732, tel. (322) 801-00 or 801-10, fax 800-68. They have a total of 36 bungalows and suites. The big beach bungalows rent from about $75 d; off-beach suites run from $60 d. Bargain for discounts and longterm rates, especially during low Jan.-Feb., May-June and Sept.-Nov. months. All rooms feature TV with HBO, phone, a/c; mini-market, two pools, credit cards accepted.

Continuing south, nearby **Bungalows Pico,** Av. Los Pico and Retorno Pontoque, Playas Huanacaxtle, Bucerías, Nayarit 63732, tel. (322) 804-70 or 801-31, shares the same palm-shadowed Bucerías beachfront. A rambling, Mexican family-style complex, Bungalows Picos clusters around a big inner pool-patio, spreading to a second bungalow tier beside a breezy beachside pool area. These units, which enjoy ocean views, are the most popular. During low season, the management offers such promotions as three nights for the price of two; discounts for long-term rentals usually available. Bargain under all conditions. The 47 bungalows, all with kitchenettes, run from about $45 d; four small units rent for about $35. With TV, a/c, and two pools; credit cards accepted.

Sharing the same beachside as Bungalows Pico and the Princess is **Suites Atlas,** a Spanish-style tile and stucco villa built around a luxurious beachside pool-patio garden. Located on Retorno Destiladeras, Bucerías, Nayarit 63732, tel. (322) 802-35 and 800-659, with 11 units renting from around $100/day; a special $1200/month rate is sometimes available during the slow low seasons. All rooms are spacious and deluxe, sleeping about six, with fully equipped kitchenettes, all with a/c. Try for one of the choice upstairs front units, which offer private balconies and ocean vistas.

Casa Blanca, on the south side of town at the corner of Galeana and L. Cárdenas, is an elegant Spanish-style villa of large, tastefully furnished kitchenette apartments beside a beachside patio garden. Amenities include a pool and a palm-thatched treehouse perched in a green rubber tree with a view of the beach. Make reservations early for one of the three upper units, which offer palm-silhouetted ocean sunset vistas. The nine luxury suites with kitchenettes rent for about $1000/month including TV, phone, a/c, and boat-launch ramp.

You can rent the Casa Blanca units through reputable and friendly agents Mina Sánchez de Gonzales and her husband Carlos, whose office is on the highway at the south edge of town. If Casa Blanca is full, Mina and Carlos will try to find you something just as good. Contact them through **Gonzales Real Estate,** P.O. Box 95 Aeropuerto, Puerto Vallarta 48300, Jalisco, tel. (329) 802-94 or 801-27, fax 802-94.

In a flowery, palm-shaded garden right on the beach is **Bucerías Trailer Park,** Calle Lázaro Cárdenas, a quarter-mile south of the business district. The property was once owned by Elizabeth Taylor; the present owners have converted the luxurious living room of the former residence into a homey restaurant and social room, which they call Restaurant Pira-pa. Ask them what it means. Make your winter reservations early through P.O. Box 39-A Aeropuerto, Puerto Vallarta, Jalisco 48300; or P.O. Box 148, Bucerías, Nayarit 63732; tel. (329) 802-65, fax 803-00. The 48 spaces rent for about $15/day or $330/month, with hookups, showers, toilets, nearby boat ramp, and good drinkable well water.

Right across the street from the trailer park is **Bungalows Arroyo,** one of Bucerías's best-buy lodgings at 500 Lázaro Cárdenas, Bucerías, Nayarit 63732, tel./fax (329) 802-88. The dozen or so roomy, two-bedroom apartments are clustered beside a green, palmy pool-garden half a block from the beach. The units are comfortably furnished, each with king-size bed, private balcony, kitchen, and living and dining room. The friendly, conscientious managers live a few doors down. Units rent for about $500 per month; weekly rentals sometimes available. They're popular; get your winter reservations in months early.

Pie in the Sky

Even if only passing through Bucerías, don't miss Pie In the Sky, the little bakery of entrepreneurs Don and Teri Murray, who've developed a thriving business soothing the collective sweet tooth of Puerto Vallarta's expatriate and retiree colony. Their chocolate-nut cookies have to be tasted to be believed. Watch for their sign on the inland side of the highway just south of town; open Mon.-Fri. 0900-1700. Or visit their store in Puerto Vallarta, at Basilio Badillo 270, tel. (322) 250-99; open 0900-2100 daily.

PUNTA MITA COUNTRY

A few miles north of Bucerías, slow down at the intersection where the Punta Mita Hwy. forks west from Hwy. 200 and stop at the local office of the **Nayarit State Tourist Information Office;** open Mon.-Fri. 0900-1300 and 1500-1700. The officer in charge, friendly, knowledgeable, and locally born José D. Elizondo, can answer most any question about the Nayarit half of the Bay of Banderas.

Drivers, mark your mileage at the Hwy. 200 turnoff before you head west along the Punta Mita Highway. Within a mile (two km), look downhill and you'll see the little drowsy town of **Cruz de Huanacaxtle** above a small fishing harbor. Although the town has stores, a good cafe, a few simple lodgings, and a protected boat and yacht anchorage, it lacks a decent beach.

Half a mile (at around Mile 2, Km 3) farther on, however, a side road to the left leads to beautiful **Playa Manzanillo** and the **Hotel and Trailer Park Piedra Blanca**. The beach itself, a carpet of fine, golden-white coral sand, stretches along a little cove sheltered by a limestone headland—thus Piedra Blanca, "White Stone." This place was made for peaceful vacationing: snorkeling at nearby **Playa Piedra Blanca** on the opposite side of the headland, fishing from the beach, rocks, or by boat launched on the beach or hired in the Cruz de Huanacaxtle harbor, camping in RV or tent in the trailer park or adjacent open field.

The hotel is a small, friendly, family-managed resort. The best of the big comfortable suites offer upstairs ocean views. All the ingredients—a good tennis court, a shelf of used novels, and a rustic *palapa*-restaurant beside an inviting beach-view pool-patio—perfect for tranquil relaxation. The 31 suites with kitchenettes and a/c rent from $40 d in the low season ($240 weekly, $700 monthly) to $60 in the high season; credit cards not accepted. Reserve by writing directly to P.O. Box 48, Bucerías, Nayarit 63732, or calling the Guadalajara agent at (361) 76-051 or faxing 76-047.

The hotel also manages the trailer park in the beachside but largely unshaded lot next door. Although trailer park residents aren't supposed to use the pool, hotel management doesn't seem to mind. This is a popular winter park, so make reservations early. The 26 spaces rent for $12/day, $80/week, $280/month; hookups, showers, toilets, pets okay.

Past Piedra Blanca, the highway winds for 12 miles (19 km) to Punta Mita through the bushy green jungle country at the foot of the Sierra Vallejo, empty except for a few scattered ranchos. Side roads draw adventurous travelers to hidden beaches for a day—or a week—of tranquil swimming, snorkeling, and beachcombing. You might want to get out and walk before your vehicle bogs down on these side roads. Campers should bring everything, including plenty of drinking water. If in doubt about anything, don't hesitate to inquire locally, or ask Jose Elizondo in the information office back at Hwy. 200.

Rock coral, the limestone skeleton of living coral, becomes gradually more common on these beaches, thus tinting the water aqua and the sand white. As the highway approaches Punta Mita the living reef offshore becomes intact and continuous.

Playa Las Destiladeras

Marked (at Mile 5, Km 8) by a pair of *palapa*-restaurants on the left is Playa Las Destiladeras, a beach-lover's heavenly mile of white sand. Two- to five-foot waves roll in gently, providing good conditions for bodysurfing and boogie-boarding. Surfing gets better the closer you get to the end of **Punta El Burro**'s (known also as Punta Veneros) headland, where good left-breaking waves make it popular with local surfers.

The intriguing label *destiladeras* (seepage) originates with the fresh water oozing from the cliffs past Punta El Burro, collecting in freshwater pools right beside the ocean. Campers who happen upon one of these pools may find their water problems solved.

Playa Pontoque and Playa Anclote

A Restaurante Paraíso Escondido sign (Mile 8, Km 13) marks the downhill, vine-draped forest road to Playa Pontoque, an intimate jungle-backed crescent of coral-white sand. Here, the living reef lies offshore, ripe for snorkeling and fishing for red snapper and *toro*. Surfing, boogie-boarding, and bodysurfing are possible when snorkeling isn't.

The restaurant specializes in seafood and steaks, catering to tourist tastes. Relatively few locals come here—the owner says they prefer a continuous shoreline to Pontoque's scenic, outcrop-dotted sand and offshore reef. The peo-

ple who do come seem to have a great time, strolling, swimming, snorkeling, and tidepooling. Acacia boughs overhang the sand, forming shady nooks perfect for lazing away the day and night. If you want to camp, ask the restaurant owner if its okay. Bring water; the restaurant has none to spare.

For a treat, stop in at the friendly, family-run **Restaurant Amapas,** across the highway from the Paraíso Escondido road turnoff. Homesteaded when the Punta Mita road was a mere path through the jungle, Restaurant Amapas still retains a country flavor. Ducks waddle around the yard, javelina (wild pigs) snort in their pen, and candles flicker during the evening twilight as the elderly owner recalls her now-deceased husband hunting food for the table: "We ate deer, javelin, ducks, coatimundi, rattlesnake, iguana . . . whatever we could catch." Although local hunters now provide most of the food, she and her daughter-in-law do all the cooking, and their many loyal customers still enjoy the same wild fare. The restaurant is open 0900 to sunset every day.

Playa Anclote ("Anchor Beach") farther west (Mile 13, Km 21) gets its name from the galleon anchor displayed at one of the beachside *palapa* restaurants. Playa Anclote is a broad, half-mile-long curving strand of soft, very fine, coral sand. The water is shallow for a long distance out and the waves are gentle and long-breaking, good for beginning surfing, boogie-boarding,

sea cucumbers out to dry at Corral de Riscos, near Punta Mita at the northwest tip of the Bay of Banderas

BRUCE WHIPPERMAN

and bodysurfing. Surfboards and boogie boards rent for about $5 on the beach.

Among the better of Playa Anclote restaurants is **Restaurant El Dorado,** tel. (329) 465-56, open daily 1100 to sunset, run by friendly Hector López. His menu is based on meat, poultry, and the bounty of super-fresh snapper, scallops, oysters, and lobsters that local fisherfolk bring onto the beach.

Tent camping is possible when not prohibited by the government because of local construction; ask at the restaurant if you can flop under big trees at both ends of the beach. Stores in the small town of Emiliano Zapata a quarter-mile away (commonly known as Punta Mita) can furnish the necessities, including drinking water.

Hard feelings have lately erupted between the local Emiliano Zapata *ejido* and the Nayarit government. The government is attempting to move the *ejido* fisherfolk who live and work on communal land at Corral de Riscos (see below) to a housing development and new anchorage at Playa Anclote. The reason is as old as Mexico: when traditional lands become worth something, powerful local interests often try to displace the poor communal owners. In this case, foreign investors—with government approval—want to build two big luxury hotels on Punta Mita, while the people continue to say they don't wish to be moved like rabbits against their will.

Punta Mita

The Punta Mita Hwy. ends at **Corral de Riscos,** an islet-enfolded aqua lagoon bordered by a long coral-sand beach. Folks relax beneath a lineup of restaurant *palapas;* boats rest at the edge of the water, while fishermen talk and laugh as they mend their nets.

The two bare-rock islets **Isla del Mono** and **Isla de las Abandonadas** shelter the lagoon. The name of the former comes from a *mono* (monkey) face people see in one of the outcroppings; the latter label springs from the legend of the fishermen who went out to sea and never returned. Las Abandonadas were their

wives, who waited on the islet for years, vainly searching the horizon for their lost husbands.

The local fisherfolk have organized themselves into a cooperative; its representative, friendly Jesus "Chuy" Casilla, welcomes tourists daily from 0900 to 1800 at his shop **Sol y Arena,** located on the beachfront directly below the parking lot. He rents boogie boards, snorkel gear, and surfboards for about $5 per day. Chuy also arranges sportfishing launches (three-hour trip, about $65 complete) and snorkeling, wildlife viewing, and photography boat tours to the pristine offshore wildlife sanctuaries of **Islas Las Marietas.** During a typical half-day trip, visitors may glimpse dolphins, sea turtles, and sometimes whales, as well as visit breeding grounds for brown and blue-footed boobies, Heerman's gulls, and other birds.

When he's not working, Chuy follows his love of surfing, which he also teaches. He claims the best surfing in the Bay of Banderas is on the left-breaks off Isla del Mono, off the lighthouse point about a quarter-mile to the south.

Plenty of open land with trees provides breezy **camping** sites—if permitted; ask Chuy. A clean basic store, **Abarrotes Las Palmeras,** can supply milk, cheese, juice, meats, groceries, and fruit. Also check out the bountiful coconut grove in the backyard.

Getting There

Transportes Pacífico buses, Insurgentes 282, tel. (322) 256-22, leave Puerto Vallarta for Tepic via Nuevo Vallarta (highway only) and Bucerías about once an hour. Small local Transportes Pacífico buses complete the **Punta Mita** roundtrip several times daily; the last bus leaves the Corral de Riscos parking lot at around 1730.

Auto Transportes Medina buses also complete several daily roundtrips between Punta Mita and the Puerto Vallarta station north of the *malecón.* The Puerto Vallarta station is at 1279 Brasil, corner of Honduras, one block south of the Buenaventura Hotel and three blocks from the beach, tel. (322) 269-43.

MIKE WELLINS

SOUTH TO MANZANILLO
ALONG THE ROAD
TO BARRA DE NAVIDAD

The country between Puerto Vallarta and Barra de Navidad is as unsullied as the new road that traverses it. Development has barely begun to penetrate its vast tracts of mountainous jungle, tangled thorny scrub, and pine-clad summit forests. Footprints rarely mark the miles of curving, golden beach.

This is a landscape ripe for adventurers—traveling by thumb, by bus, by car, or by RV—who enjoy getting away from the tourist track. Fortunately, everyone who travels south of Puerto Vallarta doesn't have to be a Daniel Boone. The coastal strip within a few miles of the highway has acquired some comforts—stores, trailer parks, campgrounds, hotels, and a scattering of small resorts—enough to become well known to Guadalajara people as the Costa Alegre, the "Happy Coast."

This modicum of amenities makes it easy for all travelers to enjoy what local people have for

years: plenty of sun, fresh seafood, clear blue water, and sandy beaches, some of which stretch for miles, while others are tucked away in little rocky coves like pearls in an oyster.

Heading Out
If you're driving, note your odometer mileage (or reset it to zero) as you pass the Pemex gas station at Km 214 on Hwy. 200 at the south edge of Puerto Vallarta. In the south, in the open country, mileage and roadside kilometer markers are a useful way to remember where your little paradise is hidden.

If you're not driving, simply hop onto one of the many southbound Transportes Cihuatlán second-class buses just before they pass at the south-end gas station or, alternatively, at their bus terminal at Madero 296. Let the driver know a few minutes beforehand where along the road you want to get off.

CHICO'S PARADISE

The last outpost on the Puerto Vallarta tour-bus circuit is Chico's Paradise, 13 miles (22 km, at Km 192) from the south edge of Puerto Vallarta in the lush jungle country. Here, the clear, cool Río Tuito cascades over a collection of smooth, friendly granite boulders. Chico's restaurant is a big multilevel *palapa* that overlooks the entire beautiful scene—deep green pools for swimming, flat warm rocks for sunning, and gurgling gentle waterfalls for splashing. Although a few homesteads and a humbler rival restaurant, Indian Paradise (see below), dot the streamside nearby, the original Chico's still dominates, although their reputation rests mainly on the beauty of the setting rather than the quality of their rather expensive menu.

Indian Paradise offers a similarly airy and scenic *palapa* setting just upstream from Chico's, at more reasonable prices. Their good soups, salads, and seafood and meat entrees go for $7-12. After refreshment, stroll across the wooden bridge to their rustic view gazebo to a perch above the beautiful scene.

The forest perfumed breezes, the gurgling, crystal stream, and the friendly, relaxed ambience are perfect for shedding the cares of the world. Although there are no formal lodgings, a number of potential **camping** spots border the river, both up- and downstream. **Stores** at Boca de Tomatlán, three miles downhill, can provide supplies.

Adventurers can hire local guides (ask at Indian Paradise) for horseback rides along the river and overnight treks into the green of the jungle **Sierra Lagunillas** that rises on both sides of the river. If you're quiet and aware, you may be rewarded with views of chattering parrots, dozing iguanas, feisty javelinas (wild pigs), clownish *tejones* (coatimundis), and wary *gatos montaña* (wildcats). If you're especially lucky, you might even get a glimpse of the fabled *tigre* (jaguar).

CABO CORRIENTES COUNTRY

El Tuito

The town of El Tuito, at Km 170 (27 miles, 44 km, from Puerto Vallarta), appears from the highway as nothing more than a bus stop. It doesn't even have a gas station. Most visitors pass by without even giving a second glance. This is a pity, because El Tuito (pop. 3,000) is a friendly little place that spreads along a long main street to a pretty square about a mile from the highway.

El Tuito enjoys at least two claims to fame: besides being the **mescal** capital of western Jalisco, it's the jumping-off spot for the seldom-visit-

Flat, friendly rocks decorate the clear River Tuito, which flows beneath the palapa at Chico's Paradise.

BRUCE WHIPPERMAN

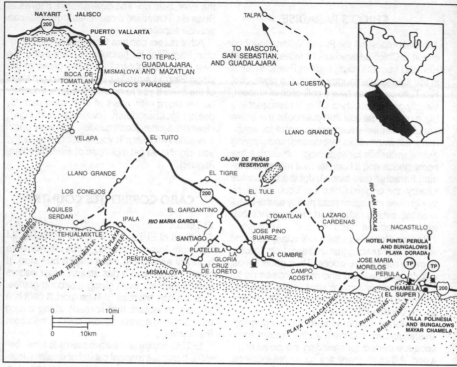

ed coastal hinterland of Cabo Corrientes, the southernmost lip of the Bay of Banderas. This is pioneer country, a land of wild beaches and forests, unpenetrated by electricity, phone, and paved roads. Wild creatures still abound: Turtles come ashore to lay their eggs, hawks soar, parrots swarm, and the faraway scream of the jaguar can yet be heard in the night.

The rush for the *raicilla,* as local connoisseurs call El Tuito mescal, begins on Saturday when men crowd into town and begin upending bottles around noon, without even bothering to sit down. For a given individual, this cannot last too long, so the fallen are continually replaced by fresh arrivals all weekend.

Although El Tuito is famous for the *raicilla,* it is not the source. *Raicilla* comes from the sweet sap of the maguey plants, a close relative of the cactus-like "century plant," which blooms once then dies. An *ejido* (cooperative farm) of

Cicatan, six miles out along the dirt road as you head to the coast west of town, cultivates the maguey.

Along the Road to Aquiles Serdán

You can get to the coast with or without your own wheels. If you're driving, it should be a strong, high-clearance vehicle (pickup, jeep, very maneuverable RV, or VW van) filled with gas; if you're not driving, trucks and VW taxivans *(kombis* or *colectivos)* make daily trips. Their destinations include the coastal hamlet of Aquiles Serdán, the storied fishing cove of Tehualmixtle, and the agricultural village of Ipala beside the wide Bahía de Tehualmixtle. Fare runs several dollars per person; inquire at the Hwy. 200 crossing or the west end of the El Tuito central plaza.

Getting there along the bumpy, rutted, sometimes steep 28-mile (45-km) dirt track is half the

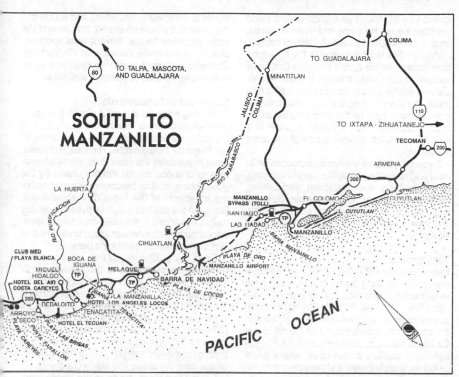

SOUTH TO MANZANILLO

TO TALPA, MASCOTA, AND GUADALAJARA

COLIMA

TO GUADALAJARA

MINATITLAN

JALISCO
COLIMA

TO IXTAPA - ZIHUATANEJO

TECOMAN

RÍO MARABASCO

ARMERIA

LA HUERTA

RÍO PURIFICACIÓN

MANZANILLO
BYPASS (TOLL)

EL COLOMO

CUYUTLAN

SANTIAGO

L. CUYUTLAN

LAS HADAS

MANZANILLO

BAHIA MANZANILLO

CIHUATLAN

CLUB MED
PLAYA BLANCA

PLAYA DE ORO

BOCA DE
IGUANA

MANZANILLO AIRPORT

MIGUEL
HIDALGO

MELAQUE

HOTEL DEL AIN
COSTA CAREYES

BARRA DE NAVIDAD

PLAYA DE COCOS

LA MANZANILLA

PEDALOITO

HOTEL LOS ANGELES LOCOS

ARROYO
SECO

TENACATITA

HOTEL EL TECUAN

PLAYA LAS BRISAS

PUNTA FARALLON

PACIFIC OCEAN

fun of Aquiles Serdán (pop. 200). About six miles (10 km) from Hwy. 200, you'll pass through the lands of the mescal cooperative, Cicatan, marked only by a whitewash-and-thatch *bodega* (storage house) in front of a tiny school on the right. On the left, you'll soon glimpse a field of maguey in the distance. A few dozen families (who live in the hills past the far side of the field) quietly go about their business of tending their maguey plants and extracting, fermenting, and distilling the precious sap into their renowned *raicilla.*

The road dips up and down the rest of the way, over sylvan hillsides dotted with oak *(robles),* through intimate stream valleys perfect for parking an RV or setting up a tent, and past the hardscrabble rancho-hamlets of Llano Grande ("Broad Plain," 15 miles, 24 km, a small store) and Los Conejos ("The Rabbits," 21 miles, 34 km).

You can't get lost, because there's only one route until a few miles past Los Conejos, where a fork (26 miles, 42 km) marks your approach to Aquiles Serdán. The left branch continues south to Maito and Tehualmixtle. A mile and a half to the north along the right branch you will arrive at the Río Tecolotlán. Aquiles Serdán stands on the far bank, across 100 yards of watery sand. Fortunately the riverbed road is concrete-bottomed, allowing you to drive right across the streambed any time other than after a storm.

Aquiles Serdán

The Aquiles Serdán villagers see so few outsiders you will become their attraction of the week. Wave and say hello, buy a *refresco,* stroll around town, and, after a while, the kids will stop crowding around and the adults will stop staring when they've found out you, too, are human. By that time, someone may even have invited you into their tree-branch-walled, clean dirt-floor house for some hot fish-fillet tacos, fresh tomatoes, and beans. Accept, of course.

Aquiles Serdán basks above the lily-edged river lagoon, which during the June-Oct. rainy season usually breaks through the beach-sandbar and drains directly into the surf half a mile below the town. During the dry season, the lagoon wanders lazily up the coast for a few miles. In any case, the white-sand beach is accessible only by boat, which you can borrow or hire at the village.

If you do, you'll have miles of untouched white sand and surf all to yourself for days of camping, beachcombing, shell collecting, surf fishing, wildlife viewing, and, if the waves permit, swimming, surfing, boogie-boarding, and snorkeling. The town's two stores can provide your necessities.

Tehualmixtle

Back at the fork (26 miles, 42 km from the highway) continue along the left branch about three miles through Maito (pop. 100, one store) to another fork (29 miles, 47 km). The right branch goes steeply up and then down a rough track to the right, which soon levels out on the cliff above the idyllic fishing cove of Tehualmixtle. Here, a headland shelters a blue nook, where a few launches float, tethered and protected from the open sea. To one side, swells wash over a submerged wreck, while an ancient, moss-stained warehouse crumbles above a rocky little beach. At the end of the road downhill, a beachside *palapa* invites visitors with drinks and fresh-out-of-the-water oysters, lobster, *dorado,* and red snapper.

Owner-operator Candelario is the moving force behind this pocket-size paradise. After your repast, and a couple more bottles of beer for good measure, he might tell you his version of the history of this coast—of legends of sunken galleons, or of the days when the old warehouse stored cocaine for legal shipment to the United States, when Coca-Cola got its name from the cocaine, which, generations ago, was added to produce "the pause that refreshes."

Nowadays, however, Tehualmixtle serves as a resting point for occasional sailboaters, travelers, fisherfolk, and those who enjoy the rewards of clear-water snorkeling and scuba diving around the sunken shrimp trawler and the rocky shoreline nearby. Several level spots beside the cove invite camping or RV parking. Candelario will gladly supply you with your stomach's delight of choice seafood and drinks.

Southeast of Tehualmixtle

Returning back up the road above the cove, glimpse southward toward the azure Bay of Tehualmixtle washing the white-sand ribbon of the Playa de Tehualmixtle. The village of **Ipala,** three miles down the road, is supply headquarters for the occasional visitors drawn by the good fishing, surfing, beachcombing, and camping prospects of the Playa de Tehualmixtle. Being on the open ocean, its waves are usually rough, especially in the afternoon. Only experienced swimmers who can judge undertow and surf should think of swimming here.

From Ipala (32 miles, 52 km), you can either retrace your path back to the highway at El Tuito, or continue down the coast (where the road gets rougher before it gets better) through the hamlet and beach of **Peñitas** (39 miles, 63 km, a few stores, restaurants), past **Mismaloya** (49 miles, 79 km), site of a University of Guadalajara turtle-hatching station. To get there, turn right onto the dirt trail just before the concrete bridge over the broad Río María Garcia.

From Mismaloya, return to the bridge, continue over the river three miles, and you will soon be back to the 20th century at **Cruz de Loreto** (52 miles, 84 km, many stores, sidewalks, electric lights and phones). From there, you can head directly to Hwy. 200 (10 miles via Santiago and Gargantino) at Km 131, just 24 miles (39 km) south of where you started at El Tuito.

CAJÓN DE LAS PEÑAS RESERVOIR

The lush farms of the Cabo Corrientes region owe much of their success to the Cajón de Peñas dam, whose waters enable farmers to profit from a year-round growing season. An added bonus is the recreation—boating, fishing, swimming, camping, hiking—which the big blue lake behind the dam makes possible.

With a car, the reservoir is easy to reach. Trucks and cars are frequent, so hikers can easily thumb rides. At Hwy. 200 Km 130, about a mile south of the Cruz de Loreto turnoff, head left (east) at a signed, paved road. After about five miles the road turns to gravel. Continue another four miles to a road fork atop the pair of earthern dams, separated by a hill. The left road continues over the smaller of the two dams. Follow the right fork, which first leads to **El Solitario,** a humble family-run restaurant *palapa* and boat landing. The friendly husband-wife team of Marcos Almanzar and Eva Olivera maintain their little outpost in hopes of serving their trickle of mostly holiday and weekend visitors. Besides their children, who help with chores, their little settlement consists of two parrots, a brood of turkeys, and a flock of chickens who fly into the nearby forest to roost at night. Eva's cooking, based mostly upon freshly caught *lobina* (largemouth bass) is basic but wholesome. Their parking lot above the lake has room for a number of self-contained RVs, while the forested knoll nearby might serve for tent camping. Marcos offers his boat for lake sightseeing and fishing excursions for about $12 an hour. Otherwise, you could swim, kayak, or launch your own motorboat right from the lakeshore below the restaurant.

Continue over the second, larger dam, counterclockwise around the forested, sloping lakeshore. Within three kilometers you'll arrive at the boat-cooperative village, where several downscale *palapa*-restaurants and boat landings provide food and recreational services for visitors. For a fee (offer to pay), they usually let you set up a tent or park your RV under a nearby lakeside tree.

PLAYA CHALACATEPEC

Playa Chalacatepec (chah-lah-kah-tay-PEK) lazes in the tropical sun just nine and a half kilometers from the highway at Km 88. Remarkably few people know of its charms except a handful of local youths and the occasional families who come on Sunday outings.

Playa Chalacatepec, with three distinct parts, has something for everyone: on the south side,

a wild, arrow-straight miles-long strand with crashing open-ocean breakers; in the middle, a low, wave-tossed, rocky point; and on the north, a long, tranquil, curving fine-sand beach.

The north beach, shielded by the point, has gently rolling breakers good for surfing, body-surfing, and safe swimming. Shells seasonally carpet its gradual white slope, and visitors have even left a pair of *palapa* shelters. These seem readymade for camping by night and barbecuing fish with by day with all of the driftwood lying around for the taking.

The point, Punta Chalacatepec, which separates the two beaches, is good for pole fishing on its surf-washed flanks and tidepooling in its rocky crevices.

Folks with RVs can pull off and park either along the approach road just above the beach or along tracks (beware of soft spots) downhill in the tall acacia scrub that borders the sand.

One of the few natural amenities that Playa Chalacatepec lacks is water, however. You'll have bring your own from the town back on the highway.

How to Get There

At Km 88, just as you're entering little José María Morelos (pop. 2,000), turn toward the beach at the corner with the auto-parts store *(refaccionaria)* marked with a big yellow Bardahl sign. Besides oil and batteries, the store sells a few snack-groceries. A number of better-stocked stores nearby sell water and more substantial supplies.

The road, although steep in spots, is easily negotiable by passenger cars in good condition and small-to-medium RVs. Owners of big rigs should do a test run.

On foot, the road is an easy two-hour hike (all of which probably won't be necessary because of the many passing farm pickups).

Mark your odometer at the highway. Continue over brushy hills and past fields and pastures, until Mile 5.2 (Km 8.4) where the road forks sharply right. You take the left track and pass a gate (close it after yourself). Atop the dune, glimpse the mangrove lagoon (bring kayak or rubber boat for wildlife-watching) in the distance to the left. Downhill, at Mile 6 (Km 9.7), you will be at Playa Chalacatepec.

CHAMELA BAY

Most longtime visitors know Jalisco's Costa Alegre through Barra de Navidad and two big, beautiful, beach-lined bays: Tenacatita and Chamela. Tranquil Bahía de Chamela, the most northerly of the two, is broad, blue, dotted with islands, and lined by a strip of fine, honey-yellow sand.

Stretching five miles south from the sheltering Punta Rivas headland near Perula village, Chamela Bay is open but calm. A chain of intriguingly labeled rocky *islas,* such as Cocinas ("Kitchens"), Negrita ("Little Black One"), and Pajarera ("Place of Birds"), scatter the strong Pacific swells into gentle billows by the time they roll onto the beaches.

Besides its natural amenities, Chamela Bay has three bungalow-complexes, one mentionable motel, two trailer parks, and an unusual campground. The focal point of this low-key resort area is the Km 72 highway corner (88 miles, 142 km, from Puerto Vallarta, 46 miles, 74 km, to Barra de Navidad). This spot, marked "Chamela" on many maps, is known simply as **"El Super"** by local people. Though the supermarket and neighboring bank have closed and are filled with the owner's antique car collection, El Super, nevertheless, lives on in the minds of the local folks.

Beaches and Activities

Chamela Bay's beaches are variations on one continuous strip of sand, from Playa Rosadas in the south through Playa Chamela in the middle to Playas Fortuna and Perula at the north end.

Curving behind the sheltering headland **Playa Perula** is the broadest and most tranquil beach of Chamela Bay. It is best for children and a snap for boat launching, swimming, and fishing from the rocks nearby. A dozen *pangas* usually line the water's edge, ready to take visitors on fishing excursions (figure $20 per hour, with bargaining) and snorkeling around the offshore islets. A line of seafood *palapas* provides the food and drinks for the fisherfolk and mostly Mexican families who know and enjoy this scenic little village-cove.

Playas Fortuna, Chamela, and Rosadas: Heading south, the beach gradually changes character. The surf roughens, the slope steepens, and the sand narrows from around 200 feet at Perula to perhaps 100 feet at the south end of the bay. Civilization also thins out. The dusty village of stores, small eateries, vacation homes, and beachfront *palapa* restaurants that line Playa Fortuna give way to farmland and scattered houses at Playa Chamela. Two miles farther on, grassy dunes above trackless sand line Playa Rosada.

The gradually varying vigor of the waves and the isolation of the beach determine the place where you can indulge your own favorite pas-

Accommodations are often available (drop in only) to the public at Centro Vacacional Chamela, the Chamela Bay teacher's resort.

BRUCE WHIPPERMAN

times: For bodysurfing and boogie-boarding, Rosada and Chamela are best; and while windsurfing is usually possible anywhere on Chamela Bay it will be best beyond the tranquil waves at La Fortuna. For surf fishing, try casting beyond the vigorous, breaking billows of Rosada. And likewise Rosada, being the most isolated, will be the place where you'll most likely find that shell-collection treasure you've been wishing for.

Beach Hiking, Jogging, and Bicycling: The five-mile curving strand of Chamela Bay is perfect for a morning hike from Rosada Beach. To get there, ride a Transportes Cihuatlán second-class bus to around the Km 65 marker, where a dirt road heads a half-mile to the beach. With the sun comfortably at your back, you can walk all the way to Perula if you want, stopping for refreshments at any one of several *palapas* along the way.

The firm sand of Chamela Bay beaches is likewise good for jogging, even for bicycling, provided you don't mind cleaning the sand out of the gears afterwards.

Accommodations

The El Super corner is hard to miss. Far removed from his homeland, a forlorn Polynesian god stands in continuous vigil across from the corner, silently directing people down the side road to Chamela Beach and **Villa Polinesia** one mile away.

Villa Polinesia's owners, who live in Guadalajara, call it a "camping club." The description fits. It is the only place in Mexico, they claim, "to allow you to meet nature." The beach and bay certainly set the mood: soft, golden sand, island-silhouetted sunsets, tranquil surf, abundant birds and fish, sometimes whales and dolphins, and occasionally great manta rays leap from the water offshore.

For a campground, Villa Polinesia's facilities are luxurious. The lovely, palm-shadowed complex has two tall, elaborate *palapa* restaurant-bars, a mini-market, drinkable water, hot water, communal showers, toilets, and a laundry.

They offer four kinds of accommodations. Most luxurious are a dozen open-air oceanfront Swiss Family Robinson-style *cabañas,* each with cooking-eating area and toilet and shower downstairs, and a pair of thatch-roofed bedrooms with soft floor-sleeping pads upstairs.

There is much more. Besides half an acre of space for **camping,** they have about three dozen concrete A-line "tents," each with a soft pair of sleeping pads, electricity, and a small screened ventilation window inside. These may be hot for sleeping during the warm half of the year; best bring your own tent, which is easier to adjust for temperature than their clever concrete installations.

In addition, they have a pleasant, shady 15-space **trailer park** with all hookups, right next to the communal showers and toilet.

A minor drawback to all this, besides there being no pool, is their somewhat steep rates: the open-air cabañas go for the same price as a moderate hotel room: about $33 for four, $25 for one or two; the trailer spaces go for about $12 per day or $250 per month; tent spaces rent for $5/day per person. These prices, however, are subject to bargaining and discounts any time other than peak holidays. Their address is simply Km 72, Carretera 200, Barra de Navidad a Puerto Vallarta, Chamela, Jalisco, no phone; for more info and reservations, write, or call Guadalajara tel. (3) 6-223-940, or Mexico City tel. (5) 5101-464.

Right next door to the Villa Polinesia stands **Bungalows Mayar Chamela** (Km 72, Carretera Puerto Vallarta, Chamela, Jalisco, tel. (328) 552-52), perhaps the most attractive moderate accommodation between Puerto Vallarta and Barra de Navidad. The 18 spacious, well-maintained kitchenette-bungalows with fans (no a/c) surround a palmy, banana-fringed pool and patio, gleaming with loving care. With the beach just steps away, no wonder people come from all over the world to stay here for months on end. Get your winter reservation in early. Rates are about $33 for two, $66 for four; monthly discounts. For reservations, write or fax the reservations manager, Arturo Javier Yañez G., at Obregón 1425 S.L., Guadalajara, Jalisco, tel. (3) 6-440-044, fax 6-439-318.

At Km 76, a sign marks a dirt road to Playas Fortuna and Perula. About two miles downhill, right on the beach, you can't miss the bright yellow stucco **Bungalows Playa Dorada,** Perula, Km 76, Carretera 200 Melaque-Puerto Vallarta, Jalisco, the biggest building on Chamela Bay. More a motel than bungalows, its three tiers of very plain rooms and kitchenette-suites are nearly empty except on weekends and Mexican holidays.

Playa Dorada's two saving graces, however, are the beach, which curves gracefully to the scenic little fishing nook of Perula, and the motel's inviting palm-edged pool-patio. The best-located rooms are on the top floor, overlooking the ocean. They rent 18 rooms sleeping two to three for about $33; 18 kitchenette units sleeping four go for about $66, all with parking. Although they routinely offer a 20% discount for weekly rentals, you might be able to bargain for an even better deal any time other than peak holidays.

It's easy to miss the low-profile **Hotel Punta Perula,** just one block inland from the Bungalows Playa Dorada, at Perula, Km 76, Carretera 200, Melaque-Puerto Vallarta, Jalisco, tel. (328) 550-20. This homey old place seems like a scene from Old Mexico, with a rustic white stucco tier of rooms enclosing a spacious green garden and venerable tufted grove. Their 14 clean, gracefully decorated, colonial-style, fan-equipped rooms go for about $27 d, except for Christmas and Easter holidays. Bargains are offered on longer stays. (Being out of Old Mexico, they have no pool, of course.)

A few blocks north of the Hotel Playa Dorada is the funky **Punta Perula Trailer Park,** Perula, Km 76, Carretera, Puerto Vallarta, Jalisco. The spare facilities include about 16 usable but shadeless spaces (out of 20) right on the beach, with all hookups, a fish-cleaning sink, and showers and toilets. Playa Perula Trailer Park residents enjoy stores nearby, good fishing, and a lovely beach for a front yard. Rates are low, but indefinite—although one of the residents said he was paying a monthly rate that amounted to about $6 a day.

The **Centro Vacacional Chamela** right on pristine Rosada Beach is a teachers' vacation retreat that rents its unoccupied units to the general public. The building is a modern, two-story apartment house with a well-maintained pool and patio. An outdoor *palapa* stands by the pool and another open room invites cards and conversation. The units themselves are large, bright, and airy one-bedrooms, sleeping four, with sea views and kitchen. They rent for $40, drop-in only. Arrive before 1700, when the manager returns home for the night. On non-holiday weekdays the place is often nearly empty. Have a look by following the upper of two side roads at the big concrete "47" monument near the Km 66 marker. Within less than a mile you'll be there. Ask one of the teachers to explain the significance of the "47."

If the teacher's retreat is full, try next door at the **Club Playa Chamela,** perhaps the most downscale timeshare in Mexico, if not the world. The manager said that, for a one-time $1000 fee, you can get one idyllic week for each of twenty years there. In the meantime, while the units are being sold, the owner is renting them out. All eight of the pink and blue bare bulb cottages have two bedrooms, a kitchenette, and small living room. Although plainly furnished, they're reasonably clean and have ceiling fans and hot water. Outside, beyond a small forest of young palms, is a blue pool, a *palapa* sometimes-restaurant, and a long, pristine, sunset-view beach. The asking rate is $50/day, $230/week, or $650/month. Try bargaining for a better price anytime other than the popular Christmas, Easter, and August seasons. Contact owner Jose A. Santana Soto, at Venezuela 719 (Colonia Moderna), Guadalajara, tel. (3) 6-101-103, or (3) 6-103-147 for information and reservations.

Camping
For RVs, the best spots are the trailer parks at **Villa Polinesia** and the **Perula Trailer Park** (see preceding). Car-camping sites are likewise available at the Villa Polinesia for $10 per day for two.

If you can walk in, you can probably set up a tent anywhere along the bay you like. One of the best places would be the grassy dune along pristine Playa Rosada a few hundred yards north of the Centro Vacacional (Km 66; see above). Water is available.

Playa Negrito, the pristine little sand crescent that marks the southern end of Chamela Bay, offers still another picnic or camping possibility. Get there by following the dirt road angling downhill from the highway at the south end of the bridge between Km 63 and Km 64. Turn left at the Chamela village stores beneath the bridge, continue about two miles, bearing left to the end of the road, where the *palapa* of an old restaurant stands at beachside. This is the southernmost of two islet-protected coves flanking the low Punta Negro headland. With clear, tranquil waters and golden-sand beaches, both coves are great for fishing from the rocks, snorkeling, windsurfing, and swimming. The south-end beach is unoccupied and has plenty of room for tenting and RV parking; a house sits back from the north-end beach about a quarter-mile away on the far side of the point. If you want to camp around there, ask them if it's okay: *"¿Es bueno acampar acá?"*

Food
Supplies are available at stores near the **El Super** corner (Km 72) or in the villages of **Perula** (on the beach, turn off at Km 76), **San Mateo** (Km 70), and **Chamela** (follow the side road at the south end of the bridge between Km 64 and 63).

Hearty country Mexican food, hospitality, and snack groceries are available at the **Tejaban** truck stop-restaurant at the El Super corner; open daily from breakfast time until 2200-2300. Two popular local roadside seafood spots are the **La Viuda** ("The Widow," Km 64) and **Don Lupe Mariscos** (Km 63). They both have their own divers who go out daily for fresh fish ($8), octopus *(pulpo)* ($8), conch, clams, oysters, and lobster ($14). Open daily 0800 until around 2100.

Services, Information, and Emergencies
The closest **bank** is 34 miles north at Tomatlán (turnoff at La Cumbre, at Km 116). *Casetas de larga distancia* operate at the El Super corner, daily 0800-1500 and 1600-2100, and at Pueblo Careyes, the village behind the soccer field at Km 52.

The **Pemex** *gasolinera* at El Super usually has unleaded Magna Sin gas. Fill up because the next ones are 27 miles north at La Cumbre (Km 116), and 50 miles (80 km) south at Melaque (Km 0).

If you get sick, go to your hotel desk. If you're not staying at a hotel, the closest clinic is in Perula (Km 76, four blocks south of the village plaza, no phone) or at Pueblo Careyes at Km 52 (doctors available daily 0800-1400; around the clock in emergencies).

Local **police,** known as the Policia Auxiliar del Estado, are stationed in a pink roadside house at Km 46, no phone, and also at the hamlet of San Mateo, one km south of El Super.

HOTEL BEL AIR COSTA CAREYES

The Hotel Bel Air Costa Careyes, one of the little-known gems of Pacific Mexico, is really two hotels in one. After Christmas and before Easter it brims with well-to-do Mexican families letting their hair down. The rest of the year the hotel is a tranquil, tropical retreat basking at the edge of a pristine, craggy cove.

The natural scene sets the tone: a majestic palm grove opens onto a petite sandy beach set between rocky cliffs. Offshore, the water, deep and crystal clear, is home for dozens of kinds of fish. Overhead, hawks and frigato birds soar, pelicans dive, and boobies and terns skim the waves. At night nearby, turtles carry out their ancient ritual by silently depositing their precious eggs on nearby beaches where they were born.

As if not to be outdone by nature, the hotel itself is an elegant, tropical retreat. A platoon of gardeners manicure lush spreading grounds that lead to gate and reception. Past the desk, tiers of ochre-hued Mediterranean lodgings enfold an elegant inner courtyard where a blue pool meanders beneath majestic, rustling palms. At night, the grounds glimmer softly with lamps. They illuminate the tufted grove, light the path to a secluded beach, and lead the way up through the cactus-sprinkled hillside thorn forest to a romantic restaurant high above the bay.

Hotel Activities
Hotel guests enjoy a plethora of sports facilities, including tennis courts, riding stables, and a polo field. Aquatic activities include snorkeling, scuba diving, kayaking, sailing, and deep-sea fishing. Boats are additionally available for picnic-excursions to nearby hidden beaches, wildlife-viewing, and observing turtle nesting in season. A luxury spa with view pampers guests with massage, facials, sauna, jacuzzi, and exercise machines. Evenings, live music brightens the cocktail and dinner hours at the elegant beach-view restaurant-bar.

The hotel was named for *carey,* (kah-RAY) the native word for an endangered species of

SAVING TURTLES

S ea turtles were once common on Puerto Vallarta beaches. Now a determined corps of hardy volunteers literally camps out on isolated beaches, trying to save the turtles from extinction. This is a tricky business, because their poacher opponents are invariably poor, determined, and ofttimes armed. Since turtle tracks lead right to the eggs, the trick is to get there before the poachers. The turtle-savers dig up the eggs and hatch them themselves, or bury them in secret locations where the eggs will hopefully hatch unmolested. The reward—the sight of hundreds of new hatchlings returning to the sea—is worth the pain for this new generation of Mexican eco-activists.

green turtle

Once featured on a thousand restaurant menus from Puerto Ángel to Mazatlán, turtle meat, soup, and eggs are now illegal. Although not extinct, Pacific Mexico's three sea turtle species— green, hawksbill, and leatherback—have dwindled to a tiny fraction of previous numbers.

The **green turtle** (Chelonia mydas), known locally as tortuga verde or caguama, is named for the color of its fat. Although officially threatened, the prolific green turtle remains relatively numerous. Females can return to shore up to eight times during the year, depositing an aggregate of 500 eggs in a single season. When not mating or migrating, the vegetarian greens can most often be spotted in lagoons and bays, especially in the Bay of Banderas, nipping at seaweed with their beaks. Adults, usually around three or four feet long and weighing 100-200 pounds, are easily identified out of water by the four big plates on either side of their shells. Green turtle meat was once prized as the main ingredient of turtle soup.

leatherback turtle

The endangered **hawksbill** (Eretmochelys imbricata) has vanished from many Pacific Mexico beaches. Known locally as the tortuga carey, it was the source of both meat and the lovely translucent tortoiseshell that has been largely supplanted by plastic. Adult careyes, among the smaller of sea turtles, usually run two to three feet in length and weigh 30-100 pounds. Their usually brown shells are readily identified by shingle-like overlapping scales. During late summer and fall, females come ashore to lay clutches of eggs (around 100) in the sand. Careyes, although preferring fish, mollusks, and shellfish, will eat most anything, including seaweed. When attacked, careyes can be plucky fighters, inflicting bites with their eagle-sharp hawksbills.

You'll be fortunate indeed if you glimpse the rare **leatherback** (Dermochelys coriacea), the world's largest turtle. "Experts" know so little about the leatherback, or tortuga de cuero, it's impossible to determine just how endangered it is. Tales are told of fisherfolk netting seven- or eight-foot leatherbacks weighing nearly a ton apiece. If you see even a small one you'll recognize it immediately by its back of smooth, tough skin, creased with several lengthwise ridges.

hawksbill turtle

sea turtle that used to lay eggs on the little beach of Careyitos that fronts the hotel. Saving the turtles at nearby Playa Teopa, accessible only through hotel property, has now become a major hotel mission. Guards do, however, allow access to serious outside visitors during hatching times; follow the dirt road between Km 49 and 50 to gate and beach; no camping, please. Check with the hotel desk for information and permission.

Hotel Information

For reservations and more information, contact the hotel at P.O. Box 24, Cihuatlán, Jalisco 48970, tel. (335) 100-00, or in the U.S. (800) 457-7676 and (800) 525-4800. Rooms, standard, superior, and deluxe, run $135, $160, and $200 low season double, and $165, $195, and $230 high; ocean-view suites run $265 low season and $320 high; all accommodations have a/c, TV, and direct-dial phones. Additional hotel facilities and services include fiber-optic telecommunications, a children's activity center, 100-person meeting room, several shops and boutiques, library, movie theater, babysitters, heliport, private landing strip, boutiques, shops, and many business services.

Getting There

The Hotel Bel Air Costa Careyes is a few minutes drive down a cobbled entrance road (bear left all the way) at Km 53.5 (100 miles, 161 km, from Puerto Vallarta; 34 miles, 55 km from Barra de Navidad; and 52 miles, 84 km from the Manzanillo International Airport).

CLUB MED PLAYA BLANCA

The Club Med Playa Blanca basks at the opposite corner of the same little bay as the Hotel Bel Air Costa Careyes. The Club Med's youngish (mostly 20-40, kids under 12 not allowed) guests enjoy an extensive sports menu, including trampoline, scuba, snorkel, a climbing wall, kayaking, racquetball and volleyball, sailing, and more. Action centers around Playa Blanca, the resort's luxuriously intimate little sand crescent, tucked beneath cactus-decorated tropical headlands. Above the beach, a verdant, tufted grove shades a platoon of reclin-

ing vacationers. From there, garden walkways lead past the pool, disco, bars, and restaurants to a hillside colony of 320 luxurious a/c view *cabañas.*

All meals, drinks, and activities (except for outside tours and deep-sea fishing) are included in a single package price. Rates run between $120 and $250 per day, depending upon season and promotions (open November to Easter only). For information and reservations call locally (335) 100-01, 100-02, or 100-03, or from the U.S. and Canada, call (800) CLUBMED.

Get there via the same Km 53.5 side road as the Hotel Bel Air Costa Careyes (see "Getting There" above). Bear right and follow signs about a mile to the gate. For security reasons, Club Med Playa Blanca doesn't take kindly to outsiders. If you simply want to look around, be sure to arrive with an appointment.

PLAYA CAREYES AND CUITZMALA

At Km 52, just south of a small bridge and a bus stop, a dirt road leads to the lovely honey-tinted crescent of Playa Careyes. Here, a car-accessible track (be careful for soft spots) continues along the dune, where you could enjoy a day or week of beach camping. Beyond the oft-powerful waves (swim with caution), the intimate, headland-framed bay brims with outdoor possibilities. Birdwatching and wildlife-viewing can be quite rewarding; notice the herons, egrets, and cormorants in the lagoon just south of the dune. Fishing is good either from the beach, by boat (launch from the sheltered north end), or the rocks on either side. Water is generally clear for snorkeling, and beyond the waves, good for either kayaking or windsurfing. If you have no boat, no problem, for the local fishing cooperative (boats beached by the food *palapa* at north end) would be happy to take you on a fishing trip. Figure about $15 per hour, with bargaining. Afterwards, they might even cook up the catch for a big afternoon dinner at their tree-shaded *palapa.* Nearby Pueblo Careyes (behind the soccer field at Km 52) has a **store,** for supplies, and a ***centro de salud*** (health center) and *larga distancia* in case of emergency.

Access to the neighboring **Playa Teopa,** is, by contrast, carefully guarded. The worthy reason is to save the hatchlings of the remaining *carey* turtles (see the special topic "Saving Turtles") who still come ashore during the late summer and fall to lay eggs. For a closer look at Playa Teopa, you could walk south along the dune-top track, although guards might eventually stop you. They will let you through (entry gate on dirt road between Km 49 and 50) if you get official permission at the desk of the Hotel Bel Air Costa Careyes.

The pristine tropical deciduous woodlands that stretch for miles around Km 45 are no accident. They are preserved as part of the **Fideicomiso Cuitzmala** (Cuitzmala Trust), the local kingdom of beach, headland, and forest held by billionaire Sir James Goldsmith. Local officials, many of whom are not privy to Sir James's grand design (which includes a sprawling seaview mansion complex), say that a team of biologists are conducting research on the property. A ranch complex, accessible through a gate at Km 45, is Fideicomiso Cuitzmala's most obvious highway-visible landmark. Another, less obvious one is the Fideicomiso Cuitzmala's pink private police headquarters at roadside between Km 46 and 47.

PLAYA LAS BRISAS

For a tranquil day, overnight, or weeklong beach adventure consider Playa Las Brisas, a few miles by the dirt road (turnoff sign near Km 36) through the village of Arroyo Seco.

About two miles long, Playa Las Brisas has two distinct sections: first comes a very broad, white sandy strand decorated by pink-blossomed verbena and pounded by wild, open-ocean waves. For shady tenting or RV parking, a regal coconut grove lines the beach. Before you set up, however, you should offer a little rent to the owner-caretaker, who may soon show up on a horse. Don't be alarmed by his machete; it's for husking and cutting fallen coconuts.

To see the other half of Playa Las Brisas, continue along the road past the little beachside vacation home subdivision (has a season-

al store and snack bar). You will soon reach an open-ocean beach and headland, backed by a big, level, grassy dune, perfect for tent or RV camping. Take care not to get stuck in soft spots, however.

The headland borders the El Tecuán Lagoon, part of the Rancho El Tecuán, whose hilltop hotel you can see on the far side of the lagoon. The lagoon is an unusually rich fish and wildlife habitat; see "Hotel El Tecuán" following, for details.

Getting There

You reach the village of Arroyo Seco, where stores can furnish supplies, 2.3 miles (3.7 km) from the highway at Km 36. At the central plaza, turn left, then immediately right at the Conasupo rural store, then left again, heading up the steep dirt road. In the valley on the other side, bear right at the fork at the mango grove, and within another mile you will be in the majestic beach-bordering palm grove.

HOTEL EL TECUÁN

Little was spared in perching the Hotel El Tecuán above its small kingdom of beach, lagoon, and palm-brushed rangeland. It was to be the centerpiece of a sprawling vacationland, with marina, golf course, and hundreds of houses and condos. Although those plans have yet to materialize, the hotel stands with an ambience more like an African safari lodge than a Mexican beach resort.

Masculinity bulges out of its architecture. Its corridors are lined with massive, polished tree trunks, fixed by brawny master joints to thick, hand-hewn mahogany beams. The view restaurant is patterned after the midships of a Manila Galleon, complete with a pair of varnished tree-trunk masts reaching into inky darkness of the night sky above. If the restaurant could only sway, the illusion would be complete.

The rooms are comfortable and continue the masculine theme. The best have private balconies, which, in addition to a luxurious ocean vista, overlook the elegantly manicured grounds and blue pool and *palapa*-patio a hundred feet below.

Hotel Activities

It is perhaps fortunate the hotel and its surroundings, part of the big **Rancho Tecuán,** may never be developed. Being private, public access has always been limited, so the Rancho has become a de facto habitat-refuge for the rapidly diminishing local animal population. Wildcats, ocelots, small crocodiles, snakes, and turtles hunt in the mangroves edging the lagoon and the tangled forest that climbs the surrounding hills. The lagoon itself nurtures hosts of waterbirds and shoals of *róbalo* (snook) and *pargo* (snapper).

Guests can easily enjoy the hotel's fishing and wildlife-viewing opportunities, first by simply walking down to the lagoon, where big white herons and egrets perch and preen in the mangroves. Don't forget your binoculars, sun hat, mosquito repellent, telephoto camera, and identification book. Launch your own boat, canoe, or inflatable raft for an even more rewarding outing.

Hotel Tecuán offers plenty of jogging and walking opportunities. For starters, stroll along the lagoonside entrance road and back (4.8 km) or south along the beach to the Río Purificación and back (6.4 km). Take water, mosquito repellent, sunscreen, a hat, and something to carry your beachcombing treasures in. There are plenty of fish in the river, so you might want to take your fishing rod, too.

Besides swimming in the pool or the lagoon, you can enjoy the hotel's tennis (bring your own racquet and balls) and volleyball courts. If you bring a bicycle you can ride it along miles of beach, lagoon, and ranch roads.

Tecuán Beach

The focal point of the long, wild, white-sand Playa Tecuán is to the north, where, at low tide, the lagoon's waters stream into the sea. Platoons of waterbirds—giant brown herons, snowy egrets, and squads of pelicans, ibises, and grebes—stalk and dive for fish trapped in the shallow, rushing current.

On the beach nearby, the sand curves southward beneath a rocky point, where the waves strew rainbow carpets of limpet, clam, and snail shells. There the billows rise sharply, angling shoreward, often with good intermediate and advanced surfing breaks. Casual swimmers beware; the surf is much too powerful for safety.

Hotel Information

For more information, contact the hotel at Km 33.5, Carretera 200, Jalisco tel. (335) 150-18, 150-26, or 150-28. Their 36 rooms and suites rent from $63 d, $75 t, suites $75 and up; with a/c, restaurant, bar, long-distance phone, heliport, credit cards accepted, and discounts during low season. For advance reservations, contact Promotora El Tecuán, Garibaldi 1676, Sector Hidalgo, Guadalajara, Jalisco 44680, tel. (3) 616-0085 or 616-0183, fax 616-6615.

Getting There

The Hotel Tecuán is six miles (10 km) along a paved entrance road marked by a white lighthouse at Km 33 (112 miles, 181 km, from Puerto Vallarta; 22 miles, 35 km, from Barra de Navidad; and 40 miles, 64 km, from the Manzanillo International Airport).

PLAYA TENACATITA

Imagine an ideal tropical paradise: free camping on a long curve of clean white sand, right next to a lovely little coral bottomed cove, with all the beer you can drink and all the fresh seafood you can eat. That describes Tenacatita, a place that old Pacific Mexico hands refer to with a sigh. Tenacatitaaahhh . . .

Folks usually begin to arrive sometime in November; by Christmas, some years, there's only room for walk-ins. Which anyone who can walk can do: carry in your tent and set it up in one of the many RV-inaccessible spots.

Tenacatita visitors enjoy three distinct beaches: the main one, Playa Tenacatita, the little one, Playa Mora, and Playa La Boca, a breezy, palm-bordered sand ribbon stretching just over three kilometers north to the *boca* (mouth) of the Río Purificación.

Playa Tenacatita's strand of fine white sand curves from the north-end of Punta Tenacatita along a long, tall packed dune to **Punta Hermanos,** a total of about two miles. The dune is where most visitors—nearly all Americans and Canadians—park their RVs. The water is clear with gentle waves, fine for swimming and windsurfing. Being so calm, it's easy to launch a boat for fishing—common catches are *huachinango* (red snapper) and *cabrilla* (sea bass)—especially at the very calm north end.

The sheltered north cove is where a village of *palapas* has grown to service the winter camping population. One of the veteran establishments is **El Puercillo**, run by longtimer José Bautista. He and several other neighbors take groups out in his launches ($60 total per half day, complete, bring your own beer) for offshore fishing trips and excursions.

Tenacatita may be headed for changes, however. The federal government has sold out to a foreign corporation to develop a hotel at Tenacatita. The trouble is the fifty-odd squatter-operators of the Tenacatita *palapas* refuse to leave. One night in November, 1991, after giving the squatters plenty of warning, federal soldiers and police burned and smashed the *palapas*. The squatters, backed by the Rebalcito *ejido*, the traditional owner of Tenacatita, have vowed to have their day in court. Meanwhile, the squatters have rebuilt their *palapas*.

Playas Mora and La Boca

Jewel of jewels Playa Mora is accessible by a dirt road running north from the Tenacatita *palapas*. The beach itself is salt-and-pepper, black sand dotted with white coral, washed by water sometimes as smooth as glass. Just 15 meters from the beach the reef begins. Corals, like heads of cauliflower, some brown, some green, and some dead white, swarm with fish: iridescent blue, yellow-striped, yellow-tailed, some silvery, and others brown as rocks. (Careful: moray eels like to hide in rock crannies; they bite. Don't stick your hand anywhere you can't see.)

If you get to Playa Mora by December you may be early enough to snag one of the roughly dozen car-accessible camping spots. If not, plenty of tenting spaces exist, also a few abandoned *palapa* thatched huts are usually waiting to be resurrected.

Playa La Boca is the overflow campground for Tenacatita. It's not as popular because of its rough surf and steep beach. Its isolation and vigorous surf, however, make Playa La Boca the best for driftwood, beachcombing, shells, and surf fishing.

Wildlife Viewing

Tenacatita's hinterland is a spreading, wildlife-rich mangrove marsh. From a landing behind the Tenacatita dune, you can float a boat, rubber raft, or canoe for a wildlife-viewing excursion. Local guides also furnish boats and lead trips from the same spot. Take your hat, binoculars, camera, telephoto lens, and plenty of repellent.

Tenacatita Bugs

That same marshland is the source for swarms of mosquitoes and *jejenes*, "no-see-um" biting gnats, especially around sunset. At that time no one sane at Tenacatita should be outdoors without having slathered on some good repellent.

Food, Services, and Information

The village of **Rebalcito**, a mile and a half away, is Tenacatita's supply and service center. It has two or three fair *abarroterias* (groceries) that carry meat and vegetables, a *caseta de larga distancia*, a *gasolinera* that sells leaded regular from drums, a water *purificadora* that sells drinking water retail, and even a bus stop. A single Transportes Cihuatlán bus makes one run a day between Rebalcito and Manzanillo, leaving Rebalcito at the crack of dawn (inquire locally) and returning from the Manzanillo central bus station around 1500.

If you want a diversion from the fare of Tenacatita's seafood *palapas* and Rebalcito's single restaurant, you can drive or thumb a ride seven miles (11 km) to **Restaurant Yoly** in Miguel Hidalgo (Km 30 on Hwy. 200) for some country-style enchiladas, tacos, chiles rellenos, tostadas, and beans. Open daily 0700-2000.

Getting There

Leave Hwy. 200 at the Tenacatita sign (Km 28) just south of the big Río Purificación bridge. Rebalcito is 3.7 miles (six km), Tenacatita 5.4 miles (8.7 km), by a wide, level dirt road.

HOTEL LOS ANGELES LOCOS

In spite of its name, the Hotel Los Angeles Locos has nothing to do with crazy people from Los Angeles. Once upon a time, a rich family built an airstrip and a mansion by a lovely little beach on pristine Tenacatita Bay and began coming for vacations by private plane. The local people, who couldn't fathom why their rich neighbors would go to so much trouble and expense to come to such an out-of-the-way place, dubbed them *los angeles locos,* the "crazy angels," because they always seemed to be flying.

The beach is still lovely and Tenacatita Bay, curving around Punta Hermanos south from Tenacatita Beach is still pristine. Now the Hotel Los Angeles Locos makes it possible for droves of sun-seeking vacationers to enjoy it en masse.

Continuous music, open bar, plentiful buffets, and endless activities set the tone at Los Angeles Locos—the kind of place for folks who want a hassle-free week of fun in the sun. The guests are typically working-age couples and singles, mostly Mexicans during the summer, Canadians and some Americans during the winter. Very few children (although they are welcome) seem to be among the guests.

Hotel Activities
Although all sports and lessons—including tennis, snorkeling, sailing, windsurfing, horseback riding, volleyball, aerobics, exercises, water-skiing—plus dancing, disco, and games cost nothing extra, guests can, if they want, do nothing but soak up the sun. Los Angeles Locos simply provides the options.

A relaxed attitude will probably allow you to enjoy yourself the most. Don't try to eat, drink, and do too much in order to make sure you get your money's worth. If you do, you're liable to arrive back home in need of a vacation.

Although people don't come to the tropics to stay inside, Los Angeles Locos's rooms are quite comfortable—completely private, in pastels and white, air-conditioned, each with cable TV, phone, and private balcony overlooking either the ocean or palmy pool-patio.

Hotel Information
For information and reservations, contact a travel agent or the hotel at Km 20, Carretera Federal No. 200, Melaque, Jalisco, tel. (335) 150-02, 150-05, or 150-06. High-season rates for the 201 rooms and suites run about $136 per person per day, double occupancy, $185 per day, single occupancy; for a bigger, better view junior suite, add $30 per room; prices include everything except transportation.

Getting There
The Hotel Los Angeles Locos is about four miles (six km) off Hwy. 200 along a signed cobbled entrance road near the Km 20 marker (120 miles, 194 km, from Puerto Vallarta; 14 miles, 23 km, from Barra de Navidad; and 32 miles, 51 km, from the Manzanillo International Airport).

If you want to simply look around the resort, don't drive up to the gate unannounced. The guard won't let you through. Instead, call ahead and make an appointment for a "tour." After your guided look-see, you have to either sign up or mosey along. They don't accept day guests.

PLAYA BOCA DE IGUANAS

Plumy Playa Boca de Iguanas curves for six miles along the tranquil inner recess of the Bay of Tenacatita. The cavernous former Hotel Bahía Tenacatita, which slumbered for years beneath the grove, is being reclaimed by the jungle and the animals that live in the nearby mangrove marsh.

The beach, however, is as enjoyable as ever: wide, level, with firm white sand, good for hiking, jogging, and beachcombing. Offshore, the gently rolling waves are equally fine for bodysurfing and boogie-boarding. Beds of oysters, free for those who dive for them, lie a few hundred feet offshore. A rocky outcropping at the north end invites fishing and snorkeling while the calm water beyond the breakers invites windsurfing. Bring your own equipment.

Accommodations
The pocket paradise, **Camping and Trailer Park Boca de Iguanas,** Km 16.5, Carretera Melaque-Puerto Vallarta, P.O. Box 93, Melaque, Jalisco, seems to be succeeding where the old hotel failed. Instead of fighting the jungle, the manager is trying to coexist with it. A big crocodile lives in the the mangrove-lined lotus marsh at the edge of the trailer park.

"When the crocodile gets too close to my ducks," the manager says, "I drive him back into the mangrove where he belongs. This end of the mangrove is ours, the other side is his."

The trailer park offers 40 sandy, shaded (but smallish) spaces for tents and RVs, including electricity, well water for showering, flushing, and laundry, bottled water for drinking, and a dump station. The manager runs a mini-market that supplies the necessities for a relaxed week or month on the beach. Many American and Canadian regulars stay here all winter. The trailer park includes a funky kitchenette bungalow that sleeps four for $45/day. To find it, follow a signed gravel road at Km 17 for 1.5 miles, 2.4 km. Reservations are generally needed only during Christmas or Easter week. Rates run about $5 per person, $4 for kids under 10.

The neighboring **Camping Tenacatita Trailer Park** also has about 50 camping and RV spaces shaded beneath a majestic, rustling grove at Km 16.5 Carretera Melaque-Puerto Vallarta, P.O. Box 18, Melaque, Jalisco; tel. (338) 103-93 (Autlán, Jalisco), or fax (3) 6-200-968 (Guadalajara). Although their layout is newer, friendly owners Michel and Bertha Billot (he's French, she's Mexican) are trying harder. Their essentials are in place: electricity, water, showers, toilets, and about 40 spaces with sewer hookups. Much of their five acres is undeveloped and would be fine for tenters who prefer privacy with the convenience of fresh water, a small store, and congenial company at tables beneath a rustic *palapa*. Rates run $9/day for two in motorhome or trailer, $8/day van or camper, $3 per extra person, tent camping $4, with discounts for weekly or monthly rentals.

A third lodging, the nearby **Hotel and Campamento Entre Palmeras** offers six plain but clean apartment-bungalows with fan for one to four persons for $26. The grounds feature much tent or RV camping space, electricity, showers, toilets, and a funky swimming pool. Their location, closer to the mangrove marsh and farther from the beach, is buggier.

PLAYA LA MANZANILLA

The little fishing town of La Manzanilla (pop. 2,000) drowses along the same long strip of sand that begins the Boca de Iguanas trailer parks. Here the beach, Playa La Manzanilla, is as broad and flat and the waves are as gentle, but the sand is several shades darker. Probably no better fishing exists on the entire Costa Alegre than at La Manzanilla. A dozen seafood *palapas* on the beach manage to stay open by virtue of a trickle of foreign visitors and local weekend and holiday patronage.

A pair of basic hotels accommodate guests. Guests at **Hotel Posada del Cazador** ("The Hunter") enjoy friendly management, a lobby for sitting and socializing, a shelf of used paperback novels, and a long-distance phone. Find it at María Asunción 183, La Manzanilla, Jalisco, tel. (335) 552-14 or 553-30. They have seven plain but clean rooms, $20 d. Kitchenette suites sleeping four rent for $30; a larger suite, sleeping eight, is $57, all with fans.

On the opposite even sleepier country edge of town, the **Hotel Puesta de Sol** ("Sunset"), Calle Playa Blanca 94, La Manzanilla, Jalisco, offers two-stories of basic rooms around a cool, leafy central patio. Rates are even lower than the Cazador; figure $16 d, with discounts for longer-term rentals.

Get to La Manzanilla by following the signed paved road at Km 13 for one mile. The Hotel Cazador is on the left, just after you turn left onto the main beachfront street. The Hotel Puesta de Sol is a quarter mile farther along; bear right past the town plaza for a few blocks along the beachfront street, Calle Playa Blanca.

BARRA DE NAVIDAD, MELAQUE, AND VICINITY

THE BAR OF CHRISTMAS

The little country beach town of Barra de Navidad, Jalisco (pop. 5,000), whose name literally means "Bar of Christmas," has unexpectedly few saloons. In this case, "Bar" has nothing to do with alcohol; it refers to the sandbar upon which the town is built. That lowly spit of sand forms the southern perimeter of the blue Bay of Navidad, which arcs to Barra de Navidad's twin town of San Patricio Melaque (pop. 10,000) a few miles to the west.

Barra and **San Patricio Melaque,** locally known as "Melaque" (may-LAI I-kay), are twin, but distinct. towns. Barra has the cobbled. shady lanes and friendly country ambience; Melaque is the metropolis of the two, with most of the stores and services.

HISTORY

The sandbar is called "Navidad" because the Viceroy Antonio de Mendoza, the first, and arguably the best, viceroy Mexico ever had, disembarked there on 25 December 1540. The occasion was auspicious for two reasons. Besides being Christmas Day, Don Antonio had arrived to personally put down a bloody rebellion raging through western Mexico that threatened to burn New Spain off the map. Unfortunately for the thousands of Indians who were torched, hung, or beheaded during the brutal campaign, Don Antonio's prayers on that day were soon answered. The rebellion was smothered, and the lowly sandbar was remembered as Barra de Navidad from that time forward.

A generation later, Barra de Navidad became the springboard for King Philip's efforts to make the Pacific a Spanish lake. Shipyards built on the bar launched the vessels that carried the expedition of conquistador Miguel López de Legazpi and Father André de Urdaneta in search of God and gold in the Philippines. Urdaneta came back

a hero one year later, in 1565, having discovered the great circle route, which was followed by a dozen subsequent generations of the renowned ship the Manila Galleon.

By 1600, however, the Manila Galleon was landing in Acapulco, with its much quicker land access to the capital to transport their priceless Oriental cargoes. Barra de Navidad went to sleep and and didn't wake up for more than three centuries.

Now Barra de Navidad only slumbers occasionally. The townsfolk welcome crowds of beachgoing Mexican families during national holidays, and during the winter a steady procession of North American and European budget vacationers.

SIGHTS

Exploring Barra and Melaque
Nearly all hotels and the fancier restaurants in Barra lie on one oceanfront street named, uncommonly, after a conquistador, Miguel López de Legazpi. Barra's other main street, Veracruz, one short block inland, has most of the businesses, groceries, and small family-run eateries.

Head south along Legazpi toward the steep Cerro San Francisco in the distance and you will soon be on the palm-lined walkway that runs atop the famous sandbar of Barra. On the right, ocean side, the Playa Barra de Navidad arcs northwest to the hotels of Melaque, which spread like white pebbles along the far end of the strand. The great blue water expanse beyond the beach, framed at both ends by jagged, rocky sea stacks, is the **Bahía de Navidad.**

Opposite the ocean, on the other side of the bar, spreads the tranquil, mangrove-bordered expanse of the **Laguna de Navidad,** which forms the border with the state of **Colima,** whose mountains (including nearby Cerro San Francisco) loom beyond it. The lagoon's calm appearance is deceiving, for it is really an *estero* (estuary), an arm of the sea, which ebbs and

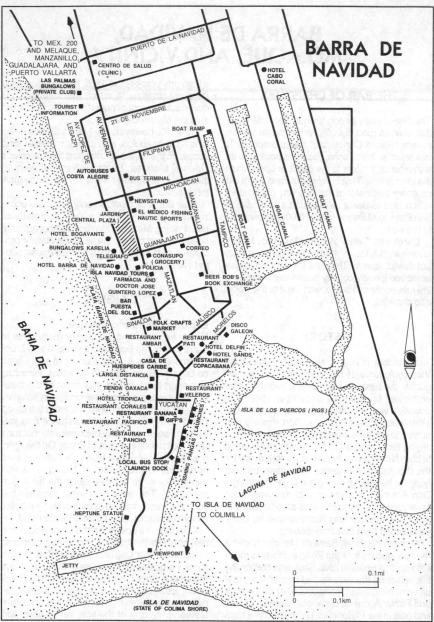

BARRA DE NAVIDAD

TO MEX. 200
AND MELAQUE,
MANZANILLO,
GUADALAJARA, AND
PUERTO VALLARTA

LAS PALMAS BUNGALOWS
(PRIVATE CLUB)

TOURIST INFORMATION

PUERTO DE LA NAVIDAD

CENTRO DE SALUD
(CLINIC)

HOTEL CABO CORAL

21 DE NOVIEMBRE

AV. VERACRUZ

AV. LOPEZ DE LEGAZPI

BOAT RAMP

FILIPINAS

AUTOBUSES COSTA ALEGRE

BUS TERMINAL

MICHOACAN

NEWSSTAND

JARDIN (CENTRAL PLAZA)

EL MEDICO FISHING NAUTIC SPORTS

MANZANILLO

TAMPICO

BOAT CANAL

BOAT CANAL

BOAT CANAL

HOTEL BOGAVANTE

BUNGALOWS KARELIA

TELEGRAFO

HOTEL BARRA DE NAVIDAD

ISLA NAVIDAD TOURS

FARMACIA AND DOCTOR JOSE QUINTERO LOPEZ

BAR PUESTA DEL SOL

GUANAJUATO

CORREO

CONASUPO (GROCERY)

POLICIA

MAZATLAN

BEER BOB'S BOOK EXCHANGE

BAHÍA DE NAVIDAD

PLAYA BARRA DE NAVIDAD

SINALOA

JALISCO

FOLK CRAFTS MARKET

RESTAURANT AMBAR

RESTAURANT PATI

MORELOS

DISCO GALEON

HOTEL DELFIN
HOTEL SANDS

CASA DE HUESPEDES CARIBE

RESTAURANT COPACABANA

LARGA DISTANCIA

TIENDA OAXACA

HOTEL TROPICAL

RESTAURANT CORALES

RESTAURANT BANANA

RESTAURANT PACIFICO

RESTAURANT PANCHO

YUCATAN

GIFF'S

RESTAURANT VELEROS

ISLA DE LOS PUERCOS (PIGS)

LOCAL BUS STOP/ LAUNCH DOCK

FISHING PANGAS (LAUNCHES)

LAGUNA DE NAVIDAD

NEPTUNE STATUE

TO ISLA DE NAVIDAD
TO COLIMILLA

VIEWPOINT

JETTY

ISLA DE NAVIDAD
(STATE OF COLIMA SHORE)

MOON

0   0.1mi
0   0.1km

© MOON PUBLICATIONS, INC.

flows through the channel beyond the rock **jetty** at the end of the sandbar. Because of this natural flushing action, local folks still dump fishing waste into the Laguna de Navidad. Fortunately new sewage plants route human waste away from the lagoon, so with care, you can usually swim safely in its inviting waters. Do not, however, venture too close to the lagoon-mouth beyond the jetty or you may get swept out to sea by the strong outgoing current.

On the sandbar's lagoon side, a local minibus stop and adjacent *panga* (fishing launch) dock hum with daytime activity. From the dock, launches ferry loads of passengers for 50 cents to the Colima shore, which is known as **Isla de Navidad,** the name of the marina and hotel development visible across the lagoon. The minibuses head in the opposite direction, along Veracruz and Hwy. 200, three miles (4.8 km) to Melaque.

The once-distinct villages of San Patricio and Melaque now spread as one along the Bay of Navidad's sandy northwest shore.

The business district, still known locally as San Patricio (follow a small San Patricio sign two blocks from the highway), centers around a plaza, market, and church bordering the main shopping street López Mateos.

Continue two blocks to beachfront Calle Gómez Farías, where a lineup of hotels, eateries, and shops cater to the vacation trade. From there, the curving strand extends toward the quiet west end, where *palapas* line a glassy, sheltered blue cove. Here, a rainbow of colored *pangas* perch upon the sand, sailboats rock gently offshore, pelicans preen and dive, and people enjoy snacks, beer, and the cooling breeze in the deep shade beneath the *palapas.*

Although a continuous strand of medium-fine golden sand joins Barra with Melaque, it changes character and names along its gentle, five-mile arc. At Barra de Navidad, where it's called **Playa de Navidad,** the beach is narrow and steep, and the waves are sometimes very rough. Those powerful swells often provide good intermediate **surfing** breaks adjacent to the jetty. **Fishing** by line or pole is also popular from the jetty rocks.

Most mornings are calm enough to make the surf safe for **swimming** and splashing, which, along with the fresh seafood of beachside *palapa* restaurants, make Barra a popular Sunday and holiday picnic-ground for local Mexican families. The relatively large number of folks walking the beach makes for slim pickings for shell collectors and beachcombers.

For a cooling midday break from the sun, drop in to the restaurant of the Hotel Tropical at the south end of Legazpi and enjoy the bay view, the swish of the waves, and the fresh breeze streaming through the lobby.

As the beach curves northwesterly toward Melaque, the restaurants and hotels give way to dunes and pasture. At the outskirts of Melaque,

BRUCE WHIPPERMAN

Seafood palapas await at Colimilla's lagoonside for visitor-filled boats from Barra de Navidad.

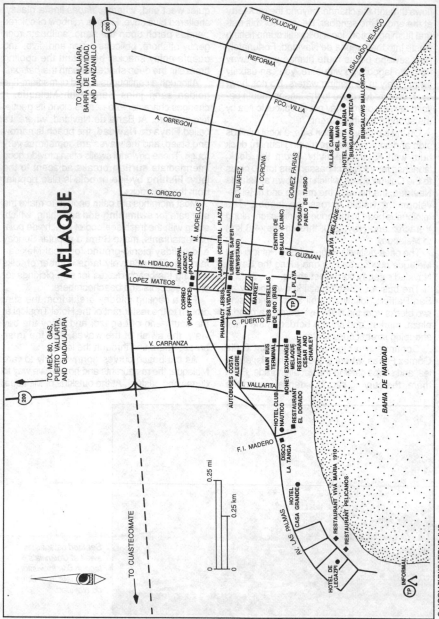

© MOON PUBLICATIONS, INC.

civilization resumes, and the broad beach, now called **Playa Melaque,** billows gently to the west.

Continuing past the town center, a lineup of rustic *palapas* and *pangas* pulled up on the sand decorate the tranquil west-end cove, which is sheltered from the open sea behind a tier of craggy sea stacks. Here, the water clears, making for good **fishing** from the rocks.

Colimilla and Isla de Navidad

A boat trip across the lagoon for super-fresh seafood at the palm-studded village of Colimilla is a primary Barra pastime. While you sit enjoying a moderately priced oyster cocktail, ceviche, or broiled whole-fish dinner, gaze out on the mangrove-enfolded glassy expanse of the Laguna de Navidad. Far away, a canoe may drift silently, while white herons quietly stalk their prey. Now and then a launch will glide in and deposit its load of visitors, or a fisherman will head out to sea.

One of the most pleasant Colimilla vantage spots is the **Restaurant Susana,** whose broad *palapa* extends out into the lagoon; open daily 0800-2000. Take mosquito repellent, especially if you're staying for dinner. Launches routinely ferry as many as six passengers to Colimilla from the Barra lagoonside docks for $10 roundtrip. Tell them when you want to return, and they'll pick you up.

From the same Barra lagoonside dock, launches also shuttle passengers for $1 roundtrip across the lagoon to the **Isla de Navidad** hotel, marina, vacation home development, and golf course (see "Tennis and Golf" below). Local **minibuses** connect with the launches at the dock and pick up passengers along Av. Veracruz as they head out of town for Melaque (30 cents one-way).

Playa de Cocos

A trip to wild, breezy Playa de Cocos, hidden just behind the Cerro San Francisco headland south of Barra, makes an interesting afternoon outing, especially when combined with the trip to Colimilla. A wide, golden sand beach curves miles southward, starting beneath a cactus-dotted jungly headland. The beach, although broad and steep, with strong shorebreakers. Although swimming is hazardous, fishing off the rocks

and beachcombing are the delights here. A feast of driftwood and multicolored shells—olives, small conches, purple-striated clams—litters the sand, especially on an intimate, spectacular hidden cove, reachable by scampering past the waves. (For more details, see "Trailer Parks and Camping" following.)

There are two ways to get to Playa de Cocos. Through Colimilla, walk uphill to the road above the La Colimilla restaurants. Head left (east) for about a quarter-mile. Turn right at the palm-lined boulevard and continue along the golf course about a mile and a quarter to the beach beneath the tip of the Cerro San Francisco headland.

You can also drive there by turning off Hwy. 200 at the Ejido La Culebra (or Isla de Navidad) sign as the highway cuts through the hills at Km 51 a few miles south of Barra. Mark your odometer at the turnoff. Follow the road about three miles (4.8 km) to a bridge, where you enter the state of Colima. From there the road curves right, paralleling the beach. After about two more miles (3.2 km), you pass through the golf course gate. After winding through the golf course another mile, fork left at the intersecting boulevard and traffic circle at the north edge of the golf course. Continue another mile to the end of the road and beach.

Playa Cuastecomate

Playa de Cocos has its exact opposite in Playa Cuastecomate (kooah-stay-koh-MAH-tay), tucked behind the ridge rising beyond the northwest edge of Melaque. The dark, fine-sand beach arcs along a cove on the rampart-rimmed big blue **Bahía de Cuastecomate.** Its very gentle waves and clear waters make for excellent swimming, windsurfing, snorkeling, and fishing from the beach itself or the rocks beneath the adjacent cliffs. A number of *palapa* restaurants along the beach serve seafood and drinks.

The Cuastecomate beachside village itself, home for a number of local fisherfolk and a few North Americans in permanently parked RVs, has a collection of oft-empty bunglows on the hillside, a small store, and about three times as many chickens as people.

For lodging, try the bungalows, or see Hotel Costa Sur under "Melaque Hotels" below. To get there, drive, taxi, or bus via the local minibus or Transportes Cihuatlán to the signed Melaque turnoff from Hwy. 200. There, a dirt side road marked "Hotel Costa Sur" heads into the hills, winding for two miles (3.2 km) over the ridge through pasture and jungle woodland to the village. If you're walking, allow an hour and take your sun hat, insect repellent, and water.

Barra-Melaque Hike

You can do this four-mile stroll either way, but starting from Barra with the sun behind you, the sky and the ocean will be at their bluest best. Take insect repellent, sunscreen, and a hat. At either end, enjoy lunch at one of the seaside restaurants (see "Food" following). At the Melaque end you can continue walking north to the cove on the far side of town. The trail beneath the cliff leads to spectacular wave-tossed tidepools and rugged sea rocks at the tip of the bay. At the Barra end, you can hire a launch to Colimilla (see preceding). End your day leisurely by taxiing or busing back from the bus station at either end.

Bird and Wildlife Viewing

The wildlife-rich upper reaches of the Laguna de Navidad stretch for miles and are only a boat ride away. Besides the ordinary varieties of egrets, terns, herons, pelicans, frigate birds, boobies, ducks, and geese, patient birdwatchers can sometimes snare rainbow flash-views of exotic parrots and bright tanagers and orioles.

As for other creatures, quiet, persistent observers are sometimes rewarded with mangrove-edge views of turtles, constrictors, crocodiles, coatimundis, racoons, skunks, deer, wild pigs, ocelots, wildcats, and, very rarely, a jaguar. The sensitivity and experience of your boatman-guide is, of course, crucial to the success of any nature outing. Ask at the dock-office of the **Sociedad Cooperativos de Servicios Turístico,** 40 Av. Veracruz on the lagoon front, tel. (335) 552-28, for a suitable person.

ACCOMMODATIONS

Barra Hotels

Whether on the beach or not, all Barra Hotels (except the four-star Cabo Coral) fall in the budget or moderate categories. One of the best,

the family-run **Hotel Sands,** offers a bit of class at modest rates at Morelos 24, Barra de Navidad, Jalisco 48987, tel. (335) 551-48. Two tiers of rooms enclose an inner courtyard lined with comfortable sitting areas opening into a lush green garden of leafy vines and graceful coconut palms. A side-corridor leads past a small zoo of spider monkeys, raccoons, and squawking macaws to a view of Barra's colorful lineup of fishing launches. On the other side, past the swim-up bar, a big curving pool and outer patio spreads to the placid edge of the mangrove-bordered Laguna de Navidad. The pool-bar (happy hour daily 1600-1800 in season) and the sitting areas afford inviting places to meet other travelers. The rooms, all with fans (but without hot water) are clean and furnished with dark varnished wood and tile. Light sleepers should wear earplugs or book a room in the wing farthest from the disco down the street, whose music thumps away till around 0200 most nights during the high season. Their 43 rooms and bungalows rent from $28 d low season, $33 high; bungalows sleeping four with kitchenette rent $50 low season, $70 high; credit cards accepted, parking.

Across the street, its loyal international clientele swears by the German family-operated **Hotel Delfín,** Morelos 23, Barra de Navidad, Jalisco 48987, tel. (335) 550-68, fax 560-20. Its four stories of tile-floored, balcony-corridor rooms (where curtains, unfortunately, must be drawn for privacy) are the cleanest and coziest of Barra's moderate hotels. The Delfín's tour de force, however, is the cheery patio buffet where guests linger over the breakfast offered every morning ($3-5, open daily 0830-1030) to all comers. Overnight guests, like those of the Sands, must put up with the moderate nighttime noise of the disco half a block away. For maximum sun and privacy take one of the top-floor rooms, many of which enjoy lagoon views. The Delfín's 30 rooms rent $24 d low season, $32 high; with fans, small pool, parking, and credit cards accepted.

One block away and a notch down the economic scale is **Casa de Huéspedes Caribe,** Sonora 15, Barra de Navidad, Jalisco, 48987, tel. 335-552-37, tucked along a side street. Unassuming elderly owner Maximino Oregon offers 11 clean, plain rooms, all with bath and hot water, for a devoted following of long-term cus-

BARRA AND MELAQUE HOTELS

Barra and Melaque (area code 335) hotels, in order of increasing high-season double-room price:

BARRA HOTELS
(POSTAL CODE 48987)

Casa de Huéspedes Caribe, Sonora 15, tel. 552-37, $18

Hotel Delfín, Morelos 23, tel. 550-68, fax 560-20, $32

Hotel Sands, Morelos 24, tel. 551-48, $33

Bungalows Karelia, Legazpi s/n, tel. 553-84 or 561-20, $33

Hotel Barra de Navidad, Legazpi 250, tel. 551-22, fax 553-03, $44

Hotel Tropical, Legazpi 96, tel. 550-20, fax 551-49, $45

Hotel Bogavante, Legazpi s/n, tel. 553-84 or 561-20, $50

Hotel Cabo Coral, P.O. Box 31, tel. 564-00, 564-01, $100

MELAQUE HOTELS
(POSTAL CODE 48980)

Hotel Santa María, Abel Salgado 85 (P.O. Box 188), tel. 556-77 or 555-53, $18

Bungalows Azteca, P.O. Box 57, tel. 551-50, $30

Hotel de Legazpi, Av. de las Palmas s/n (P.O. Box 88), tel. 553-97, $33

Hotel Villas Camino del Mar, P.O. Box 6, tel. 552-07, fax 554-98, $40

Posada Pablo de Tarso, Gómez Farías 408, tel. 551-17 or 552-68, $40

Bungalows Mallorca, Abel Salgado 133 (P.O. Box 157), tel. 552-19, $70

Hotel Club Náutico, Gómez Farías 1A, tel. 557-70 or 557-66, fax 552-95, $70

Hotel Casa Grande, Gómez Farías s/n (P.O. Box 8), tel. 550-01 or 551-95, fax 553-82, $160

Hotel Costa Sur, P.O. Box 12, tel. 550-85, 551-25, or 551-35, $100

tomers. Amenities include a secure front door (which Maximino personally locks every night), a homey downstairs garden sitting area, and more chairs and a hammock for snoozing on an upstairs porch. Rates run $9 s, $18 d, and $25 t in rooms with twin, double, or both types of beds.

Of the several Barra beachside hotels, the longtime **Hotel Tropical,** near the "bar" end of Legazpi, is the oldest and largest at Av. L. de Legazpi 96, Barra de Navidad, Jalisco 48987, tel. (335) 550-20, fax 551-49. Guests in many of its oceanfront tiers of comfortable, high-ceilinged rooms enjoy luxuriously private ocean-view balconies. Downstairs, the natural air-conditioning of an ocean breeze often floods the sea-view lobby-restaurant. The 57 rooms rent $30 s, $45 d, with fans, tiny pool, and credit cards accepted.

Sharing the same beachfront by the town plaza a few blocks away, the white stucco three-story **Hotel Barra de Navidad** encloses a cool, leafy interior courtyard at Av. L. de Legazpi 250, Barra de Navidad, Jalisco 48987, tel. (335) 551-22, fax 553-03. Guests in the seaside upper two floors of comfortable (but not deluxe) rooms enjoy palm-fringed ocean vistas from private balconies. An inviting pool-patio on one side and a dependable upstairs restaurant complete the picture. Rates for the 57 rooms run $30 s, $44 d, $51 t ocean side ($27, $35, $40 street side), with fans, credit cards accepted.

The friendly ambience and homey beachside porch of the **Hotel Bogavante** keep a steady stream of mostly North American and European travelers returning year after year to Av. L. de Legazpi s/n, Barra de Navidad, Jalisco 48987, tel. (335) 553-84 or 561-20. Eight of their 14 accommodations are roomy kitchenette suites, especially handy for groups and families weary of the hassles and expense of eating out. All units, several of which have ocean views, rent for $50 s, d, or t. Bargain for possible low-season discounts; monthly rates available, fans, no pool.

Bungalows Karelia, the Bogavante's downscale twin lodging next door, shares the same pleasant beachside porch, Av. L. de Legazpi s/n, Barra de Navidad, Jalisco 48987, tel. (335) 553-84 or 561-20. All the Karelia's rentals are kitchenette bungalows, satisfactory for many young families and travelers who don't mind cleaning up a bit in exchange for more modest rates. The 10 bungalows with fans rent for $33 d, $46 t.

Hint: If considering a beachside room in one of the several Barra oceanfront hotels, listen to the waves before you move in. They may be loud enough to interfere with your sleep. If so, use earplugs or switch to a streetside room or a hotel on the lagoon.

Barra's only deluxe lodging is the peach-hued stucco-and-tile four-star **Hotel Cabo Coral,** formerly Cabo Blanco, P.O. Box 31, Barra de Navidad, Jalisco 48987, tel. (335) 564-00, fax 564-01. The 125-room hotel anchors the vacation home development along the three marina-canals that branch from the lagoon about five blocks inland from the town. Within its manicured garden-grounds, Hotel Cabo Coral offers night-lit tennis courts, restaurants, bars, two pools, kiddie pools, and deluxe sportfishing yachts-for-hire. The accommodations, all air-conditioned, range from deluxe, pastel-decorated hotel doubles ($100 d) to fancy two-story, four-bedroom family villas ($125-250) for two to six. All with cable TV and phones; with a discotheque, many water sports, and credit cards accepted. Bring your repellent; during late afternoon and evening mosquitoes and gnats from the nearby mangroves seem to especially enjoy the Cabo Blanco's plush ambience.

Melaque Hotels

Melaque has a swarm of hotels and bungalows, many of them poorly designed and indifferently managed. They scratch along, nearly empty except during the Christmas and Easter holiday deluges when Mexican middle-class families must accept anything to stay at the beach. There are, nevertheless, several bright exceptions, which can be conveniently divided into "South" and "North of Town" groups:

Hotels South of Town: Classy in its unique way is the **Villas Camino del Mar,** whose owner doesn't believe in advertising. A few signs in the humble beach neighborhood about a quarter mile on the Barra side of the Melaque town center furnishes the only clue this gem of a lodging hides among the Melaque dross at Calle Francisco Villa, corner Abel Salgado, P.O. Box 6, San Patricio-Melaque, Jalisco 48980, tel. (335) 552-07, fax 554-98. A five-story white stucco monument draped with fluted, neoclassic columns and hanging pedestals, the Villas Camino del Mar offers a lodging assortment that varies from simple double rooms through deluxe suites with kitchenettes to a rambling penthouse. The upper three levels have sweeping ocean views, while the lower two overlook an elegant blue pool-patio bar and shady beachside palm grove. The clientele is split between Mexican middle class families who come for weekends all year around, and quiet Canadian and American couples who come to soak up the winter sun for weeks and months on end. Reserve early, especially for the winter. The 37 rooms and suites include comfortable ocean-view doubles for as little as $40 ($32 weekly, $18 monthly); one-bedroom kitchenette suites, about $73 ($59 weekly, $33 monthly); and deluxe two-bedroom, two-bath suites with kitchen, about $105 ($84 weekly, $48 monthly), all with fans only.

If the Camino del Mar is full, you can choose from a trio of acceptable lodgings around the corner that share the same golden sunset-view strand. The plain but priced-right **Hotel Santa María** offers 46 rooms with bath and kitchenette bungalows close enough to the water for the waves to lull guests to sleep at Abel Salgado 85, P.O. Box 188, San Patricio-Melaque 48980, tel. (335) 556-77 or 555-53. Rooms, popular with long-term Canadian and Americans in winter, are arranged in a pair of motel-style stucco tiers around a leafy-green inner patio. Units vary; look at a few before you move in. Prices for the Spartan but generally tidy rooms begin at about $18 d ($450/month); bungalows, including kitchenette, go for about $33 d ($600/month).

Right next door, the sky-blue and white **Bungalows Azteca** auto court-style cottages line both sides of a cobbled driveway courtyard at P.O. Box 57, San Patricio-Melaque 48980, tel. (335) 551-50, in Guadalajara, tel. (3) 6-255-118 or 6-261-191. The 14 spacious kitchenette cottages, in small (one-bedroom) or large (three-bedroom) versions, are plainly furnished but clean. The one-bedroom units rent for about $30; the three-bedrooms for about $47, with discounts available for weekly and monthly rentals. Make reservations early, especially for the winter.

Less than a block away, the open, park-like grounds, spacious blue pool, and beachside palm garden of the **Bungalows Mallorca** invite unhurried relaxation at Abel Salgado 133, Colonia Villa Obregón, P.O. Box 157, San Patricio-Melaque, Jalisco 48980, tel. (335) 552-19. Although its stacked, Motel 6-style layout is about as unimaginative and un-Mexican as you can find south of Anchorage, Alaska, groups and families used to providing their own atmosphere might find the kitchens and spacious (but dark) rooms of the Bungalows Mallorca appealing. Despite the relatively high asking rates, the management might entertain reasonable offers, especially when the place is half empty (most of the time). The 24 two-bedroom bungalows with fans rent from about $55 d ($175/week, $700/month) low-season to about $70 d high-season. A pair of beachside units with jacuzzi and view balcony are the best.

Closer toward town is the well-kept, colonial-chic **Posada Pablo de Tarso** (named after the apostle Paul of Tarsus). This unique label, along with the many classy details, including art decorated walls, hand-carved bedsteads and doors, and a flowery beachside pool-patio, demonstrate a labor of love. Located at Av. Gómez Farías 408, San Patricio-Melaque, Jalisco 48980, tel. (335) 551-17 and 552-68. The only drawback lies in the motel-style corridor layout, which requires guests to pull the dark drapes for privacy. The 27 rooms and bungalows begin at about $40 d; a kitchen raises the tariff to about $58 d; with a/c, TV, phones. You can also reserve through the owner at Justo Sierra 2354, segundo piso, Guadalajara, Jalisco, tel. (3) 6-521-425 or 6-166-688.

Hotels North of Town: If you prefer hotel high-rise ambience with privacy, a sea-view balcony, and a disco next door, you can have it right on the beach at the in-town **Hotel Club Náutico,** Av. Gómez Farías 1A, San Patricio-Melaque, Jalisco 48980, tel. (335) 557-70 and 557-66, fax 552-39. The 40 deluxe rooms, in blue, pastels, and white, angle toward the ocean in sunset-view tiers above a smallish pool-patio. The upper-floor rooms nearest the beach are likely to be quieter with the best views. The hotel also has a good beachside restaurant whose huge *palapa* both captures the cool afternoon sea breeze and frames the blue waters of the Bay of Navidad. The hotel's main drawback is lack of space, being sandwiched into a long,

narrow beachfront lot. Although the asking rate runs a steep $60 d, high season, they give discounts for three or more days occupancy and may accept less when they're near empty; with a/c, TV, phones, travel agent, restaurant-bar, and credit cards accepted.

The adjacent ponderous pink **Hotel Casa Grande** rambles for hundreds of yards along the northwest end of the Melaque beach at Calle Gómez Farías s/n, P.O. Box 8, San Patricio-Melaque, Jalisco 48980, tel. (335) 550-01, or 551-95, fax 553-82. Its bountiful all-inclusive buffets, open bars, and continuous games, sports, and entertainment are popular with package groups of North Americans who come to enjoy a week of fun in the sun. The atmosphere, however, is institutional, and the building itself, with long concrete corridors, resembles a former Soviet People's hotel. The Spartan but comfortable and private rooms have air-conditioning and ocean-view balconies overlooking the palm-lined beachside pool-patio. For no extra charge guests can enjoy snorkeling, a gym, both high- and low-impact aerobics, kayaking, volleyball, tennis, windsurfing, croquet, Spanish and dancing lessons, mini-club for kids 4-12 and a nightly show-party and a disco. The 236 rooms rent for about $80 per person, double occupancy, $120 single occupancy. Two children under 12 are free when accompanied by parents. All meals and activities are included, credit cards are accepted; for reservations, contact the hotel or your travel agent.

In contrast, the friendly, white stucco modern-funky **Hotel de Legazpi** in the drowsy beach-end neighborhood nearby offers a more personal and tranquil ambience, at P.O. Box 88, San Patricio-Melaque, Jalisco 48980, tel. (335) 553-97. A number of the hotel's spacious, clean and comfortable front-side rooms have balconies with palmy ocean and sunset views. Downstairs, guests enjoy use of a common kitchen and a rear-court pool-patio. The hotel's beachside entrance leads through a homey vegetable garden to the idyllic Melaque west-end sand crescent. Here, good times bloom among an informal club of longtime winter returnees beneath the *palapas* of the popular Pelicanos and Viva María restaurants. (See "Food" below.) The hotel's 16 fan-only rooms (two with kitchenette) rent for $27 s, $33 d, and $40 t in the high season, $18 d low.

The five-star **Hotel Costa Sur** on Playa Cuastecomate a few miles north (see under "Sights" above) offers a local, Club Med-style alternative at P.O. Box 12, San Patricio Melaque, Jalisco 48980, tel. (335) 550-85, 551-25, or 551-35. The hotel's low-rise view guest *cabañas* spread like a giant mushroom garden in the jungly palm-forest hillside above the beach. Patrons—mostly Canadians and Americans in winter, Mexicans in summer and holidays—enjoy deluxe air-conditioned view rooms with cable TV, tennis courts, sailing, windsurfing, pedalboats, snorkeling, volleyball, and a broad pool-sundeck right on the beach. Rates run about $75 per person per day, low-season double occupancy, $100 high, including all food, drinks, and in-hotel activities; credit cards are accepted.

During the low summer-fall season, both the Hotel Casa Grande and the Hotel Costa Sur may accept day guests for a set fee. Call them for details.

Trailer Parks and Camping

Barra-Melaque has one formal trailer park, **La Playa,** right on the beach in downtown Melaque at Av. Gómez Farías 250, San Patricio-Melaque, Jalisco 48980, tel. (335) 550-65. Although the park is a bit cramped and mostly shadeless, longtimers nevertheless get their winter reservations in early for the choice beach spaces. The better-than-average facilities include a small store, fish-cleaning sinks, showers, toilets, and all hookups. Their water is brackish; drink bottled. Boat launching is usually easy on the sheltered beach nearby; otherwise, use the ramp at the Hotel Cabo Coral (see "Boat Launching" following). The Trailer Park La Playa's 45 spaces rent for about $13/day.

Follow wide, bumpy Av. Las Palmas past Hotel Casa Grande to its dirt continuation above the west-end Melaque cove. There, you'll find an informal **RV-trailer park-campground** with room for about 50 rigs and tents. The cliff-bottom lot spreads above a calm rocky cove, ripe for swimming, snorkeling, and windsurfing. Other extras include super fishing and a sweeping view of the entire Bay of Navidad. All spaces are usually filled by Christmas and remain that way until March. The people are friendly, the price is certainly right, and the beer and water

trucks arrive regularly throughout the winter season. Please, however, dump your waste in sanitary facilities. Continued pollution of the cove by irresponsible occupants has led to complaints, which may force local authorities to close the campground.

Wilderness campers will enjoy **Playa de Cocos,** a miles-long golden sand beach, accessible by launch from Barra to Colimilla, or by road the long way around (see "Sights" preceding). Playa de Cocos has an intimate hidden sandy cove, perfect for an overnight or a few barefoot days of birdwatching, shell collecting, beachcombing, and dreaming around your driftwood campfire. The restaurants at the village of Colimilla or the stores (by launch across the lagoon) in Barra are available for food and water. Mosquitoes come out around sunset. Bring plenty of good repellent and a mosquito-proof tent.

FOOD

Breakfast and Snacks

An excellent way to start your Barra day is at the intimate *palapa*-shaded patio of the **Hotel Delfín,** Av. Morelos 23, tel. (335) 700-68. While you dish yourself fruit and pour your coffee from their little countertop buffet, the cook fixes your choice of breakfast options, from savory eggs and omelettes to french toast and luscious, tender banana pancakes; a complete breakfast costs $3-5, daily 0830-1030.

For an airy lagoon-front alternative, try **Banana,** the equally welcoming outpost of Barra longtimers, Av. Veracruz 55; open daily 0800-2400, and Wed.-Sun. 1830-2200. Good service and tasty juices, fruit, eggs, omelettes, hash browns, pancakes, and french toast keep the place humming, low season and high.

In Melaque, Cesar and Charley's, Club Náutico, and Pelicanos (see below) are also good places to start your day.

For evening light meals and snacks, Barra has plenty of options. Here, families seem to fall into two categories: those who sell food to sidewalk passersby, and those who enjoy their offerings. The three blocks of Av. Veracruz from Morelos to the city *jardín* (park) are dotted with tables that residents nightly load with hearty, economical food offerings, from tacos *de lengua* (tongue) and pork tamales to *pozole Guadala-jara* and chiles rellenos. The wholesomeness of their menus is evidenced by their devoted followings of longtime neighbor and tourist customers.

Restaurants

Complete dinner price key: Budget: under $7; Moderate: $7-14; Expensive: more than $14.

One such family has built their sidewalk culinary skills into a thriving Barra storefront business, the **Restaurant Pati,** at the corner of Veracruz and Jalisco, tel. (335) 707-43. They offer the traditional menu of Mexican *antojitos*—tacos, quesadillas, tostadas—plus roast beef, chicken, and very tasty *pozole* soup. Open daily 0800-2300. Budget.

Restaurant Ambar, Veracruz 101A, corner Jalisco, one of Barra's most refined eateries, stands beneath a luxuriously airy upstairs *palapa* diagonally across from the Pati. Their unusual menu features lighter fare—eggs, fish, whole-wheat *(harina integral)* tortillas and bread. Besides a large selection of sweet and nonsweet crepes, they also serve a number of seafood and vegetable salads and Mexican plates, including scrumptious chiles rellenos. Their wine list, which features the good Baja California Cetto label, is the best in town. Open daily 0800-1200 for breakfast, 1700-2200 for dinner; American Express accepted. Moderate.

Barra's class-act eatery is the new **Copa Cabana,** tucked away on side-street Morelos, next to the Hotel Delfín. In downscale Barra, the Copa Cabana's subdued tropical ambience—soft guitar melodies, whirring ceiling fans, low lights—and tasty Mexican-nouveau menu will be heartily welcomed by Barra's sophisticated world-traveling tourist cadre. Open 0700-2400 in season. Moderate.

One of Barra's most entertainingly scenic restaurants is **Veleros,** right on the lagoon at Veracruz 64, tel. 558-38. If you happen to visit Barra during the full moon, don't miss watching its shimmering reflection from the restaurant-*palapa* as it rises over the mangrove-bordered expanse. An additional Veleros bonus is the fascinating darting, swirling school of fish attracted by the spotlight shining on the water. Finally comes the food, which you can select

from a menu of carefully prepared and served shrimp, lobster, octupus, chicken, and steak entrees. Their brochettes are especially popular. Open daily 1200-2200; credit cards accepted. Moderate.

Equally brimming with scenic lagoonside ambience is nearby **Banana,** Veracruz 55. Although most renowned for their breakfasts, the American expatriate family owners also serve tasty sandwiches, Mexican specialties, and hearty vegie, meat, and seafood pastas for dinner. Open daily 0800-2400, Wed.-Sun. 0630-2200. Moderate.

For change of scene, try **Restaurant Corales,** one block away, on the beach side of the sandbar, where guests enjoy a refreshing sea breeze every afternoon and a happy-hour sunset every evening at López de Legazpi 146. Besides tempting fresh seafood selections, they feature savory pineapple chicken and succulent rib plates. Open daily 1200-2300, credit cards accepted. Moderate to Expensive.

Restaurant Pancho, three doors away at Legazpi 53, is one of Barra's original *palapas,* which old-timers can remember from the days when *all* Barra restaurants were *palapas.* The original Pancho, who has seen lots of changes in the old sandbar in his 80-odd years, still oversees the operation daily 0800-2000. Moderate.

Melaque has a scattering of good beachside restaurants. **Restaurant El Dorado,** under the big beachside *palapa* in front of the Hotel Club Náutico, provides a cool breezy place to enjoy the beach scene during breakfast or lunch at Calle Gómez Farías 1A, tel. (335) 557-70. Service is crisp and the specialties are carefully prepared. Their live amplified lunch and dinner combo would be an asset except that they sometimes play loud enough to ruin many people's digestion. If enough folks ask them to turn down the volume, they may eventually get the message. Stark lighting also detracts from the potentially lovely evenings here. You might, nevertheless, drop by to see if the atmosphere has improved. Open daily 0800-2300; credit cards accepted. Moderate to expensive.

One block along the beach toward Barra is the pleasantly picturesque little brick-and-tile **Restaurant Cesar and Charley,** Av. Gómez Farías on the beach across from the central bus terminal, tel. (335) 556-99. The family owner-operators maintain an unusually extensive international menu with an unusually small kitchen by simply not giving up. If some ingredient is lacking, out the door some child will go with instructions to buy the required item. Within 15 minutes your selection will arrive, hot and home-cooked, from the kitchen. Open daily 0730-2100. Moderate.

Restaurant Pelicanos, a beach *palapa* on the tranquil cove about five blocks northwest of the town-center, remains one of Melaque's most enduring institutions. As much as a social spot as a restaurant, they nevertheless retain their popularity with good hamburgers and very fresh fish. Open 0800-2200 daily. Moderate.

Viva María 1910 next door accomplishes about the same by specializing in good Mexican-style food. The restaurant's name is in honor of the thousands of unsung "Marías," *soldaderas* who fought and died along with their men during the Revolution of 1910-17.

SPORTS

Swimming and Surfing

The roughest surf on the Bahía de Navidad shoreline is closer to Barra, the most tranquil closest to Melaque. Swimming is consequently best and safest toward the Melaque end, while, in contrast, the only good surfing spot is where the waves rise and roll in beside the Barra jetty. Bodysurfing and boogie-boarding are best somewhere in between. Shops in Barra (see below) sell and rent surfboards and boogie boards.

Sailing and Windsurfing

Sailing and windsurfing are best near the Melaque end of the Bay of Navidad and in the Bay of Cuastecomate nearby. The only equipment available for use, however, is the windsurfing outfits for guests at the Hotels Casa Grande, tel. (335) 553-82, and Costa Sur, tel. (335) 551-35, and Hobie Cats at the Costa Sur. Call the hotels about a day membership if you want to participate.

Snorkeling and Scuba Diving

Snorkeling is good off the rocky headlands of both the Bays of Navidad and Cuastecomate.

Both the Hotel Casa Grande and Hotel Costa Sur organize tours for their guests to these spots. Although no commercial dive shops operate out of Barra or Melaque, Susan Dearing, the very professional Manzanillo-based instructor, outfits and leads dives in the Barra-Melaque area. Susan, a veteran certified YMCA-method instructor with a record of many hundreds of accident-free guided dives, can be contacted at the La Posada Hotel (Carretera Las Brisas, L. Cárdenas 201, Manzanillo, Colima 28200, tel. (333) 318-99.

For other details on surfing, snorkeling, fishing, hiking and walking, see the specific beaches under "Sights" in this chapter.

Tennis and Golf

The Hotel Cabo Coral tennis courts, tel. (335) 564-00, are customarily open for public rental. Lessons may also be available. The Hotels Casa Grande, tel. (335) 553-82, and Costa Sur, (335) tel. 551-35, have tennis courts for guests and day members.

The lovely, breezy 18-hole Isla de Navidad Golf Course is available to the public for a fee of around $100 per person. For information, call the desk at Hotel Cabo Coral, tel. (335) 564-00, whose owners also developed the golf course. Get there from Hwy. 200 at the Ejido La Culebra (or Isla de Navidad) sign as the highway cuts through the hills at Km 51 a few miles south of Barra. Follow the road about three miles (4.8 km) to a bridge, where the road curves right, paralleling the beach. After about two more miles (3.2 km), you pass through the golf course gate. After winding through the golf course another mile (1.6 km), turn right at the traffic circle at the north edge of the golf course. Continue another mile (1.6 km), between the golf course and the adjacent hillside, to the big golf clubhouse on the right.

Sportfishing

The captains of the Barra Boat Cooperative **Sociedad Cooperativa de Servicios Turístico** routinely take parties on successful marlin and swordfish hunts for about $400 per boat, per day, including bait and tackle. Contact them at their lagoonside office-dock at Av. Veracruz 40, P.O. Box 43, Barra de Navidad, Jalisco 48987, tel. (335) 552-28.

Other big-game boats are available from the El Médico Fishing Nautic Sports shop, Veracruz 230, Barra de Navidad, Jalisco 48987, tel. (335) 558-07 or 558-08, in downtown Barra. Their five well-equipped boats range from the 47-foot *Yopo* (eight passengers, $65/hour) to the launch *Neptuno* (three passengers, $25/hour).

There are many other fish in the sea besides deep-sea marlin and swordfish, both of which often make tough eating. Half-day trips (about $20/hour) arranged through the Sociedad Cooperativa de Servicios Turístico or others will typically hook several large dorado, albacore, snapper, or other delicious eating fish. Local restaurants will generally cook up a banquet for you and your friends if you give them the extra fish caught during such an outing.

Boat Launching
If you plan on mounting your own fishing expedition you can do it from the Barra boat-launching ramp at the end of Av. Pilipinas near the Hotel Cabo Coral. The fee—about $7 per day—covers parking your boat in the canal and is payable at the hotel desk, tel. (335) 564-00.

Sports Equipment Sales and Rentals
Barra has two sports shops. The smallest, the **Farmacia Zurich** on Legazpi right across Jalisco from the church, tel. (335) 505-31, doubles by selling fishing lures, poles and tackle, outboard motors, fins, snorkels, masks, surfboards, and boogie boards. They also rent surfboards and snorkel gear for very reasonable rates. Open daily 0800-2100.

The other, **El Médico Fishing Nautic Sports,** Av. Veracruz 230, at Michoacán, tel. (335) 708-08, has nearly everything you need for fishing. This usually includes fishing poles, lures and tackle, snorkel gear, water-skis, outboard motors, and even an entire jet-ski boat. Open Mon.-Sat. 0900-2000.

EVENTS AND ENTERTAINMENT

Most entertainments in Barra and Melaque are informal and local. *Corridas de toros* (bullfights) are occasionally held during the winter-spring season at the bullring on Hwy. 200 across from the Barra turnoff. Local *vaqueros* (cowboys) sometimes display their pluck in spirited *charreadas* (Mexican-style rodeos) in neighboring country villages. Check with your hotel desk or the Barra tourist information office (see below) for details.

The big local festival occurs in Melaque during the St. Patrick's day week 10-17 March. Events include blessing of the local fishing fleet, folk dancing, cake eating, and boxing matches.

Nightlife
Folks enjoy the Bahía de Navidad **sunset** colors nightly at the bar happy hours at Hotel Tropi-

The antics of dwarfs, jugglers, and acrobats were common entertainments in preconquest Mexico.

cal and its neighbor, Restaurant Corales. The same is true at the beachside Restaurant Dorado at Hotel Club Náutico in Melaque, Morelos 24, on the lagoon. You can prepare for this during the afternoons (December, January, and February mostly) at the very congenial 1600-1800 happy hour around the swim-up bar at Barra's Hotel Sands.

Lovers of tranquility, on the other hand, enjoy the breeze and sunset view from the end of Barra's rock jetty. Here, you can enjoy one of Barra's lowest-key entertainments: the unusual V-shaped waves that race along the submerged jetty-end breakwater and spend themselves, washing against the rocks.

After dinner, huge speakers begin thumping away, lights flash, and the fogs ooze from the ceilings around 2200 at disco El Galeón (of the Hotel Sands, young local crowd) and La Tanga (at the Hotel Casa Grande in Melaque, mixed young-older local and tourist crowd). Their hours vary seasonally; call the Sands, tel. (335) 551-48, or the Casa Grande, tel. (335) 553-82, for details.

Another very popular and friendly dancing hangout is Giff's bar on the sandbar end of Legazpi, across from the Hotel Tropical. Seasonally, from around 2100, couples sway to a live, medium-volume mixed soft rock and tropical music repertoire.

SERVICES AND SHOPPING

Moneychanging

Neither Barra nor Melaque has a bank; the closest ones are in Cihuatlán, on Hwy. 200, about nine miles (14 km) toward Manzanillo. Hotels, however, customarily change cash and U.S. traveler's checks. Additionally, the Liquoría Barra de Navidad, on Legazpi, across from the Hotel Barra de Navidad, exchanges both Canadian and American traveler's checks and cash; open daily 0830-2300.

The only official local moneychanger is Money Exchange Melaque, Gómez Farías 27A across from the bus terminal, tel. (335) 553-43. They exchange both American and Canadian traveler's checks and cash Mon.-Sat. 0900-1400 and 1600-1900, Sunday 0900-1400. Their tariff, however, often amounts to a steep three dollars per 100 above bank rate.

Communications

Barra and Melaque each have a small post office (correo). The Barra office, on Guanajuato (at

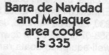

Barra de Navidad and Melaque area code is 335

Mazatlán, two and a half blocks away from the beach), is open Mon.-Fri. 0800-1300 and 1500-1800. The Melaque post office, on the plaza at López Mateos and Morelos, is open Mon.-Fri. 0900-1600, Saturday 0900-1200.

The Barra telegrafo, which also handles money orders, is right at the Av. Veracruz corner of the jardín, tel. (335) 552-62; open Mon.-Fri. 0900-1500.

Next door, at the delegación municipal (municipal agency office), you may use the 24-hour public larga distancia telephone. Another long distance telephone office, tel. (335) 562-92, fax 559-70, is open daily 0700-2300 on beachfront Av. Legazpi diagonally across from the church.

Travel Agents

For airplane tickets and other arrangements in Barra, contact Isla Navidad Tours at Veracruz 204A (between Sinaloa and Guanajuato, tel. (335) 556-65, 556-66, or 556-67; open Mon.-Sat. 0900-1400 and 1600-1900. In Melaque, contact the Costa Alegre Tours at the Hotel Club Náutico, Gómez Farías 1A, tel. (335) 557-70, ext. 125, or 552-39, ext. 125.

Grocery Shopping

There are no large markets, traditional or modern, in Barra or Melaque. However, a number of good mini-supers and fruterías stock basic supplies. In Barra, try the government Conasupo, on Veracruz at the central plaza, open Mon.-Sat. 0900-2100, Sunday 0900-1500, and the La Colmena fruit and grocery three doors away, open daily 0700-2200.

In Melaque, nearly all grocery and fruit shopping takes place at several good stores on main street López Mateos, which runs away from the beach past the west side of central plaza.

Handicrafts

While Melaque has many stores crammed with humdrum commercial tourist curios, Barra has some unusual sources. The Ambar jewelry and crafts store at Veracruz and Jalisco, beneath the upstairs *palapa* restaurant, offers an interesting collection of silver, leather, textiles, and ceremonial crafts. Most outstanding of all is the lineup of one-of-a-kind fiesta masks and artifacts from Guerrero. Open 0900-2000 daily; American Express accepted.

One block away is, for Barra, the decidedly upscale **Tienda Oaxaca**, with racks of high-quality handmade and designer cottons, mostly from Oaxaca and Guadalajara. Not cheap, they are nevertheless marked at around half of what you would expect to pay in the U.S. or Canada for similar items. Open daily 0900-1400, 1500-1830; American Express accepted.

Next door, the enterprising, friendly proprietors of **Artesanías Portal** are busily crafting and selling their convincing versions of pre-Columbian artifacts, along with a choir of goods imported from all over Mexico. **Ayotl**, their companion store, does much the same around the corner on the side street Yucatán.

Barra's small **folk-crafts market**, on Legazpi, corner of Sinaloa, behind the church, is open daily about 0900-1800. The vendors, many indigenous, offer handmade items from their own locales, which range along the Pacific from Sinaloa and Nayarit in the north to Oaxaca and Guerrero in the south. The Jalisco items especially—such as sculptures of human figures in local dress, and papier mâché parrots—are bargainable for prices significantly below Puerto Vallarta levels. Don't bargain too hard, however. Many of these folks, far from their country villages, are strangers in a strange land. Their sometimes-meager earnings often support entire extended families back home.

INFORMATION

Tourist Information Office

The small Barra-Melaque regional office of the Jalisco Department of Tourism is tucked away at bungalow 11 inside the private Las Palmas Bungalows complex at the north end of Legazpi, two blocks from the *jardín*. They distribute maps and literature and answer questions during office hours (Mon.-Fri. 0900-1900, tel. 335-551-00). They also are a good source of information about local civic and ecological issues and organizations (see "Ecology Groups" below).

Health

In Barra, the government **Centro de Salud** clinic, corner Veracruz and Puerto de La Navidad, four blocks from the town square, tel. (335) 562-20, has a doctor 24 hours a day. A local ambulance—contact through the police number, tel. (335) 553-99—is available when necessary to whisk serious emergency cases to better-equipped hospitals in Manzanillo.

For routine consultations, a number of Barra and Melaque doctors and pharmacists are available long hours at their own pharmacies. For example, in Barra, see Jose Quintero López, M.D., evenings till 2200 at Farmacia Marcela, Av. Veracruz 69, near the corner of Sinaloa; 24 hours on call, tel. (335) 554-31.

In Melaque, the trailer park residents swear by the diagnostic skill of English-speaking pharmacist Jesus Saldivar at the pharmacy on Lóopez Mateos, west corner of the *jardín*, tel. (335) 551-67.

The Melaque Centro de Salud clinic, Calle Gordiano Guzman 10, off main beachside street Gómez Farías two blocks from the trailer park, offers access to a doctor 24 hours a day.

Melaque's ambulance-equipped **paramedic** squad is on call and reachable on CB channel 9, or through the police.

Police

The Barra **police**, tel. (335) 553-99, are on 24-hour duty at the city office at 179 Veracruz, adjacent to the *jardín*.

For the Melaque police headquarters, go to the municipal office, at the *jardín* corner of L. Mateos and Morelos, or call (335) 550-80.

Publications

The Barra **newsstand**, open daily 0700-2100, at the corner of Veracruz and Michoacán, regularly stocks the Mexico City *News,* which arrives around 1500.

Perhaps the best English-language lending library in all of the Puerto Vallarta region is **Beer Bob's Book Exchange** on a Barra back street, 61 Mazatlán, near Sinaloa. Thousands of vintage paperbacks, free for borrowing or exchange, fill the shelves. Chief librarian and Scrabble devotee Bob (actually, Duane Renville, USN retired) manages his little gem of an establishment just for the fun of it. It is not a store, he says; just drop your old titles in the box and take away the equivalent from his well-organized collection. If you have nothing to exchange, simply return whatever you borrow before you leave town.

In Melaque, the **Librería Saifer,** open daily 0900-2100, on the central plaza, southwest corner, also stocks the *News*.

Ecology Groups
The private **Grupo Ecología Costa Alegre,** Juárez 64, second floor, Melaque, tel. (335) 553-48, conducts educational programs and consults with government and private agencies in an effort to preserve local endangered species and their habitats. The group's president, Juan Manuel Espinoza, welcomes exchanges with interested visitors; though, as he speaks only Spanish, come prepared with an interpreter.

The less formal **Grupo Ecobana** accomplishes similar goals through practical examples, which include weekly beach-cleaning sessions with schoolchildren and camping out at secluded local beaches in order to discourage turtle egg poachers. For more information, contact Ecobana's personable leader, Luis, who operates the Puesta de Sol bar, overlooking the beach, a block north of the church.

The University of Guadalajara also runs the local **Centro Estudios Ecologíos de la Costa,** which, through research, education, and direct action is trying to preserve local animal and

Local chapters of Mexico's grassroots Partido Ecologista ("Ecology Party") are becoming increasingly influential in municipal elections.

plant species and habitats. Now and then you may spot one of their white vans on the highway or around town. At the wheel might be their director, Emilio Michel, one of whose better-known efforts is the turtle-hatching station at Mismaloya, about 72 miles (115 km) north of Barra, near Cruz de Loreto (see "Southeast of Tehualmixtle" under "Cabo Corrientes Country" above).

GETTING THERE AND AWAY

By Air
Barra de Navidad is air-accessible either through **Puerto Vallarta** airport (see "Getting There and Away" in the previous chapter), or **Manzanillo** airport about 19 miles (30 km) south of town. Both access routes have their drawbacks. From Puerto Vallarta, you must rent a car or taxi from the airport to a bus station—preferably, Transportes Cihuatlán or Tres Estrellas de Oro—where you can catch a bus (three hours) to Barra-Melaque. Through Manzanillo, lack of direct flights from the U.S. means you must first fly from the U.S. to either Guadalajara or Mexico City, where you can connect with a flight to Manzanillo (usually Mexicana or Aeroméxico). Fortunately, either of these air connections is doable in one long day via the U.S. gateway cities of San Francisco, Los Angeles, Chicago, Houston, Dallas, and New York.

The Manzanillo (officially the Playa de Oro) airport (code ZLO) terminal is relatively small, with neither money exchange, hotel booking, nor tourist information booths. The terminal, nevertheless, has a few gift shops, snack stands, an upstairs restaurant, and a *buzón* (mailbox) just inside the front entrance.

Transportation is well organized. Car rentals—Avis, Hertz, National, and Budget—are available, as are *colectivos* or *taxis especiales* at the terminal door. *Colectivos* to Barra-Melaque are only seasonally available, so you may have to share a private taxi (figure about $20 for four) to Barra-Melaque.

Although no public buses service the Manzanillo airport, strong, mobile travelers on tight budgets could save many *pesos* by hitching or hiking the five miles to Hwy. 200 and flagging down one of the frequent Barra-Melaque-bound second-class buses (fare about $2).

By Car or RV

Three highway routes access Barra de Navidad: from the north via Puerto Vallarta, from the south via Manzanillo, and from the northeast via Guadalajara.

From Puerto Vallarta, the **Mexican National Hwy. 200** is all-asphalt and in good condition along its 134-mile (216-km) stretch to Barra de Navidad. Traffic is generally light, and there are no long steep grades. Traffic may slow a bit as the highway climbs the 2,400-foot Sierra Cuale summit near Tuito south of Puerto Vallarta, but the light traffic and the generally excellent road make safe passing relatively simple. Allow about three hours for this easy, very scenic trip.

From Manzanillo, The 38-mile (61-km) stretch of Hwy. 200 is nearly all countryside and all level. It's a snap in under an hour.

The same is not true of the winding, 181-mile (291-km) route between Barra de Navidad and Guadalajara. From Plaza del Sol at the center of Guadalajara, follow the signs for Colima, loading along the four-lane combined **Mexican National Highways 15, 54, and 80** heading southwest. Nineteen miles from the city center, as Hwy. 15 splits right for Morelia and Mexico City, continue straight ahead, following the signs for Colima and Barra de Navidad. Very soon follow the Hwy. 80 right fork for Barra de Navidad. Two miles farther, Hwy. 54 branches left to Colima; take the right branch. Hwy. 80 to Barra de Navidad. From there, the narrow, two-lane road continues through a dozen little towns, over mountain grades, and around curves for another 160 miles (258 km) to Melaque and Barra de Navidad. To be safe, allow about five hours driving time for the whole trip.

By Bus

Various regional bus lines cooperate in connecting Barra de Navidad north with Puerto Vallarta, south with Cihuatlán, Manzanillo, and Lázaro Cárdenas, and northeast with Guadalajara. They arrive and leave so often (about every half hour during the day) from the little Barra de Navidad station, on Av. Veracruz a block and a half past the central plaza, tel. (335) 552-65, that they're practically indistinguishable. Open daily 0800-2200.

Of the various lines, **Transportes Cihuatlán** and its sister line, **Autocamiones del Pacífico,** provide the most options: Super-first-class "Primera Plus" buses connect (three per day) with Guadalajara, Manzanillo, and Puerto Vallarta. In addition to this, Transportes Cihuatlán offers at least a dozen second-class buses per day in all three directions. These often stop anywhere along the road if passengers wave them down.

Another line, **Autobuses Costa Alegre,** provides similar services out of its separate little station at Veracruz 269, across and half a block up the street, tel. (335) 561-11.

The buses that stop in Barra also stop in Melaque, all except one line stop at the Melaque **Central de Autobuses** on Gómez Farías at V. Carranza, tel. (335) 550-03; open 24 hours daily. Autobuses Costa Alegre maintains its own station a block away at V. Carranza and R. Corona.

However, one line, **Tres Estrellas de Oro** (TEO), does not stop in Barra. It maintains its own little station in Melaque at Gómez Farías 257, tel. (335) 552-43. From there, TEO connects by first-class express north all the way to Tijuana, and south to Manzanillo, Zihuatanejo, and Acapulco.

Note: All Barra de Navidad and Melaque bus departures are *salidas de paso,* meaning they originate somewhere else. Reserved seats, *asientos reservados,* are generally available with the possible exception of Christmas and Easter.

MIKE WELLINS

MANZANILLO
AND INLAND TO COLIMA
MANZANILLO

Manzanillo (pop. 100,000) is a small city tucked at the southern corner of a bay so broad it has room for a pair of five-mile-wide junior bays. From the north spreads the **Bahía de Santiago,** separated by the jutting Peninsula de Santiago from its twin **Bahía de Manzanillo** on the south.

Manzanillo's importance as a port has continued since the conquest. Even its name comes from its fortunate harborfront location, where *manzanillos*—trees whose poisonous yellowish red fruit resembles a small apple, or *manzanillo*—flourished beside the orginal wharves.

Splendid local fishing led to an unexpected bonus: flocks of visitors, drawn by Manzanillo's annual International Sailfish Tournament. During three days in 1957, for example, tournament participants brought in 336 sailfish. The word soon got around. The balmy winters and the golden sand beaches drew even more visitors.

By the 1980s, a string of small hotels, condos, and resorts lined Manzanillo's long, soft strands, providing jobs and opportunities in the previously sleepy bayside communities of Santiago and Salagua.

HISTORY

Before Columbus
One of the earliest records of Manzanillo comes from a story of Ix, king of ancient Coliman, now the state of Colima. The legend states that Ix received visits from Chinese trader-emissaries at a shore village, which became the present town of Salagua, on Tzalahua Bay (now the Bay of Manzanillo). It's not surprising the dream of riches gained by trade propelled the Chinese across the Pacific hundreds of years before the Spanish conquest. The same goal drew Columbus

across the Atlantic and pushed Hernán Cortés to this gateway to the Orient a generation later.

Conquest and Colonial Times

Cortés heard of the legend of the Chinese at Manzanillo Bay from the emperor of the Tarascan kingdom in Michoacán. With the riches of China tantalizingly within his grasp, Cortés sent his lieutenants to conquer Pacific Mexico, on whose sheltered beaches they would build ships to realize Columbus's elusive quest.

In 1522, Gonzalo de Sandoval, under orders from Cortés, reconnoitered Manzanillo Bay, looking for safe anchorages and good shipbuilding sites. Before he left a year later, Sandoval granted an audience to local chieftains at the tip of the Santiago Peninsula, which to this day retains the name Playa la Audioncia.

Cortés himself visited Manzanillo Bay twice, in pursuit of a Portuguese fleet rumored to be somewhere off the coast. Cortés massed his forces at the northern bay of Manzanillo, which he christened Bahía de Santiago on 24 July 1535. Although Cortés's enemy failed to appear, the foreign threat remained. Portuguese, English, and French corsairs menaced Spain's galleons as they repaired, watered, and unloaded their rich cargoes for ten generations in Manzanillo and other sheltered Pacific harbors.

Independence

The hope generated by Independence in 1821 soon dissipated in the turbulent civil conflicts of the next half century. Manzanillo languished until President Porfirio Díaz's orderly but heavyhanded rule (1876-1910) finally brought peace. The railroad arrived in 1889; telephone, electricity, drainage, and potable water soon followed. During the 1950s and '60s the harbor was modernized and deepened, attracting ships from all over the Pacific and capital for new industries. Anticipating the demand, the government built a huge oil-fueled (but unfortunately smoky) generating plant, which powered a fresh wave of factories. By the 1970s, Manzanillo had become a major Pacific manufacturing center and port, providing thousands of local jobs in dozens of mining, agricultural, and fishing enterprises.

Recent Times

Although Mexican tourists had been coming to Manzanillo for years, international arrivals grew rapidly after the opening of the big Club Maeva and Las Hadas resorts in the 1970s. The new jetport north of town increased the steady flow to a flood; then came the 1980s, with Bo Derek starring in her fabulously successful movie *Ten*, which rocketed Las Hadas and Manzanillo to the stars as an international vacation destination.

SIGHTS

Getting Oriented

Longtimers know two Manzanillos: the old downtown, clustered around the south-end harborfront *jardín* and the rest—greater Manzanillo—spread northerly along the sandy shores of **Manzanillo and Santiago Bays**. The downtown has the banks, the government services, and the busy market district, while most of the hotels,

Charming reminders of old Mexico await visitors who stroll Manzanillo's downtown lanes.

BRUCE WHIPPERMAN

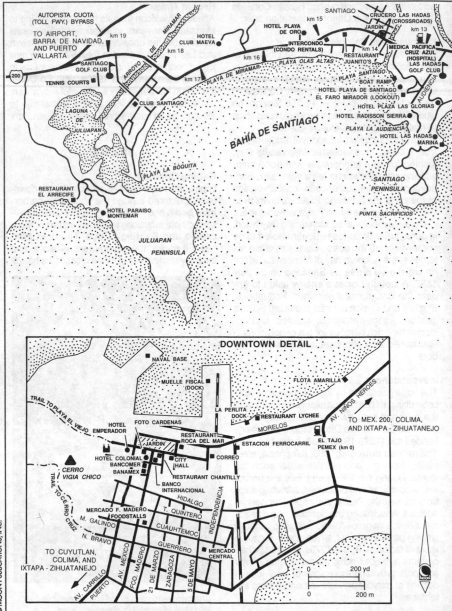

DOWNTOWN DETAIL

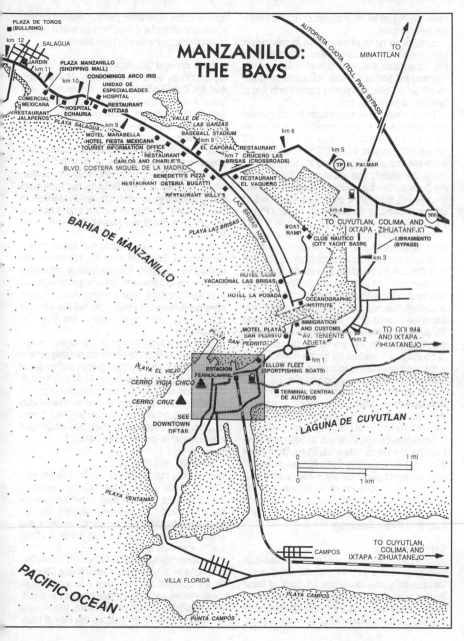

MANZANILLO:
THE BAYS

PLAZA DE TOROS
■ (BULLRING)

km 12   SALAGUA

JARDIN
km 11

PLAZA MANZANILLO
(SHOPPING MALL)

km 10   CONDOMINIOS ARCO IRIS

UNIDAD DE
ESPECIALIDADES
HOSPITAL

COMERCIAL
MEXICANA

RESTAURANT   HOSPITAL   RESTAURANT
JALAPEÑOS   ECHAURIA   KITZIAS

PLAYA SALAGUA   km 9

MOTEL MARABELLA   VALLE DE
HOTEL FIESTA MEXICANA   LAS GARZAS
TOURIST INFORMATION OFFICE   km 8   BASEBALL STADIUM

RESTAURANT   EL CAPORAL RESTAURANT
CARLOS AND CHARLIE'S   km 7 CRUCERO LAS
BLVD. COSTERA MIGUEL DE LA MADRID   BRISAS (CROSSROADS)

BENEDETTI'S PIZZA
RESTAURANT OSTERIA BUGATTI   RESTAURANT
RESTAURANT WILLY'S   EL VAQUERO

AUTOPISTA CUOTA (TOLL FWY) BYPASS

TO
MINATITLAN

km 6

km 5
TP EL PALMAR

km 4   200

BAHIA DE MANZANILLO

PLAYA LAS BRISAS

LAS BRISAS HWY

BOAT
RAMP

TO CUYUTLAN, COLIMA, AND
IXTAPA - ZIHUATANEJO

CLUB NAUTICO   LIBRAMIENTO
(CITY YACHT BASIN)   (BYPASS)

km 3

HOTEL CLUB
VACACIONAL LAS BRISAS

HOTEL LA POSADA   OCEANOGRAPHIC
INSTITUTE

IMMIGRATION   TO COLIMA
AND CUSTOMS   AND IXTAPA -
AV. TENIENTE   ZIHUATANEJO
MOTEL PLAYA   AZUETA   km 2
SAN PEDRITO

PLAYA
SAN PEDRITO

km 1

PLAYA EL VIEJO   ESTACION   YELLOW FLEET
FERROCARRIL   (SPORTFISHING BOATS)
CERRO VIGIA CHICO

CERRO CRUZ   TERMINAL CENTRAL
DE AUTOBUS

SEE
DOWNTOWN
DETAIL   LAGUNA DE CUYUTLAN

0   1 mi

0   1 km

PLAYA VENTANAS

PACIFIC OCEAN

CAMPOS   TO CUYUTLAN,
COLIMA, AND
IXTAPA - ZIHUATANEJO

VILLA FLORIDA

PLAYA CAMPOS

PUNTA CAMPOS

restaurants, and tourist businesses dot the northern beachfronts.

Everything north of downtown is measured from the **El Tajo** junction (Km 0), marked by the downtown Pemex station. Here, along bayfront **Av. Niños Héroes,** the Barra de Navidad-Puerto Vallarta highway starts north just a few blocks from the *jardín.*

The highway curves past foothills and marshland, crossing the mirror-smooth waters of the **Valle de Las Garzas** ("Valley of the Herons") between Kilometers 5 and 7. The soaring white concrete sculpture at the traffic circle (Km 7) marks the *crucero* Las Brisas, or "suicide crossing." Here, the **Las Brisas Hwy.** forks left, southward, through a quiet neighborhood of condos, homes, and small hotels fronting **Playa Las Brisas.**

Back on the main highway, now the **Boulevard Costera Miguel de la Madrid,** continue north past the hotels and restaurants that dot the long **Playa Azul** beachfront. Just after the dusty little town *jardín* of **Salagua** around Km 11, a golf course and big white gate mark the Las Hadas *crucero* (crossing) at Km 12. There, **Av. Audiencia** leads uphill along the plush, condo-dotted **Santiago Peninsula,** flanked by the Las Hadas resort on its south side and Hotel Radisson Sierra on **Playa La Audiencia** on the north.

Back on the main road, continuing north, you pass the **Pemex** gas station at Km 13. Soon comes the Río Colorado creek bridge, then the **Santiago** town *jardín,* on the right, across from the restaurants, banks, and stores of **Plaza Santiago** shopping center (Km 13.5) on the left. From there, traffic thins out, as you pass scattered beachfront condos along **Playa Olas Altas** (Km 15-16). Soon the **Club Maeva** spreads, like a colony of giant blue-and-white mushrooms, along the hill above **Playa de Miramar** at Km 17. Finally, another golf course and entrance gate at Km 19 mark the vacation-home community of **Playa Santiago.**

Getting Around
Visitors can easily drive, taxi (share to make it affordable), or bus to their favorite stops along Manzanillo's long shoreline. Dozens of **local buses** run along the highway through Las Brisas, Salagua, and Santiago (destinations marked on the windshields), all eventually returning to the downtown *jardín.* Fares (in pesos) run less than half a dollar. Hop on with a supply of small change and you're in business.

A Walk around Downtown
A pair of busy north-south streets—**Av. México** and **Av. Carrillo Puerto**—dominate the downtown. Avenida Carrillo Puerto traffic runs one way from the *jardín,* while Av. México traffic does the reverse. The corner of Av. México and Av. Juárez, adjacent to the *jardín,* is a colorful slice of old Mexico, crowded with cafes, curio shops, and street vendors. A dignified Porfirian kiosk presides nearby at the *jardín's* center, while, on the far side, bulging rail tank cars queue obediently along dockside Av. Morelos. In the distance, drab gray cutters and destroyer escorts line the **Base Naval** (BAH-say nah-VAHL) wharfs.

Walk a pair of blocks along Av. Juárez (which becomes B. Dávalos) past Av. México to the cathedral, officially the **Parroquia Nuestra Señora de Guadalupe,** after Manzanillo's patron saint. Inside, four shining stained-glass panels flanking the main altar tell the story of Juan Diego and the miracle of the Virgin of Guadalupe.

During the first 12 days of December, a colorful clutter of stalls lines the streetfront, where families bring their children, girls in embroidered *huipiles* and *chinas poblanas,* and boys in sombreros and serapes. After paying their respects to the Virgin, they indulge in their favorite holiday foods, and get themselves photographed in front of a portrait of the Virgin. (See "Entertainment and Events" below for more details.)

Town Hills and Market
Steep knolls punctuate Manzanillo's downtown. Residents climb precipitous cobbled alleyways, too narrow for cars, to their small (yet luxuriously perched) homes overlooking the city. For an interesting little detour, climb the lane that angles uphill off Av. Juárez, at the post office, two blocks east of *jardín.*

An even steeper hill rises behind the cathedral—the brushy slope of **Cerro Vigía Chico**—where colonial soldiers kept a lookout for pirates. Above and beyond that towers the cross-decorated summit of **Cerro Cruz,** the highest point (about 1,000 feet) above the Bay of Manzanillo. Every 3 May, *peregrinos* (pilgrims) climb to its summit. (See "Hikes" below.)

A Manzanillo downtown walk wouldn't be complete without including a stroll down Av. México, past a dozen old-fashioned little shops—*papelerías, farmacias, dulcerías, panaderías*—to the **Mercado** (turn left at Cuauhtémoc) at Calle 5 de Mayo. Here you can wander among the mounds of bright produce, admire the festoons of piñatas, say a good word to the shrimp-sellers, and stop to listen to the harangue of a sidewalk politician or evangelist. (See "Shopping" below.)

BEACHES

Playa San Pedrito

Playa San Pedrito is Manzanillo's closest-to-downtown beach, a tranquil little strip of sand right on the harbor along Av. Teniente Azueta (which angles off Niños Héroes half a mile from the El Tajo junction Pemex station). The perfect Mexican Sunday beach, San Pedrito has lots of golden sand, seafood *palapas,* and a few big trees for shade. Although its very gentle waves are fine for swimming and windsurfing (with your own equipment) Playa San Pedrito is too close to the harbor for much good fishing or snorkeling.

Manzanillo Bay Beaches

From either the *jardín* or the Las Brisas *crucero,* ride a Las Brisas-marked bus to end-of-the-line Hotel La Posada at the southern end of **Playa Las Brisas.** From the jetty, which marks the entrance to the Puerto Interior ("Inner Harbor"), a hundred-foot-wide sand ribbon seems to curve north without end. It changes its name to **Playa Azul,** then **Playa Salagua** along its five-mile length, ending finally at Las Hadas at the base of the Santiago Peninsula. The beach, while wide, is also steep. The usually gentle waves break suddenly at the sand, allowing little chance for surfing, bodysurfing, or boogie-boarding. Windsurfing (bring your own equipment) and surf fishing, however, are popular, as are snorkeling and scuba diving among the fish that swarm around the corals and rocks of the south-end jetty.

A number of restaurants along the beaches provide refreshments. They include the Hotel

La Posada and the Club Vacacional Las Brisas on Playa Las Brisas; Carlos and Charlie's and the big white Days Inn on Playa Azul; and Motel Marabella on Playa Salagua.

The Santiago Peninsula And Playa La Audiencia

One of Manzanillo's loveliest views is from **El Faro,** the white tower atop the Santiago Peninsula. At Las Hadas *crucero* (Km 12) turn onto the cobbled Av. Audiencia. Continue past the golf course to the top of the rise, turn right at Calle La Reyna, and keep winding upward to the summit. Although El Faro is the centerpiece of a serene condominium community atop the hill, they don't mind if you climb their tower.

The view is unforgettable. From the emerald ridge of the **Juluapan Peninsula** and the 4,000-foot (1,300-meter) **Cerro Toro** bull's hump on the north, the panorama sweeps past green sierras and the blue bays to the white downtown spread beneath the pyramid-peak of **Cerro Cruz** on the southern horizon. On the ocean side, due west, the **Hotel Radisson Sierra** rises above the diminutive sand ribbon of **Playa La Audiencia.**

Once an idyllic downscale cove, Playa La Audiencia is now dominated by the ultramodern gleaming white tower of the Hotel Radisson Sierra. Families nevertheless still come here on Sunday to play in the fine golden-black sand, drink coconut milk, eat tacos, and leave everything on the beach. The beach concessionaire, Promociones y Recreaciones Playa Audiencia, tel. (333) 381-48, rents kayaks, windsurfing boards, water skis, jet-ski boats, banana boats, and boogie boards right on the beach; open daily 0900-1800: instructors (see "Sports" below) from the hotel often guide **snorkeling and scuba diving** parties from the beach to the shoals on either side.

Santiago Bay Beaches

The beaches of Santiago Bay stretch for five golden miles north of the Santiago Peninsula to **Playa La Boquita,** the lagoon-mouth beneath the Juluapan Peninsula's headland. The beaches are all continuous variations of the same wide carpet of yellow, semi-coarse sand.

First, at around Km 14, **Playa Santiago** reaches the Río Colorado creek, where it becomes **Playa Olas Altas.** Here, although the sand drops steeply into the surf, it levels out offshore, so the waves roll in gradually, providing excellent surfing, bodysurfing, and boogie-boarding breaks.

Playa Miramar continues past Club Maeva, marked by the highway pedestrian overpass. The beach itself is popular and cluttered with umbrellas, horses for rent, and vendors. The usually gentle surf is good for bodysurfing and boogie-boarding. Concessionaires rent boogie boards for about $2 an hour.

Finally, at Club Santiago, the beach curves past a village of seafood *palapas* and fishing boats called **La Boquita** ("The Little Mouth"). The sand is wide and firm, and the surf is as tranquil as a huge kiddie pool. Offshore, a 200-foot wreck swarms with fish a few feet beneath the surface, excellent for snorkeling and scuba diving. On the other side of the beach, the **Laguna de Juluapan,** a wildlife-rich tidal wetland, winds along miles of forest-edged shallows and grassy marshes.

Hikes

The adventurous can seek out Manzanillo's many hidden corners, beginning right downtown. **Playa Viejo** is often missed, tucked in a little cove over the hill and accessible by path only. Wear walking shoes and a hat, and take your bathing suit, water, and a picnic lunch. Follow Calle Balbino Dávalos past the cathedral. Bear left up the narrow street and climb the steep concrete staircase (on the left) to the hilltop schoolyard. Continue down the other side along a wooded arroyo trail to the beach. The dark sand beach is strewn with shells and surf-rounded rocks. One dry, grassy spot for possible camping perches above the surf.

Also beginning from downtown, the steep trail to Cerro Vigía Chico and Cerro Cruz will challenge fit hikers. It leads to the top of the highest point in Manzanillo for a breezy panoramic view of the city, bay, and ocean below. Allow about an hour and a half roundtrip for Cerro Vigía Chico, about twice that for the very steep continuation to Cerro Cruz (see below). Take plenty of water, and avoid midday heat by going early in the morning or late afternoon.

Cerro Vigía Chico: Head south along Av. Carrillo Puerto from the *jardín.* Notice the *sastrería* (tailor shop) Aguayo at no. 223 on the left-hand side, where the master tailor sews suits by hand. Turn the corner at the *tortillería* at Nícholas Bravo and head along the upward lane, past little hillside-perched houses. Ask the local people if you get lost. Ask *"¿A Cerro Vigía, por favor?"* They'll help keep you on the right track.

You'll know you've arrived when you see the white "Turquoise Radio" FM transmitter station atop the hill.

Cerro Cruz: Extra-fit hikers can gather breath and push ahead, along the steep, forested uphill path from "Turqoise Radio" to the summit of Cerro Cruz. There, a majestic panorama spreads below: from the Gibraltar-like headland of Juluapan in the north, past golden beaches, over the villa-studded Santiago Peninsula, past the white city to the huge expanse of the Laguna de Cuyutlán, where power stanchions leapfrog across the lagoon from the gargantuan, smoke-spewing seaside power plant.

ACCOMMODATIONS

Downtown Hotels

Near cafes, shopping, and transportation, Manzanillo's downtown is colorful and lively, but often noisy.

The **Hotel Colonial,** Bocanegra 28, at Av. México, Manzanillo, Colima 28200, tel. (333) 210-80, 211-34, or 212-30, Manzanillo's best downtown hotel, is built around a dignified interior courtyard-restaurant. Dating from the 1940s, the Colonial is replete with old-fashioned touches—bright-hued tile staircases, stained-glass windows, and sentimental tile wall scenes. The rooms, although worn, have traditional high ceilings, hand-hewn leather chairs, and wrought-iron lamp fixtures. They open to shady, street-view corridors, lined with chairs for sitting. Try for a room on the relatively quiet Bocanegra Street side of the hotel Their 38 rooms rent for about $22 s or d with fan, $26 with a/c; one block from the *jardín,* credit cards accepted.

A prime budget stop is the **Hotel Emperador,** at B. Dávalos 69, Manzanillo, Colima 28200, tel. (333) 223-74, a stack of 28 rooms

OWNING PARADISE

Droves of once-visitors have fled their northern winters and have bought or permanently rented a part of their favorite Pacific Mexico paradise. They happily reside all or part of the year in beachside developments that have mushroomed, especially in Mazatlán, Puerto Vallarta, Manzanillo, and Acapulco. Deluxe vacation homes, which foreigners can own through special trusts, run upwards from $50,000; condos begin at about half that. Timeshares, a type of rental, start at $5000.

Trusts
Past Mexican generations have feared (with some justification) that foreigners were out to buy their country. Present laws prohibit foreigners from having direct title to property within 30 miles (50 km) of a beachfront or within 60 miles (100 km) of a national border.

Mexican law does permit *fideicomisos* (trusts), which substitute for outright foreign ownership. Trusts allow you (as beneficiary) all the usual rights to the property, such as use, sale, improvement, and transfer, in exchange for paying an annual fee to a Mexican bank (the trustee), which holds nominal title to the property. Trust ownership has been compared to owning all the shares of a corporation, which in turn owns a factory. While not owning the factory in name, you have legal control over it.

Although some folks have been bilked into buying south-of-the-border equivalents of the Brooklyn Bridge, Mexican trust ownership is a happy reality for growing numbers of American, Canadian, and European beneficiaries who simply love Mexico.

Bienes raíces (real estate) in Mexico works a lot like in the U.S. and Canada. Agents work through multiple listings, show properties, assist negotiations, track paperwork, and earn commissions for sales completed. If you're interested in buying a Mexican property, work with one of the many honest and hard-working Mexican agents, preferably recommended through a reliable back-home firm.

Once you find a good property and have a written sales agreement in hand, your agent should recommend a notary *(notaria pública)* who, unlike a U.S. notary public, is an attorney skilled and licensed in property transactions. A Mexican notary, functioning much as a title company does in the U.S., is the star actor in completing your transaction. The notary traces the title, ensuring that your bank-trustee legally receives it, and making sure the agreed-upon amounts of money get transferred between you, seller, bank, agent, and notary.

You and your agent should meet jointly with the notary early on to discuss the deal and get the notary's computation of the closing costs. For a typical trust-sale, closing costs (covering permit, filing, bank, notary, and registry fees) are considerable, typically 8-10% of the sale amount. After that, you will continue to owe property taxes and an approximately one percent annual fee to your bank-trustee.

Time-Sharing
Started in Europe, time-sharing has spread all over the globe. A time-share is a prepaid rental of a condo for a specified time period per year. Agreements usually allow you to temporarily exchange your time-share rental for similar lodgings throughout the world.

Your first contact with time-sharing will often be someone on a resort streetcorner who offers you a half-price tour for "an hour of your time." Soon you'll be attending a hard-sell session offering you tempting inducements in exchange for a check written on the spot. The basic appeal is your investment—say $10,000 cash for a two-week annual stay in a deluxe beach condo—will earn you a handsome profit if you decide to sell your rights sometime in the future. What they don't mention is the interest you could get for your $10,000 cash would go far toward renting an equally luxurious vacation condo every year without entailing as much risk.

And risk there is, because you would be handing over your cash for a promise only. Read the fine print. Shop around, and don't give away anything until you inspect the condo you would be getting and talk to others who have invested in the same time-share. It may be a good deal, but don't let them rush you into Paradise.

MANZANILLO HOTELS

Manzanillo hotels, in order of increasing approximate high-season double-room price. (The area code is 333, the postal code is 28200, and toll-free 800 numbers are reached from the U.S. and Canada only.)

Emperador, B. Dávalos 69, tel. 223-74, $14

Colonial, Bocanegra 28, tel. 210-80, 211-34, or 212-30, $20

Playa de Santiago, P.O. Box 147, tel. 300-55 or 302-70, fax 303-44, $33

Playa San Pedrito, Teniente Azueta 3, tel. 205-35, $24

Parador Marabella, Km 8.5, Playa Azul (P.O. Box 554), tel. 311-03 or 311-05, $38

Club Vacacional Las Brisas, L. Cárdenas 207, tel. 320-75 or 317-47, $37

Condominios Arco Iris, P.O. Box 359, tel. 301-68, $48

Fiesta Mexicana, Km 8.5, Blvd. Miguel de la Madrid (P.O. Box 808), tel. 321-80, $58

La Posada, L. Cárdenas 201, tel. 318-99, $80

Club Maeva, P.O. Box 440, tel. 505-95 or (800) GO-MAEVA, fax 503-95, $200 (two adults, all inclusive, two kids free)

Sierra Radisson Plaza, Av. La Audiencia 1, tel./fax 320-00 or (800) 333-3333, $143

Las Hadas, P.O. Box 158, tel. 400-00 or 420-00, fax 304-30, $200

around a dim interior patio, which, at first glance, appears uninviting. Inside, however, the grandmotherly owner, María Trinidad Bautista and her staff keep the corridors and stairways shining. The rooms too, although very plain, are very clean. Furthermore, the price is certainly right: rates run about $14 d, $21 for four, with baths, ceiling fans, and a good restaurant downstairs. Located half a block from the *jardín,* on the quiet westward extension of B. Dávalos, just before the church.

If you prefer the beach, to the north the **Motel Playa San Pedrito** offers a homey close-in alternative, right on popular Playa San Pedrito Teniente Azueta 3, Manzanillo, Colima 28200, tel. (333) 205-35. This unpretentious Mexican family hotel rambles amidst a flowery garden, edged with colorful tropical plants and centering on a bubbling, blue swimming pool. A well-kept

tennis court stands at one side, and beyond that, waves lap the sandy beach. With all those outdoor attractions, the plainness of the rooms and the dust in their corners matter little. Request one of the *piso arriba* (upper-floor) rooms for privacy and sea views from a front balcony-corridor. The 33 fan-only rooms go for about $24 d, $27 t; with parking, and credit cards are accepted.

Las Brisas-Playa Azul Hotels

The swish of the waves on the sand, long walks at dusk, and good restaurants nearby summarize the attractions of the "passionate pink" **Hotel La Posada,** a durable jewel among Manzanillo's small hotels, Av. Lázaro Cárdenas 201, P.O. Box 201, Manzanillo, Colima 28200, tel. (333) 318-99. Every memorable detail—leafy potted plants, rustling palms, brick arches, airy beach-view *sala,* resplendent bay-view sunsets—adds to La Posada's romantic ambience. La Posada's clientele, mostly middle-aged North American winter vacationers, prefer the upstairs rooms, some of which have private balconies and sea views. Get your winter reservations in early. Rates for the 24 comfortable but non-deluxe rooms run about $53 d low season, $80 high, some with a/c, all include a big breakfast. The hotel has a bar-cart, snack restaurant, comfortable sitting area, good pool, street parking, and accepts credit cards.

A few doors north along the beach, the **Club Vacacional Las Brisas** likewise enjoys platoons of repeat customers, Av. L. Cárdenas 207, Fracc. Las Brisas, Manzanillo, Colima 28200, tel. (333) 320-75 or 317-47. Good on-site management keeps the garden manicured, the pool inviting, and the beach beyond the gate clean and golden. The best rooms, white-walled and comfortable but not deluxe, are on the beach-side ocean-view upper floors. The 56 rooms and suites, all with kitchenettes, rent from about $37 d with fan, a/c available; with parking, and credit cards accepted.

The **Hotel Fiesta Mexicana,** Km 8.5, Carretera Manzanillo-Santiago, Blvd. Miguel de la Madrid, P.O. Box 808, Manzanillo, Colima 28200, tel. (333) 321-80, right on Playa Azul, appears as a big white box perched on the beach. Inside the rooms rise in tiers, which enclose a lovely patio with a meandering blue pool. On one side is a big restaurant with an ocean-vista veranda. The rooms are smallish but comfortable, with TV, phones, and a/c. The rooms on the ocean side look out on sea views. Their 190 rooms rent for about $58 d, low-season promotions are sometimes available; with street parking and pool aerobics; credit cards are accepted.

Not far away, the **Motel Parador Marabella,** Km 8.5, Playa Azul, P.O. Box 554, Manzanillo, Colima 28200, tel. (333) 311-03 or 311-05, offers a breezy beachfront location at moderate prices. All the ingredients seem to be in place—a small pool, rustling palms, a small bar-restaurant, sand and surf—for a tranquil Manzanillo week in the sun. The best of the 60 rooms, on the upper floor of the two-story wing, have private balconies and plumy sea views. Rates for the a/c rooms run about $41 d low season and $45 high; $35 low, $38 high with fans; with parking, and credit cards are accepted.

The **Condominios Arco Iris,** Km 9.5, P.O. Box 359, Manzanillo, Colima 28200, tel. (333) 301 68, half a mile north, is more a garden apartment complex than condominiums. The setting, a spacious, leafy manicured tropical park, with inviting blue pool-patio and *palapa,* nicely complements the apartments themselves. The units, all at ground level, with kitchenettes and either one or two bedrooms, are immaculate and tastefully furnished in '70s-modern style. The two-bedroom units, which sleep four, rent for about $80 low season, $90 high; the one-bedrooms, $40 low, $48 high. Discounts are generally available for monthly (or perhaps even weekly) rentals. A block from the beach and a favorite of many Manzanillo longtimers. Get your winter reservation in early.

Santiago Peninsula Hotels

The Santiago Peninsula's sea-view villas, condo developments, and resorts for the rich and famous are luxuriously isolated, generally requiring a car or taxi to get anywhere.

Hotel Las Hadas, P.O. Box 158, Manzanillo, Colima 28200, tel. (333) 400-00, 420-00, or (800) 7-CAMINO from the U.S. and Canada, fax 304-30, is a self-contained city with a host of pleasurable amenities. Las Hadas is so large only a fraction of its rooms are near the sand, and most are a small hike to the beach. Furthermore, when guests finally get there, they find no waves on the sheltered Las Hadas cove, and their views are cluttered by the white Arabian-style tents of a regiment of fellow guests.

Las Hadas nevertheless offers plenty of interest, at extra charge: three restaurants, a sportfishing marina, a sunset cruise, horseback riding, a golf course, a squadron of tennis courts, and a dozen aquatic sports. You'll have to do without parasailing, however. The approximately 300 luxurious white-and-blue motif suites, villas, and rooms rent from about $200 standard d to about $300 for a junior suite with breakfast and all amenities, including complete wheelchair access.

On the other side of the peninsula, the shining white **Hotel Sierra** (officially the Hotel Sierra Radisson Plaza), Av. La Audiencia 1, Peninsula Santiago, Manzanillo, Colima 28200, tel./fax (333) 320-00, or (800) 333-3333 from the U.S. and Canada, towers futuristically above the gemlike Playa La Audiencia. The hotel's large size, however, doesn't seem to bother the guests, whose activities focus upon the spreading ocean-view pool-patio. There, around the swim-up bar, drinks flow, music bounces, and water volleyball and polo fill the sunny days. No matter if guests tire of pool frolicking; every hotel corner, from the indulgent pastel-appointed rooms (each with sea-view balcony) to **Hidra,** the airy, rustic-chic restaurant-in-the-round, abounds with style. Bars offer nightly live music; fine crafts and designer clothes fill the boutiques, while dozens of books and the latest U.S. magazines line the shop shelves. Rates for the 350 rooms run about $143 d hill view or $195 ocean view, depending upon season; with a/c, color cable TV, phones, mini-bars, all water sports, tennis, golf, wheelchair access, and credit cards accepted.

Santiago Bay Hotels

The once-grand but now relatively humble '50s-genre **Hotel Playa de Santiago,** Balneario de

Santiago s/n, Bahía de Santiago, P.O. Box 147, Santiago, Colima, tel. (333) 300-55 or 302-70, fax 303-44, on the south side of Santiago Bay nevertheless offers much for budget-conscious travelers. Besides spacious, private balcony sea-view rooms overlooking the hotel's placid cove and beach, guests enjoy a palmy, seaside pool-sundeck, a tennis court, a boat ramp, and friendly management. Prices for the 105 rooms and suites run about $33 d for a standard room, to $50 for a split-level apartment for four, with phones and fans only; credit cards accepted.

The **Club Maeva,** P.O. Box 440, Manzanillo, Colima 28200, tel. (333) 505-95, or (800) GO-MAEVA from the U.S. and Canada, fax 503-95, Manzanillo's all-inclusive fun-in-the-sun colony, spreads for a whitewashed quarter-mile on the hillside above Santiago Bay. Club Maeva, whose summer clientele is mostly Mexican, while Canadian and American during the winter, demonstrates the power of numbers. Its staff of 700 services upwards of a thousand guests who enjoy a plethora of aquatic, field, court, and gym activities at no extra cost. Months would be needed to take full advantage of the endless sports menu, which includes pool scuba, snorkeling, tennis, horseback riding, volleyball, softball, aerobics, and basketball.

Besides sports, Club Maeva guests enjoy continuous open bar and restaurant service, nightly theme shows, a disco, a miles-long beach, sunning beside Latin America's largest pool, and a complete water-slide park.

Inclusive rather than exclusive, Club Maeva resembles a huge comfortable summer camp. Children are more than welcome, with a special 4- to 12-year-old miniclub. Club Maeva seems to offer options for everyone, such as table games—cards, backgammon, checkers, and chess—Spanish lessons, and a tranquil adults-only solarium and pool-bar.

The rooms, actually clusters of small villas, are an unusual luxurious-Spartan combination, snow white and royal blue with private view balconies and marble floors, but with no movable furniture. With the exception of stoves and refrigerators in some units, all shelves, cabinets, bed platforms, and seats are attractive but indestructible white concrete built-ins. The 550 rooms and suites rent for the all-inclusive rate of about $105 per person, double occupancy. One child free per adult; with a/c, no phones or room TV; credit cards accepted.

Apartment and Condominium Rentals

Many attractive condominium and apartment complexes dot Manzanillo's beautiful beachfronts. Owners often rent their units through agents who specialize in condo listings. Among the best organized is **Intercondos,** whom you can phone at (333) 329-04 or (333) 404-24 or write at P.O. Box 93, Santiago, Colima 28860. You can also drop by their roadside office Mon.-Sat. around Km 15 (on the beach side, north end of Santiago, just where the highway bends back to the beach.) Some of the more tranquil spots, removed from highway noise, are in Santiago and Las Brisas. They rent moderate to luxurious units, by the day, week, or month. Quality varies widely; advance as little deposit as possible on a sight-unseen rental. If it seems too good to be true, it probably is.

On the other hand, if you can't find the right condo to rent, you might look into buying one. Manzanillo's long, uncrowded beaches have many condos for sale, some for very reasonable prices.

Trailer Park and Camping

Condos, hotels, and restaurants have crowded out virtually all camping prospects along Manzanillo beaches. Authorities even discourage overnight RV parking in the remaining open space around Km 18 between Club Maeva and Club Santiago. Furthermore, **El Palmar,** Manzanillo's last trailer park, unfortunately closed in 1994. You might want to check if they've reopened: Km 4.5, Boulevard Costero Miguel de la Madrid, Manzanillo, Colima 28200, tel. (333) 232-90.

The closest good campsites are about a dozen miles north, three miles off Hwy. 200, at **Playa de Oro,** accessible by cobbled road from the signed turnoff near Km 31, five miles north of El Naranjo.

A land development turned sour, Playa de Oro has returned to the wild: an endless sandy beach with many drive-in sites, good for RVs and tents. The surf, while often not too rough, has some undertow; don't swim alone. Boogie-boarding and surfing are possible for cautious beginners and intermediates. Surf fishing is excellent, and the waves deposit carpets of shells and miles of driftwood, perfect for a week of beachcombing. You'll share the beach with a colony of sand crabs which, like a legion of arthropodic prairie dogs, jealously guard their individual sand-holes. Bring everything; the closest stores are in El Naranjo.

FOOD

Downtown Snacks and Foodstalls

The cluster of *fondas* (permanent foodstalls) at the **Mercado Francisco Madero** is the downtown mecca for wholesome homestyle cookery. Each *fonda* specializes in a few favorite dishes, which range from rich *pozole* and savory stewed pork, beef, or chicken, to ham and eggs and whole grilled fish.

One of the favorites, the **Menudería Paulita,** open daily 0500-2200, is tended by a jolly squad of women off of Av. México, at the F. Madero and Cuauhtémoc corner, five short blocks from the *jardín*. One of them enjoys the singular job of crafting and baking unending stacks of hot tortillas, which their mostly workingmen customers use to scoop up the last delectable morsels.

Besides sit-down meals, the same downtown neighborhood is a source of on-street desserts. These include *churros* (long doughnuts) and **pastries,** sold from carts late afternoons along Av. México about four blocks from the *jardín*, and velvety ice cream from the **Bing** ice cream chain's downtown branch on the east end of the *jardín*.

North-End Breakfast and Snacks

Along the north-side highway, regulars flock nightly to tiny **Pepe's,** around Km 8.5, Hwy. 200, beach side, which specializes in mouthwatering barbecued beef, roast chicken, and pork loin tacos; open daily 1900-0100.

No local vacation would be complete without breakfast or lunch at **Juanito's,** Manzanillo's friendly refuge from Mexico, in Santiago, Km 13.5, a few blocks north of Santiago Plaza, tel. (333) 313-88. The longtime American expatriate owner features tasty, modestly priced hometown fare, such as ham and eggs any style, hot-

cakes, hamburgers, milkshakes, and apple pie. For a generation of repeat customers, Juanito's is home away from home, with satellite TV, a shelf of used paperbacks, a long-distance telephone, and bottomless cups of coffee. Open daily 0800-2200.

Downtown Restaurants

Complete dinner price key: Budget: under $7; Moderate: $7-14; Expensive: over $14.

One of Manzanillo's prime people-watching cafes is the **Restaurant Chantilly** on the *jardín* corner adjacent to City Hall, tel. (333) 201-94. The completely unpretentious Chantilly offers its mostly local clientele prompt service, an extensive economical menu, and long moments lingering over several varieties of *cafe espresso*. The *comida corrida* (five-course set lunch, $4.50) highlights many patrons' downtown day. Open daily except Saturday, 0700-2200. Budget to moderate.

Doughnutlike deep-fried churros *rank among downtown Manzanillo's most popular street snacks.*

BRUCE WHIPPERMAN

The dignified, airy ambience of the **El Patio** restaurant of the Hotel Colonial on Av. México, just south of the *jardín,* offers another attractive option. Besides its high beamed ceiling, softly whirring ceiling fans, and a tranquil adjoining open-air patio, the lunch and dinner menu offers an unusually long selection of seafood, from broiled marlin and tuna to jumbo butterflied shrimp and pan-fried squid. A live duo sometimes adds to the enjoyment with soft guitar music afternoons and evenings. Open daily 0700-2200. Moderate.

The crowd of midafternoon customers alerts budget-minded eaters to the value and quality of the restaurant at the **Hotel Emperador,** at B. Dávalos 69, half a block west of the *jardín,* tel. (333) 223-74. Although *desayuno, comida* and *cena* are all good at the Emperador, the favorite is the $3 *comida corrida* set lunch, beginning around 1300.

A different cadre of loyal customers enjoys the **Cafe Roca del Mar,** at the east end of the *jardín.* With approximately the same menu and prices as the Chantilly, the Roca del Mar, whose tables spread to the shady sidewalk, is perhaps a bit more relaxed.

Around the corner, **Restaurant Lychee,** on the dockfront, two blocks east, at Niños Héroes 397, tel. (333) 211-03, serves bountiful plates of tasty Chinese-style specialties. Although their meat and fish dishes are tasty enough, it's the mounds of stir-fried broccoli, bean sprouts, snow peas, and bok choy that you can also order that spell welcome relief for vegetable-hungry palates. Open Mon.-Sat. 1200-2200. Moderate.

Las Brisas Restaurants

Several popular restaurants cluster around the *crucero* Las Brisas intersection (marked by the traffic circle and sculpture) at Km 7. Foremost among them is **Ostería Bugatti,** tel. (333) 329-99, which provides much more than its mere oyster house label suggests. As much a nightclub as a restaurant, Bugatti's is where older folks go to remember the '40s and the young find out what they missed. The scene is certainly correct: couples swaying to live dancefloor swing and bebop, a platoon of tuxedo-attired waiters scurrying to and fro beneath glimmering chandeliers, and a strictly old-fashioned mayonnaise, boiled vegetable, meat, and

spumoni menu. (Actually, it's a little better than that: you can get *ensalada* Caesar, good pastas, T-bone steak, pork chops, stuffed chicken, and fish fillet with your boiled vegetables.) Open daily 1330-2400; credit cards accepted. Moderate.

Half a block but a world away is **Restaurant El Vaquero,** Crucero Las Brisas 19, tel. (333) 316-54, Manzanillo's air-conditioned cowboy B-movie set. Its decor includes checkered tablecloths, wagon wheels, antelope-head wall trophies, and varnish-splashed plywood walls. The impression fits: an 1880s Sonora mining camp saloon-cafe, where teenage country waiters can manage little more than plopping plates onto your table and picking them up when you're finished. The cook outside hoists the ponderous steak-loaded iron grill to dump great shovels of charcoal into the fire below. You order your Vaquero steak by the kilogram—from two pounds on down. A "petite" half-pound (250-gram) T-bone or sirloin usually suffices. As an impression of the Wild West, Restaurant El Vaquero seems correct. Historians tell us that the old cowboy joints were both seedy and expensive. Vaqueros represents an improvement, however: it accepts credit cards. Open daily 1400-2300. Expensive.

Willy's nearby represents something altogether different. Casual but elegant, Willy's airy, beachside terrace is *the* place to be seen in Manzanillo, two blocks down the Las Brisas Hwy. from the *crucero,* tel. (333) 317-94. Owner Jean François LaRoche features a list of good but pricey designer appetizers, salads, seafood, meats, and desserts. Open daily 1900-2400; reservations recommended. Expensive.

The Las Brisas branch of the Mexican **Benedetti's Pizza** chain offers respectable Italian fare, good service, a friendly family atmosphere, and reasonable prices, tel. (333) 315-92, next to Ostería Bugatti. Their cool salad bar plate—carrots, tomato, beets, mushrooms, lettuce, and hot bread, $3—seems like heaven on a warm afternoon. Open daily 1400-2300. Budget to moderate.

Playa Azul-Salagua Restaurants

Restaurants dot the three-mile beach strip north of the *crucero* Las Brisas. One of the renowned is **Carlos'n Charlie's,** the Manzanillo branch of late owner Carlos Anderson's goofy worldwide chain, Hwy. 200, Km 8, across from the baseball stadium; open Mon.-Sat. 1330-0100 high season, call for low-season hours, tel. (333) 311-50. The fun begins at the entrance where a sign announces: "Colima Bay Cafe, since 1800." Inside, the outrageous decorates the ceilings while a riot of photos—romantic, poignant, sentimental, and brutal—covers the walls. Meanwhile, the waiters (who, despite their antics, are gentle sorts) entertain the customers. The menu, with items such as "Moo," "Peep," and "Pemex," cannot be all nonsense, since many of them, such as Oysters 444, TBC Salad, and their tangy barbecued ribs, are delicious. Moderate to expensive.

A sensational hors d'oeuvre and salsa plate draws customers year-round to **Restaurant Jalapeños,** at Km 10.5, a quarter mile south of Comercial Mexicana. Don't eat lunch if you want to fully appreciate it: a giant platter piled with hot, fresh chips, a trio of savory salsas, a plate of crisp pickled chiles, and a bowl of scrumptious refried beans. This comes automatically, before all the salads and entrees, and do try the luscious all-fresh cheese chiles rellenos. Since you can't possibly have room for dessert, order a Sexy Coffee instead. Open daily 1700-2400.

ENTERTAINMENT AND EVENTS

El Caporal
One of Manzanillo's unmissable entertainments starts quietly at around 1300 at El Caporal, a big *palapa* restaurant-bar specializing in *botanas* (Mexican-style hors d'oeuvres). As soon as you order a drink, the *botanas*—small plates of ceviche, beans, pickled vegetables, and guacamole—begin to flow. By 1500, mariachis begin strumming away, more bottles pop open, and more *botanas* arrive. By 1600, the place is usually packed; if you stay till 1800 you'll probably need someone to stuff you into a taxi home. El Caporal is behind the Superior beer distributor at the Km 8 post across the highway from the beach, open daily 1200-1900, tel. (333) 322-10.

Sunsets, Strolling, and Sidewalk Cafes
Playa Las Brisas and Playa Azul provide the best vantage for viewing Manzanillo's often spectacular sunsets. For liquid refreshment and atmosphere to augment the natural light show, try one of the romantic beachside spots, such as **Hotel La Posada, Restaurant Willy's, Carlos'n Charlie's,** and the **Hotel Fiesta Mexicana.** (Sunset views from the plush terraces at Santiago Peninsula and Bay hotels, such as Las Hadas, Sierra, and Club Maeva, are unfortunately obstructed by intervening headlands.)

Las Hadas provides an out, however. Their trimaran sloop *Aguamundo* departs daily from the hotel marina (at 1615) and the downtown La Perlita dock (at 1700) for a *crucero de atardecer* (sunset cruise). The $20 per-person tariff includes drinks. For tickets, contact the hotel, tel. (333) 4000-00, or their La Perlita dock office, tel. (333) 207-26, open daily 1100-1800, or a travel agent, such as Agencia Bahías Gemelas, tel (333) 310-00.

Early evenings are great for enjoying the passing parade around the downtown *jardín*. Relax over dessert and coffee at bordering sidewalk cafes, such as **Chantilly,** corner Av. México, closed Saturday, or **Roca del Mar,** east side of *jardín*, next to Bing ice cream.

North of downtown, the **Salagua** (Km 11.5) and **Santiago** (Km 14) village plazas offer similar, even more *típica*, sidewalk diversions.

Movies
After strolling a few times around the downtown *jardín*, you might enjoy taking in a movie at the adjacent **Cine Bahía.** Their double-bill programs ($2.50, beginning at 1600) often combine an American sleeper with European art-erotica. On the highway at Playa Azul, the **Cine Club Fiesta,** Km 9.5, across from Vog disco, screens first-run Mexican and U.S. films, $3 beginning around 1600. On the Santiago town *jardín,* the **Cine Marisol** offers similar programs.

Fiestas
Manzanillo's longest yearly party is the **Fiesta de Mayo,** celebrated for two weeks, beginning late April and ending around 10 May. A continuous schedule of events, including sports tournaments, art exhibitions, parades, concerts, folkloric dancing in the *jardín,* and a carnival by the downtown market, brightens Manzanillo days and nights.

The **Fiesta de Guadalupe** honors Manzanillo's—and all Mexico's—patron saint, the Virgin of Guadalupe (see "Religion" in the Introduction chapter). Shrines to the Virgin, with flower and food offerings beneath her traditional portrait, begin appearing everywhere, especially downtown, by the end of November. For 12 evenings beginning 1 December, floats parade and Indian-costumed dancers twirl around the *jardín*. Afternoons, people (women and girls, especially) proudly display their ancestry by dressing up in Indian *huipiles, enredos,* and *fajas* and heading to the cathedral. Nearing their destination, they pass through lanes crowded with stalls offering Indian food, curios, toys, souvenirs of the Virgin, and snapshots of them beside the Virgin's portrait.

Sporting Events

Manzanillo hosts an occasional winter-season *corrida de toros* (bullfight) at either the Salagua or the El Coloma bullring (on Hwy. 200, four miles south of town). Watch for posters. For dates, call a travel agent or the tourist information office, tel. (333) 322-77, fax 314-26.

The renowned Manzanillo **International Sailfish Tournament** kicks off annually during the last half of November (for details, see "Sportfishing" following).

Maycol

Singer-instrumentalist Maycol wows audiences regularly at big local hotels and clubs, such as Ostería Bugatti and the Hotel Sierra. With fingers flying over half a dozen instruments from the piano to the saxophone and his velvety voice crooning dozens of tunes a la Frank Sinatra, Stevie Wonder, Nat King Cole (and even Dionne Warwick!), Maycol radiates such charisma that you think he is performing personally for you. In fact, he will: for a private show for you and your friends, contact him or his wife Barbara at P.O. Box 726, Manzanillo 28200, tel. (333) 325-87.

Tourist Shows

The **Club Maeva** hosts a lively Saturday **Mexican Fiesta,** including swirling dancers, mariachis, rope dance, and rooster fights. Other nights, they stage theme parties where guests become part of the entertainment: International Gala Night, a journey to the world's great cities; Brazilian Night, a glittering Río de Janeiro Car-

Many small shrines to the Virgin of Guadalupe appear in Manzanillo neighborhoods prior to 12 December, the culminating day of the Virgin's fiesta.

naval; and Wednesday amateur Night of the Stars, your chance to shine on the stage. Club Maeva parties, open to the public, begin with a big buffet at 2000 and cost about $25 per person, $12 for kids under 12; for reservations, phone the hotel at (333) 505-96, ext. 145, or a travel agency, such as Agencia Bahías Gemelas, tel. (333) 301-00.

Dancing and Discoing

The **Ostería Bugatti** offers cocktails, dining, and live-music dancing nightly in season at *crucero* Las Brisas, 1940s and '50s style, beginning around 2000, tel. (333) 329-99. The **Hotel Sierra** lobby-bar has live dance music at Playa Audiencia, nightly in season 1900-2100, tel. (333) 320-00. A combo also often plays for dancing at the flashy new **Restaurant Kitzia's,** Km 10.5, beach side of highway; call (333) 314-14 for reservations.

Discomania reigns regularly at a number of clubs along Hwy. 200. Call to verify hours, which vary with season. Some of the better spots, moving from south to north:

The very popular **Bar Felix,** Km 9 on Playa Azul, tel. (333) 318-75, has relatively low volume recorded music, soft couches, and no cover, with a two drinks minimum at $3 apiece. Music is much less subdued, however, at its hot new companion club, Disco Vog, next door. There, lights begin gyrating and the woofers begin thumping around 2230; entrance fee is $10.

At **Disco Oui,** near Salagua at Km 10, tel. (333) 323-33 or 313-03, seasonally scheduled sporadic, loud heavy metal alternates with softer Latin-romantic. Lights begin around 2230, music an hour later; about $8 cover.

At disco **Enjoy,** in Santiago, Km 15, tel. (333) 325-40, patrons gather in its soaring black-walled interior to watch weird Warhol-type videos and listen to medium-volume rock until midnight, when the lights begin whirling and the blasting begins in earnest. About $8 cover, call 328-39 for info.

The round, spacy interior of **Disco Solaris,** at Km 15.5, Hotel Playa de Oro, feels like a trip in a big flying saucer. Lights begin flashing, colored fogs descend, and music begins booming around 2330; about $7 cover.

SPORTS

Walking and Jogging

All of the beaches of Manzanillo and Santiago bays are fine for walking. The sand, however, is generally too soft for jogging, except along the wide, firm, north-end **Playa de Miramar.** On the south side, the last mile of the no-outlet **Las Brisas Hwy.** asphalt serves as a relatively tranquil and popular jogging course.

Swimming and Boarding

With the usual precautions (see "Safety First" under "Sports And Recreation" in the On the Road chapter), Manzanillo's beaches are generally safe for swimming, except on occasional days of high waves, when all but the most foolhardy avoid the surf. The safest swimming beaches are **Playa San Pedrito** and **Playa de Miramar** at the protected south and north ends, respectively.

The best surfing breaks occur along **Playa Olas Altas** ("High Waves Beach"), where, most any day, a sprinkling of surfers ride the swells a hundred yards offshore.

Bodysurfing and boogie-boarding are much more common, especially on **Playas Audiencia, Olas Altas,** and **Miramar,** where concessionaires often rent boogie boards. (See "Beaches" above.)

Sailing, Windsurfing, and Kayaking

Manzanillo's waters are generally tranquil enough for kayaking, but also windy enough for good sailing and windsurfing. A few concessionaires rent equipment at fairly hefty prices. At **Playa La Audiencia,** the beach concessionaire, Promociones y Recreaciones, tel. (333) 318-48, rents windsurfers ($20/hour plus $10 lesson) and kayaks ($20/hour) to any able body. At Las Hadas beachside, Aguamundo, tel. (333) 400-00, ext. 759, rents windsurfers and kayaks to Las Hadas guests and those of hotels Plaza Las Glorias, Club Maeva, Sierra, Villa del Palmar, and certain other big hotels.

Snorkeling and Scuba Diving

Manzanillo waters are generally clear. Visibility runs from about 30 feet onshore to 60-80 feet farther out. Manzanillo has three standout shore-accessible spots: the jetty rocks (depth 5-25 feet) at the south end of **Playa Las Brisas;** the shoals on both sides of **Playa de la Audiencia;** and the wrecked ('59 hurricane) frigate 200 yards off north-end **Playa La Boquita.** All of these swarm with schools of sponge- and coral-grazing fish.

The veteran YMCA-method certified dive instructor Susan Dearing operates **Underworld Scuba** from her poolside Hotel Sierra headquarters, tel. (333) 320-00. With thousands of accident-free dives, Susan ranks among Pacific Mexico's best-qualified scuba instructors.

Susan and her assistants start you out with a free qualifying lesson at the pool. After enough free practice, they'll guide you in onshore dives (for about $50 for a two-hour outing, including one half-hour fully equipped dive). They guide experienced divers (bring your certificate) much farther afield, including super sites such as Roca Elefante at the Juluapan Peninsula's foamy tip. You can also reach her through her personal number 90-335-803-27, or through Hotel La Posada, tel. (333) 318-99, in Manzanillo.

Although Aguamundo at Las Hadas (which also services Club Maeva and guests of other hotels) has boats, scuba equipment, and experienced scuba guides, they have no professionally licensed instructors. Their guided scuba dives (sometimes cluttered with tag-along snorkelers and spectators) are limited to certified scuba divers only.

Jet- and Water-Skiing

At **Playa La Audiencia,** wave-runners and water-ski towing are available at about $40 per half hour from the beach concessionaire, Promociones y Recreaciones, tel. (333) 318-48.

Aguamundo (tel. 400-00, ext. 759) at **Las Hadas** beach offers similar equipment and services to guests of hotels Las Hadas, Plaza Las Glorias, Club Maeva, Sierra, and Villa del Palmar.

Tennis and Golf

Manzanillo has no free public tennis courts. **Hotel Sierra,** however, rents its six superb courts to outsiders for $10 hourly during the day and $20 at night. Their teaching pro offers lessons for about $26 per hour. Most other large hotels, notably Club Maeva and Las Hadas, have many courts, but do not rent them to the public.

You may also take advantage of the three excellent tennis courts of the Club Santiago golf course, tel. (333) 503-70, open about 0700-1800, about $12/hour. Get there by turning off Hwy. 200 at the side road, signed "Canchas de Tenis," just north of the golf course.

For tennis players on a budget, check in to the **Motel Playa San Pedrito,** the **Club Vacacional Las Brisas,** or the **Hotel Playa de Santiago** (see "Accommodations" above); each has a playable tennis court.

Manzanillo golfers enjoy two good golf courses. The nine-hole **Club Santiago** course (office just inside the Club Santiago gate at Hwy. 200, Km 19) is available for public use daily 0800-1700. The 18-hole greens fee runs

about $40 (half that for nine holes), clubs rent for about $15 a set, and a golf cart about $30 ($20 for nine holes). Caddies work 18 holes for about $12 ($8 for nine holes). For information and reservations, call the club at (333) 503-70.

The renowned 18-hole **Las Hadas** course, at Km 12, Hwy. 200, is generally available only for Las Hadas (and Hotel Sierra, Plaza Las Glorias, Club Maeva and other hotel) guests. Fees vary. For specifics, check with your hotel desk.

Sportfishing

Manzanillo's biggest sportfishing operation is the **Flota Amarilla (Yellow Fleet),** whose many captains operate cooperatively through their association, Sociedad Cooperativa de Prestación de Servicios Turísticos Manzanillo. You can see their bright yellow craft anchored off their dockside office on Av. Niños Héroes, a long block east (away from downtown) of the El Tajo Pemex gas station.

Their five-person boats run about $180 for a day's billfish (marlin, sailfish) hunting, completely equipped with three fishing lines. Larger, plusher eight-person, six-line boats go for about $300, complete with ice and no-host bar. All of their boats are insured and equipped with CB radios and toilets. For information and reservations, call (333) 210-31, write Flota Amarilla-Soc. Coop. de P. de Servicios Turísticos Manzanillo, Niños Héroes frente al 638, Manzanillo, Colima 28200, or drop into their dockside office.

Other alternatives are available through travel agents, such as the Agencia Bahías Gemelas, tel. (333) 310-00.

Manzanillo sponsors two annual **billfish tournaments** in early February and late November. Competing for automobiles as top prizes, hundreds of contestants ordinarily bring in around 300 big fish in three days. The complete entry fee runs about $500, which includes the farewell awards dinner. For more information, contact Fernando Adachi, tournament coordinator, at downtown Ferretería Adachi, Av. México 251, tel. (333) 327-70, or write the sponsors, the Deportivo de Pesca Manzanillo, P.O. Box 89, Manzanillo, Colima 28200.

Hopefully, sponsors of such tournaments will soon be able to devise competitions that will

(top) One of Pacific Mexico's many varieties of pea family embellishes a hillside near Barra de Navidad, Jalisco. (bottom) Any time is nap time poolside at the Hotel Bucanero in San Blas. (photos by Bruce Whipperman)

(top left) shops on Paseo Isla Cuale, Puerto Vallarta; (top right) weaver using traditional backstrap loom, Puerto Vallarta; (bottom left) an Amuzgo Indian potter poses behind her goods near Pinotepa Nacional, Oaxaca (bottom right) Florencio Gallardo, woodcarver of Huazolotitlán, Oaxaca (photos by Bruce Whipperman) preserve, rather than wipe out, the species upon which their sport depends. Some progressive captains have seen the light and encourage their clients to release the caught fish.

Yacht Berthing and Boat Launching

Las Hadas Hotel's excellent marina has about 100 berths (up to 80 feet) rentable for about 50 cents per foot per day, including potable water and 110/220-volt electrical hookup. Reservations recommended, especially during the winter; write Manager, Las Hadas Marina, P.O. Box 158, Manzanillo, Colima 28200, or call (333) 400-00 (ask for the Marina), or send your reservation request via fax (333) 419-50.

Las Hadas marina also has a boat ramp, available for a fee. Make arrangements with the marina before you arrive, however, or you might have to do some fast talking to get past the guard at the gate. At Hwy. 200, Km 12, follow Av. Audiencia past the hilltop, turn left at the Las Hadas sign. At the gate, the guard will direct you.

On the south end of Manzanillo Bay, you can either use the **Club Náutico** (Yacht Club and sailfish tournament headquarters) boat ramp (inside the cyclone fence) for about $12, or the impromptu ramp at the road's end for free. At the end of the Las Brisas Hwy., turn left at and follow the road in front of the Oceanographic Institute to the inner harbor. If a naval guard is at the gate, he will let you through; say *"Club de Yates, por favor."* (kloob day YAH-tays, por fah-VOR.)

On north-side Santiago Bay, you can also use the ramp at the **Hotel de Playa Santiago,** tel. (333) 302-55, fax 303-44, for a $5 fee. From Hwy. 200, Km 13.5, just south of the Los Colorados creek bridge, just north of the gas station, follow the side road running behind the ETN bus terminal, along the peninsula's north shore to the hotel at road's end.

SHOPPING

Markets and Downtown

Manzanillo's colorful, untouristed **Mercado Municipal** district clusters around the main market at Cuauhtémoc and Independencia (five short blocks along Av. México from the *jardín,*

turn left four blocks). Southbound "Mercado"-marked buses will take you right there.

Wander through the hubbub of fish stalls, piled with dozens of varieties, such as big, fresh-caught *sierra* (mackerel) or slippery *pulpo* (octopus). Among the mounds of ruby tomatoes, green melons, and golden papayas, watch for the exotic, such as *nopales* (cactus leaves) or spiny green *guanabanas,* the mango-shaped relative of the Asian jackfruit. On your way out, don't miss the spice stalls, with their bundles of freshly gathered aromatic cinnamon bark and mounds of fragrant dried *jamaica* flower petals (for flavoring *aguas* drinks).

Heading back toward the *jardín,* you might look through some of the *artesanías* (crafts shops) along Av. México and the *jardín,* such as **Artes Cacho,** B. Dávalos 13 for Olinalá lacquerware, Tonalá papier-mâché animals and figurines, or Tlaquepaque glass. Don't be shy about bargaining. In this part of town, it's *la costumbre.*

Shrimp sellers display their fresh offerings near Manzanillo's central market.

BRUCE WHIPPERMAN

Santiago Shopping

Every Saturday morning, folks gather for the **Santiago Market,** beneath *tianguis* (awnings) that spread along Av. V. Carranza, two blocks north of the town plaza. Although merchandise tends toward dime-store-grade clothes and hardware, it's worth a stroll if only for the color and the occasional exotica (wild fruits, antiques, bright for-sale parrots) that may turn up.

For a host of genuine folkcrafts, head to nearby **Centro Artesanal Las Primaveras,** at Juárez 40, tel. (333) 301-73, two blocks from the highway, couple of blocks north of the Santiago town *jardín.* There, scattered amidst a rambling, dusty clutter, many attractive handicrafts—blown glass, crepe flowers, pre-Columbian-motif pottery, leatherwork, papier-mâché clowns and parrots—languish, waiting for someone to rescue them. Open Mon.-Sat. 0800-2000, Sunday 0800-1400.

Back on the highway, just a few doors north of the Santiago *jardín,* take a look inside **El Palacio de Las Conchas y Caracoles** shell emporium, tel. (333) 302-60. Bring your shell book. Hosts of glistening, museum-quality specimens—iridescent silver nautiluses, luscious rose conches, red and purple corals—line a multitude of shelves. Purchase them (from $1000 on down) singly or choose from an array of jewelry—necklaces, earrings, brooches, and rings. Open Mon.-Sat. 0900-1400 and 1600-2100, Sunday 0900-1400.

Supermarket, Photo, and Health-Food Stores

The Manzanillo branch of the big **Comercial Mexicana,** tel. (333) 300-05, marked by the orange pelican sign, anchors the American-style Plaza Manzanillo shopping center at Km 11.5. They seemingly offer everything—from appliances and cosmetics to produce, groceries, and a bakery—spread along shiny, efficient aisles. Open daily 0900-2100.

At the entrance to the same Plaza Manzanillo complex, drop off your film for quick finishing at up-to-date **Foto Sol,** tel. (333) 318-60. They also sell popular films and stock some camera accessories. Open daily 0900-2100.

Downtown, **Photo Studio Cárdenas** offers three-hour photo finishing, film, and some cameras and accessories on the *jardín,* at Balvino Dávalo 52, tel. (333) 211-60; open 0930-1400 and 1630-2030, closed Sunday.

Manzanillo's health-food store, **Yacatecuhtli,** located downtown, at Av. México 249, urges customers to "watch your health" with their yogurt, granola, natural vitamins, ginseng, alfalfa tablets, soy hamburger and cheese. Open Mon.-Sat. 0800-2200, Sunday 0800-1500 and 1700-2200.

Additionally, in Santiago, a small health-food store, on the highway, about a block south of the Santiago town *jardín,* stocks a modest supply of health foods and products.

SERVICES

Money Exchange

The downtown **Banamex** (Banco Nacional de Mexico) exchanges both U.S. and Canadian traveler's checks and cash, Av. México 136, three blocks from the *jardín,* tel. (333) 204-68; open Mon.-Fri. 0900-1400. The **Bancomer** next door, Av. México 122, tel. (333) 228-88, does the same during the same hours. If they are too crowded, the **Banco Internacional,** across the street a block away, changes U.S. traveler's checks and cash, across from the Hotel Colonial, tel. (333) 208-09; money exchange Mon.-Fri. 0930-1400.

A scattering of banks along Hwy. 200 north of downtown also change money. In **Salagua,** try the Banamex, tel. (333) 414-90, in Manzanillo Plaza shopping center, or the Bancomer, tel. (333) 418-61, across the highway and north a block. In **Santiago,** you have a choice of **Banco Serfin,** tel. (333) 309-41, Mon.-Fri. 1000-1245 (U.S. traveler's checks and cash) and **Banco Internacional,** tel. (333) 303-81, Mon.-Fri. 0930-1200 (U.S. traveler's checks and cash), both on the highway across from the Santiago town *jardín.*

American Express Agency

Although they don't cash American Express traveler's checks, **Agencia de Viajes Bahías Gemelas** (Twin Bays Travel Agency), Hwy. 200 Km 9, next to Chrysler Motor, tel. (333) 310-00 or 310-53, fax 306-49, sells them to card-carrying members for personal checks (usually up to $1000). As the official Manzanillo American Express office, they also perform the usual membership services and book air tickets, local tours, and hotel reservations. Open Mon.-Sat. 0900-1400 and 1600-1800.

Communication

The downtown *correo* is at the corner of Avs. Juárez and Cinco de Mayo, one long block (parallel to the waterfront) from the *jardín;* open Mon.-Fri. 0800-1900, Saturday 0900-1300.

Nearby *telecomunicaciones,* the new high-tech telegraph office, sends telegrams, telexes, and fax messages. Open Mon.-Fri. 0900-2000, Saturday 0900-1200. *Giros* (money order) hours are shorter, however: Mon.-Fri. 0900-1300 and 1500-1700 only. Located in the Presidencia Muncipal on the *jardín,* bottom floor.

In **Santiago,** the post office, tel. (333) 411-30, and *telecomunicaciones* offices are together on side street Venustiano Carranza no. 2, across Hwy. 200 from Juanito's restaurant. Post office hours are Mon.-Fri. 0900-1300 and 1500-1800, Saturday 0900-1300, while *telecomunicaciones* hours are Mon.-Fri. 0900 1500.

Manzanillo's *larga distancia* telephone offices are conveniently spread from the downtown north along Hwy. 200. Efficient, computer-assisted **Computel** has several convenient locations: downtown, at Av. México 336, on the *malecón* at Morelos 196, one block east of the *jardín,* open daily 0800-2100; at *crucero* Las Brisas, open daily 0800-2130; and in Santiago, open Mon.-Sat. 0700-2145, Sunday 0900-1300, next to Juanito's, which, incidentally, also offers long-distance telephone and fax (tel./fax 333-320-10) service.

Immigration and Customs

Both **Migración** and the **Aduana** occupy the upper floors of the **Edificio Federal Portuario** (Federal Port Building) on San Pedrito Beach, at the foot of Av. Teniente Azueta.

The cooperative, efficient Migración staff, third floor, tel. (333) 200-30, can replace a lost tourist card. (Make a copy of it beforehand, just in case.) Open Mon.-Fri. 0800-1500 for business and around the clock for questions.

Contact the Aduana, second floor, tel. (333) 200-87, for instructions if you have to leave Mexico temporarily without your car. If your Spanish is rusty, ask your hotel desk clerk (or the tourist information office, see following) to call for you. Open Mon.-Fri. 0800-1500.

> **Manzanillo area code is 333**

INFORMATION

Tourist Information Office

The combined federal-state-city **Turismo** ("Tourism Office") answers questions and dispenses a small Colima and Manzanillo map. Located on 4960 Blvd. Miguel de la Madrid, across from Mariscos Barra de Navidad, tel. (333) 322-77, fax 314-26; open Mon.-Sat. 0800-1500.

Hospital, Police, and Emergencies

In a medical emergency, call a taxi or **Cruz Roja** (Red Cross) at (333) 428-14, and have them take you to either **Centro Médico Quirúrgico Echauri** at Km 9.7, Blvd. Miguel de la Madrid, tel. (333) 400-01, or **Médica Pacífico Cruz Azul,** at Av. Palma Real 10, Km 13, a block off, just south of the gas station, tel. (333) 403-85. Manzanillo's newest and best-equipped private hospitals, they each have round-the-clock service, including a laboratory and several specialists on call you can also visit for routine consultations.

For both medical consultations and a good pharmacy in Santiago, contact French- and English-speaking **Joseph Cadet Jr., M.D.** at his office (next to Juanito's at Hwy. 200, Km 14.5; open Mon.-Sat. 1000-1400 and 1700-2000) or his adjacent Farmacia Continental (open Mon.-Sat. 0900-1400 and 1600-2100, tel. 333-382-86).

For **police** emergencies, call the **Preventiva Municipal,** tel. (333) 210-04, in the City Hall on the *jardín.*

Publications

Downtown is **Revistas Saifer,** Av. México 117, across from the Hotel Colonial, and Av. México 207, two blocks down the street from the *jardín,* tel. (333) 229-99, which stocks the Mexico City *News* and a few American magazines, such as *Time, Life, Newsweek, Computer,* and *Brides;* open daily 0800-2200. The same is true for their Plaza Manzanillo shopping center branch in Salagua, Km 11.

The *tabaquería* shop at **Hotel Sierra,** tel. (333) 320-00, stocks U.S. newspapers, a rack of U.S. magazines, and some English-language paperbacks.

Public Library
The Manzanillo **Biblioteca Municipal** is open Tues.-Sun. 0800-1300 and 1600-2000 on the third floor of the Presidencia Municipal on the *jardín* downtown.

GETTING THERE AND AWAY

By Air
The **Manzanillo airport,** officially the Playa de Oro International Airport (code ZLO), is 28 easy highway miles (44 km) north of downtown Manzanillo, and only about 20 miles (32 km) from most Manzanillo beachside hotels. In the other direction, the airport is 19 miles (30 km) south of Barra de Navidad.

The terminal itself is small for an international destination, lacking money exchange, hotel booking, and tourist information booths. The terminal nevertheless has a few gift shops, snack stands, an upstairs restaurant, and a *buzón* (mailbox) just inside the front entrance.

Flights
Aeroméxico flights connect Manzanillo airport several times a week with Los Angeles (via Guadalajara) and Mexico City. For reservations, contact Aeroméxico's downtown offices, at Av. Carrillo Puerto 107, tel. (333) 212-67 or 217-11; for Aeroméxico flight information, contact, their airport office, tel. (333) 324-24.

Mexicana Airlines flights connect only with Mexico City. For reservations and flight information, contact their airport office, tel. (333) 323-23.

Airport Arrival
With neither airport hotel booking service nor money exchange, you should fly into Manzanillo with a day's worth of pesos and a hotel reservation. If you don't, you'll be at the mercy of taxi drivers who love to collect fat commissions on your first-night hotel tariff.

After the usually cursory immigration and customs checks, independent arrivees have their choice of a car rental (see below) or **taxi tickets** from a booth just outside the gate. *Colectivo* tickets run about $6 per person to any Manzanillo hotel, while a *taxi especial* runs about $20.

Colectivos head for **Barra de Navidad** and other northern points seasonally only. *Taxis especiales,* however, will take three passengers to Barra, Melaque, or Coastecomate for about $30 total or to Hotel Los Angeles Locos, $50, hotels El Tecuán and Costa Careyes, $70, or Chamela-El Super, $90.

No public buses service the Manzanillo airport. Strong, mobile travelers on tight budgets could save many pesos by hitching or hiking the five miles to Hwy. 200 and flagging down one of the frequent north or southbound second-class buses (fare about $2 to Barra or Manzanillo). Don't try it at night, however.

As for airport **car rentals,** you have a choice of Avis, tel. (333) 301-90, National, tel. (333) 306-11 (or at Hotel Las Hadas, tel. 400-00), and Budget, tel. (333) 314-45. Hint: Unless you don't mind paying upwards of $50 per day, shop around for your car rental by toll-free 800 numbers at home *before* you leave (see the chart in the On the Road chapter).

Airport Departure
Save money by sharing a taxi to the airport with fellow departing hotel guests. Always establish the taxi fare before you get into the taxi. If the driver insists on too much, hail another taxi.

Since airport authorities accept neither credit cards nor traveler's checks, save enough dollars or pesos to pay your **$12 international departure tax.** If you've lost your tourist card and don't have a duplicate, be prepared to pay a departure fine of around $20. You might be able to squeeze by without a fine if you have a copy of your lost tourist card and a police report of the loss.

By Car or RV
Three main highway routes connect Manzanillo with the outside world: from the north via Puerto Vallarta and Barra de Navidad; from the northeast via Guadalajara and Colima; and from the southeast via Ixtapa-Zihuatanejo and Playa Azul (Lázaro Cárdenas).

From the north, **Mexico National Hwy. 200** glides 170 smooth asphalt miles (276 km) from Puerto Vallarta via Barra de Navidad. Few steep grades or much traffic slow progress along this foothill-, forest-, and beach-studded route. Allow about four hours to or from Puerto Vallarta, about one hour to or from Barra.

The safety and ease of the new Guadalajara-Colima *autopista* (combined National Highways 15, 54, and 110) more than compensates for the tolls. Head southwest from the Glorietta Minerva circle in Guadalajara along Hwy. 15 for around 27 miles (45 km) until Acatlán de Juárez, and take the Hwy. 54 fork south for Colima. Later connect with Hwy. 110, bypassing Colima and continuing south to just before Tecomán, where Hwy. 200 splits off right, northwest, to Manzanillo. Figure about four and a half driving hours for this easy, 190-mile (311-km) trip, either way.

The same cannot be said for the winding 238 miles (390 km) of coastline Hwy. 200 between Zihuatanejo and Manzanillo. Keep your gas tank filled; the spectacularly scenic but sparsely populated 150-mile stretch from Playa Azul to the Colima border has no gas stations. Allow a full eight-hour day, in broad daylight, either way. Don't try it at night.

Drivers who want to avoid the long, sometimes congested Santiago-Salagua beachfront strip should follow the *cuota* (toll) **bypass.** (See map, "Manzanillo: The Bays.") Southbound, watch for signs around Km 20, at the village of Naranjo. Northbound, do the same after you cross the Laguna Cuyutlán bridge on the Hwy. 200 *cuota* freeway.

By Bus

Several bus lines serve Manzanillo from the **Central Camionera** ("Central Bus Terminal") at Hidalgo and Aldama, about a mile from the downtown El Tajo Pemex south along the Colima highway. The well-organized terminal has a long-distance telephone and a number of shops where savvy passengers stock up with food and water. They have no left-luggage lockers, however.

The separate ticket offices line up along one side of the terminal. All departures listed below are local *(salidas locales)* unless noted as *salidas de paso.* Choose first class whenever you can; its service, speed, and *asientos reservados* (reserved seats) far outweigh the small additional ticket cost. The bus lines divide roughly into north-south and east-west categories.

North-South Bus Lines: Tres Estrellas de Oro (TEO) and its associated lines **Elite** (EL) and **Transportes Norte de Sonora** (TNS) operate from the same office, tel. (333) 201-35. They provide luxury and first-class service north with Puerto Vallarta, Mazatlán, and Tijuana, and south with Playa Azul junction, Lázaro Cárdenas, Zihuatanejo, and Acapulco. Other first-class departures also connect northeast with Colima, Guadalajara, and Mexico City.

Transportes Cihuatlán (TCL), tel. (333) 205-15, and its two associated lines provide Manzanillo's most frequent service north and northeast. Their "Primera Plus" (super-first-class) buses connect with Puerto Vallarta directly three times a day and Guadalajara (via Melaque and Aztlán) twice. Many other second-class buses follow the same routes, stopping everywhere.

Autotransportes Sur de Jalisco second-class buses, tel. (333) 210-03, connect half-hourly 'round the clock with Guadalajara via Colima. Three buses per day also connect south with the Playa Azul junction and Lázaro Cárdenas.

The interurban second-class **Sociedad Cooperativo de Autotransportes** buses connect half-hourly with south Colima destinations of Armería, Cuyutlán, Tecomán, and Colima.

East-West Buses: More than a dozen **Autobuses del Occidente** (ADO) "Primera Plus" and first-class buses, tel. (333) 201-23, connect 'round the clock with Mexico City through Michoacán via Morelia, where you can make connections to Pátzcuaro. Many second-class buses connect daily with subsidiary Michoacán destinations of Apatzingan, Zamora, Uruapan, Pátzcuaro, and Morelia.

Flecha Amarilla, tel. (333) 202-10, and its susidiary lines combine under the "Servicios Coordinados" blanket to offer a host of departures. Many luxury-class "Primera Plus" buses connect direct with Guadalajara and Mexico City. Other "Primera Plus" connections continue past Guadalajara as far as Aguascalientes. Other departures (about a dozen a day) connect with Mexico City through Colima and Michoacán destinations of Minatatlán, Colima, Zamora, Salamanca, Irapuato, and Morelia. Still others connect north with Barra de Navidad-Melaque and Puerto Vallarta.

By Train

President Porfirio Díaz's once-plush 19th-century passenger service that carried Guadalajara's elite to frolic on Manzanillo's beaches has been reduced to a pair of scruffy second-class diesels that chug opposite ways daily between Guadalajara and Manzanillo via Colima.

Train **no. 92** departs Guadalajara daily (Guadalajara-Manzanillo fare $1.50) around 0900, arriving in Manzanillo around 1800. Meanwhile, train **no. 91** departs Manzanillo around 0600, arriving in Colima around 0800, continuing to Guadalajara, where it arrives 1400-1500.

Schedules change; verify times at the station during daylight hours.

In Guadalajara, passengers continuing east can board the connecting first-class sleeper **El Tapatío** and arrive in Mexico City the following morning (or get off en route at Morelia, where the next day they can board a Pátzcuaro-Lázaro Cárdenas-bound train).

Guadalajara train passengers continuing north can connect with the first-class coach **Estrella** around 0815, headed for Tepic (1500 arrival), Mazatlán (1800 arrival), and Mexicali (1600 succeeding day arrival) at the U.S. border.

*reproduction of Colima
pre-Columbian pottery dogs*

INLAND TO COLIMA

From atop their thrones of fire and ice high above the Valley of Colima, legends say that the gods look down upon their ancient domain. The name "Colima" itself echoes the tradition: from the Nahuatl "Colliman" (*colli:* ancestors or gods, and *maitl:* domain of).

Approaching from Manzanillo, visitors seldom forget their first view of the sacred mountains of Colima: the dignified, snowcapped 14,220-foot (4,323-meter) Nevado de Colima, above his fiery, tempestuous younger brother, the 13,087-foot (3,980-meter) Volcán de Fuego ("Volcano of Fire"). The heat from that heavenly furnace rarely reaches down the green slopes to the spring-fed valley, where the colonial city invites coastal visitors to its more temperate (1,400-foot) heights for a refreshing change of pace.

HISTORY

Before Columbus

Although Colima (pop. 180,000) is the smallish capital of a diminutive agricultural state, it is much more than a farm town. Visitors can enjoy the residents' obvious appreciation of their arts and their history—twin traditions whose roots may extend as far south as Ecuador and Peru and as far west as the Gulf coast's mystery-shrouded monument builders, the Olmecs.

Colima's museums display a feast of ceramic treasures left behind by the many peoples—Nahua, Tarascan, Chichimec, Otomi—who have successively occupied the valley of Colima for upwards of 3,000 years. Much more than mere utilitarian objects, the Colima pottery bursts with whimsy and genius. Acrobats, musicians, and dancers frolic, old folks embrace, mothers nurse, and most of all, Colima's famous dogs scratch, roll, snooze, and play in timeless canine style, as if they could come alive at any moment.

Conquest and Colonization

By 1500, the ruler of Colima, in order to deter his aggressive Tarascan neighbors to the north, had united his diminutive kingdom with three neighboring coastal provinces. This union, now known as the Chimalhuacan Confederation, did not prevail against Spanish horses and steel. Many local folks take ironic pride Colima is one of Mexico's earliest provinces. Their ancestors fell to the swords of conquistador Gonzalo de Sandoval and his 145 soldiers, who, in an anticlimax to their bloody campaign, founded the city on 25 July 1523.

Two years later, Cortés appointed his nephew, Francisco Cortés de Buenaventura, mayor and head of a settlement of about 100 Spanish colonists and 6,000 Indian tributaries.

Cortés himself, in search of Chinese treasure in the Pacific, repeatedly visited Colima on his way to and from the Pacific coast during the 1530s, most notably during January 1535, en route to his exploration of Baja California.

Sparsely a generation after the route to the Orient was finally discovered in the 1560s, the Spanish king bypassed Colima by designating Acapulco as the prime Pacific port. This, along with a series of disasters—earthquakes, volcanic eruptions, hurricanes, and pirates—kept Colima in slumber until President Porfirio Díaz built the railroad to the beaches and new port of Manzanillo during the 1880s.

Modern Times

The destructive 1910-17 Revolution and the hard economic times of the 1930s kept Colima quiet until the 1950s, when burgeoning mining and Pacific Rim shipping, fishing, and tourism brought thousands of new jobs. Manzanillo became a major port and manufacturing center, boosting Colima to a government and university headquarters and trading hub for the bounty (meat, hides, milk, fruit, vegetables, copra, sugar) of rich valley and coastal plantations, farms, and ranches.

IN-TOWN SIGHTS

Getting Oriented

Colima's central district is a simple, one-mile square. The street grid runs north-south (north, toward the volcanoes; south, toward the coast)

COLIMA

LIBRAMIENTO A GUADALAJARA

TO COLIMA VOLCANOES AND GUADALAJARA

TO COLIMA REGIONAL FAIRGROUND

TO GUADALAJARA

54

UNIVERSITY OF GUADALAJARA

HOTEL LOS CANDILES

HOTEL MARIA ISABEL

CENTRAL CAMIONERA (BUS STATION)

0.2 mi
0.2 km

BLVD. CAMINO REAL

AV. DE LOS INSURGENTES

AV. FELIPE SEVILLA DEL RIO

TO COMALA, CARRIZALILLO, AND LAGUNA LA MARIA

PLAZA COUNTRY (SHOPPING CENTER)

MUSEUM OF THE CULTURES OF THE WEST (ARCHAEOLOGY)

EJERCITO NACIONAL

PEDRO GALVAN

AV. NIÑOS HEROES

VIPS RESTAURANT AUERRERA (DEPARTMENT STORE)

LIBRAMIENTO A MANZANILLO

TO MANZANILLO AND IXTAPA- ZIHUATANEJO

GALLARDO

IGNACIO SANDOVAL

GRAL. NUÑEZ

FILOMENO MEDINA

AV. DE LOS MAESTROS

HOSPITAL CIVIL

CARRANZA

BOMBEROS

ALDAMA

IGNACIO ALLENDE

VICENTE GUERRERO

FCO. I. MADERO

HIDALGO

MORELOS

BRAVO

CROTOS GRILL

LAGUNA CARRIZALILLO, AND LAGUNA LA MARIA

PALACIO FEDERAL (POST OFFICE AND TELEGRAPH)

AV. REY COLIMAN

20 DE NOVIEMBRE

MUSEO DE CULTURAS POPULARES (MASCARA Y DANZA)

CONSTITUCION

A. OBREGON

Restaurant FONDA SAN MIGUEL

DOWNTOWN PARKING

CAFE CISNES

PLAZA TORRES QUINTERO

PLAZA NUÑES

BANAMEX (BANK)

JUAREZ

REVOLUCION

CORREGIDORA

MATAMOROS

V. CARRANZA

NIGROMANTE

ARTESANIAS

Hotel CEBALLOS

JARDIN DE LIBERTAD

MUSEO DE HISTORIA

PALACIO DE GOBIERNO

HOTEL AMERICA

ABASOLO

VICTORIA

REFORMA

SUAREZ

MACLOVIO HERRERA

HOSPITAL CENTRO MEDICO

IGLESIA DE LA SALUD

Restaurant CHARCO DE LA HIGUERA

BOMBEROS

TURISMO (TOURIST INFO.)

MERCADO CONSTITUCION

DEGOLLADO

AV. CORONEL A. BRIZUELA

MUNICIPAL POLICE (PREVENTIVA)

ESTACION FERROCARRIL

TO VILLA DE ALVAREZ AND COMALA

DR. MIGUEL GALLARDO

TORRES QUINTERO

IGLESIA SAN JOSE

TO LO DE VILLA AND COQUIMATLAN

TO MANZANILLO

© MOON PUBLICATIONS, INC.

BRUCE WHIPPERMAN

At Colima's downtown Jardín de Libertad, a procession of revelers heads to the festival of Villa Alvarez.

and east-west. Nearly all sights are reachable by a few minutes' walk or short taxi ride from the central plaza, the **Jardín de Libertad.**

A Walk around Downtown

An ambience of refined prosperity—fashionable storefronts, shady portals, and lush, manicured greenery—blooms in the blocks that spread from Jardín de Libertad. The landmark *catedral* and **Palacio de Gobierno** statehouse stand side by side on Av. Constitución, bordering the *jardín.* For a colonial town, the buildings are not old, having replaced the original earthquake-weakened colonial-era structures generations ago. A number of local celebrations begin from the *jardín,* the hub of commercial and community activities. The mayor shouts the Grito de Dolores (independence cry, evening of 15 September), and crowds celebrate the Fiesta Charrotaurina (7-23 February). (See "Entertainment and Events" following.)

Other landmarks dot the portals around the square. First, as you move counterclockwise from the cathedral, comes the renovated **Hotel Ceballos,** corner of Constitución and Av. Francisco I. Madero. At the succeeding corner (Madero and north-south Av. V. Carranza) rises the **Presidencia Municipal.** And finally, on the south side, stands the state and city **Museo de Historia** on Av. 16 de Septiembre, corner of Constitución. Step into the museum, tel. (331) 29-228, for excellent examples of Colima's famous pre-Columbian pottery and a good book-

store offering a number of excellent local art, history, and picture-guidebooks. Open Tues.-Sat. 1000-1400 and 1600-1800, Sunday 1700-2000.

Back outside, for information and a Colima map, step to the adjacent, west side of the plaza to the **Portal Hidalgo** arches to the helpful state **Turismo** information office; open Mon.-Fri. 0900-1900, Saturday 0900-1300.

Then stroll across the *jardín* to the Palacio de Gobierno, head through its big, open front door, and enjoy the calm, classic elegance of the cloistered inner patio. Continue out the other side and into Colima's second square, named after **Torres Quintero** (1866-1934), a beloved Colima teacher whose statue decorates the tree-shaded park.

Back at the Jardín de Libertad corner of Constitución and Madero explore the little block-long **Andando Constitución** pedestrian mall, one of Colima's charming little corners. Here you will find several interesting shops, a good Italian restaurant, and, at the far end, a friendly coffee-break cafe and a good crafts store with a bountiful selection of reasonably priced folkcrafts. These include fine ceramic reproductions of Colima's dogs. (For more details, turn ahead to the "Food" and "Shopping" sections.)

Two Good Museums

For more excellent regional crafts, continue along Constitución four blocks north to Aldama, then east a block and a half to the **Museo de Culturas Populares,** tel. (331) 268-69. Besides a folk-art sales shop (pottery, gourds, baskets, a loom, glassware) and several intriguing displays of masks (don't miss the scary horned crocodile-man) and ceremonial costumes, you can often watch potters and other artisans at work in the little house to the right of the museum entrance on Aldama. The museum, the full name of which is Museo Universitario de Culturas Populares María Teresa Pomar, is located at Avs. Aldama and 27 de Septiembre; open Mon.-Sat. 0900-1400 and 1600-1900.

The prime repository of Colima's archaeological treasures is the landmark **Museo de Culturas del Occidente** ("Museum of Cultures of the West"). Walk or taxi along the diagonal street E. Carranza to side street Ejercito Nacional, about a mile from the town center. Inside the modern building, a spiral walkway leads you past artifact-illustrated displays of the history of Colima and surrounding regions. The exposition climaxes on the top floor with choirs of delightful classical Colima figurines: musicians tapping drums and fingering flutes, dancers circling, wrestlers grappling, and hosts of animals, including the all-time favorites, Colima dogs. Open Tues.-Sun. 0900-1800.

OUT-OF-TOWN SIGHTS

The valley and mountainsides surrounding the city offer a variety of scenic diversions, from relaxing in colonial villages and camping on sylvan mountainsides to exploring tombs, examining petroglyphs, and descending into limestone caverns.

Northside Foothill Country:
Comalá and Lakes María and Carrizalillos
Head out the Comalá road toward the foothills northwest of the city, where your first reward will be ever-closer views of the volcanoes. **Comalá** town, nestling above a lush stream valley about six miles from Colima, has always been a local Sunday favorite. Here, cares seem to float away in the orange-scented air around the plaza. Mariachis stroll every afternoon and restaurants (try Los Portales right on the plaza) serve *botanas* free with drinks, which should

include at least one obligatory glass of local *ponche* fruit wine.

The road winding uphill past Comalá leads past green pastures and groves through the village of Cofradía de Suchitán. Soon the road divides. Take the left fork and continue down a jungly, lava-cliffed canyon to ex-hacienda **San Antonio** about 20 miles (32 km) from Colima. Here, water gurgles from the ancient aqueduct, the stone chapel stands intact, and a massive gate and wall, like a medieval keep, still protect the inhabitants from long-forgotten marauders. The owners have recently been renovating the hacienda into a hotel and soon may be ready to receive guests.

A gravel road continues uphill from San Antonio a few miles farther to the mountainside Shangri-La **Ejido La María.** Past a gate (where you pay a small admission to park), a walking trail downhill leads past tidy vegetable fields to the idyllic shoreline of natural **Laguna La María.** Here, weekend and holiday visitors enjoy creekside picnicking and camping beneath the spreading boughs of a venerable lakeside grove. At other times, walk-in campers often enjoy nearly complete solitude. Bring everything, including water-purifying tablets, insect repellent, and tents for possible rain, especially during the summer. The 4,000-foot (1,215-meter) elevation produces usually balmy days and mild nights.

For noncampers, the *ejido* (communal farm) offers five clean bungalows on the hillside above the lake, with complete kitchens (bring your food), flush toilets, and hot water for about $30 per night. Additionally, self-contained RVs can park hereabouts for a fee. Given the general friendliness of the local *ejido* folks, visitors who enjoy the outdoors by day and mountain stillness by night could spend a very enjoyable few days at Laguna La María.

Centro Turístico Carrizalillos ("Little Reeds") offers yet another outdoor possibility. Back at the fork, two miles uphill past Cofradia de Suchitán, head right. After about two more miles, follow the driveway off to the right. The Carrizalillos campsites spread for about a mile around the circumference of an oak-studded ridge that encloses a small natural lake. The few dozen developed campsites (picnic tables, water, pit toilets), some suitable for small-to-medium RVs,

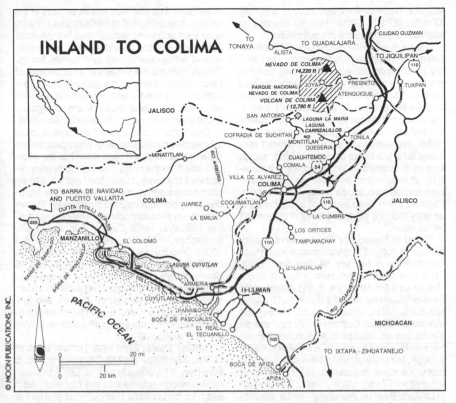

INLAND TO COLIMA

rent for about $4 a day. A rustic view restaurant occupies a lakeside hilltop and a dozen housekeeping cabins overlook the lake. (The cabins may be in usable shape; the tariff is about $14 for two; take a look before paying.) In season—Easter and Christmas weeks, and August—horses ($14/hour) and boats ($4/hour) are available. Given the magnificent mountain and valley views, the blue lake (if the water level is up), and the fresh air, Carrizalillos might be just right for a cool, restful change of pace.

The Volcanoes
Although taller by 1,133 feet, Nevado ("Snowy One") de Colima is far quieter than his younger brother, Volcán de Fuego, one of the world's most active volcanoes. The **Volcán de Fuego** has erupted dozens of times since the conquest,

continuously belching a stream of smoke and ash and frequently burping up red-hot boulders. The government seals the access road when a serious eruption is imminent.

If you want a close-up look at Volcán de Fuego, check with the state tourism office, 20 Portal Hidalgo, downtown Colima, tel. (331) 243-60 and 283-60, for advice, pack everything you're going to need, and head out along Hwy. 54 *libre* (old non-toll route) northeast of Colima. Drive a high-clearance truck or van or ride a second-class bus from the Central Camionera Bus Station (see "Getting There and Away" below). Pass Tonila (19 miles, 30 km from Colima) to a dirt turnoff road 35 miles (near the Km. 56 marker) from Colima. There, at a Teléfonos de Mexico *microndas* (microwave relay station) sign, take a sharp left toward the mountain. The

Volcanic National Park boundary is a bumpy 17 miles (27 km) farther. How far you can go after that depends upon the authorities. The approach to the much quieter **Nevado de Colima** is considerably more certain. The clear, dry winter months, when the views and the weather are the best, are the Colima climbers season of choice. The ascent, which begins at La Joya hut at around the 11,000-foot level, is not particularly difficult for experienced, fit hikers. The trail starts out leading for an easy hour to the microwave station at the tree line. Then it continues for a few hours of steep walking, except for a bit of scrambling at the end. Ice is a possibility all year round, however, so carry crampons and ice axes and be prepared to use them. Climbers often sleep overnight at La Joya, get an early morning start, and arrive at the summit before noon.

To get to Nevado de Colima, drive a jeep, pickup, or rugged, high-clearance van. Head out northeast along Hwy. 54 *libre*, past Tonila. Thirty-nine miles (63 km) from Colima (a couple of miles past the Atequique mining village), Hwy. 54 *libre* interchanges with the Colima-Guadalajara *cuota* (toll) freeway. Fork left on Hwy. 54 *libre* toward Ciudad Guzmán (rather than straight ahead, toward Jiquilipan). After paralleling the freeway for about four miles, a small sign marks a rough, but dry-weather passable uphill track (about six miles) to Fresnito. At Fresnito, head left another 17 very rough miles (27 km) farther to La Joya. Pack up everything—winter sleeping bags, tents, alpine equipment, water, and food—that you'll need.

Southern Excursion: Tampumachay

The valley of Colima has a number of important archaeological sites, one of the most accessible and scenic of which is near the village of Los Ortices, eight miles south of Colima city.

The **Centro Turístico Tampumachay,** a shady green mini-resort, accommodates visitors with a modest five-room hotel, two swimming pools, a restaurant, and a camping area. Developed originally by archaeologist Fidencio Perez of Colima, the present owners continue his policy of careful custodianship of the nearby ruins.

The archaeological zone spreads along both edges of a deep, rocky gorge about a mile south of the hotel. The staff lead visitors on tours of the brushy, cactus-dotted cliffside plateau. Paths wind past intriguing animal- and human-motif petroglyph-sculptures and descend into tombs littered with grave pottery and human bones. Guides point out the remains of an unexcavated ceremonial platform on the opposite side of the canyon. The tombs and petroglyphs are well preserved, since local people, fearing dire ghostly consequences, generally leave the site alone.

Other local excursions include exploration of a limestone cave a couple of miles past the archaeological zone and hikes down into the gorge by a trail near the hotel. The Tampumachay resort itself is a lovely, tree-shaded garden, with artifact-dotted paths, a rope bridge, view gazebos, and pool-decks perfect for snoozing. Reservations are probably not necessary except during holidays; write Centro Turístico Tampumachay, P.O. Box 149, Colima, Colima 28000. You can also contact them through the Los Ortices local operator, tel. (331) 472-25 (in Spanish), who will forward your message to Tampumachay. Their accommodations, a four-room cabin, with communal kitchen, and five plain, clean fan-only rooms, rent for about $24 d. Campsites for tents and (self-contained) RVs are also available.

Getting There: Eight miles (13 km) south of Colima city, follow the Los Ortices turnoff road from Hwy. 110, officially signed "Los Asmoles," for the village adjacent to the highway. Also watch for the unofficial "Tampu" hotel sign on the highway. More signs on the side road direct you about three more miles to Tampumachay.

COLIMA ACCOMMODATIONS

Untouristed Colima has, nevertheless, a sprinkling of hotels. Some are city-style, downtown near the central plaza, and others are motel-style, in the suburbs. The prices quoted may be subject to discounts, which, under any conditions, you should always ask for: Say *"¿Hay discuentos?"*

Downtown Hotels
Many business travelers stay at **Hotel America,** Morelos 162, Colima, Colima 28000, tel. (331) 295-96 or 203-66, fax 444-25, three blocks from

the city center. Outside, the facade is colonial; inside a two-story warren of rooms hides among a maze of glass-and-steel tropical terrariums. The rooms are spacious, carpeted, and comfortable. Lack of a pool is partially compensated by a sauna (use of which is limited to mornings, however). One of Hotel America's plusses is its good restaurant, where patrons enjoy snappy service and tasty food at reasonable prices. Their 70 rooms rent for about $55 s or d with TV, a/c, phones, and parking, but no pool; credit cards are accepted, and there is limited lower-level wheelchair access.

Hotel Ceballos, Portal Medillin 12, Colima, Colima 28000, tel. (331) 244-44, right on the central plaza, offers a more economical alternative. Although recently renovated, the hotel retains its high ceilings and graceful colonial ambience. They offer two grades of accommodations: tastefully decorated, clean, and comfortable air-conditioned rooms with TV, and slightly worn fan only *económico* rooms. During hot weather especially, the a/c rooms are worth the price difference. Rates for the 83 rooms run about $24 economy s or d, $42 deluxe with a/c; credit cards accepted, parking.

Suburban Hotels

Hotel María Isabel, Blvd. Camino Real at Av. Felipe Sevilla del Rio, Colima, Colima 28010, tel. (331) 264-64 or 262-62, a motel about a mile from the city-center, appeals to families and RV and car travelers. The double-story room tiers line a long parking lot edged on one side by a lawn and tropical foliage. A large pool and (mediocre) airy restaurant occupy one side near the entrance. The rooms come in economy and deluxe versions. The economy are very plain, the deluxe have tonier decor. Both have air-conditioning and TV. Although the María Isabel is attractive enough at first glance, general cleanliness and service leave something to be desired. The 90 rooms go for about $36 economy s or d, $55 deluxe s or d; credit cards accepted, parking.

Neighboring **Hotel Los Candiles,** Blvd. Camino Real 399, Colima, Colima 28010, tel. (331) 232-12, avoids the usual cluttered motel parking lot atmosphere by putting the swimming pool-patio at the center and the cars off to the side. An attractive tropical garden-style hotel is

the result. The rooms, in economy (fan only) and deluxe (a/c) options are clean, comfortable, and tastefully furnished. The 60 rooms rent for about $40 economy s or d, $65 deluxe; credit cards accepted, with TV and a restaurant.

FOOD

Breakfast and Snacks

A good place to start out the day is the restaurant at the **Hotel America,** Morelos 162, tel. (331) 295-96, open daily at seven for breakfast, dinner served till ten, where the servers greet you with hot coffee and a cheery *"Buenos dias."* The menu affords plenty of familiar fare, from fresh eggs any style to pancakes and fruit, at reasonable prices.

After a few hours among the downtown sights, take a break at one of the **sidewalk cafes** bordering the Jardín de Libertad. First choice goes to the airy **Cafe de la Plaza,** open 0700-2100 daily, at the Hotel Ceballos on the Jardín de Libertad. Here, high ceilings, graceful arches, and, if you choose, sidewalk tables, add a touch of leisurely refinement to your breakfast or mid-day lunch break. The relatively short menu, of breakfasts, sandwiches, tacos, *tortas,* juices, desserts, and expresso coffees is crisply served and reasonably priced.

Another good sidewalk cafe is **Cisnes,** tucked around the corner (away from traffic noise) at the end of Andando Constitución, the pedestrian-mall continuation of Av. Constitución; open Mon.-Sat. 0800-1500 and 1600-2200.

Restaurants

Complete dinner price key: Budget: under $7; Moderate: $7-14; Expensive: over $14.

Starting downtown, by the *jardín,* **Livorno's,** tel. (333) 450-30, serves good pizza and other Italian specialties, complete with atmosphere, on Andando Constitución, right off Jardín de Libertad. Livorno's is one of the few spots for a late meal on the *jardín.* Open Tues.-Sat. 1200-2300; credit cards accepted. Moderate.

The popularity of **Restaurant Fonda San Miguel** is due to its good regional food, refined ambience, and very correct service, at 129 Av. 27 de Septiembre, near corner of Allende, tel. (331) 448-40. Patrons enjoy shady seating beneath a hacienda roof beside a sun-splashed fountain-patio. Although they serve good breakfasts, the house specialties are Colima regional lunch and early dinner dishes, such as Pepena roast beef in sauce and Tatemado roast pork. Vegetable lovers, on the other hand, order their excellent tomato, onion, and avocado salad. Open daily 0730-1800. Moderate.

Unpretentiously lovely restaurant **El Charco de la Higuera,** tel. (331) 310-92, is a perfect spot for soaking up the charm of traditional Mexico. Its graceful amenities—at the leafy edge of an old church plaza, a bubbling fountain, a shady veranda—and its long list of *típico* Mexican specialties provide all the ingredients for a leisurely breakfast, lunch, or dinner. Located at old San José church, six blocks from the *jardín,* along the westward extension of Madero. Open daily 0800-2400.

Crotos Grill, tel. (331) 494-94, near the eastern edge of downtown, is another local favorite, partly due to its airy, tropical setting. Lush vines hang from huge trees nearby, a big-beamed red-tile roof canopy soars overhead, and piano music plays softly in the background. Waiters move briskly about, serving delectable house specialties such as Parrillada (grill) for two, Sopa de Croto, or Ostiones de Chef. Open daily 0800-0100, Calzado Pedro A. Galvan 207; follow Av. Morelos from the city center east about a mile to wide Calzado Galvan, where Crotos will be one block south, downhill, across the street. Moderate to expensive.

If, however, you hanker for familiar food in modern, air-conditioned surroundings, head for the local branch of **Vips,** the Mexican (although classier) version of Denny's. Also on east-side Calzado Galvan, just a block downhill from Allende, in front of the big, shiny Auerrera department store. Open Sun.-Thurs. 0700-2300, Fri.-Sat. 0700-0200. Moderate.

Horse-on-a-stick toys appeared among the Mexicans not long after the conquest and the introduction of horses.

ENTERTAINMENT AND EVENTS

Local folks compensate for the lack of nightlife by whooping it up during Colima's three major local festivals. Don't miss them if you happen to be in town.

For nine days beginning 23 January, people celebrate the **Fiesta de La Virgen de La Salud,** which climaxes on 2 February. The church (Iglesia de La Salud) neighborhood near Avs. Gallardo and Corregidora blooms with colorful processions and food and crafts stalls, and the church plaza resounds with music, folk dancing, and fireworks.

Ever since 1820, the Villa de Alvarez (a suburb a few miles northwest of the city center) has staged **Fiesta Charrotaurina,** a 10-day combination rodeo-bullfight-carnival. The celebration wouldn't be as much fun if the Villa de Alvarez people stayed to themselves. Every day, however, 7-23 February around noon, a troupe of Villa Alvarez musicians, cowboys, cowgirls, papier-mâché bulls, and a pair of *mojigangos* (giant effigies of the Colima governor and spouse) assemble on Colima's downtown Jardín de Libertad. The music begins, the *mojigangos* start whirling, and a big crowd of bystanders follows them back to Villa de Alvarez.

Visitors who miss the Virgen de La Salud in January can get in on the similar **Fiesta de San José,** which culminates on 19 March in the west-side neighborhood of the Iglesia de San José (corner Quintero and Suárez), with a host of traditional foodstalls, regional folk dancing, and religious processions.

The Casa de Cultura (at the history museum on the Jardín de Libertad downtown) organizes a yearly monthlong (last half of Nov. to first half of Dec.) fine arts festival. Performances and exhibits—including classic and folkloric ballet, orchestral and solo music, theater, operas, sculpture, and painting—occur daily. Check with the tourist office, tel. (331) 243-60, or the history museum, tel. (331) 29-228, on the *jardín* for schedule details.

ERIN DWYER

SHOPPING

Two good downtown sources sell reproductions of Colima's charming pre-Columbian animal and human figurines. The state-operated **Casa de Las Artesanías**, Av. Zaragoza and Andando Constitución, tel. (331) 447-90, near the Jardín de Libertad, stocks a number of locally made figurines, plus shelves of handicrafts gathered from all over Mexico, such as sombreros, *huipiles,* serapes, toys, and Christmas decorations. Other local items include Colima coffee beans, regional cuisine cookbooks, and coconut candy. Open Mon.-Fri. 1000-1400 and 1700-2000, Saturday 1000-1400.

If you prefer to buy your figurines directly from the artisan, go to the **Museo de Culturas Populares**, Avs. Aldama and 27 de Septiembre, tel. (331) 268-69, four blocks north of the *jardín.* The potters work in the little house to the right of the museum entrance on Av. Aldama. If no artisan is available, the museum shop inside sells figurines, plus many other folkcrafts, both local and national. Open Mon.-Sat. 0900-1400 and 1600-1900.

SERVICES AND INFORMATION

Money Exchange
The **Banamex** downtown branch, at Hidalgo 90, just two blocks east of the *jardín,* tel. (331) 209-16 or 298-20, exchanges U.S. currency and traveler's checks Mon.-Fri. 0900-1200.

Communication
The main *correo* is open Mon.-Fri. 0900-1400 and 1600-1800, Saturday 0900-1200 in the Palacio Federal on Plaza Nuñez (corner Madero and Nuñez) about six blocks east of the Jardín de Libertad.

Colima area code is 331

The Farmacia Colima (on Jardín de Libertad, across Madero from the cathedral) operates a *larga distancia* telephone Mon.-Sat. 0830-2130. On Sunday, you can use the *larga distancia* and fax in the little office (open daily

0700-2200) beneath the portal on the south side of the *jardín.*

Tourist Information Office
The efficient and helpful staff of the *oficina de turismo* at 20 Portal Hidalgo, on the west side of the Jardín de Libertad, tel. (331) 243-60 or 283-60, answers questions and offers a Colima map and an excellent tourist attractions guide. For out of the ordinary or detailed questions, ask for friendly, English-speaking Alejandro Cano. Open Mon.-Fri. 0900-1800, Saturday 0900-1300.

Hospital, Police, and Emergencies
The respected private hospital, **Centro Médico** at Maclovio Herrera 140, a quarter-mile north of Jardín de Libertad, tel. (331) 240-44, 240-45, or 240-46, has emergency service and many specialists on 24-hour call.

The **Farmacia Colima**, tel. (331) 200-31 or 255-37, on the *jardín,* offers a large stock of medicines and drugs. Open Mon.-Sat. 0900-2100.

The **Caberca Policía** (police headquarters), tel. (331) 314-34 or dial 06, is on the south side of town, south side of Av. 20 de Noviembre, between Juárez and Revolución.

For **fire** emergencies, call the *bomberos* (fire fighters), tel. (331) 258-58, off of Ejercito Nacional, by the west side of the Museum of the Cultures of the West.

Newsstand
English newspapers and magazines are rare in Colima. The newsstand next to the Hotel Ceballos stocks the English-language Mexico City *News,* however; open daily 0800-2100.

GETTING THERE AND AWAY

By Car or RV
The Manzanillo-Colima combined Highways 200 and 110 *autopista* makes Colima safely accessible from Manzanillo in an hour. From Manzanillo, follow the *cuota* (toll) Hwy. 200 (34 miles, 54 km) southeast to the Hwy. 110 junction near Tecomán. Branch north, continuing on 110 for another 25 miles (40 km) to Colima. (See Manzanillo "Getting There and Away" above for highway routes from Guadalajara and Zihuatanejo.)

By Bus

Several excellent first-class bus lines, such as **Tres Estrellas de Oro**, tel. (331) 284-48 or 284-99, **Ómnibus de Mexico**, tel. (331) 290-50 or 471-90, and **Autobuses de Occidente**, tel. (331) 205-08 or 481-79, provide frequent connections to Manzanillo to the south and Guadalajara to the north. All of these operate out of the big Nueva Central Camionera on the Hwy. 110 *libramiento* (bypass) east of town.

By Train

The Colima train station is at the end of Av. Medellin in the southern suburbs, about a mile from the town center. Reservations are not generally necessary. Simply buy tickets at the station prior to departure. One Guadalajara-bound second-class diesel coach departs daily around 0800; one similar Manzanillo-bound train departs daily in the opposite direction around 1500. Call the ticket office, tel. (331) 292-50, to verify times.

Colima ceramic, mother with child at a metate

BOB RACE

SOUTH TO
IXTAPA-ZIHUATANEJO
AND INLAND TO PÁTZCUARO

ALONG THE ROAD TO PLAYA AZUL

Heading southeast out of Manzanillo, the Mexican Pacific coast highway winds for 200 miles, hugging the shorelines of two states. First, it follows the southern Colima coast, well known for its beaches, surf, and abundant fresh seafood. After that the road pierces the little-traveled wild coast of Michoacán.

That last lonely Michoacán coastal link was completed in 1984. Local people still remember when, if they wanted to travel to Manzanillo, they had to walk half the way. What they saw along the path is still there: mountainsides of great vine-draped trees and seemingly endless pearly, driftwood-strewn beaches, fringed by verdant palm groves and enfolded by golden sandstone cliffs. From ramparts high above the foaming surf, gigantic headlands seem to file in procession along the shore and fade into the sea-mist a thousand miles away. Along the highway, coatimundis peer from beneath bushes, iguanas scurry along the shoulder, and a rainbow of blossoms—yellow, red, pink, and violet—blooms from the roadside.

HISTORY

Before Columbus

The great Río Balsas, whose watershed includes Michoacán and five other Mexican states, has repeatedly attracted outsiders. Some of the first settlers to the Río Balsas basin came thousands of years ago, from perhaps as far away as Peru. They left remains—pottery, of unmistak-

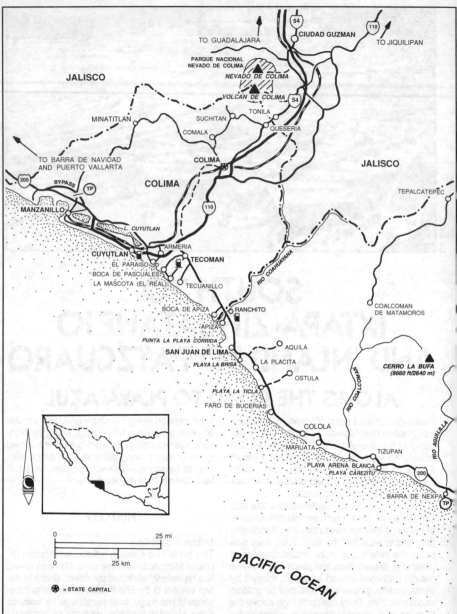

= STATE CAPITAL

0   25 mi
0   25 km

© MOON PUBLICATIONS, INC.

PACIFIC OCEAN

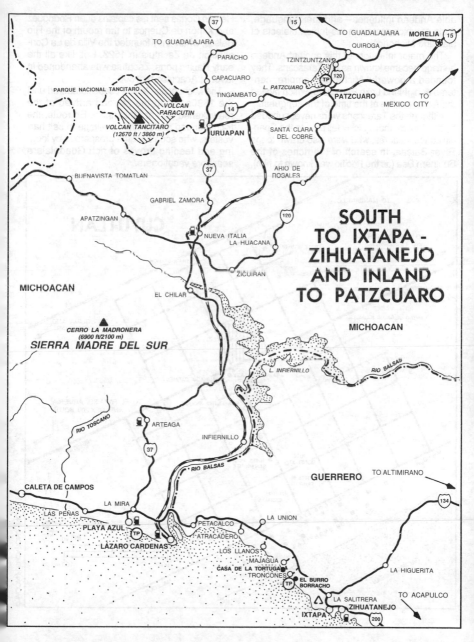

able Andean influence—and their language, roots of which remain in the Indian dialects of highland Michoacán.

The major inheritors of this ancient Andean heritage became known as the Tarascans. They founded a powerful Michoacán empire, centered at highland Lake Pátzcuaro, which rivaled the Aztec empire at the time of the conquest.

Although the Tarascans were never subdued by the Aztecs, they quickly fell prey to the Spanish conquistadores, who were also drawn to the River Balsas. In search of the riches of the Southern Sea (as the Pacific was known to him),

Hernán Cortés sent his captains Juan Rodríguez and Ximón de Cuenca to the mouth of the Río Balsas, where they founded the Villa de La Concepción de Zacatula in 1523. But, like all the early Pacific ports, Zacatula was abandoned in favor of Acapulco by 1600.

The Michoacán-Colima coast slumbered until the 1890s, when the railroad arrived at the reawakened port of Manzanillo. En route, the train stopped at Cuyutlán, a village of salt harvesters, who soon became prosperous by lodging and feeding droves of rich Guadalajara seashore vacationers.

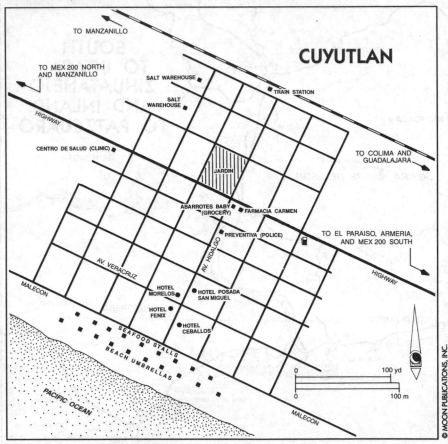

© MOON PUBLICATIONS, INC.

Neighboring coastal Michoacán had to wait for the dust of the 1910-17 Revolution to settle before getting its own development project. Again the Río Balsas drew outsiders. Dam builders came to harness the river's hydropower to make steel out of a mountain of Michoacán iron ore. In succession came the new port, Lázaro Cárdenas, the railroad, the dam, then finally the huge Las Trucas (curiously, "The Trout") steel mill. Concurrently, Playa Azul, Michoacán's planned beach resort on the Pacific, was developed nearby.

The new facilities, however, never quite lived up to expectations. Although a few ships and trains still arrive, and some tourists come weekends and holidays, Lázaro Cárdenas and Playa Azul drowse fitfully, dreaming of their long-expected awakening.

CUYUTLÁN

Little Cuyutlán (pop. 2,000) is heaven for lovers of nostalgia and tranquility. No raucous hangouts clutter its lanes, no rock music bounces from its few cafes. Sun, sand, and gentle surf are its prime amenities. Rickety wooden walkways lead across its hot dark sands to a line of beachfront umbrellas, where you can rent a chair for the day, enjoy the breeze, and feast on the seafood offerings of seaside kitchens.

Virtually all of Cuyutlán's hotels, restaurants, and services lie along a single street: Hidalgo, which runs from the *jardín* (on the Manzanillo-Armería road) a few blocks, crossing Av. Veracruz and ending at the beachfront *malecón*.

The shady, cobbled side streets of Cuyutlán invite impromptu exploring. Near the beach, lanes lead past weathered wooden houses and *palapas* (some for rent). On the inland side of the *jardín* near the rail station, kerosene lamps flicker at night through the walls of bamboo village houses. The station itself is an antique out of the Porfirian age, with cast-iron benches and original filigreed columns still supporting its moss-streaked, gabled platform roof. Nearby, hulking wooden (exotically unusual in Mexico) salt warehouses line an earthen street. Those ancient repositories are reminders of the 300-year tradition of salt harvesting at the edges of nearby Cuyutlán lagoon.

The Green Wave

Cuyutlán's latter-day claim to fame is the mysterious Green Wave, which is said to occasionally rise offshore and come crashing down from a height of 20, 30, or even 50 feet. (The later at night the story is told, it seems, the greater the height.)

The source of the Green Wave's color is also a mystery, although some local aficionados speculate that an offshore algae bloom might be responsible.

Although several faithful still carefully scan the horizon (during the most-likely month of May), few folks seem to remember when the last Green Wave rolled shoreward. Some suggest that the 1978 local earthquake may have shifted the ocean bottom and quieted the Green Wave (temporarily, at least). The Hotel Morelos, at the corner of Hidalgo and Veracruz, displays, in addition to its lobby gallery of James Dean and Marilyn Monroe photos, a snapshot of an alleged 30 foot Green Wave by local photographer and enthusiast Eduardo Lolo.

Beach Activities

Cuyutlán's wide and seemingly endless beach invites a number of activities and sports. The nearly level offshore slope produces little undertow, so wading and swimming conditions are ideal. The waves, which roll in gradually, are fine for boogie-boarding, bodysurfing, and all levels of surfing, depending on the size of the swells. Bring your own surfboard, although boogie board rentals are available on the beach. Shells become more common the farther you stroll away from the few picked-over blocks of beach.

As for fishing, the shallow slope decreases the chances for successful surf-casts. Best hire or launch your boat (easy in calm weather) and head to the happy fishing grounds beyond the waves.

Cuyutlán Accommodations

The **Hotel Morelos,** Hidalgo 185, Cuyutlán, Colima 28350, tel. (332) 418-10, local ext. 107, founded in the 1890s, continues Cuyutlán's turn-of-the-century tradition with a long (quaintly downhill-sloping) lobby festooned with plastic flowers and green Grecian columns. Although the family-run restaurant serves hearty local-style food, some of the rooms are dark and dank. Look at several before moving in. The Morelos's 36 rooms rent for about $7 s, $13 d, with hot water and fans.

Across Av. Veracruz stands the equally venerable but plainer **Hotel Fénix**, Hidalgo 201, Cuyutlán, Colima 28350, tel. (332) 418-10, local ext. 147, whose patrons likewise enjoy an open-air street-level restaurant. Although many of the rooms, scattered along upstairs corridors, are clean and airy, they tend toward the scruffy and have no hot water. Rates for the 17 rooms with fan run about $7 per person.

Hotel Posada San Miguel, Av. Hidalgo, Cuyutlán, Colima 28350, tel. (332) 418-10, local ext. 135, across Hidalgo from the Morelos, has bright, comfortable upstairs rooms that open onto a shady sitting porch overlooking the street. The eight rooms run about about $9 per person, with hot water and fans.

Fourth choice goes to Cuyutlán's newest and biggest, **Hotel Ceballos**, Veracruz 10, Cuyutlán, Colima 28350, tel. (332) 418-10, local ext. 101, fronting the beach at the foot of Hidalgo. Inside, the cavernous atrium-lobby more resembles a bus station than a hotel. At night, guests sit watching a huge TV that echoes over the entire lobby. But that needn't bother you, especially if you rent one of the many Spartan but clean rooms, which, on the oceanfront side, enjoy private, breezy sea-view balconies. The Ceballos is open seasonally, 15 Dec.-31 May only. Their 80 rooms rent for about $18 per person with hot water and some fans. Try bargaining for a discount during times of low occupancy, such as weekdays and January and February.

Camping and RV Parking
Although Cuyutlán has no established campground, dirt roads lead to miles of open beach, good for camping or parking, on both sides of town. (Be careful of soft sand, however.) Cuyutlán, being a generally friendly, upright country place, will ordinarily present no security problem. If in doubt, however, don't hesitate to ask local shopkeepers. Say, "¿Es bueno acampar acá?" (EHS boo-WAY-noh ah-kam-PAHR ah-KAH?).

Food
Besides the good Hotel Morelos restaurant and its rival at the Hotel Fénix across the street, the main good Cuyutlán eateries are the many seafood vendors, whose semipermanent umbrella-covered establishments do big business on holidays and weekends. Quality of the fare—oyster cocktails, grilled or boiled shrimp and lobster, and fried fish—is generally excellent, since many of them depend on loyal repeat customers.

Shopping, Services, and Information
Most of Cuyutlán's businesses are spread along Hidalgo between the beach and the jardín. For groceries, try Abarrotes Baby, on the jardín, corner Hidalgo. At the same corner is the **Farmacia Carmen,** open daily 0900-1400 and 1600-2100. Up the street, at 144 Hidalgo, the *preventiva* (police) are on duty round the clock. Downhill, a block from the jardín, Manzanillo direction, is the **Centro de Salud** (health center), open routinely till 1700, but only in emergencies after that. **Unleaded gasoline** is usually available at the Pemex station, on the local road (not the toll superhighway), just south of town.

Cuyutlán
area code
is 332

Getting There and Away
By car or RV from Manzanillo, follow the Hwy. 200 *cuota* (toll) branch superhighway 17 miles (28 km) to Cuyutlán. Or, for a more scenic alternative, follow main street Av. Carrillo Puerto past the jardín through downtown Manzanillo and continue along the west end of placid Laguna Cuyutlán. This route curves past the power plant, through miles of ciruela orchards, then along a breezy barrier dune and wild beach, eventually joining the toll highway before Cuyutlán. At one point, upon crossing a narrow estuary bridge, the highway asphalt joins with the railroad track. Don't forget to look for the train before starting across.

Manzanillo taxis take passengers to Cuyutlán for about $20, one way. If this is too expensive, local **buses** connect with Cuyutlán every half hour until around 2000 from Armería (transfer point on Hwy. 200, half an hour by bus from Manzanillo's Central Camionera bus station).

Second-class diesel coach **no. 91** leaves Manzanillo every morning around 0600, arriving in Cuyutlán around 1830, then continuing to Colima and Guadalajara. In the opposite direction, **no. 92** arrives at Cuyutlán from Guadalajara and Colima around 1640 and continues to Manzanillo. Check at the station, three blocks inland from the *jardín*, for service or schedule changes.

SOUTH COLIMA BEACHES

El Paraíso

El Paraíso (pop. 1,000), just seven miles (via the local road, follow the right fork, four miles from the *jardín*) south of Cuyutlán, is popular on Sundays and holidays with families, who fill the dozen beachfront seafood *palapas* lining the bumpy main street. El Paraíso's long strand, which extends for miles on both sides, is similar to Cuyutlán's: hot, dark sand and generally gentle, rolling surf, with little or no undertow, excellent for safe wading, swimming, bodysurfing, boogie-boarding, and surfing.

The good beach and seafood account for the success of the **Hotel Paraíso** and restaurant, Playa Paraíso, Armería, Colima 28300, tel. (332) 810-09, which perches above the surf at the south end (left as you arrive) of the beachfront street. Many of the hotel's plain but clean rooms enjoy the same airy oceanfront vista as their popular restaurant. The adjacent pool and sundeck is yet another reason for spending a day or two there. The 54 rooms (none with hot water) rent from $22 d, $25 t; credit cards are accepted. Reserve, especially during holidays and weekends, by writing or calling the hotel, or contacting their agent in Colima, tel. (331) 210-32.

Boca de Pascuales, El Real, Tecuanillo, And Boca de Apiza

Although none of this quartet of downscale beachside *palapa* heavens has an acceptable hotel, local folks know them well for their gentle surf, abundant seafood, and wide-open spaces for tent and RV camping. Drivers can access them along good paved roads from Hwy. 200. For bus travelers, Tecomán Camionera Central is the point of departure for local buses, which run frequently until around 1800. After that, you might have to take a taxi.

Boca de Pascuales, eight paved miles (13 km) from Hwy. 200, is literally the *boca* (mouth) of the Armería River, whose waters, which begin on the snowy slope of Nevado de Colima, widen to a broad estuary. Here, they nourish schools of fish and flocks of seabirds—pelicans, cormorants, herons—which dive, swoop, and stalk for fry in the rivermouth lagoon. Fishermen wade in and catch the very same prey with thrownets.

The beach itself is broad, with semicoarse gray sand. The waves roll gradually shoreward over a near-level, sandy shelf, and recede with little or no undertow. Consequently, swimming, boogie-boarding, and bodysurfing are relatively safe, and surfing is not uncommon. A lot of driftwood litters the sandbar, and several rentable fishing *lanchas* lie pulled up along the beach. A quarter-mile lineup of seafood *ramadas* (semitemporary flat palm thatch roofs) provide shade and food for the local families who crowd in on Sundays and holidays. Find Boca de Pascuales by heading south on Hwy. 200 to just before Tecomán. Follow the signed turnoff road about eight miles to the beach, turn right, and continue a quarter mile past the *ramadas* to the lagoon and sandbar.

For more lovely beach and surf, head from Boca de Pascuales along the two miles of beachfront road to El Real (marked La Mascota on some maps). The paved road passes a file of hurricane-battered shoreline homes, separated by open spaces, good for camping or RV parking (if you don't mind occasional company). Ask if it's okay before setting up camp. Bring all of your supplies, including water; the few stores along this stretch are meagerly stocked.

Three or four restaurants (notably, the popular En Ramada Boca de Río) dot the two miles to El Real. There, a few more more rustic seafood *ramadas* crowd the corner where the road heads back about seven miles (11 km) to Hwy. 200 at Tecomán.

For Tecuanillo, head seaward at the paved Hwy. 200 turnoff road about a mile south of the Tecomán (south end) Pemex station. Continue about six miles to the roadside ponds of the

La Granja restaurant, open Tues.-Sun. 1200-1800, just before the beach. About six acres of ponds supply loads of *langostinas* (prawns) and *pargo* (sea bass) for on-the-spot consumption—broiled, boiled, Ranchera, Garlic, Diabla, ceviche—any way you prefer, $4-8.

Besides its long, wide beach and good surf fishing, visitors to the hamlet of Tecuanillo enjoy the protection of some of the few official lifeguards on the south Colima coast. The friendly staff of the small road's-end naval detachment volunteers for the duty. They don't mind, since the beach is nearly empty except for weekends and holidays. Tecuanillo is a good tenting or RV parking spot for lovers of seafood and solitude who appreciate the added security of the nearby naval detachment. Beach *palapa* restaurants and a local store can supply food and drinks and the village has a water supply.

Boca de Apiza, at the mouth of the Coahuayana River (which forms the Colima-Michoacán border), has surfing potential, driftwood, and possible tenting spots next to a wild, mangrove jungle-lined beach. Get there by following Colima Hwy. 185, the signed, paved turnoff road about 21 miles (34 km) south of Tecomán. About three miles from the highway, past a mangrove channel, the road splits. Ahead is a beach with some informal camping spots; left about a mile down the dry-weather-only dirt road dead-ends at a second beach, where powerful surfing waves rise sharply and break both left and right.

Although the fishing hamlet of Apiza is in Michoacán, it's barely so, being just south of the Río Coahuayana. It's reachable by the paved side road about a mile south of the river bridge. A dozen seafood *ramadas,* complete with tables and hammocks, spread along the road's end 2.5 miles from the highway. The long dark-sand beach spreads seemingly without limit on the south side, while on the other, a bamboo-hut village spreads quaintly along the boat-lined estuary bank. With a store for supplies, tenters and self-contained RV campers could fish, beachcomb, and bodysurf here for a month of Sundays.

Tecomán Services

Tecomán (pop. 50,000), on Hwy. 200, 37 miles (59 km) southeast of Manzanillo, three miles south of the Colima (Hwy. 110) junction, is south Colima's service center. All services are not far from the Hwy. 200 through-town main boulevard, which splits, diverting city-center traffic around the main plaza Manzanillo direction, one-way south, and Michoacán direction, one-way north.

Accommodations: If you're going to stay overnight, Tecomán's best lodging is the refined and comfortable **Real Motel,** at Av. Insurgentes, corner of Lic. M. Gudiño, Tecomán, Colima 28110, tel. (332) 401-00, about six blocks north of the city center. Rates for the 80 rooms run about $30 s, $37 d, with a/c, phones, satellite TV, pool, and parking.

For **money exchange:** Try Banamex, north side of the main plaza, at López Mateos and Hidalgo, tel. (332) 433-57; Banco Serfin, on the south side of the main plaza, at 20 de Noviembre 119, tel. (332) 419-96; or Bancomer, about three blocks north of the main plaza, on Av. Insurgentes, the Hwy. 200 boulevard. For a **doctor,** go to 24-hour diagnostic Clínica Centro Médico, at 592 E. Zapata, a block off Insurgentes, about seven blocks north of the main plaza, tel. (332) 435-60.

Communication: The *correo,* tel. (332) 419-39, is at B. Dávalos 35, two blocks north of the main plaza. Computel **long-distance telephone** and public fax, tel. (332) 438-99, open 0700-2200, is at the Camionera Central (main bus terminal).

Bus Info: A pair of cooperating bus networks operate out of the Camionera Central about four blocks west and two blocks north of the main plaza. Autotransportes Sur de Jalisco and Autobuses del Occidente, tel. (332) 407-95, have many daily departures connecting north with Colima and Ciudad Guzmán and east-west with Manzanillo and Lázaro Cárdenas. Companion line Autobuses del Occidente connects north with Mexico City via Toluca and Morelia, Michoacán and intermediate destinations. In an adjacent booth, sharing the same phone number, tel. (332) 407-95, Servicios Coordinados agents sell tickets for Flecha Amarilla (FA) and "Primera Plus" departures, which connect, along northern routes, with Colima, Guadalajara, Michoacán, Celaya, Querétaro, and Mexico City.

Tres Estrellas de Oro (TEO) maintains a separate, smaller station (at Constitución 251, tel.

(332) 402-82, about three blocks across the Hwy. 200 boulevard, west, from the landmark Real Motel. Several *salidas de paso* connect daily along the Hwy. 200 corridor, south with Acapulco (via Playa Azul, Zihuatanejo) and north with the U.S. border (via Manzanillo, Melaque, Puerto Vallarta, and Mazatlán).

NORTHERN MICHOACÁN BEACHES

Adventure often draws travelers along the thinly populated, pristine northwestern Michoacán coast. Without telephones and electricity, most people live by natural rhythms. They rise with the sun, tend their livestock, coconuts, and papayas, take shady siestas during the heat of the day, and watch the ocean for what the tides may bring.

Outsiders often begin to enjoy the slow pace. They stop at little beaches, sit down for a soda beneath a *ramada,* ask about the fishing, the waves, and stroll along the beach. They wander, picking up shells and driftwood and saying hello to the kids and fisherfolk along the way. Charmed and fully relaxed, they sometimes linger for months.

On the Road

If driving, fill up with unleaded Magna Sin gas at the Tecomán (north side) Pemex or the Playa Azul Pemex (if traveling in the opposite direction). The road runs 165 miles (267 km) between them with only one gas station—at Ranchito, just south of the Colima-Michoacán border—and a few stores selling leaded regular from drums. If you're driving south, note your odometer mileage at the Río Coahuayana bridge (Hwy. 200, Km 231) at the Colima-Michoacán border. (The kilometer markers, incidentally, begin with zero at the junction near Playa Azul, thus giving the distance directly from that point.) In such undeveloped country, road mileage will help you find and remember your own favorites among Michoacán's dozens of lovely beach gems.

Bus travelers enjoy the best connections at Manzanillo Central Camionera bus station, Armería, or Tecomán in the northwest, or Lázaro Cárdenas or La Mira (near Playa Azul) in the

southeast. Bus lines, such as Autotransportes Sur de Jalisco, Ruta Paraíso, Flecha Amarilla, Tres Estrellas, and de Oro Transportes Norte de Sonora, run a few daily first-class local departures from both Manzanillo and Lázaro Cárdenas. Second-class Autotransportes Galeana buses run from the same terminals approximately hourly during the day, stopping everywhere and giving adventurers the option of getting off wherever they spot the palmy little heaven they've been looking for.

San Juan de Lima

Although its number of hotels has recently doubled from two to four, San Juan de Lima (or Alima; residents say it doesn't matter) is small and sleepy. A scattering of small houses with neither phones nor good store, San Juan de Lima's popularity comes from its long, creamy sand beach, framed between a pair of rocky headlands. Very surfable breakers roll in gently from about 50 yards out and recede with little undertow. All beach sports are safe, except during the fall hurricane season, when the waves are 10 or 15 feet tall and surfers are as common as coconuts.

Fishing is probably best off the rocks at the sheltered north-end beach, **Playa La Punta Corrida,** where the very gentle waves allow easy boat launching. (Be on your guard for soft sand.) The same spot appears ripe for RV or tent camping. For access, see "Getting There" below.

Accommodations: The side-by-side southend hotels **Parador** and **Miramar,** each with about a dozen rooms and its own sea-view *palapa* restaurant, manage to stay open all year. Mutual rivalry keeps their standards and prices on an approximate par. About $10 gets you a very plain but clean bare-bulb room with toilet and shower (sorry, no hot water).

The Hotel Parador (the one on the right) has the largest and most popular *palapa* in town. The family who runs it takes special pride in the cooking, which invariably includes the fresh catch of the day. They're friendly, and the view from their shady tables is blue and breezy.

Slightly higher up the scale is the newcomer motel-style **Hotel San Juan** and beach *palapa* restaurant, which has gained a niche at the north end of town. Their 10 Spartan but clean rooms with (room-temperature-only) baths rent for about $13 d. If you want an advance reservation, call the owner in Colima at (332) 416-81.

Getting There: San Juan de Lima is at Km 211, 12 miles southeast of the Colima border. Get to the north-end beach via the dirt road at Km 212.5 south of town. After a third of a mile (half km), follow the left fork. Continue past the oceanography station at Mile 1.6 (Km 2.6) to the beach a half mile farther.

Playa La Brisa

At Km 207, 16 miles south of the Colima line, the highway reaches a breezy vista summit, where a roadside *mirador* (viewpoint) affords a look southeast. Far below, a foam-bordered white strand curves from a little palm grove, past a lagoon to a distant misty headland. This is Playa La Brisa, where, beneath the little grove, the Renteria-Alvarez family members manage their miniature Utopia.

Their shady grove is made for either tent or self-contained RV camping. People often ask them how much they charge. "Nothing," they say. "As long as you have a little lunch or dinner in our *palapa* here, stay as long as you like."

On the very broad beach beyond the grove, the waves roll in, breaking gradually both right and left. With little or no undertow, the surf is good for swimming, boogie-boarding, and body-surfing. Furthermore, taking your clue from the name "La Brisa," you know that windsurfing is frequently good here, too.

Additionally, the lagoon a mile down the beach affords opportunities for wildlife viewing, aided by your own kayak or portable rubber boat. Fishing is also often rewarding either from the rocks beneath the headland, or by boat (your own or local *panga*) launched from the beach. Get there by following the dirt road at Km 205 at the base of the hill one mile to the palm grove.

La Placita Services

The dusty town of La Placita (pop. 5,000) sits at Km 199 four miles south of La Brisa. Rent a room in the **Reina,** a small hotel next to the bridge. Pharmacies are located on the highway at the central plaza, a government *centro de salud* (health center) is on the street that borders the south edge of the plaza, and a *larga distancia* phone is on the plaza.

Playa La Ticla

The broad, gray-white sands of La Ticla attract visitors—mostly surfers—for two good reasons: its big, right-breaking rollers, and an ice-cream van, which arrives daily at three. The specialties are fruit-flavored ices, which many La Ticla visitors seem to plan their day around.

Besides the surfing waves, a clear, sandy-banked river, fine for freshwater swimming, divides the beach in two. The town has both stores and a centro de salud (health center). The beach has plenty of room for RV parking and tents and would seem fine for camping. Unfortunately, drugs have led to problems, such as a gun-point robbery during the early '90s. Check locally at a store to see if things have improved.

Getting There: Turn off at the dirt side road (southbound-facing sign only) at Km 183, 31 miles from the Colima border. At mile 1.7 (Km 2.7), follow the left, more-traveled fork; at the village basketball court, jog right, then left. Continue to the beach at Mile 2.2 (Km 3.5).

Faro de Bucerías

Idyllic perfectly describes Faro de Bucerías: a crystalline yellow-sand crescent and clear blue waters protected by offshore islets. The name Bucerías ("Divers") suggests what local people already know: Faro de Bucerías is a top snorkeling location. Favorable conditions, such as minimal local stream runoff and a nearly pure silica-sandstone shoreline combine to produce unusually clear water. Chance has even intervened to make it better, in the form of a wreck beside the offshore Morro Elefante ("Elephant Moor") islet, where multicolored fish swarm amongst the corals.

Several petite sandstone bays and beaches dot the coast around the main beach, Playa de Faro de Bucerías, which has all the ingredients for a relaxing stay. The beach itself is a lovely half-mile arc, where the waves rise and crash immediately at the water's edge and recede with strong undertow. Wading is nevertheless safe and swimming ideal in a calm south-end nook, protected by a rocky, tidepool-laced outcropping.

For food and accommodations, beachside *palapas* serve seafood during holidays, while the **Parador Turístico** restaurant-campground on the northwest side of the bay serves visitors on a daily basis. You set up your tent or park your RV (sorry, motor homes are probably too big to get in) beneath their beachfront camping *ramada* for $1 per person, per night, showers included.

This is heaven for fresh seafood lovers. Local divers (their spots marked by their floating offshore inner tubes) bring up daily troves of octopus, conches, clams, oysters, and lobsters, which you can purchase on the spot and have cooked in the restaurant. If you prefer, catch your own from the rocks or hire a local fisherman to take you out for half a day.

For more local diversions, you can poke around in tidepools or climb to the white lighthouse *(faro)*, which is perched atop the southeast rocky point. Another day you can walk in the opposite direction and explore little Playa Manzanilla and other hidden coves beyond the stony northeast headland.

Getting There: A big (southbound-facing) El Faro sign over the highway at Km 173 marks the Faro de Bucerías turnoff, 37 miles (58 km) from the Colima border. Just before the village store (yellow, on the right), at Mile 1.9 (Km 3), turn right, pass the school, and continue about 300 yards to a "T." Turn left and continue another 200 yards to the Parador Turístico, at the north end of the beach.

Playa Maruata

This unique seaside refuge has formed where a mountain river tries to empty into the sea but is partially blocked by a pair of big rocks. Sand has collected, so the rocks appear as islands in sand rather than water. The ocean has worn away sea tunnels, which surging waves penetrate, pushing air and water, gushing and spouting onto the shore. At times, a dry sand beach builds up next to the rocks, where campers can build an evening fire and be soothed to sleep by the gurgling, booming, and whistling lullaby of Maruata.

Besides plenty of beach for camping, the Nahua-speaking *ejido* owners of Playa Maruata run a pair of good *palapa* restaurants beneath the sleepy beachfront grove and maintain a few shady palm-frond *ramadas* on the sand for visitors. During the popular winter season, several tenters and self-contained RVers usually camp there. Water is scarce, so bring a supply if you plan to join them.

Maruata visitors enjoy three distinctly different beaches. On the northwest, right side, thunderous, open-ocean breakers (advanced surfing) pound a long, steep beach. A small middle beach, protected between the rocks, has oft-swimmable (with caution) water. The southeast, left-side beach is long and sheltered by the sea rocks, enclosing a shallow rivermouth lagoon. Its usually gentle waves are generally safe for wading, swimming, and boat launching. In addition, snorkeling off the rocks is often very good during the winter-spring dry season.

Getting There: Playa Maruata is 50 miles (80 km) southeast of the Colima line at Km 150.

The lagoon provides a sheltered anchorage and a rest for fishermen at Maruata.

BRUCE WHIPPERMAN

Rustic beach houses at Barra de Nexpa are popular accommodations, especially during the fall surfing season.

BRUCE WHIPPERMAN

Just south of a big bridge, the dirt turnoff road descends steeply from the northbound lane and crosses *under* the bridge. At the airstrip, bear left and follow for about a hundred yards and turn right at a wide gravel road, heading through the village. Continue through a stream (low water only) to the palm grove and beach. If, on the other hand, you want to fly in, the airstrip is smooth asphalt about half a mile long.

Playas Arena Blanca and Carezitu

Near Km 93, the rugged coastal mountains open to a stream valley, where (by a small roadside Conasupo store) a narrow dirt lane winds down from the highway through a small village to Playa Arena Blanca. Here a creamy strand faces a broad blue bay, which arcs gracefully a mile to a wave-splashed south-end headland. Prospects appear excellent for swimming, beachcombing, and surf- and rock-casting. During calm mornings boat-launching wouldn't be difficult, as evidenced by the *pangas* pulled up on the beach. Seafood lovers are in heaven here, with the fish, octupi, and oysters that local fisherfolk and divers bring in and sell right on the beach. For water and limited additional supplies, small stores and restaurants in the village and on the highway (a half mile north at the bus stop) are available.

Even prettier and more intimate is neighboring Playa Carezitu, a crescent of yellow sand, enfolded by sandstone cliffs, which is accessible either from Playa Arena Blanca, by ducking around

the north-end cliff corner, or by a steep downhill track near Km 94. Big rolling surfable breakers rise in the middle of a petite bay, while tranquil billows lap the sand on the sheltered northwest end. The sand curves a few hundred yards past scattered shoreline rocks, where snorkeling and fishing (by either surf or rock casting) appear promising, while shells, driftwood, and even a volleyball net enrich the beach possibilities. On one side, a semipermanent food *palapa* is set up to serve holiday visitors.

Playa Carezitu might be good for at least a pleasant afternoon, perhaps more. Temporary palm-thatch *ramadas,* apparently ready for new camper-occupants, stand on the beach. The entrance track, while too steep and rough for big RVs, is negotiable in dry weather by jeeps, pickups, and high-clearance vans.

Barra de Nexpa

While well known as one of Pacific Mexico's best surfing beaches, Barra de Nexpa's appeal is not limited to surfers. Don Gilberto, the grandfatherly founder of this pocket Utopia, will gladly tell you all about it (in Spanish, of course). As more people arrived, facilities were added. First, Don Gilberto built *palapas* (now rentable at $2 per person), a well, and showers. Then he built a restaurant, which his son now runs. Next, an informal RV and tenting park spread along the palmy shoreline of the adjacent freshwater lagoon. Finally, a line of Robinson Crusoe-like rustic beach houses sprouted along the sandbar.

Don Gilberto's enterprise grew, but the natural setting remained unchanged. The breakers (10-footers are common) still roll in, often curling into tubes, to the delight of both surfers and surf-watchers. Nexpa's big waves, however, need not discourage waders and swimmers, who splash and paddle in the freshwater lagoon instead. Beachcombers savor many hours picking through driftwood and shells while bird-watchers enjoy watching dozens of species preen, paddle, stalk, and flap in the lagoon. And finally, when tired of all of these, everyone enjoys the hammocks, which seem to hang from every available Nexpa post and palm.

At the height of the fall-winter season, when lots of surfers and campers crowd in, the atmosphere is generally communal and friendly. At the *palapa* restaurant, on the beach, or in the shade beneath the palms and the *ramadas,* you won't lack company.

Getting There: At Km 56, 109 miles (175 km) southeast of the Colima border, follow the unmarked dirt road, which curves sharply, following an uphill slope. It continues, bumping and winding downhill about half a mile to the beach. The road appears negotiable, when dry, by cars and RVs, even perhaps big motorhomes. If in doubt, do a preliminary run.

Caleta de Campos

Caleta de Campos (pop. 2,000) is at the signed turnoff of Km 50, 112 miles (181 km) southeast of the Colima border. Sometimes called Bahía de Bufadero ("Blowhole"), Caleta de Campos is the metropolis and service center for this corner of Michoacán. Although it has a sandy beach beside a blue bay, the beach is a haven primarily for commercial fishing launches rather

than tourist visitors. Fishing *pangas* may be rented on the beach. A half-day excursion (about $50) typically returns with 50 pounds of *huachinango* (snapper), *cabrilla* (sea bass), *sierra* (mackerel), *róbalo* (snook), and *atún* (tuna). Anyone can launch a boat on the bay's protected northwest end, provided a strong truck is available to lug it up the moderately steep beach-access road, turn right just after the Hotel Yuritza.

Caleta's one hotel, the **Hotel Yuritza,** perches on the hill above the beach. Plain but clean, the Yuritza is fine for an overnight stay. A big yard within the fenced hotel compound can also accommodate large RVs. Reserve by writing the hotel, address simply Caleta de Campos, Michoacán. Their 19 rooms rent $13 s, $17 d, and include fans and baths, but lack hot water.

The good **Torta and Burger Bahía** *lonchería* occupies the corner across from the hotel. Their *liquados, tortas,* hamburgers, and ham and eggs taste delicious after a hard day riding the waves.

Most of Caleta's stores and institutions are scattered along its single main street, which leads from the highway. There you'll find a *larga distancia* telephone office, tel. (753) 601-92, a **farmacia,** a grocery, and a *centro de salud* (health center) on a side street nearby.

Buses stop frequently at both the Hwy. 200 crossing and the small station on the dirt main street a block uphill. Paraíso first-class and Galeana second-class run between Manzanillo and Lázaro Cárdenas; Tres Estrellas de Oro run the entire Pacific coast down to Acapulco; and local microbuses run to and from Lázaro Cárdenas. Drivers of micro- and second-class buses will generally let you off anywhere along the highway you request.

PLAYA AZUL

It's easy to see how Playa Azul ("Blue Beach") got on the map of Pacific Mexico. The beach is long and level, the sand is yellow and silky. The waves roll in slowly, swish gently, and stop, leaving wet, lazy arcs upon the sand. At sunset, these glow like medallions of liquid gold.

Around Town

Playa Azul (pop. 5,000) is a small town on a big beach with a mile of *palapa* seafood restaurants. Three bumpy streets, Carranza, Madero, and Independencia, parallel the beachfront *malecón* walkway. Much of the activity clusters on or near a fourth street (actually a dirt lane), Aquiles Serdán, which bisects the other three and ends at the *malecón*. Here the atmosphere—piquant aromas of steaming *pozole* and hot tacos, the color of mounds of papayas and tomatoes, the language and laughter of the people—is uniquely and delightfully Mexican.

Beach Activities

The Playa Azul beach is good for just about everything. The waves, big enough for surfing as they break far offshore, roll shoreward, picking up boogie-boarders and bodysurfers along the way, finally rippling around the ankles of waders and splashers at the sand's edge. Concessionaires rent chairs, umbrellas, and boogie boards, but few, if any, surfboards. The weekend crowds keep the beach relatively free of shells and driftwood, although pickings will be better farther out along the beach (which stretches many miles in either direction).

Eating is another major Playa Azul beach occupation. Fruit vendors stroll the sand, offering luscious cut pineapple, watermelon, and mangos-on-a-stick, while semipermanent beach stands and dozens of *malecón* restaurants offer fresh *cóctel de ostión* (oyster cocktail, $4), *langostina al gusto* (prawns any style, $6), and *langosta al vapor* (steamed lobster, $10).

ACCOMMODATIONS

Playa Azul has half a dozen hotels, one with a trailer park. Three of them stand out. One block from the beach, the triple-tiered main building of the **Hotel Playa Azul and Trailer Park,** Av. V. Carranza s/n, Playa Azul, Michoacán 60982, tel. (753) 600-88 or 600-93, fax 600-92, surrounds a lovely pool-patio of tall palms, rubber trees, and big-leafed vines. A spacious blue swimming pool curves artfully in the middle, while the bar and restaurant are tucked beneath a soaring beamed *palapa* on one side. The shady patio invites quiet relaxation; other rooms offer TV and Ping-Pong. Families especially enjoy the hotel's water-slide minipark (beachside, behind the main building past the trailer park).

The 55 rooms, spacious and comfortable but not luxurious, come in economy and standard versions. Economy rooms (with fan only, on the ground floor by the parking lot) rent for about $13 s and $20 d; standard rooms go for about $18 and $28, with fan only; add about $5 for a/c; parking is available, credit cards are accepted, and there is limited wheelchair access.

The trailer park, with about a dozen spaces cramped behind the hotel, is nevertheless popular, since guests have access to hotel facilities. Spaces (up to about 30 feet) rent for about $12 per day with all hookups, including power for air-conditioning, toilets, and hot showers. Discounts for lower power and weekly and monthly stays are available. Contact the hotel for reservations, which are mandatory for the trailer park during the winter.

The **Hotel María Teresa,** Av. Independencia 626, Playa Azul, Michoacán 60982, tel. (753) 600-05 or 601-50, and fax 600-55, three blocks south of Aquiles Serdán and three short blocks from the beach, stands within an airy garden compound, with parking on one side and an attractive *palapa* restaurant and sunny pool patio tucked on the other. Their discotheque, Playa Azul's only one, rocks seasonally Friday and

Saturday. If you desire tranquility, however, request a room on the relatively *tranquilo* wing farthest from the disco. Their 42 comfortable, near-deluxe rooms, all with TV, phones, and a/c, rent for about $23 s, $28 d, and $33 t; credit cards accepted, limited wheelchair access.

Playa Azul's cheaper accommodations lack hot water, a serious defect for many winter vacationers. One good budget lodging *with* hot water, however, is the **Hotel Costa de Oro**, Av. F. Madero s/n, Playa Azul, Michoacán 60982, tel. (753) 600-86, on Madero, one block east of Serdán, two blocks from the beach. Their 14 rooms, Spartan but clean, rent from about $10 s, $14 d.

FOOD

Avenida Aquiles Serdán (at the Hotel Playa Azul corner) offers several possibilities. The friendly **Super del Centro** grocery has a little bit of everything, from cheese and milk to mops and *espirales mosquitos* (mosquito coils). Open daily 0730-2100.

Evenings, on the adjacent curbside, a squad of taco stalls open up. Their steaming tacos—of *res* (roast beef), *chorizo* (spicy sausage), and *lengua* (tongue)—wrapped in hot tortillas and spiced with piquant salsas make perfect appetizers.

Next door, the family owners of the newcomer **Restaurant Coco** offers good breakfasts, lunches and dinners in their shady outdoor patio.

For an equally tasty third course, step down Serdán past the corner of Madero and take a streetside table at **Restaurant Galdy.** The all-woman cadre of cooks and waitresses tries harder than anyone in town, especially with hearty *pozole* (soup), *pierna* (roast pork), and *platos mexicanos* (combination plates). Open daily 0700-2300.

For dessert, step back to the Madero corner to **Frutería Berenice** for a succulent selection of fruit. Local mangos (spring, early summer), pineapple, and *platanos* (bananas) will be familiar, but *guanabanas* (green and scaly, like an artichoke) and *ciruelas* (yellow and round, like a plum) probably will not. Open daily 0630-2100.

To top everything off, cross Serdán to the *panadería* and pick up some cake, cookies, or *donas;* open Mon.-Sat. 0700-2200.

ENTERTAINMENT AND SHOPPING

Playa Azul's evening entertainment begins with the sunset, views of which are unobstructed year-round. The effect is doubly beautiful, for the sky's golden glow is reflected from both the ocean and Playa Azul's shoreline swaths of flat wet sand. Sunset is also an excellent time for joggers and walkers to take advantage of the cool sea breeze and Playa Azul's level, firm sand.

Playa Azul's one regular dance spot, the **discotheque** at the Hotel María Teresa, on Independencia three blocks east of Aquiles Serdán, is generally open Friday and Saturday.

The **tourist market,** beneath the awnings stretched over Aquiles Serdán next to the Hotel Playa Azul, has several stands that offer beach balls, T-shirts, and bathing suits. Some of the more common crafts, such as painted ceramic animals and papier-mâché, may be available also.

SERVICES AND INFORMATION

Playa Azul has only a few services. Go to Lázaro Cárdenas (see below), 14 miles (22 km) southeast along Hwy. 200, for what Playa Azul lacks.

Playa Azul
area code
is 753

The town **doctor,** Horacio Soto-Mayor, has an office (phoneless) next to the Pemex gasoline station at the highway entrance to town. If he's closed, and it's an emergency, take a taxi to the *centro de salud,* tel. (753) 500-04, in La Mira (five miles, at the Hwy. 200 and Hwy. 37 intersection). If they're closed, continue to the General Hospital in Lázaro Cárdenas (see below).

For routine drugs and medications, try the **Farmacia Dios,** corner of Independencia and Aquiles Serdán, tel. (753) 601-85; open Mon.-Sat. 0900-2100, Sunday 0900-1400 and 1700-2000.

The *larga distancia* Cuqui (KOO-kee) is on Independencia, one block west of Aquiles Serdán.

GETTING THERE AND AWAY

By car or RV, paved Hwy. 200 connects Playa Azul with Manzanillo in the northwest (195 miles, 314 km). Although the route is in good condition and lightly traveled most of the way, its twists and turns through rugged oceanside canyons and along spectacular shoreline ridges make it considerably slow going. Allow at least six hours for safety. Fill up with gasoline as you start out, since the last available Magna Sin (unleaded) heading southeast is in Tecomán, about 167 miles (269 km) from the Playa Azul Pemex, which also stocks Magna Sin.

Between Playa Azul and Ixtapa-Zihuatanejo in the southeast, the route is relatively short and straight, although trucks sometimes slow progress. Allow two and a half hours for the 76-mile (122-km) trip.

With Pátzcuaro and central Michoacán in the north, Highways 37 and 14 connect with Playa Azul over 191 miles (307 km) of winding mountain highway. Although paved all the way, this route—through fertile valleys and over pine-shadowed crests—is potholed in places and occasionally congested. Allow at least seven hours for safety. Magna unleaded gasoline is only available at Arteaga, Nueva Italia, and Uruapán, so keep filled. As for "bandidos," stick to the main highway for security. Many mountain folks cultivate marijuana and opium. They're understandably suspicious of wandering strangers.

Upon bus arrival, ask your driver to drop you at the Hwy. 200 Playa Azul junction (three miles from Playa Azul, two miles from La Mira), where a taxi or local minivan can take you the rest of the way.

For bus departure from Playa Azul, go to La Mira (five miles by local minivan or taxi) and wait at the intersection of Highways 200 and 37. Although most Manzanillo-, Pátzcuaro-, and Zihuatanejo-bound buses stop hourly at La Mira during daylight, reserved seats are only available from the Lázaro Cárdenas stations. See "Lázaro Cárdenas and along the Road to Ixtapa-Zihuatanejo" below.

INLAND TO PÁTZCUARO

The high road from Playa Azul leads inland to Pátzcuaro (pop. 70,000), a city brimming with inspirations. Pine- and cedar-brushed mountains ring it; an islet-studded lake borders it. Its air is fresh and clean and the sky always seems blue. Visitors come from all over the world to wander through narrow colonial lanes, buy fine copperware and cloisonné, and gaze at grand, mystery-shrouded monuments of long-forgotten emperors.

HISTORY

Before the Conquest

The valley and lake of Pátzcuaro, elev. 7,500 feet (2,280 meters), have nurtured civilizations for millenia. The Tarascans, whose king, Tariácuri, rebuilt the city during the 1370s, were the last and the greatest dynasty. To them the lake and surrounding grounds were sacred: the door to their land of the ancestors. They chose the venerated foundation stones of already-ancient temples as the new city's cornerstones, marking the symbolic door to the land of the dead: tza-capu-amúcutin-pátzcuaro, the "stone door where all changes to blackness." The last part of that original name remains in use today.

The founders of Pátzcuaro did not call themselves Tarascans. This was from the Spanish label, meaning "son-in-law." Before the conquest, Pátzcuaro people called (and still call) themselves the Purépecha (poo-REH-pehchah). After the Spanish arrived in 1521, they increasingly applied their own label as they intermarried with the Pátzcuaro people.

Prior to the conquest, the Valley of Pátzcuaro was the center of a grand Purépecha empire, which extended beyond the present-day borders of the state of Michoacán. Local folk are still proud that their ancestors were never subjects of the Aztecs, whose armies they defeated and slaughtered by the tens of thousands on the eve of the conquest.

Conquest and Colonization

As Cortés approached the Valley of Mexico, the jittery Aztec emperor Moctezuma sent ambassadors to Tzintzuntzán (seen-soon-SAHN),

(top left) Plaza de Armas, Guadalajara; (top right) Hotel Radisson Sierra, Manzanillo; (bottom) village church decorations near La Salina, Guerrero (photos by Bruce Whipperman)

(top) bringing in the catch at Rincón de Guayabitos, Nayarit;
(bottom) cooking tortillas atop a traditional adobe stove (photos by Bruce Whipperman)

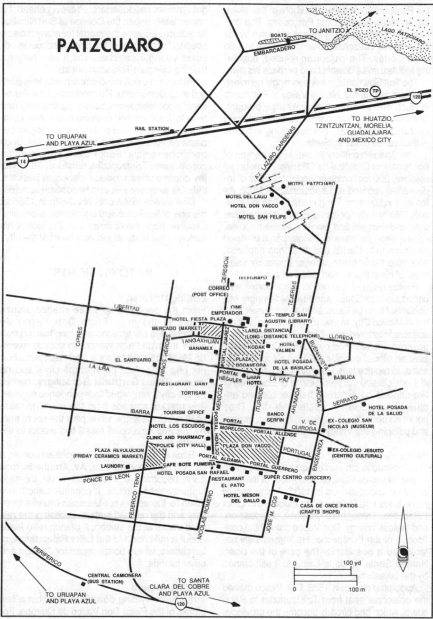

PATZCUARO

TO JANITZIO

BOATS

EMBARCADERO

LAGO PATZCUARO

EL POZO (TP)

120

TO IHUATZIO,
TZINTZUNTZAN, MORELIA,
GUADALAJARA,
AND MEXICO CITY

RAIL STATION

TO URUAPAN
AND PLAYA AZUL

14

AV. LAZARO CARDENAS

MOTEL PATZCUARO

MOTEL DEL LAGO

HOTEL DON VASCO

MOTEL SAN FELIPE

CEREGON

TELEGRAFO

CORREO
(POST OFFICE)

LIBERTAD

CINE
EMPERADOR

HOTEL FIESTA PLAZA

MERCADO (MARKET)

CIPRES

TANGAXHUAN

NINOS HEROES

BANAMEX

EL SANTUARIO

LA ERA

PORTAL JUAREZ

EX - TEMPLO SAN
AGUSTIN (LIBRARY)

LARGA DISTANCIA
(LONG-DISTANCE TELEPHONE)

KODAK

PLAZA
BOCANEGRA

HOTEL
VALMEN

HOTEL POSADA
DE LA BASILICA

TEJERIAS

BUENVISTA

LLOREDA

PORTAL
NEGUELS

GRAN
HOTEL

LA PAZ

BASILICA

RESTAURANT DANY

TORTISAM

IBARRA

TOURISM OFFICE

HOTEL LOS ESCUDEROS

CLINIC AND PHARMACY

POLICE (CITY HALL)

PLAZA REVOLUCION
(FRIDAY CERAMICS MARKET)

LAUNDRY

PONCE DE LEON

PORTAL MENDOZA

ITURBIDE

AHUMADA

ARCIGA

SERRATO

HOTEL POSADA
DE LA SALUD

PORTAL
MORELOS

BANCO
SERFIN

V. DE
QUIROGA

EX - COLEGIO SAN
NICOLAS (MUSEUM)

CAFE BOTE FUMEIRA

PORTAL HIDALGO

PORTAL ALDAMA

PLAZA DON VASCO

PORTAL ALLENDE

PORTAL GUERRERO

PORTUGAL

ENSENADA

EX-COLEGIO JESUITO
(CENTRO CULTURAL)

HOTEL POSADA SAN RAFAEL

RESTAURANT
EL PATIO

SUPER CENTRO (GROCERY)

FEDERICO TENO

NICOLAS ROMERO

HOTEL MESON
DEL GALLO

JOSE M. COS

CASA DE ONCE PATIOS
(CRAFTS SHOPS)

0   100 yd

0   100 m

MOON

PERIFERICO

TO URUAPAN
AND PLAYA AZUL

CENTRAL CAMIONERA
(BUS STATION)

TO SANTA
CLARA DEL COBRE

120

TO SANTA
CLARA DEL COBRE
AND PLAYA AZUL

© MOON PUBLICATIONS, INC.

the Purépecha capital on the shore of the lake a dozen miles northwest of Pátzcuaro. The ambassadors implored King Zuanga, known by his imperial title *caltzonzin,* to send an army to help repel Cortés. The *caltzonzin* refused, hastening Moctezuma's downfall and perhaps his own.

The first Spaniards, a few seemingly harmless travelers, wandered into the Valley of Pátzcuaro in 1521. The smallpox they unwittingly brought, however, was far from harmless. Zuangua soon succumbed to the ugly disease, along with tens of thousands of his subjects.

The Spanish military threat, in the person of conquistador Cristóbal de Olid and 70 mounted soldiers, 200 foot soldiers, and thousands of Indian allies, arrived at Tzintzuntzán in 1522. As the new *caltzonzin,* Tangaxoan II, fled to Uruapán, Olid quickly appropriated the imperial treasure and the gold and jewels from the temples. After a short resistance, Tangaxoan II pledged his homage to Cortés and was soon baptized, accepting the Christian name of Pedro. By 1526, most of his subjects had followed suit.

Peace reigned, but not for long. Cortés was called back to Spain, and the gold-hungry opportunist Nuño de Guzmán took temporary control in Mexico City. In late 1528, Guzmán had the *caltzonzin* tortured and killed. The Spanish royal government, alarmed by Guzmán's excesses, sent an official panel, called the Second Audiencia, to replace him. Guzmán, one jump ahead of them, cleared out in command of a battalion of like-minded adventurers, hell-bent to find another Tenochtitlán in western Mexico. They pounced upon the Purépecha, burning, raping, and pillaging the Valley of Pátzcuaro.

Vasco de Quiroga

The Purépecha fortunes began to improve when Father Vasco de Quiroga, a member of the Second Audiencia, arrived in 1533. At the age of 63 he began his life's work on the shore of Lake Pátzcuaro. Through his kindness, compassion, and tireless energy, Don Vasco gained the confidence of the Purépecha. He immediately established a hospital for the care of the poor. Named Santa Fe de la Laguna, it still stands by the lakeshore.

Appointed bishop in 1538, Don Vasco moved the episcopal seat from Tzintzuntzán to Pátzcuaro, which had already become the provincial government headquarters. Pressing ahead, he immediately began the College of San Nicolas. Its features became the model for many more: a hospital for the care of the poor, a school to educate young Tarascans, and a seminary for training bilingual Tarascan priests.

Pátzcuaro's rich handicrafts heritage is partly due to Don Vasco. He moderated the Tarascans' *encomienda* obligations so that they had time to become self-sustaining on their communal and individual plots. Entire villages became centers of specific skills and trades. Such traditions remain: Santa Clara turns out fine copperware; Tzintzuntzán, furniture. Other valley communities produce elaborate baskets, delicate lacquerware, and handsome saddles.

Don Vasco toiled until his death in 1565 at the age of 95. Pátzcuaro people still adore him. Children often leave flowers at the foot of his statue in the plaza at the very heart of the city.

IN-TOWN SIGHTS

Getting Oriented

From the good bishop's tree-shaded bronze image in the main **Plaza Don Vasco de Quiroga,** the city spreads out along half a dozen north-south and east-west main streets. **Avenida Mendoza** runs from the northwest plaza corner one long block north to the city's second square, **Plaza Gertrudis Bocanegra,** named for the city's renowned Independence heroine. The **market** spreads from the northwest side of Plaza Bocanegra, while past the south end, Av. La Paz runs uphill (east) two blocks to the **basilica.**

Back at the main plaza's northeast corner, a second main thoroughfare, **Av. Amuhada,** runs north, becoming Av. Lázaro Cárdenas, the main highway-access route. It continues about two miles to the east-west Uruapán-Morelia highway and the railroad station. Crossing the railroad tracks at the station, a branch road leads about a mile north to the **Lake Pátzcuaro** embarcadero, where boats depart for Janitzio and other islands.

Getting Around

Virtually everything downtown is within a few blocks of the Plaza Don Vasco de Quiroga. For

The facade of the Colegio San Nicolas (1540), a cherished national treasure, graces a quiet Pátzcuaro street corner.

BRUCE WHIPPERMAN

trips out of the city, hail a taxi or ride a white *colectivo* van from in front of the Hotel Los Escudos (Ibarra and Mendoza plaza corner) to the Central Camionera (main bus station) on the *periférico* boulevard on the west side of town.

A Walk around Old Pátzcuaro

The natural place to start is at the center of the main plaza, beneath the statue of the revered Don Vasco de Quiroga (1470-1565). As first bishop of Pátzcuaro (see "History" above) he reversed the despair and destruction wrought by the conquistadores.

Colonial buildings, some dating back to the 17th century, rise behind the portals that spread around the square. The portals are themselves named and localize individual addresses (such as the Hotel Los Escudos, Portal Hidalgo 73).

Walk east, uphill, one block to Pátzcuaro's oldest building, the former **Colegio San Nicolas,** begun by Don Vasco in 1540. Pass inside beneath its quaint three-bell Spanish classic facade to the venerable inner garden. Now called the Museo de Arte Popular, tel. (434) 210-29, its portaled corridors lead past rooms filled with fine regional crafts. In a rear courtyard, be sure to see the stairstep foundations of the original Tarascan temple, exposed on the hillside. Turn around and inspect a wall inscribed with the marks of prisoners counting the days. Open Tues.-Sat. 0900-1900, Sunday 0900-1500.

As you exit the museum, glance left at the curious little doorway emerging from the out-side uphill lane. Behind that door, Pátzcuaro people say, is an aqueduct that Don Vasco built to supply the poor with water during times of drought.

Walk ahead past the big courtyard and church on the left, a former Jesuit College, now being restored as a community cultural center. Plans include a museum, and classes in theater, painting, drawing, and music, both instrumental and choral. Watch for announcements of events. Continue along Calle Enseñanza. After two blocks, turn right, downhill, to the former Dominican Convent of Santa Catarina de Sena, commonly known as the **Casa de Once Patios** ("House of Eleven Patios") on the left. Most of its inner labyrinth of gardens, corridors, and rooms is restored and open to the public. Dozens of artisans have set up display-workshops where they paint, weave, polish, and carve handicrafts for sale. Open daily 0900-1400 and 1600-1900. (See "Shopping" below for details.)

Return past the former Colegio San Nicolas and continue two blocks along Calle Arciga to the big **Basilica María Inmaculada de la Salud,** begun by Don Vasco during the mid-16th century. In addition to Don Vasco's tomb, the basilica is noted for its four-century-old main altar image of the Virgin, made according to a pre-Columbian recipe of cornstalk paste and orchid glue.

Follow diagonal Av. Buenavista downhill and continue a block along Lloreda to the former monastery, **Ex-Templo San Agustín,** now the Biblioteca (public library), at the northeast corner of Plaza Bocanegra; open Mon.-Fri. 0900-1900, Saturday 0900-1300. The library's main attraction is its huge mural, the first by Juan O'Gorman, completed in 1942. In this panorama of the history of the Valley of Pátzcuaro, O'Gorman is nearly as critical of the Tarascans' slaughtering of 30,000 Aztec prisoners as of Nuño de Guzmán (scowling like a demon in armor) as he tortures the last *caltzonzin* (emperor). All is not lost as O'Gorman shows the murdered emperor's niece, Erendira, riding out (and becoming the first Native American to ride a horse) to warn the people. Don Vasco, the savior, appears at the bottom, assuring a happy ending as he brings Utopia to Pátzcuaro.

The librarian has a Spanish copy of the mural guide, signed by O'Gorman, who appears with his wife at the mural's left side. The library also has a respectable book collection, including many Spanish-language reference works and several shelves of English language fiction and nonfiction.

JANITZIO

An excursion to the island of Janitzio (hah-NEET-seeoh) is de rigueur in Pátzcuaro. The breezy launch trip takes about half an hour. Waves splash, spray, and rock the bow; gulls wheel above the stern as the pyramidal vol-

canic island-village of Janitzio grows upon the horizon. The Janitzio villagers believe themselves to be the purest of the Purépecha. Only the young speak Spanish; the old—some of whom have never visited the mainland—hold fast to their language and traditional ways.

Fishing for the tasty Pátzcuaro *pescado blanco* (whitefish) is the major Janitzio occupation. Overfishing has unfortunately reduced the famous *mariposas* (butterfly nets), which Don Vasco introduced long ago, to mere ceremonial objects. Long, cumbersome nets are now needed for the increasingly meager catches. The price (about $10) of a succulent whitefish platter—the specialty of the dozen-odd embarcadero restaurants—has inflated beyond the reach of most Pátzcuaro families.

Fortunately, government and local cooperative conservation measures show promise of eventually replenishing the whitefish population. Meanwhile, the *mariposas* come out for display only during tourist-show regattas on weekends and holidays.

A steady procession of handicrafts shops lines the steep lane that winds to the island's summit. Although most items (baskets, masks, papier-mâché, lacquerware, cottons and woolens) are cheap and common, some unusual buys await those willing to look and bargain.

At the top, the still more isolated islets of Tecuen, Yuñuen, and La Pacanda dot the lake's northern reaches, while in the opposite direction, the city of Pátzcuaro basks at the foot of a distant pine-tufted green sierra. If you have the energy, climb to the tip-top of the colossal José María Morelos statue, lined inside with a continuous mural of scenes from the fiery Independence hero's life.

Getting to Janitzio: If you're driving, head downhill (north) a couple of miles along Av. Lázaro Cárdenas and turn left at the Uruapán-Morelia highway. Within a few hundred yards, turn right at the road crossing the rail tracks at the rail station. After about half a mile, bear right at a fork, and soon you'll see the parking lot (about $1). If you're not driving, taxi or ride the white *colectivo* VW van (about 60 cents, from the corner by the Hotel Los Escudos on Plaza Don Vasco, or the Mercado corner, Plaza Bocanegra) to the embarcadero. Roundtrip boat tickets, available from a dockfront booth, cost about $2 in advance to departure. The last return boat leaves the island at 1800.

Eerie local-style Pátzcuaro, Michoacán masks are common sale items in Janitzio shops.

ERIN DWYER

IHUATZIO

Pre-Columbian ruins dot the Pátzcuaro Valley. Most remain unexcavated grassy mounds except the most famous: Ihuatzio (ee-WAHT-seeoh) and Tzintzuntzán, both near the lakeshore northeast of the city.

Pátzcuaro dominated the valley during the latter-1300s golden-era reign of King Tariácuri. When he died the valley was divided between his younger son and his nephews, Hiripan and Tangaxoan (ancestor of Tangaxoan II, the last Tarascan emperor). According to Vasco de Quiroga's 16th-century narrative, *Relación de Michoacán,* squabbling broke out among the heirs. Hiripan won out, and, by 1400, had concentrated power at Ihuatzio.

IHUATZIO ARCHAEOLOGICAL ZONE

WALL-CAUSEWAY

WALL-CAUSEWAY

WALL-CAUSEWAY

OBSERVATORY

RECONSTRUCTED PYRAMIDS

YACATAS

KING'S CAUSEWAYS

WALL-CAUSEWAY

PARADE GROUND

AREA OPEN TO THE PUBLIC

PARKING

TO PATZCUARO

0   150 yd

0   150 m

© MOON PUBLICATIONS, INC.

Exploring Ihuatzio

The remains of Ihuatzio, literally, "Place of the Coyotes," spread over a rectangular area about half a mile long by a quarter mile wide. Nearly all ruins are mound-dotted unexplored fields, closed to the public. The open part, the so-called **Parade Ground,** is about the size of four football fields and enclosed by a pair of ceremonial stepped-wall raised causeways. These lead toward a pair of hulking truncated pyramids that tower above the Parade Ground's west end. These, Ihuatzio's most prominent structures, lost nearly all of their original stone sheathing to colonial construction projects, although a remnant appears on the right pyramid's face as you approach from the Parade Ground.

Climb carefully (the steps are steep) to the top for a view of the surrounding unexcavated ruins. Along the Parade Ground's north and south sides, notice the **King's Causeways,** a pair of long stepped mounds, presumably used as the *caltzonzin's* ceremonial approach road.

About a quarter mile due south rises another mound, which marks the **Observatory,** a mysterious 100-foot-wide cylindrical structure whose

name merely represents an educated guess about its possible function. In nearly the same direction as the Observatory, but much closer, stands the rubbly mound of the **yácatas,** three half-cylindrical truncated pyramids, whose original forms are unrecognizable due to repeated ransackings. Their shapes, however, are certain, due to a number of other excavated local examples, most notably, Tzintzuntzán, five miles to the north. The Ihuatzio site is open daily around 0900-1600; entry fee about $2, no facilities except a lavatory; don't forget your hat and drinking water.

For directions to Ihuatzio, see "Getting There" under Tzintzuntzán following.

TZINTZUNTZÁN

Ihuatzio's power waned during the 1400s, gradually giving way to nearby Tzintzuntzán ("Place of the Hummingbirds"). Within a generation, Tzintzuntzán (seen-soon-SAHN) became the hub of an expanded Tarascan empire, which included nearly all of present Michoacán and half of Jalisco and Guanajuato. When the Spanish arrived in 1521, authority was concentrated entirely in Tzintzuntzán, an imperial city whose population had swelled to perhaps as much as 100,000.

The present town (pop. 5,000) a dozen miles northeast of Pátzcuaro is a mere shadow of its former glory. The Great Platform, although long abandoned, still towers, in proud relief, on the hill above the dusty modern town.

Exploring the Archaeological Site

The entire archaeological zone—of which the Great Platform occupies a significant but very small area—spreads over nearly three square miles. The excavated part, open to the public, comprises only a fiftieth of the total, being confined within a rectangle perhaps 500 yards long and half that in width. Visitors approach the rear of the Great Platform from the east through a grassy park. They first see the Great Platform spreading from right (north) to left, with the town and lake below the far front side.

The Great Platform is singularly intriguing, because of its five side-by-side *yácatas:* massive, semicylindrical ceremonial platforms. The *yácatas* are built of huge cut basalt (lava) stones, like a giant child's neat stacks of black building blocks. When the Spanish arrived, a temple to the legendary god-king Curicaueri perched upon the *yácata* summit.

Although the Great Platform itself was purely ceremonial in function, excavations in outer portions of the zone reveal that imperial Tzintzuntzán was an entire city, housing all classes from kings to slaves. Within the city, people lived and worked according to specialized occupations—farmers, artisans, priests, and warriors. Most experts agree that such urban organization required a high degree of sophistication, including excess wealth, laws and efficient government, and a reliable calendar.

Tzintzuntzán grew through a number of stages from its founding around A.D. 900. Excavations beneath the Great Platform masonry reveal earlier *yácatas* overlaid, like layers of an onion, above earlier constructions with similar, but smaller, features. (Look, for example, at the archaeological test hole between *yácatas* 4 and 5.)

Other intriguing structures dot the Great Platform. **Entrance ramps,** apparently built as boat-traffic terminals, appear beneath the Great Platform's 20-foot-high stepped retaining wall. (Records reveal that, at the time of the conquest, lake waters lapped beaches at the foot of these ramps.)

The Palace, a group of rooms surrounding an inner patio, stands about a hundred yards northeast of the first *yácata.* Because thousands of human bones and an altar were found here, some archaeologists speculated that it may have been a ceremonial depository for the remains of vanquished enemies.

About 75 yards in front of *yácatas* 4 and 5 is Building E, a puzzling L-shaped group of rooms. Although archaeolgists speculate that they may have been storerooms or granaries, excavations, curiously, revealed no entrances.

The site is open daily about 0900-1700; facilities include a picnic park and lavatories. Entry fee is about $3: bring your hat and drinking water.

A sample of the huge selection of colonial-style woodcrafts for sale at Tzintzuntzán carver's shops.

BRUCE WHIPPERMAN

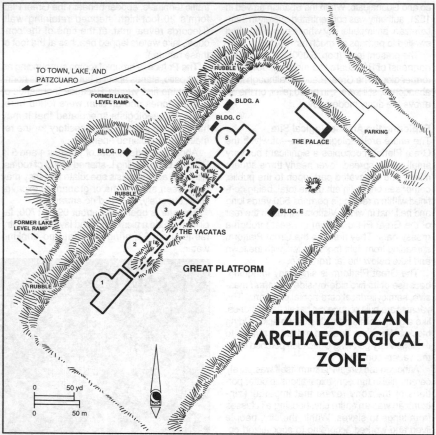

TO TOWN, LAKE, AND
PATZCUARO

RUBBLE

FORMER LAKE
LEVEL RAMP

BLDG. A

BLDG. C

5

BLDG. D

THE PALACE

PARKING

RUBBLE

3

BLDG. E

FORMER LAKE
LEVEL RAMP

THE YACATAS

2

GREAT PLATFORM

RUBBLE

1

0   50 yd

0   50 m

TZINTZUNTZAN
ARCHAEOLOGICAL
ZONE

© MOON PUBLICATIONS, INC.

Modern Tzintzuntzán

The buildings the Spanish colonials erected still
stand at the far (west) end of the town park,
which spreads from the crafts stalls bordering
the Hwy. 120-main street. Clustered at the park's
far end you will find the **Franciscan monastery
and church.** Inside the church are several paintings and murals dedicated to the Señor de
Rescate, whose festival the townspeople celebrate with Purépecha music and regional
dances. The adjacent monastery, dedicated to
Santa Anna, is known for its plateresque facade and courtyard, containing some of the
world's oldest olive trees (which somehow survived the royal ban on olive trees in Mexico).

Back on the main street, handicrafts stores
and shops offer some unusual woodwork. Especially noteworthy are the **Artesanías Lupita** and the warren of shops behind it. Wander
among their riots of wooden crafts—giant
masks, baskets, headboards, cabinets—where
you can select from a potpourri of pre-
Columbian, Gothic, baroque, and neoclassic
motifs.

Getting There

Drive Hwy. 120 from Pátzcuaro northeast
(Morelia direction) about five miles (eight km)
to the signed Ihuatzio turnoff. Turn left and continue about two more miles to a signed road on

the right, which bumps for about another mile to the site parking lot. For Tzintzuntzán, continue about five miles on the highway past Ihuatzio to the right fork, which leads to the ruins on the hill above the highway.

By bus, from the Pátzcuaro Central Camionera (south side of town) ride either the Ihuatzio or Tzintzuntzán blue-and-white *urbano* buses. Tell the driver *"ruinas"* and, at Ihuatzio, the driver will drop you within a mile of the site. At Tzintzuntzán, the driver will stop on the highway fork to the ruins (or, if you're lucky, at the ruins parking lot a quarter mile farther on).

EXCURSIONS SOUTH AND WEST OF PÁTZCUARO

An auto excursion to the copper-crafting town of **Santa Clara de Cobre** can be conveniently extended into a half-day loop that includes tranquil mountain lake Zirahuén and the mysterious pre-Tarascan ruins at the Tinganio archaeological site.

Santa Clara de Cobre (pop. 5,000) is tucked on a gently sloping mountainside about half an hour (13 miles by Hwy. 120) south of Pátzcuaro. The town clusters around an intimate plaza, where most everything you see—the benches, the bandstand, and the lampposts—seems to be made of copper. A look at the shiny contents of the plaza shops—galaxies of gleaming utensils, curios, and art objects—confirms the impression. Although their old mines are all played out, the livelihoods of many Santa Clara families are still based on the fine copperware (made from copper from other parts of Mexico), which they turn out in their workshop-homes. If you decide to linger, attractive colonial-style built restaurants and hotels on the plaza can provide food and lodging.

From Hwy. 120, just past the southern fringe of Santa Clara, a cobbled road forks right about seven miles (12 km) to reed-lined **Lake Zirahuén.** According to Purépecha legend, the lake resulted from the river of tears that Princess Zirahuén wept after losing her true love. Although Zirahuén died of sorrow, her spirit still lives in the lake. Men who set out upon the water in their canoes must beware, for the spirit appears as a lovely, beckoning young maiden. And alas for the one who cannot resist, as the spirit will take him never to be seen again.

Ghosts notwithstanding, Lake Zirahuén is a jewel set amongst emerald, pine-clad mountains and lush communal fields ripe for relaxed exploring. Fisherfolk paddle dugout canoes across its mirror surface; local-style wooden houses known as *trojas* cluster near the lakeshore. A rough but passable road circles the lake, and excursion boats take parties out from a pair of wharves near **Zirahuén** town (pop. 1,000). Restaurants at both wharves offer whitefish dinners for very reasonable prices. The more upscale of the two wharves, Embarcadero Ala, whose entrance you pass en route from Santa Clara, has a very attractive restaurant-lodge, and rustic, clean housekeeping cabins sleeping two to six persons. For information and reservations, telephone or fax Operadora Lago de Zirahuén at their office in Morelia, Michoacán: tel. (431) 545-19, 544-16, 543-64, fax 512-81. Rates run about $60 per night and up. If this is too rich for you, a motel at the edge of the town nearby offers clean rooms for about $15.

Besides the road from Santa Clara, you can get there two miles along the well-signed turnoff road at Km 17 (10 miles from Pátzcuaro) on Hwy. 14 to Uruapán. Stay on the same Hwy. 14 and you'll arrive at **Tingambato**, at Km 37 (23 miles from Pátzcuaro, 16 miles from Uruapán). Turn at the small roadside archaeological sign and continue through the town about a mile to the Tinganio archaeological site parking lot.

The excavated section, uncovered during the late 1970s, constitutes a small, albeit very important part of the entire archaeological zone. Modern dating methods show construction occurred in two phases, the first beginning around A.D. 450 and the second continuing between A.D. 600 and A.D. 900. The second stage culminated in the visible reconstructions, which surround a central sunken plaza: on the east side, a 25-foot, six-step pyramid; a tomb complex on the north; and a sunken ball court on the west. The pyramid, accessed by a ritual stairway, is reminiscent of classic Teotihuacán style. Opposite is the ceremonial ball court (see special topic "*Tlatchtli:* The Ball Game") in which players tried to bat a solid, natural rubber ball past their opponents with their torsos, shoulders, and heads. Stakes for ritually important contests sometimes ran as high as the lives of the participants.

Although much of the site had been looted before the arrival of the Spanish, excavators discovered an unopened tomb (note the descending staircase) on the north side. Finds included a host of skulls and skeletons—although only one complete, seated at the entrance—and a trove of artifacts, enough for a generation of archaeologists to sort out.

ACCOMMODATIONS

Downtown Hotels

Pátzcuaro visitors enjoy a number of good, reasonably priced colonial-decor hotels clustered near the plazas. Because of the mild, dry climate, rooms generally have neither air-conditioning nor central heating. Fans and *chimeneas* (fireplaces, a cozy winter plus) are sometimes available.

The family-managed **Hotel Los Escudos,** Portal Hidalgo 73, Pátzcuaro, Michoacán 61600, tel. (434) 201-38 and 212-90, right on the plaza, is a longtime Pátzcuaro favorite. Its rooms rise in three tiers around a cool, serene inner patio, wrapped in wrought iron, tile, and bright green-

ery. The homey, dark-paneled rooms come with lacey curtains, wood floors, and fireplaces (wood included). The wood-paneled cafe downstairs, one of Pátzcuaro's favorite meeting places, is a good spot for lingering over dessert with friends or with a good book after a hard day on the lake. The hotel's 30 rooms rent for about $25 s and $32 d, with TV, parking, and credit cards accepted. Reservations, recommended any time, are mandatory weekends and holidays.

Hotel Posada San Rafael, Portal Aldama 13, Plaza Vasco de Quiroga, Pátzcuaro, Michoacán 61600, tel. (434) 207-70 or 207-79, on the adjacent plaza-front block, offers an alternative. Greatly expanded during the 1980s from an original colonial mansion core, its 104 rooms spread along three stories of corridors facing a narrow inner parking courtyard. While the parked cars detract, the neocolonial decor—traditional tile, big-beamed ceilings, and hand-carved oak doors—lend a touch of charm. The paneled rooms, with throw rugs, wood floors, and fluffy curtains, if not deluxe, are at least clean and comfortable. Hot-water hours are limited to 0700-1100 and 1830-2130. Rates run about $21 s, $26 d, $32 t; no fireplaces.

One of Pátzcuaro's best-buy lodgings, **Hotel Meson del Gallo,** Dr. Coss 20, Pátzcuaro, Michoacán 61600, tel. (434) 215-11 or 214-74, is around the corner just a block south of the plaza Don Vasco. Clean, tastefully appointed colonial-decor rooms with bath, manicured green gardens on both sides of the building, a pool, and a restaurant add a touch of luxury unusual in such moderately priced lodging. The 25 rooms and suites rent for about $20 s, $25 d, with parking, limited wheelchair access, and no TV; credit cards are accepted.

The plainer but well-managed modern-style **Gran Hotel on Plaza Bocanegra,** Portal Regules 6, Plaza Bocanegra, Pátzcuaro, Michoacán 61600, tel. (434) 204-43, offers an

---

PÁTZCUARO HOTELS

Pátzcuaro (area code 434, postal code 61600) hotels, in order of increasing high-season double-room price:

DOWNTOWN

Hotel Valmen, Lloreda 34, tel. 211-61, $15

Hotel Posada de la Salud, Av. Serrato 9, tel. 200-58, $15

Gran Hotel, Portal Regules 6, Plaza Bocanegra, tel. 204-43, $16

Hotel Meson del Gallo, Dr. Coss 20, tel. 215-11 or 214-74, $25

Posada San Rafael, Portal Aldama 13, tel. 207-70 or 207-79, $26

Hotel Fiesta Plaza, Plaza Bocanegra 24, tel. 225-15 or 225-16, $26

Posada de la Basilica, Arciga 6, tel. 211-08, $27

Hotel Los Escudos, Portal Hidalgo 73, tel. 201-38 or 212-90, $32

AV. LÁZARO CÁRDENAS

Motel Del Lago, L. Cárdenas 509, tel. 214-71, $20

Motel Pátzcuaro, L. Cárdenas 506, tel. 207-67, $21

Motel San Felipe, L. Cárdenas 321, tel. 212-98, $32

Hotel Don Vasco, L. Cárdenas 450, tel. 202-27, fax 202-62, $65

even more economical alternative. Its 20 rooms, stacked in two stories, are clean, comfortable, and thoughtfully decorated in '60s motel style. For minimum noise, get a room away from the busy street. Rates run about $14 s, $16 d, and $23 t, with restaurant but no phones, parking, or TV.

The **Hotel Fiesta Plaza,** Plaza Bocanegra 24, Pátzcuaro, Michoacán 61600, tel. (434) 225-15 or 225-16, on the opposite, north side of Plaza Bocanegra, is a 1990 newcomer among Pátzcuaro hotels. A former landmark colonial mansion, the hotel's three tiers of comfortable rooms enfold a fountain-decorated inner patio. Their restaurant, convenient for breakfast, spreads into the patio, while just outside the door the colorful Plaza Bocanegra hubbub—the market, the movie theater, a dozen taco stands, bus and minivan traffic—buzzes from morning to midnight. Guests who require relief should pick an upper-tier room away from the street. Rooms rent for about $21 s, $26 d, $32 t; with TV, phones, and parking; credit cards accepted.

Hotel Valmen, Lloreda 34, Pátzcuaro, Michoacán 61600, tel. (434) 211-61, on the corner of Lloreda and Ahumada two blocks up the street, offers a budget alternative. Plants and attractive tile soften the Valmen's otherwise Spartan (to the point of being un-Mexican) ambience. Two upper tiers of plain but tidy rooms, with hot showers, spread around the interior patio. Avoid the street noise by choosing an interior room. Rates run about $12 s, $15 d, $18 t.

Guests at the very popular **Posada de la Basilica,** Arciga 6, Pátzcuaro, Michoacán 61600, tel. (434) 211-08, one block farther uphill, across from the basilica, enjoy a very attractive view restaurant. The panorama (also visible from the hotel's adjoining patio) of colonial city, lake, and mountains adds a bit of luxury to the hotel's authentically colonial atmosphere. The rooms, furnished in hand-carved, hand-woven, and hand-wrought 17th-century chic, add even more. The 11 rooms, all with hot water, run about $21 s, $27 d, and $32 t; six rooms have fireplaces; reservations are generally necessary.

The **Hotel Posada de la Salud,** Av. Serrato 9, Pátzcuaro, Michoacán 61600, tel. (434) 200-58, on the basilica's south side, is especially popular with female basilica visitors. The 15 plain but very clean rooms spread around a sunny, conventlike courtyard. The typical guest, while not saintly, is at least probably in bed reading, by nine at the latest. Rooms rent for about $12 s, $15 d, and $18 t; reservations recommended, especially during religious holidays, such as the Fiesta de la Virgen de La Salud (first two weeks in December) and Semana Santa (week preceding Easter Sunday).

Avenida Lázaro Cárdenas Hotels

A number of acceptable motel-style accommodations cluster along Av. Lázaro Cárdenas, about half a mile from the Uruapán-Morelia Highway.

The **Motel del Lago,** Av. L. Cárdenas 509, Pátzcuaro, Michoacán 61600, tel. (434) 214-71, is just a few blocks from the highway. The budget choice of families with wheels, the del Lago's 12 brick units surround a central parking area garden, bordered by leafy avocado, rubber, and peach trees. Although the cottages have fireplaces (wood $2 extra) and hot water, they're plain, a bit worn, and could be cleaner. Rooms run $18 s, $20 d, and $25 t; credit cards accepted and limited wheelchair access.

Cross Av. Lázaro Cárdenas to **Motel Pátzcuaro,** Av. L. Cárdenas 506, Pátzcuaro, Michoacán 61600, tel. (434) 207-67, a homey cluster of a dozen cottages, set half a block back from the road. Owned and operated by long-time lovers of Pátzcuaro, Obdulia and Arturo Pimentel Ramos, the units are attractively furnished in rustic browns, knotty-pine paneling, and brick fireplaces. The grassy grounds spread past a swimming pool (not maintained in winter) and a tennis court to an acre of tent and RV (self-contained only) sites on the adjacent gentle hillside. A kitchen is available for use of guests. The cottages rent for about $18 s, $21 d, and $24 t. Tent and RV guests pay about $4 per person, per night. The cottages are often filled; it's best to make reservations. Limited wheelchair access.

Guests of the sprawling 103-room resort-style **Hotel Don Vasco,** Av. Lázaro Cárdenas 450, Pátzcuaro, Michoacán 61600, tel. (434) 202-27, fax 202-62, enjoy neocolonial decor, comfortable, high-beamed rooms, spreading lawns, quiet patio nooks, a chapel, a big pool, tennis, billiards, bowling, a bar, and a fancy restaurant.

The rooms in the newer wing are large and luxurious, with private garden-view balconies. Rooms begin at about $55 s, $65 d; with TV, phones, electric heat, seasonal discotheque, credit cards accepted, parking, and limited wheelchair access to lower floors.

A more economical alternative is the **Motel San Felipe**, a few blocks uphill on Av. L. Cárdenas 321, Pátzcuaro, Michoacán 61600, tel. (434) 212-98. Behind the roadside restaurant, 11 motel-style cottages surround a patio parking lot. Clean, comfortable, and carpeted, the units have colonial-style wrought-iron fixtures and brick fireplaces. The rooms rent for about $25 s, $32 d, and $38 for three or more; credit cards accepted, limited wheelchair access.

RV and Camping Park

Visitors who enjoy staying near the lakeside opt for **Trailer Park El Pozo** ("The Well"). Watch for the sign on the highway about a mile in the Morelia direction past the Av. Lázaro Cárdenas intersection. The 20 spaces spread downhill in a grassy park about a quarter mile from the reed-lined lakeshore. The friendly, family-run park provides all hookups, a picnic table with each space, some shade, toilets, and hot showers for about $10 per day (longer-stay discounts available). Tenters are also welcome, at about $3 per person. While reservations are not necessary year-round, it's best to call or write ahead of time for weekends and holidays: Trailer Park El Pozo, P.O. Box 142, Pátzcuaro, Michoacán 61600, tel. (434) 209-37.

FOOD

Breakfast and Snacks

A good spot to start out the day is **Restaurant Dany** at Mendoza 30 (the street connecting the west sides of Plazas Don Vasco and Bocanegra). Although they serve good food 0800-2200 daily, the American breakfast ($4) in their shiny upstairs section tastes especially good on a crisp Pátzcuaro morning.

For quick cooling energy during the heat of the day, try the no-name *nevería* (ice-cream stand) in front of the Hotel Los Escudos on Plaza Vasco de Quiroga. Their fruit ices are so popular you may have to wedge your way in. Just

point to what you want. Eat without worry, their offerings are pure; they depend on repeat customers. Open daily 0900-1800.

For a hot pick-me-up, try a cup of freshly ground Michoacán mountain-grown coffee at **Cafe Bote Fumeira** ("Smoking Boat") beneath Portal Aldama at the adjacent corner of the plaza. They also sell fresh-roasted beans for around $4 per pound ($8 per kilo). Open daily 0900-1400 and 1600-2000.

At night at the market corner of Plaza Bocanegra, a very professional lineup of taco stands steams with hearty offerings. Among the best is **Tacos Rápido,** run by Jorge, whose fingers fly as if they could wrap a thousand *chorizo* (spiced sausage), *res* (roast beef), *pastor* (roast pork or beef), and *lengua* (tongue) tacos a night.

For a late snack, go to **Tortisam** at Mendoza 12, tel. (434) 224-06, between Plazas Vasco de Quiroga and Bocanegra. Juicy hamburgers, hot dogs, *tortas,* french fries, and malts plus lots of friendly cheer are the secret to the success of the paradoxically young proprietor Viejo ("Old") Sam. Open daily 1000-2300.

For tasty late-night Mexican-style fare, try the popular **Cenaduría Equipales,** open daily 1700 to about midnight on the north side of Plaza Don Vasco, next to Banco Serfin.

Restaurants

Pátzcuaro has a sprinkling of good, moderately priced restaurants, nearly all on or near the Plaza Vasco de Quiroga.

At the **Cafetería Los Escudos** in the Hotel Los Escudos, northwest plaza corner of Mendoza and Ibarra, tel. (434) 201-38, conversation and cafe espresso sometimes seem as important as the menu. A broad list of regional and international favorites (try the taco soup) keeps customers satisfied. Open daily 0800-2130; credit cards accepted.

Whitefish is the house specialty at the **Restaurant El Patio,** at 19 Plaza Vasco de Quiroga, near the Hotel Posada San Rafael, tel. (434) 204-84, where soft music, muted lighting, and tasteful handicraft decor set the tone. Despite the mostly tourist clientele, many are longtime repeat customers (who know to start out with the excellent Tarascan soup). Open daily 0800-2130; credit cards accepted.

Romantics congregate at the restaurant of the **Hotel Posada de la Basílica** on Arciga, opposite the basilica, tel. (434) 211-08. They enjoy Pátzcuaro's famous whitefish and wine (ask for Cetto label sauvignon blanc) while feasting on the gleaming view of the old city, the lake, and the mountains beyond. Open daily 0800-2100; credit cards not accepted.

ENTERTAINMENT AND EVENTS

Pátzcuaro's one unmissable entertainment is the famous **Viejecitos** ("Little Old Men") dance. Said to have been invented during the early colonial period to mock the conquerors, a troupe of men put on wrinkle-faced masks and *campesino*-style dress and dance as if every stumbling step were about to send them to the hospital. Hotels, such as the Don Vasco (tel. 434-202 27), often stage regular dance shows in season.

Local people celebrate a number of fiestas and holidays. During the first two weeks in December, dance, music, processions, fireworks, and foodstalls fill Pátzcuaro streets and plazas in celebration of the **Fiesta de La Virgen de La Salud,** the city's patron saint.

Later, Semana Santa festivities climax on **Viernes Santa** (Good Friday), when townsfolk carry big Christ-figures through the packed downtown streets.

Finally, on 2 November, Pátzcuaro (and many neighboring towns) stage Mexico's most spectacular **Día de los Muertos** ("Day of the Dead") festivals. Crowds converge on the *panteón* (cemetery) on the old Morelia road with loads of food offerings and decorations for the graves of their beloved deceased. To get there take a taxi a half mile northeast of the basilica. They keep the candles burning next to the tombstones all night, illuminating their ancestors' return path to feast with the family once again.

The big movie house and theater **Cine Emperador** screens Mexican and American movies and stages occasional concerts and cultural events. Drop by (north end of Plaza Bocanegra, next to the Hotel Fiesta Plaza) and check the schedule.

SHOPPING

The Valley of Pátzcuaro is rich in handicrafts. Visitors need only travel to the **Mercado** (which extends a long block, beginning at the Plaza Bocanegra) to find good examples. Copperware from the village of Santa Clara de Cobre and locally crafted woolens are among the most plentiful and bargainable items.

In the fish stalls, you'll see mounds of Pátzcuaro whitefish (at about $2 a kilo); and farther on, among the piles of produce, unusual fruits from around Uruapán (such as the brown, sour-tasting *mamey* and the greenish-pink *anona,* which is creamy like a Southeast Asian custard apple).

For a uniquely rich selection of fine handicrafts, don't miss the former convent, **Casa de Once Patios,** one block east and one block south of the Plaza Don Vasco de Quiroga. In a dozen separate shops, artisans paint, carve,

anona fruits (foreground) for sale at the Pátzcuaro market

BRUCE WHIPPERMAN

weave, and polish excellent work for sale. In the *local de paja* (straw shop), for example, workers fashion Christmas decorations—candy canes, trees, wreaths, bells—entirely of strands of colored straw. Nearby, the *local de cobre* (copper shop) displays shelves and cases of brilliant copper and silver plates, vases, cups, and jewelry.

Although other *locales* craft and display fine furniture, textiles, papier-mâché, and masks, the climax comes in the *local de laca,* with lacquerware so fine it rivals the rich cloisonnés of Europe and Asia. In the especially fine shop of the brothers Alozo Meza, artisans finish wares in a myriad of animal, human, and floral motifs in sizes and complexities to fit every pocketbook. Open daily 0900-1400 and 1600-1900.

On Friday the small plaza, **Jardín Revolución,** blooms with ceramics from all over Michoacán (corner Ponce de Leon and Tena, one block west of the Plaza Don Vasco de Quiroga).

Grocery Store and Camera Shop

The **Super Centro** *abarrotería* grocery-liquor at Plaza Vasco de Quiroga 120, near the Hotel Posada San Rafael, tel. (434) 208-47, conveniently stocks a little bit of everything; open daily 0830-1500 and 1700-2030.

The local Kodak dealer is at Plaza Bocanegra 21, tel. (434) 216-45, on the plaza's south side. Besides a fair stock of film and photo equipment, they offer 24-hour color, three-day transparency, and five-day black-and-white photofinishing services. Open Mon.-Fri. 0900-1400 and 1600-2000, and Sat.-Sun. 0900-1400.

SERVICES AND INFORMATION

Although the **Michoacán Tourism Office,** tel. (434) 212-14, is supposed to supply maps and answer questions, your hotel desk clerk will probably be more

Pátzcuaro
area code
is 434

helpful. If you ask to see the *jefe* (chief, say HAY-fay), however, you may get a satisfactory response. They're located at Av. Ibarra 2, corner Av. Mendoza, on the Plaza Don Vasco de Quiroga; open Mon.-Sat. 0900-1400 and 1600-1900.

Banamex changes U.S. traveler's checks and cash Mon.-Fri. 0900-1300 at their Plaza Bocanegra (Portal Juárez, west side) headquarters, tel. (434) 215-50 or 210-31.

The **Clínica San Marcos,** tel. (434) 219-98, provides 24-hour emergency medical service (gynecologist, surgeon, pediatrician, and internist on call). Their pharmacy (the El Portal, open 1000-1400 and 1700-2100, tel. (434) 204-13) and adjacent hospital are located right on the Plaza Don Vasco de Quiroga at Portal Hidalgo 76, three doors from the Hotel Los Escudos.

For **police** emergencies, contact the *preventiva,* tel. (434) 200-04 or 218-89, in the Presidencia Municipal, next to the Clínica San Marcos.

The *correo,* tel. (434) 201-28, is open Mon.-Fri. 0800-1900, Saturday 0800-1300, at Obregón 13, one block north of the Plaza Bocanegra.

For computer-assisted *larga distancia* and public fax, go to Computel, on the Plaza Bocanegra next to the Cine Emperador movie house.

Among the very few sources of English-language news is the newsstand on the Plaza Bocanegra (at Portal Juárez 32, next door to Banamex) which, around noon, gets the *News* from Mexico City and sometimes stocks *Time* magazine.

GETTING THERE AND AWAY

By Car or RV

North-south National Highways 14 and 37 connect Pátzcuaro with the Pacific coast Hwy. 200 at Playa Azul. The 192-mile (307-km) scenic but winding and sometimes potholed route requires around seven hours of careful driving. Fill with gasoline, especially unleaded. Magna Sin is available only at Uruapán, Nueva Italia, and Arteaga en route.

In the opposite direction, National Hwy. 120 will connect you with the state capital Morelia (in an hour and a half); from there Hwy. 15 will set you to Mexico City in about eight hours.

By Bus

From the south-side **Central Camionera,** a number of lines, such as first-class Ruta de

Paraíso and Tres Estrellas de Oro and second-class Galeana, connect with the Pacific coast destinations of La Mira (five miles from Playa Azul) and Lázaro Cárdenas, where buses connect farther to Zihuatanejo and Manzanillo. Tres Estrellas de Oro and Autobuses del Occidente connect to north and east destinations of Guadalajara, Morelia, and Mexico City.

By Train

Pátzcuaro lies on the rail line connecting Lázaro Cárdenas on the Pacific coast to Morelia. A northbound first- and second-class coach train departs Lázaro Cárdenas daily around 0700, arriving at Pátzcuaro about 1600 and Morelia about an hour and a half later. The opposite train departs Morelia daily around 0600, arriving at the Pátzcuaro rail station around 0700. It continues (via Uruapán and Nueva Italia), arriving at Lázaro Cárdenas about 1800. Verify schedules and buy tickets at the station, tel. (434) 208-03, just off the highway at the north side of town. Get there by *colectivo* or taxi from the plazas.

Train connections may be made in Morelia for Mexico City, Guadalajara, Manzanillo, Mazatlán, and the U.S. border.

LÁZARO CÁRDENAS AND ALONG THE ROAD TO IXTAPA-ZIHUATANEJO

The new industrial port city of Lázaro Cárdenas, named for the Michoacán-born president famous for expropriating American oil companies, is Michoacán's Pacific transportation and service hub. Most of its businesses, including banks, bus stations, hotels, and restaurants, are clustered along north-south Av. Lázaro Cárdenas, the main ingress boulevard, about three miles from its Hwy. 200 intersection.

SERVICES

Money Exchange

Banamex, at Av. L. Cárdenas 1646, tel. (753) 220-20, exchanges U.S. dollar traveler's checks Mon.-Fri. 0900-1200. If they're too crowded, try **Bancomer** on the diagonally opposite corner (of Corregidora) or **Banco Promex,** on the same side, a block farther south (corner of Constitución de 1814). After hours, try the **Casa de Cambio Las Truchas,** a few doors south of Banamex, which changes both U.S. and Canadian money Mon.-Fri. 0900-1400 and 1600-1900, Saturday 0900-1400 tel. (753) 244-37.

Hospitals and Communications

The **General Hospital** is at Comonfort 202, tel. (753) 226-42, on the boulevard into town,

left side, just before the big right side traffic circle. The private hospital, Clínica Santa Lucia, is at Melchor Ocampo 71 (about five blocks south of Banamex, left on Ocampo, tel. (753) 213-70.

The **correo,** tel. (753) 205-47, is on Av. N. Bravo, in the middle of the big town plaza; look for it on the left as you head into town, two long blocks after the big right-side traffic circle. **Telecomunicaciones** (telegraph, money orders, telephone, and public fax), tel. (753) 202-73, is next door to the post office. **Computel,** the computer-assisted long-distance telephone and fax agency, operates Mon.-Sat. 0700-2400, Sunday 0700-2200, tel./fax (753) 248-06, next to the Galeana bus terminal, at 1810 L. Cárdenas.

Bus Terminals

A pair of long-distance bus terminals serves Lázaro Cárdenas. From the Galeana terminal at 1810 Av. L. Cárdenas, tel. (753) 202-62, Galeana and Ruta Paraíso first- and second-class local-departure buses connect daily north with Uruapán, Pátzcuaro, and Morelia. Additionally, many more first- and second-class departures connect northwest with Manzanillo and intermediate points.

The Estrella Blanca-Tres Estrellas de Oro terminal is at F. Madero 15, on the street behind the Galeana terminal, one block from Av. L. Cárdenas. From there, first-class Tres Estrellas de Oro (tel. 82-117) local departures connect north with Michoacán destinations of Uruapán,

Lázaro Cárdenas
area code is 753

Pátzcuaro, and Morelia. Other buses stop, en route southeast to Zihuatanejo-Acapulco and northwest to Manzanillo, Puerto Vallarta, Mazatlán, and the U.S. border. Similarly, first-class Autotransportes Cuauhtémoc—a subsidiary of Estrella Blanca, tel. (753) 211-71—local departures connect southeast with Zihuatanejo, Acapulco, and intermediate points.

Trains

A combined first- and second-class coach train departs Lázaro Cárdenas daily at noon, northbound for Uruapán, Pátzcuaro, and Morelia, arriving in Pátzcuaro at 2100. The opposite train departs Morelia at around 0600, Pátzcuaro at around 0730, arriving in Lázaro around 1800. Call the station, tel. (753) 228-36, for information, although a travel agent (see below) may be more helpful. Since you're saving so much money by train (tickets are only around $10 first class to Pátzcuaro), have a taxi take you to the train station, which is on the outskirts of town. At Morelia, train connections to Mexico City and Guadalajara (and thence Manzanillo, Mazatlán and the U.S. border) are available.

Travel Agents

Since the train station is out of the downtown area, they've commissioned city-center **Chinameca Viajes,** Javier Mina 278, tel. (753) 22-117, to sell train tickets. Another good and conveniently located travel agency (and possible information source) is **Viajes Reyna Pio,** on L. Cárdenas, right across from the Galeana bus station and Banamex, tel. (753) 238-68.

ALONG THE ROAD TO IXTAPA-ZIHUATANEJO

It's hard to remain unimpressed as you cross over the **Río Balsas Dam** for the first time. The dam, which marks the Michoacán-Guerrero state boundary, is huge and hulking. Behind it a grand lake mirrors the Sierra Madre mountains, while on the opposite side, Mexico's greatest river spurts from the turbine exit gates hundreds of feet below. The river's power, converted into enough electric energy for millions of light bulbs, courses up great looping transmission wires, while the spent river meanders toward the sea.

On the Road

The middle of the dam (Hwy. 200, Km 103 north of Zihuatanejo) is a good point at which to reset your odometer. Your odometer and the roadside kilometer markers may be your best way to find the several little hideaways between the Río Balsas and Zihuatanejo.

As for bus travelers, having gotten aboard at La Mira or Lázaro Cárdenas (or Zihuatanejo, if traveling northwest), ask the driver to let you off at your destination.

Playas Atracadero and Los Llanos

Both of these little havens are especially for shellfish lovers who yearn for their fill of swimming, surfing, splashing, fishing, and beachcombing. Atracadero is the less frequented of the two. The several beach *palapa* restaurants operate only seasonally. Crowds must gather sometimes, however: one of the *palapas* has a five-foot pile of oyster shells! Another thing is certain; the local folks supplement their diet with plenty of iguanas, judging from the ones boys offer for sale along the road.

The beach sand itself is soft and gray. The waves, with good surfing breaks, roll in from far out, arriving gently on the beach. Boat launching would be easy during calm weather. Little undertow menaces casual swimmers, bodysurfers, or boogie-boarders. Lots of driftwood and shells—clams, limpets, snails—cover the sand. The beach extends for at least three miles past palm groves on the northwest. A fenced grove and house with pigs occupies the southeast. Although tenters could find camping space, RVers would be hard-pressed. Bring your own food and water.

To get to Playa Atracadero, turn off at Km 64, 24 miles (39 km) from the Río Balsas and 40 miles from Zihuatanejo. Bear left all the way, 1.7 miles (2.8 km) to the beach.

At Los Llanos ("The Plains"), the day climaxes when the oyster divers bring in their catches around 1430. They combine their catches into big 100-pound (45-kg) bags, which wait for trucks to take them as far as Mazatlán. On the spot, one dozen in a cocktail go for $3-4. On the other hand, if you prefer to shuck your own oysters, you can buy them unshucked $2 a dozen. The divers also bring in octopus and lobsters, which, broiled and served with fixings, sell for about $7 for a one-pounder. You can also do your own fishing via rentable (offer $15/hour) beach *pangas,* which go out daily and routinely return with three or four 20-pound fish.

The beach itself is level far out, with rolling waves fine for surfing, swimming, boogie-boarding, and bodysurfing. There's enough driftwood and shells for a season of beachcombing. The beach spreads for hundreds of yards on both sides of the road's end. Permanent *palapa* restaurants supply shade, drinks, and seafood. Beach camping is common and popular, especially during the Christmas and Easter holidays. Other times, you may have the whole place to yourself. A north-end grove provides shade for camping. Bring your own food and water, although the small store at the highway village may help add to your supplies.

To get to Los Llanos, at Km 40, 39 miles (63 km) southeast of the Río Balsas and 25 miles northwest of Zihuatanejo, turn off at the village of Los Llanos. (Notice the pharmacy at the highway and the Conasupo store about one-tenth of a mile farther on.) At two-tenths of a mile, turn right, at the church, just before the basketball court, and continue another 2.5 miles (4 km) to the beach.

Playa Majagua and Playa Troncones

This pair of palmy nooks basks on a pristine coastal stretch, backed by a jungly, wildlife-rich hinterland.

Playa Majagua, at Km 32.5 north of Zihuatanejo, is a fishing hamlet with palmy shade, stick-and-wattle houses, and about half a dozen hammock-equipped *ramadas* scattered along the beach. One of the *ramadas* is competently run by a friendly family who call it Restaurant Los Angeles. Camping is safe and welcomed by local folks (although space, especially for RVs, is limited). Water is available, but campers should bring purifying tablets and food.

The beach curves from a rocky south-end point, past a lagoon of Río Lagunillas, and stretches miles northwest past shoreline palm and acacia forest. The sand is soft and dark yellow, with mounds of driftwood but few shells. Waves break far out and roll in gradually, with little undertow. Fine left-breaking surf rises off the southern point. Boats are easily launchable

(several *pangas*) lie along the beach) during normal good weather.

To get to Playa Majagua, turn off at the sign just south of the Río Lagunillas bridge, at Km 32.5, 44 miles (70 km) southeast of Río Balsas, 20 miles northwest of Zihuatanejo. Continue 2.9 miles to the beach.

Nearby Playa Troncones has a little bit of everything: shady seafood *ramadas* on the left as you enter from the highway; next, a half-mile beach with several spots to pull off and camp. At the southern end, a lagoon spreads beside a pristine coral-sand beach, which curls around a low hill toward a picture-perfect little bay. A small store can supplement your food. Water is available.

But that's just the beginning. Troncones has both **El Burro Borracho** and **Casa de la Tortuga** (formerly Dewey's Dew-Drop Inn). Friendly owners Dewey and Karolyn McMillin began pioneering their small retreat in the late 1980s. Now, Casa de Tortuga guests enjoy a clean room with bath and breakfast in their modern beach house, a restful patio with plenty of shade, quiet, and opportunities for delighting in the outdoors. Guests swim, surf, bodysurf, and boogie board the waves, jog and beachcomb along the sand, and hike the adjacent jungle hinterland. Wildlife—fish, whales, dolphins, and swarms of herons, boobies, egrets, and cormorants—abound in the ocean and in nearby lagoons.

Their six inside rooms and a separate guest cottage rent for about $25 s and $35 d (shared bath), $40 s and $50 d (with bath); all with breakfast. The whole layout (sleeping a dozen or more) rents for about $200 per day, $1200 per week. Discounts are negotiable for longer stays. A kitchen is available for guest use. No children under 12, unless you rent the whole place. Write or fax them for reservations (mandatory during the winter) at P.O. Box 37, Zihuatanejo, Guerrero 40880, fax (755) 432-96. If business is slow, they close June, July, and August.

Dewey manages the restaurant at **El Burro Borracho,** ("The Drunken Burro"), on the heavenly beachfront, a couple of miles south. Besides the shady ocean-view *palapa* restaurant, a favorite of both in-house guests and Zihuatanejo vacationers, Burro Borracho offer six "simply elegant" airy rooms, each with bath, in three stone duplex beachfront cottages. Extras include king-size bed, rustic-chic native decor, and fans. Cooking facilities are also available. Sports and activities include all those listed above, plus kayaks, for use of guests. Winter-season rentals run about $40 d, $50 d, including continental breakfast. Facilities also include five (shadeless) **RV spaces,** with all hookups, adjacent to the cottages for $8-12 per night. Discounts are available for long-term and low season rentals. Write/fax for reservations (winter-mandatory) at P.O. Box 277, Zihuatanejo, Guerrero 40880, fax (755) 432-96.

Get to Playa Troncones by following the (signed southbound) paved turnoff around Km 30, about 42 miles (73 km) south of the Río Balsas (about 18 miles north of Zihuatanejo). Continue 2.2 miles to the Playa Troncones beachfront *ramadas*. Turn left for the camping spots, the main part of the beach and El Burro Borracho; turn right for Casa de la Tortuga, which is about a mile farther along a beachfront forest road. From there, the car-negotiable dry-weather track continues about a mile and a half along the beach to Playa Majagua.

*Nayarit ceramic,
old man singing*

BOB RACE

IXTAPA-ZIHUATANEJO AND SOUTH TO ACAPULCO

IXTAPA-ZIHUATANEJO

The Costa Grande, the "Big Coast," of the state of Guerrero angles 200 miles southeast from the Río Balsas to Acapulco. Before the highway came in the 1960s, this was a land of corn, coconuts, fish, and fruit. Although it's still that, the road added a new ingredient: a trickle of visitors seeking paradise in Zihuatanejo, a sleepy fishing village on a beautiful bay.

During the 1970s, planners decided to create the best of all possible worlds by building Ixtapa, a luxurious resort on a pearly beach five miles away. Now, Ixtapa-Zihuatanejo's clear, rich waters, forested eco-sanctuaries, pearly little beaches, pristine offshore islets, good food, comfortable hotels, and friendly local folks offer visitors the ingredients for memorable stays any time of the year.

HISTORY

Zihuatanejo's azure waters attracted attention long before Columbus. Local legend says the Tarascans (whose emperor ruled from now-Michoacán and who was never subject to the Aztecs) built a royal bathing resort on Las Gatas Beach in Zihuatanejo Bay.

That was sometime around 1400. People had been attracted to the Costa Grande much earlier than that: Archaic pottery has been uncovered at a number of sites, left by artists who lived and died as long as five thousand years ago. Later, around 1000 B.C., the Olmecs (famous for their monumental Gulf coast sculptures) came and left their unmistakable stamp on local ceramics. After them came waves of set-

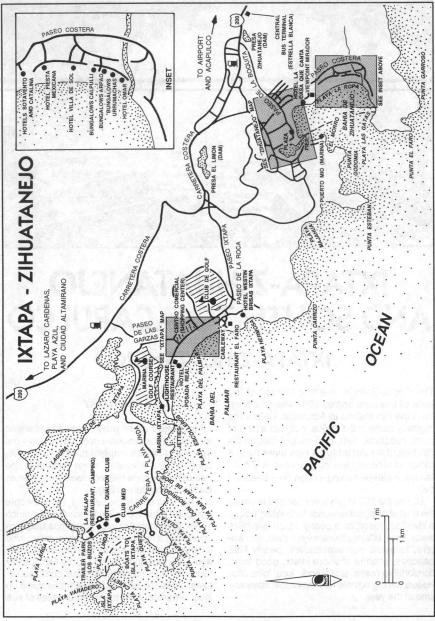

IXTAPA - ZIHUATANEJO

TO LAZARO CARDENAS,
PLAYA AZUL,
AND CIUDAD ALTAMIRANO

200

CARRETERA COSTERA

CARRETERA COSTERA

TO AIRPORT
AND ACAPULCO

200

PRESA
ZIHUATANEJO
(DAM)

CENTRAL
BUS TERMINAL
(ESTRELLA BLANCA)

PRESA EL LIMON (DAM)

PRESA EL LIMON (DAM)

PASEO COSTERA

SEE INSET ABOVE

PLAYA LA ROPA

HOTEL LA
CASA QUE CANTA

VIEWPOINT MIRADOR

BAHIA DE
ZIHUATANEJO

SEE "ZIHUATANEJO" MAP

PLAZA

PIER

PUERTO MIO (MARINA)

EL MORRO

PUNTA
GODOMA

PLAYA LAS GATAS

PUNTA EL FARO

PUNTA GARROSO

PLAYA ESTEBAN

PLAYA
MAJAHUA

PUNTA ESTEBAN

LAGUNA IXTAPA

PASEO DE LAS GARZAS

SEE "IXTAPA" MAP

PASEO IXTAPA

PASEO DE LA ROCA

PASEO IXTAPA

CLUB DE GOLF

CENTRO COMERCIAL
(SHOPPING CENTER)

HOTEL WESTIN
BRISAS IXTAPA

MARINA IXTAPA

MARINA IXTAPA
(GOLF COURSE)

LIGHTHOUSE
RESTAURANT

HOTEL
POSADA REAL

PLAYA DEL PALMAR

PLAYA ESCOLLERA

JETTIES

RESTAURANT EL FARO

CABLEWAY

PLAYA HERMOSA

BAHIA DEL
PALMAR

PUNTA CARRIZO

PACIFIC OCEAN

CARRETERA A PLAYA LINDA

LA PALAPA
(RESTAURANT, CAMPING)

LOS BUZOS

TRAILER PARK

HOTEL QUALTON CLUB

CLUB MED

PLAYA LARGA

PLAYA VARADERO

ISLA IXTAPA

BOATS TO
ISLA IXTAPA

PLAYA LINDA

PLAYA QUIETA

CABLE

PLAYA CUATA

PLAYA DON RODRIGO

SAN JUAN DE DIOS

INSET

PASEO COSTERA

HOTELS SOTAVENTO
AND CATALINA

HOTEL FIESTA
MEXICANA

HOTEL VILLA DE SOL

BUNGALOWS CALPULLI

BUNGALOWS ARPAO

BUNGALOWS
URRUMICHAS

HOTEL OMAR

© MOON PUBLICATIONS, INC.

0   1 mi

0   1 km

tlers, including the barbaric Chichimecs ("Drinkers of Blood"), the agricultural Cuitlatecs, and an early invasion of Aztecs, perhaps wandering in search of their eventual homeland in the Valley of Mexico.

None of those peoples were a match for the armies of Tarascan emperor Hiripan, who during the late 1300s invaded the Costa Grande and established a coastal province, headquartered at Coyuca, between Zihuatanejo and present-day Acapulco.

Three generations later the star of the Aztec emperor Tízoc was rising over Mexico. His armies invaded the Costa Grande and pushed out the Tarascans. By 1500 the Aztecs ruled the coast from their provincial own capital at Zihuatlán, the "Place of Women" (so named because the local society was matriarchal), not far from present-day Zihuatanejo.

Conquest and Colonization

Scarcely months after Hernán Cortés conquered the Aztecs, he sent an expedition to explore the "Southern Sea" and hopefully find a route to China. In November 1522 Captain Juan Alvarez Chico set sail with boats built in Tehuantepec and reconnoitered the coast to the Río Balsas, planting crosses on beaches, claiming the land for Spain.

An oft-told Costa Grande story says when Chico was exploring at Zihuatanejo, he looked down on the round tranquil little bay, lined with flocks of seabirds and women washing clothes in a freshwater spring. His Aztec guide told him that this place was called Zihuatlán. When Chico described the little bay, Cortés tacked *"nejo"* (little) on to the name, giving birth to "Zihuatlanejo," which later got shortened to the present Zihuatanejo.

Cortés, encouraged by the samples of pearls and gold that Chico brought back, sent out other expeditions. Villafuerte established a shipyard and town at Zacatula at the mouth of the Balsas in 1523. Then, in 1527, Captain Alvaro Saavedra Cerón set sail for China from Zihuatanejo Bay. Not knowing any details of the Pacific Ocean and its winds and currents, it is not surprising that (although he did arrive in the Philippines) Saavedra Cerón failed to return to Mexico. A number of additional attempts would be necessary until finally, in 1565, Father André de Ur-

daneta coaxed the Pacific to give up its secret and returned, in triumph, from the Orient.

hieroglyph of Zihuatanejo ("the Place of Women")

By royal decree, Acapulco became Spain's sole port of entry on the Pacific in 1561. Except for an occasional galleon (or pirate caravel) stopping for repairs or supplies, all other Pacific ports, including Zihuatanejo, slumbered for hundreds of years.

Zihuatanejo was one of the last to wake up. The occasion was the arrival of the highway from Acapulco during the 1960s. No longer isolated, Zihuatanejo's headland-rimmed aqua bay attracted a small colony of paradise-seekers.

Zihuatanejo had grown to perhaps 5,000 souls by the late '70s when FONATUR, the government tourism-development agency, decided Ixtapa ("White Place," for its brilliant sand beach five miles north of Zihuatanejo) was a perfect site for a world-class resort. Investors agreed, and the infrastructure—drainage, roads, and utilities—was installed. The jetport was built, hotels rose, and by the '90s the distinct but inseparable twin resorts of Ixtapa and Zihuatanejo (combined pop. 70,000) were attracting a steady stream of Mexican and foreign vacationers.

SIGHTS

Getting Oriented

Both Ixtapa and Zihuatanejo are small and easy to know. Zihuatanejo's little **Plaza de Armas** town square overlooks the main beach, **Playa Municipal,** just beyond the palm-lined pedestrian walkway, **Paseo del Pescador.** From the plaza looking out toward the bay, you are facing south. On your right is the *muelle* (moo-AY-yay), and on the left, the bay curves along the outer beaches Playas la Ropa, la Madera, and finally las Gatas beneath the far Punta El Faro ("Lighthouse Point").

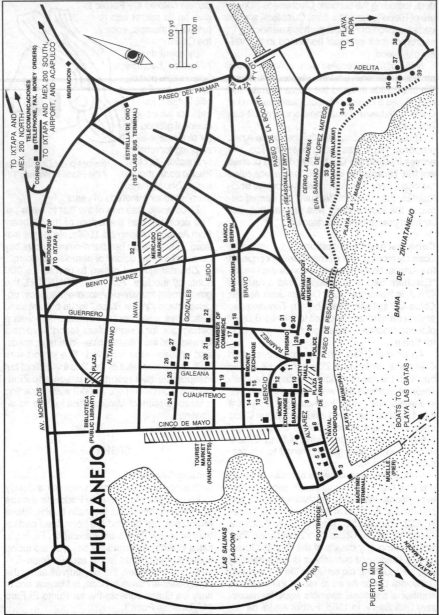

ZIHUATANEJO

1. Hotel Tres Marías
2. Equipos y Embarcaciones (sporting goods)
3. Sociedad Cooperativa Teniente Azueta (sportfishing)
4. Sirena Gorda
5. Servicios Sociedad Cooperativa Juárez (sportfishing)
6. Servicios Turísticos Aquaticos (sportfishing)
7. Hotel Raoul Tres Marías
8. Casa Elvira
9. Casa Marina
10. Zihuatanejo Scuba Center
11. Librería Byblos (books)
12. Super El Dorado
13. Deli Cafe
14. Cine Paraíso
15. Alberto's Jewelry
16. Galería Maya
17. Restaurant El Picolo
18. Deportes Naútico (sporting goods)
19. Cafetería Nova Zelandia
20. Natural Foods
21. Restaurant Los Braseros
22. Restaurante Tamales y Atoles "Any"
23. Lavandería Aldam (laundry)
24. Super Foto La Palma
25. Laundry Super Clean
26. bakery
27. Hotel Imelda
28. Cerámicas Tonalá
29. Hotel Avila
30. Hotel Susy
31. Posada Citlali
32. Super El Globo
33. Bungalows Pacífico
34. Bungalows Allec
35. Bungalows Ley
36. Hotel Palacio
37. Hotel Villas Miramar
38. Bungalows Milagro
39. Hotel Irma

Turning around and facing inland (north), you see a narrow waterfront street, **Juan Alvarez,** running parallel to the beach past the plaza, crossing the main business streets (actually tranquil shady lanes) **Cuauhtémoc** and **Guerrero.** A third street, busy **Benito Juárez,** one block to the right of Guererro, conducts traffic several blocks to and from the shore, passing the market and intersecting a second main street, Av. Morelos. There, a right turn will soon bring you to Hwy. 200 and, within five miles, Ixtapa.

Nearly everything in Ixtapa lies along one three-mile-long boulevard, **Paseo Ixtapa,** which parallels the main beach, hotel-lined **Playa del Palmar.** Heading westerly from Zihuatanejo, you first pass the Club de Golf Ixtapa, then the big Sheraton on the left, followed by a succession of other high-rise hotels. Soon come the **Zona Comercial** shopping malls and the **Paseo de las Garzas** corner on the right. Turn right for either Hwy. 200 or the outer beaches, Playas Cuata, Quieta, Linda, and Larga. At Playa Quieta, boats continue to heavenly Isla Ixtapa.

If, instead, you had continued straight ahead back at the Paseo de las Garzas corner, you would have soon reached the **Marina Ixtapa** condo development and yacht harbor.

Getting Around

In downtown Zihuatanejo, shops and restaurants are within a few blocks' walking distance of the plaza. For the beaches, walk along the beachfront *andador* (walkway) to La Madera, take a taxi ($2) to La Ropa, and a launch from the pier ($2) to Las Gatas. For Ixtapa, ride one of the very frequent microbuses, which leave from the east corner of Juárez and Morelos. A taxi ride between Ixtapa and Zihuatanejo runs about $4. In Ixtapa itself, walk, or ride the microbuses that run along Paseo Ixtapa. For the Ixtapa outer beaches, take a taxi, about $4.

Zihuatanejo Museum

The small **Museo Arqueología de la Costa Grande** on the beachfront side of Alvarez, near the Guerrero corner, details the archaeological history of the Costa Grande. Maps, drawings, small dioramas, and artifacts—many donated by local resident and innkeeper Anita Rellstab—illustrate the development of local cultures, from

A rental Windsurfer rests on Zihuatanejo Bay's Playa la Ropa.

BRUCE WHIPPERMAN

early hunting and gathering to agriculture and, finally, urbanization by the time of the conquest. Open Tues.-Sun. 0900-2000).

Beaches around Zihuatanejo Bay

Ringed by forested hills, edged by steep cliffs, and laced by rocky shoals, Zihuatanejo Bay would be beautiful even without its beaches. Five of them line the bay. On the west side is narrow, tranquil Playa El Almacén ("Warehouse Beach"), mostly good for fishing from its nearby rocks. Moving past the pier toward town comes the colorful, bustling **Playa Municipal.** Its sheltered waters are fine for wading, swimming, and boat launching (which fishermen, their motors buzzing, regularly do) near the pier end.

For a maximum of sun and serenity, walk away from the pier along Playa Municipal past the usually dry creek outlet where a concrete *andador* winds a hundred yards along the beachfront rocks that mark the beginning of **Playa La Madera.** If you prefer, you can also hire a taxi to take you to Playa la Madera, about $2.

Playa la Madera ("Wood Beach"), once a loading point for lumber, stretches about 300 yards, decorated with rocky nooks and outcroppings, and backed by the lush hotel-dotted hill, **Cerro La Madera.** The beach sand is fine and gray-white. Swells enter the facing bay entrance, breaking suddenly in two- or three-foot waves, which roll in gently and recede with little undertow. Madera's calm waters are good for

child's play and easy swimming. Bring your mask and snorkel for glimpses of fish in the clear waters. Beachside restaurant-bars, La Bocana and La Madera, and the Hotel Irma, above the far east end, serve drinks and snacks.

Zihuatanejo Bay's favorite resort beach is **Playa La Ropa** ("Clothes Beach"), a mile-long crescent of yellow-white sand washed by oft-gentle billows. The beach got its name centuries ago from the apparel that once floated in from an offshore Chinese wreck. From the bay's best *mirador* (viewpoint) at the summit of **Paseo Costera,** the La Ropa approach road, the beach sand, relentlessly scooped and redeposited by the waves, appears as an endless line of half-moons.

On the 100-foot-wide beach, vacationers bask in the sun, jet-ski beetles buzz beyond the breakers, rental sailboats ply the waves, and windsurf outfits recline on the sand. The waves, generally too gentle and and quick-breaking for surf sports, break close-in and recede with little undertow. Joggers come out mornings and evenings. Restaurants at the several beachfront hotels provide food and drinks.

Isolated **Playa Las Gatas,** ("Cat Beach"), reachable on foot or easily by launch from the town pier, lies sheltered beneath the south-end Punta El Faro headland. Once a walled-in royal Tarascan bathing pool, the beach got its name from a species of locally common, small, whiskered nurse sharks. Generally calm and quiet, often with super-clear offshore waters,

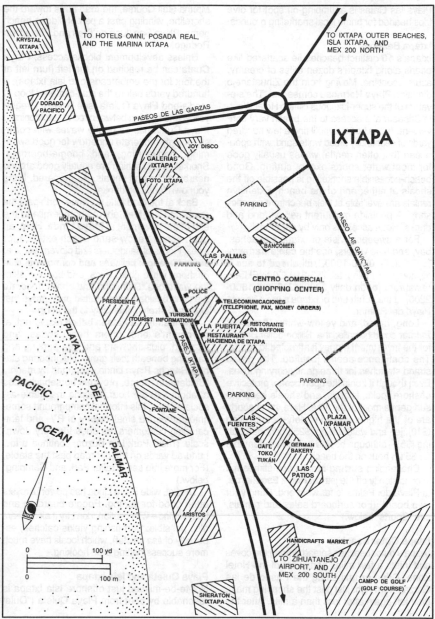

IXTAPA

TO HOTELS OMNI, POSADA REAL,
AND THE MARINA IXTAPA

TO IXTAPA OUTER BEACHES,
ISLA IXTAPA, AND
MEX 200 NORTH

KRYSTAL
IXTAPA

DORADO
PACIFICO

PASEOS DE LAS GARZAS

JOY DISCO

GALERIAS
IXTAPA

FOTO IXTAPA

HOLIDAY INN

PARKING

BANCOMER

LAS PALMAS

PARKING

PASEO LAS GAVIOTAS

PRESIDENTE

POLICE

CENTRO COMERCIAL
(SHOPPING CENTER)

TELECOMUNICACIONES
(TELEPHONE, FAX, MONEY ORDERS)

TURISMO
(TOURIST INFORMATION)

RISTORANTE
DA BAFFONE

LA PUERTA

RESTAURANT
HACIENDA DE IXTAPA

PLAYA DEL PALMAR

PACIFIC

OCEAN

FONTANE

PARKING

PARKING

PLAZA
IXPAMAR

LAS
FUENTES

CAFÉ
TOKO
TUKÁN

GERMAN
BAKERY

LAS PATIOS

ARISTOS

HANDICRAFTS MARKET

0   100 yd

0   100 m

© MOON PUBLICATIONS, INC.

SHERATON
IXTAPA

TO ZIHUATANEJO
AIRPORT, AND
MEX 200 SOUTH

CAMPO DE GOLF
(GOLF COURSE)

Playa las Gatas is a jumping-off spot for dive trips headed for prime local snorkeling grounds.

Ixtapa Beaches

Ixtapa's 10 distinct beaches lie scattered like pearls along Ixtapa's dozen miles of creamy, azure coastline. Moving from the Zihuatanejo direction **Playa Hermosa** comes first. The elevators of the super-luxurious clifftop Hotel Westin Brisas make access to the beach very convenient. At the bottom you'll find a few hundred yards of seasonally broad white sand, with open-ocean (but often gentle) waves usually good for most water sports except surfing. Good beach-accessible snorkeling is possible off the shoals at either end of the beach. Extensive rentals are available at their beachfront aquatics shop. A poolside restaurant serves food and drinks. Hotel access is only by car or taxi.

For a sweeping vista of Ixtapa's beaches, bay, and blue waters, ride the **cable tramway** (open daily 0700-1900, call ahead to see if tramway is running, tel. 755-310-27) to El Faro restaurant (open daily 0800-1200 and 1800-2200) at the south end of Ixtapa's main beach, Playa del Palmar.

Long, broad, and yellow-white, **Playa del Palmar** could be called the "Billion-dollar Beach" for the investment money it attracted to Ixtapa. The confidence seems justified. The broad strand stretches for three gently curving miles. Even though it fronts the open ocean, protective offshore rocks, islands, and shoals keep the surf gentle most of the time. Here, most sports are of the high-powered variety—parasailing ($10), jet- and water-skiing ($25), banana-boating ($5)—although boogie boards are rentable for $5 an hour on the beach.

Challenging **surfing** breaks sometimes roll in consistently off the jetty at **Playa Escolleros,** at Playa del Palmar's far west end. Bring your own board. (For surfboard sales and rentals, see "Sports" below.)

Ixtapa Outer Beaches

Ixtapa's outer beaches spread among the coves and inlets a few miles northwest of the Hotel Zone. Drive or taxi along the Paseo de las Garzas (turn right just past the shopping mall), then left again after less than a mile. After the Marina Golf Course, the road turns toward the shoreline, winding past a pair of hidden beach gems, Playa San Juan de Dios and Playa Don Rodrigo.

Unless development blocks access, **Playa Cuata** can be reached on the left (turn left at the fork for the embarcadero to Isla Ixtapa), a hundred yards before the stall-cluttered loop at road's-end Playa Quieta (see below). Cream-yellow and nestling between rocky outcroppings, Playa Cuata has oft-gentle waves with correspondingly moderate undertow for good swimming, bodysurfing, and boogie-boarding. Snorkeling and fishing are equally good around nearby rocks and shoals. Be prepared, bring your own food and drinks.

Back at the road fork, continue north past the rambling Club Med about another mile to the end of the pavement at **Playa Linda.** Here, an open-ocean yellow-sand beach extends for miles. Flocks of sandpipers and plovers skitter at the surf's edge; pelicans and cormorants dive offshore, while gulls, terns, and boobies skim the wavetops. Driftwood and shells decorate the sand beside a green-tufted palm grove that seems to stretch endlessly to the north.

The friendly **La Palapa** beach restaurant, at pavement's end, offers beer, sodas, and seafood, plus showers and free parking and camping beneath their grove. Neighboring stables Rancho Playa Linda, managed by friendly "Spiderman" Jorge, provides horseback rides at about $20 per hour. Despite the stable-associated flies, this informal campground sometimes attracts a small colony of RV- and tent-camping customers, as does the very downscale Trailer Park Los Buzos, continue a few hundred yards on the dirt road past the stable. (For more info see "Trailer Park and Camping" below.)

The flat, wide Playa Linda has powerful rollers often good for surfing. Boogie-boarding and bodysurfing—with caution, don't try it alone—are also possible. Surf fishing yields catches, especially of *lisa* (mullet), which locals have much more success netting than hooking.

Playa Quieta and Isla Ixtapa

Not-to-be-missed just offshore Isla Ixtapa is reachable by boat from Playa Quieta ("Quiet

Beach"), a place that lives up to its name. A ribbon of fine yellow sand arcs around a smooth inlet dotted by a regatta of Club Med kayaks and sailboats plying the water. A few sunbathers and families laze on the sands, while several *palapas* beneath the shoreline trees offer rentals, food, and drinks.

Every few minutes a boat heads from the beach dock to mile-long Ixtapa Island daily 0900-1700; $2 roundtrip. Upon arrival, you soon discover the secret to the preservation of the island's pristine beaches, forests, and natural underwater gardens. "No trash here," the *palapa* proprietors say. "We bag it up and send it back to the mainland."

It shows. Great fleshy green orchids and bromeliads hang from forest branches, multicolored fich dart among offshore rocks, shady native acacias hang lazily over the shell-decorated sands of the island's little beaches. Boats from Quieta arrive at **Playa Cuachalatate** (koo-ah-chah-lah-TAH-tay), the island's most popular beach, named for a local tree whose bark relieves liver ailments. Many visitors stay all day, splashing, swimming, and eating fresh fish, shrimp, and clams cooked at any one of a dozen *palapas*. Visitors also enjoy the many sports rentals: water skis, banana rides, boats for fishing, aquatic bicycles ($15/hour), snorkel gear ($5/hour), and kayaks ($7/hour).

For a change of scene, follow the short path over the west-side (right as you arrive) forested knoll to **Playas Varadero and Carey** on opposite flanks of an intimate little isthmus. Varadero's yellow-white sand is narrow and tree-shaded, its waters are calm and clear. Behind it lies Playa Carey, a steep coral-sand beach fronting a rocky blue bay. Named for the sea-turtle species (see the special topic "Saving Turtles" in the preceding "South to Manzanillo" chapter), Playa Carey is a magnet for beach lovers, snorkelers, and the scuba divers who often arrive by boat to explore the waters around the offshore coral reef.

Scuba diving is so rewarding here the Escuela de Buceos ("Diving School") Oliverio maintains headquarters near the west end of Playa Cuachalatate. Others in Ixtapa and Zihuatanejo (see "Sports" below) are more competent and better equipped to provide the same services.

ACCOMMODATIONS

Ixtapa or Zihuatanejo?

Your choice of local lodging sharply determines the tone of your stay. Zihuatanejo still resembles the colorful seaside village that visitors have enjoyed for years. Fishing *pangas* decorate its beachside, while *panaderías, taquerías,* and *papelerías* line its narrow shady lanes. Many of its hotels—budget to moderate, with Spartan but clean fan-only rooms—reflect the tastes of the bargain-conscious travelers who "discovered" Zihuatanejo during the 1960s.

Ixtapa, on the other hand, mirrors the fashion-wise preferences of new-generation Mexican and international vacationers. A broad boulevard fronts your Ixtapa hotel, while on the beach side, thatch-shaded chairs on a wide strand, a palmy garden, blue pool, and serene outdoor restaurant are yours to enjoy. Upstairs, your air-conditioned room—typically in plush pastels, with private sea-view balcony, marble bath, room service, and your favorite TV shows by satellite—brings maximum convenience and comfort to a lush tropical setting.

Actually, you needn't be forced to choose. Split your hotel time between Ixtapa and Zihuatanejo and enjoy both worlds.

Zihuatanejo Downtown Hotels

Zihuatanejo's hotels divide themselves by location and (largely by price) between the budget downtown and more pricy Playas La Madera-La Ropa.

Starting on the west side near the beach, begin at the **Hotel Tres Marías,** across the lagoon-mouth by footbridge from the end of Paseo Pescador, at Noria 4, Colonia Lázaro Cárdenas, Zihuatanejo, Guerrero 40880, tel. (755) 423-91. Its longtime popularity derives from its low prices and the colorful lagoon-front boat scene, visible from porches outside some of its 25 rooms. Otherwise, it's a strictly bare-bones place, without even hot water. Rooms rent for about $18 s, $23 d, and $31 t, with fan.

Guests at the hotel's sister branch, **Hotel Raoul Tres Marías,** Juan Alvarez and Cinco de Mayo, Zihuatanejo, Guerrero 40880, tel. 755-429-77 (owned by brother Raoul, near the end of

IXTAPA-ZIHUATANEJO HOTELS

Ixtapa-Zihuatanejo (area code 755, postal code 40880) hotels, in order of approximate high-season double-room price:

ZIHUATANEJO DOWNTOWN

Hotel Susy, Guerrero and Alvarez, tel. 423-39, $20

Hotel Tres Marías, Noria 4, Col. Lázaro Cárdenas, tel. 423-91, $23

Posada Citlali, Guerrero 3, tel. 420-43, $25

Hotel Raoul Tres Marías, Alvarez and Cinco de Mayo, tel. 429-77, $28

Hotel Avila, Alvarez 8, tel. 420-10, $75

ZIHUATANEJO PLAYAS MADERA AND LA ROPA

Hotel Palacio, Av. Adelit (P.O. Box 57), tel. 420-55, $22

Bungalows Milagro, Av. Marina Nacional s/n, tel. 430-45, $33

Bungalows Ley, Cerro La Madera, tel. 445-63 or 440-87, $38

Bungalows Allec, Cerro La Madera, tel. 445-10, $40

Hotel Irma, Av. Adelita, tel./fax 437-38, $40

Hotel Fiesta Mexicana, tel. 437-76 or 436-36, $40

Hotel Sotavento and Catalina, P.O. Box 2, tel. 420-32 or 420-24, fax 468-70, $40

Bungalows Pacífico, Cerro La Madera (P.O. Box 12), tel. 421-12, $50

Hotel Villas Miramar, Av. Adelita (P.O. Box 211), tel. 421-06 or 426-16, $60

Hotel Villa del Sol, Playa La Ropa (P.O. Box 84), tel. 422-39 or 432-39, U.S. (800) 223-6510, Canada (800) 424-5500, fax 427-58, $280

Hotel La Casa Que Canta, Carretera Escénica a Playa La Ropa, tel. 470-30, fax 470-40, U.S. (800) 525-4800, Canada (800) 424-5500, $410

IXTAPA

Hotel Posada Real, Paseo Ixtapa s/n, tel. 316-25, 317-45, or (800) 528-1234 from the U.S. and Canada, fax 318-05, $75

Hotel Dorada Pacífico, Paseo Ixtapa s/n (P.O. Box 15), tel. 320-25, fax 301-26, $105

Krystal Ixtapa, Paseo Ixtapa s/n, tel. 303-33, or (800) 231-9860 from the U.S. and Canada, fax 302-16, $135

Hotel Sheraton Ixtapa, Paseo Ixtapa s/n, tel. 318-58, or (800) 325-3535 from the U.S. and Canada, fax 324-38, $140

Hotel Westin Las Brisas Ixtapa, Paseo de la Roca (P.O. Box 97), tel. 321-21, or (800) 228-3000 from the U.S. and Canada, fax 307-51, $205

Alvarez) enjoy a few more amenities and the long-popular Restaurant Garrobos downstairs. A few of the 18 rooms have air-conditioning and/or private balconies looking out on the usually quiet street below. Being close to the pier, the new branch is popular with fishing parties. Newcomers might pick up some local fishing pointers around the tables after dinner. Rooms go for about $18 s, $22 d or t low season, $23 s, $28 d or t high, with hot water and fans; add about $7 for a/c.

A few blocks east on Alvarez is the **Hotel Avila,** Juan Alvarez 8, Zihuatanejo, Guerrero 40880, tel. (755) 420-10, downtown Zihuatanejo's only beachfront hostelry. Popular for its location rather than its management, which seems to be content with the dirt in the corners, the Avila has 27 rooms, some of which enjoy luxurious private-terrace bay views. Try for an upper-floor beachside room, while avoiding those that front the noisy street. Rooms rent for about $60 s, $75 d high season with view, $50 and $60 without; with fans, TV, phones, hot water, and some with a/c at extra cost; credit cards accepted.

Hotel Susy, Guerrero and Alvarez, Zihuatanejo, Guerrero 40880, tel. (755) 423-39, across the street, has three tiers of rooms surrounding a shady inner patio. The seven upper-floor bayside rooms have private view balconies. Inside corridors unfortunately run past room windows, necessitating closing curtains for privacy, a drawback in these fan-only rooms. Avoid traffic noise by requesting an upper-floor room away from the street. The 20 clean but very plain rooms go for $15 s, $20 d, including fans and hot water.

A better choice next door is the popular **Posada Citlali,** Av. Guerrero 3, Zihuatanejo, Guerrero 40880, tel. (755) 420-43, built in a pair of triple tiers, which rise around a shady, plant-decorated inner courtyard. The 20 plain, rather small but clean rooms are all thankfully removed from direct street noise. Guests on the upper floors have less corridor traffic and consequently enjoy more privacy. Reservations are mandatory during the high winter season and strongly recommended at other times. Rates run about $15 s, $25 d, with hot water and fans.

Zihuatanejo Playa La Madera and Playa La Ropa Hotels

The other half of Zihuatanejo's lodgings spreads along Playas La Madera and La Ropa on the east side of the bay. Several of them cluster on Cerro La Madera, the bayside hill just west of town. Due to Zihuatanejo's one-way streets (which fortunately direct most noisy traffic away from downtown) getting to Cerro La Madera is a bit tricky. The key is **Plaza Kyoto,** the traffic circle-intersection of Paseo de la Boquita and Paseo del Palmar a quarter mile east of downtown. If you're driving, keep a sharp eye out and follow the small Zona Hotelera signs. At Plaza Kyoto, marked by a big Japanese *torii* gate, bear right across the canal bridge and turn right at the first street. Straight ahead for another block to Av. Adelita, the address of several Playa la Madera hotels, which runs along the base of Cerro La Madera.

By location, moving eastward, start at **Bungalows Pacífico,** Cerro la Madera, Calle Eva Samano de López Mateos, P.O. Box 12, Zihuatanejo, Guerrero 40880, tel. (755) 421-12, the labor of love of longtime local resident Anita Rellstab. Superlatives can only describe what her guests enjoy: six spacious, comfortable, art-decorated hillside apartments with broad bay-view patios and complete furnishings, including kitchenettes and daily maid service. Anita, herself an amateur archaeologist, ecologist, birdwatcher and community leader, is a friendly, forthright, and knowledgeable hostess. She's more than

happy to inform other bird and animal-watching enthusiasts of good local viewing spots.

Flower-bedecked and hammock-draped, Anita's retreat is ideal for those seeking quiet relaxation. No matter for lack of a pool; lovely Playa La Madera is a short walk down the leafy front slope. Get your reservations in early, especially for winter. The apartments rent for about $50 d, $60 t; with hot water, fans only, and street parking; monthly discount possible during the 1 May -1 Dec. low season; get there via the short street uphill from Av. Adelita.

Along the same rustic-scenic hilltop street, guests of **Bungalows Allec,** Cerro La Madera, Calle Eva Samano de López Mateos, Zihuatanejo, Guerrero 40880, tel. (755) 445-10, enjoy luscious bay views from their private balconies. Comfortable but not luxurious, the 12 light, clean apartments have hot water and fans. Six of the apartments are very large, sleeping up to six, with completely equipped kitchenettes. The others are small, cozy doubles. No pool, but Playa La Madera is a few steps downhill. The kitchenette apartments go for about $50 low season, $80 high; the smaller doubles go for about $30 low, $40 high. Longer term and low-season discounts may be available; street parking.

Next door is **Bungalows Ley,** Calle Eva Samano de López Mateos s/n, Playa La Madera, P.O. Box 466, Zihuatanejo, Guerrero 40880, tel. (755) 445-63, 440-87, six white stucco studio apartments that stairstep directly downhill to heavenly Playa Madera. Although the Spartan apartments, with baths, hot water, kitchenettes, and king-size beds, are clean and comfortable enough, it is the beachfront location—looking out on a luxurious, palm-fringed bay vista, and a short, scenic shoreline walk to town restaurants and shopping—that provides all the ingredients for a season of tropical relaxation. Rates are about $45 d with a/c, $38, with fan only.

Downhill on Av. Adelita is the family-run **Hotel Palacio,** Av. Adelita, Playa La Madera, P.O. Box 57, Zihuatanejo, Guerrero 40880, tel. (755) 420-55, a beachfront maze of rooms connected by meandering, multilevel walkways. Room windows along the two main tiers face corridor walkways, where curtains must be drawn for privacy. Upper units fronting the quiet street avoid this drawback. The rooms themselves are plain, but clean and comfortable, with fans and hot water. Guests enjoy a small but very pleasant bay-view pool-sundeck, which perches above the waves at the hotel beachfront. The 25 rooms rent for about $15 s, $22 d, $27 t; street parking.

The **Hotel Villas Miramar,** Playa la Madera, Av. Adelita, P.O. Box 211, Zihuatanejo, Guerrero 40880, tel. (755) 421-06 or 426-16, next door clusters artfully around gardens of pools, palms, and leafy potted plants. The gorgeous, mani-cured layout makes maximum use of space, creating both privacy and intimacy in a small setting. The designer rooms have high ceilings, split levels, built-in sofas, and large, comfort-able beds. The street divides the hotel into two different but equally lovely sections, each with its own pool. The restaurant, especially convenient for breakfast, is in the shore-side section, but still serves guests who sun and snooze around the luxurious, beach-view pool-patio garden on the other side of the street. The 16 rooms rent for about $45 d low season, $60 high; with phones and a/c; credit cards accepted; additional dis-counts may be available during May-June and Sept.-Oct. low seasons. Reservations strongly recommended during the winter season.

The **Hotel Irma,** Av. Adelita, Playa Madera, Zihuatanejo, Guerrero 40880, tel./fax (755) 437-38, half a block farther uphill, is a favorite of longtime lovers of Zihuatanejo, if for no reason other than its location. Although details are not the Irma's strong suit, the basics are there: clean rooms, a passably pleasant sunset-view ter-race restaurant and bar, and a pair of blue pools perched above the bay. A short walk downhill and you're at beautiful Madera beach. Best of all, most of the simply furnished but comfortable rooms have private balconies with just about the loveliest view in town. The 70 rooms go for $40 s or d high season, with a/c, TV, and hot water.

Nearby, a couple of blocks off the beach, is the downscale but homey **Bungalows Mila-gro,** Av. Marina Nacional s/n, Playa la Madera, Zihuatanejo, Guerrero 40880, tel. (755) 430-45, the project of local doctor Klaus Bührer and his wife Lucina Gomes. A haciendalike com-pound of cottages and apartments clustering around a shady pool, the Bungalows Milagro is winter headquarters for a cordial group of Ger-man longtime returnees. The friendly atmos-phere and the inviting pool-garden account for the Milagro's success, rather than the plain but clean kitchenette lodgings, which vary in style from ramshackle-rustic to 1940s motel. Look at several before you choose. The 10 rooms rent, high season, for about $25 s, $33 for two or three, a bit less during low season. Additional discounts may be negotiated for longer stays; all with fans and parking; hot water in only some of the units.

A few hundred yards farther south along the Paseo Costera is **La Casa Que Canta,** Camino Escénico a Playa La Ropa, Zihuatanejo, Gue-rrero 40880, tel. (755) 470-30, fax 470-40, which is as much a work of art as a hotel. The pageant begins at the lobby, a luxurious soaring *palapa* that angles gracefully down the cliffside to an intimate open air view dining-room. Suite-clus-ters of natural adobe sheltered by thick *palapa* roofs cling artfully to the craggy precipice deco-rated with riots of bougainvillea and gardens of cactus. From petite pool terraces perched above foamy shoals, guests enjoy a radiant aqua bay panorama in the morning and brilliant ridge-sil-houetted sunsets in the evening.

The 18 art-bedecked, rustic-chic apartments, all with private view balconies, come in two grades: spacious "grand suites" and even larg-er versions with their own small pools. Rentals run about $310 and $410 s or d high season, $225 and $300 low, with a/c, fan, phone, no TV, and no kids under 16. Make winter reser-vations very early; from the U.S., call (800) 525-4800 or (800) 223-6510, from Canada, (800) 424-5500.

About a mile farther along the road to Playa La Ropa, the twin **Hotels Sotavento and Catali-na,** Playa la Ropa, P.O. Box 2, Zihuatanejo, Guerrero 40880, tel. (755) 420-32 or 420-24, fax 468-70, perch together on a leafy hillside above La Ropa Beach. Good management by the owners, a savvy husband-wife team, keeps the rambling complex healthy. The twin hotels contrast sharply. The Sotavento is a 70-room mod-style warren that stairsteps five stories down the hillside. Each floor of rooms opens to a broad, hammock-hung communal terrace overlooking the beach and bay. By contrast, the Hotel Catalina's 30 *cabañas* lie scattered beneath shady hillside trees all the way down to the beach. A pair of restaurants, a mediocre breakfast-lunch cafeteria at the beach level, and a fancier dinner restaurant upstairs service the guests, many on vacation packages.

The Sotavento's rooms are '60s modern, clean and comfortable, opening onto the view terrace, with king- or queen-size beds and ceiling fans. The Catalina's comfortably appointed tropical-rustic *cabañas* are more private, being separate units with individual view terraces and hammocks. At the bottom of the hill, the hotel aquatics shop offers sailing, windsurfing, snorkeling, and other rentals; those who want to rest enjoy chairs beneath the shady boughs of a beachside grove. Standard rooms rent during high season for $65 s or d, deluxe terrace suites $85, and deluxe bungalows $85. A few small "student" units rent for about $30; discounts possible May through mid-November; no pool, fans only, parking, credit cards accepted.

Half a dozen hotels and bungalow complexes spread along La Ropa Beach. The **Hotel Fiesta Mexicana**, Playa la Ropa, Zihuatanejo, Guerrero 40880, tel. (755) 437-76 or 436-36, seems to be popular for nothing more than its stunning location right in the middle of the sunny beach hubbub. Its 60 rooms, in low-rise stucco clusters, while comfortable and air-conditioned, are (like the entire hotel) neither fancy nor particularly tidy. This, however, doesn't seem to bother the mostly North American winter clientele, who jetski, parasail, and boogie-board from the beach, snooze around the pool, and socialize beneath the *palapa* of the beachside restaurant. Asking rates for standard rooms are $40 d high season; $60 for room with private view patio, $70 for deluxe. Low-season discount runs about 20%; parking; credit cards accepted.

German expatriate Helmut Leins sold out in Munich and came to create paradise on Playa la Ropa in 1978. The result is Playa la Ropa's luxury **Hotel Villa del Sol,** Playa la Ropa, P.O. Box 84, Zihuatanejo, Guerrero 40880, tel. (755) 422-39 or 432-39, (800) 223-6510 from the U.S., (800) 424-5500 from Canada, fax 427-58, an exquisite beachside mini-Eden. A corps of well-to-do North American, European, and Mexican clients return yearly to enjoy tranquility and the elegance of the Villa del Sol's crystal-blue pools, palm-draped patios, and classic *palapas.* The lodgings themselves are spacious, with shining floor tile, handcrafted wall art, tropical-canopy beds, and private hammock-hung patios. The plethora of extras includes a restaurant, bars, pools, night tennis courts, a newsstand, boutique, beauty salon, and meeting room for about 30 people. The approximately 50 accommodations begin at $180 s, $220 d low season, $230 and $280 high. Super-plush options include more bedrooms and baths, ocean views, and jacuzzis for $500 and up; with a/c and parking; credit cards accepted.

Ixtapa Hotels

Ixtapa's dozen-odd hotels line up in a luxurious strip between the beach and boulevard Paseo Ixtapa. Among the most reasonably priced is the Best Western **Hotel Posada Real,** Paseo Ixtapa s/n, Ixtapa, Guerrero 40880, tel. (755) 316-25, 317-45, (800) 528-1234 from the U.S. and Canada, fax 318-05, at the far west end. Get there via the street, beach side, just past the Lighthouse Restaurant. With a large grassy football field instead of tennis courts, the hotel attracts a seasonal following of soccer enthusiasts. Other amenities include three restaurants (one of them the attractive Los Cocos), two pools, and a disco. The 110 smallish rooms are clean and comfortable, but lack ocean views. Rooms rent for about $75 d, often with big discounts for longer stays. Kids under 12 with parents are free; with a/c, satellite TV, phones and parking; credit cards accepted.

Nearer the middle of the hotel zone, the Mexican-owned **Krystal Ixtapa,** Paseo Ixtapa s/n, Ixtapa, Guerrero 40880, tel. (755) 303-33, or (800) 231-9860 from the U.S. and Canada, fax 302-16, towers over its spacious garden compound. Its innovative wedge design ensures an ocean view from each room. A continuous round of activities—a Ping-Pong tournament, handicrafts and cooking classes, and aerobics and scuba lessons—fills the days, while buffets, Mexican fiestas, dancing, and discoing fill the nights. Unscheduled relaxation centers on the blue pool, where guests enjoy watching each other slip from the water slide and duck beneath the waterfall all day. The 260 tastefully appointed deluxe rooms and suites have private view balconies, satellite TV, a/c, and phones. Rooms rent from $90 d low season, about $135 high. Check for additional discounts through extended-stay or other packages. Extras include tennis courts, racquetball, an exercise gym, parking, and wheelchair access; credit cards accepted.

If the Krystal is full, try the nearly-as-good **Hotel Dorado Pacífico,** Paseo Ixtapa s/n, P.O. Box 15, Ixtapa, Guerrero 40880, tel. (755) 320-25, fax 301-26, next door. Although fewer organized activities fill the day, three palm-shaded blue pools, water slides, a swim-up bar, and three restaurant-bars seem to keep guests happy. Upstairs, the rooms, all with sea-view balconies, are pleasingly decorated with sky-blue carpets and earth-tone designer bedspreads. The 285 rooms rent from $105 d high season, with a/c, phones, and TV; low season and extended-stay discounts may be available. Extras include tennis courts, parking, and wheelchair access; credit cards accepted.

The **Hotel Sheraton Ixtapa,** Paseo Ixtapa s/n, Ixtapa, Guerrero 40880, tel. (755) 318-58, or (800) 325-3535 from the U.S. and Canada, fax 324-38, across from the golf course at the east end of the beach, rises around a soaring lobby-atrium. A worthy member of the worldwide Sheraton chain, the Sheraton Ixtapa serves its mostly American clientele with complete resort facilities, including pools, all sports, an exercise gym, several restaurants and bars, cooking and arts lessons, nightly dancing, and a Fiesta Mexicana. The 332 rooms in standard (which include mountain-view balconies only), deluxe, and junior suite grades, are spacious and tastefully furnished in designer pastels and include a/c, phones, and satellite TV. Standard non-deluxe rooms run from $90 d low season, $140 high; deluxe from $110 d low season, $165 high; parking, credit cards accepted, and wheelchair access.

From the adjacent jungle hilltop, the **Hotel Westin Brisas Ixtapa,** Paseo de la Roca, P.O. Box 97, Ixtapa, Guerrero 40880, tel. (755) 321-21, or (800) 228-3000 from the U.S. and Canada, fax 307-51, slopes downhill to the shore like a latter-day Mexican pyramid. The monumentally stark hilltop lobby, open and unadorned except for a clutch of huge stone balls, contrasts sharply with its surroundings. The hotel's severe lines immediately shift the focus to the adjacent jungle. The fecund forest aroma wafts into the lobby and terrace restaurant, where, at breakfast, guests sit watching iguanas munch hibiscus blossoms in the nearby treetops.

The hotel entertains guests with a wealth of resort facilities, including pools, four tennis courts, a gym, aerobics, an intimate shoal-enfolded beach, restaurants, bars, and nightly live dance music. The standard rooms, each with its own spacious view patio, are luxuriously Spartan, floored with big designer tiles, furnished in earth tones and equipped with big TVs, small refrigerators, phones, and a/c. More luxurious options include suites with individual pools and jacuzzis. The 427 rooms begin at about $175 for a standard low-season double, $205 high, and run about twice that for super-luxury suites. June through October, bargain packages can run as low as $70 d per night, including buffet breakfast, tennis, and a local tour for two.

Trailer Park and Camping
Ixtapa-Zihuatanejo has a very basic trailer park toward the north-end of Playa Linda. Visitors enjoy breezy palm-shaded spaces right on the beachcombing and surf-fishing haven of Playa Linda. **Los Buzos** offers camping and basic showers and toilets (but no electricity) for about $3 per night. The owner arrives in the morning around eight, tends his downscale *palapa* restaurant, and leaves before sunset. He does a brisk business between Christmas and New Year and the week before Easter; other times a few RVs and tenters remain keeping each other company. No telephone and no reservations taken.

House, Apartment, and Condo Rentals
Zihuatanejo residents sometimes offer their condos and homes for temporary lease through agents. Among the better known is **Elizabeth Williams,** a longtime local realtor. Contact her at P.O. Box 169, Zihuatanejo, Guerrero 40880, tel. (755) 426-06, fax 447-62, for a list of possible rentals.

Also, O.J.B. Real Estate, tel. (755) 443-74 (contact Julie), in Zihuatanejo is highly recommended for finding rentals.

FOOD

Snacks, Bakeries, and Breakfasts
For something cool in **Zihuatanejo,** stop by the **Paletería y Nevería Michoacana** ice shop

across from the plaza. Besides ice cream, popcorn, and safe *nieves* (ices) they offer delicious *aguas* (fruit-flavored drinks, 50 cents), which make nourishing, refreshing Pepsi-free alternatives.

The **Panadería Francesa** bakery, tel. (755) 427-42, four short blocks up Cuauhtémoc from the beach, turns out a daily acre of fresh goodies, from *pan integral* (whole wheat) and black bread loaves to doughnuts and rafts of Mexican-style cakes, cookies, and tarts. With coffee, chairs, and tables, they are open daily 0700-2100, on C. González, corner of Galeana, the lane paralleling Cuauhtémoc.

Tasty, promptly served breakfasts are the specialty of the downtown **Cafetería Nova Zelandia** on Cuauhtémoc, corner of Ejido. Favorites include hotcakes, eggs any style, fruit, juices, and espresso coffee. They serve lunch and supper also. Open daily 0800-2200.

For hot sandwiches and good pizza on the downtown beach, try the friendly **Cafe Marina.** The friendly, hardworking owner features a spaghetti—either bolognesa, pesto, or primavera—party Wednesday night and chili Friday. Their shelves of books for lending or exchange are nearly as popular as their food. Open Mon.-Sat. 1200-2200, closed approximately June to mid-September; on Paseo del Pescador, just west of the plaza.

A local vacation wouldn't be complete without dropping in to the **Sirena Gorda** ("Fat Mermaid"), Thurs.-Tues. 0700-2200, tel. (755) 426-87, near the end of Paseo de Pescador across from the naval compound. Here the fishing crowd relaxes, trading stories after a tough day hauling in the lines. The other unique attractions, besides the well-endowed sea nymphs who decorate the walls, are tempting shrimp-bacon and fish tacos, juicy hamburgers, fish *mole,* and conch and cactus plates.

In **Ixtapa,** the **Cafe Toko Tucán** offers a refreshing alternative to hotel breakfasts. White cockatoos and bright toucans in a leafy patio add an exotic touch as you enjoy the fare, which, besides the usual juices, eggs, hotcakes, and french toast, includes lots of salads, vegie burgers, and sandwiches. Open daily 0800-2200, on the west front corner of the Los Patios shopping complex, across the boulevard from Hotel Aristos.

The perfume wafting from freshly baked European-style yummies draws dozens of the faithful to the nearby **German Bakery,** tel. (755) 303-10, brainchild of local longtimers Helmut and Esther Walter. He, a German, and she, an East Indian from Singapore, satisfy homesick palates with a continuous supply of scrumptious cinnamon rolls, pies, and hot buns. Open daily 0800-1400, on the inner patio, upper floor of the Los Patios shopping complex.

Restaurants

Complete dinner price key: Budget: under $7; Moderate: $7-14; Expensive: more than $14.

Local chefs and restaurateurs, long accustomed to foreign tastes, operate a number of good local restaurants, mostly in Zihuatanejo (where, in contrast to Ixtapa, most of the serious eating occurs *outside* of hotel dining rooms).

In **Zihuatanejo,** all trails seem to lead to **Deli Cafe,** on Cuauhtémoc a block from the plaza. Here the atmosphere is refined but friendly, and the food—hot dogs, hamburgers, potato salad, eggs Benedict, T-bone, guacamole, and milkshakes—is familiar. Open daily 0800-2200; credit cards accepted. Moderate.

Zihuatanejo has a pair of good, genuinely local-style restaurants in the downtown area. **Tamales y Atoles "Any,"** Zihuatanejo's clean, well-lighted place for Mexican food, is the spot to find out if your favorite Mexican restaurant back home is serving the real thing. Tacos, tamales, quesadillas, enchiladas, chiles rellenos, and such goodies are called *antojitos* in Mexico. At Tamales y Atoles "Any," they're savory enough to please even demanding Mexican palates. Open Wed.-Mon. 0700-2200, corner Guerrero and Ejido. Budget to moderate.

Restaurant Los Braseros, half a block along Ejido, at Ejido 21, between Cuauhtémoc and Guerrero, tel. (755) 448-58, is similarly authentic and popular. Waiters are often busy after midnight even during low season serving seven kinds of tacos and specialties such as "Gringa," "Porky," and "Azteca" from a menu it would take three months of dinners (followed by a six-month diet) to fully investigate. Open daily 1600-0100. Moderate.

Italian restaurant and bar **El Picolo,** on Bravo, northwest corner of Guerrero, open daily mid-afternoon till around 2300, holds its own with good salads, crepes, pizza, and pasta. If you're in the mood for dessert, don't miss their house-specialty caramel crepes. Moderate.

Casa Elvira, founded long ago by now-octogenarian Elvira, is as popular as ever, still satisfying the palates of a batallion of loyal Zihuatanejo longtimers. Located on Paseo del Pescador, by the naval compound, tel. (755) 420-61. Elvira's continuing popularity is easy to explain: a palm-studded beachfront, strumming guitars, whirling ceiling fans, and a list of super-fresh salads, soups, fish, meat and Mexican specialties, expertly prepared and professionally served. Open daily 1300-2200; reservations recommended during the high season.

Ixtapa restaurants have to be exceptional to compete with the hotels. One such, the **Belle Vista,** *is* in a hotel, being the Westin Ixtapa's view-terrace cafe. Breakfast is the favorite time to watch the antics of the iguanas in the adjacent jungle treetops. These black, green, and white miniature dinosaurs crawl up and down the trunks, munch flowers, and sunbathe on the branches. The food and service, incidentally, are quite good. Open daily 0700-2300; call ahead to reserve a terrace-edge table, tel. (755) 321-21; credit cards accepted. Moderate to expensive.

The **Hacienda de Ixtapa,** right on the boulevard next to the Presidente, tel. (755) 306-02, offers good food and service in an airy patio setting. Fruit plate, eggs any style, and hotcakes breakfasts run about $2 each, while fish fillet ($6), T-bone ($9), and lobster ($14) dinners are similarly reasonable and tasty. Open daily 0700-2300; credit cards accepted. Moderate.

Those hankering for Italian-style pastas and seafood head to **Ristorante Da Baffone,** at the back side of the La Puerta shopping complex on Paseo Ixtapa, tel. (755) 311-22. Here, Mediterranean-Mex decor covers the walls while marinara-style shrimp and clams with linguini, calamari, ricotta and spinach-stuffed canelloni, and glasses of Chianti and chardonnay load the tables. Open daily about 1200-2400 during high season; call for reservations. Moderate to expensive.

Other Ixtapa restaurants, also popular for their party atmosphere, are described below.

ENTERTAINMENT AND EVENTS

In Zihuatanejo, visitors and residents content themselves mostly with quiet pleasures. Afternoons, they stroll the beachfront or the downtown shady lanes and enjoy coffee or drinks with friends at small cafes and bars. As the sun goes down however, folks head to Ixtapa for its sunset vistas, happy hours, shows, clubs, and dancing.

Sunsets
Sunsets are tranquil and often magnificent from the **Restaurant-Bar El Faro,** tel. (755) 310-27, which even has a cableway, south end of the Ixtapa beach, open 0700-1900, leading to it. Many visitors stay to enjoy dinner and the relaxing piano bar. Open daily around 1730-2200; reservations recommended winter and weekends. Drive or taxi via the uphill road toward the Westin Brisas Ixtapa at the golf course; at the first fork, head right for El Faro.

For equally brilliant sunsets in a lively setting, try either the lobby-bar or Belle Vista terrace restaurant of the **Westin Brisas Ixtapa.** Lobby-bar happy hour runs 1800-1900; live music begins around 1930. Drive or taxi, following the signs, along the uphill road at the golf course, following the signs to the crest of the hill just south of the Ixtapa beach.

Sunset and Sunshine Cruises
Those who want to experience a sunset party while at sea ride the trimaran *Tri Star,* which leaves from the Zihuatanejo pier around 1700 daily, returning around 1930. The tariff runs about $40 per person, including open bar.

The Tri Star also heads out daily on a "Sunshine Cruise" around 1000, returning around 1630. Included are open bar, lunch, and snorkeling, for about $58 per person. Book tickets for both of these cruises, which include transportation to and from your hotel, through a hotel travel agent, such as American Express, tel. (755) 308-53, at Hotel Krystal in Ixtapa. Tickets are also available at the Tri Star office, tel. (755) 435-89, at Puerto Mío. Located at the small marina about half a mile across the bay from town. Get there via the road that curves around the western, right-hand shore of Zihuatanejo Bay.

Tourist Shows

Ixtapa hotels regularly stage **Fiesta Mexicana** extravaganzas, which begin with a sumptuous buffet and go on to a whirling skirt-and-sombrero folkloric ballet. Afterward, the audience usually gets involved with piñatas, games, cockfights, dancing, and continuous drinks from an open bar. In the finale, fireworks often boom over the beach, painting the night sky in festoons of reds, blues, and greens.

Entrance runs about $30-35 per person, with kids under 12 usually half price. Shows on Tuesday at the **Presidente**, tel. (755) 300-18, seasonally at the **Dorado Pacífico**, tel. (755) 320-25, and Wednesday at the **Sheraton**, tel. (755) 318-58, are the most reliable and popular. Usually open to the public, call ahead for confirmation and reservations.

Clubs and Hangouts

Part restaurant and part wacky nightspot, the **Restaurant-Bar Cocos** at Ixtapa's Hotel Posada Real offers hamburgers and seafood in a Robinson Crusoe chic setting. Patrons recline in ceiling-hung chairs, while waiters try to outdo each other's zany tricks, and lively tropical music bounces out of the speakers. Open daily 0700-2300.

Next door, **Carlos'n Charlie's**, tel. (755) 300-85, is as wild and as much fun as all of the other Carlos Anderson restaurants from Puerto Vallarta to Paris. Here in Ixtapa you can have your picture taken on a surfboard in front of a big wave for $3, or have a fireman spray out the flames from the chili sauce on your palate. You can also enjoy the food, which, if not fancy, is innovative and tasty. Loud rock music ($10 minimum) goes on 2200-0400 during the winter season. The restaurant serves daily 1200-2400. Located on the beachfront about half a block on the driveway road west past the Hotel Posada Real.

Dancing and Discoing

Nearly all Ixtapa hotel lobbies blossom with dance music from around 1900 during the high winter season. Year-round, however, good medium-volume groups usually play for dancing nightly 1930-2400 at the **Westin**, tel. (755) 321-21, the **Sheraton**, tel. (755) 318-58, and the **Krystal**, tel. (755) 303-33, lobby bars.

Christine, Ixtapa's big-league discotheque, offers fantasy for a mere $12 cover charge. From 2200, the patrons warm up by listening to relatively low-volume rock, watch videos, and talk while they can still hear each other. That stops around 2330, when the fogs descend, the lights begin flashing, and the speakers boom forth their 200-decibel equivalent of a fast freight roaring at trackside. Located at the Hotel Krystal, call (755) 303-33, ext. 429, to verify times.

SPORTS

Walking and Jogging

Zihuatanejo Bay is strollable from the Playa la Madera all the way west to Puerto Mío. A relaxing half-day adventure could begin by taxiing to the Hotel Irma, Av. Adelita, on Playa la Madera, for breakfast. Don your hats and follow the stairs down to Playa la Madera and walk west toward town. At the end of the Playa la Madera sand, head left along the *andador* walkway that twists along the rocks, around the bend toward town. Continue along the beachfront Paseo del Pescador; at the west end, cross the lagoon bridge, head left along the bayside road to **Puerto Mío** for a drink at the hotel cafe and perhaps a dip in their pool. Allow three hours, including breakfast, for this two-mile walk; do the reverse trip during late afternoon for sunset drinks or dinner at the Irma.

Playa del Palmar, Ixtapa's main beach, is good for similar strolls. Start in the morning with breakfast at the Restaurant-Bar El Faro, tel. (755) 310-27, atop the hill at the south end of the beach; open daily 0600-1100, 1800-2200. Ride the cableway or walk downhill. With the sun at your back stroll the beach, stopping for refreshments at the hotel pool-patios en route. The entire beach stretches about three miles to the marina jetty, where you can often watch surfers challenging the waves and where taxis and buses return along Paseo Ixtapa. Allow about four hours, including breakfast. The reverse walk would be equally enjoyable during the afternoon. Time yourself to arrive at the El Faro cableway (call ahead, tel. 755-310-27, to make sure the cableway is running) about half an hour before sundown to enjoy the sunset over drinks or dinner. Get to El Faro by driving or taxiing via Paseo de la Roca, which heads uphill off the Zihuatanejo road at the golf course. Follow the first right fork to El Faro.

Adventurers who enjoy ducking through underbrush and scrambling over rocks might enjoy exploring the acacia forest and pristine beaches of the uninhabited west side of **Isla Ixtapa.** Take water, lunch, and a good pair of walking shoes. (For Isla Ixtapa access, see under "Sights" above. Your exploration should begin at the far end of Playa Varadero.)

Joggers often practice their art either on the smooth, firm sands of Ixtapa's main beachfront or on Paseo Ixtapa's sidewalks. Best avoid crowds and midday heat by jogging early mornings or late afternoons. For even better beach jogging, try the flat, firm sands of uncrowded **Playa Quieta** about three miles by car or taxi northwest of Ixtapa. Additionally, mile-long **Playa la Ropa** can be enjoyed by early morning and late afternoon joggers.

Golf and Tennis

Ixtapa's 18-hole, professionally designed **Campo de Golf** is open to the public. In addition to its manicured, 6,898-yard course, patrons enjoy full facilities, including pool, restaurant, pro shop, lockers, and tennis courts. Greens fee runs $32, cart $25, club rental $15, 18 holes with caddy $8 ($5 for nine), and golf lessons, $23 an hour. Play goes on daily 0600-1630. The clubhouse, P.O. Box 105, Zihuatanejo, Guerrero, 40880, tel. (755) 310-30, is off Paseo Ixtapa, across from the Sheraton. No reservations are accepted; morning golfers, get in line early during the high winter season.

The Marina Golf Course, west side of Ixtapa, on the way to Isla Ixtapa (see "Ixtapa Outer Beaches" above), although professionally designed, is too new for much shade, and is, as yet, too hot for most golfers.

Ixtapa has nearly all of the local **tennis** courts, all of them private. The Campo de Golf (see above) has some of the best. Rentals run about $5/hour days, $6 nights. Reservations, tel. (755) 310-30, may be seasonally necessary. A pro shop rents and sells equipment. Teaching professional Luis Valle offers lessons for about $17 per hour.

Several hotels also have tennis courts, equipment, and lessons. Call the **Sheraton,** tel. (755)

318-58), **Omni,** tel. (755) 300-03, **Dorado Pacifico,** tel. (755) 320-25, **Krystal,** tel. (755) 303-33, and the **Westin,** tel. (755) 321-21, for rental information.

Horseback Riding

Rancho Playa Linda on Playa Linda (see under "Ixtapa Outer Beaches" above) rents horses daily for beach riding for about $20 per hour. Travel agencies and hotels offer the same, though for considerably higher prices.

Swimming and Surfing

Calm Zihuatanejo Bay is fine for swimming but too calm for surfing, bodysurfing, and boogie-boarding, except marginally at Playa la Ropa.

Heading northwest to more open coast, waves improve for bodysurfing and boogie-boarding along Ixtapa's main beach **Playa del Palmar,** while usually remaining calm and undertow-free enough for swimming beyond the breakers. As for surfing, good breaks sometimes rise off the Playa Escolleros jetty at the west end of Playa del Palmar.

Along Ixtapa's outer beaches, swimming is great along very calm Playa Quieta, while surfing, bodysurfing, and boogie-boarding are correspondingly good, but hazardous in the sometimes mountainous surf of farther north Playa Larga. See "Sights" above for more beach details.

Snorkeling and Scuba Diving

Clear offshore waters (sometimes up to 100-foot visibility during the Nov.-May dry season) have drawn a steady flow of divers and nurtured professionally staffed and equipped dive shops. Just offshore, good snorkeling and scuba spots, where swarms of multicolored fish graze and glide among rocks and corals, are accessible from Playa las Gatas, Playa Hermosa, and Playa Carey (on Isla Ixtapa). For access details and beach snorkeling prospects, see the various beach headings under "Sights" above.

Many boat operators take parties for offshore snorkeling excursions. On Playa la Ropa, contact the aquatics shop at the foot of the hill beneath Hotel Sotavento. Playa las Gatas, easily accessible by boat for $2 from the Zihuatanejo pier, also has a scuba shop and snorkel and excursion boat rentals. In Ixtapa, similar services are available at beachside shops at the **Westin Ixtapa, Sheraton, Krystal,** and seasonally at other hotels.

Other even more spectacular offshore sites, such as Morros de Potosí, El Yunque, Bajo de Chato, Bajo de Torresillas, Piedra Soletaria, and Sacramento, are accessible with the help of professional guides and instructors.

One local dive shop stands out. In downtown Zihuatanejo, marine biologist-instructor Juan M. Barnard Avila coordinates his **Zihuatanejo Scuba Center,** at Cuauhtémoc 3, Zihuatanejo, Guerrero 40880, tel. (755) 421-47. Licensed for instruction through NAUI (National Association of Underwater Instructors), Avila is among Pacific Mexico's best-qualified professional instructors. Aided by loads of state-of-the-art equipment and several experienced licensed assistants, his shop has accumulated a long list of repeat customers.

Avila's standard resort scuba package, including a morning pool instruction session and an afternoon offshore half-hour dive, runs about $70 per person ($60 with your own gear) complete. Other services for beginners include open-water certification (one week of instruction, $350) and more rigorous NAUI certification (price negotiable). For certified divers (bring your certificate), Avila offers night, shipwreck, deep-water, and marine-biology dives at more than three dozen coastal sites. The dive shop is open Mon.-Sat. 0830-2030.

Sailing, Windsurfing, and Kayaking

The tranquil waters of Zihuatanejo Bay, off Ixtapa's Playa del Palmar, and the quiet strait off Playa Quieta (see "Sights" above) are good for these low-power aquatic sports. Shops on Playa La Ropa in Zihuatanejo Bay and in front of Ixtapa hotels, such as the Westin Ixtapa, the Sheraton, and the Krystal, rent small sailboats, sailboards, and sea kayaks hourly.

Fishing

Surf or rock casting with bait or lures, depending on conditions, is generally successful in local waters. Have enough line to allow casting beyond the waves (about 50 feet out on Playa la Ropa, 100 feet on Playa del Palmar and Playa Linda).

The rocky ends of Playas la Ropa, la Madera, del Palmar, and Cuata on the mainland, and Playa Carey on Isla Ixtapa are also good for casting. (For details and access, see "Sights" above.)

For deep-sea fishing, you can launch your own boat (see below) or rent one. *Pangas* are available for rent from individual fishermen on the beach, the boat cooperative (see below) at Zihuatanejo pier, or aquatics shops of the Hotel Sotavento on Playa la Ropa or the Hotels Westin Ixtapa, Sheraton, Krystal, and others on the beach in Ixtapa. Rental for a seaworthy *panga*, including tackle and bait, should run $20-25 per hour, depending upon the season and your bargaining skill. An experienced boatman can help you and your friends hook, typically, six or eight big fish, which local restaurants are often willing to serve as a small banquet for you in return for your extra fish.

Big-Game Sportfishing

Zihuatanejo has long been a center for billfish (marlin, swordfish, and sailfish) hunting. Most local captains have organized themselves into cooperatives, which visitors can contact either directly or through town or hotel travel agents. Trips begin around 0700 and return 1400-1500. Fishing success depends on seasonal conditions. If you're not sure of your prospects, go down to the Zihuatanejo pier around 1430 and see what the boats are bringing in. During good times they often return with one or more big marlin or swordfish per boat (although captains are increasingly asking that billfish be set free after the battle has been won). Although fierce fighters, the sinewy billfish do not make the best eating and are often discarded after the pictures are taken. On average, boats bring in two or three other large fish, such as *dorado* (dolphinfish or mahimahi), yellowfin tuna, and roosterfish, all more highly prized for the dinner table.

The biggest local sportfishing outfitter is the blue-and-white fleet of the **Sociedad Cooperativa Teniente Azueta,** tel. (755) 420-56, named after the naval hero Lieutenant José Azueta. You can see adjacent to the Zihuatanejo pier many of their several dozen boats bobbing at anchor. Arrangements for fishing parties can be made through hotel travel desks or at their office, open daily 0600-1800, at the foot of the pier. The largest 36-foot boats, with four or five lines, go out for a day's fishing for about $250. Twenty-five-foot boats with three lines run about $120 per day.

The smaller (18-boat) **Servicios Sociedad Cooperativa Juárez,** tel. (755) 437-58, tries harder by offering similar boats for lower prices. Their 36-foot boats for six start around $200; their 25-foot for four, about $100. Contact them at their office across from the naval compound near the end of Paseo de Pescador, open daily 0900-2000.

Next door, the private **Servicios Turísticos Aquaticos,** tel. (755) 441-62, also provides boats and captains for similar prices; open daily 0900-1800.

Prices quoted by providers often (but not necessarily) include fishing licenses, bait, tackle, and amenities such as beer, sodas, ice, and on-board toilets. Such details should be pinned down (ideally by seeing the boat) before putting your money down.

Sportfishing Tournament

Twice a year, usually in May and January, Zihuatanejo fisherfolk sponsor their **Torneo de Pez Vela,** with prizes for the biggest catches of sailfish, swordfish, marlin, and other varieties. Entrance fee runs around $450, and the prizes usually include a new Dodge pickup, cars, and other goodies. For information, contact the local sportfishing cooperative, Sociedad Cooperativa Teniente José Azueta, Muelle Municipal, Zihuatanejo, Guerrero 40880, tel. (755) 420-56.

Marinas and Boat Launching

Marina Ixtapa, at the north end of Paseo Ixtapa, offers excellent boat facilities. The slip charge runs about 50 cents per foot, per day, subject to a minimum of $15 per day. This includes use of the boat ramp, showers, pump-out, electricity, trash collection, mailbox, phone, fax, and satellite TV. For reservations and info, contact them Mon.-Sat. 0800-1400 and 1600-1800 at the harbormaster's office in the marina-front white building on the right a block before the big white lighthouse, or write Harbormaster, Marina Ixtapa, Ixtapa, Guerrero 40880, or call or fax them at tel./fax (755) 321-80.

The smooth, gradual Marina Ixtapa **boat ramp,** open to the public for a $10 fee, is on the right-hand side street leading to the water, just past the big white lighthouse. Get your ticket beforehand from the harbormaster (see above).

Puerto Mío, Zihuatanejo's small private boat harbor at the end of the western curve of Zihuatanejo Bay, rents boat slips for about $1.50 per foot, per day. The fee includes toilets, water, electricity, and use of their swimming pool, showers, and adjacent restaurant. The usefulness of Puerto Mío's boat-launching ramp (fee $50) is reduced, however, by its rapid drop-off. Although they state that minimum contract slip-rental period is for six months, they may negotiate if they have extra space, Paseo del Morro, Playa del Almacén, Zihuatanejo, Guerrero 40880, tel./fax (755) 427-48.

Sports Equipment Shops

Deportes Naúticos Adidas, tel. (755) 444-11, corner of N. Bravo and Guerrero in downtown Zihuatanejo, sells snorkel equipment, boogie boards, tennis rackets, balls, and a load of other general sporting goods. Open Mon.-Sat. 1000-1400 and 1600-2000.

Equipo and Embarcaciones, tel. (755)432-29, at the pier end of Alvarez, has a more specialized stock of equipment, including fishing tackle, fins and snorkels, waterskis, jet-ski boats, and surfboards. Open Mon.-Sat. 0900-1400 and 1600-1900.

SHOPPING

Zihuatanejo

Every day is market day at the Zihuatanejo **Mercado** on Av. Benito Juárez, four blocks from the beach. Behind the piles of leafy greens, round yellow papayas, and huge gaping sea bass, don't miss the sugar and spice stalls. There you will find big, raw brown sugar cones, thick golden homemade honey, mounds of fragrant jamaica petals, crimson dried chiles, and forest-gathered roots, barks, and grasses sold in the same pungent natural forms as they have been for centuries.

For more up-to-date merchandise, go to the nearby **Super El Globo** on the side street next to the market, tel. (755) 427-40. Their well-organized aisles have most of what you'll need, including Cocoa Puffs cereal, Canada Dry soda,

BRUCE WHIPPERMAN

*Fresh fruit is among
the big bargains at the
Zihuatanejo* mercado.

Nucoa margarine, spaghetti, a few wines, and J & B scotch. Open Mon.-Sat. 0800-1930, Sunday 0800-1500.

For convenience shopping, the **Super El Dorado,** tel. 427-25, one block from the beach, is one of the only stores in downtown Zihuatanejo with much food. Open daily 0900-1400 and 1600-2100.

Zihuatanejo's small **Health Food Store,** corner Galeana and Ejido, three blocks from the beach, open Mon.-Sat. 0900-1400 and 1600-2000, stocks a little bit of everything from frozen yogurt and organic honey to shark cartilage and herbal shampoo.

Ixtapa Shopping

Ixtapa's **Centro Comercial** complex stretches along the midsection of Paseo Ixtapa across from the hotels. It has four viable (of about 10 still forthcoming) and attractive subcomplexes, all fronting the boulevard. Moving east to west, first come the Los Patios and Fuentes subcomplexes, where mini-marts, T-shirt and trinket shops, and super-expensive designer stores—Bill Blass, Ralph Lauren, and Gucci—occupy the choice boulevard frontages. Behind them, dozens of mostly small and ordinary crafts and jewelry shops languish along back lanes and inside patios. More of the same occupies the La Puerta subcomplex a hundred yards farther on. Next comes the police station, and, after that, the Galerías Ixtapa subcomplex at the corner of Paseo Las Garzas.

Handicrafts

Although some stores in the Ixtapa Centro Comercial shopping center and the adjacent tourist market (across from the Sheraton) offer handicrafts, Zihuatanejo offers the best selection and prices.

The Zihuatanejo **tourist market** stalls display a flood of crafts brought by families who come from all parts of Pacific Mexico. Their goods—delicate Michoacán lacquerware, bright Tonalá birds, gleaming Taxco silver, whimsical Guerrero masks, rich Guadalajara leather—spread for blocks along Av. Cinco de Mayo on the downtown west side. Compare prices; although bargaining here is customary, the glut of merchandise makes it a one-sided buyer's market, with many sellers barely managing to scrape by. If you err in your bargaining, kindly do it on the generous side.

Prominent among **downtown shops** nearby is the **Casa Marina,** a family project of community leader Helen Krebs Posse. She and her adult children and spouses separately own and manage stores in the complex, just west of the beachfront town plaza.

Helen's store, the **Embarcadero,** on the lower floor, street side, has an unusually choice collection of woven and embroidered finery, mostly from Oaxaca. In addition to walls and racks of colorful, museum-quality traditional blankets, flower-embroidered dresses, and elaborate crocheted *huipiles,* she also offers wooden folk-figurines and a collection of intriguing masks.

Guerrero basket

ERIN DWYER

Other stores in the Casa Marina complex include **La Zapoteca** on the bottom floor, specializing in weavings from Teotitlán del Valle in Oaxaca. Farther on and upstairs are El Jumil (silver and masks), Latzotil (Mayan art), El Calibria (leather), and the Cafe El Marina (pizza and used paperbacks). Local weavers demonstrate in the Embarcadero and La Zapoteca stores mornings and afternoons. The entire complex is open Mon.-Sat. 0900-1300 and 1600-2000, tel. (755) 423-73, credit cards accepted.

Cerámicas Tonalá, a block east, on the opposite side of the plaza, has one of the finest Tonalá pottery collections outside of the renowned source itself. Here, graceful glazed vases and plates, decorated in traditional plant and animal designs, fill the cabinets, while a menagerie of lovable owls, ducks, fish, armadillos, and frogs, all seemingly poised to spring to life, crowd the shelves. Open Mon.-Sat. 0900-1400 and 1600-2000; credit cards accepted.

A few steps up Cuauhtémoc, **Alberto's** two shops, on opposite sides of the street, tel. (755) 439-90, offer an extensive silver jewelry collec-

tion. As with gold and precious stones, their silver prices can be reckoned approximately by weighing, at about $1 per gram. Their cases and cabinets of shiny earrings, chains, bracelets, rings, and much more, are products of a family of artists, taught by a master craftsman, now semi-retired, in Puerto Vallarta. Many of the designs are original, and, with bargaining, reasonably priced. Open Mon.-Sat. 0900-1430 and 1600-2030; credit cards accepted.

At **Galería Maya** nearby at Nicolas Bravo 31, between Cuauhtémoc and Guerrero, tel. (755) 446-06, Tania, the friendly American expatriate owner, has accumulated a multitude of one-of-a-kind folk curios from many parts of Mexico. Her wide-ranging, carefully selected collection includes masks, necklaces, sculptures, purses, blouses, *huipiles*, ritual objects, and much more. Open Mon.-Sat. 1000-1400 and 1700-2100.

Photography

In Zihuatanejo, one-hour photofinishing, popular film varieties, and some photo supplies are available at local Fuji film dealer **Feconde Laboratorio** at the corner of Alvarez and Cuauhtémoc, adjacent to the beachfront plaza, tel. 433-78. Open Mon.-Sat. 1000-1900.

Super-Fotografía La Palma, four blocks up the street, offers approximately the same services and plenty of Kodak film. Located on Cuauhtémoc, corner of Gonzáles, tel. (755) 433-28. Open Mon.-Sat. 0900-1400 and 1530-2000.

SERVICES

Money Exchange

To change money in Zihuatanejo, go to **Banamex,** tel. (755) 421-81, a few doors up Cuauhtémoc from the plaza. Open for money exchange Mon.-Fri. 0900-2300. If the Banamex lines are too long, go to their **teller machine** (MasterCard, Visa, Cirrus, and Plus) a few doors away, or to **Bancomer,** or **Banco Serfin,** at Bravo and Juárez, a few blocks east, across from the market.

After hours, go around the corner to the **Casa de Cambio Ballestros,** at Galeana and Bravo, two blocks from the beach, to change U.S., Canadian, French, German, Swiss, and other currencies and traveler's checks. For the convenience, they offer you significantly less for your money than the banks. Open daily 0800-2100.

In Ixtapa, change money at your hotel desk; or, for better rates, go to **Bancomer** in the El Portal complex behind the shops across the boulevard from the Presidente. Open for traveler's checks and currency exchange Mon.-Fri. 0930-1130, tel. (755) 305-64 or 306-24.

The local **American Express** branch in the Hotel Krystal issues and cashes American Express traveler's checks and provides travel agency services to the public. For card-carrying members, they provide full money services, such as check-cashing. They're open Mon.-Sat. 0900-1400 and 1600-1800; money services hours may be shorter. Call for confirmation, tel. (755) 308-53, fax 312-06.

Communication

The only **post office** serving both Zihuatanejo and Ixtapa is in Zihuatanejo

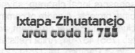

Ixtapa-Zihuatanejo area code is **755**

at the Centro Federal. Open Mon.-Fri. 0900-1900, Saturday 0900-1300, a couple of blocks east of the Ixtapa minibus stop at Juárez and Morelos, five blocks from the beach.

Next door is **Telecomunicaciones,** which offers long-distance telephone, public fax (fax 755-421-63), telegrams, and money orders Mon.-Fri. 0900-1700. Another similar office serves Ixtapa, in the La Puerta shopping center (rear side) across Paseo Ixtapa, from the Hotel Stouffer Presidente.

Not far away about two blocks closer to the beach at 69 Paseo del Palmar, tel. (755) 431-65, is the upgraded very reliable government **Mexpost** (like U.S. Express Mail) mail service.

The small **Cruise Ship Terminal** office on the Zihuatanejo pier sells stamps and has a mailbox, long-distance telephone, and public fax; open Mon.-Sat. 0900-1500.

Downtown Zihuatanejo's private *larga distancia* telephone office also changes both U.S. and Canadian currency and traveler's checks; open daily 0800-2100, on Galeana, the lane parallel to Cuauhtémoc, corner of Bravo, tel. (755) 428-00.

In both Ixtapa and Zihuatanejo, streetside public phone booths handle international long distance calls. For best rates, call collect or with a credit card. Dial 95-800-462-4240 for the English-speaking AT&T international operator, 95-800-674-6000 for MCI, or 95-800-877-8000 for Sprint.

Immigration and Customs

If you lose your tourist card, go to **Migración** on Paseo del Palmar, about five blocks past Plaza Kyoto, on the northeast edge of downtown, tel. (755) 427-95; open Mon.-Fri. 0900-1500. Bring your passport and some proof of the date you arrived in Mexico, such as your airline ticket, or a copy of your lost tourist permit.

The **Aduana** office, tel. (755) 432-62, is at the airport, off Hwy. 200 about seven miles south of Zihuatanejo, open daily 0800-1900. If you have to temporarily leave the country without your car, have someone fluent in Spanish call them about the required paperwork.

Laundromats

In Zihuatanejo, take your laundry to **Laundry Super Clean** at Gonzáles and Galeana, just off Cuauhtémoc, four blocks from the plaza, tel. (755) 423-47; open Mon.-Sat. 0800-2000. If you also need dry-cleaning, take both it and your laundry items to **Lavandería Alda,** on Cuauhtémoc, a few doors away, tel. (755) 450-46; open Mon.-Sat. 0830-1400 and 1500-2000.

INFORMATION

Tourist Information Offices

The helpful staff of the Zihuatanejo municipal office of tourism, tel. (755) 420-01, ext. 121, answers questions and hands out maps and brochures at their small office behind the city hall, on the beachfront plaza. Open Mon.-Sat. 0900-1400 and 1600-1900.

The Ixtapa federal office of **Turismo** appears to function more as a regulatory agency rather than an information office. You may do better by seeing the travel agent in your hotel lobby. Open Mon.-Fri. 0900-1500 in the La Puerta shopping complex, across the boulevard from the Hotel Presidente.

An excellent alternative local information source is the *cámara de comercio* (chamber of commerce) in downtown Zihuatanejo, on Bravo, near corner of Guerrero, tel. (755) 425-75. Friendly director Gilda Soberanis and her staff are ready and able to answer questions, suggest contacts, and provide whatever local maps and literature they have. Open Mon.-Fri. 0900-1400 and 1600-1900.

Hospital, Police, and Emergencies

Zihuatanejo has no well-equipped private hospitals. Many local people recommend the state of Guerrero **general hospital,** on Av. Morelos, corner of Mar Egeo, just off from Hwy. 200, tel. (755) 438-48 or 439-65, for its generally competent, dedicated, and professional staff.

For medicines and drugs in Ixtapa, try your hotel shop, or call one of the many Zihuatanejo pharmacies in downtown Zihuatanejo, such as the **Farmacia Zihuatanejo,** at Cuauhtémoc 10, one block from the beachfront plaza, tel. (755) 420-30.

For **police emergencies** in Ixtapa and Zihuatanejo, contact the *caberca de policía* headquarters in Zihuatanejo, on Calle Limón near the post office, tel. (755) 420-40. You can also go directly to the *caseta de policía* on-duty police booth behind the Zihuatanejo plaza-front city hall, or the same in Ixtapa on the boulevard across from the Hotel Presidente.

Publications

The best local English-language selection lines the many shelves in the bookshop of the **Hotel Westin Ixtapa.** Besides dozens of new paperback novels and scores of popular U.S. magazines, they stock *USA Today* and the *News* of Mexico City newspapers and a thoughtful selection of Mexico guides and books of cultural and historical interest. Open daily 0900-2100.

The newsstand on Cuauhtémoc, at the Zihuatanejo plaza, is a sometimes source of popular U.S. magazines, such as *Vogue, Time,* and *Sports Illustrated,* plus the newspapers *News* of Mexico (around 1300) and *USA Today.* Open daily 0800-2000. A similar small selection is sometimes available at the newsstand on Cuauhtémoc, two blocks from the plaza, corner of Ejido. Open daily 0800-1900.

The friendly, small Zihuatanejo bookstore **Librería Byblos,** despite its mainly Spanish inventory, does have some used English-language paperbacks. They also stock English-Spanish dictionaries and a good map of Guerrero. Open Mon.-Sat. 1000-1500 and 1700-2200, Sunday 1700-2200; at Asencio 11, off Cuauhtémoc, one block from the plaza, tel. (755) 422-81. Many more used paperbacks line the walls of friendly **Cafe Marina** adjacent to the beach just west of the plaza; open Mon.-Sat. till 2200, closed June to mid-September.

The small Zihuatanejo **Biblioteca** (public library) also has some shelves of English-language paperbacks. Open Mon.-Fri. 0900-1400 and 1600-2000, Saturday 0900-1300; on Cuauhtémoc, at the little plaza five blocks from the beach.

Ecological Association And Humane Society

The grassroots **Asociación de Ecologistas** sponsors local cleanup, save-the-turtles, and other projects. A cadre of community leaders, including the former president, Jorge Luis Reyes, tel. (755) 437-04, Anita Rellstab, owner of Bungalows Pacífico, tel. (755) 421-12, and marine biologist Juan M. Barnard Avila, owner of Zihuatanejo Scuba Center, tel. (755) 421-47 are dedicated to preserving the Ixtapa-Zihuatanejo coast. They welcome volunteers to join their efforts.

Helen Krebs Posse is the guiding light of the **Sociedad Protectora de Animales,** which is working hard to educate people about animal issues. Contact her at her shop, Embarcadero, just west of the Zihuatanejo plaza, tel. (755) 423-73.

GETTING THERE AND AWAY

By Air

Three major carriers connect Ixtapa-Zihuatanejo directly with U.S. and Mexican destinations.

Aeroméxico flights connect with Houston daily via Mexico City. Many other flights connect directly to Mexico City. For flight information and reservations, call (755) 420-22.

Mexicana Airlines flights connect directly with Los Angeles via Guadalajara four times a week. For reservations and information, call (755) 322-08, 322-09, or toll-free 91-800-50-220.

Delta Air Lines flights connect directly with Los Angeles on Saturday, and Sunday. For flight information and reservations, call toll-free 91-800-902-21.

Air Arrival and Departure

Ixtapa-Zihuatanejo is quickly accessible, only seven miles (11 km) north of the airport via Hwy. 200. Arrival is generally simple—if you come with a day's worth of pesos and hotel reservations. The terminal has no money exchange, information booth, or hotel-reservation service. It's best not to leave your hotel choice up to your taxi driver, for he will probably deposit you at the hotel that pays him a commission on your first night's lodging.

Transportation to town is usually by taxi or *colectivo* van. Tickets are available at booths near the terminal exit for about $4-6 per person (depending on destination) for a *colectivo*, or $15-25 for three persons in a taxi. Mobile budget travelers can walk the few hundred yards to the highway and flag down one of the frequent daytime Zihuatanejo bound buoco (vory fow, if any, continue on to Ixtapa, however). At night, ride a *colectivo*.

Several major **car rentals** operate airport booths. Avoid problems and save money by negotiating your rental through the agencies' toll-free yellow-page 800 numbers (see chart in the "On the Road" chapter) before departure: Hertz, tel. (755) 430-50 or 425-90; Dollar, tel. (755) 430-66; Avis, tel. (755) 429-32; Quick, tel. (755) 448-37 or 318-30.

Departure is quick and easy if you have your passport, tourist permit (which was stamped on arrival), and $12 cash (or the equivalent in pesos) international departure tax. Departees who've lost their tourist permits can avoid trouble and a fine by either getting a duplicate at Zihuatanejo Immigration (see "Information" above) or (perhaps) by having a police report of the loss.

For last-minute postcards and shopping, the airport has a mailbox and a few gift shops.

By Car or RV

Three routes, two easy and one unsafe and not recommended, connect Ixtapa-Zihuatanejo with Playa Azul and Michoacán to the northwest, Acapulco to the southeast, and Ciudad Altamirano and central Guerrero to the northeast.

Traffic sails smoothly along the 76 miles (122 km) of Hwy. 200, either way, between Zihuatanejo and Lázaro Cárdenas/Playa Azul. The same is true of the 150-mile (242-km) Hwy. 200 southern extension to Acapulco. Allow about two and a half hours to or from Playa Azul, four hours to or from Acapulco.

The story is much different, however, for the winding, sparsely populated, cross-Sierra Hwy. 134 (intersecting with Hwy. 200 nine miles north) from Zihuatanejo to Ciudad Altamirano. Rising along spectacular, jungle-clad ridges, the paved but sometimes potholed road leads over cool, pine-clad heights and descends to the Altamirano high valley after about 100 miles (160 km). The continuing leg to Iguala on the Acapulco-Mexico City highway is longer, about 112 miles (161 km), equally winding, and often busy. Allow about eight hours westbound and nine hours eastbound for the entire trip. Keep filled with gasoline, and be prepared for emergencies, especially along the Altamirano-Zihuatanejo leg, where no hotels and few services exist. **Warning:** This route, unfortunately, has been plagued by robberies and nasty drug-related incidents. Inquire locally—your hotel, the tourist information office, the bus station—to see if authorities have secured the road before attempting this trip.

By Bus

Zihuatanejo's big, shiny long-distance **Central de Autobús** is on Hwy. 200, Acapulco-bound side, about a mile south of downtown Zihuatanejo. Travelers enjoy a restaurant-cafeteria, a public long-distance phone, left-luggage lockers, and a snack stand, but no food store. You'd best prepare by stocking up with water and goodies before you depart.

Estrella Blanca (EB), tel. (755) 434-77, the major carrier, computer-coordinates its service with the service of its subsidiaries Flecha Roja (FR) and Transportes Cuauhtémoc. Tickets are available with cash or credit cards for all departures from computer-assisted agents. In total, they offer "Primera Plus" (infrequent, super-first-class, reserved), first class (frequent, reserved), and second class (very frequent, unreserved) service.

Most buses run along the Hwy. 200 corridor, connecting with Lázaro Cárdenas/Playa Azul and northwestern points, and with Acapulco and points south and east.

Dozens of "Primera Plus" and first-class buses and many (every half hour) second-class buses connect daily with Acapulco. Several of them continue on to Mexico City. In the opposite direction, many "Primera Plus" and first- and second-class buses (at least one an hour) connect daily with Lázaro Cárdenas/Playa Azul and northwest points.

A number of **Tres Estrellas de Oro** departures connect from the same terminal, along the Pacific coast Hwy. 200 corridor, south to Acapulco, and north via Manzanillo, Puerto Vallarta, and Mazatlán, to the U.S. border at Mexicali and Tijuana. Others departures connect north with Uruapán and Morelia, via Playa Azul.

Another major bus carrier **Estrella de Oro,** tel. (755) 438-02 offers a few competing long-distance first-class departures from their station on Paseo del Palmar, four blocks from Plaza Kyoto.

ALONG THE ROAD TO ACAPULCO

Although the 150-mile (242-km) Zihuatanejo-Acapulco stretch of Hwy. 200 is smooth and easy, resist the temptation to hurry through. Your reward will be a bright string of little pearls—idyllic south-seas villages, miles of stroll-able, fishable beaches, wildlife-rich *esteros*, lovely small hotels, and a tranquil little beach resort on the hidden edge of Acapulco.

On the Road

If you're driving, mark your odometer at the Zihuatanejo southside Pemex, near Km 240 on Hwy. 200. Or, if driving north, do the same at the Acapulco *zócalo* (old town square) Km zero, and head out on the northbound coast road past Pie de la Cuesta. Road mileages and kilometer markers are helpful in finding the paths to hidden little beaches.

Bus travelers, take a second-class bus from the Zihuatanejo or the Acapulco Estrella Blanca Central de Autobús. Ask the driver to drop you at your chosen haven.

PLAYA LAS POZAS

This surf-fishing paradise is reachable via the Zihuatanejo airport turnoff road. The reward is a lagoon full of bait fish, space for RV or tent camping (be careful of soft sand), a wide beach, and friendly beachside *palapa* restaurants.

The beach itself is 100 yards wide, of yellow-white sand, and extends for miles in both directions. It has driftwood but not many shells. Fish thrive in its thunderous, open-ocean waves. Consequently, casts from the beach can routinely yield five- and 10-pound catches by either bait or lures. Local folks catch fish mostly by net, both in the surf and the nearby lagoon. During the June-Sept. rainy season, the lagoon breaks through the bar. Big fish, gobbling prey at the outlet, can be netted or hooked at the same spot themselves.

Camping is popular here on weekends and holidays. Other times you may have the place to yourself. As a courtesy, ask the friendly Netos family, who runs the best of the *palapa* restaurants, if it's okay.

Get there by following the well-marked airport turnoff road at Km 230. After one mile, turn right at the cyclone fence just before the terminal and follow the bumpy but easily passable straight level road 1.1 miles (1.8 km) to the beach.

BARRA DE POTOSÍ

At Achotes, nine miles (15 km) south of Zihuatanejo, a Laguna de Potosí sign points right to Barra de Potosí, a picture-perfect fishing hamlet at the sheltered south end of the Bahía de Potosí. After a few miles through green, tufted groves, the road parallels the bayside beach, a crescent of fine white sand, virtually undeveloped except for one hotel.

The **Hotel Resort Barra de Potosí** perches right on the beach. With eight air-conditioned apartments (with hot water and fans), a pretty beachfront pool, palms, a bar, and a restaurant, it appears perfect for a tranquil week's rest. Reservations are probably necessary only during the post-Christmas and pre-Easter weeks; try writing for information at simply Barra de Potosí, Guerrero, or calling tel. (755) 434-45 or 433-19.

The surf is generally tranquil and safe for swimming near the hotel, although the waves, which do not roll but break rather quickly along long fronts, are not good for surfing.

The waves become even more tranquil at the south end, where a sheltering headland rises beyond the village and the lagoon. Beneath its swaying palm grove, the hamlet of Barra de Potosí (pop. 1,000) has the ingredients for weeks of tranquil living. Several broad, hammock-hung *palapa* restaurants (here called *enramadas*) front the bountiful lagoon.

Home for swarms of birds and waterfowl and shoals of fish, the **Laguna de Potosí** stretches for miles to its far mangrove reaches. Adventure out with your own boat or kayak, or go with **Orlando,** who regularly takes parties out for fishing or wildlife-viewing tours.

Bait fish, caught locally with nets, abound in the lagoon. Fishing is fine for bigger catches (jack, snapper, mullet) by boat or casts beyond the waves. Launch your boat easily in the lagoon, then head, like the local fishermen, past the open sandbar.

Camping is common by RV or tent along the uncrowded edge of the lagoon. Village stores can provide basic supplies.

Get there by taking the signed turnoff road at Km 225, nine miles south of Zihuatanejo, just south of the Los Achotes River bridge. Continue along the good (trailer-accessible) dirt road for 5.5 miles (8.9 km) to the hotel and the village half a mile farther south.

PAPANOA

The small town of Papanoa (pop. 3,000) straddles the highway 47 miles (75 km) south of Zihuatanejo and 103 miles (165 km) north of Acapulco. Local folks tell the tongue-in-cheek story of its Hawaiian-sounding name. It seems that there was a flood, and the son of the local headman had to talk fast to save his life by escaping in a *canoa.* Instead of saying "Papa . . . canoa," the swift-talking boy shortened his plea to "Papa . . . noa."

The town itself has a few snack restaurants, a pharmacy, a doctor, groceries, a *gasolinera* that stocks unleaded gas, first-class bus stops, a long-distance telephone, and one resort-style lodging, the **Hotel Club Papanoa,** Papanoa, Guerrero 40907, tel. (742) 201-50.

Near the beach about a mile south of town, the hotel has about 30 large rooms, a restaurant, and a big pool set in spacious ocean-view garden grounds. Intended to be luxurious but now a bit worn around the edges, the hotel remains popular on weekends and holidays but is nearly empty most other times. Rooms run about $25 s, $37 for two to four, with hot water and fans.

The hotel grounds adjoin the beach, **Playa Cayaquitos.** The wide, breezy, yellow-gray

Pelicans, tidepools, a garden of sandstone, and gourmet surf fishing attract adventurers to Playa Piedra Tlacoyunque.

BRUCE WHIPPERMAN

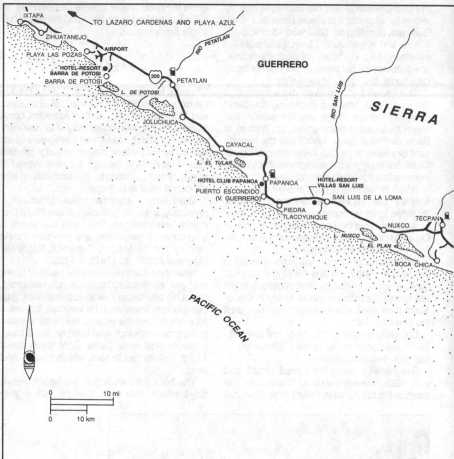

strand stretches for two miles, washed by powerful open-ocean rollers with good left and right surfing breaks. Additional attractions include surf fishing beyond the breakers and driftwood along the sand. Beach access is via the off-highway driveway just north of the hotel. At the beach, a parking lot borders a seafood restaurant. Farther on, the road narrows (but is still motor home accessible) through a defunct beachside home development, past several brush-bordered informal RV parking or tenting spots.

PIEDRA TLACOYUNQUE

At Km 150 (56 miles, 90 km from Zihuatanejo, 94 miles from Acapulco) a signed "Zona Reserva Protección de Tortugas" side road heads seaward to Piedra Tlacoyunque and the Carabelas Restaurant. One mile down the good dirt road, the restaurant appears, perching on a bluff overlooking a monumental sandstone

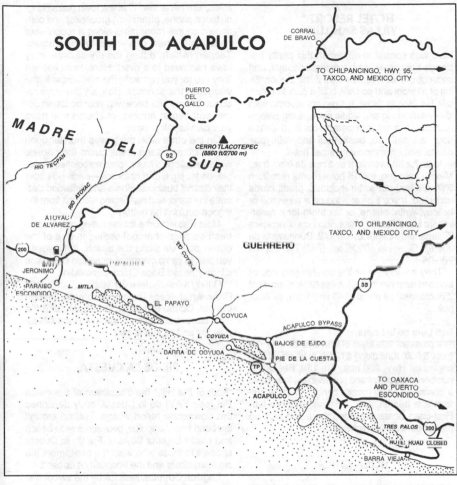

SOUTH TO ACAPULCO

CORRAL
DE BRAVO

TO CHILPANCINGO, HWY 95,
TAXCO, AND MEXICO CITY

PUERTO
DEL
GALLO

MADRE

DEL

SUR

CERRO TLACOTEPEC
(8860 ft/2700 m)

RIO TECPAN

92

RIO ATOYAC

GUERRERO

ATOYAC
DE ALVAREZ

TO CHILPANCINGO,
TAXCO, AND MEXICO CITY

200

JERONIMO

TO COYUCA

38

PARAISO
ESCONDIDO

L. MITLA

EL PAPAYO

COYUCA

ACAPULCO BYPASS

L. COYUCA

BAJOS DE EJIDO

BARRA DE COYUCA

PIE DE LA CUESTA

TP

ACAPULCO

TO OAXACA
AND PUERTO
ESCONDIDO

L. TRES PALOS

200

NOTE: ROAD CLOSED

BARRA VIEJA

rock, Piedra Tlacoyunque. Below, a wave-tossed strand, ripe for beachcombing and surf fishing, stretches for miles. Powerful breakers with fine right-hand surfing angles roll in and swish up the steep beach. For fishing, buy some bait from the net fishermen on the beach and try some casts beyond the billows crashing into the south side of the Piedra. Later, stroll through the garden of eroded rock "sea stacks" on the north side. There you can poke among the snails and seaweeds in a big sheltered

tidepool, under the watchful guard of the squads of pelicans roosting on the surrounding pinnacles.

At the Carabelas Restaurant on the bluff above, you can take in the whole breezy scene while enjoying the recommended catch of the day. For an overnight or a short stay, ask the restaurant owners if it's okay to park your (self-contained) RV in the restaurant lot or in the beach-level grove down below.

HOTEL RESORT
VILLAS SAN LUIS

Little was spared to embellish this pretty hacienda-like corner of a big mango, papaya, and coconut grove. It appears as if the owner, tiring of all work and no play, built a park to entertain his friends. Now, his project blooms with lovely swimming and kiddie pools, a big *palapa* restaurant, a smooth *palapa*-covered dance floor, a small zoo, basketball and volleyball courts, and an immaculate small hotel.

Ideal for an overnight or a respite from hard Mexico traveling, the 15 hotel rooms rent from $37, a/c and hot water included, credit cards accepted. If you'll be arriving on a weekend or holiday, write, phone, or fax them for a reservation: Hotel Resort Villas San Luis, Carretera Zihuatanejo-Acapulco, Km 142, Buenavista de Juárez, Guerrero 40906, tel. (742) 703-28, fax 700-08.

They are located on the southbound side of the road near Km 142, 61 miles (98 km) south of Zihuatanejo, 89 miles (143 km) north of Acapulco.

San Luis de la Loma

The pleasant little town of San Luis de la Loma (pop. 3,000) runs along a hilltop main street that angles off Hwy. 200 near Km 140. Besides a number of groceries and pharmacies, they have a *centro de salud* (health center), a *larga distancia*, a dentist, and a clinical analysis lab. First-class buses also stop there and pick up passengers on the highway.

BOCA CHICA

For the fun and adventure of it, visit Boca Chica, a beach village accessible by boat only. Here, camping is de rigueur, since even permanent residents are doing it. It makes no sense to pour concrete on a sandbar where palm fronds are free and the next wave may wash everything away anyway.

The jumping-off spot is near Km 98 (88 miles, 142 km south of Zihuatanejo, 61 miles, 98 km north of Acapulco), where a sign marks the dirt road to Tetitlán (pop. 2,000). In about three

miles, turn left at the "T" at the town plaza (long-distance phone, pharmacy, groceries) and continue a couple more miles along a rough—but negotiable when dry—road to the Laguna Tecpán (which, during the dry season, may have narrowed to a river). Here, launches will ferry you (or you can walk) the mile across to the village on the sandbar. Bargain the *viaje redondo* (return-trip) price with your boatman before you depart (unless, of course you have your own kayak or boat).

On the other side, the waves thunder upon the beach and sand crabs guard their holes, while the village's four separate societies—people, dogs, pigs, and chickens—each go about their distinct business. Shells and driftwood decorate the sand, and surf fishing with bait from the lagoon couldn't be better.

Most visitors come for the eating only: super-fresh seafood charcoal-broiled in one of the dozen *palapas* along the beach. If, however, you plan to camp overnight, bring drinking water, a highly prized Boca Chica commodity.

During the summer rainy season, the Tecpán River, which feeds the lagoon, breaks through the bar. Ocean fish enter the lagoon, and the river current sometimes washes Boca Chica, *palapas* and all, out to sea.

PIE DE LA CUESTA

"Foot of the Hill," the translation of the name Pie (pee-YAY) de la Cuesta, aptly describes this downscale resort village. Tucked around the bend from Acapulco, between a wide beach and placid Laguna Coyuca, Pie de la Cuesta appeals to those who want the excitement the big town offers and the tranquility it doesn't.

Laguna Coyuca, kept full by the sweet waters of the Río Coyuca, has long been known for its fish, birdlife, and tranquil, palm-lined shores. During the early 1400s, the Tarascans (who ruled from the Michoacán highlands) established a provincial capital near the town of Coyuca. After the Aztecs drove out the Tarascans a century later (and the Aztecs in turn were defeated by the Spanish) Pie de la Cuesta and its beautiful Laguna Coyuca slumbered in the shadow of Acapulco.

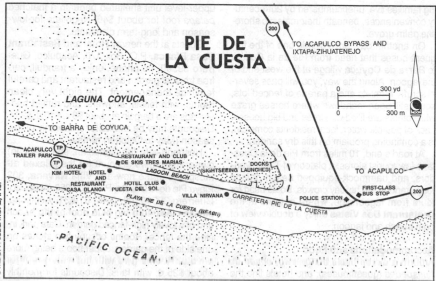

Sights

Laguna de Coyuca is a large sandy-bottomed lake, lined by palms and laced by mangrove channels. It stretches 10 miles along the shoreline, west from Pie de la Cuesta, which occupies the southeast (Acapulco) side. The barrier sandbar, wide Playa Pie de la Cuesta, separates the lagoon from the ocean. It extends a dozen miles west to the river outlet, which is open to the sea only during the rainy season. A road runs along the beach west the length of Laguna Coyuca to the tourist hamlet of Barra de Coyuca. There, *palapas* line the beach and serve seafood to busloads of Sunday visitors.

Playa Pie de la Cuesta, a seemingly endless, hundred-yard-wide stretch of yellow sand, is fine for surf fishing, beachcombing, jogging, and long sunset walks. However, its powerful open-ocean waves are unsuited for surfing and frequently hazardous for swimming. They often break thunderously near the sand and recede with strong, turbulent undertow.

On the other side of the bar, the east end of Laguna Coyuca is an embarkation point for lagoon tours and center for water-skiing and jet-skiing. Among the best equipped of the shoreline clubs that offer powerboat services is the

Restaurant and Club de Skis Tres Marías. Besides a pleasant lake-view shoreline *palapa* restaurant, they offer water-skiing at about $35/hour and jet-ski boats for about $50/hour.

If you want to launch your own boat, you can do so easily at Club Tres Marías and others for about $10. The boat traffic, which confines itself mostly to mid-lagoon, does not deter **swimming** in the lagoon's clear waters. Slip on your bathing suit and jump in anywhere along the sandy shoreline.

Lagoon tours begin from several landings dotting the Pie de la Cuesta end of the lagoon. Half-day regular excursions (maximum 10 persons, about $14 per person) push off daily around 1100, 1200, and 1330. Along the way, they pass islands with trees loaded with nesting cormorants, herons, and pelicans. In mid-lake, gulls dip and sway in the breeze behind your boat while a host of storks, ducks, avocets, and a dozen other varieties paddle, preen, and forage in the water nearby. Other times, your boat passes through winding channels hung with vines and lined with curtains of great mangrove roots. At midpoint, tours usually stop for a bite to eat at Isla Montosa. Here, roosters crow, pigs root, bougainvillea blooms, and a colony of fishing families live, unencumbered by 20th-century conveniences, beneath their majestic shoreline palm grove.

On another day, drive or ride one of the frequent buses that head from Pie de la Cuesta to **Barra de Coyuca** village at the west end of the lagoon. Along the way, you will pass several scruffy hamlets and a parade of fenced lots, some still open meadows where horses graze while others are filled with trees and big houses. Lack of potable water, local residents complain, is a continuing problem on this dry sandbar.

At road's end, 10 miles from Pie de la Cuesta, a few tourist stores, a platoon of T-shirt vendors, and hammock-equipped beach *palapa* restaurants serve holiday crowds. Boats head for tours from lagoonside, where patrons at the **Restaurant Dos Vistas** enjoy a double view of both beach and lagoon.

Accommodations and Food

Around a dozen basic bungalows, *casas de huéspedes* (guesthouses), and hotels line the Pie de la Cuesta's single beachside road. Competition keeps cleanliness high, management sharp, and prices low. They all cluster along a quarter mile of roadfront, enjoying highly visible locations extending directly to the beach. Write for reservations, especially for the winter season and holidays. Most of them have tepid, room-temperature bath water only, and do not accept credit cards; exceptions are noted below.

In order of increasing price, first comes **Casa de Huéspedes Leonor,** which is very popular with a loyal cadre of Canadian winter returnees, 63 Carretera Pie de la Cuesta, Guerrero 39900, tel. (746) 00-348. They enjoy camaraderie around the tables of the *palapa* restaurant that occupies the beachside end of a large leafy parking-lot garden. The several breezy, more private upper-floor units are most popular. All 10 rooms have two beds, showers, and fans, and rent for about $17 d daily, $14 monthly.

More picturesque are the **Bungalows María Cristina,** P.O. Box 607, Acapulco, Guerrero 39300, nine units (six rooms, three kitchen-equipped bungalows) set between a streetside parking lot and a palmy beachside restaurant-garden. The very plain rooms, with toilets and showers, rent for about $22 d. The most charming of the bungalows is a big, breezy, and private

upper-level unit sheltered beneath a thatched *palapa* roof for about $40. Negotiate for low-season and long-term discounts.

Guests at the nearby **Hotel and Restaurant Casa Blanca,** P.O. Box 370, Acapulco, Guerrero 39300, no phone, enjoy a tranquil, car-free tropical garden and restaurant and careful feminine management. The eight very clean rooms, with toilets, showers, and ruffled bedspreads are a bargain at about $8 s, $15 d, $23 t. Discounts may be available for monthly or low season (May to October) rentals.

Husband-wife (he Canadian, she Mexican) owner-managers account for the relaxed atmosphere of the new-age **Villa Nirvana,** 302 Playa Pie de la Cuesta, P.O. Box 950, Acapulco, Guerrero 39300, tel. (746) 01-631. Additional plusses include a big blue pool at the beach end of a lovely high-fenced garden. Cars park inside the fence. Rooms occupy two stories on one side of the garden, upper floors being more private. Rooms (two with hot water) rent for about $25 d, with fans. Discounts for monthly rentals run about 15%.

Among the prettiest of Pie de la Cuesta accommodations is the **Hotel Club Puesta del Sol,** P.O. Box 1264, Acapulco, Guerrero 39300, tel. (746) 00-412, where guests enjoy a good restaurant, a blue pool, and a tennis court within spacious, sculpture-decorated garden grounds. Tasty food from the kitchen of the amiable co-manager and friendly hours spent around the restaurant tables account for the hotel's loyal North American, European, and Mexican clientele. The 24 Spartan but clean rooms are spread among two double-story buildings, one at beachfront. Doubles by the beach go for about $30 high-season and $24 low; away from the beach, the same run $24 and $16. Kitchen-equipped beachside bungalow apartments for six rent for about $50 high season, $37 low. All accommodations come with fans, warm-water showers, and include parking.

Trying hard to be luxurious is the **Ukae Kim Hotel Club de Playa y Ski,** Playa Pie de la Cuesta 336, Pie de la Cuesta, Guerrero 39900, tel. (746) 02-187, fax 02-188. Unfortunately, the builder crammed the 31 rooms into a small space, rendering them private but generally dark. Amenities include a small but artful pool and *palapa* restaurant at the hotel's beachfront end. They also have a water-sports marina across the street, which provides water-skiing for $50 per hour. For maximum light, try for an upper, seafront room. The clean, tastefully decorated rooms go for about $45 s or d; $55 for more luxury with jacuzzi; with hot water; credit cards accepted.

RV-equipped Pie de la Cuesta vacationers enjoy the excellent **Acapulco Trailer Park,** with about 60 palm-shaded beachfront and lagoonside spaces, with all hookups, P.O. Box 1, Acapulco, Guerrero 39300, tel. (746) 00-010, fax 02-457. A friendly atmosphere, good management, and many extras, including a secure fence and gate, keep the place full most of the winter. Facilities include a boat ramp, a store, a security guard, and clean restrooms and showers. Spaces rent (low season) for about $10 beach side, $9 lagoon side; one free day per week. Get your winter reservation in early.

The security guard at the Acapulco Trailer Park is a reminder of former times, when muggings and theft were occurring with some frequency on Playa Pie de la Cuesta. Although bright new night lights on the beach and a local police station have greatly reduced the problem, local folks still warn against camping or walking on the beach at night.

As for **food,** most folks either do their own cooking, eat at their Pie de la Cuesta lodgings, or go into Acapulco. Of the few restaurants along the Pie de la Cuesta road, the best is the lakeview *palapa* of the Club de Skis Tres Marías (see above).

Information and Services
Nearly all services are concentrated 20 minutes away in Acapulco. Pie de la Cuesta does have a doctor (who understands both English and French), a pharmacy, a few mini-markets, and a **long-distance telephone** (in front of the Acapulco Trailer Park). In emergencies, go to the *policía,* at the small station near the intersection of the Pie de la Cuesta road and the highway to Acapulco.

Getting There and Away
Pie de la Cuesta is accessible via the fork from Hwy. 200 near Km 10, 144 miles (232 km) southwest of Zihuatanejo. First-class buses drop passengers at the roadside, where they can either walk, taxi, or ride one of the very frequent Acapulco microbuses half a mile to the hotels.

From the same intersection, Acapulco is six miles (10 km) by car, taxi ($5), or local bus.

MIKE WELLINS

ACAPULCO
AND INLAND TO TAXCO

ACAPULCO

All over Mexico and half the world, Acapulco (pop. 1,500,000) means merrymaking, good food, and palm-shaded beaches. Despite 50 years of continuous development, its reputation is as deserved as ever. The many Acapulcos—the turquoise bay edged by golden sands and emerald hills, the host of hotels, humble and grand, the spontaneous entertainments, the colorful market, and shady old town square—continue to draw millions of yearly visitors from all over the world.

HISTORY

Before Columbus
Despite its modern facade, Acapulco has been well known as a traveler's crossroads for at least a millennium. Its name comes from the

Nahuatl (Aztec) words that mean "place of dense reeds."

The earliest-discovered local remains, stone metates and pottery utensils, were left behind by seaside residents around 2500 B.C. Much later, sophisticated artisans fashioned curvaceous female figurines, which archaeologists unearthed at Las Sabanas near Acapulco during the mid-20th century. Those unique finds added fuel to speculation of early Polynesian or Asian influences in Pacific Mexico as early as 1,500 years before Columbus.

Other discoveries, however, resemble artifacts found in highland Mexico. Although undoubtedly influenced by Tarascan, Mixtec, Zapotec, and Aztec civilizations and frequented by their traders, Acapulco never came under their direct control, but instead remained subject to local chieftains until the conquest.

Conquest and Colonization

The Aztecs had scarcely surrendered when Cortés sent expeditions south to build ships and find a route to China. The first such explorers sailed out from Zacatula, near present-day Lázaro Cárdenas on the coast 250 miles northwest of Acapulco. They returned, telling Cortés of Acapulco Bay. By a royal decree dated 25 April 1528, "Acapulco and her land . . . where the ships of the south will be built . . . " passed directly into the hands of the Spanish Crown.

Voyages of discovery set sail from Acapulco for Peru, the Gulf of California, and to Asia. None returned from the across the Pacific, however, until Father Andrés de Urdaneta discovered the northern Pacific tradewinds, which propelled him and his ship, loaded with Chinese treasure, to Acapulco in 1565.

From then on, for more than 200 years, a special yearly trading ship, renowned as Nao de China or in England as the Manila Galleon, not only from Acapulco for the Orient. Its return sparked an annual merchant fair, swelling Acapulco's population with traders jostling to bargain for the Manila Galleon's shiny trove of silks, porcelain, ivory, and lacquerware.

Acapulco's yearly treasure soon attracted marauders, too. In 1579, Francis Drake threatened, and in 1587, off Cabo San Lucas, Thomas Cavendish was the first to capture the Manila Galleon, the *Santa Anna*. The cash booty alone, 1.2 million gold pesos, severely depressed the London gold market.

After a Dutch fleet invaded Acapulco in 1615, the Spanish rebuilt their fort, which they christened Fort San Diego in 1617. Destroyed by an earthquake in 1776, the fort was rebuilt by 1783. But Mexico's War of Independence (1810-21) stopped the Manila Galleon forever, sending Acapulco into a century-long slumber.

Modern Acapulco

In 1927, the government paved the Mexico City-Acapulco road; the first cars arrived on 11 November. The first luxury hotel, the Mirador, at La Quebrada, went up in 1933; soon airplanes began arriving. During the 1940s President Miguel Alemán (1946-52) fell in love with Acapulco and thought everyone else should have the same opportunity. He built new boulevards, power plants, and a superhighway. Investors responded with a lineup of high-rise hostelries. Finally, in 1959, presidents Eisenhower and Adolfo López Mateos convened their summit conference in a grand Acapulco hotel.

Thousands of Mexicans flocked to fill jobs in the shiny hotels and restaurants. They built shantytowns, which climbed the hills and spilled over into previously sleepy communities nearby. The government responded with streets, drainage, power, and schools. By the 1990s more than a million people were calling Acapulco home.

SIGHTS

Getting Oriented

In one tremendous sweep, Acapulco curves around its big half-moon bay. Face the open ocean and you are looking south. West will be on your right hand, east on your left. One continuous beachfront boulevard, appropriately named the **Costera Miguel Alemán** (the "Costera," for short), unites old Acapulco, west of Parque Papagayo amusement zone, with new Acapulco, the lineup of big beach hotels that stretches around the bay to the Las Brisas condo headland. There, during the night, a big cross glows and marks the hilltop lookout, Mirador La Capilla, above the bay's east end.

On the opposite, old-town side of Parque Papagayo, the Costera curves along the palmy, uncluttered *playas* Hornos and Hamacas to the steamship dock. Here the Costera, called the *malecón* as it passes the *zócalo* (town square), continues to the mansion-dotted hilly jumble of **Península de las Playas.**

Getting Around

Buses run nearly continuously along the Costera. Fare averages the equivalent of about 20 cents, rarely more than 40 cents. Bus routes—indicated by such labels as "Base" (BAH-say, the naval base on the east end), "Centro" *(zócalo),* "Caleta" (the beach, at the far west end), "Cine" (movie theater near the beach before the *zócalo*), "Hornos" (the beach near Parque Papagayo)—run along the Costera.

Taxis, on the other hand, cost between $2 and $5 for any in-town destination. They are not metered, so agree upon the price *before*

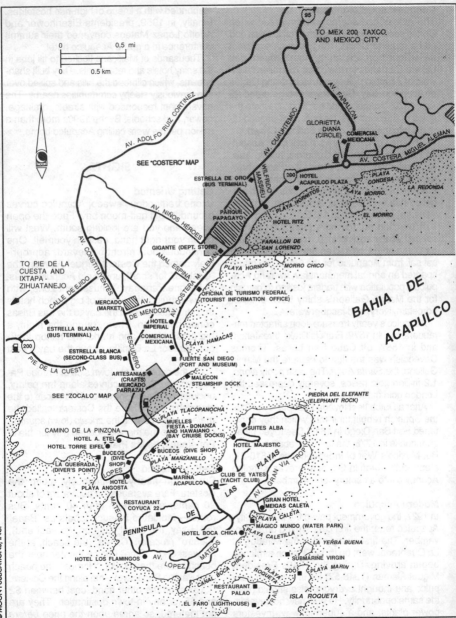

Map labels:

TO MEX 200 TAXCO AND MEXICO CITY
95
AV. FARALLON
AV. ADOLFO RUIZ CORTINEZ
AV. CUAUHTEMOC
WILFRIDO MASSIEU
GLORIETTA DIANA (CIRCLE)
COMERCIAL MEXICANA
AV. COSTERA MIGUEL ALEMAN
PLAYA CONDESA
LA REDONDA
PLAYA MORRO
SEE "COSTERO" MAP
ESTRELLA DE ORO (BUS TERMINAL)
200
HOTEL ACAPULCO PLAZA
PLAYA HORNITOS
EL MORRO
AV. NIÑOS HÉROES
PARQUE PAPAGAYO
HOTEL RITZ
FARALLON DE SAN LORENZO
GIGANTE (DEPT. STORE)
AMAL ESPINA
AV. CONSTITUYENTES
CALLE DE EJIDO
TO PIE DE LA CUESTA AND IXTAPA-ZIHUATANEJO
PLAYA HORNOS
MORRO CHICO
MERCADO (MARKET)
AV. DE MENDOZA
OFICINA DE TURISMO FEDERAL (TOURIST INFORMATION OFFICE)
BAHIA DE ACAPULCO
ESTRELLA BLANCA (BUS TERMINAL)
HOTEL IMPERIAL
COMERCIAL MEXICANA
PLAYA HAMACAS
200
ESTRELLA BLANCA (SECOND-CLASS BUS)
PIE DE LA CUESTA
ESCUDERO
AV. COSTERA M. ALEMAN
FUERTE SAN DIEGO (FORT AND MUSEUM)
ARTESANIAS (CRAFTS) MERCADO PARRAZAL
MALECON STEAMSHIP DOCK
PIEDRA DEL ELEFANTE (ELEPHANT ROCK)
SEE "ZOCALO" MAP
PLAYA TLACOPANOCHA
MUELLES FIESTA - BONANZA AND HAWAIIANO (BAY CRUISE DOCKS)
SUITES ALBA
CAMINO DE LA PINZONA
HOTEL A. ETEL
HOTEL TORRE EIFEL
BUCEOS (DIVE SHOP)
HOTEL MAJESTIC
LAS PLAYAS
LA QUEBRADA (DIVER'S POINT)
LOPES
BUCEOS (DIVE SHOP)
PLAYA MANZANILLO
HOTEL PLAYA ANGOSTA
MARINA ACAPULCO
CLUB DE YATES (YACHT CLUB)
AV. GRAN VIA TROPICAL
RESTAURANT COYUCA 22
GRAN HOTEL MEIGAS CALETA
PLAYA CALETA
PENINSULA
DE
MATEOS
HOTEL BOCA CHICA
MAGICO MUNDO (WATER PARK)
PLAYA CALETILLA
LA YERBA BUENA
HOTEL LOS FLAMINGOS
AV. LOPEZ
MATEOS
CANAL BOCA CHICA
PLAYA ROQUETA
SUBMARINE VIRGIN
ZOO
PLAYA MARIN
RESTAURANT PALAO
EL FARO (LIGHTHOUSE)
ISLA ROQUETA
TRAIL

0   0.5 mi
0   0.5 km

MOON

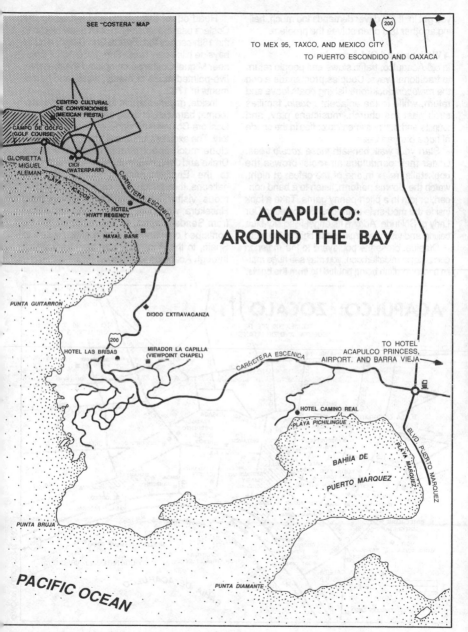

you get in. If the driver demands too much, hailing another taxi often solves the problem.

A Walk around Old Acapulco

In old Acapulco, traffic slows and people return to traditional ways. Couples promenade along the *malecón* dockfront, fishing boats leave and return, while in the adjacent *zócalo*, families stroll past the church, musicians play, and tourists and businessmen sip coffee in the shade of huge banyan trees.

Start your walk beneath those *zócalo* trees. Under their pendulous air roots, browse the bookstalls, relax in one of the cafes; at night, watch the clowns perform, listen to a band concert, or join in a pitch-penny game. Take a look inside the mod-style **cathedral** dedicated to Our Lady of Solitude. Admire its angel-filled sky-blue ceiling and visit the Virgin to the right of the altar.

Outside, cross the boulevard to the *malecón* dockside; in midafternoon, you may see huge marlin and swordfish being hauled up from the boats.

Head out of the *zócalo* and left along the Costera past the steamship dock a few blocks to the 18th-century fort, **Fuerte San Diego**, atop its bayside hill; open Tues.-Sun. 1030-1630. Engineer Miguel Costansó completed the massive, five-pointed maze of moats, walls, and battlements in 1783.

Inside, galleries within the original fort storerooms, barracks, chapel, and kitchen illustrate local pre-Columbian, conquest, and colonial history. The excellent, unusually graphic displays include much about pirates (such as Francis Drake and John Hawkins, known as "admirals" to the English-speaking world); Spanish galleons, their history and construction; and famous visitors, notably Japanese Captain Hasekura, who in 1613 built a ship and sailed from Sendai, Japan, to Acapulco; thence he continued overland to Mexico City, by sea to Spain, to the Pope in Rome, and back again through Acapulco to Japan.

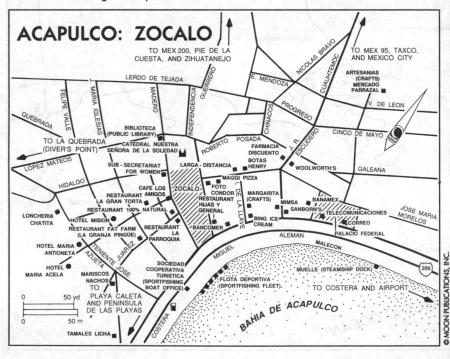

ACAPULCO: ZOCALO

La Quebrada

Head back to the *zócalo* and continue past the cathedral. After three short blocks to Av. López Mateos, continue uphill to the La Quebrada diver's point, marked by the big parking lot at the hillcrest. There, Acapulco's energy focuses five times a day (at 1300 and evenings hourly 1930-2230) as tense crowds watch the divers plummet more than a hundred feet to the waves below. Admission is about $1.50, collected by the divers' cooperative. Performers average about $100 per dive from the proceeds. The adjacent Hotel Plaza Las Glorias (the former Hotel Mirador) charges about $7 cover to view the dives from their terrace.

Old Town Beaches

These start not far from the *zócalo*. At the foot of the Fuerte San Diego, the sand of **Playa Hamacas** begins, changing to **Playa Hornos** ("Ovens") and continuing north a mile to a rocky shoal line called Farallón de San Lorenzo. Hornos is the Sunday favorite of Mexican families, where boats buzz beyond the very tranquil waves and retirees stroll the wide, yellow sand while vendors work the sunbathing crowd.

Moving south past the *zócalo* and the fishing boats, you'll find **Playa Tlacopanocha,** a petite strip of sand beneath some spreading trees. Here, bay-tour launches (see "Isla Roqueta" below) wait for passengers, and kids play in the glassy water, which would be great for swimming if it weren't for the refuse from nearby fishing boats.

From there, cross the Costera and hop on a bus marked "Caleta" to gemlike **Playa Caleta** and its twin **Playa Caletilla** on the far side of the hilly pensinsula (named, appropriately, Peninsula de las Playas). With medium-coarse yellow sand and blue ripples for waves, Caleta and Caletilla are for people who want company. They are often crowded, sometimes nearly solid on Sunday. Boats offer banana-tube rides, and snorkel gear is rentable from beach concessionaires. Dozens of stalls and restaurants serve refreshments.

Mágico Mundo water park, tel. (74) 831-215—with an aquarium, museum, restaurant, water slides, cascades, and more—perches on the little peninsula between the beaches. Open daily 0900-1700; admission $5 adult, $3.50 child.

Isla Roqueta

A Roqueta Island ticket tout will often try to snare you as you get off the Caleta bus. The roundtrip, which runs around $4, is usually in a boat with a glass bottom, through which you can peer at the fish as they peer back from their aqua underwater world. On the other side, you can sunbathe on sunny little Playa Roqueta, have lunch at one of several beachside *palapas,* swim, snorkel, and quaff the thirst of the famous Roqueta beer-drinking burros (who are said to prefer Corona).

The burros are the island's sole inhabitants, except for the lighthouse keeper, for whom the burros haul supplies weekly. For those with the energy, the gradual lighthouse trail, only a few hundred yards long, begins at Playa Roqueta. Open Wed.-Mon.; admission $1. Take drinks and a hat.

Other island attractions include a good small zoo in the shady mixed acacia-deciduous hillside forest above Playa Roqueta. Animals include many endangered local varieties, such as howler monkeys, and a jaguar, mountain lion, coatimundi, peccary, crocodile, and ocelot. Past the zoo hillcrest, a trail leads steeply downhill to tiny, secluded **Playa Marin,** where you can loll to your heart's content in the waves, which funnel into the narrow channel. (Be prepared to avoid sunburn, however.)

A **boat tour** from Playa Tlacopanocha (see above) is another way to get to Isla Roqueta. The glass-bottomed boats *Maryvioli, Santa María,* and *Tequila* leave several times daily for hour-and-a-half tours (about $5 per person). Trips include viewing underwater life, shoreline vistas, the *Virgen Submarina* (a statue submerged in the Isla Roqueta channel), a stop on the island, and snorkeling. Beer and soft drinks are sold onboard.

Playa Angosta

Back on the mainland, you can visit another hidden beach nearby, Playa Angosta ("Narrow Beach"), the only Acapulco strand with an unobstructed sunset horizon. A breezy dab of a beach, sandwiched between a pair of sandstone cliffs, Angosta's ocean waves roll in, swishing upon the sand. A hotel *palapa* (see Hotel Playa Angosta under "Accommodations" below) occupies one side of the beach and a few fishing launches and nets are on the other. With caution, swimming, bodysurfing, and boogie-boarding are sometimes possible here; otherwise, Angosta is best for scenery and picnics.

Costera Beaches

These are the hotel-lined golden shores where affluent Mexicans and foreign visitors stay and play in the sun. They are variations on one continuous curve of sand. Beginning at the west end with **Playa Hornitos** (also known as Playa Papagayo), they continue, changing names from **Playa Morro** to **Playa Condesa** and finally, **Playa Icacos,** which curves and stretches to its sheltered east end past the naval base. All of the same semicoarse golden silica sand, the beaches begin with fairly broad 200-foot-wide Playas Papagayo and Morro. They narrow sharply to under 100 feet at Playa Condesa, then broaden again to more than 200 feet along Playa Icacos.

Beach palapas *spread like a field of buttons on Playa Hornitos, as seen from the upper floors of the Hotel Ritz.*

BRUCE WHIPPERMAN

Their surf is mostly very gentle, breaking in one- or two-foot waves and receding with little undertow. This makes for safe swimming within float-enclosed beachside areas, but it's too tranquil for bodysurfing, boogie-boarding, or surfing. Beyond the swimming floats, motorboats hurry along, pulling parasailors and banana-tube riders, while jet-ski boats cavort and careen over the swells.

Such motorized hubbub lessens the safety and enjoyment of quieter sports off most new town beaches. Sailboaters and windsurfers with their own equipment might try the remote, more tranquil east end of Playa Icacos, however.

Water-skiing, officially restricted to certain parts of Acapulco Bay, has largely moved to Coyuca Lagoon northwest of the city. Coyuca Lagoon has enough space for many good motorboat-free spots for sailboaters and windsurfers (see "Pie de la Cuesta" in the preceding chapter).

Rocky outcroppings along Playas Papagayo, Morro, and Condesa add interest and intimacy to an already beautiful shoreline. The rocks are good for tidepooling and fishing by pole-casting (or by line, as locals do) above the waves.

Beaches Northwest of Town:
Pie de la Cuesta and Laguna Coyuca

For details on this downscale little resort and beautiful lagoon northwest of Acapulco, see "Pie de la Cuesta," the last section of the preceding chapter. Get there from Acapulco by "Pie de la Cuesta"-marked buses, which leave frequently from the *zócalo* area (on Av. Escudero adjacent to Sanborn's and Woolworth's).

Beaches Southeast of Town

Ride a "Puerto Marquez" or "Lomas" bus or drive along the Costera eastward. Past the naval base entrance on the right, the road climbs the hill, passing a number of panoramic bay viewpoints. After the Las Brisas condo-hotel complex, the road curves around the hill shoulder and heads downward past picture-perfect vistas of **Bahía de Puerto Marquez.** At the bottom-of-the-hill intersection and gas station, a road forks right to Puerto Marquez.

The little bayside town is mainly a Sunday seafood and picnicking retreat for Acapulco families. Dozens of *palapa* restaurants line its motorboat-dotted sandy beach. One ramshackle hotel, at the far south end of the single main beachfront street, offers lodgings.

If you're driving, mark your odometer at the hill-bottom intersection and head east toward the airport. If traveling by bus, continue via one of the "Lomas" buses, which continue east from Acapulco about once an hour. About a mile farther, a turnoff road goes right to the Acapulco Princess and the Pierre Marquez hotels and golf course on **Playa Revolcadero.** (For hotel details, see under "Accommodations" below.)

Beach access is by side roads or by walking directly through the hotel lobbies. If you come by bus, hail a taxi from the highway to the Hotel Princess door for the sake of a good entrance.

Playa Revolcadero, a broad, miles-long yellow-white strand, has the rolling open-ocean billows that Acapulco Bay doesn't. The sometimes-rough waves are generally good for boogie-boarding, bodysurfing, and even surfing near the rocks on the northwest end. Because of the waves and sometimes hazardous currents, the hotel provides lifeguards for safety. The Playa Revolcadero breeze is also brisk enough for sailing and windsurfing with your own boat or board. Some rentals may be available from the hotel beach concession.

Barra Vieja

About seven miles (11 km) from the Puerto Marquez traffic intersection, the Barra Vieja road forks right and heads along a breezy wild beach. About two miles from the fork, you will pass the **Marparaíso Queen condo-hotel.** The 100 two-bedroom luxury apartments surround a spacious pool-garden with beachside restaurant. Sleeping four, the air-conditioned kitchenette apartments rent for about $95. Filled with mostly Canadian clients during the winter, the apartments may be bargainable for less during slack periods. Although they have no phone, write them for reservations: Km 9.6, Carretera Barra Vieja, Acapulco, Guerrero.

About 18 miles (32 km) from the traffic intersection (11 miles from the fork) a sign marks **Playa Encantada,** an airy downscale beachside restaurant beside a big blue pool, garden, and large parking lot. The owner, Gloria Ríoja de Reyes, and her manager-son invite visitors to park in their lot and set up tents on the beach. If they don't mention any fee, parking and tenting will probably be gratis if you eat a few meals in their restaurant. On the wide, breezy strand, the rolling waves, with ordinary precautions, would be good for boogie-boarding, bodysurfing, and possibly surfing. The sun sets on an unobstructed horizon, and the crab-rich beach is good for surf fishing (or by boat if you launch during morning calm). Additionally, the firm, level sand is excellent for jogging, walking, and beachcombing. Tenters could set up comfortably and securely in the shade of the little beachside palm grove.

About a mile farther on, the stores (groceries and long-distance phone) and modest houses of fishing village Barra Vieja dot the roadside. Many seafood *palapas* line the beachside. The better among them include the upscale Beto's Condesa (with pool) and Gloria del Mar, with no pool. The latter is a family operation, run by a friendly woman who stretches out in a hammock reading her Bible when she has no customers.

Besides the beach, Barra Vieja visitors enjoy access to the big **Laguna Tres Palos** mangrove lagoon from the *estero* at the east end of town before the bridge. From there, boatmen take parties on fishing and wildlife-viewing excursions.

The road (which maps routinely show going through) ends about two miles farther east at scruffy Lomas de Chapultepec village.

ACCOMMODATIONS

Location largely determines the price and style of Acapulco hotels. In the old town, most hotels are either clustered around the *zócalo* or perched on the hillsides of Peninsula de las Playas. They are generally not on the beach and are cheaper and less luxurious. Most new town hotels, by contrast, lie mostly along the Costera Miguel Alemán right on the beach. Guests often enjoy numerous resort amenities and luxury view rooms at correspondingly luxurious prices.

Many lodgings, however, defy categorization. Acapulco offers numerous choices to suit individual tastes and pocketbooks. In all cases, and especially in the luxury hotels, you can often

ACAPULCO HOTELS

Acapulco (area code 74, postal code 39300 unless otherwise noted) hotels, in order of increasing approximate high-season double-room price:

ZÓCALO AND PENINSULA DE LAS PLAYAS HOTELS

Hotel María Acela, La Paz 19, tel. 820-661, $14

Hotel Asturias, Quebrada 45, tel. 836-548, fax 822-076, $15

Hotel María Antioneta, Teniente Azueta 15, tel. 825-024, $25

Hotel Misión, Felipe Valle 12, tel. 823-643, $25

Hotel Torre Eifel, Inalambrica 110, tel. 821-683, $25

Hotel Amuebalados Etel, Pinzona 92, tel. 822-240 or 822-241, $34

Hotel Playa Angosta, P.O. Box 88, tel. 821-629 or 822-785, $40

Hotel Majestic, Pozo del Rey 73, tel. 820-655, $45

Suites Alba, Gran Via Tropical 35, tel. 830-073, fax 838-378, $55

Hotel Los Flamingos, P.O. Box 70, tel. 820-690, 820-691, or 820-692, fax 839-806, $65

Hotel Boca Chica, Playa Caletilla s/n, tel. 836-601 or 836-741, $105

Gran Hotel Meigas Caleta, Cerro San Martin 325, tel. 837-536 or 837-538, $120 (all inclusive, for two)

COSTERA HOTELS

Hotel Del Valle, G. Gomez Espinosa 150 (P.O. Box C-14), tel. 858-336 or 858-388, $25

Hotel Sands, Calle Juande la Cosa 178 (P.O. Box 256), tel. 841-024, fax 841-053, $40

Auto-Hotel Ritz, P.O. Box 157, tel. 858-023, fax 855-647, $60

Hotel Romano Days Inn, Costera M. Alemán 130, tel. 845-332, fax 845-822, $65

Hotel Maris, Costera M. Alemán 59, tel. 858-440 or 858-492, $70

Hotel Howard Johnson Maralisa, El Esclavo s/n, tel. 856-677, fax 859-228, $90

Hotel Fiesta Americana Condesa, Costera M. Alemán 1220, tel. 842-828, or (800) 1-FIESTA from the U.S. and Canada, $110

Hotel Ritz, Costera M. Alemán, P.O. Box 259, tel. 857-544, 857-336, or (800) 237-7487, fax 857-076, $120

Hyatt Regency Acapulco, Costera M. Alemán 1, postal code 39860, tel. 691-234, or (800) 233-1234 from the U.S. and Canada, fax 843-087, $192

Hotel Villa Vera and Racquet Club, Lomas del Mar 35, tel. 840-333, (800) 223-6510 in U.S., (800) 424-5500 in Canada, fax 847-479, $200

Hotel Acapulco Princess, Playa Revolcadero, tel. 691-000, or (800) 223-1818 from the U.S. and Canada, $300

save money by requesting low-season, package, and weekly or monthly discounts. For winter high-season lodgings, call or write for early reservations. (See the chart below for a listing according to price.)

Hotels near the Zócalo

A number of clean, economical hotels cluster in the colorful neighborhood between La Quebrada and the zócalo. Among the most popular is the colonial-chic **Hotel Misión,** Felipe Valle 12, Acapulco, Guerrero 39300, tel. (74) 823-643, fax 822-076, built in two stories around a plant-decorated patio, shaded by a spreading mango tree, corner of La Paz, two blocks from the zócalo. When the mangos ripen in April guests get their fill of the perfumy fruit. The 24 attractively decorated rooms rent for about $15 per person during the Nov.-Dec. and March-April high months, $12 otherwise; with fans, hot water, and parking.

One block farther along La Paz, the '60s-modern **Hotel María Antioneta** fronts the lively shop- and restaurant-lined Av. Azueta, Teniente Azueta 15, Acapulco, Guerrero 39300, tel. (74) 825-024. The 34 plainly furnished but comfortable rooms are light and pleasant, especially on the upper floor. Most rooms are fortunately recessed along the leafy inner courtyard, away from street noise. Rates run about $25 d, with hot water and fans.

A block away, on the quiet cul-de-sac end of Av. La Paz, stands the Spartan three-story

Hotel María Acela, Av. La Paz 19, Acapulco, Guerrero 39300, tel. (74) 820-661. Its family management lends a homey atmosphere more like a guesthouse than a hotel. The austerely furnished rooms, although clean, lack hot water. The 21 rooms rent for around $7 s, $14 d, with fan.

The **Hotel Asturias,** Quebrada 45, Acapulco, Guerrero 39300, tel. (74) 836-548, on Av. Quebrada a few blocks uphill from the *zócalo,* offers a relaxing atmosphere at budget rates. Its two stories of plain but tidy rooms surround a plant-decorated pool-patio with chairs for sunning. Get an upper room for more light and privacy. Rates for the 15 rooms cost about $10 s, $15 d, and $20 t year-round, with fans; four short blocks from the cathedral, between Ramirez and Ortiz.

A few blocks farther uphill, **Hotel Torre Eifel,** Inalambrica 110, Acapulco, Guerrero 39300, tel. (74) 821-683, rises above its hillside garden overlooking the La Quebrada diver's point tourist mecca. The 25 simply but comfortably furnished rooms rise in four motel-modern tiers above an inviting pool and patio. Guests in the uppermost rooms enjoy breezy sea views and a sunset horizon. Rooms rent for about $20 s, $25 d, and $30 t, with fans, hot water, and parking; at the corner of Av. Pinzona, one block uphill from the La Quebrada parking lot.

Two more blocks up winding Av. Pinzona, the hotel **Amuebalados Etel** ("Ethel's Furnished Apartments") stands on the hillside above old Acapulco, Av. Pinzona 92, Acapulco, Guerrero 39300, tel. (74) 822-240 or 822-241. Well managed by friendly owner Etel (great-granddaughter of renowned California pioneer John A. Sutter), the three-building complex stairsteps downhill to a luxurious view garden and pool. Its airy hillside perch lends the Amuebalados Etel a tranquil, deluxe ambience unusual in such an economical lodging. Chairs and sofas in a small street-level lobby invite relaxed conversation with fellow guests. The primly but thoughtfully furnished and well-maintained rooms range from singles to multibedroom view apartments. The dozens of rooms and suites rent from about $14 per person low season, $17 high, with fans, a/c, and hot water. Completely furnished view apartments with kitchens go for about $55 low season, $80 high, with approximately 25% discount for monthly rentals, some parking, and credit cards accepted.

Peninsula de las Playas Hotels

Many of these lodgings are spread along one continuous boulevard that winds through this plush hillside neighborhood. The boulevard starts as the Costera Miguel Alemán as it heads past the *zócalo* toward the peninsula. There it veers left as the Gran Via Tropical, rounding the peninsula clockwise. Passing Caleta and Caletilla beaches, the boulevard changes to Av. López Mateos and continues along the peninsula's sunset (southwest) side past Playa Angosta and La Quebrada diver's point before ending back in the *zócalo* neighborhood.

First along that path comes the big hillside **Hotel Majestic,** Av. Pozo del Rey 73, Acapulco, Guerrero 39300, tel. (74) 820-655, winter headquarters for crowds of youthful American, Canadian, and German vacationers. Guests enjoy breezy bay views from the spacious grounds that spread downhill to a bayside beach club. Tennis, beach, and pool sports fill the days, while dining in the restaurants, theme parties, and disco dancing enliven the nights. The Spartan but comfortable tile-floored rooms come with a/c, cable TV, and telephones. The 210 rooms and suites rent from about $30 d low season, $45 high; credit cards accepted, with parking. Sports opportunities include windsurfing, kayaking, a gym, aerobics, and more.

A couple of blocks farther along Gran Via Tropical the multistory **Suites Alba,** Gran Via Tropical 35, Acapulco, Guerrero 39300, tel. (74) 830-073, fax 838-378, apartment-style complex rambles through its well-kept hilltop garden of palms and pools. The mostly Canadian and American middle-class guests enjoy many facilities, including a pair of pools, a jacuzzi, a restaurant, tennis courts, a mini-mart, and a downhill bayside beach club with its own saltwater pool. The comfortably furnished apartments have kitchenettes, a/c, and private garden-view balconies. The 292 apartments begin at about $55 d, $65 t, with about 10% discount for monthly and low-season rentals; credit cards accepted, parking.

On the opposite side of the peninsula, guests at the **Hotel Boca Chica,** Playa Caletilla s/n, Acapulco, Guerrero 39300, tel. (74) 836-601or 836-741, enjoy views of Playa Caletilla on one hand and the green Isla Roqueta beyond an azure channel on the other. The hotel perches on a rocky point, invitingly close to the clear

ACAPULCO: COSTERA

aqua water from the pool deck and surrounding garden paths. The light, comfortably furnished rooms vary; if you have the option, look at two or three before you choose. Early reservations year-round are strongly recommended. Rates for the 45 rooms with phones and a/c run about $105 d with breakfast; credit cards accepted, parking.

If you like the location but can't get into the Hotel Boca Chica immediately, try the best-buy

Gran Hotel Meigas Caleta, Cerro San Martin 225, Playa Caleta, Acapulco, Guerrero 39300, tel. (74) 837-536 or 837-538, on the other side of nearby Playa Caleta. Hotel guests enjoy a big blue pool and view sundeck, lush green garden, and deluxe, comfortable rooms, each with private panoramic view balcony. Rates for the 260 rooms run about $60 per person double occupancy, including all meals, drinks, and in-house sports and entertainment; with a/c,

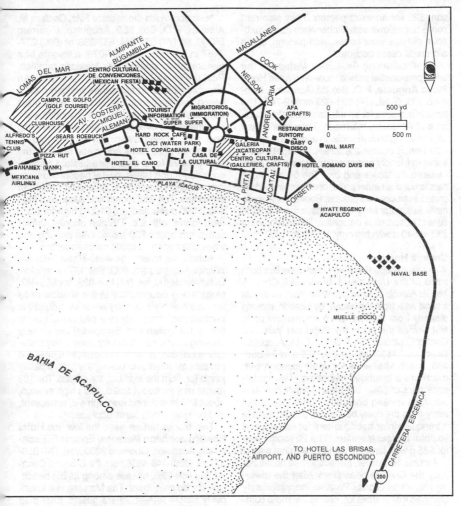

phones, cable TV, parking, credit cards accepted.

Hotel Flamingos, P.O. Box 70, Acapulco, Guerrero 39300, tel. (74) 820-690, 820-691, 820-692, fax 839-806, uphill about a mile along Av. López Mateos, is where oldsters reminisce and youngsters find out who John Wayne, Johnny Weissmuller, and Rory Calhoun were. Faded Hollywood photos decorate the open-air lobby walls, while nearby pathways wind through a hilltop jungle of palm, hibiscus, and spreading mangoes. The rooms, several with private, ocean-view balconies, perch on a cliffside that plummets into foaming breakers hundreds of feet below. Soft evening guitar music in an open-air sunset view restaurant and a luxurious cliffside pool-patio complete the lovely picture. The 40 rooms, in standard, superior, and junior suite grades, run about $50, $60, and $70 d low season, respectively. Add about $10 for high season, $25 for an extra person. They also rent some bungalows with kitchenettes and a luxurious cliffside view house; with parking, some a/c; credit cards accepted.

Continue along Av. López Mateos to the once-presidential palace, now-renovated **Hotel Playa Angosta,** P.O. Box 88, Acapulco, Guerrero 39300, tel. (74) 821-629 or 822-785. The hotel is a mecca for an informal club of Canadian and American returnees. They spend their days relaxing both at poolside and on the scenic little beach across the street. At night, many linger in friendly conversation around the hotel restaurant's tables and bar. The 50 rooms, in tiers around an inner patio, are charmingly decorated in stucco and pastels. Rooms vary; some have luxurious king-size beds, others private sunset ocean-view balconies. Rates run about $30 s, $40 d with fan only, higher for a/c.

Costera Hotels

With few exceptions, these hostelries line both sides of the busy beach boulevard, Costera Miguel Alemán. Hotels are either right on or just a short walk from the beach. By location, moving easterly from the Papagayo amusement park, first comes the economy **Hotel del Valle,** G. Gomez Espinosa 150, P.O. Box C-14, Acapulco, Guerrero 39300, tel. 74-858-336 and 74-858-388, which shares its fortunate location with much more luxurious neighbors. Two motel-style tiers of plain but clean rooms border a small but inviting pool-patio. On a side street away from the noisy boulevard, the del Valle is a tranquil winter headquarters for retirees and youthful budget travelers. The 20 rooms rent for $25 d with fan, $33 with a/c; with hot water.

Around the corner, three high-rise hotels occupy the Costera beachfront. After the towering Plaza Las Glorias Paraíso, inappropriately cramped into a small lot, comes the more comfortably sized **Hotel Maris,** Av. Costera M. Alemán 59, Acapulco, Guerrero 39300, tel. (74) 858-440 or 858-492, where guests get spacious rooms with private view balconies for surprisingly reasonable rates. Lobby-level amenities include a small pool above the beach club with bar and restaurant (where you may have to ask them to turn down the TV volume). No parking is available. Rates for the 84 rooms run about $50 d and $65 t low season, $70 d and $90 t high; with a/c, TV, and phones.

Next door rises the midsize **Ritz,** Costera M. Alemán, P.O. Box 259, Acapulco, Guerrero 39300, tel. (74) 857-544, 857-336, or (800) 237-7487 in the U.S., fax 857-076, a favorite of a generation of upper-class Mexican families. Past the plush lobby, you soon see why. An airy, broad *palapa* restaurant looks out on a beach and bay panorama, as Latin music plays softly in the background. Nearby a wooden walkway meanders over an intimate blue swimming pool. Live music plays nightly, while on weekends a riot of balloons and crepe festoons the plumy grove for a beachside fiesta. Upstairs, onyx floors and baths, pastel bedspreads and drapes, and private view balconies embellish the rooms. The 252 rooms and suites rent from about $90 d low season, $120 d high for standard rooms with a/c, TV, and phones. Junior suites run about $20 more. With parking and wheelchair access; credit cards accepted.

Across the street, the **Auto-Hotel Ritz,** Av. Wilfrido Massieu s/n, P.O. Box 157, Acapulco, Guerrero 39300, tel. (74) 858-023, fax 855-647, plugs along successfully in the shadow of its upscale neighbor. Activity revolves around the verdant pool-patio, where a platoon of guests (many Canadian and European) are usually soaking up the sun. Upstairs, they enjoy tastefully appointed, recently redecorated rooms and private balconies overlooking the patio's palmy jungle (or, from the top floor, the ocean). The 103 rooms rent for about $60 d, $70 t high season, about $10 less during low; with a/c, restaurant, and parking; credit cards accepted.

Two blocks farther east, the low-rise **Hotel Howard Johnson Maralisa,** Enrique El Esclavo s/n, Acapulco, Guerrero 39300, tel. (74) 856-677, or (800) 446-4656 from the U.S. and Canada, fax 859-228, nestles among its big beachside condo neighbors. The Maralisa is a luxuriously simple retreat, where guests, after their fill of sunning beside the big palm-lined pool-patio, can walk a few steps for a jog or stroll along the beach. Later, they might dine in the hotel's beachside restaurant or go out for dancing in nearby resort hotels. Several of the Maralisa's 90 comfortable rooms, tastefully decorated in whites and warm pastels, have private balconies. Standard rooms rent for about $65 d low season, $90 high; superior go for about $10 more. Up to two kids under 12 stay free; with a/c, TV, phones, and parking; credit cards accepted.

Several blocks farther east the low-rise **Hotel Sands,** Calle Juan de la Cosa 178, P.O. Box 256, Acapulco, Guerrero 39300, tel. (74) 841-024, fax 841-053, contrasts sharply with the monumental Acapulco Plaza across the boulevard. In addition to a pool-patio and restaurant next to the main '60s-modern building, the deceivingly spacious grounds encompass a shady green park in the rear that leads to an attractive hidden *cabaña*-enclosed garden. Of the main building rooms, the uppers are best, with private balconies and light, comfortable if a bit tattered and less than immaculate furnishings. *Cabaña* guests, on the other hand, enjoy tasteful browns, tile decor, and big windows looking out into a leafy garden. Bungalows 1-8 are the most secluded. The 59 rooms and 34 *cabañas* run about $40 d, $50 t high season, about $10 less low season. Additional 33% discounts for three-, six-, and nine-night stays are often available. All with a/c, cable TV, and phones; parking, squash courts, and jeep rental; credit cards accepted.

The super-luxury **Hotel Fiesta Americana Condesa,** Av. Costera M. Alemán 1220, Acapulco, Guerrero 39300, tel. (74) 842-828, or (800) 1-FIESTA from the U.S. and Canada, presides atop its rocky shoreline perch smack in the middle of new Acapulco. Boulevard traffic roars nonstop past the front door and nightclubs rock all night nearby. By day, ranks of middle-class American and Canadian vacationers sun on the hotel's spacious pool-deck and downstairs at its *palapa*-shaded beach club. Resort facilities include multiple restaurants and bars, nightly live music, shops, rentals, tennis, golf, and all aquatic sports. Rooms, most with private bay-view balconies, are furnished in luscious pastels, rattan, and designer lamps. Rooms rent from $110 d, with a/c, TV, phones, parking, and full wheelchair access; credit cards accepted.

In exclusive isolation several blocks uphill, guests at the **Hotel Villa Vera and Racquet Club** enjoy what seems like their own Acapulco country club, Lomas del Mar 35, Acapulco, Guerrero 39300, tel. (74) 840-333, (800) 223-6510 from the U.S., (800) 424-5500 from Canada, fax 847-479. Overlooking the entire city and bay, the hotel's dozens of bungalows nestle in a manicured garden around an elegant hillside pool and terrace restaurant. The lodgings, which range from one-room doubles to suites, are decorated in creams, pastels, and earth tones and tastefully appointed with handicrafts and one-of-a-kind wall art. No children admitted, however. Rates for the 80 rooms and suites run about $130 d low season, $200 high for superior grade; $165 and $240, respectively, for suite; with a/c, cable TV, phones, parking, clay tennis courts, massage, and sauna; credit cards accepted. Get there via the street between the Pizza Hut and the golf course, continuing uphill at each fork. The Villa Vera gate will appear on the left after about a quarter mile.

Back on the Costera, many folks who want a reasonably priced ocean-view room a block from the beach go to the **Romano Days Inn,** Costera M. Alemán 130, Acapulco, Guerrero 39300, tel. (74) 845-332, fax 845-822, not to be confused with the Romano Palace. The youngish, mostly single clientele also like the lively late-night bar and the big pool-deck where they can rest and recover during the day. The 279 light and comfortable rooms come with a/c, TV, views, and phones. Rooms rent for about $55 d low season, $65 high; parking available, credit cards accepted.

Next door rises the 20-story tower of the **Hyatt Regency Acapulco,** Costera M. Alemán 1, Acapulco, Guerrero 39860, tel. (74) 691-234, (800) 223-1234 from the U.S. and Canada, fax 040-007, everything resort, with spacious gardens, blue lagoon swimming pool, a Tarzan jungle waterfall, a squadron of personal beach *palapas,* restaurants, bars, nightly music till midnight, shops, all aquatic sports, and tennis and golf. The 690 rooms, all with private view balconies, are large and luxurious. Low season prices, furthermore, can be surprisingly reasonable. Standard rooms rent from about $83 d low season, $192 high, with a/c, cable TV, phones, parking, and full wheelchair access; credit cards accepted.

Out-of-Town Hotels

The sleepy **Pie de la Cuesta** resort village on placid Coyuca Lagoon (about six miles by road northwest from the Acapulco *zócalo*) has several reasonably priced beachside lodgings. Drive (see map, "Acapulco: Around the Bay"), taxi (about $5), or ride a "Pie de la Cuesta"-marked bus from Av. Escudero in front of Sanborn's and Woolworth's near the *zócalo*. For many more details, see the "Pie de la Cuesta" section at the end of the the previous chapter.

Past the southeast end of town near the airport, the showplace **Hotel Acapulco Princess** provides a plethora of resort facilities (including an entire golf course) spreading from luscious beachfront garden grounds at Playa Revolcadero, Acapulco, Guerrero 39300, tel. (74) 691-000, (800) 223-1818 from the U.S. and Canada, fax 691-015. Although the hotel centers on a pair of hulking neopyramids (1,019-room total), the impression from the rooms themselves is of super-luxury; from the garden it is of Eden-like jungle tranquility—meandering pools, gurgling cascades, strutting flamingos, swaying palms—which guests seem to soak up with no trouble at all. Rooms rent from about $200 d low season, $300 high; all facilities, all sports, full wheelchair access, credit cards accepted.

Trailer Parks and Camping
Although condos and hotels have replaced virtually all of Acapulco's in-town trailer parks, good prospects exist nearby. Among the best is the **Acapulco Trailer Park** right on the beach in Pie de la Cuesta resort village, six miles by the coast highway northwest of the *zócalo*. For details, see the "Pie de la Cuesta" section at the end of the preceding chapter.

And although development and urbanization have likewise squeezed out in-town camping, possibilities exist in the trailer park in Pie de La Cuesta, and also at Playa Encantada beach restaurant near Barra Vieja (see under "Sights" above).

FOOD

Breakfast and Snacks near the *Zócalo*
Sidewalk cafe **Maggi Pizza** on the opposite side of the *zócalo*, end of Carranza, beneath a venerable shady tree, is a friendly source of afternoon and wee-hour snacks. You will have to be up late indeed to outlast the club of domino aficionados who own the place.

Eat well for under $3 at **Lonchería Chatita**, Av. Azueta, corner of Hidalgo, open daily 0800-2200, where a friendly female kitchen squad serves mounds of wholesome, local-style specialties. On a typical day, these may include savory chiles rellenos, rich *puerco mole de Uruapán, pozole* (savory hominy soup), or potato pancakes.

For something creamy and cool, go to **Bing** ice cream, open daily 0900-2300, one block from the *zócalo* toward the steamship dock.

Continue another block to **Sanborn's**, *malecón* corner of Escudero, open daily 0730-2300, where you can escape the heat and enjoy home-style ham and eggs, hamburgers, roast beef, and apple pie, although prices are fairly high.

Woolworth's, one block from the Costera, behind Sanborn's, also offers air-conditioned ambience and similar fare at more reasonable prices.

Costera Breakfast and Snacks
Snack food concentrates in Acapulco, as in many places, around **McDonald's**, corner Esclavo and Av. Costera M. Alemán, a few blocks east of Hotel Ritz, tel. (74) 860-777. Except for breakfast, which they don't serve, you'll find everything from Chicken McNuggets to the Big Mac, priced about a third higher than back home. Open daily 0930-2400.

For an interesting contrast, visit **Taco Tumbra** across the street from McDonald's. Here, piquant aromas of barbecued chicken, pork, and beef and strains of Latin music fill the air. For a treat, order three of their delectable tacos, along with a refreshing fruit juice *(jugo)* or fruit-flavored *agua*. Open Sun.-Thurs. 1800-0200, Fri.-Sat. 1800-0400.

About three blocks east, **Gran Fogon,** corner Costera M. Alemán and Sandoval, despite its soaring modern canopy, takes pride in its country Mexican cooking, served with a flourish that makes even a bowl of *pozole* seem like a party. If you're hankering for something a bit out of the ordinary, try their house specialty, a *molcajete* (mohl-kah-HAY-tay), big stone bowl draped with succulent cooked *nopales* (cactus leaves) and filled with big green onions and savory stewed beef, pork, or chicken. Enough for two or three. Open daily about 0900-2400.

Denny's next door is a little bit of Council Bluffs, Seattle, and Denver all rolled into Acapulco. This is where, round the clock, you can have it all, especially breakfasts: blueberry pancakes, three-egg omelettes drowned in American cheese with hash browns, or the Grand Slam—two eggs, pancakes, sausage, bacon, toast, and all the coffee you can drink.

100% Natural, in 24-hour competition directly across the Costera from Denny's, offers appropriately contrasting fare: many vegie and fruit drinks (try the Conga—made of papaya, guava, watermelon, pineapple, lime, and spinach), several egg breakfasts, breads, sandwiches, tacos, and enchiladas.

The diminutive **Cafe Viena,** a half mile farther along the Costera, offers still more options, on the Costera next to American Express, between the Diana Circle and the Hotel Fiesta Americana Condesa. You can start out with familiar egg and toast breakfasts, or enjoy sampling the strudels, bear claws, pies, and cakes, which friendly owner Sophia crafts in her small bakery upstairs. Open daily 0830-2300.

Sanborn's oooond Acapulco branch occupies an ocean-view perch on the bottom floor of the high-rise a block east of the Fiesta Americana Condesa, Av. Costera M. Alemán 1226, tel. (74) 844-465. Service is crisp, entrees are tasty, and the ocean view from either an airy outside terrace or cool air-conditioned inside dining room is lovely. Open daily 0730-2300.

Zócalo and Peninsula de las Playas Restaurants

Complete dinner price key: Budget: under $7; Moderate: $7-14; Expensive: more than $14.

Even though Acapulco has seemingly zillions of restaurants, only a fraction may suit your expectations. Local restaurants come and go like the Acapulco breeze, though a handful of solid longtime eateries continue, depending on a steady flow of repeat customers.

For plain good eating and homey sidewalk atmosphere morning and night, try outdoor **Cafe Los Amigos,** Calle La Paz, a few steps off the *zócalo.* Shady umbrellas beneath a spreading green tree and many familiar favorites, from tuna salad and chili, to waffles, T-bone steak, and breaded shrimp attract a friendly club of Acapulco Canadian and American longtimers. Open daily 0930-2200. Budget to Moderate.

Good food and atmosphere keep customers flocking to the German-Mexican **Restaurant La Parroquia,** overlooking the *zócalo,* corner Juárez, tel. (74) 839-463. Not that the plaza

views from the restaurant's open-air upper floors aren't interesting, but the old-Europe specialties, such as roast pork Dubrovnik, Wiener schnitzel Vienna, and sauerbraten are too tasty to be ignored. Open Mon.-Sat. 1200-2400, Sunday 1700-2400. Moderate.

Two blocks from the *zócalo,* along Juárez, the **Fat Farm** (La Granja Pingüe) would be unique even without the name, Juárez 10, at Felipe Valle, tel. (74) 835-339. It's a cooperative, run by graduates of a local orphanage. The relaxed atmosphere, service, and food are made to please. Breakfasts are the high point of many a longtimer's day. Fare also includes several flavors of ice cream and sandwiches (such as their giant tuna, $2.50). Budget.

La Gran Torta at La Paz 6, one block from the *zócalo,* tel. (74) 838-476, is an old town headquarters for hearty local-style food at local-style prices. Specialties here are *tortas* (big sandwiches), often of *pierna* (roast pork), *chorizo,* or *pollo* (chicken) with tomato and avocado stuffed in a *bolillo.* Additional favorites include hearty *pozole,* on Thursday and Friday. Open daily 0900-2200. Open daily 0800-2400. Budget.

Good, reasonably priced seafood restaurants are unexpectedly hard to come by in Acapulco. An important exception is the lineup of local-style seafood eateries along Av. Azueta three blocks from the *zócalo.* Located right where the boats come in, they get the freshest morsels first. Among the best and friendliest is **Mariscos Nachos,** corner Juárez and Azueta, where continuous patronage assures daily fresh shrimp, prawns, half a dozen kinds of fish, and lobster (big, $17, smaller, $10). Open daily 1000-2130. Moderate.

If you prefer something a bit fancier, head a block farther from the *zócalo,* to tourist favorite **Mariscos Pipos,** at 3 Almirante Breton, tel. (74) 822-237. The freshest of everything, cooked and served to please. Open daily around 1200-2100. Moderate to expensive.

A few steps away on Costera M. Alemán 322, corner of Almirante Breton, seekers of home-style Mexican cooking need go no farther than **Tamales Licha,** tel. (74) 822-021. Here, appetizing south-of-the-border specialties—succulent tamales, savory *pozole,* crunchy tostadas, and tangy enchiladas—reign supreme. Portions are generous, ambience is relaxed, and hygiene standards are impeccable. Open nightly 1800-2400. Budget.

Many visitors' Acapulco vacations wouldn't be complete without a dinner at the luxurious clifftop palapa-restaurant at the **Hotel Flamingos,** Av. López Mateos s/n, tel. (74) 820-690, about a mile uphill, west from Playa Caleta. Here all the ingredients for a memorable evening—attentive service, tasty seafood, chicken, and meat entrees, airy sunset view, and soft strumming of guitars—come together. Open daily 0800-2230; credit cards accepted. Moderate.

Coyuca 22 is both the name and the address of the restaurant so exclusive and popular it manages to close half the year. The setting is a spacious hilltop garden, where tables spread down an open-air bay- and city-view terrace. Arrive early (around 1845) to enjoy the sunset sky light up and paint the city ever-deepening colors, ending in a deep rose as finally the myriad lights shimmer and stars twinkle overhead. After that, the food (specialties, such as prime rib and lobster tails) and wines seem like dessert. Open daily 0700-2230 1 Nov.-30 April; credit cards accepted. Expensive; entrees run about $30. Reservations are required, tel. (74) 823-468 or 835-030. Dress is elegant resort wear, coat not necessary.

Costera Restaurants
The Hotel Ritz's **La Cava,** Av. Costera M. Alemán and Wilfrido Massieu, tel. (74) 857-544, restaurant is a longtime favorite of serious eaters. Atmosphere—candlelight and roses, tuxedoed waiters and wine steward—enhances the enjoyment of their carefully prepared and presented specialties. Start with a Caesar salad, continue with a cream of spinach soup, and end with a seafood pasta, such as clam linguini, all accompanied with a Baja California Cetto-label sauvignon blanc. Open nightly 1800-2330; credit cards accepted. Expensive. Reservations recommended.

At **Vips,** tel. (74) 868-574, right across the street, you can glimpse the Mexico of the future. Here, Mexican middle-class families flock to a south-of-the-border-style Denny's that beats Denny's at its own game. Inside, the air is as fresh as a spring breeze, the windows, water glasses, and utensils shine like silver, the food is tasty and reasonably priced, and the staff is

both amiable and professional. Open Sun.-Thurs. 0700-2400, Friday and Saturday 0700-0200; credit cards accepted. Moderate.

Although a relative newcomer in Acapulco, **La Cuisine Canadienne** about a block east of the Diana fountain, upper floor, tel. (74) 840-058, appears headed for success. The reason seems to be a solidly eclectic menu and a wine list distinguished enough to satisfy a growing legion of loyal French-speaking customers. Open daily 0800-1200 and 1700-2300. Moderate.

One of Acapulco's most atmospheric and palate-pleasing Italian restaurants is **Dino's,** nearby on the Costera a block west of the Fiesta Americana Condesa. Located on Costera M. Alemán, next to Hotel Tortuga, tel. (74) 840-037. Guests can choose to sit on a bay-view terrace in front or an intimate fountain patio in back. From the menu, select among antipastos, salads, meats, and many seafood and meat pastas smothered in sauces, made with a flourish right at the table. Open daily 1800-2330; credit cards accepted. Moderate to expensive.

No tour of Acapulco restaurants would be complete without a stop at **Carlos'n Charlie's,** which, like all of the late Carlos Anderson's worldwide chain, specializes in the zany. On the Costera, across and a block east of the Hotel Fiesta Americana Condesa, tel. (74) 840-039. The fun begins with the screwy decor, continues via the good-natured, tongue-in-cheek antics of the staff, and climaxes with the food and drink, which is organized by categories, such as "Slurp," "Munch," "Peep," "Moo," and "Zurts," and is very tasty. Open daily 1800-2400; credit cards accepted. Moderate to expensive.

Another successful culinary experiment is the Acapulco branch of the worldwide **Suntory** Japanese restaurant chain, across from the Oceanic 2000 building, east end of the Costera, tel. (74) 848-088. Although a Japanese restaurant in Mexico is as difficult to create as a Mexican restaurant in Japan, Suntory, the giant beer, whiskey, and wine manufacturer, carries it off with aplomb. From the outside, the clean-lined wooden structure appears authentically classic Japanese, seemingly lifted right out of 17th-century Kyoto. The impression continues in the cool interior, where patrons enjoy a picture-perfect tropical Zen garden, complete with moss, a stony brook, sago palm, and feathery festoons of bamboo. Finally comes the food, from a host of choices, vegetables, rice, fish, and meat—which chefs (who, although Mexican, soon begin to look Japanese) individually prepare for you on the grill built into your table. Open daily 1400-2300; credit cards accepted. Moderate to expensive.

The Acapulco bent for restaurant fantasy continues right across the street, at **Raul's Wharf.** Inside, you enter a dim, Disney-esque world. A jungle waterfall cascades behind you while a rickety bridge leads you over a misty lagoon, where, at any moment, you fear that a crocodile or a pirate is going to grab you. If you cross over safely your reward will be a cool salad bar, and a choice of several intriguing specialties, such as Siamese chicken, Blackbeard's shrimp, or alligator steak. Credit cards accepted. Expensive.

ENTERTAINMENT AND EVENTS

Strolling and Sidewalk Cafes
The old *zócalo* is the best place for strolling and people-watching. Bookstalls, vendors, band concerts, and, on weekend nights especially, pitch-penny games, mimes, and clowns are constant sources of entertainment. When you're tired of walking, take a seat at a sidewalk cafe, such as Maggi's Pizza, or Cafe Los Amigos, and let the scene pass *you* by for a change.

Movies
A number of cinemas dot the Costera. The movies usually begin around 1600 or 1630. The second screening generally starts around 2030 and finishes around midnight. From lower-brow to high, first comes the **Cine Variedades,** admission about $2, at Mendoza and Cuauhtémoc, tel. (74) 852-753, where visitors can enjoy viewing a double-whammy bill of Mexican and American action potboilers.

Farther up the scale is the **Cine Hornos,** admission $2, Nuñez de Balboa 10, tel. (74) 851-731, on the Costera, corner of de Ulloa, which shows mostly American first-run action flicks. Topping the list is the Cine Plaza Bahía, admission $3, in the Plaza Bahía shopping center, next to the Hotel Acapulco Plaza, which screens first-run American action and drama.

Tourist Shows
The **Mexican Fiesta,** Acapulco's dance performance extravaganza, goes on Tuesday, Thursday, and Saturday at the sprawling Centro Internacional (formerly Convention Center) just east of the golf course. The all-Mexico sombrero and whirling-skirt folkloric dance show is highlighted by a replica performance of the wheeling Papantla flyers. Tickets, available from travel agents, can include either the show only ($17), the show and two drinks ($24), or the show, drinks, and buffet ($42, kids half price). The buffet customarily begins around 1900, followed by the performance at 2015. Book your tickets through a travel or tour agent.

Sunsets
West-side hills block Acapulco Bay's sunset horizon. Sunset connoisseurs remedy the problem by gathering at certain points on the Peninsula de las Playas, such as **La Quebrada, Playa Angosta,** and the cliffside restaurant and gazebo-bar of the **Hotel Flamingos** before sunset.

Bay Cruise Parties
One popular way to enjoy the sunset and a party at the same time is on a cruise aboard either of the steel excursion ships *Bonanza* or *Hawaiano.* They leave from the pair of bayside docks on the Costera half a mile (toward the Peninsula de las Playas) from the *zócalo.* Both excursions leave about 1630, return around 1900, and include live music, dancing, and open bar. Tickets are available from hotels, travel agents, or at the dock. *Bonanza* reservations, tel. (74) 831-803, *Hawaiano,* tel. (74) 822-199 or 820-785, for about $18 per person, kids half price. They also offer midday cruises (*paseo matutino,* 1100-1400, with snorkeling) and moonlight cruises (*lunada,* 2230-0100) for similar prices.

Bullfights
Bullfights are staged every Sunday at 1730 at the arena near Playa Caletilla. Avoid congestion and parking hassles by taking a taxi. Get tickets (about $20) through a travel agent or the ticket office, tel. (74) 839-561.

Jai-Alai and Offtrack Betting
About $12 gains you entrance to Acapulco's new big jai-alai *frontón,* an indoor stadium, on the Costera, east end, across from the Hotel

Hyatt, open Tues.-Sun. 2100-0100. Here, it's hard not to ooh and aah at the skill of players competing in the ancient Basque game of jai-alai. With a long narrow, curved basket tied to one arm, players fling a hard rubber ball, at lethal speeds, to the far end of the court, where it rebounds like a pistol shot, and must be returned by an opposing player. You can place wagers on your favorite player, or, downstairs, bet on horseraces and other sports events taking place far away.

Dancing and Discoing

Several of the Costera hotels have live music for dancing at their lobby-bars. Moving east along the Costera, the better possibilities are: the **Ritz,** tel. (74) 857-544; **Acapulco Plaza,** tel. (74) 859-700; the **Fiesta Americana Condesa,** tel. (74) 842-828; the **Presidente,** tel. (74) 841-700; and the **Hyatt Regency,** tel. (74) 691-234. Call to verify times.

Many restaurant-bars along the Costera have nightly dance music, both recorded and live. A pair of favorites of both longtime tourists and local people are the **Tropicana** (on beach side, across the Costera from Cine Hornos) and the **Copacabana** (on beach side, near corner of Amal Espina). Both have cocktails and live Latin (sometimes called "Tropical") music for dancing till around 0300. Call ahead—Copacabana tel. (74) 851-051, Tropicana tel. (74) 853-050— to verify times.

A lively band also plays nightly at the restaurant-club **Paradise** (across from the Hotel Romano), tel. (74) 845-988, on the Costera beachside entertainment strip (see below) just west of the Hotel Fiesta Americana Condesa. Zany waiters, a lively, varied musical repertoire, and good-enough food all spell happy times at the Paradise.

Discotheques usually monitor their entrances carefully and are consequently safe and pleasant places for a night's entertainment (provided you either are either immune to the noise or bring earplugs). They open their doors around 2200 and play relatively low-volume music and videos for starters until around 2300, when fogs descend, lights flash, and the thumping begins, continuing sometimes till dawn. Admission runs about $7 to $15 or more for the tonier joints.

Acapulco's discos and dance hangouts concentrate in two major east-side spots. Moving east, between the Diana Circle and the Fiesta Americana Condesa, a solid lineup of clubs, hangouts, and discos occupies the Costera's beach side. During peak seasons, the dancing crowds spill onto the street. Stroll along and pick out the style and volume that you like.

Of the bunch, **Beach** disco is the loudest, brashest, and among the most popular. For the entrance fee of $10 ($17 Wednesday, open bar included) the music and the lights go till dawn. Other neighboring discos, such as Taboo, Baby Lobster, Corona, Blackbeard's, and Beto Safari, while sometimes loud, are nevertheless subdued in comparison.

Another mile east, the Hard Rock Cafe, which actually serves food, signals the beginning of a second lineup on both sides of the street of about a dozen live-music or disco clubs. The energy they put out, trying to outdo each other (with brighter lights, louder music, and larger and flashier facades) is only exceeded by the frequency at which they seem to go in and out of business. More or less permanently fixed are **Hard Rock Cafe,** "Save the Planet," live music, 2230-0200, no cover, tel. (74) 840-047; **Baby 'O** disco and concert hall, "There's only one Acapulco and only one Baby 'O," 2200-0400, cover, tel. (74) 847-474; and **Atrium,** "Too hot fun," disco, 2200-0400, cover, tel. (74) 841-900.

Reigning above all of these lesser centers of discomania is **Extravaganza,** visible everywhere around the bay as the pink neon glow on the east-side Las Brisas hill. Go there, if only to look, though call for a reservation beforehand, tel. (74) 847-164, or they won't let you in. Inside, the impression is of ultramodern fantasy—a giant spaceship window facing outward on a galactic star carpet—while the music explodes, propelling you, the dancing traveler, through inner space. A mere $10-15 cover gets you through the door; inside, drinks are $5-10, while French champagne runs $300 a bottle.

Child's Play

CICI (short for Centro Internacional de Convivencia Infantil) is the biggest of Acapulco's water parks. An aquatic paradise for families, CICI has acres of liquid games, where you can swish along a slippery toboggan run, plummet down a towering kamikaze slide, or loll in a gentle wave pool. Other pools contain performing whales, dolphins, and sea lions. Patrons also enjoy a restaurant, a beach club, and much more. CICI is on the east end of the Costera between the golf course and the Hyatt Regency; open daily 1000-1800, adult admission $7, kids $6, sea mammal performances occur at 1230, 1530, and 1730.

Mágico Mundo, tel. (74) 831-215, Acapulco's other water park, is on the opposite side of town at Playa Caleta. Includes an aquarium, museum, restaurant, water slides, cascades, and more; open daily 0900-1700, admission $5 adult, $3.50 child.

SPORTS

Walking and Jogging
The most interesting beach walking in Acapulco is along the two-mile stretch of beach between the Hotel Fiesta Americana Condesa and the rocky point at Parque Papagayo. Avoid the midday heat by starting early for breakfast along the Costera (such as Sanborn's, Av. Costera M. Alemán 1226, tel. 74-844-465, open from 0730) and walking west along the beach with the sun to your back. Besides the beach itself, you'll pass rocky outcroppings to climb on, tidepools to poke through, plenty of fruit vendors, and *palapas* to rest in from the sun. Bring a hat, shirt, and sunscreen and allow two or three hours. If you get tired, ride a taxi or bus back. You can do the reverse walk just as easily in the afternoon after about 1500 from Playa Hamacas just past the steamship dock after lunch on the *zócalo* (try the Cafe Los Amigos).

Soft sand and steep slopes spoil most **jogging** prospects on Acapulco Bay beaches. However, the green open spaces surrounding the Centro Cultural de Convenciones, just east of the golf course, provide a good in-town substitute.

Tennis and Golf
Acapulco's tennis courts are all private and mostly at the hotels. Try the Acapulco Plaza, tel. (74) 859-050, Fiesta Americana, tel. (74) 842-828, Villa Vera, tel. (74) 840-333, Presidente, tel. (74) 841-700, and the Hyatt, tel. (74) 691-234. The Hyatt, for example, has five night-

lit hard courts which, for visitors, rent for $16 per hour during the day and $21 at night. If, however, you live in Acapulco, or play with someone who does, courts run only $5 by day and $10 by night. Lessons by the in-house teaching pro cost about $25 an hour.

If you prefer clay courts, located in the Costera the **Hotel Villa Vera and Racquet Club,** Lomas del Mar 35, tel. (74) 840-333, has three of them for about $21 per hour by day and $24 by night.

One of the coziest places for tennis in town is **Alfredo's Tennis Club,** literally the home of former tennis champion Alfredo Millet. He has two night-lit courts, rentable for $10 per hour during the day, $15 at night, including towel, refreshment, and use of his swimming pool. Lessons run $50 an hour. Located at Av. Prado 29, tel. (74) 840-004 or 847-070 (call first); get there via Av. Deportes, next to the Pizza Hut. Go uphill one block, then left another to Alfredo's, at the corner of Prado.

If Alfredo is all booked up and you can't afford $20 an hour for a tennis court, call some of the less plush hotels with courts (ee "Accommodations" above), such as the Gran Motel Acapulco, $9/hour days, $16 nights, Costera near the Hotel Acapulco Plaza, tel. (74) 855-437; Las Hamacas, tel. (74) 837-709; Majestic, tel. (74) 834-710; and Suites Alba, tel. (74) 830-073.

The Acapulco **Campo de Golf,** tel. (74) 840-781 or 840-782, right on the Costera, is open daily to the public, first-come first-served, 0630-1730 daily. Exceptions are Wednesday and Saturday after 1300, when the course is limited to foursomes. Greens fee for nine holes runs about $25, 18 holes $40, caddy $14, club rental $15.

Much more exclusive and better maintained is the Club de Golf at the hotels Acapulco Princess and Pierre Marques (tel. 74-691-000), about five miles past the southeast edge of town (see "Out-of-Town Hotels" preceeding). Here, the 18-hole greens fee runs $60 if you're a hotel guest and $80 if you're not. Caddies, carts, and club rentals are correspondingly priced.

Swimming, Surfing, and Boogie-boarding
Acapulco Bay's tranquil (if not pristine) waters generally allow safe swimming from hotel-front beaches. The water is too tranquil for surf sports, however. Strong waves off open-ocean Playa Revolcadero southeast of the city often give

good bodysurfing, boogie-board, and surfboard rides. Be aware, the waves can be dangerous. The Acapulco Princess on the beach provides lifeguards. Check with them before venturing in. Bring your own equipment; rentals may not be available.

Snorkeling and Scuba Diving

The best local snorkeling is off **Roqueta Island.** Closest access point is by boat from the docks at Playa Caleta (and Playa Tlacopanocha, see "Old Town Beaches," and "Isla Roqueta" under "Sights" previous). Such trips usually run about $20 per person for two hours, equipment included. Snorkel trips can also be arranged through beachfront aquatics shops at hotels such as the Ritz, Acapulco Plaza, Fiesta Americana Condesa, and the Hyatt Regency.

Although local water clarity is often not ideal, Acapulco does have some professional dive instructors. NAUI-licensed diver Mario Trevino Diaz, who works out of his shop at the Hotel San Francisco, 219 Costera M. Alemán (about three blocks west of the Hawaiano tour boat dock), tel. (74) 820-045, offers everything from brief resort courses and beginning dives to complete NAUI open-water certification and advanced dives to choice local spots. Figure on paying about $60 for beginning training, including an easy local dive. Open-water certification averages about five days and may cost around $300.

Another instructor, NAUI-certified José Vasquez, offers approximately the same thing. Contact José through the Acapulco Marina, tel. (74) 837-505, fax 831-026.

Sailing and Windsurfing

Close-in Acapulco Bay waters are too congested with motorboats for tranquil sailing or windsurfing. Nevertheless, some beach concessionaires at the big hotels, such as the Acapulco Plaza and Hyatt Regency do rent (or take people sailing in) simple boats from $20 per hour.

Limited windsurfing is also possible at the Hotel Majestic beach club in the little sub-bay sheltered by the Peninsula de las Playas.

Outside of town, tranquil Laguna Coyuca, on the coast about 20 minutes' drive northwest of the *zócalo,* offers good windsurfing and sailing prospects (see the last section of the previous chapter, "Pie de la Cuesta,").

Jet-Skiing, Water-Skiing, and Parasailing

Power sports are very popular on Costera hotel beaches. Concessionaires (recognized by their lineup of beached boats) operate from most big hotel beaches, notably at the Radisson, Ritz, Acapulco Plaza, Fiesta Americana Condesa, and the Hyatt Regency. Prices run about $60 per hour for jet-ski boats, $50 per hour for water-skiing, and $20 for a 10-minute parasailing ride.

Sailfish, which sportfishing boats frequently bring in at Acapulco's zócalo-front malecón, make tough eating and should be released when caught.

BRUCE WHIPPERMAN

Sportfishing

Fishing boats line the *malecón* dockside across the boulevard from the *zócalo*. Activity centers on the dockside office (see the "Acapulco: Zócalo" map) of the 20-boat blue-and-white fleet run by **Sociedad Cooperativa Turísticas,** whose dozens of licensed captains regularly take visitors for big-game fishing trips. Although some travel agents may book you individually during high season, the Sociedad Cooperativa Turísticas office, tel. (74) 821-099, open daily 0800-1800, rents only entire boats, including captain, equipment, and bait.

Rental prices and catches depend on the season. Drop by the dock after 1400 to see what they are bringing in. During good times, boats might average one big marlin or sailfish apiece. Best months for sailfish *(pez vela)* are said to be November, December, and January; for marlin, February and March.

Big 40-foot boats with live or six fishing lines rent from $150 per day. Smaller boats, with three or four lines and holding five or six passengers, rent from $120 or less. All of the Cooperativa boats are radio-equipped, with toilet, life preservers, tackle, bait, and ice. Customers usually supply their own food and drinks. Although the Cooperativa is generally competent, look over the boat and check its equipment before putting your money down.

You can also arrange fishing trips through a travel agent or your hotel lobby tour desk.

Sailfish and marlin are neither the only nor necessarily the most desirable fish in the sea. Competently captained *pangas* can typically haul in three or four large 20- or 30-pound excellent-eating *róbalo* (snook), *huachinango* (snapper) or *atún* (tuna) in two hours just outside Acapulco Bay.

Such lighter boats are rentable from the cooperative for about $30 per hour or less from individual fishermen on Playa Hamacas (past the steamship dock at the foot of Fort San Diego).

Marina and Boat Launching

A safe place to launch or dock your boat is the 150-slip **Marina Acapulco** on the Peninsula de las Playas's sheltered inner shoreline, Av. Costera M. Alemán 215, Fracc. Las Playas,

Acapulco, Guerrero 39300, tel. (74) 837-505, fax 831-026. Boat launching runs about $25 per day. The slip rate is around $600 per month for the first 30 feet, plus $20 per additional foot per month, including 110/220-volt power, potable water, pump-out, satellite disk TV connection, toilets, showers, ice, and access to the marina pool, restaurant, hotel, and repair facilities. Get there via the driveway past the suspension bridge over the Costera about a mile from the *zócalo*.

SHOPPING

Market

Acapulco, despite its modern glitz, has a very colorful traditional market, which is fun for strolling through even without buying anything. It is open daily, dawn to dusk. Vendors arrive here with grand intentions: mounds of neon-red tomatoes, buckets of *nopales* (cactus leaves), towers of toilet paper, and mountains of soap bars. As you wander through the sunlight-dappled aisles, past big gaping fish, bulging rounds of cheese, and festoons of huaraches, don't miss **Piñatas Amanda,** one of the market's friendliest shops. You may even end up buying one of her charming paper Donald Ducks, Snow Whites, or Porky Pigs. The market is at the corner of Mendoza and Constituyentes, a quarter mile inland from Hornos Beach. Ride a "Mercado"-marked bus, or taxi.

Supermarkets and a Natural-Food Store

In the *zócalo* area, **Woolworth's** is a good source of a little bit of everything at reasonable prices, on Escudero, corner of Morelos, behind Sanborn's; open daily 0930-2030. Their lunch counter, furthermore, provides a welcome refuge from the midday heat.

Comercial Mexicana, with two Acapulco branches, is a big Mexican Kmart, which, besides the expected film, medicines, cosmetics, and housewares, also includes groceries and a bakery. On the Costera, at Cinco de Mayo, just east of the Fort San Diego; and on Farallones, a couple of blocks uphill from the Costera's Diana Circle, both open daily 0900-2100.

If you can't find what you want at Comercial Mexicana, try the huge **Sam's Club,** just uphill from the Farallones Comercial Mexicana, and the giant **Wal-Mart,** at the far east end, across from the Hyatt Regency.

Super-Super, also near the Costera's east end, is an American-style refuge from Acapulco, if only for its ice-cream-cool air-conditioning, on the Costera across from CICI water park; open daily 0800-2300, tel. (74) 846-961: Besides groceries and notions, its big newsstand carries loads of U.S. magazines, paperback novels, records, and some Mexico guides.

Photography

Foto Condor, tel. (74) 822-112, right on the *zócalo,* does photofinishing and sells photo supplies and several popular film varieties. Find it on the corner of J. Carranza; open daily 0800-2100.

One of the best-stocked photo shops in town is **Super Foto Económica,** Costera M. Alemán 82, not far from Hotel Fiesta Americana Condesa, tel. (74) 840-643 or 841-194, Torre Acapulco condo tower. In addition to one-hour color service, they rent cameras and stock and develop professional films, including black and white and transparencies.

Handicrafts

Despite much competition, asking prices for Acapulco handicrafts are relatively high. Bargaining, furthermore, seldom brings them down to size. **Sanborn's,** two blocks from the *zócalo* (with another branch on the Costera a block from the Fiesta Americana Condesa), is a good starting point for comparison shopping, since their prices are both fixed and fairly reasonable. Located at Costera M. Alemán and Escudero; open daily 0730-2300, with bookstore and restaurant, tel. (74) 826-167. Sanborn's all-Mexico selection includes, notably, black Oaxaca *barra* pottery, painted gourds from Uruapán, Guadalajara leather, Taxco silver jewelry, colorful plates from Puebla, and Tlaquepaque pottery and glass.

With Sanborn's prices in mind, head one block toward the *zócalo* to **Margarita,** where, in the basement of the big old Edificio Oviedo, glitters an eclectic fiesta of Mexican jewelry. Find it at I. de la Llave and Costera M. Alemán,

local 1, tel. (74) 820-590 or 825-240; open Mon.-Sat. 0900-2100, Sunday 0900-1500. Never mind if the place is empty; cruise-line passengers regularly fill the aisles. Here you'll be able to see artisans adding to the acre of gleaming silver, gold, copper, brass, fine carving, and lacquerware around you. Don't forget to get your free margarita (or soft drink) before you leave.

Another bountiful handicrafts source near the *zócalo* is the artisans' market **Mercado de Parrazal.** From Sanborn's, head away from the Costera a few short blocks to Vasquez de Leon and turn right one block. There, a big plaza of semipermanent stalls offers a galaxy of Mexican handicrafts: Tonalá and Tlaquepaque papier-mâché, brass, and pottery animals; Bustamante-replica eggs, masks, and humanoids; Oaxaca wooden animals and black pottery; Guerrero masks; and Taxco jewelry. Sharp bargaining is necessary, however, to cut the excessive asking prices down to size.

The new side of town has a number of interesting handicrafts sources. Along the Costera sidewalk bordering the shady Centro Cultural (galleries, auditorium, library open Mon.-Sat. 0900-1400 and 1600-1900, and small archaeological museum) grounds, vendors often pile tables with crafts. Among the most intriguing are the originals of Juan Silviera, who, with his wife, Blanca, has built a thriving business fashioning fanciful painted animals. Fluent in English (he lived for years in Canada) and very well informed, Juan also leads private insider's-eye tours of Acapulco. If you can't find them there, stop by their handicrafts shop **Albrijes** (ahl-BREE-hays), in the shopping Plaza Bahía, just west of the Acapulco Plaza Hotel.

The biggest crafts store in Acapulco, **AFA** (Artesanías Finas de Acapulco), is tucked a block off the Costera near the Hyatt Regency on Horacio Nelson, corner of James Cook, tel. (74) 848-039 or 848-040, fax 842-448; open Mon.-Sat. 0900-1930, Sunday 0900-1500. Although jewelry is their strong suit, they have plenty more from most everywhere in Mexico. Items include pottery, papier-mâché, lacquerware, onyx, and much leather, including purses, belts, and saddles.

SERVICES

Money Exchange

In the *zócalo* neighborhood, go to the **Bancomer,** fronting the Costera, tel. (74) 848-055, to change U.S. (0900-1330) or Canadian (1100-1330) cash or traveler's checks. Although the lines at **Banamex** nearby on the Costera, two blocks from *zócalo* next to Sanborn's, are usually longer, they exchange major currencies (including French, Spanish, British, German, Swiss, and Japanese) and are likely to have longer hours.

On the new side of town, change money at **Banamex** across from McDonald's, open Mon.-Fri. 0900-1700, tel. (74) 859-020; or at the **Bancomer,** Glorietta Diana (Diana Circle) office, open Mon.-Fri. 0900-1300 for U.S. currency and traveler's checks and 1030-1300 for Canadian, tel. (74) 843-455.

After hours on the Costera, the **Consultorio International** (tel. 843-108) in Galería Picuda shopping center, across the street and west from the Hotel Fiesta Americana Condesa, exchanges currency and traveler's checks daily 0900-2100.

American Express Offices

The only Acapulco American Express branch, at Costera M. Alemán 1628, tel. (74) 691-124, cashes American Express traveler's checks at near-bank rates and provides member financial services and travel agency services. They're open Mon.-Sat. 1000-2100, although check-cashing hours may be shorter.

Communications

The Acapulco main *correo* is in the Palacio Federal across the Costera from the steamer dock three blocks from the *zócalo.* They provide Mexpost fast

Acapulco
area code
is 74

mail and philatelic services, Mon.-Fri. 0800-2000, Saturday 0900-1300, tel. (74) 822-083. A **branch post and telegraph office** at the Estrella de Oro bus terminal, Cuauhtémoc and Massieu, is open Mon.-Fri. 0900-2000, Saturday 0900-1200.

Telecomunicaciones next to the main post office provides money order, telegram, telex,

and fax services, Mon.-Fri. 0900-1800 and Saturday 0900-1200, tel. (74) 822-622 or 822-621.

Near the *zócalo,* you can call *larga distancia* daily 0800-2200 from the small office on J. Carranza at Calle de la Llave.

Round-the-clock long-distance telephone is available at **Larga Distancia Tel-plus** across from at the Estrella Blanca Central de Autobús (central bus terminal) at Ejido 47, about a mile northwest from the *zócalo* on the road to Pie de la Cuesta.

Immigration and Customs

If you lose your tourist card go to **Migración,** on the Costera, around the traffic circle from Super Super, same side of the Costera, tel. (74) 867-024, with proof of your identity and some proof (such as your passport, airline ticket, or a copy of your lost tourist card) of your arrival date in Mexico. If you try to leave Mexico without your tourist card, you may face trouble and a fine. Also report to Migracion if you arrive in Acapulco by yacht.

The **Aduana** (customs), tel. (74) 820-931, is in the Palacio Federal, on the Costera, *zócalo* area, next to Sanborn's. If you have to temporarily leave your car in Mexico, check with state Turismo (see below), tel. (74) 869-167, to see what paperwork, if any, must be completed.

Consulates

Acapulco has several consulates. The U.S. consular officer, Bob Urbanek (Hotel Club del Sol mezzanine), tel. (74) 856-600, ext. 7348, or 857-297, holds office hours Mon.-Fri. 1000-1400. He's a busy man, and asks that you kindly have your problem written down, together with a specific request for information or action.

The **Canadian** consul, Diane McLean de Huerta, is also at the Hotel Club del Sol, tel. (74) 856-600 or 856-621.

For the **British** consul, Derek Gore, call (74) 846-605 at the Hotel Las Brisas.

Call the **German** consul, Mario Wichtendahl, at (74) 847-437.

The **Netherlands** consul, Ángel Diaz Acosta, is at (74) 846-179.

The **French,** Vidal Mendoza, at (74) 823-394; and **Spanish,** Tomas Lagar Alonso, may be reached at (74) 857-205.

INFORMATION

Tourist Information Office
The helpful federal **Turismo** information office staff answers questions and gives out maps and written materials at their office on the beach side of the Costera, corner of Amal Espina, across from Banamex on Av. M. Alemán 187, tel. (74) 869-167, 869-164, or 869-168; open Mon.-Fri. 0800-2000, Sat.-Sun. 1000-1800.

Medical, Police, and Emergencies
If you get sick, see your hotel doctor or go to the **Hospital Magellanes,** one of Acapulco's most respected private hospitals, for either office calls or round-the-clock emergencies. Facilities include a lab, 24-hour **pharmacy,** and an emergency room with many specialists on call, at W. Massieu 2, corner of Colón, one block from the Costera and the Hotel Ritz; tel. (74) 856-544 or 856-597, pharmacy 856-706.

For routine medications near the *zócalo,* go to one of many pharmacies, such as at Sanborn's, corner of Escudero and the Costera, tel. (74) 826-167, or the big **Farmacia Discuento** (discount pharmacy), tel. (74) 820-804, open daily 0800-2200, at Escudero and Carranza, across the street from Woolworth's.

For police emergencies, contact one of the many **tourist police** (on the Costera, in safari pith helmets), or call the **Policía Preventiva** station, tel. (74) 850-490, 850-862 or 850-650, at the end of Av. Caminos, on the inland side of Papagayo Park.

In case of fire, call the *bomberos,* tel. (74) 844-122, on Av. Farallon, behind Comercial Mexicana, two blocks off the Costera from the Glorietta Diana.

Publications
One of the best book sources in town is **Sanborn's** on the Costera, tel. (74) 844-465, ground floor of the Condo Estrella tower, one block east of the Hotel Fiesta Americana Condesa. They stock hundreds of magazines, paperback novels, maps, Mexico guides, and coffee-table art and archaeological books. Open 0730-2300. The *zócalo* branch, on the Costera across from the steamship dock, same hours, tel. (74) 826-167, is equally good.

English-language international newspapers, such as the Mexico City *News,* the *Los Angeles Times,* and *USA Today,* are often available in the large hotel bookshops, especially the Acapulco Plaza, Fiesta Americana Condesa, and the Hyatt Regency. On the other end of town, newsstands around the *zócalo* regularly sell the *News.*

A local English-language newspaper, the Acapulco *Heat,* specializes in social events, Mexico travel, and restaurants, and lists houses and apartments for sale or rent. Pick up a copy at their office, tel. (74) 812-625, or at the Fat Farm restaurant or Super-Super grocery store.

Public Library
The small, friendly Acapulco *biblioteca* is near the *zócalo* adjacent to the cathedral. Their collection, used mostly by college and high school students in their airy reading room, is nearly all in Spanish. Find it at Madero 5, corner of Quebrada, tel. (74) 820-388; open Mon.-Fri. 0900-2100, Saturday 0900-1400.

Guide and Language Instruction
Sculptor and art teacher Juan Silviera offers personalized tours of Acapulco for small groups, P.O. Box 112, Acapulco, Guerrero 39300. Personable and well informed, Silviera also speaks fluent English, having lived in Canada for many years. "They may pay whatever they want," he replies, when asked about his fee. You also may be able to contact him at his handicrafts store, Las Albrijes, in the big Plaza Bahía shopping center, just west of the Acapulco Plaza Hotel.

The long-established **Harmon Hall** school of languages offers Spanish instruction. Their four-week package includes 20 hours of intensive study and runs around $180. They're located at 59 Costera M. Alemán, Fracc. Las Playas, Acapulco, Guerrero 39300, tel. (74) 867-005 or 867-006, or at 138 Av. Farallon, tel. (74) 843-000 or 841-883.

Service Club and Women's Meeting
The **Friends of Acapulco** charitable club holds fund-raising fiestas and fashion shows to support the Acapulco Children's home and other local good works. For information, write P.O. Box C-54, Acapulco, Guerrero 39300.

The Guerrero state **Sub Secretaría de Mujer** provides counseling and help for problems such as rape, domestic abuse, abandonment, and birth control at their small Acapulco office at Hidalgo 1, at the *zócalo,* open Mon.-Fri. 0900-1500 and 1800-2100, tel. (74) 826-311.

The Sub Secretaría also sponsors a public meeting on the first Thursday (verify by calling) of each month in the evening at the small auditorium in the park-like grounds of the **Centro Cultural,** on the Costera, a block or two west of CICI water park. Local leaders, such as the Sub Secretaría's local *directora,* Rudolfina Soriano Gasga, and Inez Huerta Pegueros, former *directora* of the Acapulco chapter of the nationwide Movimiento Social Contra la Violencia Sexual, often attend.

GETTING THERE AND AWAY

By Air
Soveral airlines connect the Acapulco airport (code-designated ACA, officially the Juan N. Alvarez International Airport) with U.S. and Mexican destinations.

Aeroméxico flights connect directly with **Houston** (via Mexico City) four times weekly. For reservations, contact them at their Torre Acapulco office, tel. (74) 851-625, 851-600, 851-705 or 851-706. For flight information, call the airport at 669-296 or 668-014.

Delta Air Lines flights connect daily with Dallas; others connect daily with Los Angeles, continuing to Portland. For reservations, call a travel agent, or toll-free tel. 91-800-902-21.

Mexicana Airlines flights connect with Chicago daily and with Mexico City five times daily. For reservations, call (74) 846-890 or 841-215; for flight information, call the airport at (74) 669-121.

American Airlines flights connect twice daily with Dallas. For reservations, call a travel agent, or toll-free 91-800-90-460; for flight information, call the airport at (74) 669-227.

Continental Airlines charter flights connect with Houston. For reservations, call a travel agent or 91-800-9050; for flight information, call (74) 669-051 or 669-063.

MEXICO CITY DRIVING RESTRICTIONS

In order to reduce smog and traffic gridlock, authorities have limited which cars can drive in Mexico City, depending upon the last digit of their license plate. If you violate these rules, you risk getting an expensive ticket: On Monday, no vehicle may be driven with final digits 5 or 6; Tuesday, 7 or 8; Wednesday, 3 or 4; Thursday, 1 or 2; Friday, 9 or 0. Weekends, all vehicles may be driven.

Air Arrival and Departure
After the usually perfunctory immigration and customs checks, Acapulco arrivees enjoy airport car rentals, efficient transportation for the 15-mile trip to town, and money exchange service (U.S. and Canadian cash and traveler's checks, Mon.-Fri. 1000-1500). If you'll be arriving after money-exchange hours or on weekends, change a day's worth of money before arrival.

Airport **car rental** agents usually include Hertz, tel. (74) 858-947 or 856-889; Avis, tel. (74) 841-633 or 842-581; National, tel. (74) 848-234 or 844-348; Budget, tel. (74) 810-592 or 810-596; Economovil, tel. (74) 842-828 or 858-050; and SAAD jeep rentals, tel. (74) 843-445 or 845-325. You can ensure availability and often save money by bargaining with agencies via their national toll-free numbers (see chart in the On the Road chapter).

Tickets for **ground transport** to town are sold by agents near the terminal exit. Options include collective GMC Suburban station wagon (about $5, kids half price) or microbus (about $2.50, kids half price), both of which deposit passengers at individual hotels. *Taxis especiales* run about $17 to a $30 maximum, depending on distance. Plush limousines are $21-38. GMC Suburbans can be hired "especial" as private taxis for about $32 for up to seven passengers.

On your departure day, save money by sharing a taxi with fellow departees. Don't get into the taxi until you settle the fare. Having already arrived, you know what the airport ride should cost. If the driver insists on greed, hail another taxi.

Simplify your departure by having US$12 or its peso equivalent (they don't take traveler's checks or credit cards) for your international departure tax. If you lost your tourist card (which Immigration stamped upon your arrival), don't pass Go; return to Migración (see "Services" above) prior to your departure date.

The Acapulco air terminal building has a number of shops for last-minute handicrafts purchases, a *buzón* (mailbox) for postcards, long-distance telephones, and a restaurant.

By Bus

Major competitors Estrella Blanca and Estrella de Oro operate separate long-distance Centrales de Autobús (central bus terminals) on opposite sides of town.

Estrella Blanca, tel. (74) 692-028, 692-029, or 692-030, coordinates its service with subsidiary lines Flecha Roja, Autotransportes Cuauhtémoc, and Gacela at its big northwest-side terminal at Av. Ejido 47. The airy station is so clean you could sleep on the polished onyx floor and not get dirty; bring an air mattress and blanket. Other conveniences include inexpensive left-luggage lockers, food stores across the street, and a 24-hour *larga distancia* and fax office (Tel-plus, fax 74-829-117), across the street.

Scores of Estrella Blanca *salidas locales* (local departures) connect with destinations in three directions: northern interior, Costa Grande (northwest), and Costa Chica (southeast) coastal destinations.

Most connections are first class or "Primera Plus" (super first class). Specific northern interior connections include Mexico City (dozens daily, some via Taxco), Toluca, Morelia via Chilpancingo and Altimirano (six daily), and Guadalajara (three daily).

Many first- (about 10 per day) and second-class (hourly) departures connect northwest with Costa Grande destinations of Zihuatanejo and Lázaro Cárdenas. Southeast Costa Chica connections, terminating in Puerto Escondido, include four first-class daily (one via Ometepec) and approximately one second-class connection per hour.

Also from the Estrella Blanca terminal, a few Tres Estrellas de Oro daily arrivals and departures connect with the U.S. border (Mexicali and Tijuana) via the Pacific coast route (Zihuatanejo, Manzanillo, Puerto Vallarta, and Mazatlán).

The busy, modern Estrella de Oro bus terminal on the east side, at Cuauhtémoc and Massieu, tel. (74) 858-705, provides connections with Mexico City corridor (Chilpancingo, Iguala, Taxco, Cuernavaca) and northwest (Zihuatanejo direction) Costa Grande destinations. Services include left-luggage lockers ($4 per day), snack bars, food stores, restaurant, and *correo* and *telégrafo* offices on the outside upstairs walkway, west end; open Mon.-Fri. 0900-2000, Saturday 0900-1200.

Estrella de Oro connections include dozens of first and super first class with Mexico City and intermediate points. Only a few, however, connect directly with Taxco. Four departures connect daily with Costa Grande (three with Zihuatanejo, one only with Lázaro Cárdenas). Estrella de Oro offers no Costa Chica (Puerto Escondido) connections southeast.

Estrella Blanca also maintains a **second-class terminal** at Cuauhtémoc 97, tel. (74) 822-220; from Sanborn's near the *zócalo*, walk or taxi about seven blocks along Escudero, which becomes Cuauhtémoc. Many departures head to Guerrero, ranging east to Ometepec, north to Chilpancingo, and west to Pie de la Cuesta and Tecpán.

By Car or RV

Good highways connect Acapulco north with Mexico City, northwest with the Costa Grande and Michoacán, and southeast with the Costa Chica and Oaxaca.

The Mexico City Hwy. 95 *cuota* (toll) super-highway would make the connection via Chilpancingo easy (83 miles, 133 km, about two hours) if it weren't for the Acapulco congestion (see below). The uncluttered extension (125 miles, 201 km) to Cuernavaca via Iguala is a breeze in two and a half hours. For Taxco, leave the superhighway at Iguala and follow the winding but scenic old Hwy. 95 cutoff 22 miles (35 km) northwest. From Cuernavaca, the over-the-mountain leg to Mexico City (53 miles, 85 km) would be simple except for Mexico City gridlock, which might lengthen it to two hours. Better allow a minimum of around five and a half driving hours for the entire 261-mile (420-km) Acapulco-Mexico City trip.

The Costa Grande section of Hwy. 200 northwest toward Zihuatanejo is generally uncluttered and smooth (except for some potholes). Allow about four hours for the 150-mile (242-km) trip.

The same is true for the Costa Chica stretch of Hwy. 200 southeast to Pinotepa Nacional (157 miles, 253 km) and Puerto Escondido (247 miles, 398 km total). Allow about four driving hours to Pinotepa, six and a half total to Puerto Escondido.

Acapulco's most congested ingress-egress bottleneck is the over-the-hill leg of Hwy. 95 from the middle of town. You can bypass this by driving east along the Costera past Las Brisas as if you were heading to the airport. At the big cloverleaf intersection near Puerto Marques, head north. When you reach Hwy. 200, head right for the Costa Chica, or left for Hwy. 95 and northern points.

INLAND TO TAXCO

As Acapulco thrives on what's new, Taxco (pop. 150,000) luxuriates in what's old. Nestling among forest-crowned mountains and decorated with monuments of its silver-rich past, Taxco now enjoys an equally rich flood of visitors who stop en route to or from Acapulco. They come to enjoy its fiestas and clear, pine-scented air and to stroll the cobbled hillside lanes and bargain for world renowned silver jewelry.

And despite the acclaim, Taxco preserves its diminutive colonial charm *because* of its visitors, who come to enjoy what Taxco offers. They stay in venerable, family-owned lodgings, walk to the colorful little *zócalo*, where they admire the famous baroque cathedral, and wander among the awning-festooned market lanes just downhill.

hieroglyph of Taxco ("Place of the Ball Game")

cingo, now known as Taxco Viejo ("Old Taxco"), seven miles downhill from present-day Taxco. The Spanish Crown appropriated the mines and worked them with generations of Indian forced labor.

Eighteenth-century enlightenment came to Taxco in the person of José Borda, who, arriving from Spain in 1716, modernized the mine franchise his brother had been operating. José improved conditions and began paying the miners, thereby increasing productivity and profits. In contrast to past operators, Borda returned the proceeds to Taxco, building the monuments that still grace the town. His fortune built streets, bridges, fountains, arches, and his masterpiece, the church of Santa Prisca, which included a special chapel for the miners, who before had not been allowed to enter the church.

HISTORY

The traditional hieroglyph representing Taxco shows a pair of athletes in a court competing in a game of *tlachtli* (still locally played) with a rubber ball. "Tlachco," the Nahuatl name representing that place which had become a small Aztec garrison settlement by the eve of the conquest, literally translates as "Place of the Ball Game." The Spanish, more interested in local minerals than in linguistic details, shifted the name to Taxco.

Colonization

In 1524, Hernán Cortés, looking for tin to alloy with copper to make bronze cannon, heard that people around Taxco were using bits of metal for money. Prospectors hurried out, and within a few years they struck rich silver veins in Tetel-

Independence and Modern Times

The 1810-21 War of Independence and the subsequent civil strife, within a generation, reduced the mines to but a memory. They were nearly forgotten when William Spratling, an American artist and architect, moved to Taxco in 1929 and began reviving Taxco's ancient but moribund silversmithing tradition. Working with local artisans, Spratling opened the first cooperative shop, Las Delicias, which remains today.

Spurred by the trickle of tourists along the new Acapulco highway, more shops opened, increasing the demand for silver, which in turn led to the reopening of the mines. Soon silver demand outpaced the supply. Silver began streaming in from other parts of Mexico to the workbenches of thousands of artisans in hundreds of family- and cooperatively owned shops dotting the still-quaint hillsides of a new, prosperous Taxco.

SIGHTS

Getting Oriented

Although the present city, elev. 5,850 feet (1,780 meters), spreads much farther, the center of town encompasses the city's original seven hills, wrinkles in the slope of a towering mountain.

For most visitors, the downhill town limit is the Carretera Nacional (National Highway), named after John F. Kennedy. It contours along the hillside from **Los Arcos** ("The Arches") on the north, Mexico City, end of town about two miles, passing the Calle Pilita intersection on the south, Acapulco, edge of town. Along the *carretera,* immediately accessible to a steady stream of tour buses, lie the town's plusher hotels and many silver shops.

The rest of the town is fortunately insulated from tour buses by its narrow winding streets. From the *carretera,* the most important of them climb and converge, like bent spokes of a wheel, to the *zócalo* (main plaza). Beginning with the most northerly, the main streets (and the directions they run) are La Garita (uphill), Alarcón (downhill), Veracruz (downhill), Santa Ana (downhill), Salubridad (uphill), Morelos (downhill), and Pilita (downhill).

Getting Around

Although walking is Taxco's most common mode of transport, taxis go anywhere within the city limits for about $2. White *kombi* collective vans (fare about 30 cents) follow designated routes, marked on the windshields. Simply tell your specific destination to the driver. For side trips to nearby towns and villages, a fleet of **Flecha Roja** second-class local buses leave frequently from their *carretera* terminal near the corner of Veracruz.

TAXCO

1. Cableway to Hotel Monte Taxco
2. tourist information (two locations)
3. Hotel Borda
4. Biblioteca Taxco-Canoga Park
5. Banamex
6. Hotel Posada de la Misión (Cuauhtémoc Mural)
7. Restaurant Taberna
8. Hotel Agua Escondida
9. Hotel Posada Los Castillo
10. Hotel Los Arcos
11. Casa Ayja (grocery)
12. Casa Humboldt (Art and History Museum)
13. Restaurant La Parroquia
14. Hotel Rancho Taxco Victoria
15. Restaurant El Adobe
16. Hotel Casa Grande
17. Tienda la Misión
18. La Gruta (silver)
19. Casa Dominguez (bookstore)
20. Museo Spratling (Archaeology Museum)
21. Hotel Santa Prisca
22. market
23. Hotel Hacienda del Solar
24. Restaurant La Ventana de Taxco

Around the Zócalo

All roads in Taxco begin and end on the *zócalo* at **Santa Prisca** church. French architect D. Diego Durán designed and built it between 1751 and 1758 with money from the fortune of silver king Don José Borda. The facade, decorated with pedestaled saints, arches, and spiraled columns, follows the baroque *churrigueresque* style (after Jose Churriguera, 1665-1725, the "Spanish Michelangelo"). Interior furnishings include an elegant pipe organ, brought from Germany by muleback in 1751, and several gilded side altars. The riot of interior elaboration climaxes in the towering gold-leaf main altar, which seems to drip with ornamentation in tribute to Saint Prisca, the Virgin of Guadalupe, and the Virgin of the Rosary, who piously preside above all.

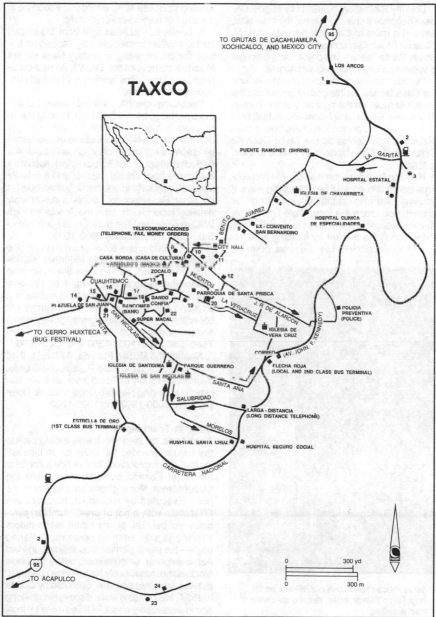

TAXCO

TO GRUTAS DE CACAHUAMILPA
XOCHICALCO, AND MEXICO CITY

95

LOS ARCOS

1

2

LA GARITA

PUENTE RAMONET (SHRINE)

HOSPITAL ESTATAL

3

6

IGLESIA DE CHAVARRIETA

4

BENITO JUAREZ

HOSPITAL CLINICA
DE ESPECIALIDADES

EX - CONVENTO
SAN BERNARDINO

TELECOMUNICACIONES
(TELEPHONE, FAX, MONEY ORDERS)

7   5

8

CITY HALL

10

CASA BORDA (CASA DE CULTURA)
ARNOLDO'S (MASK)

11

ZOCALO

9

12

CUAUHTEMOC

13

16

14   15

1/

DANOD
CONFIA

18

PLAZUELA DE SAN JUAN

BANCOMER
(BANK)

MUERTOS

PARROQUIA DE SANTA PRISCA

19   20

LA VERACRUZ

J. R. DE ALARCON

POLICIA
PREVENTIVA
(POLICE)

21

SAN NICOLAS

SUPER MACAL

22

PILITA

IGLESIA DE
VERA CRUZ

TO CERRO HUIXTECA
(BUG FESTIVAL)

CORREO
(AV. JOHN F. KENNEDY)

IGLESIA DE SANTISIMA

PARQUE GUERRERO

FLECHA ROJA
(LOCAL AND 2ND CLASS BUS TERMINAL)

IGLESIA DE SAN NICOLAS

SANTA ANA

SALUBRIDAD

LARGA - DISTANCIA
(LONG DISTANCE TELEPHONE)

ESTRELLA DE ORO
(1st CLASS BUS TERMINAL)

MORELOS

HOSPITAL SANTA CRUZ

HOSPITAL SEGURO SOCIAL

2

CARRETERA NACIONAL

95

TO ACAPULCO

24

23

0   300 yd

0   300 m

© MOON PUBLICATIONS, INC.

Dreamy Bible-story paintings by Miguel Cabrera decorate a chamber behind the main altar, while in a room to the right, portraits of Pope Benedict IV, who sanctioned all this, and Manuel Borda, Santa Prisca's first priest, hang amongst a solemn gallery of subsequent padres.

Outside, landmarks around the plaza include the **Casa Borda,** visible (facing away from the church facade) on the right side of the *zócalo.* This former Borda family town house, built concurrently with the church in typical baroque colonial style, now serves as the Taxco Casa de Cultura, featuring exhibitions by local artists and artisans.

Heading from the church steps, you can continue downhill in either of two interesting ways. If you walk left immediately downhill from the church, you reach the lane, Calle Los Arcos, running alongside and below the church. From there, reach the **market** by heading right before the quaint archway over the street, down the

Santa Prisca church, built in 1758 with profits from Taxco's silver mines, remains the center of town activities.

winding staircase-lane, where you'll soon be in a warren of awning-covered stalls.

If, however, you head right from the church steps, another immediate right leads you beside the church along legendary **Calle de los Muertos** ("Street of the Dead"), named partly because of the many workmen who died constructing the church.

Continuing downhill, you'll find **Museo Guillermo Spratling,** tel. (762) 216-60, fronting the little plaza behind the church. On the main and upper floors, the National Institute of Archaeology displays intriguing carvings and ceramics (including unusual phallic examples), such as a ball-game ring, animal masks, and a priestly statuette with knife in one hand, human heart in the other. Basement-floor displays interestingly detailed local history from the Aztecs through William Spratling. The museum is open Tues.-Sat. 1000-1700, Sunday 0900-1500.

Back outside, one block down Alarcón (the downhill extension of Calle Muertos), stands **Casa Humboldt,** named after the celebrated geographer (who is said to have stayed only one night, however). Now the state maintains it as a fine arts museum, featuring a permanent collection of classical and contemporary works and temporary exibitions by local artists. Open Tues.-Sat. about 1000-1300 and 1500-1800.

Nearby, the **Museo Platería,** 4 Alarcón, third floor, next door to the Hotel Posada Los Castillo, illustrates a history of Taxco silver-craft and displays outstanding pieces by local artisans. Open Mon.-Fri. 1000-1300 and 1500-1700.

Other In-Town Sights

A short ride, coupled with a walk circling back to the *zócalo,* provides the basis for an interesting half-day exploration. Taxi or ride a *kombi* to the Hotel Posada de la Misión, where the **Cuauhtémoc Mural** glitters on a wall near the pool. Executed by renowned muralist Juan O'Gorman with a riot of pre-Columbian symbols—yellow sun, pearly rabbit-in-the-moon, snarling jaguar, writhing serpents, fluttering eagle—the mural glorifies Cuauhtémoc, the last Aztec emperor. Cuauhtémoc, unlike his uncle Moctezuma, tenaciously resisted the conquest, but was captured and later executed by Cortés in 1524. His remains were discovered not long ago in Ixcateopan, about 24 miles away by local

TLATCHTLI: THE BALL GAME

Basketball fever is probably a mild affliction compared to the enthusiasm of pre-Columbian crowds for *tlatchtli*, the ball game played throughout (and still played in some parts of) Mesoamerica. Contemporary accounts and latter-day scholarship have led to a partial picture of *tlatchtli* as it was played centuries ago. Although details varied locally, the game's basis was a hard natural rubber ball, which players batted back and forth across a center dividing line with leg-, arm-, and torso-blows.

Play and scoring was vaguely similar to tennis. Opponents, either individuals or small teams, tried to smash the ball past their opponents into scoring niches at the opposite ends of an I-shaped, sunken court. Players could also garner points by forcing their opponents to make a wild shot that bounced beyond the court's retaining walls.

Courts were often equipped with a pair of stone rings fixed above opposing ends of the center dividing line. One scoring variation awarded immediate victory to the team who could manage to bat the *tlatchtli* through the ring.

Like tennis, players became very adept at smashing the ball at high speed. Unlike tennis, however, the ball was solid and perhaps as heavy as two or three baseballs. Although protected by helmets and leather, players were usually bloodied, often injured, and sometimes even killed from opponents' punishing *tlatchli*-inflicted blows. Matches were sometimes decided like a boxing match, with victory going to the opponent left standing on the court.

As with everything in Mesoamerica, tradition and ritual ruled *tlatchli*. Master teachers subjected initiates to rigorous training, prescribed ritual, and discipline not unlike those of a medieval monastic brotherhood.

Potential rewards were enormous, however. Stakes varied in proportion to a contest's ritual significance and the rank of the players and their patrons. Champion players could win fortunes in gold, feathers or precious stones. Exceptional games could result in riches and honor for the winner, and death for the loser, whose heart, ripped from his chest on the centerline stone, became food for the gods.

---

bus or car. Follow the fork from the *carretera* about two miles south of town. In Ixcateopan, a small museum and memorial document and enshrine the remains.

Continue your walk a few hundred yards along the *carretera* (Mexico City direction) from the Hotel Posada de la Misión. There, a driveway leading right just before the gas station heads to the Hotel Borda grounds. Turn left on the road just after the gate and you'll come to an antique brick smelter chimney and cable-hung derrick. These mark an inactive **mineshaft** descending to the mine-tunnel honeycomb thousands of feet beneath the town. (The mines are still being worked from another entrance, but for lead rather than silver. You can see the present-day works from the hilltop of the Hotel Hacienda del Solar on the south edge of town.)

Now, return to the *carretera,* cross over and stroll the **Calle la Garita** about a mile back to the *zócalo*. Of special interest, besides a number of crafts stores and stalls, are the **Iglesia de Chavarrieta,** the **Biblioteca** (open weekdays), **Taxco-Canoga Park,** and the **ex-Convento San Bernardino.**

Farther on, a block before the *zócalo,* pause to decipher the colored stone mosaic of the **Taxco Hieroglyph,** which decorates the pavement in front of the Palacio Municipal.

Cableway to Hotel Monte Taxco
On the north side of town, where the *carretera* passes beneath Los Arcos ("The Arches"), a cableway above the highway lifts passengers to soaring vistas of the town on one side and ponderous, pine-studded mesas on the other.

Open daily 0730-1930; one-way tickets about $2, kids half price; return by taxi if you miss the last car. The ride ends at the Hotel Monte Taxco, where you can make a day of it golfing, horseback riding, playing tennis, eating lunch, and sunning on the panoramic-view pool deck.

Town Vistas

You needn't go as far afield as the Hotel Monte Taxco to get a good view of the city streets and houses carpeting the mountainside. Vistas depend not only on vantage point but time of day, since the best viewing sunshine (which frees you from squinting) should come generally from *behind*. Consequently, spots along the highway (more or less *east* of town), such as the pool-patios of the **Hotel Posada de la Misión** and the **Hotel Borda,** provide good morning views, while afternoon views are best from points west of town, such as the restaurant balcony or the hilltop of the **Hotel Rancho Taxco Victoria.**

SIGHTS OUT OF TOWN

The monumental duo, the Grutas de Cacahuamilpa caves and the ruins of ancient Xochicalco, combine for an interesting day-trip. Don't get started too late; the Grutas are 15 miles (25 km) north (Mexico City direction) of town and Xochicalco is 25 miles (40 km) farther.

Grutas de Cacahuamilpa

They're worth the effort. The Grutas de Cacahuamilpa are one of the world's great caverns. Forests of stalagmites and stalactites, in myriad shapes—Pluto the Pup, the Holy Family, a desert caravan, asparagus stalks, cauliflower heads—festoon a series of gigantic limestone chambers. The finale is a grand, 30-story hall that meanders for half a mile, like a fairyland in stone. The caves are open daily; hourly three-mile, two-hour walking tours in Spanish are included in the $4 admission and begin at 1000. A few gift shops sell souvenirs; snack bars supply food.

Getting There: *Kombi* collective vans go hourly, beginning at 0830, from the Flecha Roja bus station on the *carretera* to the caves for a one-way fare of about $3. By car, get to the caves via Hwy. 95 north from Taxco; after 10

miles (16 km) from the northside Pemex station, fork left onto Hwy. 55 toward Toluca. Continue five more miles (eight km) and turn right at the signed Cacahuamilpa junction. After a few hundred yards, turn right again into the entrance driveway.

Xochicalco

Xochicalco (soh-shee-KAHL-koh), an hour farther north, although little publicized, is a fountainhead of Mesoámerican legend. The ruin itself spreads over a half a dozen terraced pyramid hilltops above a natural lake-valley, which at one time sustained a large population. Xochicalco flowered during the late-classic period around A.D. 800, partly filling the vacuum left by the decline of Teotihuacán, the previously dominant Mesoamerican classic city-state. Some archaeologists speculate that Xochicalco at its apex was the great center of learning, known in legend as Tamanchoan, where astronomer-priests derived and maintained calendars and where the Quetzalcoatl legend was born.

Exploring the Site: Walk about 100 yards directly west, uphill, from the parking lot, where the **Pyramid of Quetzalcoatl** ("The Plumed Serpent") rises on the hilltop. Vermilion paint remnants hint of its original appearance, which was perhaps as brilliant as a giant birthday cake. In bas-relief around the entire base a serpent writhes, intertwined with personages, probably representing chiefs or great priests. Above these are warriors, identified by their helmets and *atlatl,* or lance-throwers.

Most notable, however, is one of Mesoámerica's most remarkable sculptures, to the left of the staircase. It shows the 11th week sign, *ozomatli* (monkey), being pulled by a hand (via a rope) to join with the fifth week sign, *calli* (house). Latter-day scholars generally interpret this as describing a calendar correction that resulted from a grand conclave of chiefs and sages from all over Mesoámerica, probably at this very spot.

About 150 feet south rises the **Temple of the Steles,** so named for three large stone tablets found beneath the floor. They narrate the events of the Quetzalcoatl legend, wherein Quetzalcoatl (discoverer of corn and the calendar) was transformed into the morning star (the planet Venus), and who continues to rule the

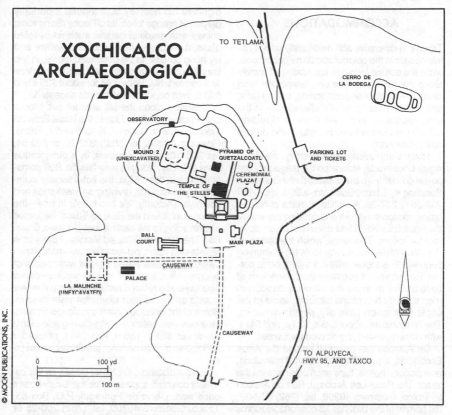

XOCHICALCO
ARCHAEOLOGICAL
ZONE

TO TETLAMA

CERRO DE
LA BODEGA

OBSERVATORY

MOUND 2
(UNEXCAVATED)

PYRAMID OF
QUETZALCOATL

PARKING LOT
AND TICKETS

CEREMONIAL
PLAZA

TEMPLE OF
THE STELES

BALL
COURT

MAIN PLAZA

CAUSEWAY

PALACE

LA MALINCHE
(UNEXCAVATED)

CAUSEWAY

TO ALPUYECA,
HWY 95, AND TAXCO

0   100 yd
0   100 m

© MOON PUBLICATIONS, INC.

heavens as the brightest star and the Lord of Time.

About 100 yards farther south, the **Main Plaza** was accessible to the common people via roads from below. This is in contrast to the sacrosanct **Ceremonial Plaza** nearby. A faintly visible causeway once connected the yet-unexplored La Malinche pyramid, 200 yards to the southwest, with the Ceremonial Plaza.

That causeway passed the **Ball Court,** which is strikingly similar to ball courts as far away as Toltec Tula in the north and Mayan Copan, in Honduras far to the south. On the opposite side of the causeway from the Ball Court lies the **Palace,** a complex marked by many rooms with luxury features such as toilet drainage, fireplaces, and steam baths.

On the opposite side of the complex is the **Observatory,** a room hollowed into the hill and stuccoed and fitted with a viewing shaft for timing the sun and star transits essential for an accurate calendar.

Get to Xochicalco by continuing past the Grutas (see directions above) driveway entrance. Continue northeast via Hwy. 160 toward Alpuyeca. After 25 miles (40 km) from the caves, a signed road heads left uphill to the Xochicalco ruins, which are open daily 1000-1700. Admission runs about $3.50, Sundays and holidays free. Since caretakers shoo all visitors out by 1700, arrive early enough to allow a couple of hours to explore the ruins. Bring food, drinks, a hat, and comfortable walking shoes.

ACCOMMODATIONS

Taxco's inexpensive and moderately priced hotels cluster in the colorful *zócalo* neighborhood, while the deluxe lodgings are scattered mostly along the *carretera*. The dry, temperate local climate relegates air-conditioning, ceiling fans, and central heating to frills offered only in the most expensive hotels. All of the hotel recommendations below have hot water and private baths, however.

Taxco's only *zócalo*-front hostelry, the **Hotel Agua Escondida,** stands on the diagonally opposite corner from the church, Calle Guillermo Spratling 4, Taxco, Guerrero 40200, tel. (762) 207-26 or 207-36. A multilevel maze of hidden patios, rooftop sundecks and dazzling city views, the Agua Escondida has dozens of clean, comfortable rooms. The name, which translates as "Hidden Water," must refer to its big swimming pool, which is tucked away in a far rooftop corner. Rooms vary; if you have the choice, look at several. Try to avoid the oft-noisy streetfront rooms. If you don't mind climbing, some of the upper-floor rooms have airy, penthouse views. The 76 rooms run about $23 s, $35 d, and $41 t, with limited parking; credit cards accepted.

On Alarcón just downhill behind the Agua Escondida, a pair of former colonial mansions, now popular hotels, face each other across the street. The **Hotel Los Arcos,** J. Ruiz de Alarcón 2, Taxco, Guerrero 40200, tel. (762) 218-36, the homier of the two, has 28 comfortable rooms in tiers around an inviting fountain patio and restaurant. Rooms rent for about $20 s, $25 d. The **Hotel Posada Los Castillo,** J. R. Alarcón 7, Taxco, Guerrero 40200, tel. (762) 213-96, across the street is small and intimate, with plants, carved wood, paintings, and sculptures gracing every wall and corner. Rooms, in neocolonial decor, are clean and comfortable. The owners also run a nearby silver boutique, whose displays decorate the downstairs lobby. The 14 rooms rent for about $17 s, $23 d, and $30 t, with credit cards accepted.

Heading past the opposite side of the plaza, follow Cuauhtémoc to the Plazuela de San Juan and the adjacent **Hotel Santa Prisca,** Cena Obscura 1, P.O. Box 42, Taxco, Guerrero 40200, tel. (762) 200-80 or 209-80. A tranquil, dignified old hostelry built around a perfumy garden of orange trees, its off-lobby dining room shines with graceful details, such as beveled glass, a fireplace, blue-white stoneware and ivy-hung portals. Its tile-decorated rooms, in two tiers around the garden just outside, are clean and comfortable. Rooms go for about $25 s and $40 d, with parking; credit cards accepted.

Continue along the hill another two blocks past Plazuela de San Juan to the **Hotel Rancho Taxco Victoria,** Carlos J. Nibbi 5 and 7, Taxco, Guerrero 40200, tel. (762) 202-10 or 200-04, fax 200-10, which rambles, in a picturesque state of decay, along its view hillside. Built sometime back in the 1920s, the hotel usually slumbers on weekdays, reviving on weekends and holidays. (Actually, it's two hotels in one—the Victoria uphill and the Rancho Taxco, neglected and returning to the earth across the road, downhill.) The better-maintained Victoria, however, is replete with rustic, old-world extras—hand-hewn furniture, whitewashed stucco walls, riots of bougainvillea, a spreading view garden—plus a big pool and a relaxed restaurant and bar where guests enjoy the best afternoon vista in town. Some of the spacious, comfortable rooms have luxurious view balconies. Standard-grade rooms run about $25 s, $30 d, and $40 t; deluxe for $35 s, $40 d, with parking; credit cards accepted.

From a distance, the **Hotel Borda** off the *carretera* downhill, appears to be the luxury hotel it once was, Cerro de Pedregal, P.O. Box 83, Taxco, Guerrero 40200, tel. (762) 200-25 or 202-25, fax 206-17. Lackluster management, however, detracts from the hotel's magnificent assets—a grand vista, spacious garden, luxurious pool-patio shaded by great, vine-draped trees. Check to see if your room is clean and in working order before you move in. The 110 rooms rent for about $38 s, $40 d, with restaurant, bar, live music nightly, and parking; credit cards accepted.

The **Hotel Posada de la Misión** decorates a hillside nearby, Cerro de la Misión 32, Taxco, Guerrero 40200, tel. (762) 200-63 or 205-33, fax 221-98. Its guests, many on group tours, enjoy cool, quiet patios, green gardens, plant-lined corridors, a sunny pool-patio, and a view restaurant. Many of the luxurious rooms have panoramic city views; some have fireplaces. All rooms have color TV and phones. Rooms rent for about $70 s, $75 d with breakfast, Christmas-New Year's prices higher; with parking, credit cards accepted. Just off the *carretera,* 200 yards south of the Pemex gas station.

The luxuriously exclusive **Hotel Hacienda del Solar,** P.O. Box 96, Taxco, Guerrero 40200, tel. (762) 203-23, spreads over a tranquil hilltop garden on the south edge of town. Guests in many of the 22 airy and spacious rooms enjoy private patios, fireplaces, and panoramic valley and mountain views. Rooms, in standard, deluxe, and junior suite versions, vary individually but are all artfully furnished with appointments including hand-woven rugs, colorful tile, paintings, and folk art. The standard rooms share a spacious living area near the lovely view pool-patio; deluxe and junior suite rooms have huge beds and deep tile bathtubs. Other amenities include a view restaurant, the Ventana ("Window") de Taxco, and a cocktail lounge. Adults 22 years and over only, however. Rooms for two go for about $50 standard, $75 deluxe, and $100 junior suite. During certain busy seasons, meals may be required with rentals, which will consequently rise to about $100, $120, and $150.

Vacationers who want resort amenities stay at the **Hotel Monte Taxco,** Lomas de Taxco, Taxco, Guerrero 40200, tel. (762) 213-00, 213-01, or (800) 929-9394 from Canada and the U.S., fax 214-28, atop a towering mesa accessible by either a steep road or cableway from the highway just north of town. On weekends, the hotel is often packed with well-heeled Mexico City families, whose kids play organized games while their parents enjoy the panoramic poolside view or play golf and tennis. The 156 deluxe rooms, many with view balconies, rent from about $85 d, with a/c, phones, and TV; facilities include restaurants, a piano bar, disco, parking, a gym, sauna, spa, nine-hole golf course, and tennis courts; credit cards accepted.

FOOD

Stalls and Snacks

The score of *fondas* (foodstalls) atop the *artesanías* (ar-tay-sah-NEE-ahs) handicrafts section of the market is Taxco's prime source of wholesome country-style food. The quality of their fare is a matter of honor for the proprietors, since among their local patrons word of a little bad food goes a long way. It's very hard to go wrong, moreover, if your selections are steaming hot and made fresh before your own eyes (in contrast, by the way, to most restaurant and hotel fare).

You can choose from a potpourri that might include steaming bowls of *menudo* or *pozole,* or maybe plates of pork or chicken *mole,* or *molcajetes* (big stone bowls) filled with steaming meat and broth and draped with hot nopal cactus leaves.

Stalls offering other variations appear evenings on the *zócalo.* A family sells tacos and *pozole,* while another, which labels itself La Poblana, sometimes arrives in a truck and offers french-fried bananas, *churros,* and potato chips fried on the spot until about 2230, next to the church.

Restaurants

Complete dinner price key: Budget: under $7; Moderate: $7-14; Expensive: more than $14.

Of the *zócalo* restaurant options, the upstairs **La Parroquia,** tel. (762) 230-96, a half block from the church steps, ranks among the best; open 0830-2200, credit cards accepted. The front balcony tables are ideal perches for the view or watching the parade below while enjoying a good breakfast, lunch, or dinner. Moderate.

Two blocks downhill from the *zócalo,* just past the post office, **La Taberna,** Juárez 12, tel. (762) 252-26, offers tasty light lunches and dinners in a cool, intimate patio setting. The friendly European owner's specialties include pastas (spinach lasagna, clam linguini), salads, desserts, and wines. Open daily 1300-2400; credit cards accepted. Moderate to expensive.

A block on the opposite side of the *zócalo,* overlooking Plazuela de San Juan, the Mexican-style **Restaurant El Adobe,** Plazuela de San Juan 13, opposite Bancomer, tel. (762) 214-16, is a good place for breakfast or lunch while sightseeing or shopping. For breakfast, you can enjoy juice, eggs, and hotcakes; for lunch, hamburgers, tacos, enchiladas, and guacamole. Open daily 0800-2300. Budget to moderate.

A classy spot where you can enjoy the view, a swim, and lunch after seeing the Cuauhtémoc Mural is the adjacent **Restaurant El Mural,** at the Hotel Posada La Misión on the *carretera;* see "Accommodations" above; open daily for breakfast 0700-0930, lunch 1300-1530, dinner 1900-2300. If the place is packed with tours, have a drink, enjoy the mural, and go somewhere else. Expensive.

For good food in an elegant view setting, go to **Restaurant La Ventana de Taxco,** tel. (762) 205-87, at the Hotel Hacienda del Solar two blocks off the highway, south end of town. Open daily for breakfast 0830-1030, lunch 1300-1630, and dinner 1900-2300, when the whole town appears like a shimmering galaxy through the windows; reservations recommended. Their mostly Italian and Mexican specialties include salads, lasagna, scallopini, saltimbocca, *mole* chicken, enchiladas, and wines. Expensive; figure about $30 per person.

ENTERTAINMENT, EVENTS, AND SPORTS

Around the *Zócalo*

Taxco people mostly entertain each other. Such spontaneous diversions are most likely around the *zócalo,* which often seems like an impromptu festival of typical Mexican scenes. Around the outside stand the monuments of the colonial past, while on the sidewalks sit the Indians who come in from the hills to sell their onions, tamales, and pottery. Kids run between them, their parents and grandparents watching, while young men and women flirt, blush, giggle, and jostle one another until late in the evening.

Three restaurant-bars on the side adjacent to the church provide good perches for viewing the hubbub. Visitors can either join the locals at **Bar Serta,** on the church corner, or take a balcony seat and enjoy the bouncy music with the mostly tourist crowd at **Bar Paco** next door. For more tranquility, head upstairs to **Restaurant La Parroquia** a few steps farther on.

For a glimpse of a different slice of Taxco life, head downhill on Alarcón a half block past the Casa Borda (city hall). There, at a no-name video parlor, a dozen boys are usually honing their reflexes in nonstop bashing of electronic skinheads and extraterrestrials (although three vintage manual table-soccer games remain the most popular).

Dancing and Discoing

Seasonally and on weekends the larger hotels have music for evening dining and dancing. Call the hotels Borda, tel. (762) 200-25 or 202-25, Posada de la Misión, tel. (762) 200-63 or 205-33, and the Monte Taxco (which also has a discotheque), tel. (762) 200-63 or 205-33, for details.

Festivals

Many local fiestas provide the excuses for folks to celebrate, starting on 17 and 18 January, with the Festival of Santa Prisca. On the initial day, kids and adults bring their pet animals for blessing at the church. At dawn the next day, pilgrims arrive at the *zócalo* and sing *Mañanitas* in honor of the saint, then head for folk dancing inside the church.

During the year Taxco's many neighborhood churches celebrate their saints' days (such as Chavarrieta, 4 March; Veracruz, the four weeks before Easter; San Bernardino, 20 May; Santísima Trinidad, 13 June; Santa Ana, 26 July; Asunción, 15 August; San Nicolas, 10 September; San Miguel, 19 September; San Francisco, 4 October; and Guadalupe, 12 December) with food, fireworks, music, and dancing.

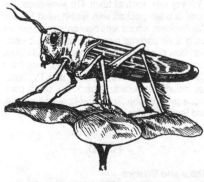

Taxco people celebrate their festival of the jumil *(a type of grasshopper) on the first Monday after the 2 November Day of the Dead.*

MIKE WELLINS

Religious fiestas climax during Semana Santa (Easter week), when, on Jueves and Viernes Santa (Thursday and Friday before Easter), cloaked penitents proceed through the city, carrying gilded images and bearing crowns of thorns.

On the Monday after the 2 November Día de los Muertos ("Day of the Dead"), Taxco people head to pine-shaded **Parque Huixteco** atop the Cerro Huixteco behind town to celebrate their unique **Fiesta de los Jumiles.** In a ritual whose roots are lost in pre-Columbian legend, people collect and feast on *jumiles* (small crickets)—raw or roasted—along with music and plenty of beer and fixings. Since so many people go, transportation is easy. Ask a taxi or *zócalo* van driver or your hotel desk clerk for details.

Sports
Most local people go everywhere by foot; Taxco's streets and side lanes seem to always lead somewhere interesting. And since all roads return to the *zócalo*, getting lost is rarely a problem.

The Hotel Monte Taxco, tel. (762) 213-00 or 213-01 (for access, see "Sights" above), has **horses** ready for riding, three good **tennis** courts, and a **nine-hole golf course** available for fee use by nonguests. Informal *sendas* (hiking paths; ask directions from the horse-rental man) branch from the horse paths to the surrounding luscious pine- and cedar-forested mesa country. Take sturdy shoes, water, and a hat.

SHOPPING

Market
Taxco's big market day is Sunday, when the town is loaded with people from outlying villages selling produce and live animals. The market is located just downhill from Los Arcos, the lane that runs below the right side of the *zócalo* church (as you face that church). From the lane, head right before the arch and down the staircase. Soon you'll be descending through a warren of market stalls. Pass the small Baptist church on Sunday and hear the congregation singing like angels floating above the market. Don't miss the spice stall, **Yerbería Castillo,** piled with the intriguing wild remedies collected by owner Elvira Castillo and her son Teodoro.

Farther on you'll pass mostly scruffy meat stalls but also some clean juice stands, such as **Liquados Memo,** open daily 0700-1800, where you can rest with a delicious fresh *zanahoria* (carrot), *toronja* (grapefruit), or *sandía* (watermelon) juice.

Before leaving the market, be sure to ask for *jumiles* (hoo-MEE-lays), live crickets that sell in bags for about a penny apiece, ready for folks to pop them into their mouths.

If *jumiles* don't suit your taste, you may want to drop in for lunch at one of the *fondas* above the market's *artesanías* section.

Handicrafts
The submarket **Mercado de Artesanías** (watch for a white sign above an open area by the staircase) offers items for mostly local consumption, such as economical belts, huaraches, wallets, and inexpensive silver chains, necklaces, and earrings.

As you head out for tonier shops, don't miss the common but colorful and charming ceramic cats, turtles, doves, fish, and other figurines that local folk sell very cheaply. If you buy, bargain—but not too hard, for the people are poor and have often traveled far.

Masks are the prime attraction at **Arnoldo,** where the friendly proprietors, Arnoldo Jacobo and his son Raoul, are more than willing and able to explain every detail about their fascinating array of merchandise. Located on Palma no. 1, upstairs, across the uphill lane, next to Hotel Agua Escondida, tel. (762) 212-72. Hundreds of masks from all over Guerrero—stone and wood, antique and new—line the walls like a museum. All of the many motifs, ranging from black men puffing cigarettes and blue-eyed sea goddesses to inscrutable Aztec gods in onyx and grotesque lizard-humanoids, are priced to sell. Open Mon.-Sat. 0900-2030, Sunday 1000-1930.

Other shops nearby have similar offerings. Arnoldo's neighbor, **Celso,** 4 Palma, just uphill, tel. (762) 228-48, closed Wednesday, but open other days 1000-1400 and 1600-2000, except Sunday 1000-1600; and **D'Avila Ofebres** shop on Plazuela de San Juan just past the end of Cuauhtémoc, Plazuela de San Juan 7, tel. (762) 211-08, in the courtyard of Hotel Casa Grande across from Bancomer, open daily 0900-2100.

Silver Shops

Good silver shops cluster around the *zócalo* and downhill on the highway. Perhaps the favorite of all is the friendly, family-owned **Los Castillo** on the little plaza downhill behind the Hotel Agua Escondida, Plazuela de Bernal 10, tel. (762) 206-52 or 219-88. Run by the industrious and prolific Castillo family, the shop offers a big variety of all original work at reasonable prices. Here you can watch silversmiths at work, and, unlike at many shops, bargain a bit. Open daily 0900-1300 and 1500-1900; credit cards accepted.

One of the more interesting silver shops, if for only a look around, is **La Gruta**, on Cuauhtémoc between the *zócalo* and Plazuela de San Juan, Cuauhtémoc 10, tel. (762) 206-95. Inside, plaster stalagmites hang above small mountains of silver-decorated quartz crystals. Open Mon.-Sat. 1000-2000, Sunday 1000-1600; credit cards accepted.

Enough silver stores for a week of shopping line the *carretera* John F. Kennedy downhill. The original shop, **Las Delicias**, begun by William Spratling in cooperation with local silversmiths in 1931, is still a good place to buy silver, especially if you're looking for more elaborate pieces, set with semiprecious turquoise and lapis lazuli. At 28 Carretera JFK, across from Hotel Posada de la Misión; open Mon.-Sat. 0930-1930.

A Camera Store and a Couple of Groceries

Unusually well-stocked **Tienda la Misión**, half a block from the *zócalo*, offers many cameras, lenses, accessories, and much Kodak film, including professional Vericolor 120, Tri-X Pan, Plus-X, and Ektachrome. Located on Cuauhtémoc 6, tel. (762) 201-16. They also do photocopying, including enlargement and reduction. Open Mon.-Sat. 0900-1400 and 1600-2000, Sunday 0900-1400.

A grocery store, **Casa Ayja**, Benito Juárez 7, tel. (762) 203-64, a rarity in silver-rich Taxco, three blocks down Juárez from the *zócalo*, stocks a bit of everything, including wines, cheeses, and milk on its clean, well-organized shelves and aisles. Open Mon.-Sat. 0900-2200. If they're closed, go to the similarly efficient **Super Macal**, open daily, on San Nicolas, two blocks downhill from Plazuela de San Juan.

SERVICES AND INFORMATION

Money Exchange

Banks near the *zócalo* are Taxco's best source of pesos. **Banco Confia**, tel. (762) 202-37, at the *zócalo* corner of Cuauhtémoc, changes U.S. currency and traveler's checks Mon.-Fri. 0900-1200. Likewise do **Banco Mexicano** and **Bancomer**, tel. (762) 202-87 or 202-88, Mon.-Fri. 1000-1230, a few doors farther along Cuauhtémoc.

Communication

The *correo*, on the highway a few steps from Estrella de Oro bus station, is open weekdays and Saturday morning. **Telecomunicaciones**, off the *zócalo*, behind Casa Borda, tel. (762) 248-85, fax 200-01, offers telex, money order, long-distance, and public fax services; open Mon-Fri. 0900-1500. For later and Saturday long-distance telephone and fax service, go to the little *larga distancia* office two blocks downhill at 13 Juárez, across from the Restaurant Taberna.

Taxco
area code
is 762

Medical and Police

Taxco has a pair of respected private hospitals, both on the *carretera*. The **Clínica de Especialidades**, 33 Carretera JFK, tel. (762) 211-11 or 245-80, has a 24-hour emergency room, a good pharmacy, and many specialists on call. The similar **Clínica Santa Cruz**, tel. (762) 230-12, offers the same services at the corner of Morelos, across from the government Seguro Social hospital.

For routine drugs and medicines, go to one of many local pharmacies, such as **Farmacia Lourdes**, tel. (762) 210-66, at Cuauhtémoc 8, half a block from the *zócalo*; open 8 a.m.-10 p.m.

For **police** emergencies, contact the *policía*, either on duty on the *zócalo*, or at the city hall (two blocks downhill, at Juárez 6, tel. 762-200-07), or at the substation on the side street one block below the *carretera* near the corner of Alarcón.

Tourist Information Offices

Taxco has two tourist information offices, both beside the highway at opposite ends of town, open daily approximately 0900-1400 and 1500-1900. The knowledgeable and English-speaking officers readily answer questions and furnish whatever maps and literature they may have. The north office, tel. (762) 207-98, is next to Pemex at the Av. La Garita corner. The south office is about a quarter mile south of the south-end Pemex station.

Publications

English-language books and newspapers are hard to find in Taxco. Nevertheless, the bookstore **Casa Dominguez,** tel. (762) 201-33, usually has the Mexico City *News,* and sometimes *Newsweek, Time, Life, Vogue, Sports Illustrated,* and a U.S. newspaper or two. They are open daily 0900-1400 and 1630-2000 on the Los Arcos lane adjacent and below the church.

GETTING THERE AND AWAY

By Car or RV

National Hwy. 95 provides the main connection south with Acapulco in a total of about 167 miles (269 km) of easy driving via Iguala, accessible to/from Taxco via the winding, 22-mile (36-km) old Hwy. 95 cutoff. Allow about five hours' driving time for the entire Taxco-Acapulco trip, either direction.

Highway 95 also connects Taxco north via Cuernavaca with Mexico City, a total of about 106 miles (170 km). All driving except the 20-mile (32 km) leg of old Hwy. 95 north of Taxco is by the Hwy. 95 superhighway. Congestion around Mexico City lengthens the driving time to about three hours in either direction.

Authorities limit driving your car in Mexico City according to the last digit of your license plate. See the special topic "Mexico City Driving Limits" in the Acapulco section, above.

Highway 55 (junction at Cacahuamilpa, see "Grutas de Cacahuamilpa" above) gives drivers the desirable option of avoiding Mexico City by connecting Taxco north-south with **Toluca.** The two-lane road, although paved and in fair-to-good condition for the 74 miles (119 km), is winding and sometimes narrow. Southbound, allow about two hours driving time; northbound, steep grades stretch this to about three hours.

By Bus

The competing lines **Flecha Roja,** tel. (762) 201-31, highway corner near Veracruz, and **Estrella de Oro,** tel. (762) 206-48, highway corner of Pilita, operate out of separate terminals on the *carretera.* Although both have many luxury- and first-class connections north with Mexico City via Cuernavaca and south with Acapulco via Iguala and Chilpancingo, Flecha Roja additionally provides frequent first- and second-class connections with local and intermediate destinations.

crouching man and suns motif
(from impression of clay seal, Guerrero)

BOB RACE

MIKE WELLINS

THE COSTA CHICA AND INLAND TO OAXACA

In reality, the Costa Chica, the "Little Coast," which includes the state of Guerrero south of Acapulco and the adjoining coast of Oaxaca, isn't so small after all. Hwy. 200, heading out of the Acapulco hubbub, requires 400 miles to traverse it. Traffic thins out, passing scattered groves, fields, and villages along the Costa Chica southern bulge, where the coast curves, like the belly of a dolphin, to its most southerly point near Puerto Ángel.

In the main resorts of the Costa Chica—Puerto Escondido, Puerto Ángel, and Bahías de Huatulco—the beaches face south, toward the Mar del Sur, the Pacific Ocean. On the other hand, if travelers head inland, they go north, over the verdant, jungle-clad Sierra Madre del Sur and into the Valley of Oaxaca, the Indian heartland of southern Mexico.

To about a million Oaxacan native peoples, Spanish is a foreign language. Many of them—Zapotecs, Mixtecs, and a score of smaller groups—live in remote mountain villages, subsisting as they always have on corn and beans,

without electricity, sewers, schools, or roads. Those who live near towns often speak the Spanish they have learned by coming to market. In the Costa Chica town markets you will brush shoulders with them—mostly Mixtecs, Amusgos, and Chatinos—men sometimes in pure-white cottons and women in colorful embroidered *huipiles* over wrapped hand-woven skirts.

Besides the Indians, you will often see Afro-Mexicans—*morenos,* brown ones—known as Costeños because their isolated settlements are near the coast. Descendants of African slaves imported hundreds of years ago, the Costeños subsist on the produce from their village gardens and the fish they catch.

Costa Chica Indians and Costeños have a reputation for being unfriendly and suspicious. If true in the past (although it's certainly less so in the present), they have had good reason to be suspicious of outsiders, who in their view have been trying to take away their land, gods, and lives for 300 years.

Communication is nevertheless possible. Your arrival, for the residents of a little mountain or shoreline end-of-road village, might be the event of the day. People are going to wonder why you came. Smile and say hello. Buy a soda at the store or *palapa*. If kids gather around, don't be shy. Draw a picture in your notebook. If a child offers to do likewise, you've succeeded.

ALONG THE ROAD TO PUERTO ESCONDIDO

If driving from Acapulco, mark your odometer at the traffic circle where Hwys. 95 and 200 intersect over the hill from Acapulco. If, on the other hand, you bypass that congested point via the Acapulco airport road, set your odometer to zero when you get to Hwy. 200, then add three miles (five km). Mileages and kilometer markers along the road are sometimes the only locators of turnoffs to hidden villages and palmy little beaches.

Fill up with gas before starting out In Acapulco. After that, both regular and Magna Sin (unleaded) are available at Pinotepa Nacional (157 miles, 253 km), Puerto Escondido (247 miles, 398 km), and near Puerto Ángel (291 miles, 469 km).

If you're going by bus, ride one of the several daily first-class buses from the **Estrella Blanca** terminal in Acapulco. Or ride a second-class bus from the Estrella Blanca terminal at Cuauhtémoc 97 in Acapulco, or simply wave one down on the road.

PLAYA VENTURA

Three miles east of the small town of Copala, 77 miles (Km 123) from Acapulco, a roadside sign points toward Playa Ventura. Four miles down a good dirt road, which a truck-bus from Copala traverses regularly, you arrive at Ventura village. From there, a mile-long golden-sand beach arcs gently east. Past a lighthouse, the beach leads to a point, topped by a stack of granite rocks, known locally as Casa de Piedra ("House of Stone").

Playa Ventura can provide nearly everything for a restful day or week in the sun. Several good tenting or RV (maneuverable medium rigs, vans, or campers) spots sprinkle the inviting, outcropping-dotted shoreline. Shady *palapas* set up by former campers stand ready for rehabilitation and reuse by new arrivees.

Surf fishing (with net-caught bait fish) is fine from the beach, while *pangas* go out for deep-sea catches. Good **surfing** breaks angle in from

Oxcarts—slow but dependable and cheap—still do their part in rural Pacific Mexico.

BRUCE WHIPPERMAN

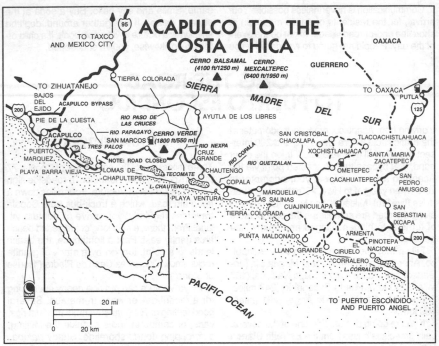

ACAPULCO TO THE COSTA CHICA

TO TAXCO
AND MEXICO CITY

OAXACA

CERRO BALSAMAL
(4100 ft/1250 m)

CERRO
MEXCALTEPEC
(6400 ft/1950 m)

GUERRERO

TIERRA COLORADA

SIERRA

TO ZIHUATANEJO

BAJOS
DEL
EJIDO

ACAPULCO BYPASS

MADRE

TO OAXACA

PUTLA

AYUTLA DE LOS LIBRES

DEL

PIE DE LA CUESTA

RIO PASO DE
LAS CRUCES

SUR

RIO PAPAGAYO CERRO VERDE

ACAPULCO

SAN MARCOS (1800 ft/550 m)

SAN CRISTOBAL
CHACALAPA

TLACOACHISTLAHUACA

L. TRES PALOS

RIO NEXPA

XOCHISTLAHUACA

SANTA MARIA
ZACATEPEC

PUERTO
MARQUEZ

NOTE: ROAD CLOSED

CRUZ
GRANDE

RIO COPALA

RIO QUETZALAN

OMETEPEC

PLAYA BARRA VIEJA

LOMAS DE
CHAPULTEPEC

L.
TECOMATE

CHAUTENGO

CACAHUATEPEC

SAN
PEDRO
AMUSGOS

L. CHAUTENGO

COPALA

MARQUELIA

PLAYA VENTURA

LAS SALINAS

TIERRA COLORADA

CUAJINICUILAPA

SAN
SEBASTIAN
IXCAPA

PUNTA MALDONADO

ARMENTA

EL
CIRUELO

PINOTEPA
NACIONAL

LLANO GRANDE

CORRALERO

L. CORRALERO

PACIFIC OCEAN

0   20 mi

0   20 km

PACIFIC OCEAN

TO PUERTO ESCONDIDO
AND PUERTO ANGEL

© MOON PUBLICATIONS, INC.

the points, and, during the rainy season, the behind-the-beach lagoon is good for fishing, shrimping, and **wildlife viewing.** (Bring your kayak or inflatable raft.)

The palm-lined beach stretches southeast for miles. Past the picturesque Casa de Piedra outcropping, an intimate *palapa-* and *panga-*lined sandy cove curves invitingly to yet another palmy point, Pico del Monte. Past that lies still another, even more pristine, cove and beach.

Food and Accommodations

Besides the village store, food is available at a number of beach *palapa* restaurants, foremost of which is the **Restaurant-Cabaña Perez.** If anyone dispels the rumor that Costeño folks are unfriendly, it's the hospitable father-son team of Bulmaro and Luis Perez, who have put together the modest beginnings of a little retreat. Bulmaro and Luis invite visitors to park in their small lot, where they offer a friendly word,

showers, and a bit of palmy shade for nothing more than the price of a meal at their restaurant. "If more people come," Luis says, "maybe we can build some hotel rooms."

SAN MARCOS, OMETEPEC, AND CUAJINICULAPA

A few larger towns along the road can provide a number of essential services. Thirty-six miles (58 km) east of Acapulco, **San Marcos** (pop. 10,000, tel. area code 745) has a bank (Banamex, tel. 745-300-36), Seguro Social (health center, tel. 745-303-39), pharmacies (El Rosario, tel. 745-300-08), a motel (Le Carma Inn, tel. 745-300-37, 20 rooms around a small pool-patio), and post, telephone, and telegraph offices.

Ometepec (pop. 15,000), a couple of hours' drive farther east, is accessible via a 10-mile paved road, which branches off Hwy. 200 at a well-marked intersection 110 miles (175 km) from Acapulco. Besides being an important service center, Ometepec (elev. 2,000 feet) enjoys a cooler climate, drawing crowds of native peoples, notably Amusgos, from outlying villages to its big morning market. Many local buses follow dirt and gravel roads from Ometepec to more remote centers, such as **Xochistlahuaca** (so-chees-tlah-hoo-AH-kah, pop. 3,000), the Amusgo town about 30 miles northeast. Not far off the Xochistlahuaca road you can visit **Cochoapa,** the partially excavated archaeological site where a number of very ancient Olmec-

style stelae and sculptures have been unearthed. Ask around for a local guide.

In Ometepec itself (tel. area code 741), banks (Banamex, tel. 741-201-22; Banco Mexicano, tel. 741-201-13), a private hospital (De la Amistad, tel. 741-202-24), a public health center (Centro de Salud, tel. 741-202-16), hotels (such as the Montero, tel. 741-201-00), and post, telephone, and telegraph offices provide essential services.

Back on Hwy. 200, **Cuajiniculapa** (kwah-hee-nee-koo-LAH-pah), pop. 10,000, area code

THE MIXTECS

Sometime during the 1980s, the Mixtecs regained their preconquest population of about 350,000. Of that total, around one-third speak only their own language. Their villages and communal fields spread over tens of thousands of square miles of remote mountain valleys north, west, and southwest of Oaxaca City. Their homeland, the Mixteca, is divided into three distinct regions: Mixteca Alta, Mixteca Baja, and the Costera.

The **Mixteca Alta** centers in the mountains about 100 road miles north of Oaxaca City, in the vicinity of small towns such as San Juan Bautista Cuicatlán, on Hwy. 131, and Jocotipac and Cuyamecalco, several miles along local branch roads from the highway.

Mixteca Baja communities, such as San Miguel El Grande, San Juan Mixtepec, and Santiago Juxtlahuaca, dot the western Oaxaca mountains and valleys in a broad region centering roughly on Tlaxiaco on Hwy. 125.

In the **Costera,** important Mixtec communities exist in or near Pinotepa Nacional, Huaxpaltepec, and Jamiltepec, all on Hwy. 200 in southwestern Oaxaca.

The Aztec-origin name Mixtecos ("People of the Clouds") was translated directly from the Mixtecs' name for their own homeland: Áunyuma ("Land of the Clouds"). The Mixtecs' name for themselves, however, is Nyu-u Sabi ("People of the Rain").

Compare this pre-Colombian Mixtec birth scene with the Huichol birth scene depicted in the special topic "The Huichol."

When the conquistadores arrived in Oaxaca, the Mixtecs were under the thumb of the Aztecs, who, after a long, bitter struggle, had wrested control of Oaxaca from combined Mixtec-Zapotec armies in 1486. The Mixtecs naturally resented the Aztecs, whose domination was transferred to the Spanish during the colonial period, and, in turn, to the mestizos during modern times. The Mixtecs still defer to the town Moxioano, but they don't like it. Consequently, many rural Mixtecs, with little state or national consciousness, have scant interest in becoming Mexicanized.

In isolated Mixtec communities, traditions still rule. Village elders hold final authority, parents arrange marriages through go-betweens, and land is owned communally. Catholic saints are thinly disguised incarnations of old gods such as Tabayukí, ruler of nature, or the capricious and powerful *tono* spirits which, lurk everywhere.

In many communities, Mixtec women exercise considerable personal freedom. At home and in villages, they often still work bare breasted. And while their men get drunk and carry on during festivals, women dance and often do a bit of their own carousing. Whom they do it with are their own business.

741, 125 miles (199 km) from Acapulco, also has a Banamex (tel. 741-400-11), a Centro de Salud (health center, tel. 741-401-42), a pharmacy (Nueva, tel. 741-402-07), a very basic hotel (Marin, tel. 741-400-11), and post, telephone, and telegraph offices.

Cuajiniculapa is a major market town for the scattering of Costeño communities, such as San Nicolas (pop. 5,000, eight miles south), along the beach road (at Km 201) to Punta Maldonado, the local fishing port.

PINOTEPA NACIONAL

Pinotepa Nacional (pop. about 25,000; 157 miles, 253 km, east of Acapulco; 90 miles, 145 km, west of Puerto Escondido) and its neighboring communities comprise an important indigenous region. Mixtec, Amusgo, Chatino, and other peoples stream into town for markets and fiestas in their traditional dress, ready to combine business with pleasure. They sell their produce and crafts—pottery, masks, handmade clothes—at the market, then later get tipsy, flirt, and dance.

The Name

So many people have asked the meaning of their city's name that the town fathers wrote the explanation on a wall next to Hwy. 200 on the east side of town. Pinotepa comes from the Aztec-language words *pinolli* (crumbling) and *tepetl* (mountain); thus "Crumbling Mountain." The second part of the name came about because, during colonial times, the town was called Pinotepa Real (Royal). This wouldn't do after Independence, so the name became Pinotepa Nacional, reflecting the national consciousness that emerged during the 1810-21 struggle for liberation.

The Mixtecs, the dominant regional group, disagree with all this, however. To them, Pinotepa has always been Ñii Yu-uku ("Place of Salt"). Only within the town limits do the Mexicans (mestizos), who own most of the town businesses, outnumber the Mixtecs. The farther from town you get, the more likely you are to hear people conversing in the Mixtec language, a complex tongue that relies on many subtle tones to make meanings clear.

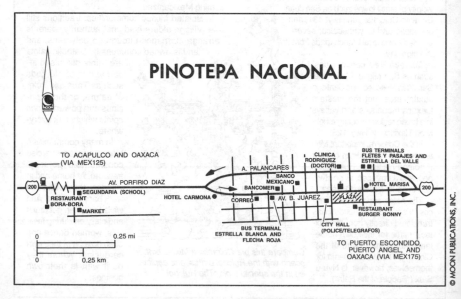

PINOTEPA NACIONAL

TO ACAPULCO AND OAXACA (VIA MEX125)

AV. PORFIRIO DIAZ

SEGUNDARIA (SCHOOL)

RESTAURANT BORA-BORA

MARKET

HOTEL CARMONA

A. PALANCARES

BANCO MEXICANO

BANCOMER

CORREO

AV. B. JUAREZ

CLINICA RODRIGUEZ (DOCTOR)

BUS TERMINALS FLETES Y PASAJES AND ESTRELLA DEL VALLE

HOTEL MARISA

PLAZA

RESTAURANT BURGER BONNY

BUS TERMINAL ESTRELLA BLANCA AND FLECHA ROJA

CITY HALL (POLICE/TELEGRAFOS)

TO PUERTO ESCONDIDO, PUERTO ANGEL, AND OAXACA (VIA MEX175)

0   0.25 mi
0   0.25 km

© MOON PUBLICATIONS, INC.

Market

Highway 200, called Av. Porfirio Díaz on the west side (B. Juárez on the east) of town, is Pinotepa's one main business street. It passes the main market (behind the big secondary school) on the west side and continues about a mile to the central plaza.

Despite the Pinotepa market's oft-exotic goods—snakes, iguanas, wild mountain fruits, forest herbs and spices—its people, nearly entirely Mixtec, are its main attraction, especially on the big Wednesday and Sunday market days. Men wear pure-white loose cottons, topped by a woven straw hat. Women wrap themselves in their lovely striped purple, violet, red, and navy blue *pozahuanco* sarong-like skirts. Many women carry a polished tan *ticara* gourd bowl atop their heads, which, although it's not supposed to, looks like a whimsical hat. Older women (and younger ones with babies at their breasts) go bare-breasted with only their white *huipil* draped over their chests as a concession to mestizo custom. Others wear an easily removable *mandil*, a light cotton apron-halter above their *pozahuanco*. A number of women can ordinarily be found at any given time selling beautiful handmade *pozahuancos*.

Festivals

Although the Pinotepa market days are big, they don't compare to the week before Easter (Semana Santa). People get ready for the finale with processions, carrying the dead Christ through town to the church each of the seven Fridays before Easter. The climax comes on Good Friday (Viernes Santa), when a platoon of young Mixtec men paint their bodies white to portray Jews, and while intoning ancient Mixtec chants shoot arrows at Christ on the cross. On Saturday, the people mournfully take the Savior down from the cross and bury him, and on Sunday gleefully celebrate his resurrection with a riot of fireworks, food, and folk dancing.

Although not as spectacular as Semana Santa, there's plenty of merrymaking, food, dancing, and processions around the Pinotepa *zócalo* church on 25 July, the day of Pinotepa's patron, Saint Santiago.

Accommodations and Food

The motel-style **Hotel Carmona,** Av. Porfirio Díaz 127, Pinotepa Nacional, Oaxaca 71600, tel. (954) 322-22, on Hwy. 200 about three blocks west of the central plaza, offers three stories of clean, non-fancy rooms, a big pool-sundeck, and a passable restaurant. For festival dates, make advance reservations. The 50 rooms run about $18 s, $23 d, $27 t; for a/c-equipped kitchenette suites, add $10-15; credit cards accepted.

If the Carmona is full, there are a couple of more basic hotels in town you can take a look at: Hotel Marisa, Av. Juárez 134, tel. (954) 321-01; and Hotel Tropical, Av. 3 Poniente and Progreso, tel. (954) 320-10.

Campers enjoy a tranquil spot on the **Río Arena** about two miles east of Pinotepa. Continue east past the river bridge a few hundred yards to a pumphouse, where a dirt track forks down to the riverbank. You will often find neighbors—in RVs or tents—set up on the riverside beneath oft-closed Restaurant La Roca a few hundred yards down the smooth stream, which is very good for kayaking.

For **food,** Pinotepa has at least two recommendable restaurants. East of town is the country-club-style **Bora Bora,** moderately priced outside *palapa* dining, open daily till about 2100, beyond the arch and uphill, just across the street from the westernmost Pemex gas station.

For a nighttime snack, try the very clean and friendly family run **Burger Bonny,** at the southeast corner of the main plaza, open daily 1100-2200. Besides six varieties of the best hamburger on the Costa Chica, they offer *tortas,* nachos, french fries, hot dogs, microwave popcorn, fruit juices, and sodas, at very reasonable prices.

Services

For **money exchange,** go to either the Bancomer (U.S. traveler's checks and cash, open 1000-1330, tel. 954-326-44) on main street Porfirio Díaz about two blocks west of the central plaza, or the Banco Mexicano (tel. 954-323-63) a block east, around the corner.

The *correo,* tel. (954) 322-64, is by the bus station, about two blocks west and across the street from Bancomer. The *telégrafo* is on the central plaza, and is open Mon.-Sat. 0900-1300 and 1500-1700 for money orders, and 0900-2100 for telegrams. There is also a *larga distancia* telephone office on the central plaza. For a **doctor,** go to the Clínica Rodriguez at 503 Aguirre Palancares, tel. (954) 323-30, one block north of the central plaza. Get routine medications at one of several town **pharmacies,** such as Farmacia Jesus on the central plaza.

Getting There and Getting Away

By **car or RV,** Hwy. 200 connects west to Acapulco (157 miles, 253 km) in an easy four hours driving time. The 90-mile (145-km) eastward continuation to Puerto Escondido can be done safely in about two and a half hours. Additionally, the 229-mile (368-km) Hwy. 125-Hwy. 190 route connects Oaxaca and Pinotepa Nacional. Although winding most of the way, the road is in good condition and generally uncongested. It's safely driveable from Oaxaca in about seven hours; add an hour for the 5,000-foot climb the opposite way.

Three long-distance **bus** lines connect Pinotepa Nacional with destinations north, east, and west. **Estrella Blanca** and subsidiary Flecha Roja have several daily first- and second-class *salidas de paso* (buses passing through) departures from their station, tel. (954) 322-54, on Porfirio Díaz about three blocks west of the *zócalo.*

The smaller lines **Fletes y Pasajes** and **Estrella del Valle** operate out of a pair of small stations one block north of the central plaza on side street Aguirre Palancares. Fletes y Pasajes, tel. (954) 321-63, connect daily with Oaxaca via Highways 125 and 190. Estrella de Valle buses, tel. (954) 326-97, also connect with Oaxaca, but in the opposite direction: first east to Pochutla (Puerto Ángel), then continuing north over the Sierra to Oaxaca via Hwy. 175.

EXCURSIONS NORTH OF PINOTEPA

The festival year at Pinotepa Don Luis begins early, on 20 Jan., with the uniquely Mixtec festival of San Sebastian. Village bands blare, fireworks pop and hiss, and penitents crawl, until the finale, when dancers whirl the local favorite dance, Las Chilenas.

Yet another exciting time around Pinotepa is during **Carnaval** when nearby communities put on big extravaganzas. Pinotepa Don Luis, sometimes known as Pinotepa Chica ("Little Pinotepa," about 15 miles by side road northeast of Pinotepa Nacional), is famous for wooden masks the people make for their big Carnaval festival. The celebration usually climaxes on the Sunday before Ash Wednesday, when everyone seems to be in costume and a corps of performers gyrates in the traditional dances: Paloma ("Dove"), Tigre ("Jaguar"), Culebra ("Snake"), and Tejón ("Badger").

Pinotepa Don Luis bubbles over again with excitement during Semana Santa, when the faithful carry fruit- and flower-decorated trees to the church on Good Friday, explode Judas effigies on Saturday, and celebrate by dancing most of Easter Sunday.

San Juan Colorado, a few miles north of Pinotepa Don Luis, usually appears as just another dusty little town until Carnaval, when its festival rivals that of its neighbors. Subsequently, on 29 November, droves of Mixtec people come into town to honor their patron, San Andres. After the serious part at the church, they celebrate with a cast of favorite dancing characters such as Malinche, Jaguar, Turtle, and Charros (cowboys).

Amusgo Country

Cacahuatepec (pop. about 3,000; on Hwy. 125 about 25 miles north of Pinotepa) and its neighboring community San Pedro Amusgos are important centers of the Amusgo people. Approximately 20,000 Amusgos live in a roughly 30-mile-square region straddling the Guerrero-Oaxaca state border. Their homeland includes, besides the above towns, Xochistlahuaca, Zacoalpán, and Tlacoachistlahuaca on the Guerrero side.

The Amusgo language is linguistically related to Mixtec, although it's unintelligible to Mixtec speakers. Before the conquest, the Amusgos were subject to the numerically superior Mixtec kingdoms until the Amusgos were conquered by the Aztecs in 1457, and later by the Spanish.

Now, most Amusgos live on as subsistence farmers, supplementing their diet with occasional fowl or small game. Amusgos are best known to the outside world for the lovely animal-, plant-, and human-motif *huipiles*, which Amusgo women always seem to be hand-embroidering on their doorsteps.

Although **Cacahuatepec** enjoys a big market each Sunday, that doesn't diminish the importance of its big Easter weekend festival and the day of Todos Santos (All Saints' Day) and Day of the Dead, 2 November, when, at the cemetery, people welcome their ancestors' return to rejoin the family.

San Pedro Amusgos celebrations are among the most popular regional fiestas. On 29 June, the day of San Pedro, people participate in religious processions, and costumed participants dressed as Moors and Christians, bulls, jaguars, and mules dance before crowds of men in traditional whites and women in beautiful heirloom *huipiles*. Later, on the first Sunday of October, folks crowd into town to enjoy the traditional processions, dances, and sweet treats of the fiesta of the Virgen de la Rosario ("Virgin of the Rosary").

Even if you miss the festivals, San Pedro Amusgos is worth a visit to buy *huipiles* alone. Two or three shops sell them along the main street through town. Look for the sign of **Trajes Regionales Elia,** the little store run by Elia and Edin Guzmán, tel. (955) 300-45. Besides dozens of beautiful embroidered garments, they stock a few Amusgo books and offer friendly words of advice and local information. (Edin has traveled in the U.S. and understands some English.)

EXCURSIONS EAST OF PINOTEPA

For 30 or 40 miles east of Pinotepa, where road kilometer markers begin at zero again near the central plaza, Hwy. 200 stretches through the coastal Mixtec heartland, intriguing to explore, especially during festival times. The population of San Andres Huaxpaltepec (oo-wash-pahl-tay-PAYK), about 10 miles east of Pinotepa, sometimes swells from about 4,000 to 20,000 or more during the three or four days before the day of Jesus the Nazarene (the fourth Friday before Good Friday). The entire town becomes a spreading warren of shady stalls, offering everything from TVs to stone metates. (Purchase of a corn-grinding metate, which, includ-

ing stone roller, sells for about $25, is as important to a Mixtec family as a refrigerator is to an American. Mixtec husband and wife usually examine several of the concave stones, deliberating the pros and cons of each before deciding.)

The Huaxpaltepec Nazarene fair is typical of the larger Oaxaca country expositions. Even the highway becomes a lineup of stalls; whole Indian clans camp under the trees; and mules, cows, and horses wait patiently around the edges of a grassy trading lot as men discuss prices. (The fun begins when a sale is made, and the new owner tries to rope and harness his bargain steed.)

Even sex is for sale within a quarter of very tightly woven no-see-through grass houses, patrolled by armed guards. Walking through, you may notice that, instead of the usual women, one of the houses offers men, dressed in low-cut gowns, lipstick, and high-heeled shoes.

Huazolotitlán Masks

Nearby Huazolotitlán (pop. 3,000) has several woodcarvers who craft excellent masks. Among them is Florencio Gallardo, whose house is on the left just before the town edge creekbottom, Arroyo Barrio. Florencio often can be found working in his woodchip-littered front-yard *palapa*, fashioning a handsome wooden owl or fierce jaguar mask. Specializing in human likenesses, Florencio will carve a mask or sculpture of anyone of whom he has a photo. His fee begins around $35. For more examples, visit other carvers nearby, such as José Luna, Lázaro Gómez, and the master Idineo Gómez.

Huazolotitlán (ooah-shoh-loh-tee-TLAN) is about two miles via the graded gravel road that forks south uphill from Hwy. 200 in Huaxpaltepec. To get there, hitchhike with a local, ride the bus, or hire a taxi for $2-3.

Santiago Jamiltepec

About 18 miles (at Km 30) east of Pinotepa is the hilltop town of Santiago Jamiltepec (hah-meel-teh-PAYK, for short). Two-thirds of its 20,000 inhabitants are Mixtec. A grieving Mixtec king named the town in memory of his infant son, Jamilly, who was carried off by an eagle from this very hilltop.

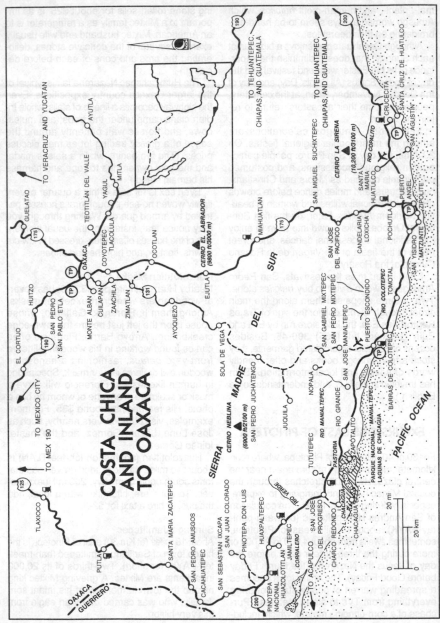

COSTA CHICA AND INLAND TO OAXACA

© MOON PUBLICATIONS, INC.

The market, while busy most any day, is biggest and most colorful on Thursday. The town's main fixed-date festivals are celebrated on 1 September, 1 January, and 15 February. In addition, Jamiltepec celebrates its famous pre-Easter (week of Ramos) festival, featuring neighborhood candlelight processions accompanied by 18th-century music. Hundreds of the faithful bear elaborate wreaths and palm decorations to the foot of their church altars.

Jamiltepec is well worth a stop if only to visit the handicrafts shop, **Yu-uku Cha-kuaa** ("Hill of Darkness"), of Santiago de la Cruz Velasco. Personable Santiago runs his shop, one of the few such local outlets, because the government cluster of shops (Centro Artesanal de la Costa, on the highway) was closed down, victim of a dispute over control. The local Mixtec artisans wanted to manage their own handicrafts sales, while the Jamiltepec branch of the INI (Instituto Nacional Indigenista) preferred to manage instead. The Mixtecs stuck together and refused to bring their handicrafts, closing the government operation. Fortunately, it has reopened under local control; stop by, on the highway, north side, at the Pinotepa edge of town.

Some of those crafts—masks, *huipiles,* carvings, hats—occupy the shelves and racks in Santiago's small store, which he keeps open till 1900 or 2000 each night except Sundays and holidays. Located on main street Av. Principal at Franciso Madero, by Seguro Social, the government health clinic. If you don't want to miss him, write Santiago a letter at his shop, Av. Principal, Barrio Grande, Sec. 5, Jamiltepec, Oaxaca 71700.

LAGUNAS DE CHACAGUA NATIONAL PARK AND VICINITY

The Lagunas de Chacagua National Park spreads for about 20 miles of open-ocean beach shoreline and islet-studded jungly lagoons midway between Pinotepa Nacional and Puerto Escondido. Tens of thousands of birds typical of a host of Mexican species fish the waters and nest in the mangroves of the two main lagoons, Laguna Pastoría on the east side, and Laguna Chacagua on the west.

The fish and wildlife of the lagoons, overfished and overhunted during recent years by local people, are now recovering. Commercial fishing is now strictly licensed. A platoon of Marines patrols access roads, shorelines, and the waters themselves, making sure catches are within legal limits. Crocodiles were hunted out during the 1970s, but the government is trying to restore them with a hatchery on Laguna Chacagua.

For most visitors, mainly Mexican families on Sunday outings, access is by boat, except for one rugged road. (See details below.) From east-side Zapotalito village, the local fishing cooperative offers full- and half-day boat excursions to the beaches, Playa Hermosa on the east side and Playa Chacagua on the west.

Exploring Lagunas de Chacagua
Zapotalito, on the eastern shore of Laguna Pastoría, is the sole easy access point to the Lagunas de Chacagua. Get there from the "Za-

---

LAGUNAS DE CHACAGUA ALTERNATIVES

Few roads penetrate the thick tropical deciduous forest surrounding the lagoons. Well-prepared adventurers can try to thumb a ride or drive a rugged high-clearance vehicle along the very rough 18-mile forest (dry season only) track to Chacagua village from San Jose del Progreso, which is located on Hwy. 200, 36 miles, 58 km, from Pinotepa Nacional. Before setting out, check with local residents or storekeepers about safety and road conditions.

If you have a boat or kayak, you can try launching your own excursion on Laguna Pastoría. The Cooperativa members, being both poor and jealous of their prerogatives, may ask you for a "launching fee," whether they're entitled to it or not.

Some of the islands in Laguna Pastoría are high and forested, and might be bug-free enough during the dry Nov.-Feb. months for a relaxing few days of wilderness camping, kayaking, and wildlife-viewing. Another alternative is to pay a boatman to drop you at your choice of islands and pick you up at a specified later time. Take everything, especially drinking water and insect repellent.

potalito" signed turnoff at Km 82, 51 miles from Pinotepa and 41 miles from Puerto Escondido. (Local buses run from Río Grande all the way to Zapotalito on the lagoon, while second-class buses from Puerto Escondido and Pinotepa Nacional will drop you on the highway.)

From the Zapotalito landings, the fishing cooperative, Sociedad Cooperativa Turística Escondida, enjoys a monopoly for transporting visitors on the lagoons. The boatmen used to make their livings fishing; now they mostly ferry tourists. Having specialized in fishing, they are generally neither wildlife-sensitive nor wildlife-knowledgeable. Canopied powerboats, seating about 10, make long, full-day trips for about $50 per boat. Cheaper half-day excursions take visitors to nearby Playa Hermosa at the mouth of Laguna Pastoría for a couple of hours' beach play and snorkeling—if you bring your own snorkeling gear.

The full-day destination, Playa Chacagua, about 14 miles distant, unfortunately seems to necessitate a fast trip across the lagoon. It's dif-ficult to get them to slow down. They roar across broad Laguna Pastoría, scattering flocks of birds ahead of them. They wind among the islands, with names such as Scorpios (scorpion), Venados (deer), or Culebra (snake), sometimes slowing for viewing multitudes of nesting pelicans, herons, and cormorants. They pick up speed again in the narrow jungle channel between the lagoons, roaring past idyllic, somnolent El Corral village, and break into open water again on Laguna Chacagua.

The **crocodile hatchery** is at Chacagua village on the west side of the lagoon, home to about two dozen local Costeño families, a shabby hotel, and a pair of lagoonside *palapa* restaurants. Past the rickety crocodile caretaker's quarters are a few enclosures housing about a hundred crocodiles segregated according to size, from hatchlings to six-foot-long toothy green adults.

The tour climaxes at the west half of Chacagua village across the estuary. Here, palms line the placid lagoon, shading the **Hotel Siete Mares** ("Seven Seas") bamboo tourist *cabañas*. The hotel, a quiet rustic tropical re-

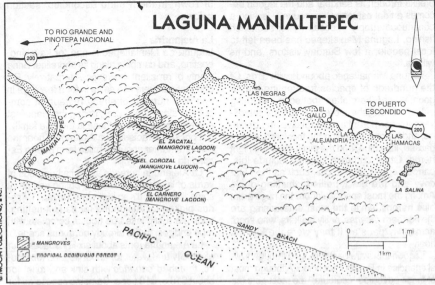

LAGUNA MANIALTEPEC

TO RIO GRANDE AND
PINOTEPA NACIONAL

LAS NEGRAS

EL
GALLO

TO PUERTO
ESCONDIDO

LA
ALEJANDRIA

LAS
HAMACAS

EL ZACATAL
(MANGROVE LAGOON)

EL COROZAL
(MANGHOVE LAGOON)

EL CARNERO
(MANGROVE LAGOON)

LA SALINA

PACIFIC
OCEAN

SANDY BEACH

= MANGROVES

= TROPICAL DECIDUOUS FOREST

0   1 mi

0   1km

© MOON PUBLICATIONS, INC.

sort, offers a small restaurant, showers and toilets, a few cabins (rent negotiable from about $15, depending upon season), and a beautiful beach a short walk away.

Playa Chacagua is lovely *because* of its isolation. The unlittered golden-white sand, washed by gently rolling waves, seems perfect for all beach activities. You can snorkel off the rocks nearby, fish in the breakers, and surf the intermediate breaks that angle in on the west side. A few *palapas* provide food and drinks, and, for beachcombers, wildlife viewers, and backpackers (who bring their own water), the breezy, jungle-backed beach spreads for 10 miles both ways.

Río Grande

Río Grande (pop. 5,000, area code 958), a few miles east of the Lagunas Chacagua, is a transportation, supply, and service point for the region. They have several *abarroterías* (groceries), a bank (Bancomer, tel. 958-260-42), several pharmacies and doctors, a *larga distancia* telephone (tel. 958-260-00, fax 260-02), and a pair of hotels.

The **Hotel Santa Monica,** Av. Puebla, Río Grande, Oaxaca 71830, tel. (958) 260-33, on the

north side of the highway in the center of town, has 22 rooms in two floors, encircling a spacious parking courtyard. With fans, toilets, and hot water, the rooms rent for about $9 s, $13 d. (They're not too clean, but will do for a night.)

The friendly, family-run **Restaurant Río Grande** across the street provides good cheer and hearty meals daily from 0700-2200.

On the east edge of town, the modern-standard, clean **Hotel Paraíso Río Grande,** Carretera 200, Río Grande, Oaxaca 71830, no phone, offers a big swimming pool and a kiddie pool in a spreading, grassy patio, plus comfortable neo-colonial-style rooms with either fans or a/c. The 20 rooms rent for about $15 s or d, $20 t with fan, $30 d with a/c.

LAGUNA MANIALTEPEC

Sylvan, mangrove-fringed Laguna Manialtepec, about 10 miles west of Puerto Escondido, is a repository for a trove of Pacific Mexico wildlife. Unlike Lagunas de Chacagua, Laguna Manialtepec is relatively deep and fresh most of the year, except occasionally during the rainy season when its main source, the Río Manialtepec, breaks through its sandbar and the lagoon becomes a tidal estuary. Consequently lacking a continuous supply of ocean-fry for sustained fishing, Laguna Manialtepec has been left to local people, a few Sunday visitors, and its wildlife.

Laguna Manialtepec abounds with birds. Of the hundreds of species frequenting the lagoon, 40 or 50 are often spotted in a morning outing. Among the more common are the olivaceous cormorant and its relative, the *anhinga;* and herons, including the tricolored, green-backed, little blue, and the black-crowned night heron. Other common species include ibis, parrots, egrets, and ducks, such as the Muscovy and the black-bellied whistling duck. Among the most spectacular are the huge great blue herons, while the most entertaining are the northern *jacanas,* or lily walkers, who scoot across lily pads as if they were the kitchen floor.

Lagoon tours are best arranged through travel agencies in Puerto Escondido. Although most of these advertise "ecotours," the most genuine is **Hidden Voyages Ecotours,** tel. (908) 207-34, led by Canadian ornithologist Michael Malone and arranged through the very competent travel agency Turismo Rodemar (see "Sights out of Town" in the "Puerto Escondido" section below).

La Alejandria

Laguna de Manialtepec is ripe for kayaking, boating, and camping along its shoreline. Bring plenty of repellent, however. Alternatively, RV and tent campers can settle in for a few days in one of a number of shady restaurant compounds along the shore. Among the friendliest and best organized of these is the little family-run pocket paradise of La Alejandria, near the Km 125 marker about 10 miles from Puerto Escondido.

La Alejandria spreads along its hundreds of yards of lakefront, shaded by palms and great spreading trees. It's so idyllic the "Tarzan" TV series picked La Alejandria for its film setting, adding a rustic lake tree house, complete with rope bridges, to the already gorgeous scene.

La Alejandria rents about six RV spaces with electricity and water for about $8, and four rustic, thatched *cabañas* with sink and toilet for about $13 d, $18 t or q. Camping spaces go for about $7. The homey centerpiece restaurant-bar, screened-in from bugs and embellished with animal trophies, is reminiscent of a venerable East African safari lodge.

PUERTO ESCONDIDO

Decorated by intimate coves, sandy beaches, and washed by jade-tinted surf, Puerto Escondido enjoys its well-deserved popularity. Despite construction of a jet airport in the 1980s, Puerto Escondido remains a place where everything is within a short walk, no high-rise blocks anyone's sunset view, and moderately priced accommodations and good food remain the rule.

Puerto Escondido, "Hidden Port," got its name from the rocky Punta Escondida, which shelters its intimate half-moon cove, which perhaps would have remained hidden if local farmers had not discovered that coffee thrives beneath the cool forest canopy of the lush seaward slopes of the Sierra Madre del Sur. They began bringing their precious beans for shipment when the port of Puerto Escondido was established in 1928.

When the coast highway was pushed through during the 1960s, Puerto Escondido's then-dwindling coffee trade was replaced by a growing trickle of vacationers, attracted by the splendid isolation, low prices, and high waves. With some of the best surfing breaks in North America, a permanent surfing colony soon got established. This led to more nonsurfing visitors, who, by the 1990s, were enjoying the comfort and food of a string of small hotels and restaurants lining Puerto Escondido's still-beautiful but no longer hidden cove.

SIGHTS

Getting Oriented

Puerto Escondido (pop. 30,000) seems like two small towns, separated by Hwy. 200, which runs along the bluff above the beach. The upper town is where most of the local folks live and go about their business, while in the town below the highway, most of the tourist restaurants, hotels, and shops spread along a single, mile-long beachfront street, **Av. Pérez Gasga.**

Av. Pérez Gasga runs east-west, mainly as a pedestrian mall, where motor traffic is allowed only before noon. Afternoons, the *cadenas* (chains) go up, blocking cars at either end.

Beyond the west-end *cadena,* Pérez Gasga leaves the beach, winding uphill to the highway, where it enters the upper town at the *crucero,* Puerto Escondido's only signaled intersection. From there, Pérez Gasga continues into the upper town as Av. Oaxaca, National Hwy. 131.

Getting Around

In town, walk or take a taxi, which should run no more than $2 to anywhere.

For longer local excursions, such as Lagunas Manialtepec and Chacagua (westbound), and as far as Pochutla (near Puerto Ángel) eastbound, ride one of the very frequent *urbano* microbuses that stop at the *crucero.*

BEACHES AND ACTIVITIES

Puerto Escondido bayfront begins at the sheltered rocky cove beneath the wave-washed lighthouse point, Punta Escondida. The shoreline continues easterly along Playa Principal, the main beach, curving southward at Playa Marineros, and finally straightening into long, open-ocean Playa Zicatela. The sand and surf change drastically, from narrow sand and calm ripples at Playa Principal to a wide beach pounded by gigantic rollers at Zicatela.

Playa Principal

Playa Principal is where Mexican families love to frolic on Sundays and holidays and sun-starved winter vacationers doze in their chairs and hammocks beneath the palms. The sheltered west side is very popular with local people who arrive afternoons with nets and haul in small troves of silvery fish. The water is great for wading and swimming, clear enough for casual snorkeling but generally too calm for anything else in the cove. However, a few hundred yards east

around the bay, the waves are generally fine for bodysurfing and boogie-boarding, with a minimum of undertow. Although not a particularly windy location, windsurfers do occasionally bring their own equipment and practice their art here. Fishing is fine off the rocks or by small boat, easily launched from the beach. Shells, generally scarce on Playa Principal, are more common on less-crowded Playa Zicatela.

Playa Marineros

As the beach curves toward the south, it increasingly faces the open ocean. Playa Marineros begins about 100 yards from the "Marineros," the eastside rocky outcroppings in front of the Hotel Santa Fe. The rocks' jutting forms are supposed to resemble visages of grizzled old sailors. Here the waves can be rough. Swimmers beware; appearances can be deceiving. Intermediate surfers practice here, as do daring boogie-boarders and bodysurfers.

Playa Zicatela

Past the Marineros rocks you enter the hallowed ground of **surfers,** Playa Zicatela. The wide beach, of fine golden-white sand, stretches south for miles to a distant cliff and point. The powerful Pacific swells arrive unimpeded, crashing to the sand with awesome, thunderous power. Both surfers and nonsurfers congregate year-round, waiting for the renowned Escondido "pipeline," where grand waves curl into whirling liquid tunnels, which expert surfers skim through like trains in a subway. At such times, the watchers on the beach outnumber the surfers by as much as 10 or 20 to one. Don't try surfing or swimming at Zicatela unless you're expert at both.

Playas Puerto Angelito, Carrizalillos, And Bachoco

About a mile west of town, the picture-postcard blue little bays of Puerto Angelito and Carrizalillos nestle beneath the seacliff. Their sheltered gold-and-coral sands are perfect for tranquil picnicking, sunbathing, and swimming. Here, **snorkeling and scuba diving** are tops, among shoals of bright fish grazing and darting among the close-in coral shelves and submerged rocky outcroppings. Get there by launch from Playa Principal or by taxi. On foot (take a sun hat and water) follow the street that angles from Pérez

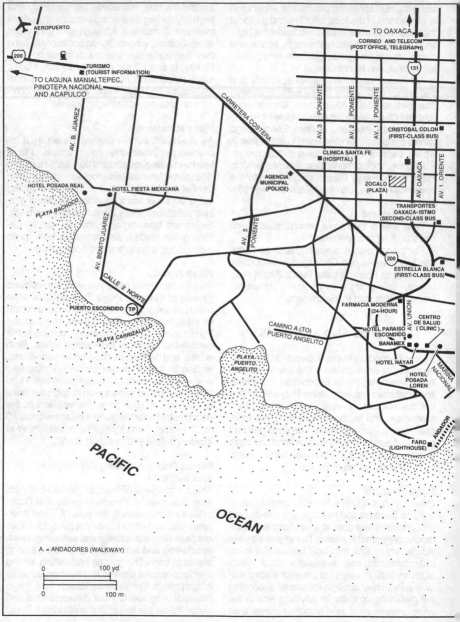

A. = ANDADORES (WALKWAY)

0 — 100 yd

0 — 100 m

© MOON PUBLICATIONS, INC.

PUERTO ESCONDIDO

AV. 8 NORTE
AV. 7 NORTE
AV. 6 NORTE
AV. 5 NORTE
AV. 4 NORTE
AV. 3 NORTE
AV. 2 NORTE
AV. 1 NORTE
AV HIDALGO

AV. 2 ORIENTE
AV. 3 ORIENTE
AV. 4 ORIENTE

ESTRELLA DEL VALLE
AND OAXACA-PACIFICO
(SECOND-CLASS BUSES)

AV. BENITO JUAREZ

200

A. SOLEDAD
LIBERTAD
REVOLUCION
MARIS

CARRETERA COSTERA

RESTAURANT
HACIENDA

RESTAURANT
LA GALERIA

HOTEL CASA BLANCA
RODEMAR TOURS

BANCOMER   CHAIN

CHAIN

HOTEL LAS
PALMAS

HOTEL RINCON
DEL PACIFICO

RESTAURANT
NAUTILUS

RESTAURANT
PERLA FLAMEANTE

CAPITAN DEL PUERTO

CRAFTS STALLS

PEREZ GASGA

LAGUNA
AGUA
DULCE

PLAYA PRINCIPAL

CARMEN'S LA
PATISSERIE

(WALKWAY)

HOTEL SANTA FE

PLAYA MARINEROS

CASAS DE
PLAYA ACALI

VILLA TEMAZCALLI
(MASSAGE STUDIO)

INFRAGANTE

ABARROTES MERLIN
(GROCERY)

HOTEL ARCO IRIS

AV. DEL MORRO

CENTRAL SURF (RENTALS)

CAFECITO

BEACH HOTEL INES

PLAYA ZICATELA

ROCKAWAY
SURFER'S VILLAGE
ART AND
HARRY'S SURF INN

TO PUERTO ANGEL,
BAHIAS DE HUATULCO,
AND TEHUANTEPEC

200

Gasga uphill across from the Hotel Nayar. Continue a few hundred yards and angle left again at Camino a Puerto Angelito ("Road to Puerto Angelito") and follow the trail down the cliff. Carrizalillos is another quarter mile west, before the trailer park.

Playa Bachoco, a mile farther west, down the bluff from the Hotel Posada Real, is a long, scenic strip of breeze-swept sand, with thunderous waves and correspondingly menacing undertow. Swimming is much safer in the inviting pool of the adjacent Hotel Posada Real beach club.

If you're strong, experienced, and can get past the breaking waves, **snorkeling** is said to be good around the little surf-dashed islet a hundred yards offshore.

Although Playa Bachoco's rock-sheltered nooks appear inviting for camping, local people don't recommend it, because of occasional *rateros* (thugs and drunks) who roam Puerto Escondido beaches at night.

Trouble in Paradise

Occasional knifepoint robberies and muggings have marred the once-peaceful Puerto Escondido nighttime beach scene. Walk alone and you invite trouble, especially along the unlit stretch of Playa Principal between the east end of Pérez Gasga and the Hotel Santa Fe. If you have dinner alone at the Hotel Santa Fe, avoid the beach by returning by taxi or walking along the highway to Pérez Gasga back to your hotel.

Fortunately, such problems seem to be confined to the beach. Visitors are quite safe on the Puerto Escondido streets themselves, often more so than on their own city streets back home.

Beach Walking

The *andador* concrete walkway, which circles the lighthouse point, provides a pleasant, breezy afternoon (or sunset) diversion. From the west chain, follow the street that heads toward the lighthouse. Soon, on the left, stairs head left down on to the beach cove, where, in front of the "Capitania del Puerto" building, the *andador* heads left along the rocks. It continues, above the splashing surf, for a few hundred yards. Return by the same route, or loop back through side streets to Pérez Gasga.

For a longer walk, you can stroll as far out of town along on Playa Zicatela as you want, in outings ranging from an hour to a whole day. Best to avoid the heat of midday, and bring along a sun hat, shirt, drinks, and snacks (and perhaps sunglasses) if you plan on walking more than a mile past the last restaurant down the beach. Your rewards will be the acrobatics of surfers challenging the waves, rafts of shorebirds, and occasional finds of driftwood and shells. After about three miles you will reach a cliff and a sea arch, which you can scamper through at low tide to the beach on the other side, **Playa Barra de Colotepec.**

Playa Barra de Colotepec's surf is as thunderous as Zicatela's and the beach even more pristine, being a nesting site for sea turtles. About a quarter mile past the point you will come to **Campamento Ecologio Ayuda Las Tortugas** ("Campamento Tortugas" for short), where volunteers work to get to the turtle eggs before the poachers do. See "Trailer Parks and Camping" following.

Playa Barra de Colotepec continues for another mile to the jungle-fringed lagoon of the Río Colotepec, where a host of birds and wildlife, both common and rare, paddle and preen in the clear, fresh water.

You could break this eight-mile roundtrip into a pair of more leisurely options: Hike A could cover Zicatela only. On Hike B you could explore Barra de Zicatela and the Laguna de Colotepec by driving, taxiing, or busing straight to Campamento Tortugas: from Hwy. 200 about three miles south of town, turn off, or have the local microbus drop you, at the signed side road. After about half a mile, follow the left fork to the campground and Playa Barra Colotepec.

Beach Boat Tours

Travel agencies and the local boat cooperative, Sociedad Cooperativa Punta Escondida, offer trips for parties of several passengers to beautiful local bays, including Carrizalillo and Puerto Ángelito (see above), plus Manzanillo, Puesta del Sol, and Coral. The minimum hour-and-a-half trip runs about $40 for an entire (eight-person) boat. Trips can be extended (about $20 per additional hour) to your heart's content of beach picnicking, snoozing, and snorkeling.

SIGHTS OUT OF TOWN

Whether you go escorted (see "Tours" below) or independently, outings away from the Puerto Escondido resort can reveal rewarding glimpses of flora and fauna, local cultures, and idyllic beaches seemingly half a world removed from the Pérez Gasga tourist hubbub.

To the west of Puerto Escondido are the festivals, markets, and handicrafts of Mixtec Indian towns and villages around Jamiltepec and Pinotepa Nacional. For wildlife lovers and beachgoers there are the jungly lagoons and pristine strands of the Laguna de Manialtepec and Parque Nacional Lagunas de Chacagua. (For details, see previous sections.)

Also on the west side, the **Aguas Termales Atotonilco** hot springs, a Chatino Indian sacred site, provides an interesting focus for a day's outing. The jumping-off point is the village of San José Manialtepec, about half an hour by bus or car west of Puerto Escondido.

At the village, you should hire someone to show you the way, up the semi-wild canyon of the Río Manialtepec. The trail winds along cornfields, beneath forest canopies and past Chatino Indian villages. Finally you arrive at the hot springs, where a clear bathtub-sized rock basin bubbles with very hot (bearable for the brave), clear, sulfur-smelling water. **Get there** by driving or busing to the Hwy. 200 turnoff for San José Manialtepec, around Km 116, just east of the Río Manialtepec. Village stables provide horses and guides to the hot springs. It's a very easy two-mile walk, except in times of high water on the river, which the trail crosses several times.

Tours

Puerto Escondido agencies conduct outings to all of the above and more. Among the very best are the **Hidden Voyages Ecotours** of the Canadian husband-wife team of Michael Malone and Joan Walker. Working through the competent Turismo Rodimar Travel Agency, Av. Pérez Gasga 906, P.O. Box 122, Puerto Escondido, Oaxaca 71980, tel. (958) 207-34, ornithologist Michael and artist-ecologist Joan lead unusually informative beach, lagoon, and mountain tours seasonally, late fall through Easter. In addition, they also offer a sunset lagoon wildlife and

beach excursion, plus a two-day trip to Nopala, center of Chatino Indian culture, including a coffee plantation in the cool Sierra Madre del Sur mountain jungle. Their trips ordinarily run $40 per day, per person.

ACCOMMODATIONS

Hotels and Bungalows

The successful hotels in Puerto Escondido are appropriate to the town itself: small, reasonably priced, and near the water. They dot the beachfront from Playa Zicatela around the bay and continue up Av. Pérez Gasga to the highway. Most are either on the beach or within a stone's throw of it, which makes sense, because it seems a shame to come all the way to Puerto Escondido and not stay where you can soak up the beauty.

Downhill along Pérez Gasga from the *crucero* is the **Hotel Paraíso Escondido** on a short side street to the left, Calle Union 1, Puerto Escondido, Oaxaca 71980, tel. (958)-204-44. A tranquil colonial-chic refuge, the hotel abounds in unique artistic touches—Mixtec stone glyphs, tiny corner chapels, stained glass, and old-world antiques—blended into the lobby, corridors, and patios. The two levels of rooms nestle around a lovely view pool and restaurant patio. The rooms themselves are large, with view balconies and designer tile bathrooms, wrought-iron fixtures, and handcrafted wooden furniture. Very popular with North American and German winter vacationers; get reservations in early. Their 24 rooms rent from $40 s, $65 d, with a/c, pool, kiddie pool, and parking, but *no* credit cards are accepted.

Just downhill is the motel-style **Hotel Nayar**, Pérez Gasga 407, Puerto Escondido, Oaxaca 71980, tel. (958) 201-13 or 203-19, spreading from its inviting pool-patio past the reception to a viewpoint restaurant. Its spacious and comfortable but Spartan air-conditioned rooms have private balconies, many with sea views. A potentially beautiful hotel, the Nayar suffers from lackluster management. This often results in sullen desk personnel, dirt in the corners, torn drapes, and bare-bulb lighting. The Nayar's 36 rooms run about $18 s, $23 d, $27 t low season, and $20, $26, and $30 high.

PUERTO ESCONDIDO HOTELS

Puerto Escondido (area code 958, postal code 71980) hotels, in ascending order of approximate high-season double-room price:

Casas de Playa Acali, Calle del Morro (P.O. Box 11), tel. 207-54 or 202-78, $20

Rockaway Surfer's Village, Calle del Morro, tel. 206-68, $22

Hotel Casa Blanca, Pérez Gasga 905, tel. 201-68, $23

Hotel Rincón del Pacífico, Pérez Gasga 900, tel. 200-56 or 201-93, $25

Hotel Nayar, Pérez Gasga 407, tel. 201-13 or 203-19, $26

Hotel Arco Iris, Calle del Morro, Colonia Marinero, tel. 214-94, fax 204-32, $27

Hotel Posada Loren, Pérez Gasga 507, tel. 200-57, $27

Hotel Las Palmas, Pérez Gasga s/n, tel. 202-30 or 203-03, $30

Beach Hotel Inés, P.O. Box 44, tel. 207-92, $35

Hotel Paraíso Escondido, Calle Union 1, tel. 204-44, $65

Hotel Santa Fe, P.O. Box 96, tel. 201-70 or 202-66, fax 202-60, $70

The more popular **Hotel Posada Loren,** Av. Pérez Gasga 507, Puerto Escondido, Oaxaca 71980, tel. (958) 200-57, downhill half a block farther, is as good as it first appears, from its leafy pool-patio and its private balcony view rooms to its rooftop sundeck. Intelligent clerks staff the desk while *camaristas* scrub the rooms spotless every day. (They also assiduously spray with DDT; tell them "no DDT" if you'd prefer they didn't.) The rooms spread through two three-story buildings; the front building rooms have better views. Reserve a *cuarto con vista* if you want a view room. Reservations are often necessary, especially in the winter. The 24 basic but comfortable rooms rent for about $20 s, $24 d, $27 t low season; $23, $27, and $33 high; with parking, fans, and some a/c; credit cards accepted.

Right on the beach amidst the tourist-mall hullabaloo is the longtime favorite, **Hotel Las Palmas,** Av. Pérez Gasga s/n, Puerto Escondido, Oaxaca 71980, tel. (958) 202-30 or 203-03. Its main plus is the palmy, vine-strewn patio where you can sit for breakfast every morning, enjoy the breeze, and watch the boats, the birds, and families frolicking in the billows. The big drawback, besides sleepy management and no

pool, is lack of privacy. Exterior walkways pass the room windows, which anyone can see through. Closing the curtains unfortunately makes the (fan-only) rooms very dark and hot. This doesn't bother the legions of return customers, however, since they spend little time in their rooms anyway. Tariffs for the 40 smallish rooms run about $24 s, $30 d, and $36 t, with phones, no parking, credit cards accepted.

The **Rincón del Pacífico** next door offers about the same, but for lower prices, Av. Pérez Gasga 900, Puerto Escondido, Oaxaca 71980, tel. (958) 200-56 or 201-93. The two tiers of clean, comfortable rooms enfold a shady patio that looks out onto the lively beachfront. As at the Hotel Las Palmas above, a stay in one of their glass-front rooms feels like life in a fishbowl. This is nevertheless a very popular hotel. Reserve early. Rates for the 28 rooms run about $20 s, $25 d, $30 t; four suites with TV and a/c rent for about $40 s or d; with a restaurant, but no parking or pool; credit cards accepted.

Although it's not right on the beach like its neighbors across the street, the rooms of the **Hotel Casa Blanca,** Av. Pérez Gasga 905, Puerto Escondido, Oaxaca 71980, tel. (958) 210-68, are larger, cooler, and much more private. Some rooms even have private balconies, fine for people-watching on the street below. Guests report noise is not a problem since cars and trucks are banned on Gasca 1500-0700. Other amenities include hot water, a shelf of used paperback books, and, beyond graceful arches that border the lobby, a petite, inviting pool patio. The 21 clean, comfortable rooms rent for about $18 s, $23 d, and $28 t, with fans.

Puerto Escondido's class-act hostelry is the newish **Hotel Santa Fe,** Calle del Morro, Playa Marinero, Puerto Escondido, P.O. Box 96, Puerto Escondido, Oaxaca 71980, tel. (958) 201-70 or 202-66, fax 202-60, built in graceful neocolonial style, appealing to both Mexican and foreign vacationers. With curving staircases, a palm-shaded pool-patio, and flower-decorated walkways, the Santa Fe achieves an ambience both intimate and luxuriously private. Its restaurant is outstanding (see "Food" below). The rooms are spacious, comfortable, and thoughtfully appointed with handpainted tile, rustic wood furniture, and regional handicrafts. Get your reservation in early. Their 50 rooms rent for about $55 s or d, $60 t, low season, and $65 and $80 high; with TV, a/c, phones, and parking; credit cards accepted.

A few hundred yards south along the beach is the **Casas de Playa Acali**, Calle del Morro, P.O. Box 11, Puerto Escondido 71980, tel. (958) 202-78 or 207-54, a colony of rustic *cabañas*, clustered around a blue pool in a banana, palm, and mango mini-jungle. The *cabañas* themselves, like a vision out of a romantic southseas tale, are built with walls from sticks (nonsee-through) and sturdy plank floors, raised above ground-level. Units are clean, equipped with fans, mosquito nets, and good bathrooms. Rentals cost about $15 s, $20 d, $25 t, with hot water and small refrigerator.

Farther south on Calle del Moro, which runs along Playa Zicatela, rises the two story **Hotel Arco Iris**, Calle del Morro s/n, Colonia Marinero, Puerto Escondido, Oaxaca 71980, tel. (958) 214-94, fax 204-32. A flowery, shady green garden surrounds the hotel, leading to an attractive pool-patio. For those who love sunsets, sand, and waves (and don't mind their sometimes insistent pounding), one of the spacious, simply furnished top-floor view rooms might be just right. The Arco Iris's proximity to the famous Puerto Escondido "pipeline" draws both surfers and surf watchers to the second-floor restaurant La Galera, which seems equally ideal for wave-watching at breakfast and sky-watching at sunset. The rates for the 26 rooms run about $23 s, $27 d; suites with kitchen, about $33 d, $40 t; with fans and parking.

Next comes **Beach Hotel Inés**, Calle del Morro, P.O. Box 44, Playa Zicatela, Puerto Escondido, Oaxaca 71980, tel. (958) 207-92, the life project of German expatriate Peter Voss and his daughter, Inés. Their collection of 20 units occupy the palmy periphery of a flowery, pool cafe-garden layout, which climaxes with an attractive, stuccoed, two-story collection of rooms at the back side. Here, longtime repeat guests linger for coffee and conversation after late-morning breakfasts, stroll the beach in the afternoon, and return for balmy sunset happy hour. Most of the rentals are hotel-style rooms, with clean, light interiors, comfortable furnishings, and well-maintained bathrooms. Additionally, they rent six downscale second floor (popular with surfers) shared-bath *cabañas*, and a pair of bungalows with outdoor kitchens, sleeping four to six. Rooms go for about $35 d, *cabañas* about $13 d, and the bungalows $50, all with discounts available for long-term rentals.

Farther along Playa Zicatela is the very tidy **Rockaway Surfer's Village**, Calle del Morro, Playa Zicatela, Puerto Escondido, Oaxaca 71980, tel. (958) 206-68, a fenced-in cluster of about 15 clean, concrete-floored bamboo-and-thatch *cabañas*. Spacious and fan-equipped, they sleep about four and have private showers and toilets, mosquito nets, and shady, hammock-hung front porches. An attractive, leafy pool-patio occupies the center, while the manager's *cabaña*, offering beach, surfing, and snorkeling rentals and supplies, stands to one side. For equipment rental details, see "Sports" below. *Cabaña* rentals run about $11 per person, per night; weekly or monthly discounts are possible; parking.

Trailer Parks and Camping

Trailer Park Puerto Escondido, Puerto Escondido, Bahía Carrizalillo, Oaxaca 71980, tel. (958) 200-77, occupies a breezy lot overlooking little blue Carrizalillo Bay on the west side of town. Their acre of around 100 spaces blooms with green grass during the popular winter season, when dozens of Canadians and Americans pull in and stay for two or three months. The congenial company, all hookups, a large swimming pool, clean showers and toilets, some shaded spaces, and good fishing keep them returning. Figure on paying about $12 per day, discounts available for monthly rentals. **Get there** from Hwy. 200, via Av. Benito Juárez (look for the Tourist Information Sign) a few hundred yards (westbound) past the airport. The avenue bends left near the Hotel Posada Real, then bends right again at the Hotel Fiesta Mexicana. It ends at Calle 2, which you should follow by turning left, and continuing to the trailer park gate about a hundred yards farther on.

For safety reasons, local people do not recommend camping in isolated spots along Puerto Escondido beaches. The **Campamento Ecologio Ayuda Las Tortugas** ("Help the Turtles Ecological Campground") solves this problem by providing a safe camping place on a pristine beach.

Engineer Jorge Gutiérrez, who works in Oaxaca City, thought something ought to be done to save the turtles of Barra de Colotepec. He bought the land, dug a well, equipped it with an old-fashioned windmill, and recruited volunteers to build and maintain a campground.

Now, his volunteers maintain the campground when Jorge has to be in Oaxaca. They welcome visitors to stay free at one of the several shaded campsites and help (they need donations of food and supplies) with the ecological effort. They have had some success keeping the turtle eggs from poachers, having released hundreds of hatchlings which they and other volunteers personally saved.

"I have no official permission to do this," Jorge says. "The government could kick us out of here at any time." He hopes, however, that more volunteers and visitors will add fuel to the flickering little ecological flame he's started on Playa Barra de Colotopec.

FOOD

Breakfast and Snacks
Mornings you can smell the aroma of Carmen's **La Patisserie** along Playa Marinero, on the little street that heads toward Playa Marinero from Hwy. 200, just past the bridge. Follow the fragrance to the source, a small homey shop with a few tables for savoring the goodies. Before noon you'll usually find owner Carmen Arizmendi in the kitchen or behind the counter; afternoons, however, you'll often glimpse her swimming across the bay. Open Mon.-Sat. 0700-2000.

You don't have to walk all the way to Carmen's store to enjoy her pastries. She's opened a little branch right on Zicatela beach called **Cafecito** (next to Bungalows Acuario), where you can enjoy a cappuccino and one of her goodies as you watch the surfers conquering the waves.

Right in the middle of the Av. Pérez Gasga bustle, **Cafe Il Capuchino** is a gathering place for tourists and local folks who enjoy good

desserts and coffee with their conversation. Furthermore, the best homesickness remedy in town is their apple pie, a slice of which enables you to endure a minimum of one more hard week on the local beaches. Open daily 0800-2300.

Restaurants
Complete dinner price key: Budget: under $7; Moderate: $7-14; Expensive: more than $14.

Most of Puerto Escondido's reliable restaurants line Av. Pérez Gasga; beginning just outside the west-end chain, first comes the streetside patio of **Restaurant Hacienda y Sardina de la Plata,** Av. Pérez Gasga 512, tel. (958) 203-28, formerly two restaurants now combined into one. The present establishment is the brainchild of Barcelona-born owner-chef Fernando de Abascal López, who enjoys orchestrating a unique seafood repertoire. His list includes Catalan specialties such as Txanguro de Jaiva (snails, shrimp, and octupus in a white sauce), or Mero a la Sol (a sea bass feast for a party of four to 10). Besides such exotica, he also serves good pasta, steaks, lobster, Mexican plates, and breakfasts. Open daily 0730-2300; credit cards accepted. Moderate.

Across the street, the vegetarian restaurant **La Gota de Vida** presents an entirely different option. Here, hearty meat-free fare is king, from delicious soups and crisp salads to fresh fruit and vegie drinks and savory plates of pasta. Open daily 0800-2200. Budget to moderate.

Just inside the chain, on the uphill side of Pérez Gasga, **Restaurant La Galería** usually has customers, even when most other local eateries are empty. The reason is the exellent Italian fare—crusty, hot pizzas, rich pastas and lasagna, bountiful salads, and satisfying soups—which the European-expatriate owner puts out for her growing battalion of loyal customers. Open daily 0800-2400. Moderate.

A creation of the same owner-chef as the Galería, the upstairs *palapa* of the **Restaurant Nautilus** across the street affords a cool, palm-fringed bay view that makes even a simple lunch seem luxurious. Furthermore, she adds the adventure of sushi, smoked ham with melon, and vegetables Hindu style to an already eclectic list of salads, pastas, and seafoods. Open daily 0800-2400, credit cards accepted. Moderate.

Restaurant Crotos, arguably the best beach-front eatery on Pérez Gasga, is among the most pleasant for breakfast, lunch, or dinner. Located across from Farmacia Cortés, open daily 0700-2300. Beneath a luxurious, palm-fringed *palapa,* patrons enjoy shade, cooling breezes, and the ever-fascinating beach scene. In such a lovely setting, the food (super-fresh seafood is their specialty)—attractively presented, competently served, and tasty—seems like an added bonus. Moderate.

Near the east end of the Pérez Gasga mall, the **Restaurant Perla Flameante** offers good food, incense, new-age jazz, and a beach view from beneath a big, cool *palapa.* The friendly, conscientious staff take pride that they make everything in-house, from the mayonnaise to the potato chips that come with their big fish burger. Fish fillets rule their menu. The varieties, such as sierra, tuna, yellowtail, and mahimahi, are exceeded only by the number of styles—Cajun, teriyaki, wine and herbs, pepper-mustard, butter and garlic, orange—in which they are served. Open daily 0700-2300; no credit cards. Budget to moderate.

If you have dinner at the restaurant of the **Hotel Santa Fe,** on Calle del Morro, east side of the bay, tel. (958) 201-70, you may never go anywhere else. Savory food, impeccably served beneath a luxurious *palapa* and accompanied by softly strumming guitars, brings travelers from all over the world. Although everything on their menu is good, they are proudest of their Mexican favorites, such as rich tortilla soup, bountiful plates of chiles rellenos, or succulent snapper, Veracruz style. Open daily 0730-2300. Moderate to expensive.

Farther south along Zicatela beach, **Bruno's** is headquarters for a loyal platoon of local surfers and Canadian and American residents. Breakfasts, hamburgers, and fresh seafood plates are bountiful, tasty, and won't cost you a bundle. Open daily, about 0800-2200. Budget to moderate. "Bruno," by the way, is not the name of the restaurant's owner, but of a large hammerhead shark who used to swim in the waves near the surfers but never harmed anyone.

At the far end of Calle del Morro on Zicatela Beach is friendly **Art and Harry's Surf Inn,** named after the Canadian expatriate owners' grandfathers, open daily, noon till about 2200.

The restaurant, a big, breezy upper-floor *palapa,* is best around sunset when patrons enjoy "Frisbee golf" and more unobstructed sunsets per year than any other *palapa* in Puerto Escondido. Personable co-owner Patty Mikus keeps customers coming with her fresh salads, soups, and tasty (honey, garlic, teriyaki, Hawaiian, or marinera) fish plates.

ENTERTAINMENT AND EVENTS

Sunsets and Happy Hours
Many bars have sunset happy hours, but not all of them have good sunset views. Since the Oaxaca coast faces south (and the sun sets in the west), bars along eastside Zicatela Beach, such as the Hotel Santa Fe, Hotel Arco Iris, Bruno's and Art and Harry's are the only ones that can offer unobstructed sunset horizons.

If, on the other hand, you prefer solitude, stroll the bayfront *andador* walkway to near the lighthouse. Start on the beach side of the Capitán del Puerto office. There, from breezy perches above the waves, you'll enjoy an equally panoramic sunset.

Strolling Pérez Gasga
Strolling the Pérez Gasga mall is Puerto Escondido's prime after-dinner entertainment. By around 2100, however, people get weary of walking and, since there are few benches, begin sitting on the curb and sipping bottles of beer near the west-end chain. (If you don't drink, however, you could probably qualify for a curbside spot with a beer bottle filled with water.)

The main attraction of this curb-sitting is watching other people sitting on the curb, while listening to the music blasting nightly from the tiny open-air bars of **Barfly** and **Bar Coco** 50 feet away. The music is so loud little can be gained except hearing impairment by actually taking a seat in the bars themselves.

Those who prefer to dance with their music go to some of the few **discotheques** in town. Most popular are the Disco Paraíso at the Hotel Fiesta Mexicana (tel. 958-201-15, above Playa Bachoco) and the La Bahía (with a bay view) in town above the highway, three blocks east of the *crucero*).

Festivals

Puerto Escondido pumps up with a series of fiestas during the low-season, but excellent for vacationing, month of November. Scheduled "Fiestas de Noviembre" events invariably include surfing and usually sportfishing, culinary, and beauty contests.

If instead you hanker for the old-fashioned color of a traditional fiesta, make sure you arrive in Puerto Escondido before 18 December, when seemingly the whole town takes part in the fiesta of the **Virgen de Soledad.** Besides being the patron saint of the state of Oaxaca, the Virgen de Soledad is also protectress of fishermen. To honor her, the whole town accompanies the virgin by boat out to the bay's far reach, and then returns with her to the church plaza for dancing, fireworks, and bullfights.

If you can't be in Puerto Escondido in time to honor the virgin in December, perhaps you may be able to take a day-trip one hour west of Puerto Escondido to enjoy a fiesta at one of the small towns around Pinotepa Nacional. For dates and details, see above.

SPORTS

Walking, Jogging, Gym, and Tennis

Playa Zicatela is Puerto Escondido's most interesting walking course. (See "Beach Walks" above.) Early mornings, before the heat and crowds, are good for jogging along the level section of Av. Pérez Gasga. Calle del Morro on Playa Zicatela is good for jogging anytime it isn't too hot.

The **Acuario Gym,** on Playa Zicatela, between the Hotels Arco Iris and Inés, has a roomful of standard exercise equipment. Single visits run about $2.50, one-month passes about $23.

One of the better night-lit **tennis** courts in town available for public rental is at the Hotel Fiesta Americana. Call (958) 201-15 for details.

Surfing, Snorkeling, And Scuba Diving

Although surfing is *de rigueur* for the skilled in Puerto Escondido, beginners often learn by bodysurfing and boogieboarding first. Boogie boards and surfboards are for sale and rent ($7/day) at a number of shops along Pérez Gasga, and at **Central Surf** on Playa Zicatela

(open daily 0900-1400 and 1700-2130), below the Acuario Gym. **Rockaway Surfer's Village,** a few hundred yards farther south along the beach, rents surfboards ($7/day) and boogie boards ($5/day) and sells related supplies.

Beginners practice on the gentler billows of Playa Principal and adjacent Playa Marinero (see above) while advanced surfers go for the awesome waves of Playa Zicatela, which regularly slam foolhardy inexperienced surfers onto the sand with backbreaking force.

Clear blue-green waters, coral reefs, and droves of multicolored fish make for good local snorkeling and diving, especially in little Puerto Ángelito and Carrizalillo bays just west of town (see "Beaches and Activities" above). A number of Av. Pérez Gasga stores sell serviceable amateur-grade snorkeling equipment.

If you want to do some local scuba diving, best contact the professional **Buceos Triton** shop at the Hotel Marlin (tel. 958-700-55) an hour and a half drive south, in Santa Cruz de Huatulco. (For more details, see the "Bahías de Huatulco" section below.) No dive shop currently operates in Puerto Escondido.

Sportfishing

Puerto Escondido's offshore waters abound with fish. Launches go out mornings from Playa Principal and routinely return with an assortment including big tuna, mackerel, snapper, sea bass, and snook. The sheltered west side of the beach is calm enough to easily launch a mobile boat with the help of usually willing beach hands.

The local **Sociedad Cooperativa Punta Escondida,** which parks its boats right on Playa Principal, regularly takes fishing parties of three or four out for about $25 an hour, including bait and tackle. Additionally, travel agencies, such as Turismo Rodimar, Av. Pérez Gasga 905, tel. (958) 207-34, arrange such trips at about the same prices.

SHOPPING

Market and Handicrafts

As in most Mexican towns, the place to begin your Puerto Escondido shopping is at the local **Mercado,** on Av. 10 Norte one block west of the electric station on Av. Oaxaca. Although produce occupies most of the space, a number of stalls at the south end offer authentic handicrafts. These might include Guerrero painted pottery animals; San Bartolo Coyotepec black pottery; masks from Guerrero and Oaxaca with jaguar, devil, and scary human-animal motifs; the endearing multicolored pottery animals from Iguala and Zitlala in Guerrero; and beautiful crocheted *huipiles* from San Pedro Amusgos and Pinotepa Nacional.

Back downhill on Av. Pérez Gasga, the prices increase along with the selection. Perhaps the most fruitful time and place for handicraft shopping is at night, when it is less warm, within the illuminated-at-night cluster of crafts stalls just beyond the Gasga east chain.

One shop at that spot, the **Ruiz** textile stand, with genuine handmade rugs and serapes from Teotitlán del Valle near Oaxaca city, stands out. Fine-quality rugs are the most tightly woven—typically about 20 strands per inch.

Another good, authentic shop is **Creaciones Alberto,** next to Farmacia Cortes, tel. (958) 202-84, named for the elderly master craftsman in Puerto Vallarta, whose sons and daughters sell his fine handiwork (and that of associated craftspersons) in a number of Pacific Mexico centers. Open Mon.-Sat. 0900-1400 and 1700-2230. For hints, see "Buying Silver and Gold," in the "Shopping" section of the On the Road chapter.

Groceries and Photography
Abarrotes Lupita, a fairly well-stocked grocery, offers meats, milk, ice, and vegetables. In addition, it stocks a few English-language publications, such as the *News* of Mexico City and magazines such as *Time, Life,* and *Newsweek,* on the inland side of Gasga, outside of the east-end chain. Open daily 1000-2300.

Out on Playa Zicatela, where stores are not nearly so common, the friendly **Abarrotes Merlin** offers a small grocery selection; open daily 0900-2200.

Foto Express Figueroa, tel. (958) 205-26, on Gasga next to Turismo Rodimar, offers fast photofinishing services, Kodak color print and slide film, and a moderate stock of accessories, including point-and-shoot cameras. Open daily 0930-1400 and 1630-2000.

SERVICES

Money Exchange
Banamex, at Pérez Gasga 314, uphill from the Hotel Nayar, tel. (958) 206-26 and **Bancomer,** in the middle of the Gasga tourist zone, across from Hotel Rincón del Pacífico, tel. (958) 204-11, changes U.S. and Canadian cash and traveler's checks Mon.-Fri. 0900-1200.

After hours, the small *casa de cambio* (money exchange) office across the street changes a larger range of foreign currencies for a correspondingly larger fee, tel. (958) 205-92, across from Farmacia Cortés. Open Mon.-Sat. 0900-1400 and 1700-2000.

Communication
The *correo* and *telégrafo* are side by side on Av. 7 Norte, corner Av. Oaxaca, seven blocks into town from the *crucero.* The post office is open Mon.-Fri. 0800-1900, Saturday 0900-1300; the *telégrafo,* which has public fax (tel. 958-202-32), is open Mon.-Fri. 0900-1300 and 1500-1900, Saturday 0900-1200, Mon.-Fri. 0900-1300 and 1500-1700 for money orders.

Puerto Escondido area code is 958

More conveniently located on Pérez Gasga, a *larga distancia* offers both telephone and fax service, daily 0800-2300, tel./fax (958) 204-48, adjacent to the Restaurant Nautilus.

INFORMATION

Tourist Information Office
The friendly, well-informed *oficina de turismo,* tel. (958) 201-75, provides a very clear map which, besides an overall state highway map, has detailed maps of Puerto Escondido, Puerto Ángel, Bahías de Huatulco, and Oaxaca City and its environs. They are open Mon.-Fri. 0900-1400 and 1700-2000. Find it on Hwy. 200, in the little office on the beach side of the highway, corner of Av. Benito Juárez, in the Bachoco subdivision, a couple of blocks (westbound) past the Pemex gas station by the airport. The staff, especially the director Yvonne Alonso and her English-

speaking assistant Marco Antonio Zavala, are unusually conscientious and knowledgeable.

Hospital, Police, and Emergencies
For medical emergencies, go to the 24-hour Hospital Santa Fe, which has an internist, pediatrician, gynecologist, and a dental surgeon on call. For more routine consultations, office hours are Mon.-Fri. 0900-1400 and 1600-2000, Saturday 0900-1400. Find them three blocks west of the *crucero,* uphill from the highway on Calle 3 Poniente between Calles 2 and 3 Norte.

The government health clinic, **Centro de Salud,** is on Av. Pérez Gasga, just uphill from the Hotel Loren.

A couple of good tourist-zone pharmacies, including the 24-hour **Farmacia La Moderna,** tel. (958) 205-49, on Gasga a block below the *crucero,* and **Farmacia Cortés** (open 0800-1400 and 1700-2200), tel. (958) 201-12, on the Pérez Gasga mall, can fill prescriptions and supply many common over-the-counter remedies.

For **police** emergencies, call the municipal police at (958) 201-55, or go to the headquarters in the Agencia Municipal on Hwy. 200, about four blocks west of the Pérez Gasga *crucero.*

Publications
One of the few outlets of any English-language newspaper is the Abarrotes Lupita, on Pérez Gasga, outside the east-end chain. The *News* from Mexico City usually arrives around 1530. Pre-pay to assure yourself a copy. Sometimes they may have a few copies of popular magazines, such as *Time, Newsweek,* and *People.*

GETTING THERE AND AWAY

By Air
The small jetport, officially the **Aeropuerto Puerto Escondido** (code-designated PXM), is just off the highway a mile west of town. Only a plain waiting room with check-in desks, the airport has no services save a small snack bar. *Colectivos* to hotels in town run $2 per person. With a minimum of luggage, however, arrivees can walk a block to the highway and flag down a

local microbus to the town highway stop. Arrive with a hotel in mind, unless you prefer letting your taxi driver choose one, where he will probably collect a commission for depositing you there.

The international **departure tax** is $12 or its Mexican peso equivalent. If you lose your tourist card, avoid trouble or a fine by going to the *turismo* for help *before* your day of departure.

A few regularly scheduled airlines connect Puerto Escondido with other Mexican destinations.

Mexicana Airlines flights, tel. (958) 200-98, connect daily except Tuesday with Mexico City.

Aero Morelos flights (local agent, Turismo Rodimar, tel. 958-207-34 or 207-37) connect with Oaxaca daily and Huatulco four times a week.

If the above flights cannot take you where you want to go fast, try **Aerovega,** the dependable local air-taxi service. See Turismo Rodimar, on Gasga, near Bancomer, tel. (958) 207-34 or 207-37, for information and reservations.

Puerto Escondido is also accessible via the Puerto Ángel-Huatulco airport, one hour away by road. See "Getting There and Away" in the "Bahías de Huatulco" section following.

By Car or RV
National Hwy. 200, although sometimes winding, is generally smooth and uncongested between Puerto Escondido and **Acapulco,** 247 miles (398 km) to the west. Allow about eight hours' driving time. Regular gasoline is available at three or four towns along the way; Magna Sin is available in Pinotepa Nacional.

Traffic sails between Puerto Escondido and **Puerto Ángel,** 44 miles (71 km) apart, in an easy hour. Actually, Pochutla is immediately on the highway; Puerto Ángel is six miles downhill from the junction. **Santa Cruz de Huatulco** is an easy 22 miles (35 km) farther east.

To or from **Oaxaca City,** all-paved National Hwy. 175 connects at Pochutla junction with Hwy. 200 via its winding but spectacular 148-mile (238-km) route over the pine-clad Sierra Madre del Sur. The route, which rises 7,000 feet through Chatino and southern Zapotec Indian country, can be chilly in the winter, and has few services along the lonely 100-mile middle stretch. Take water and blankets, and be prepared for emergencies. Allow about eight hours from Puerto Escondido, seven hours the other way.

By Bus

Five long-distance bus lines serve Puerto Escondido; at least three of them offer first-class service. **Estrella Blanca** buses, at the station-lot on Av. Oaxaca just uphill from the *crucero,* tel. (958) 204-27, travel the Hwy. 200 Acapulco-Huatulco route. More than a dozen daily *salidas de paso* come through en route both ways between Acapulco and Pochutla and Huatulco (Crucecita). Other additional buses pass through, connecting with Mexico City via Acapulco.

Cristóbal Colón, another first-class bus line, corner of 2 Norte and 1 Oriente, about three blocks directly uphill from the *crucero,* tel. (958)210-73, covers the south coast, beginning in Puerto Escondido, connecting all the way to San Cristóbal las Casas in Chiapas. Intermediate destinations include Pochutla, Huatulco

(Crucecita), Salina Cruz, Tuxtla Gutiérrez (Chiapas), and Tapachula, at the Guatemala border. At Pochutla, passengers can transfer to Oaxaca-bound buses. One of these continues, via Puebla, to Mexico City.

The best-organized second-class bus line is **Autobuses Oaxaca-Istmo** on Hidalgo one block east of Av. Oaxaca, corner of 1 Oriente, tel. (958) 203-92. Several daily local departures connect Puerto Escondido with Oaxaca via Salina Cruz on the Isthmus of Tehuantepec. Intermediate destinations include Pochutla and Huatulco (Crucecita).

Camiones Oaxaca Pacífico and **Autobuses Estrella del Valle,** on Hidalgo, corner of 3 Oriente, tel. 202-50, provide more or less the same second-class service and cover the same Isthmus route as Autobuses Oaxaca-Istmo above.

Finally, for a real backcountry bus adventure, ride one of the scruffy red machines of **Autobuses Estrella Roja del Sureste** to Oaxaca. Traversing some of Mexico's most undeveloped mountain country via gravel Hwy. 131, they depart daily from the dusty lot at Calle 10 Norte and Av. Oaxaca, adjacent to the Mercado.

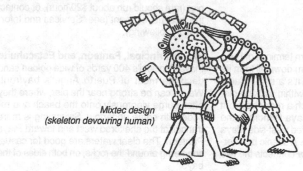

*Mixtec design
(skeleton devouring human)*

PUERTO ÁNGEL

During his presidency in the 1860s, Oaxaca-born Benito Juárez shaped many dreams into reality. One such dream was to better the lot of his Indian brethren in the isolated south of Oaxaca by developing a port for shipping the lumber and coffee they could harvest in the lush Pacific-slope jungles of the Sierra Madre del Sur. The small bay of Puerto Ángel, directly south of the state capital, was chosen, and by 1870 it had become Oaxaca's busiest port.

Unfortunately, Benito Juárez died a year later. New priorities and Puerto Ángel's isolation soon wilted Juárez's plan and Puerto Ángel lapsed into a generations-long slumber.

In the 1960s, Puerto Ángel was still a sleepy little spot connected by a single frail link—a tortuous cross-Sierra dirt road—to the rest of the country. Adventure travelers saw it at the far south of the map and dreamed of a south-seas paradise. They came and were not disappointed. Although that first tourist trickle has grown steadily, it's only enough to support the sprinkling of modest lodgings and restaurants that now dot the beaches and hillsides around Puerto Ángel's tranquil, little blue bay.

SIGHTS

Getting Oriented
Puerto Ángel is at the southern terminus of Hwy. 175, about six miles (nine km) downhill from its intersection with Hwy. 200. It's a small place, where nearly everything is within walking distance along the beach, which a rocky bayfront hill divides into two parts: **Playa Principal**, the main town beach, and sheltered west-side **Playa Panteón**, the tourist favorite. A scenic boulder-decorated shoreline *andador* connects the two beaches.

A paved road winds west from Playa Panteón along the coastline a couple of miles to **Playa Zipolite**, lined by a colony of rustic hammock-and-bamboo beachfront *cabañas,* popular with an international cadre of budget-minded seekers of heaven on earth. Continuing west,

the road passes former turtle-processing village beaches of **Playa San Agustín** and **Playa Matzunte**. From there it goes on another four miles, joining with Hwy. 200 at San Yisidro village at Km 198.

The major local service and transportation center is **Pochutla** (pop. 20,000), a mile north along Hwy. 175 from its Hwy. 200 junction.

Getting Around
Local buses run frequently between Pochutla and Puerto Ángel from about 0700-2100, stopping at the Hwy. 200 intersection. Some buses continue on to Zipolite and Matzunte from Boulevard Uribe, Puerto Ángel's main bayfront street. Also from Boulevard Uribe a local shuttle bus runs frequently to Zipolite, San Agustín, Matzunte and back about every half hour during daylight hours, stopping everywhere en route. Taxis also routinely make runs between Puerto Ángel and either Zipolite or Pochutla for about $3-4.

You can also get around by boat. Captains routinely take parties of up to eight for sightseeing, snorkeling, and picnicking to a number of nearby beaches. Bargain at the Puerto Ángel pier (rate should run about $20/hour), or contact the local travel agent (see "Services and Information" following).

Playas Principal, Panteón, and Estacahuite
Playa Principal's 400 yards of wide golden sand decorate most of Puerto Ángel's bayfront. Waves can be strong near the pier, where they often surge vigorously onto the beach and recede with some undertow. Swimming is more tranquil at the sheltered west end toward Playa Panteón. The clear waters are good for casual snorkeling around the rocks, on both sides of the bay.

Sheltered Playa Panteón is Puerto Ángel's sunning beach, lined with squadrons of beach chairs and umbrellas in front of beachside restaurants. **Playa Oso** ("Bear Beach") is a little dab of sand beside a rugged seastack of rock beyond Playa Panteón, fun to swim to or walk to

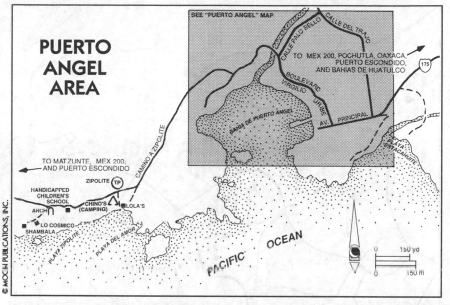

PUERTO ANGEL AREA

SEE "PUERTO ANGEL" MAP

TO MEX 200, POCHUTLA, OAXACA, PUERTO ESCONDIDO, AND BAHIAS DE HUATULCO

CALLE PALO BELLO

CALLE DEL TRAJO

BOULEVARD VIRGILIO URIBE

AV. PRINCIPAL

BAHIA DE PUERTO ANGEL

175

PLAYA ESTACAHUITE

CAMINO A ZIPOLITE

TO MATZUNTE, MEX 200, AND PUERTO ESCONDIDO

ZIPOLITE (TP)

HANDICAPPED CHILDREN'S SCHOOL

AHCH

CHINO'S (CAMPING)

LOLA'S

LO COSMICO SHAMBALA

PLAYA ZIPOLITE

PLAYA DEL AMOR

PACIFIC OCEAN

© MOON PUBLICATIONS, INC.

0   150 yd
0   150 m

from the road above the beach. Follow the uphill dirt road behind Restaurant Leyvis y Vicente about 200 yards to a blue metal gate. Go through, pass the house—if the occupants are there, ask if it's okay to pass—and carefully descend the steps and steep trail down to Playa Oso.

Playa Estacahuite, just outside the opposite (east) side of the bay, is actually two beaches in one: a pair of luscious coral-sand nooks teeming with fish grazing the living reef just offshore. (Don't put your hands in crevices. A moray eel may mistake your finger for a fish and bite.) A pair of *palapa* restaurants perched picturesquely above the beaches provide food and drinks. Get there in less than a mile by taxi or on foot via the dirt road that forks right off the highway. about 400 yards uphill from beachfront Boulevard Uribe.

Playa Zipolite

Playa Zipolite is a wide, mile-long strand of yellow-white sand enfolded by headlands and backed by palm groves. It stretches from the intimate little cove and beach of **Playa del Amor**

tucked on its east side to towering seacliffs rising behind the new-age Shambala retreat on the west end. The Playa Zipolite surf, although usually tranquil in the mornings (but always with significant undertow), can turn thunderous by the afternoon, especially when offshore storms magnify the swells. Experienced surfers love these times, when everyone but experts should stay out.

Good surfing notwithstanding, Zipolite's renown stems from its status as one of the very few (if not the only) nude beaches in Mexico. Bathing au naturel, practiced nearly entirely by visitors and a few local young men, is tolerated only grudgingly by local people, many of whose livelihoods depend on the nudists. If you're discreet and take off your clothes at the more isolated west end, no one will appear to mind (and women will avoid voyeuristic attentions of Mexican boys and men).

Visitors' nude sunbathing habits may have something to do with the gruffness of some local people. Many of them probably prefer their former occupations in turtle fishing rather than serving tourists, who often seem to be in short

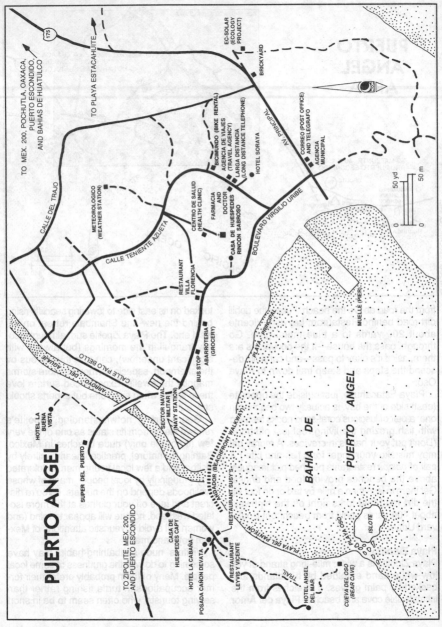

PUERTO ANGEL

TO MEX. 200, POCHUTLA, OAXACA, PUERTO ESCONDIDO, AND BAHIAS DE HUATULCO

175

TO PLAYA ESTACAHUITE

CALLE DEL TRAJO

METEOROLOGICO (WEATHER STATION)

CALLE TENIENTE AZUETA

CENTRO DE SALUD (HEALTH CLINIC)

FARMACIA AND DOCTOR

CASA DE HUESPEDES RINCON SABROSO

RESTAURANT VILLA FLORENCIA

BICIMUNDO (BIKE RENTAL)

AGENCIA DE VIAJES (TRAVEL AGENCY)

LARGA DISTANCIA (LONG DISTANCE TELEPHONE)

HOTEL SORAYA

EC-SOLAR (ECOLOGY PROJECT)

BRICKYARD

CORREO (POST OFFICE) AND TELEGRAFO

AGENCIA MUNICIPAL

AV. PRINCIPAL

BOULEVARD VIRGILIO URIBE

50 yd
50 m
0
0

PUERTO ANGEL

ARROYO DEL AGUAJE

CALLE PALO BELLO

BUS STOP

ABARROTERIA (GROCERY)

SECTOR NAVAL MILITAR (NAVY STATION)

MUELLE (PIER)

PLAYA PRINCIPAL

BAHIA DE PUERTO ANGEL

HOTEL LA BUENA VISTA

SUPER DEL PUERTO

ANDADOR (BEACHFRONT WALKWAY)

RESTAURANT SUSY'S

TO ZIPOLITE, MEX. 200, AND PUERTO ESCONDIDO

HOTEL LA CABAÑA

POSADA CAÑON DEVATA

CASA DE HUESPEDES CAPY

RESTAURANT LEVIS Y VICENTE

PLAYA DEL PANTEON

TRAIL

PLAYA OSO

ISLOTE

CUEVA DEL OSO (BEAR CAVE)

HOTEL ANGEL DEL MAR

© MOON PUBLICATIONS, INC.

supply compared to the battalion of beachfront *palapas* competing for their business.

Most Zipolite visitors stay in the palm-shaded trailer park or in one of the score of hammock-equipped stick-and-thatch beachfront *cabaña* hotels. Often with fans and outside cold-water showers and privies, *cabañas* rent for about $10 double per night. Although many are indifferently managed, some, such as Lola's, Lo Cosmico, and Shambala (see "Accommodations" below), are unique.

Playas San Agustín and Matzunte

About a mile west of Zipolite, a wide, mile-long, yellow-sand beach curves past the village of San Agustín. On the open ocean but partly protected by offshore rocks, its surf is much like that of Zipolite, varying from gentle to rough, depending mostly upon wind and offshore swells. Small village groceries and beachside *palapa* restaurants supply food and drinks to the occasional Zipolite overflow and local families on weekends and holidays. **Fishing** is excellent, either in the surf, from nearby rocks, by rented *panga*, or your own boat launched from the beach. Beach camping is customary, especially at a pull-in roadside *ramada* at the east, Zipolite, end of the beach.

Remnants of the local turtle industry can be found at the rusting former processing factories on Playa San Agustín (west end) and Playa Matzunte two miles farther west. The former turtle plant (follow the side road, east end of the beach) at Matzunte lives on as a turtle **aquarium, research center, and turtle hatchery.** Here, you can peruse displays illustrating the ongoing turtle research and conservation program, and see members of most of Mexico's turtle species, paddling in tanks overlooking the beach where their ancestors once swarmed. The center is open Tues.-Sat. 1000-1630, Sunday 1000-1430. For more information contact the Centro Mexicano de la Tortuga, P.O. Box 16, Puerto Ángel, Oaxaca 70902, tel. (958) 401-22.

The half-mile-long yellow-sand Matzunte Beach, like San Agustín, is semisheltered and varies from tranquil to rough. Fishing is likewise good, camping is customary (as a courtesy, ask if it's okay), and local stores and seafood *palapa* restaurants sell basic supplies and food.

ACCOMMODATIONS

Puerto Ángel Hotels: Around the Bay

Although none of Puerto Ángel's dozen-odd lodgings are directly on the beach, all except one are within a stone's throw of it. The successful ones have given their legion of savvy repeat customers what they want: clean, basic, cool-water accommodations in tranquil, television-free settings where Puerto Ángel's natural isolation and tropical charm set the tone for long, restful holidays.

Moving west around the bay from the pier, first comes the motel-style **Hotel Soraya**, perched on the bluff above Playa Principal, Priv. José Vasconcelos 2A, Puerto Ángel, Oaxaca 70902, tel. (958) 430-09. Well managed by a personable woman who is also the owner, the hotel includes a restaurant with an airy bay view, fine for bright morning breakfasts and sunset-glow dinners. Outside, two tiers of Spartan but light and comfortable rooms enclose a parking-patio. Although some rooms have a/c, the fan-only ones are generally better. Rent on the upper tier for more privacy. The 32 rooms rent for about $20 s, $22 d, $27 t, credit cards accepted.

Atop the adjacent hill is the **Casa de Huéspedes Rincón Sabroso**, Puerto Ángel, Oaxaca 70902, no phone, a labor of love of its family-owners. Here, guests enjoy lodgings that open onto a hammock-hung view breezeway adorned by luscious tropical greenery. Inside, rooms are very clean (but dark), with white walls, tile floors, shiny bathrooms, and natural wood furnishings. Guests have the additional option of good food and each other's company in a breezy cafe, perched above a heavenly bay and sunset panorama. Rates for the eight rooms run about $13 s, $18 d, and $23 t, with fans.

Another Puerto Ángel gem is **Hotel La Buena Vista**, P.O. Box 48, Puerto Ángel, Oaxaca 70902, tel./fax (958) 451-04, tucked on the hillside just west of the Arroyo del Aguaje. The hotel's four tiers stairstep artfully up the jungly slope, with guests in a number of rooms enjoying private hammocks and view balconies. Lower-level rooms open to shady view porches with hammocks. On the third level, a luxuriously airy restaurant *palapa* opens to a picture-perfect bay vista. The climax is a pair of large onyx-tile-floored fourth-floor rooms that share an entire private view patio with hammocks. All rooms are immaculate, light, and plainly but tastefully furnished, with spotless bathrooms. Rates for the approximately 20 rooms run about $20 s or d for standard, $25 s or d for room with private balcony, $30 for the top-floor room with double-size onyx bathtub; with fans, good restaurant, and (unusual for Puerto Ángel) hot water.

Heading around the curve of the bay to the Playa Panteón ("Cemetery") neighborhood, you'll find one of Puerto Ángel's best cheaper lodgings, **Casa de Huéspedes Capy**, Playa Panteón, P.O. Box 44, Puerto Ángel, Oaxaca 70902, tel. (958) 430-02, sitting on the bay-view hillside by the road fork to Zipolite. Rooms, in two tiers with views toward Playa Panteón, are basic but clean with fans and cool-water private baths. Good family management is the Capy's strong suit. This shows in the shady view restaurant, Arcely, where good food in a friendly atmosphere encourages guests to linger, reading or talking, for hours. The 10 rooms rent for about $7 s, $10 d.

The unusually well-kept **Hotel La Cabaña**, Playa Panteón, Calle Pedro Sainz de Barada, Puerto Ángel, Oaxaca 70902, tel. (958) 431-05, downhill, is just a few steps from Playa Panteón. Past the lobby is a verdant, plant-decorated patio, while upstairs, guests enjoy chairs and shady tables on a breezy bay-vista sundeck. Marble shines in the baths and the floors of the 23 comfortable, very clean rooms, some with private view balconies. Several beachfront restaurants are conveniently nearby. Rooms rent for about $18 s, $20 d, or $30 t; credit cards accepted.

Hidden in the leafy canyon a hundred yards uphill from the beach is **Posada Cañon Devata**, life-project of local ecological leaders Mateo and Suzanne López, P.O. Box 74, Pochutla, Oaxaca 70900, tel. (958) 430-48. Artists Mateo and Suzanne (he's Mexican, she's American) have become an example to local people, having reforested their originally denuded canyon property over a period of several years. They have gradually added on land, so their now-lush arroyo encompasses an entire watershed-ecosystem.

Their accommodations, a multiroom lodge and several luxury/rustic detached cabins, dot the slopes of their sylvan jungle retreat. All are comfortably furnished and thoughtfully decorated with handicrafts and Mateo's expressive primitivist oil paintings. Lodge rooms rent from $20, cabins $30, with fans and parking.

Their restaurant (see "Food" below) serves all-organic fruits and vegetables and whole-wheat bread and tortillas, while their gift shop, Sueños de Amusgo (see "Shopping" below), offers one-of-a-kind handicrafts, including many Amusgo Indian *huipiles* and a gallery of Mateo's paintings.

Atop the hill via the adjacent steep road, the **Hotel Ángel del Mar**, Puerto Ángel, Oaxaca 70902, tel. (958) 430-14 or 430-08, offers a sharply contrasting style of lodging. Rates for the 42 rooms run from $20 s, $25 d low-season; credit cards accepted. Guests enjoy a big open-air dining room, swimming pool, and large light rooms with private balconies looking down upon a panoramic bay vista. Mornings, guests can enjoy sunrise over the bay and evening sunsets over the ocean. Tired management, however, has unfortunately contributed to sometimes bad food, unresponsive desk staff, dusty halls, and rusty fixtures.

Zipolite Accommodations

Zipolite's line of rustic (bring your own towel and soap) lodgings starts at **Lola's** on the east end of the beach, Playa Zipolite, Puerto Ángel, Oaxaca 70902. The friendly, elderly owner continues her decades-long good management of her thatch-shaded restaurant and beach *cabañas*. For customers who hanker for a bit better lodging, Lola has broken new ground with Zipolite's first modern-standard units, eight new rooms with hot water and ceiling fans.

The scene at Lola's resembles a mini-resort, with the restaurant right on the beach, where guests enjoy late breakfasts, stroll out for swims, read thick novels, and kick back and enjoy convivial conversation with their mostly North American and European fellow vacationers. *Cabañas* rent for about $9 d with fan, shared showers and toilets, the more deluxe rooms, with private baths, for about $18.

The **Lo Cosmico** *cabañas* nestle on a cactus-dotted rocky knoll at the opposite end of the beach, Playa Zipolite, P.O. Box 37, Puerto

Ángel, Oaxaca 70902. White spheres perched on their thatched roof peaks lend a mystical Hindu-Buddhist accent to the *cabañas*' already picturesque appearance. In the restaurant on the rise you're likely to find Regula and Antonio Nadurille, Lo Cosmico's European-Mexican owners. Regula manages the restaurant, specializing in a dozen varieties of tasty crepes, while Antonio supervises the hotel. Their hillside and beach-level *cabañas* are clean, candle-lit, and equipped with hammocks and concrete floors. Showers and toilets are outside. *Cabañas* rent for about $5 per person.

Shambala, on the adjacent forested hillside, is as it sounds—a tranquil Buddhist-style retreat, Puerto Ángel, Playa Zipolite, Oaxaca 70902. Shambala's driving force is the friendly owner-community leader, Gloria Esperanza Johnson, who arrived in Zipolite by accident in 1970 and decided to stay, eventually adopting Mexican citizenship. She built the place from the ground up, gradually adding on until now about 50 primitive-rustic *cabañas*, a macrobiotic beach-view restaurant, and a spiritual center occupy her hilltop. Shambala is a quiet, alcohol-free haven for lovers of reading, sunbathing, hiking, yoga, and meditation. It sits atop an enviable few acres at the edge of a sylvan hinterland. Adjacent cactus-studded cliffs plummet spectacularly to surf-splashed rocks below, while trails fan out through lush tropical deciduous forest. The very simple candle-lit thatched concrete-floored *cabañas* with hammocks rent for about $5 per person. Toilets and showers are shared.

Gloria welcomes lovers of the outdoors to camp (about $2.50 per person, per day) in Shambala's get-away-from-it-all jungle "El Retiro" retreat, in a pristine mountain river valley about an hour away by car or local bus. For more information and directions, ask Gloria or her staff assistants.

Get to both Shambala and Lo Cosmico by turning from the main road onto the dirt driveway just west of the arch at Zipolite's west end. Bear right at the first fork, then left at the next for Lo Cosmico, right for Shambala.

Trailer Parks and Camping

The rustic **Zipolite Trailer Park** has about 20 parking (big rigs possible) or camping spaces

beneath a shady, tufted grove by the road at the east end of Playa Zipolite, Playa Zipolite, Puerto Ángel, Oaxaca 70902. A spirit of camaraderie often blooms among the tents and assorted RVs of travelers from as far away as the Klondike, Kalispell, and Khabarovsk. About $5 gets you a space for an RV, including a shower, toilet, electricity and satellite dish (if you have your own hookup). No sewer connections, however. Bottled drinking water is available in local stores.

If you prefer being nearer the beach, take a look at the very downscale **Trailer Park Chano,** Playa Zipolite, Puerto Ángel, Oaxaca 70902, by Lola's at Zipolite's east end. Chano, the friendly owner, offers about six spaces, a shower, and a toilet for vans, campers, or tents. Sorry, too cramped for big trailers or rigs. The tariff runs about $5 for RVs, including electricity, about $1 per person for tents.

One of Zipolite's best tenting spots is the forested hilltop behind **Shambala.** The friendly owner, Gloria Johnson, will probably allow you to use her showers and toilets for a small fee. Ask at the Shambala office first for permission to camp.

FOOD

Complete dinner price key: Budget: under $7; Moderate: $7-14; Expensive: more than $14.

For a small place, Puerto Ángel has good food, starting with the **Villa Florencia,** right on the main beachfront street. The Italian-born owner-chef specializes in antipasti, salads, and meat and seafood pastas. Like a good country Italian restaurant, service is crisp; presentations are attractive. Their modest wine list includes some good old-country imports, and the cappuccino is probably the best on the Costa Chica. Open daily 0800-2300. Moderate.

The unpretentiously elegant view *palapa*-restaurant at the **Hotel La Buena Vista,** tel. (958) 451-04 (see "Accommodations" above), is the best spot in town for a leisurely, intimate dinner. Here, the prodigious effort that owner/managers Lourdes and Carrie Díaz have invested in their kitchen and staff comes together beautifully. The servers, fetchingly attired in colorful Oaxaca *huipiles*, glide gracefully between kitchen and tables with a bounty of crisp salads, savory soups, tender pastas, and fresh broiled fish and meats. Moderate.

For a homey change of pace, get in on the family-style dinner at the macrobiotic restaurant at the **Posada Cañon Devata,** tel. (958) 430-48. Their fare is all fresh, organic, and high in vegetables and grains and low in meat. Reserve for the 1900 dinner by early afternoon. Moderate. (See "Accommodations" above for more info.)

Four or five restaurants line Playa Panteón. Here, the main attraction is the beach scene rather than the food. **Susy's** and **Leyvis y Vicente** seem to be the best of the bunch; fish will generally be the best choice; make sure it's fresh. Open seasonally about 0800-2100. Moderate.

Zipolite also has some good eating places. For hearty macrobiotic-style fare and a breezy beach view, go to the restauraurant at **Shambala** (see "Accommodations" above) at the west end of Playa Zipolite. Personable owner Gloria Johnson runs a very tidy kitchen, which serves good breakfasts, soups, salads, and sandwiches. Open daily 0800-2000. No alcohol. Budget to Moderate.

Regula, the European co-owner of **Lo Cosmico** on the knoll just east of Shambala, cooks from a similar macrobiotic-style menu, although she specializes in several variations of crepes, including egg, meat, cheese, and vegetable. Open daily from around 0800 to about 1900.

ENTERTAINMENT AND SPORTS

Puerto Ángel's entertainments are mostly spontaneous. If anything exciting is going to happen, it will most likely be on the beachfront Boulevard Uribe where people tend to congregate during the afternoon and evenings. A small crowd may accumulate in the adjacent restaurant Villa Florencia for talk, TV, coffee, or something from the bar.

Sunset-watchers get their best chance from the unobstructed hill perch of the **Hotel Ángel del Mar,** where the bar and restaurant can provide something to enliven the occasion if clouds happen to block the view.

The same spot sometimes provides music for dancing at their discotheque during the highest seasons, most likely between Christmas and New Year and the week before Easter.

Another spot for good company around sunset time is **El Cielo,** Posada Cañon Devata's canyon-side view perch (see "Accommodations" above). Owners Mateo and Suzanne López invite guests and visitors to join them around sunset time (1700-1900) for snacks and liquid refreshments.

For additional diversions, head to Puerto Escondido, about an hour west by car, for more and livelier entertainments. See the previous section.

Bicycling and Jogging
Mountain bike rentals (about $6/day) have come to Puerto Ángel, at **Bicimundo,** the downscale little shop (follow signs) uphill on Azueta past the *farmacia.* A fun option would be to pack a lunch and ride out to the turtle museum in

Puerto Ángel children use hand power when necessary.

BRUCE WHIPPERMAN

Matzunte. Traffic is light and the only serious grade is just west of Puerto Ángel. Figure around four hours for the entire 15-mile outing.

"Holey" streets, rocky roads, and lack of grass sharply curtail Puerto Ángel jogging prospects. The highway, however, which runs gradually uphill from near the pier, does provide a continuous, more or less smooth surface. Confine your jogging, however, to early morning or late afternoon, and take water.

Swimming and Surfing

Swimming provides more local exercise opportunities, especially in the sheltered waters off of Playa Panteón. Bodysurfing, boogie-boarding, and surfing are rewarding, depending on wind and swells, off Playa Zipolite. Be careful of undertow, which is always a threat, even on calm days at Zipolite. If you're inexperienced, don't go out alone. Alcohol and surf, moreover, don't mix. On rough days, unless you're an expert, forget it. Bring your own board; few, if any, rentals are available.

Sailing and Windsurfing

If you have your own carryable boat or windsurfing gear, sheltered Playa Panteón would be a good place to put it into the water, although the neighboring headland may decrease the available wind. Calm mornings at Playas Zipolite, San Agustin, or Matzunte (see above), with more wind but rougher waves, might also be fruitful.

Snorkeling and Scuba Diving

Rocky shoals at the edges of Puerto Ángel Bay are good for casual snorkeling. Playa Estacahuite (see above), on the open ocean just beyond the bay's east headland, is even better. Best bring your own equipment. If you don't, you can rent a snorkel and mask from Vicente, at his restaurant, Leyvis y Vicente, on Playa Panteón, for about $3 an hour.

Vicente likewise takes experienced scuba divers to local sites for about $40 per person for a one-tank dive, basic equipment furnished.

Beginners who want to learn diving contact the well-equipped and certified dive instructors of **Buceos Triton** dive shop 45 minutes' drive south in Santa Cruz de Huatulco. (See "Sports" in the following "Bahías de Huatulco" section.)

Fishing

The bayfront pier is the best place to bargain for a boat and captain to take you and your friends out on a fishing excursion. Prices depend on season, but you can figure on paying about $20 an hour for a boat for four or five persons with bait and two or three good rods and reels. During a three-hour outing a few miles offshore, a competently captained boat will typically bring in three or four big, good-eating *róbalo* (snook), *huachinango* (snapper), *atún* (tuna), or pompano. If you're uncertain about what's biting, go down to the dock around 1400 or 1500 in the afternoon and see what the boats are bringing in.

Vicente, of Leyvis y Vicente restaurant on Playa Panteón, takes out fishing parties of up to six persons for around $20 an hour, bait and tackle included. You can also arrange fishing trips through the **Gambusino Travel Agency,** tel. (958) 430-80, open Mon.-Sat. 0900-1400 and 1600-2000, in the office across the street from the doctor and pharmacy on Av. Teniente Azueta, just uphill from Uribe.

SHOPPING

Market

The biggest local market spreads along the Pochutla main street, Hwy. 175, about seven miles from Puerto Ángel, one mile inland from the Hwy. 200 junction. Mostly a place for looking rather than buying, throngs of vendors from the hills line the sidewalks, even crowding into the streets, to sell their piles of onions, mangoes, forest herbs, carrots, cilantro, and jicama.

Groceries

The best-stocked Puerto Ángel local store is the **supermarket** at the west end of beachfront street Uribe, uphill past the arroyo bridge. Also, little-bit-of-everything store **Mar Alex,** with branches in both Zipolite and on Uribe in the middle of Puerto Ángel, sells cheese, milk, bread, some vegetables, and other essentials.

Handicrafts

Sueños ("Dreams") **de Amusgos,** at Posada Cañon Devata (see "Accommodations" above), is one of the Costa Chica's most interesting handicrafts shops. Owners Suzanne and Mateo

López have assembled a quality collection of Amusgo, Mixtec, and Chatino Indian crafts, including many fine hand-crocheted *huipiles* from San Pedro de Amusgos.

SERVICES AND INFORMATION

Money Exchange
Bancomer in the center of Pochutla, corner main street Lázaro Cárdenas and Av. 3A Norte, tel. (958) 400-63, changes U.S. dollar traveler's checks and Canadian cash Mon.-Fri. 0900-2200. Call to confirm hours.

Communication and a Travel Agent
The Puerto Ángel *correo* and *telecomunicaciones* stand side by side with the Agencia Municipal at the foot of Hwy. 175. Both are open Mon.-Fri. 0900-1500.

Puerto Ángel area code is 958

The Puerto Ángel *larga distancia* telephone and fax office (tel. 958-430-46 or 430-54, fax 430-38) is on Av. Teniente Azueta, just uphill from Uribe. Hours are daily 0700-2200.

Puerto Ángel's travel agent, **Agencia de Viajes Gambusino,** tel. (958) 430-80, arranges tours and fishing trips and sells reserved air and bus tickets at the small office on Azueta next door, uphill from the *larga distancia.*

Medical and Police
Puerto Ángel's respected private **doctor,** Dr. Constancio A. Juárez, holds consultation hours (Mon.-Sat. 0700-1400 and 1700-2100) and also runs the pharmacy on Av. Teniente Azueta across from the *larga distancia.* For serious illness or a diagnostic specialist, Dr. Juárez recommends you go to the government hospitals in Pochutla or Crucecita.

Another option is to go to the small government **Centro del Salud** (health clinic, which concentrates on preventive medicine) on the hill behind the church. Go up Azueta a long curving block, go left at the first corner, and continue another block to the health center.

For **police emergencies,** ask your hotel or the *larga distancia* (see above) to call the *policía preventiva* in Pochutla.

Ecological Projects
Community leaders, such as Suzanne and Mateo López, owners of Posada Cañon Devata, and Gloria Esperanza Johnson, owner of Shambala in Zipolite, are trying to awaken local awareness of ecological issues. Suzanne and Mateo, by restoring their entire canyon ecosystem property, and Gloria, by spearheading efforts to prevent the deforestation of coastal lands, hope to serve as examples of the benefits that simple efforts can yield.

In parallel but separate action, **EC-Solar,** the semiprivate ecological "Peace Corps," works with local *campesinos* to build environmentally appropriate solutions to village sewage, water, health, and agricultural problems.

GETTING THERE AND AWAY

By Air
Scheduled flights to Mexican destinations connect daily with airports at **Huatulco,** 19 miles (30 km), or **Puerto Escondido,** 44 miles (71 km) by road from Puerto Ángel. For details see "Getting There and Away" in the "Puerto Escondido" and "Bahías de Huatulco" sections of this chapter.

By Car or RV
Good roads connect Puerto Ángel to the west with Puerto Escondido and Acapulco, north with Oaxaca, and east with the Bahías de Huatulco and Tehuantepec.

Highway 200 connects westward with Puerto Escondido in an easy 44 miles (71 km), continuing to Acapulco in an additional seven hours (247 miles, 398 km) of driving. In the opposite direction Bahías de Huatulco (actually Crucecita) is a quick 22 miles (35 km). The continuation to Tehuantepec stretches another 92 miles (148 km), or around two additional hours' driving time.

To **Oaxaca** north, paved but narrow and winding National Hwy. 175 connects 148 miles (238 km) over the Sierra Madre del Sur from its junction with Hwy. 200 at Pochutla. The road climbs to around 9,000 feet through cool (chilly in winter) pine forests and hardscrabble Chatino and Zapotec Indian villages. Fill up with gas in Pochutla. Magna Sin unleaded is available at both the Pochutla Pemex stations, both on through-town Hwy. 175: about 300 yards toward town from Hwy. 200, and on the north, uphill, edge of town. Carry water and blankets, and be prepared for emergencies. The first gas station and services are in Miahuatlán, 90 miles north. Allow about seven driving hours from Puerto Ángel to Oaxaca, about six in the opposite direction.

By Bus

A number of first- and second-class bus lines in Pochutla connect to points north, east, and west. The three separate stations cluster less than a mile from the Hwy. 200 junction along Av. Lázaro Cárdenas, the Hwy. 175 main street into Pochutla (before the town center near the taxi stand).

Many first-class **Estrella Blanca** buses at L. Cárdenas 94, tel. (958) 403-80 connect daily with Puerto Escondido, continuing to Acapul-

co. They also connect east (more than a dozen per day) with Bahías de Huatulco destinations of Crucecita and Santa Cruz de Huatulco. One "plus" (say "ploos") luxury-class bus connects daily, all the way to Mexico City.

All first-class **Cristóbal Colón** buses (L. Cárdenas 84, tel. 958-402-03) connect east with Crucecita (several per day). One bus per day connects with Tehuantepec, continuing to Tuxtla Gutiérrez in Chiapas and Tapachula, at the Guatemala border. Three buses connect north with Oaxaca via Tehuantepec; one bus daily connects with Puebla and Mexico City. Two buses connect daily west with Puerto Escondido.

Frequent second-class service (station in the same vicinity) is offered by **Autobuses Estrella del Valle** (tel. 958-403-49) and **Autobuses Oaxaca Pacífico** (tel. 958-401-38), connecting with Oaxaca, Crucecita, Puerto Ángel, and Puerto Escondido.

BAHÍAS DE HUATULCO

The nine azure Bays of Huatulco decorate a couple of dozen miles of acacia-plumed rocky coastline east of Puerto Ángel. Between the bays, the ocean joins in battle with jutting, rocky headlands, while in their inner reaches the ocean calms, caressing diminutive crescents of coral sand. Inland, a thick hardwood forest seems to stretch in a continuous carpet to the Sierra.

Ecologists shiver when they hear these bays are going to be developed. FONATUR, the government tourism development agency, says however, it has a plan. Relatively few (but all upscale) hotels will occupy the beaches; other development will be confined to a few inland centers. The remaining 70% of the land will be kept as pristine ecological zones and study areas.

Although this story sounds sadly familiar, FONATUR, which developed Ixtapa and Cancún, seems to have learned from its experience. Up-to-date sewage treatment is being installed *ahead of time;* logging and homesteading have been reversed, and soldiers patrol the beaches, stopping turtle poachers. If all goes according to the plan, the nine Bahías de Huatulco and their 100,000-acre forest hinterland will be both a

tourist and ecological paradise, in addition to employing thousands of local people, when complete in 2020. If this Huatulco dream ends as well as it has started, Mexico should take pride while the rest of the world should take heed.

HISTORY

Long before Columbus, the Huatulco area was well-known to the Aztecs and their predecessors. The name itself, from Aztec words meaning "land where a tree is worshipped," reflects one of Mexico's most intriguing legends—of the Holy Cross of Huatulco.

When the Spanish arrived on the Huatulco coast, the local Indians showed them a huge cross they worshipped at the edge of the sea. A contemporary chronicler, Ignacio Burgoa, conjectured the cross had been left by an ancient saint—maybe even the Apostle Thomas—some 15 centuries earlier. Such speculation notwithstanding, the cross remained as the Spanish colonized the area and established headquarters and a port, which they named San Agustín, at the westernmost of the Bays of Huatulco.

Spanish ports and their treasure-laden galleons from the Orient attracted foreign corsairs—Francis Drake in 1579 and Thomas Cavendish in 1587. Cavendish arrived at the bay now called Bahía Santa Cruz, where he saw the cross the Indians were worshiping. Believing it was the work of the devil, Cavendish and his men tried to chop, saw, and burn it down. Failing at all of these, Cavendish looped his ship's mooring ropes around the cross and with sails unfurled tried using the force of the wind to pull it down. Frustrated, he finally sailed away, leaving the cross of Huatulco still standing beside the shore.

In 1612, Bishop Juan de Cervantes managed to bring the cross (or a part of it) to the cathedral in Oaxaca. With a piece cut from that, he made a copy of the original, which the faithful still venerate at the main altar on each Friday of Lent.

SIGHTS

Getting Oriented

With no road to the outside world, the Bahías de Huatulco remained virtually uninhabited and undeveloped until 1982, when coastal Hwy. 200 was pushed through. A few years later, Huatulco's planned initial kernel of infrastructure was complete, centering on the brand-new residential-service town, Crucecita (pop. 10,000), and nearby Santa Cruz de Huatulco boat harbor and hotel village on Bahía Santa Cruz.

The Bays of Huatulco embellish the coastline both east and west of Santa Cruz. To the east, a paved road links Bahías Chahue, Tangolunda, and Conejos. To the west lie Bahías El Organo, El Maguey, and Cacaluta, all road-accessible from Santa Cruz. Isolated farther west are Bahías Chachacual and San Agustín, with no road from Santa Cruz (although a good dirt

BAHIAS DE HUATULCO

TO SANTA MARIA HUATULCO

TO TEHUANTEPEC, OAXACA, CHIAPAS, AND GUATEMALA

RIO COPALITA

200

TO PUERTO ANGEL, OAXACA, AND PUERTO ESCONDIDO

200

CAMPO DE GOLF (GOLF COURSE)

HOLIDAY INN

PUBLIC BEACH ACCESS

HOTEL SHERATON

HOTEL ROYAL MAEVA

MAGALLITOS

BAHIA CONEJOS

PLAYA ARENA

CRUCECITA

MANGOS TP

HOTEL CLUB MED

OMNI ZAASHILA RESORT

BAHIA TANGOLUNDA

SANTA CRUZ DE HUATULCO (BOAT HARBOR)

BAHIA CHAHUE

BAHIA SANTA CRUZ

PLAYA LA ENTREGA

RIO SAN AGUSTIN

RIO CACALUTA

BAHIA EL ORGANO

BAHIA EL MAGUEY

BAHIA CACALUTA

PACIFIC OCEAN

BAHIA CHACHACUAL

SAN AGUSTIN

BAHIA SAN AGUSTIN

0   2 mi

0   2 km

© MOON PUBLICATIONS, INC.

road runs to San Agustín from Hwy. 200 near the airport.

Besides Bahía Santa Cruz, the only other bay of Huatulco that has been extensively developed is Tangolunda, five miles east. Its golf course, small restaurant-shopping complex, and five resort hotels (Club Med, Sheraton, Club Maeva, Holiday Inn, and Omni Zaashila) have all been fully operational since the early 1990s.

Getting Around

Frequent public **minibuses** connect Crucecita and Bahías Santa Cruz, Chahue, and Tangolunda. Taxis make the same trips for about $3 by day, $4 at night. No public transportation is available to the other bays. Taxi drivers might take you for a look at west-side bays El Organo, El Maguey, and Cacalute for about $25 roundtrip from Crucecita or Tangolunda, perhaps $5 to Bahía Conejos.

For an extended day-trip to all eight road-accessible bays, figure on $50 for either a taxi or a rental car. Call Dollar at the Sheraton, tel. (958) 100-38, ext. 787; National, in Tangolunda, tel. (958) 102-92; or Budget in Crucecita at Octillo and Jazmín, tel. (958) 700-34 or 700-10.

Another option is to go by boat. The local boat cooperative (Sociedad Cooperativa Turístico Tangolunda) runs a daily excursion—around 1030, $20 per person, kids half price—to all nine bays. Included are free hotel pickup, open bar, bilingual guide, and snacks; snorkeling is $8 extra. Reserve directly through their dock office, tel. (958) 700-81, or through a travel agent (see "Services" below).

The same cooperative also rents entire boats for up to 10 people. Full day excursions run about $120, while drop-off runs to the nearest beach are about $10; to the more remote, around $30.

Local travel agents (see "Services" below) offer other tour options: several hours of sunning, swimming, picnicking, and snorkeling at a couple of Bahías de Huatulco beaches runs around $20 per person. Trips to Puerto Ángel, Puerto Escondido, and wildlife-rich lagoons go for $40-60 per person.

Crucecita and Santa Cruz

Despite its newness **Crucecita** ("Little Cross," pop. 10,000) resembles a traditional Mexican town, with life revolving around a central plaza and market nearby. Crucecita is where the people who work in the Huatulco hotels, businesses, and government offices live. Although pleasant enough for a walk around the square and a meal in a restaurant, it's nothing special—mostly a place whose modest hotels and restaurants accommodate business travelers and weekenders who can't afford the plush hotels near the beach.

The two deluxe hotels and the few travel-oriented businesses of **Santa Cruz de Huatulco** (on Bahía Santa Cruz about two miles from Crucecita) cluster near the boat harbor. Fishing and tour boats come and go; vacationers sun themselves on the tranquil yellow-sand **Playa Santa Cruz** (beyond the restaurants adjacent to the boat harbor), while T-shirt and fruit vendors and boatmen hang around the quay watching for prospective customers. After the sun goes down, tourists quit the beach for their hotels, workers return to their homes in Crucecita, leaving the harbor and streets empty and dark.

Exploring the Bays of Huatulco

Isolation has left the Huatulco waters blue and unpolluted, the beaches white and clean. Generally, the bays are similar: deciduous (green July-Feb.) forested rocky headlands enclosing generally steep, soft yellow-coral sand crescents. The water is clear and good for snorkeling, scuba diving, sailing, kayaking, and windsurfing during the often-calm weather. Beaches, however, are typically steep, causing waves to break quickly near the sand, unsuitable for body-surfing, boogie-boarding, or surfing.

The six undeveloped Huatulco bays have neither water nor much shade, since they're so pristine that even coconut palms haven't gotten around to sprouting there. When exploring, bring food, drinks, hats, sunscreen, and mosquito repellent. When camping (which is permitted everywhere except Tangolunda) bring everything.

East Side: Chahue, Tangolunda, And Conejos

Bahía Chahue, about a mile from Santa Cruz, is wide, blue, and forest-tufted, with a steep yellow dune growing to a huge pile that stretches to

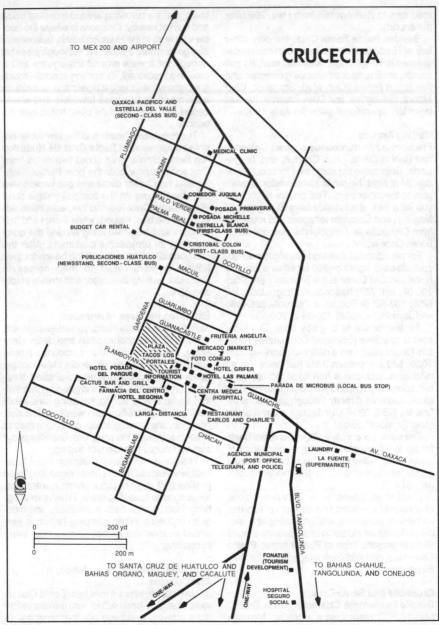

CRUCECITA

TO MEX 200 AND AIRPORT

PLUMBAGO

JAZMIN

MEDICAL CLINIC

OAXACA PACIFICO AND
ESTRELLA DEL VALLE
(SECOND - CLASS BUS)

COMEDOR JUQUILA

PALO VERDE

PALMA REAL

POSADA PRIMAVERA

POSADA MICHELLE

ESTRELLA BLANCA
(FIRST-CLASS BUS)

BUDGET CAR RENTAL

CRISTOBAL COLON
(FIRST - CLASS BUS)

PUBLICACIONES HUATULCO
(NEWSSTAND, SECOND - CLASS BUS)

MACUIL

OCOTILLO

GUARUMBO

GARDENIA

GUANACASTLE

FRUTERIA ANGELITA

FLAMBOYAN

PLAZA
TACOS LOS
PORTALES

MERCADO (MARKET)

FOTO CONEJO

HOTEL POSADA
DEL PARQUE

TOURIST
INFORMATION

HOTEL GRIFER

HOTEL LAS PALMAS

CACTUS BAR AND GRILL

FARMACIA DEL CENTRO

HOTEL BEGONIA

PARADA DE MICROBUS (LOCAL BUS STOP)

CENTRA MEDICA
(HOSPITAL)

GUAMACHIL

LARGA - DISTANCIA

RESTAURANT
CARLOS AND CHARLIE'S

COCOTILLO

CHACAH

BUGAMBILIAS

AGENCIA MUNICIPAL
(POST OFFICE,
TELEGRAPH, AND POLICE)

LAUNDRY

LA FUENTE
(SUPERMARKET)

AV. OAXACA

BLVD. TANGOLUNDA

0   200 yd

0   200 m

FONATUR
(TOURISM
DEVELOPMENT)

TO SANTA CRUZ DE HUATULCO AND
BAHIAS ORGANO, MAGUEY, AND CACALUTE

ONE-WAY

ONE-WAY

HOSPITAL
SEGURO
SOCIAL

TO BAHIAS CHAHUE,
TANGOLUNDA, AND CONEJOS

© MOON PUBLICATIONS, INC.

the marina jetty at the east end. Chahue is uncrowded even on weekends and holidays and nearly empty the rest of the time.

About four miles farther east is the breezy and broad **Bahía Tangolunda**. Although hotels front much of the beach, a signed "Playa Pública" public access road borders the western edge of the golf course (turn right just past the creek bridge). Except for its east end, the Tangolunda beach is steep and the waves break quickly right at the sand. *Palapa* restaurants at the beach serve food and drinks; or if you prefer, stroll a quarter mile for refreshments at the luxurious poolside beach clubs of the Sheraton and Club Maeva resorts.

Over the headland about two miles farther, **Punta Arena** ("Sand Point"), a forested thumb of land, juts out into wide **Bahía Conejos**. Three separate steep beaches spread along the inner shoreline. The main entrance road arrives at high-duned Playa Punta Arena. Playa Tejoncito ("Little Badger") is beyond the rocks for to the right; Playa Conejos ("Rabbits") is to the left on the other side of Punta Arena. A few palm-front *ramadas* for shade and a saltwater flush toilet lavatory occupy the Playa Punta Arena dune. Trees behind the dunes provide a few shady spots for RV or tent campers. A stables (see "Sports" below) takes visitors on horseback rides along a trail that heads east from there.

Beyond tiny **Magallitos** fishing village, less than a mile farther on, a long, broad, beach with oft-powerful surfing rollers (novices beware) stretches for at least a mile east. Beach *palapas* serve drinks and very fresh seafood. A lagoon behind the village (bring your kayak) appears ripe for wildlife viewing.

After Magallitos, the road bends inland, paralleling the **Río Copalito** wildlife sanctuary, perfect for adventure-exploring. José Assencac, owner of Hotel Posada Michelle, leads groups on a **"Tour Ecológico"** along the riverbank. Included are dugout canoeing, wildlife-viewing, swimming in the river, and a mud bath at José's family ranch across the river. The all-day tour costs $25 per person, drinks and transportation included; information and reservations at Posada Michelle, tel. (958) 705-35 (see "Accommodations" below).

West Side:
Playa Entrega and Bahías El Organo, El Maguey, Cacaluta, and San Agustín
Playa Entrega is a little dab of sand slipped into the west side of Bahía Santa Cruz. It is the infamous spot where, on 20 January 1831, Vicente Guerrero, president and Independence hero, was brought ashore in custody of archvillain Francisco Picaluga and sent to be murdered in Oaxaca a few months later.

Quarter-mile-long Playa Entrega is the ideal Sunday beach, with calm, clear water and clean yellow sand. Swimming, kayaking, and often snorkeling, sailing, and windsurfing possibilities are excellent. Some trees provide shady spots for tenting and RV camping. No facilities exist except for seasonal and holiday food and drink stands.

Get there via the main street, Bulevar Benito Juárez, which passes the Santa Cruz boat harbor. Continue west, bearing left, at the "Y," at the Hotel Binnoguendo (mark your odometer) on the right. After a few hundred yards, the road curves left and winds uphill, past panoramic viewpoints of Bahía Santa Cruz. Follow the signs and you'll soon be at Playa Entrega.

If, instead of curving left to La Entrega, you follow the rough dirt road that forks right at the same spot, you'll be headed for the Bahías El Organo, El Maguey, and Cacaluta. The roads to these bays have deteriorated in recent years. Until authorities get around to paving them, land access may only be achievable by experienced drivers, preferably in maneuverable, high-clearance vehicles. If in doubt, hire a taxi, or take the boat tour described above in "Getting Around."

El Organo is first; after about half a mile along the dirt road, look for a rough dirt track angling sharply left. The beach is isolated, intimate, and enfolded by rocky shoals on both sides. Some trees behind the dune provide shade.

Continuing straight ahead, the road forks again (about 1.3 miles from the hotel). Continue straight ahead downhill to El Maguey, or fork sharply right to Cacaluta. The sandy crescent of **El Maguey** is bordered by tidepools tucked beneath forested headlands. Facing a protected fjordlike channel, the Maguey beach is virtually waveless and fine for swimming, snorkeling, diving, windsurfing, and sailing. It would be a snap to launch a boat here for fishing in the bay. During weekends and holidays, picnickers arrive and banana towboats and *aguamotos* (mini-motorboats) buzz the beach and bay. Although camping is possible, room is limited.

Bahía Cacaluta, two miles past the El Maguey fork, spreads along a mile-long, heart-shaped beach, beckoningly close to a cactus-studded offshore islet. Swimmers beware, for waves break powerfully, surging upward and receding with strong undertow. Many shells—limpets and purple- and brown-daubed clams—speckle the beach. Surf fishing prospects, either from the beach itself or from rocks on either end, appear excellent. Although the sand directly behind the beach is too soft for vehicles, space exists farther back for RV parking and camping. Tenters could have their pick anywhere along the dune.

Bahía Chachacual, past the Río Cacaluta about four miles farther west, is a sand-edged azure nook accessible only via forest trails.

Bahía San Agustín, by contrast, is well known and easily reachable (taxi $5) by the good dirt road just across the highway from the fork to Santa María Huatulco (at Km 236, a mile west of the airport). After about seven miles along a firm track, accessible by all but the bulkiest RVs, bear right to the modest village of *palapas* at the bay's sheltered west end. From there, the beach stretches eastward along a mile of forest-backed dune. Besides good swimming, sailing, windsurfing, shell-collecting, and fishing prospects, San Agustín has a number of behind-the-dune spots (follow the left fork shortly before the road's end) for RV and tent camping. Beachside *palapas* can, at least, supply seafood and drinks and maybe some basic groceries.

ACCOMMODATIONS

In Huatulco, as in other resorts, hotels on the beach are the most expensive. Crucecita's hotels are cheapest, Tangolunda's are most expensive, and the Santa Cruz hotels are in between.

Most of the **Crucecita** lodgings are near the central plaza. The **Grifer,** at Guamachil and Carrizal, would be nothing special in most resorts of Pacific Mexico, but in hotel-poor Huatulco, it is often full, P.O. Box 159, Crucecita, Oaxaca 70980, tel. (958) 700-48. Three tiers of nondescript modern rooms enclose a TV-dominated atrium; a passable street-level restaurant is convenient for breakfast. The 16 rooms rent for about $25 s or d, with ceiling fans; no credit cards.

Across Guamachil in mid-block, the **Hotel Las Palmas,** Calle Guamachil 15, Crucecita, Oaxaca 70980, tel. (958) 700-60, offers small, plain but clean a/c rooms on the two floors above its good street-level restaurant (see "Food" below). The eight rooms rent for about $23 s or d, $30 t; only Mexican credit cards are accepted.

The **Hotel Suites Begonias,** at the southeast plaza corner, offers a more deluxe, family-run alternative, Bugambilias 503, P.O. Box 289, Crucecita, Oaxaca 70980, tel. (958) 703-90 or 700-18. The rooms, although clean and comfortable, have motel-style walkways passing their windows, decreasing privacy. Rates for the 13 rooms run about $22 s, $25 d, $33 t, with fan and TV; credit cards are accepted.

Half a block away, you might consider taking one of the relatively attractive rooms on the very top floor of the **Hotel Posada del Parque,** Flamboyan 16, Crucecita, Oaxaca 70980, tel. (958) 702-19, on the south side of the plaza. Although not especially large, the top-floor rooms have high rustic beamed ceilings, window views, and surround a cheery inner balcony-corridor. An airy sidewalk cafe downstairs serves breakfast, lunch, and dinner. All 14 rooms rent for about $23 s or d with TV and a/c; $20 with fan only, no TV.

A pair of simple but attractive *posadas* near the bus stations on Gardenia, north of the plaza, offer another option. The **Hotel Posada Michelle,** Gardenia 8, Crucecita, Oaxaca 70980, tel./fax (958) 705-35, run by friendly eco-tour guide José Aussenac has nine smallish but clean and comfortable rooms with big beds, baths, and good satellite TV. Although the rooms are dark because of their half-mirrored windows (for privacy), they do have white walls and open to a light, airy second-story walkway that leads to a pleasant, hammock-hung and shady view porch. High season rates run about $25 s, $28 d, $30 t; $20, $23, and $25 low, with both a/c and fans.

Posada Primavera, just around the corner, at Palo Verde 5, Crucecita, Oaxaca 70980, tel. (958) 711-67, offers six simply furnished but clean, light, high-ceilinged upstairs rooms with bath. Windows look out onto the palmy, bougainvillea-adorned surrounding neighborhood. Rates are about $25 s or d high season, $18 low, with fans and cool water only.

Santa Cruz Hotels
A block from the beach in Santa Cruz, first choice goes to the **Hotel Binneguenda,** Benito Juárez 5, Santa Cruz de Huatulco, Oaxaca 70900, tel. (958) 700-77, fax 702-84. Neocolonial arches, pastel stucco walls, and copper and ceramics handicrafts decorate the interiors, while in the adjacent leafy patio, guests sun themselves around the pool. In the restaurant, the customers seem as well fed and satisfied as the waiters are well trained and attentive. Upstairs, the colonial/modern-decor rooms are spacious, comfortable, and equipped with phones, TV, and a/c. Rates for the 75 rooms run about $50 s or d, $60 t, with parking; credit cards accepted.

Hotel Castillo Huatulco, Benito Juárez, P.O. Box 354, Santa Cruz de Huatulco 70980, tel. (958) 701-26 or 02-51, fax 701-31, down the street a couple of blocks amounts to a poor second choice, unless you can get in for prices substantially less than the Binneguenda. Loosely managed and often noisy, with recorded salsa music often thumping away in the bar, its 106 rooms, although comfortable, are crowded into a smaller space than the Binneguenda's 75. They are nevertheless popular with families on weekends and holidays but nearly empty (and perhaps bargainable) during quieter seasons. High-season rates run from $65 s or d, $75 t, with phones, TV, a/c, pool, and parking; credit cards accepted.

Tangolunda Luxury Resorts
Five luxury resort hotels spread along the Tangolunda shoreline. The Club Med dominates the sheltered western side-bay, with four stacked towers that make the place appear as a big ocean liner. The smaller Sheraton and Club

Royal Maeva stand side by side on the bay's inner recess next to the golf course. The Omni Zaashila spreads gracefully to its east end cove, while the hot-pink Holiday Inn stairsteps up the hillside, away from the beach.

The emphasis of all five resorts is on facilities, such as multiple pools, bars, and restaurants, full wheelchair access, music, discos, shows, and sports such as tennis, golf, sailing, kayaking, windsurfing, snorkeling, diving, and swimming. Other amenities may include shops, baby-sitting, children's clubs, and arts and crafts instruction.

In contrast to the Sheraton and the Zaashila, which operate in usual hotel style, the rates at the Maeva, Club Med, and Holiday Inn include everything—all food, sports, lessons, and entertainment. Their cuisine, although tasty and bountiful, is not fancy. The atmosphere resembles a big upscale summer camp, with hosts of options, even for those who want to do nothing.

The **Sheraton Huatulco** is a generic (but worthy) member of the worldwide chain, Paseo Benito Juárez, Bahía Tangolunda, Oaxaca 70989, tel. (958) 100-55, 100-05, 100-39, or toll-free at (800) 325-3535 from the U.S. and Canada. Rooms are comfortable, deluxe, and decorated in soothing pastels, with private bay-view balconies, phones, cable TV, and a/c. Rates for its 360 rooms and suites begin at $185 s, $190 d with ocean view, $150, $155 without.

If the **Omni Zaashila Resort,** Bahía de Tangolunda Huatulco, Oaxaca 70989, tel. (958) 104-60, fax 104-61, hasn't yet gotten an architectural award, it should soon. Builders have succeeded in creating a modern luxury hotel that has an intimate feel. This begins right at the reception, a plush round *palapa,* where arriving guests are graciously invited to sit in soft chairs while being attended to by personable clerks, who are also seated, behind rustic, designer desks. Outside, you walk to your room through manicured tropical gardens, replete with gurgling fountains, splashing brooks, and cascading, green lawn terraces.

If the Zaashila has a drawback, it's in some of the 120 rooms, which, although luxurious and comfortable, are entirely tile-floored and could use more color and warmth. However, the arrangement of separate units, nested like a giant child's building blocks, resembles a space-age Hopi Indian pueblo, each unit being uniquely perched among the whole, affording much privacy and light, especially in upper-floor units. Outside, a few steps downhill, past the big, meandering blue pool, comes the superb beachfront: acres of luscious, wave-washed yellow sand, intimately enclosed between wave-sculpted rocks on one side and a jungly headland on the other. Rentals run from about $220 d, or $250 if you must have your own little private pool; with access to water sports, tennis, golf, three restaurants, and nightly live music.

If you're activity-oriented, you'll likely get more for your money at either the Club Med, the Royal Maeva, or the Holiday Inn. The 300-room Maeva is very well managed and smaller; consequently it's likely to be more personalized than both the sprawling 554-room Club Med or the Holiday Inn (which, although it has relatively few rooms, rambles up the hillside in 10 separate buildings, accessible from below via either shuttle or a funicular elevator).

Of the three hotels, the Holiday Inn has the largest rooms. Perhaps the size of the Holiday Inn's rooms is meant to compensate for the fact it's not actually on the beach: guests must either walk or shuttle a couple of blocks to the beach club.

The biggest plus of the Holiday Inn is the price, which, low season, runs only about $115 s, $185 d (two kids in room with parents go free), including all meals, drinks, sports, kid's mini-club, and in-house entertainment. No fans, all air-conditioned. Reserve directly at Holiday Inn Crowne Plaza Resort, Boulevard Benito Juárez 8, Bahía Tangolunda, Bahías de Huatulco, Oaxaca 70989, tel. (958) 100-44 or 102-21. Save money by paying your hotel bill in pesos, if at all possible.

All-inclusive packages at the **Club Med** vary according to season, but begin at about $1500 d per week ($216 d per day), plus around $100 in "membership" fees. Child (6-11 years) rates run about $600 per week. High season rates often run nearly double that. Call (800) CLUBMED for information and reservations in the U.S. and Canada.

Club Maeva rates run about $250 d low season, $300 high, kids with parents, $60. Reserve directly at Club Royal Maeva, P.O. Box 227, Bahías de Huatulco, Oaxaca 70989, tel. (958) 100-00, 100-48, or 100-64, fax 102-20. For information and reservations in the U.S. and Canada, call (800) GOMAEVA.

Trailer Parks and Camping
In Santa Cruz, the **Trailer Park Mangos** rents about 30 spaces in a shady mango grove about a quarter mile east (toward Tangolunda) of the Hotel Castillo. The sparse facilities include toilets, showers, and electricity, but no sewer hookup. RVs pay $12 daily, tenters about $3 per person. When the place is empty, which is most of the time, you could probably bargain for a much better rate.

Authorities generally permit **camping** at all of the Bahías de Huatulco except Tangolunda. For details, see "Exploring the Bays of Huatulco" above. You might also save time by checking with FONATUR (see "Information" below) for any access changes or recommendations. The soldiers who guard the beaches against turtle poachers and squatters also make camping much more secure. They usually welcome a kind word and maybe a cool drink as a break from their lonely and tedious vigil.

FOOD

Aside from the Tangolunda hotels, nearly all good Huatulco eateries are near the **Crucecita** plaza.

Breakfast and Snacks
For inexpensive homestyle cooking, try the *fondas* at the Crucecita Mercado, between Guamachil and Guanacastle, half a block off the plaza.

The Mercado stalls are good for fresh fruit during daylight hours, as is the **Frutería Angelita,** open daily 0600-2000, just across Guanacastle.

Also nearby, the **Panadería San Alejandro,** on Flamboyan (east side of the market), tel. (958) 700-70, offers mounds of fresh baked goodies.

The crowds will lead you to Crucecita's best-bet snack shop, **Los Portales Taco and Grill,** corner of Guamachil and Bugambilias, right on the plaza. Breakfasts, a dozen styles of tacos, Texas chili (or, as in Mexico, *frijoles charros*— "cowboy beans"), and barbecued ribs are their specialties. Beer is less than a dollar. Open daily 0600-0200, tel. 700-70.

Restaurants

Equally successful is **Restaurante Sabor de Oaxaca,** tel. (958) 700-60, on the bottom floor of the Hotel Las Palmas on Guamachil, half a block from the plaza. Wall art, folk crafts, and quiet conversation set the tone, while tasty country specialties fill the tables. Try their Oaxacan-style tamales, or *botanas Oaxaqueñas*—cheese, sausage, pork, beef, and guacamole snacks. Open Tues.-Sun. 0800-2300, Monday 1300-2300.

Travelers weary of the plaza tourist scene can find authentic Mexican cooking at **Comedor Juquila,** which does quite well on nearly exclusively local patronage. Tasty regional specialties—*moles, pozole, chiles rellenos, tamales*—are the key to their popularity. Open daily 0700-2200; off of Gardenia, five blocks north of the plaza, corner of Palo Verde.

The local edition of the **Carlos'n Charlie's** worldwide chain is on Carrizal, near the corner of Flamboyan, tel. (958) 700-05. Late owner Carlos Anderson's formula of tasty specialties, outrageous decor, brash music, and zany waiters is a safe bet to brighten the evening of visitors who want a party. Hours vary seasonally.

ENTERTAINMENT

Hangouts and Discos

Huatulco entertainments center on the Crucecita plaza. Although the hubbub quiets down during low seasons, some spots are reliable amusement sources year-round. The **Cactus Bar and Grill,** on the Flamboyan side of the plaza, livens up with videos, music, and the antics of its "Cucharachas" and "Muppets" nightly 1900-0300.

On the other hand, you can get swept up nightly by the Salsa and Latin rock repertoire of the band at the **Bar Iguana,** next to Tacos Los Portales, Bugambilias side of the plaza. Open about 2000-2400, in season.

In Santa Cruz, lights flash, fogs descend, and customers gyrate to the boom-boom at **Magic Circus** disco in the old Marlin Hotel on Calle Mitla, two blocks behind Banamex off the main boulevard. Admission (from around 2200) runs about $10. Call (958) 700-17 to confirm.

Hotel Music and Dancing

The **Sheraton** in Tangolunda is among the most reliable sources of hotel nightlife. Live music plays before dinner (about 1800-2000) in the lobby-bar, guests dance to a live Latin band in the Banquet Salon (about $30 with dinner, $7 without), and decorations overflow at theme-night parties (Italian, French, Mixteca, Chinese; about $25 per person with dinner). Call (958) 100-55, 100-05, or 100-39 for details and reservations. Other hotels, such as the Holiday Inn, Maeva, and Omni Zaashila (see "Accommodations" above) may provide similar entertainments, in season.

SPORTS

Walking, Jogging, Tennis, and Golf

Huatulco's open spaces and smooth roads and sidewalks afford plenty of walking and jogging opportunities. One of the most serene spots is along the Tangolunda Golf Course mornings or evenings. Also, an interesting **trail** takes off from the stables at Bahía Conejos (see "Horse-back Riding" below).

If you're planning on playing lots of tennis, best stay at one of the Tangolunda luxury resorts. Otherwise, the Sheraton, tel. (958) 100-55, 100-05 or 100-39, and the Tangolunda Golf Course, tel. (958) 100-37 or 100-59, have tennis courts. Call for rental information.

The breezy green **Tangolunda Golf Course,** tel. (958) 100-37 or 100-59, designed by the late architect Mario Chegnan Danto, stretches for 6,851 yards down Tangolunda Valley to the bay. The course starts from a low building complex (watch for bridge entrance) off the Santa Cruz-Tangolunda highway across from the sewage plant. Greens fee runs about $26, cart $26, club rental $13, caddy $12. The tennis courts, maintained by the same government corporation that owns the golf course, are next to the clubhouse on the knoll at the east side of the golf course.

Horseback Riding

Rancho Caballo del Mar at Bahía Conejos guides horseback trips along the ocean-view forest trail that stretches from their corral to the eco-preserve zone by the Río Copalita. The four-mile tour, which costs about $40 per person, returns via Magallitos shoreline village for swimming and lunch. Adventurers can also walk the same four-mile roundtrip in around three hours. Take a hat, water, and a bathing suit, and start early (around 0800) or late (around 1500) to avoid the midday heat.

Swimming, Snorkeling, and Diving

Swimming is ideal in calm corners of the Bahías de Huatulco. Especially good swimming beaches are at Playa Entrega in Bahía Santa Cruz and Bahía El Maguey (see "Sights" above). Generally clear water makes for rewarding snorkeling off the rocky shoals of all of the Bays of Huatulco. Local currents and conditions, however, can be hazardous. Novice snorkelers should go on trips accompanied by strong, experienced swimmers or professional guides (see below). Bring your own equipment; gear purchased locally will be expensive at best and unusable at worst.

Huatulco snorkelers and divers enjoy the services of well-equipped and professional **Buceos Triton** dive shop at the Hotel Marlin, on Andador Huatulco, three blocks west of the boat dock in Santa Cruz. Contact them at the hotel, tel. (958) 700-55, fax 705-46. Owner and certified instructor Enrique La Clette has had extensive training in France, the U.S., and Mexico City. He starts novices out with a pool mini-course, followed by a three-hour ($50) trip in a nearby bay. Snorkelers go for about $20, with good equipment furnished. Open Mon.-Sat. 0900-1400 and 1600-1900.

Buceos Triton's PADI open-water certification course takes about five days and runs about $300, complete. After that, you are qualified for more advanced tours, which include local shipwrecks, night dives, and marine flora, fauna, and ecology tours.

La Clette's interests reach much deeper than the commercial. A marine biologist by training, he is a leader in the local ecological association that watchdogs FONATUR's Huatulco development work. (See "Information" below.)

A woodcarver displays his unique wares in the Crucecita market.

BRUCE WHIPPERMAN

Fishing and Boat Launching

The local boat cooperative **Sociedad Servicios Turísticos Bahía Tangolunda** takes visitors out for fishing excursions from the Santa Cruz boat quay. For a launch with two lines and bait, figure on paying about $25 an hour, although during low seasons you may be able to bargain them down a bit. More reasonable prices might be obtainable by asking around among the fishermen at Santa Cruz, or at mini-villages San Agustín and Magallitos (see "Sights" above).

You can leave the negotiation up to a travel agent, who will arrange a fishing trip for you and your friends. You'll stop afterward at a beachside *palapa*, which will cook up a feast with your catch. Save money by bringing your own tackle. Rates for an approximately three-hour trip run about $85 without tackle, $170 with. Contact an agent such as Servicios Turísticos del Sur (at the Sheraton, tel. 958-100-55, ext. 784; or Hotel Castillo, tel. 958-700-46, ext. 620) for reservations.

Some of the Huatulco bays offer easy boat-launching prospects, especially at the protected beaches of La Entrega, Bahía El Maguey, and San Agustín.

SHOPPING

Market and Handicrafts

Crucecita has a small traditional market (officially the Mercado 3 de Mayo) off the plaza between Guanacastle and Guamachil. Although produce, meats, and clothing occupy most of the stalls, a few offer Oaxaca handicrafts. Items include black *barra* pottery, hand-crocheted Mixtec and Amusgo *huipiles*, wool weavings from Teotitlán del Valle, and whimsical duck-motif wooden bowls carved by an elderly, but sharp-bargaining, local gentleman.

Steep rents and lack of business force many local silver, leather, art and other handicraft shops to hibernate until tourists arrive in December. The few healthy shops with good selections cluster either around the Crucecita plaza, the Santa Cruz boat quay, or in the Tangolunda shopping complex adjacent to the Sheraton (or in the hotel itself). Prices are generally high.

Supermarket, Laundry, and Photo Supplies

The supermarket **La Fuente** in Crucecita on east-side Av. Oaxaca offers a large stock of groceries, an ice machine, and a little bit of everything else, a block east of the Pemex station, tel. (958) 700-22. Open daily 0600-2100.

Take your washing to the **Lavandería St. Germain** next door to the supermarket; open Mon.-Sat. 0800-2100.

For film and quick develop-and-print, go to **Foto Conejo**, tel. (958) 700-54, just off the Crucecita plaza, across Guamachil from the market. Besides a photo-portfolio of the Bays of Huatulco, the friendly owner stocks supplies, point-and-shoot cameras, and Kodak, Fuji, and Konica slide and print film. Open Mon.-Sat. 0900-2000.

SERVICES

Money Exchange

Huatulco banks are on the Benito Juárez main street in Santa Cruz, corner of Pochutla. **Ba-**

namex, tel. (958) 702-66, exchanges both U.S. and Canadian traveler's checks Mon.-Fri. 0900-1500; **Bancomer** across the street, tel. (958) 703-85, does the same Mon.-Fri. 0900-1200.

Communication

The Huatulco *correo* and *telégrafo* stand side by side in the Agencia Municipal (across the east-side Blvd. Tangolunda from the Pemex station). Post office (tel. 958-798-99) hours are Mon.-Fri. 0900-1300 and 1500-1800, Saturday 0900-1300; *telégrafo* (tel. 958-708-94) is open Mon.-Fri. 0900-1300 and 1500-1800, Saturday 0900-1200.

Immigration and Customs

Both Migración and the Aduana are at the Huatulco airport. If you lose your tourist card, avoid trouble or a fine at departure by presenting Migración with proof of your date of arrival (an airline ticket, or preferably a copy of your lost tourist card) at least a day before your scheduled departure.

Medical and Police

Among the best of Huatulco private clinics is **Central Médica**, at Flamboyan 5, tel. (958) 701-04, 706-87, or 707-34, in Crucecita half a block from the plaza. They have 24-hour emergency service and several specialists on call.

Alternatively, you can go to the big **Seguro Social** hospital, tel. (958) 701-24, 702-64, or 703-83, on the boulevard to Tangolunda a quarter mile south of the Pemex gas station.

For routine medications, Crucecita has many pharmacies, such as **Farmacia del Centro,** plaza corner of Flamboyan and Bugambilias, tel. (958) 702-32, beneath the Hotel Begonias.

For **police** emergencies, call the Crucecita *policía,* tel. (958) 702-10, in the Agencia Municipal behind the post office across the Tangolunda boulevard from the Pemex *gasolinera*.

INFORMATION

Tourist Information Offices

At least three information offices serve Huatulco visitors. In downtown Crucecita, a small private office (on Guamachil just off the plaza) answers questions. The local federal tourist information office, tel. (958) 100-94, 103-83, or 103-26, is on the road into Tangolunda just before the shopping complex. If the preceding are seasonally closed, try the FONATUR office (National Tourism Development and Promotion), tel. (958) 700-30, 702-47, or 702-62, on the boulevard to Tangolunda, right side, heading beachward from the Pemex station; open Mon.-Fri. 0900-1500 and 1700-1900. '

Publications

The bookshop at the Sheraton (tel. 958-100-55) in Tangolunda stocks English-language paperback novels, Mexico art and guidebooks, newspapers such as USA Today, and many magazines.

In Crucecita, the small Publicaciones Huatulco newsstand and bus station sells the English-language News of Mexico City, corner of Gardenia and Macuil, three blocks north of the plaza; open daily 0600-2100.

Ecology Association

Local ecologists and community leaders monitor Huatulco's development through their Asociación Pro Desarrollo y Sociocultural y Ecologíos de Bahías de Huatulco. Association president, marine biologist Enrique La Clette and his associates are working earnestly to assure the government's plan—that 70% of Huatulco will remain pristine—continues in force as development proceeds. One of their initial victories was to dissuade Club Med from dumping its raw sewage into Tangolunda Bay. Enrique, who is friendly and fluent in English, enjoys talking to fellow ecologists. Drop into his dive shop, Buceos Triton, at the Hotel Castillo (tel. 958-700-55, fax 705-46) in Santa Cruz.

GETTING THERE AND AWAY

By Air

The Huatulco airport (officially the Aeropuerto Internacional Bahías de Huatulco, code-designated HUX) is just off Hwy. 200 eight miles (13 km) west of Crucecita and 19 miles (31 km) east of Puerto Ángel. The terminal is small, with only check-in booths, a few snack bars, and handicrafts and trinket shops.

Currently, regular scheduled flights connect only with domestic destinations:

Mexicana Airlines flights connect twice daily with Mexico City. For flight information, call (958) 702-23 or 702-43; for reservations, tel. (958) 102-28 or 102-08.

Aeromexico flights connect twice a week with Mexico City. For flight information and reservations, call (958) 103-29 or 103-36.

Aeromorelos flights connect daily with Oaxaca, and four times a week with Puerto Escondido. For flight information, call (958) 104-44.

Charter flights, such as American Airlines (Dallas) and Canadian Holiday Airlines (Toronto, Montreal, Chicago), do connect with North American destinations during the winter season.

Huatulco arrival is usually simple. Since the terminal has no money-exchange counter, come loaded with sufficient pesos to last until you can get to the bank in Santa Cruz. After the typically quick immigrations and customs checks, arrivees have a choice of efficient ground transportation to town. Agents sell tickets for collective "ichivan" vans or GMC Suburbans to Crucecita or Santa Cruz (about $7) or the Sheraton, Club Maeva, or Club Med (for about $8). A private taxi especial for three, possibly four passengers, runs about $23. Prices to Puerto Escondido are about double these.

Mobile travelers on a budget can walk the couple of blocks from the terminal to Hwy. 200 and catch one of the frequent public microbuses headed either way to Crucecita (east, left) or the Pochutla (Puerto Ángel) junction (west, right).

Car rental agents are usually on duty for flight arrivals. If not, call them: Budget in Crucecita tel. (958) 700-10 or 700-34; National in Tangolunda tel. (958) 102-92; Dollar at the Sheraton tel. (958) 100-55, ext. 787. Best make reservations by U.S. and Canadian toll-free numbers prior to departure. (See chart in the On the Road chapter.)

By Car or RV

Paved highways connect Huatulco east with Tehuantepec, west with Puerto Ángel and Puerto Escondido, and north with Oaxaca.

Highway 200, the east-west route, runs an easy 72 miles (113 km) to Tehuantepec, connecting with Mex. 190 northwest with Oaxaca, and continuing east to Chiapas and the

Guatemala border. In the opposite direction, the route is equally smooth, connecting with Puerto Escondido in 66 miles (106 km), continuing to Acapulco in a long 273 miles (440 km). Allow about an hour and a half to Tehuantepec, the same to Puerto Escondido, and to Acapulco, a full eight hours' driving time, either direction.

Highway 175, the cross-Sierra connection north with Oaxaca, although paved, is narrow and winding, with few services for the lonely 80-mile stretch between its junction with Hwy. 200 at Pochutla (22 miles west of Crucecita) and Miahuatlán in the Valley of Oaxaca. The road climbs to 7,000 feet into pineclad, winter-chilly Chatino and Zapotec Indian country. Be prepared for emergencies. Allow eight hours northbound, seven hours southbound, for the entire 170-mile (273-km) Huatulco-Oaxaca trip.

By Bus
Four bus lines connect Huatulco with destinations east, west, and north. They depart from small separate terminals in Crucecita scattered mostly along Calle Gardenia north of the plaza.

More than two dozen daily **Cristóbal Colón** first-class buses, at the corner of Ocotillo, tel. (958) 702-61, connect west with the four per day **Puerto Escondido** line. Buses also connect east with Tehuantepec, continuing either to Tapachula on the Guatemala border, Villahermosa (Tabasco), or Oaxaca and Mexico City via Puebla (one per day).

Estrella Blanca first- and second-class buses, one block up the street at the corner of Palo Verde, tel. (958) 701-03, connect about once every half hour west, via the Hwy. 200 coast route, all the way to Lázaro Cárdenas, Michoacán, via Acapulco and Zihuatanejo. One departure connects directly with Mexico City, via Acapulco, once a day.

Several second-class **Oaxaca-Istmo** buses connect by the long Salina Cruz-Tehuantepec route with Oaxaca daily from their station at the newsstand Publicatciones Huatulco, corner of Macuil.

A few second-class and one luxury-class **Estrella del Valle** and **Autobuses Oaxaca-Pacífico** buses connect daily with **Oaxaca via Pochutla**, from Jazmin, corner Sabali, nine blocks north of the plaza, tel. (958) 701-93.

*Mixtec man motif
from pictorial manuscript*

INLAND TO OAXACA

The Valley of Oaxaca is really three valleys, which diverge, like the thumb, index finger, and middle finger of a hand, from a single strategic point. Aztec conquerors called that spot Huaxyacac (yoo-AHSH-yah-kahk, "Point of the Calabash") Hill for a forest of gourd-bearing trees, which once carpeted its slopes. The Spanish, who founded the city at the foot of the hill, shifted that name to the more-pronounceable Oaxaca.

The people of the Valley of Oaxaca, walled by mountains from the rest of Mexico, both benefit and suffer from their long isolation. They are poor but proud inheritors of rich traditions that live on despite 300 years of Spanish occupation.

A large proportion of Oaxacans are pure Indian and speak one of a dozen different tongues. Significant numbers speak no Spanish at all. Even in and around Oaxaca city itself they make up a sizable fraction of the people. Far out in the country, they *are* the people. Mostly speaking the Zapotec or Mixtec languages, they harvest their corn for tortillas and their maguey for *pulque* and *aguardiente* (fire water). They spin their wool, hoe their vegetables, then go to market and sit beside their piles of blankets and mounds of onions, wondering if their luck is going to change.

HISTORY

Before Columbus
Evidence of human prehistory litters the riverbottoms and hillsides of the Valley of Oaxaca. Cave remains not far from the ancient city-state of Mitla tell of hunters who lived there as long as 8,000 years ago. Several thousand years later, their descendants, heavily influenced by the mysterious Olmecs of the Gulf coast, were carving gods and glyphs on stone monuments in the Valley of Oaxaca. Around 600 B.C., people speaking a Zapotec mother tongue, similarly influenced by the Olmecs, founded Monte Albán on a mountaintop above the present city of Oaxaca.

Monte Albán ruled the Valley of Oaxaca for more than a millennium, climaxing as a sophis-

ticated metropolis of perhaps 40,000, controlling a large and populous area of southern Mexico and enjoying diplomatic and trade relations with distant kingdoms. But, for reasons unknown, Monte Albán declined to a shadow of its former glory by A.D. 1000.

Mixtec-speaking people filled the vacuum. They took over Monte Albán, using it mostly as a burial ground. Their chiefs divided up the Valley of Oaxaca and ruled from separate feudalistic city-states, such as Mitla, Yagul, Matatlán, and Zaachila, for hundreds of years.

The Mixtecs in turn gave way to the Aztecs whose invading warriors crossed the mountains and threatened Oaxaca during the 1450s. In 1486 the Aztecs established a fort on the hill of Huaxyacac (now called El Fortín), overlooking the present city of Oaxaca, ruling their restive Zapotec and Mixtec subjects for barely a generation. On 21 November 1521, conquistador Francisco de Orozco and his soldiers replaced them on the hill of Huaxyacac scarcely four months after the Spanish tide had flooded the Aztecs' Valley of Mexico homeland.

Conquest and Colonization
Spanish settlers began arriving soon after the conquistadores. At the foot of the hill of Huaxyacac, they laid out their town, which they christened Antequera after the old Spanish Roman city. Soon, however, the settlers came into conflict with Cortés, whom the king had named marquis of the Valley of Oaxaca, and whose entire valley domain surrounded the town. Townspeople had to petition the queen of Spain for land on which to grow vegetables: they were granted a one-league square in 1532.

For hundreds of years, Cortés's descendants reigned, the church grew fat, the colonists prospered, and the Indians toiled—in cane and corn, in cattle pastures and silk mulberry groves.

Independence, Reform, and Revolution
In contrast to its neighbors in the state of Guerrero, conservative Antequera was a minor and grudging player in the (1810-21) War of Independence. But as the *insurgente* tide swept the

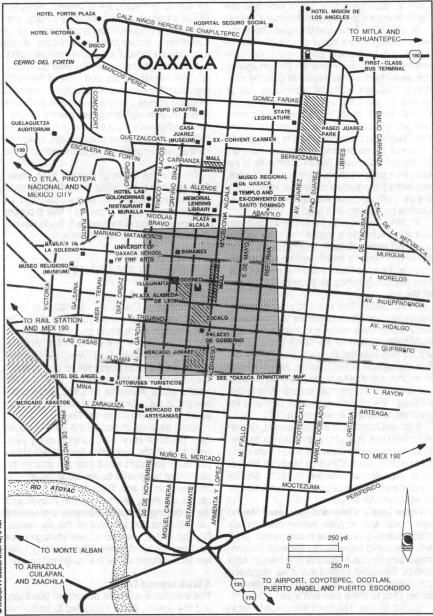

OAXACA

HOTEL FORTIN PLAZA
CALZ. NIÑOS HEROES DE CHAPULTEPEC
HOSPITAL SEGURO SOCIAL
HOTEL MISIÓN DE LOS ANGELES
HOTEL VICTORIA
DISCO
TO MITLA AND TEHUANTEPEC
CERRO DEL FORTIN
MARCOS PEREZ
190
FIRST - CLASS BUS TERMINAL
GOMEZ FARIAS
COMONFORT
ARIPO (CRAFTS)
STATE LEGISLATURE
GUELAGUETZA AUDITORIUM
CASA JUAREZ (MUSEUM)
QUETZALCOATL
EX - CONVENT CARMEN
PASEO JUAREZ PARK
100
ESCALERA DEL FORTIN
CARRANZA
MALL
BERNOZABAL
LIBRES
EMILIO CARRANZA
TO ETLA, PINOTEPA NACIONAL, AND MEXICO CITY
CRESPO
TINOCO Y PALACIOS
PORFIRIO DIAZ
I. ALLENDE
MUSEO REGIONAL DE OAXACA
AV. JUAREZ
PINO SUAREZ
CALZ. DE LA REPUBLICA
HOTEL LAS GOLONDRINAS
RESTAURANT LA MURALLA
MACEDONIA ALCALA
TEMPLO AND EX-CONVENTO DE SANTO DOMINGO
NICOLAS BRAVO
MEMORIAL LENDING LIBRARY
ABASOLO
J. DE TACUBAYA
MARIANO MATAMOROS
PLAZA ALCALA
5 DE MAYO
REFORMA
BASILICA DE LA SOLEDAD
UNIVERSITY OF OAXACA SCHOOL OF FINE ARTS
BANAMEX
MURGUIA
MUSEO RELIGIOSO (MUSEUM)
MIER Y TERAN
DIAZ ORDAZ
TELEGRAFO
CORREO
MORELOS
VICTORIA
GALEANA
PLAZA ALAMEDA DE LEON
MALL
AV. INDEPENDENCIA
TO RAIL STATION AND MEX 190
V. TRUJANO
ZOCALO
AV. HIDALGO
LAS CASAS
J. P. GARCIA
PALACIO DE GOBIERNO
V. GUERRERO
I. ALDAMA
MERCADO JUAREZ
V. DIEGO
SEE "OAXACA DOWNTOWN" MAP
HOTEL DEL ANGEL
AUTOBUSES TURISTICOS
MINA
I. L. RAYON
MERCADO ABASTOS
I. ZARAGOZA
MERCADO DE ARTESANIAS
ARTEAGA
PROL. DE VICTORIA
MANUEL DOBLADO
G. ORTEGA
TO MEX 190
NUÑO EL MERCADO
M. FIALLO
XICOTENCATL
MOCTEZUMA
RIO ATOYAC
20 DE NOVIEMBRE
MIGUEL CABRERA
BUSTAMANTE
ARMENTA Y LOPEZ
PERIFERICO
0   250 yd
0   250 m
TO MONTE ALBAN
TO ARRAZOLA, CUILAPAN, AND ZAACHILA
131
175
TO AIRPORT, COYOTEPEC, OCOTLAN, AND PUERTO ESCONDIDO

country, local nationalist fervor switched the city's name back to the original Mexican Oaxaca. By the 1850s, times had changed. Oaxacans were leading a new national struggle. Benito Juárez, a pure Zapotec Indian, was rallying liberal forces in the civil War of the Reform against the oligarchy that had replaced colonial rule. Born in Guelatao, northeast of the valley, Juárez at age 12 was an orphan sheepherder. A Catholic priest, struck by the boy's intelligence, brought him to the city as a servant and taught him Spanish in preparation for the priesthood.

Instead, Benito became a lawyer. He hung out his shingle in Oaxaca, first as a defender of the poor, then state legislator, governor, chief justice, and finally the president of Mexico. In his honor, the city's official name was again changed—to Oaxaca de Juárez—in 1872.

In 1861, after winning the three-year civil war, Juárez's Reformista forces had their victory snatched away. France, taking advantage of the United States's preoccupation with its own civil war, invaded Mexico and installed an Austrian Hapsburg prince as Emperor Maximilian of Mexico.

It took Juárez five years to prevail against Maximilian and his conservative Mexican backers. Although Maximilian and Juárez paradoxically shared many of the same liberal ideas, Juárez had Maximilian executed after his defeat and capture in 1867. Juárez bathed Mexico in enlightenment as he promulgated his "Laws of the Reform" (which remain essentially in force). Although the country rewarded him with re-election, he died of exhaustion in 1871.

Another Oaxacan of Indian-descent, General Porfirio Díaz, vowed to carry Juárez's banner. Díaz, the hero who defeated the French in the battle of Puebla on "Cinco de Mayo" (5 May) of 1862, was elected president in 1876. *"No Re-elección"* was his campaign cry. He subsequently ruled Mexico for 34 years.

Under Diaz's "Order and Progress," Mexico was modernized at great human cost. As railroads, factories, and mines mushroomed, property ownership increasingly became concentrated among rich Mexicans and their foreign friends. Smashed protest marches, murdered opposition leaders, and rigged elections returned Díaz to office time and again.

But not forever. The revolt that ousted Díaz in 1910 has, in theory, never ceased. Now, the PRI, the Institutional Revolutionary Party, presides over a uniquely imperfect Mexican form of democracy. Under three generations of PRI rule, Oaxaca Indians' lives have improved gradually. Although Indian families now go to government health centers and more of their children attend government rural schools, the price for doing so is to become less Indian and more Mexican. Although the government's INI (National Indigenous Institute) claims to represent Indians' welfare, its director always seems to be a Spanish-speaking mestizo member of the PRI.

Times in the Valley of Oaxaca have nevertheless gotten better. When tens of thousands of Zapotec and Mixtec men, women, and children parade in the Oaxaca *zócalo* on 1 May to protest the assassination of their leaders, the thousands of police on hand do not interfere.

CITY SIGHTS

Getting Oriented

The streets of Oaxaca (pop. 300,000, elev. 5,110 feet, 1,778 meters) still run along the same simple north-south grid the city fathers laid out in 1529. If you stand at the center of the old *zócalo* and look out toward the **catedral** across the Av. Hidalgo, you will be looking north. Diagonally left, to the northwest, you'll see the smaller plaza, **Alameda de León**, and directly beyond, in the distance, the historic hill of Huaxyacac, now called **Cerro del Fortín.**

Along the base of that hill the Pan American Hwy. (National Hwy. 190) runs generally east-west through the northern suburbs. Behind you (although you can't see it from the *zócalo*) the **periférico** peripheral boulevard loops around the town's south end. There it passes the yawning but oft-empty wash of the **Río Atoyac** and the sprawling **Mercado Abastos** market and second-class bus terminal on the southwest. Beyond that, if you find a clear vantage point you'll see the hill of **Monte Albán** looming 1,000 feet (450 meters) above the southwest horizon.

A Walk around Town

The venerable restored downtown buildings, and the streets, some converted to traffic-free

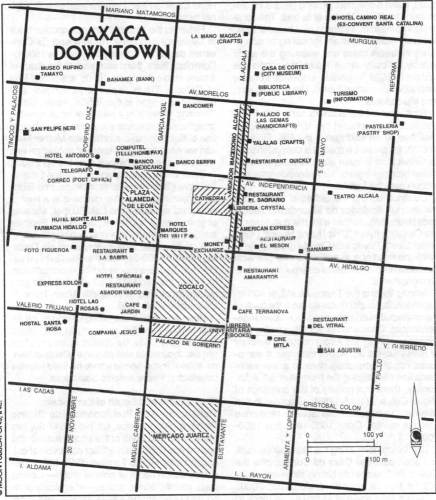

OAXACA DOWNTOWN

MARIANO MATAMOROS

MUSEO RUFINO TAMAYO

BANAMEX (BANK)

LA MANO MAGICA (CRAFTS)

HOTEL CAMINO REAL (EX-CONVENT SANTA CATALINA)

MURGUIA

CASA DE CORTES (CITY MUSEUM)

AV. MORELOS

SAN FELIPE NERI

BANCOMER

BIBLIOTECA (PUBLIC LIBRARY)

TURISMO (INFORMATION)

PALACIO DE LAS GEMAS (HANDICRAFTS)

PASTELERIA (PASTRY SHOP)

HOTEL ANTONIO'S

COMPUTEL (TELEPHONE/FAX)

BANCO MEXICANO

BANCO SERFIN

YALALAG (CRAFTS)

RESTAURANT QUICKLY

TELEGRAFO
CORREO (POST OFFICE)

AV. INDEPENDENCIA

TEATRO ALCALA

PLAZA ALAMEDA DE LEON

CATHEDRAL

RESTAURANT EL SAGRARIO

LIBRERIA CRYSTAL

HOTEL MONTE ALBAN
FARMACIA HIDALGO

HOTEL MARQUES DEL VALLE

AMERICAN EXPRESS

RESTAURANT EL MESON

FOTO FIGUEROA

RESTAURANT LA BABITA

MONEY EXCHANGE

BANAMEX

EXPRESS KOLOR

HOTEL SEÑORIAL

RESTAURANT ASADOR VASCO

RESTAURANT AMARANTOS

AV. HIDALGO

ZOCALO

VALERIO TRUJANO

HOTEL LAS ROSAS

CAFE JARDIN

CAFE TERRANOVA

HOSTAL SANTA ROSA

COMPANIA JESUS

LIBRERIA UNIVERSITARIA (BOOKS)

PALACIO DE GOBIERNO

RESTAURANT DEL VITRAL

CINE MITLA

V. GUERRERO

SAN AGUSTIN

LAS CASAS

CRISTOBAL COLON

MERCADO JUAREZ

I. ALDAMA

I. L. RAYON

0   100 yd

0   100 m

MARIANO ALCALA
M. ALCALA
GARCIA VIGIL
PORFIRIO DIAZ
TINOCO Y PALACIOS
ANDADOR MACEDONIO ALCALA
5 DE MAYO
REFORMA
20 DE NOVIEMBRE
MIGUEL CABRERA
BUSTAMANTE
ARMENTA Y LOPEZ
M. FIALLO

© MOON PUBLICATIONS, INC.

malls, make a delightful strolling ground for discovering traditional Mexico at its best. The *zócalo* itself sometimes seems to be a place of slow, leisurely motion, perfect for sitting at one of many sidewalk cafes and watching the world float by. Officially Jardín Juárez, the *zócalo* was laid out in 1529. Its portals, clockwise from the west side, are named Flores, Clavería, Juárez, and Mercaderes.

Prominent off the *zócalo's* north side is the cathedral that replaced the 1550 original, demolished by an earthquake in 1696. Finished in 1733, the present cathedral is distinguished by its Greek marble main altar, where a polished Italian bronze Virgin of the Ascension presides piously over the faithful.

Continue behind the cathedral north along the tranquil **Andador de Macedonio Alcalá** pedestrian mall, named after the composer of the Oaxacan hymn "Dios Nunca Muere" ("God Never Dies"). Paved with Oaxaca green stone in 1985 and freed of auto traffic, the mall connects the *zócalo* with a number of distinguished Oaxaca monuments.

Among them is the **Teatro Alcalá,** at 900 Independencia, tel. (951) 629-69 (from the back of the cathedral head right one block along Independencia). Christened by a 1909 opening performance of *Aida,* the Alcalá houses a treasury of Romantic-era art. Above the foyer, a sumptuous marble staircase rises to a bas-relief medallion allegorizing the triumph of art. Additionally, there is a gallery of the paintings of Miguel Cabrera (1695-1768), a Zapotec Indian who rose to become New Spain's renowned baroque painter. Open 1000-1400 and 1600-2000.

Continuing north along the Alcalá street mall, you soon pass the **Casa de Cortés,** now the **Museo de Oaxaca** city history museum, at no. 202, tel. 684-99; open Wed.-Mon. 1030-2000.

Detour right again at Murguia one block to the **Ex-Convento de Santa Catalina,** the second-oldest convent in New Spain, founded in 1576. Although the quarters of the first initiates were spare, the convent grew into a sprawling chapel and cloister complex decorated by fountains and flower-strewn gardens. Juárez's reforms drove the sisters out in 1862; the building has since served as city hall, school, and movie theater. Now, it stands beautifully restored as the

Hotel Camino Real. Note the native-motif original murals.

Return to the mall and continue another block to Oaxaca's pride, the **Templo and Ex-Convento de Santo Domingo.** Begun in 1531 by Dominican friars, the church sank to the status of a mere stable during the 1860s' anticlerical War of Reform. Times, however, changed, and restoration began in the 1950s. Inside, Santo Domingo glows with a wealth of art. Above the antechamber spreads the entire genealogical tree of Saint Dominic, starting with Mother Mary and weaving through a score of noblemen and women to the saint himself over the front door.

Continuing inside, the soaring, Sistine Chapel-like nave glitters with saints, cherubs, and Bible-story paintings. The altar climaxes in a host of cherished symbols—the Last Supper, sheaves of grain, loaves and fishes, Jesus and Peter on the Sea of Galilee—in a riot of gold leaf.

Next door, the **Museo Regional de Oaxaca,** tel. (951) 629-91, occupies the restored ex-convent. Upstairs rooms exhibit major artifacts, including the turquoise skull and the solid gold masks recovered from Monte Albán Tomb 7. Open daily 1000-1800.

Head west one block (along Carranza, off Alcalá across from the museum) to 609 Garcia Vigil and the **Casa de Juárez** museum. Here are the documents and personal effects of Benito Juárez, in the house where he lived with his benefactor, Padre Antonio Salanueva.

Sights West and South of the *Zócalo*
The **Museo Arte Prehispánico de Rufino Tamayo,** 503 Morelos, tel. (951) 647-50, two blocks west and north of the *zócalo* exhibits the brilliant pre-Columbian artifact collection of celebrated artist Rufino Tamayo (1899-1991). Displays include hosts of animal motifs—Colima dogs, parrots, ducks, snakes—whimsically crafted into polychrome vases, bowls, and urns. Open Monday and Wed.-Sat. 1000-1400 and 1600-1900, Sunday 1000-1500.

Continue three blocks west, past the University of Oaxaca School of Fine Arts and the airy Plaza of Dances, to the baroque **Basilica de Nuestra Señora de la Soledad.** Inside, the Virgin of Solitude, the patron of Oaxaca, stands atop the altar with her five-pound solid golden crown, encrusted with 600 diamonds.

Step into the **Museo Religioso,** tel. (951) 675-66, at the downhill side of the church, rear end. A host of objects of adornment—shells, paintings, jewelry—crowd cabinets, shelves, and aisles of musty rooms. Large stained-glass panels tell of the images of Jesus and the Virgin that arrived miraculously in 1620, eventually becoming Oaxaca's patron symbols. Open Mon.- Sat. 0900-1400, 1600-1900, Sunday 0900-1400.

The traditional **Juárez Market** occupies the one-block square that begins just one block south of the *zócalo*. Stroll around there for fun and perhaps a bargain in the honeycomb of traditional leather, textile, and clothing stalls. (See "Shopping" below for more details.)

ACCOMMODATIONS

Oaxaca offers a wide range of good hotels. Air-conditioning is not particularly necessary in temperate Oaxaca, although hot-water showers (furnished by all hotels listed below) feel especially comfy during cool winter evenings. The less expensive hotels are generally near the colorful, traffic-free *zócalo*. With one exception, Oaxaca's plush, resort-style hostelries dot the northern edge of town. See the accompanying chart for hotels listed in order of price.

Hotels near the Zócalo
Along with an enviable *zócalo* location, guests of **Hotel Señorial,** Portal de Flores 6, Oaxaca, Oaxaca 68000, tel. (951) 639-33, fax 636-68, enjoy clean rooms, efficient management, a reliable restaurant, and an unheated swimming pool and patio. The hotel's only drawback is that its many interior rooms have louvered (non-soundproof) windows on hallways and communal air shafts. This, combined with the hard, shiny vinyl floors, results in noise that can't be shut out. Light sleep-

ers, bring earplugs, especially on weekends and holidays, when the popular Señorial will be brimming. The 107 rooms rent for about $30 s, $35 d, $40 t, with TV, limited wheelchair access, and parking $5 extra; credit cards are *not* accepted.

A number of good budget-to-moderately-priced hotels cluster beside or behind the Hotel Señorial, within a block or two of the *zócalo*. Moving clockwise, first comes the petite **Hotel Las Rosas,** Trujano 112, Oaxaca, Oaxaca 68000, tel. (951) 422-17, half a block from the *zócalo*. Climb a flight of stairs to the small lobby, relatively tranquil by virtue of its second-floor location. Beyond that, a double tier of rooms surrounds a homey, plant-decorated inner patio. Adjacent to the lobby is a cheery sitting room with a TV, which is kept at subdued volume. The rooms themselves, although plainly furnished, are clean and tiled (except some bathrooms, which could use an extra scrubbing). Prices, moreover, at about $19 s, $27 d, $33 t (and which are usually discounted even more), are certainly right. No credit cards, parking, or wheelchair access.

The new, family-managed **Hostal Santa Rosa,** just half a block away at the corner of Trujano and Porfirio Díaz, Trujano 201, Oaxaca, Oaxaca 68000, tel. (951) 467-14 or 467-15, offers a modern-style alternative. The streetside lobby leads past an airy restaurant to the rooms, recessed along a meandering inner passageway and courtyard. Inside, the rooms are very clean, comfortably furnished, and decorated in pastels. Rentals run about $22 s, $28 d, and $33 t, with TV, phones, parking, limited wheelchair access, and an in-house travel-tour agency.

Newly renovated, authentically colonial **Hotel Antonio's,** at Díaz and Independencia, two blocks north, offers colorful streetfront ambience, a restaurant, friendly management, and more than a bit of old Mexico charm within its quiet inner courtyard. Located at Independencia 601, Oaxaca, Oaxaca 68000, tel. (951) 672-27, fax 636-72. The 15 thoughtfully decorated, comfortable, and very clean rooms rent for about $23 s, $26 d, and $30 t; parking (four blocks away) included.

On the leafy Alameda de León square just off the zócalo stands the very popular **Hotel Monte Albán,** Alameda de León 1, Oaxaca, Oaxaca 68000, tel. (951) 627-77. The hotel centers on a big patio-restaurant that hosts folkdance shows nightly 2030-2200. During the first evening this could be understandably exciting, but after a week you might feel as if you were living in a three-ring circus. The 20 rooms, which surround the patio in two tiers, are genuinely colonial, with soaring beamed ceilings, big bedsteads, and the requisite few cockroaches per room. (When a cockroach was pointed out, the bellman promptly crushed it underfoot and nudged it into a corner with the toe of his shoe.) For such a nicely located hotel, rates run a reasonable $23 s, $26 d, and $30 d; credit cards accepted.

For a fancier option, head for the old standby, the **Hotel Marques del Valle** on the north side of the zócalo, Portal Clavería, P.O. Boxes 13 and 35, Oaxaca, Oaxaca 68000, tel. (951) 636-77 or 634-74, fax 699-61. Managers have recently restored the lobby with bright chandeliers, mirrors, and shiny dark wood paneling. Upstairs, however, massive wrought-iron fixtures cast gloomy nighttime shadows through the soaring, balconied central atrium. The 96 rooms, nevertheless, retain their original 1940s polish, with handcrafted cedar furniture and marble-finished baths. Deluxe rooms have TV, carpets, and some balconies looking out on to the zócalo. Rooms rent for about $45 s or d, with restaurant-bar, limited wheelchair access, and credit cards accepted.

The '80s-mod **Hotel Gala,** Bustamante 103, Oaxaca, Oaxaca 68000, tel. (951) 422-51 or 413-05, fax 636-60, half a block south of the zócalo's southeast corner, is for those who want comfortable, modern-standard deluxe accommodations at relatively moderate prices. Rooms, although tastefully decorated and carpeted, are small. Get one of the quieter ones away from the street. The 36 rooms rent for about $36 s, $41 d, and $55 for junior suite; with phones, TV, fans, a restaurant; credit cards are accepted, but there is no parking.

Oaxaca's classiest hotel, the **Camino Real,** Calle 5 de Mayo 300, Oaxaca, Oaxaca 68000, tel. (951) 606-11, or (800) 7-CAMINO from the U.S. and Canada, fax 607-32, occupies the lovingly restored ex-Convent Santa Catalina, four blocks north of the zócalo. Flowery hidden courtyards, massive arched portals, soaring beamed ceilings, a big blue pool and impeccable bar and restaurant service combine to create a refined but relaxed old-world atmosphere. Rooms are large, luxurious, and exquisitely decorated with antiques and folk crafts and furnished with modern-standard conveniences. If street noise is likely to bother you, get a room away from bustling Calles Abasolo and 5 de Mayo. Rates run about $170 s or d; with phones and TV, but parking not included; credit cards accepted.

Although a long six blocks (four north, two west) away from the zócalo, **Hotel Las Golondrinas,** at Tinoco y Palacios 411, Oaxaca, Oaxaca 68000, tel. (951) 687-26 or 421-26, is nearly always full. Step inside and you'll immediately see why. Rooms enfold an intimate garden lovingly decorated with festoons of hothouse verdure. Leafy bananas, bright bougainvillea, and platoons of potted plants line pathways, which meander past an intimate fountain patio in one corner, and lead to an upstairs panoramic vista sundeck on the other. The care also shows in the rooms, which are immaculate and adorned with Spartan-chic pastel earth-toned curtains and bedspreads and natural wood furniture.

Guests additionally enjoy use of laundry facilities, a TV sitting room, a shelf of paperback books, and a breakfast restaurant 0800-1000. All this for only about $19 s, $24 d, and $27 t. In addition to the 27 regular rooms, a pair of honeymoon suites rent for about $27 and $33, respectively.

Northside Luxury Hotels
Three upscale suburban hostelries dot the north side of Hwy. 190. The **Hotel Victoria,** Km 545, Carretera Panamericana, Oaxaca, Oaxaca 68070, tel. (951) 526-33, fax 524-11, choicest of the three, spreads over a lush hillside garden of panoramic vistas and luxurious resort ambience. The '50s-style lobby extends from an upstairs view bar downhill past a terrace restaurant to a flame tree and jacaranda-decorated poolpatio. As for rooms, the best ones are in the newer view wing detached from the lobby building. There, the junior suites are spacious, comfortable, and luxuriously appointed, with double sized bathrooms and private view balconies. The 150 rooms, bungalows, and junior suites rent for about $83, $103, and $125 d, respectively; with TV, phones, a/c, tennis court, disco, handicrafts shop, and parking; credit cards accepted.

The **Hotel Fortín Plaza,** Av. Venus 118, Colonia Estrella, Oaxaca, Oaxaca 68040, tel. (951) 577-77, fax 513-28, next to the highway two blocks downhill, is hard to miss, especially at night. Its blue-lit six-story profile tops everything else in town. The hotel offers the usual modern facilities—restaurant-bar, pool, disco, and parking—in a compact, attractively designed layout. Upstairs, guests enjoy deluxe, clean, and comfortable rooms with private view balconies (whose tranquility is reduced, however, by considerable highway noise). Room rates run about $55 s or d, with phones, TV, and parking; credit cards accepted. Discounts are sometimes available.

Hotel Misión de Los Angeles, Calz. Porfirio Díaz 102, Oaxaca, Oaxaca 68050, tel. (951) 515-00, fax 516-80, half a mile farther east (on the prolongation of Juárez), rambles like a hacienda through a spreading oak- and acacia-dotted garden-park. With an ambience akin to an elite suburban junior college, the hotel conducts cooking, language, and cultural classes and arranges bus tours of ruins, crafts villages, and

markets. If you tire of all the activity, kick back beside the big pool or enjoy a set or two of tennis. The rooms and suites are spacious and comfortable, with big garden-view windows or balconies. Upper rooms are quieter and more private. The 162 rooms and suites rent from about $72 d for standard, $152 d for suite; with phones, parking, disco, restaurant, and a folkloric performance; credit cards accepted.

Trailer Parks and Camping
Oaxaca has a pair of reliable trailer and camping parks; one, the **Oaxaca Trailer Park,** is at the far northeast side of town, 900 Av. Violetas, Oaxaca, Oaxaca 68000, tel. (951) 527-92. Their 100 all-hookup spaces include showers, toilets, laundromat, recreation hall, a fence, and a night watchman. Spaces rent for about $11 per night, with discounts for extended stays. Pets okay.

Get there by turning left at Violetas, several blocks east of the first-class bus terminal on Hwy. 190. The street is marked by the big green "Col Reforma" sign over the highway and the red-white-and-blue "Pepsi"-marked building on the right corner just after you make the turn. Continue uphill six long blocks to the trailer park on the left.

The **Rosa Isabel,** Km 539, Carretera Nacional, Colonia Loma del Pueblo, Oaxaca, Oaxaca 68000, tel. (951) 272-10, trailer park is on Hwy. 190, on the east (Mexico City) side of town in the Loma del Pueblo Nuevo suburb. It features hookups, toilets, showers, and a recreation hall, with the Brenamiel tennis and sports club nearby. The 50 spaces rent for about $10 a night, with discounts for extended stays. **Get there,** on Hwy. 190, by turning right (heading south) about a quarter mile past the Hotel Villas Del Sol.

FOOD

Snacks and Foodstalls
During fiestas, snack stalls along Hidalgo at the cathedral-front Alameda de León square abound in local delicacies. Choices include *clayudas,* giant crisp tortillas loaded with avocado, tomato, onions, and cheese, and *empanadas de amarillo,* huge tacos stuffed with cheese and red salsa. For dessert, have a *buñuelo,* a crunchy, honey-soaked wheat tortilla.

At nonfiesta times, you can still fill up on the sizzling fare of taco, *torta*, hamburger, and hot dog (eat 'em only when they are served hot) stands that set up in the same vicinity. For sinful desserts, go to the *pastelería* (pastry shop) at Morelos and Reforma, three blocks northeast of the *zócalo;* open Mon.-Sat. 0800-2100, Sunday 1200-1900.

Cafes and Restaurants

Complete dinner price key: Budget: under $7; Moderate: $7-14; Expensive: more than $14.

Oaxaca visitors enjoy many good eateries right on or near the *zócalo*. Besides the interesting passing scene, the *zócalo*-front sidewalk cafes usually offer passable, and in some cases quite good, food and service at moderate prices. They all are open long hours, from about 0800-2400, and serve from very recognizable standard menus.

The better cafes, clockwise around the *zócalo*, are the Jardín (southwest corner), the Marques (north side), the Amarantos (northeast corner), and the Terranova (southeast corner). Of these, the best are the **Amarantos** (four stars for service and fresh, appetizingly presented food) and the **Terranova** (where entrees are made to order, and the service is as crisp as the salads).

Serious-eating longtimers return to **El Asador Vasco** restaurant on the second-floor balcony above the Restaurant Jardín, Portal Flores 11, tel. (915) 697-19. The menu specializes in hearty Basque-style country cooking: salty, spicy, and served in a decor of a medieval Iberian manor house. Favorites include fondues (bean, sausage, and mushroom), garlic soup, salads, veal tongue, oysters in hot sauce, and the *carnes asadas* (roast meats) house specialties. Open daily 1300-2300. Expensive; expect to pay about $20 per person.

For a tasty meal or snack, try **La Casita** around the corner upstairs on Hidalgo at the plaza Alameda de León, Hidalgo 612, tel. (951) 629-17. You can order either a hearty *comida corrida* multi-course lunch or one of their tasty "mystery" offerings, such as tortilla, "cat," or "nothing" soup. Open daily 1300-1800 only. Moderate.

Also on Hidalgo, just past the *zócalo's* opposite (east) side, the intimate and friendly little **El Mesón** specializes in a lunch buffet, Hidalgo 805, tel. (951) 627-29. For about $4, diners select and eat their fill of fresh fruit, salads, chili beans, and several entrees, including roast beef and pork, chicken, *moles*, tacos, tamales, and enchiladas. Open daily 0800 till midnight. Budget.

More good eating, in a refined but relaxed atmosphere, awaits you at the very popular **Restaurant El Sagrario**, around the corner behind the church at 120 Valdivieso, tel. (951) 404-03. Here mostly local, youngish upper-class customers enjoy either a club-bar atmosphere (lower-level), pizza parlor booths (middle-level), or restaurant tables (upper-level). At the restaurant level during the evening, you can best take in the whole scene around you—chattering, upbeat crowd, live guitar, flute, or jazz melodies, elegantly restored colonial details. Then, finally, will come the food: beginning, perhaps, with an appetizer, continuing with a soup or salad, then an international or regional specialty, which you finally top off with a light dessert and a savory expresso coffee. Open daily 0800. Credit cards accepted; moderate to expensive.

On the other hand, a legion of American, Canadian, and European budget travelers swear by **Restaurant Quickly,** half a block farther from the *zócalo,* 100 Alcalá, tel. (951) 470-76, on the Alcalá pedestrian mall. Once you taste their giant hamburgers, chocolate milkshakes, or pancakes (or vegies, if you prefer), you'll understand why. Open daily 0800-2300.

Although Chinese food from **Restaurant La Muralla** ("The Wall") is a lengthy six-block walk (four north, two west from the *zócalo*), your effort will be amply rewarded. Located at the corner of Tinoco y Palacios and M. Bravo, tel. (951) 622-68, Visa accepted. After a few minutes inside, you'll be convinced you've been transported to a country eatery somewhere outside Xi'an or Guangzhou. Besides the standard but tastily prepared dishes (such as wonton soup, chicken chow mein, barbecued spareribs), you will be entertained by the occupants—wriggling parrot fish, flowery tube worms, spindly spider stars—of a gorgeous, mid-room aquarium. Open daily 1300-2000.

ENTERTAINMENT, EVENTS, AND SPORTS

Around the Zócalo
The Oaxaca *zócalo*, years ago relieved of traffic, is ideal ground for spontaneous diversions. A concert or performance seems to be going on nearly every evening. When it isn't, you can run like a kid over the plaza, bouncing a 10-foot-long *aeroglobo* into the air. (Get them from vendors in front of the cathedral.) If you're in a sitting mood, watch the world go by from a *zócalo* sidewalk cafe. Later, take in the folk-dance performance at the Hotel Monte Albán on the adjacent Plaza Alameda de León, nightly 0830-2200, about $4.

Fiestas
There seems to be a festival somewhere in the Valley of Oaxaca every week of the year. Oaxaca's wide ethnic diversity explains much of the celebrating. Each of the groups celebrates its own traditions. Sixteen languages, in hundreds of dialects, are spoken within the state. Authorities recognize around 500 distinct regional costumes.

All of this ethnic ferment focuses in the city during the July **Lunes de Cerro** festival. Known in pre-Hispanic times as the Guelaguetza (gay-lah-GAY-tzah, "Offering"), tribes reunited for rituals and dancing in honor of Centeotl, the god of corn. The ceremonies, which climaxed with the sacrifice of a virgin who had been fed hallucinogenic mushrooms, were changed to tamer mixed Christian-Indian rites by the Catholic Church. Lilies replaced marigolds, the flower of death, and saints sat in for the Indian gods.

Now, for the weeks around the two Mondays following 16 July, the Virgin of Carmen day, Oaxaca is awash with Indians in costume from all seven traditional regions of Oaxaca. The festivities, which include a crafts and agricultural fair, climax with dances and ceremonies at the Guelaguetza auditorium on the Cerro del Fortín hill northwest of the city. Entrance to the events runs about $5; bring a hat and sunglasses. Make hotel reservations months ahead of time. For more information, write the local tourist information office (see "Information" below) or call the auditorium office at (951) 678-33.

Note: If the first Monday after 16 July happens to fall on July 18, the anniversary of Juárez's death, the first Lunes del Cerro shifts to the following Monday, 25 July.

On the Sunday before the first Lunes del Cerro, Oaxacans celebrate their history and culture at the Plaza de Danzas adjacent to the Virgen de la Soledad church. Events include a big sound, light, and dance show and depictions in tableaux of the four periods of Oaxaca history.

Besides the usual national holidays, Oaxacans celebrate a number of other locally important fiestas. The first day of spring, 21 March, kicks off the **Flower Games** ("Juegos Florales"). Festivities go on for 10 days, including crowning of a festival queen at the Teatro de Alcalá, poetry contests, and performances by renowned artists and the National Symphony.

On the second Monday in October, residents of Santa María del Tule venerate their ancient tree in the **Lunes del Tule** festival. Locals in costume celebrate with rites, folk dances, and feats of horsemanship beneath the boughs of their beloved great cypress.

Oaxaca people venerate their patron, the Virgin of Solitude, 16-18 December. Festivities, which center on the Virgin's basilica (on Independencia six blocks west of the *zócalo*), include fireworks, dancing, food, and street processions of the faithful bearing the Virgin's gold-crowned image decked out in her fine silks and satins.

For the Fiesta of the Radishes ("Rábanos") on 23 December, celebrants fill the Oaxaca *zócalo*, admiring displays of plants, flowers, and figures crafted of large radishes. Ceremonies and prizes honor the most original designs. Foodstalls nearby serve traditional delicacies, including *buñuelos* (honey-soaked fried tortillas), plates of which are traditionally thrown into the air before the evening is over.

Oaxaca people culminate their Posada week on **Nochebuena** (Christmas Eve) with candle-lit processions from their parishes, accompanied by music, fireworks, and floats. They converge on the *zócalo* in time for a midnight cathedral Mass.

Folkloric Dance Shows
If you miss the Lunes del Cerro festival, some localities stage smaller Guelaguetza celebrations

year-round. So do a number of hotels, the most reliable of which occurs nightly at 2030 at the Monte Albín Hotel, on Plaza de León, tel. (951) 627-77, adjacent to the *zócalo*. At other hotels, days may change, so call ahead to confirm: Hotel Camino Real, tel. (951) 606-11, Friday, $30 show with dinner, not including drinks; Hotel Misión de los Angeles, tel. (951) 515-00, daily, free to watch, dinner at regular prices; Hotel Fortín Plaza, seasonally, tel. (951) 577-77.

Nightlife
When lacking an official fiesta, you can create your own at a number of nightspots around town.

The big hotels are most reliable for **live dance music**. Call to confirm programs: Camino Real, tel. (951) 606-11; Victoria, tel. (951) 526-33; Fortín Plaza, tel. (951) 501-00; and Misión de los Angeles, tel. (951) 515-00.

The Victoria, Misión de los Angeles, and Misión San Felipe hotels also operate **discotheques** separate from their lobby-bar entertainment. Call them for details.

Additionally, the Restaurant El Sagrario (see "Cafes and Restaurants" above) offers live music for listening, nightly from about 2000.

Sports
For **jogging,** try the public **Ciudad Deportiva** ("Sports City") fields on the west side of Hwy. 190 about two miles north of the town center.

For an invigorating in-town **walk,** climb the **Cerro del Fortín** hill. Your reward will be a breezy city, valley, and mountain view. The key to getting there through the maze of city streets is to head to the **Escalera del Fortín** (staircase), which will lead you conveniently to the in-step of the hill. For example, from the northeast *zócalo* corner walk north along the Alcalá mall (see "City Sights" above). After five blocks, in front of the Santo Domingo church turn left onto Allende, continue four blocks to Crespo, and turn right. After three blocks, you'll see the staircase on the left. Continue uphill, past the Guelaguetza open-air auditorium, to the road (Nicolas Copernicus) heading north to the **Planetarium.** After that, enjoying the panorama, you can keep walking along the hilltop for at least another mile. Take a hat and water. The roundtrip from the *zócalo* is a minimum of two miles; the

hilltop rises only a few hundred feet. Allow at least a couple of hours.

Swimmers do their thing at **Balneario La Bamba,** about 2.5 (four km) south of town along Hwy. 175 before the airport. The pool is open daily 1000-1700, tel. (951) 409-25. Serious lap swimmers should choose days and hours in order to avoid crowds, Sundays being the worst.

For **tennis,** stay at either the Hotel Victoria or the Misión de los Angeles (see "Accommodations" above), which have courts. Otherwise, call the Club de Tenis Brenamiel, next to the Hotel Villas del Sol, Km 539.5 on Hwy. 190, about three miles north of the center of town, tel. (951) 268-11 or 268-22, and reserve a court; about $12 for the whole day.

A pretty fair general **sporting goods** selection is available at **Super Ahorro de Oaxaca** sports store, downtown, at Hidalgo 814, between Valdivieso and Armenta y López, tel. (951) 631-84.

SHOPPING

Market and Groceries
The traditional town market, **Mercado Juárez,** covers the entire square block just one block south of the *zócalo*. Although the hundreds of stalls offer everything, cotton and wool items—such as dresses, *huipiles,* woven blankets, and serapes—are among the best buys. Despite the festoons and overwhelming piles of merchandise, bargains are there for those willing to search them out.

The Juárez Market got so crowded the city built a bigger one—the **Mercado Abastos**—which sprawls beside the *periférico* southwest of the city. The main market day is Saturday, when folks can find everything the Juárez has, and in even greater quantities (which also means you may have to dig harder through lots of cheap items to find what you're looking for).

For simple, straightforward grocery shopping, stop by **Abarrotes Lonja** on the *zócalo* next to the Hotel Señorial; open daily 0800-2130.

Handicrafts
Oaxaca is famous for handicrafts. Among them are *huipiles,* the most renowned from San Pedro de Amusgos; wool blankets, carpets, and serapes from Teotitlán del Valle; embroidered cot-

ton "wedding dresses," originally from San Antonio, near Ocotlán; pottery—black from San Bartolo Coyotepec and green from Atzompa; carved animals from Arrazola; whimsical figurines by the Aguilar sisters of Ocotlán; mescal from Tlacolula, and some masks. If you somehow can't make it to the source villages (see "Around the Valley of Oaxaca" below), try the Juárez and Abastos markets or the sprinkling of tourist shops along the Alcalá street mall north of the *zócalo.*

Shoppers serious about getting the most for their money can get prices in perspective at the government-run **Mercado de Artesanías** three blocks south and three blocks west of the *zócalo.* Although it lacks Juárez Market's colorful bustle, the Mercado de Artesanías has a little bit of everything in relatively uncrowded displays. The fixed prices, although often a bit high, provide a good yardstick. They're open Mon.-Sat. 0900-1400 and 1600-2000, corner of Zaragoza and Carola.

Shops North of the Zócalo: Head north along the Alcalá mall from the northeast corner of the *zócalo.* Soon comes **Yalalag,** at Alcalá 104, tel. (951) 621-08, among the biggest and most expensive of Oaxaca's handicrafts stores. Quality is high, and selection, from all over Oaxaca and much of Mexico, is extensive. Open Mon.-Sat. 0930-1330 and 1630-2000.

A few doors farther on, the **Palacio de las Gemas,** corner of Morelos and Alcalá, tel. (951) 695-96, although specializing in semiprecious stones and jewelry, has much more, including a host of charming handpainted tinware Christmas decorations, Guerrero masks, and pre-Columbian reproductions in onyx and turquoise. Open Mon.-Sat. 1000-1400 and 1630-2030.

The store in the **Museo de Oaxaca,** at M. Alcalá 202, tel. (951) 684-99, has a small but good-quality all-Oaxaca selection, including *huipiles,* masks, and weavings. Open Wed.-Mon. 1030-2000.

Walk one block west to **Artesanías Cosijo,** at Garcia Vigil 202, tel./fax (951) 614-00, for a big selection of Guerrero masks, carved animals, and some Aguilar sisters pottery. Open Mon.-Sat. 0900-1300 and 1600-2000.

Back on Alcalá, **La Mano Mágica** is on the west side, just below Murguia, at Alcalá 203,

tel./fax (951) 642-75. The shop offers both a colorful exposition of crafts from all over Mexico and a patio workshop, where artisans work, dyeing wool and weaving examples of the lovely, museum-quality rugs and serapes which adorn the walls. Find them open Mon.-Sat. 1000-1330 and 1400-1930.

Across the street at the northwest corner of Alcalá and Murguia, **Creart Artesanías,** tel. (951) 614-87, has a quality selection of stoneware, pottery, Arrazola wooden animals, and masks. Open Mon.-Sat. 1100-1400 and 1700-2000.

A block farther on, the **Plaza Alcalá** complex, west corner of M. Bravo, has a tranquil courtyard restaurant and some good shops. Notable among them is **Corazón del Pueblo,** on the second floor, which, besides a select all-Mexico folk crafts assortment, offers a discriminating selection of English-language books about Mexico: guides, literature, ethnography, archaeology, history, cookbooks, maps, postcards, and more. Located at Alcalá 307, tel. (951) 305-47; open Mon.-Sat. 1000-2000.

Continue up Alcalá past venerable Santo Domingo church on the right (see "A Walk around Town" above) and turn left and stroll a block along the **Jesús Carranza** street-plaza. There, you can appreciate the offerings of the many local vendors, often including Zapotec women in traditional dress, weaving on their backstrap looms.

Rewards await shoppers who are willing to walk a few long blocks farther uphill, to the state-run **ARIPO** (Artesanías y Industrias Populares de Oaxaca) at 809 Garcia Vigil, tel. (951) 413-54. There, masks, wedding dresses, carved animals, ceramics, and tinware fill the rooms. Prices vary: cheap on some items and high on others. Open Mon.-Sat. 0930-1900, Sunday 0900-1300.

Photography
Downtown has a pair of good camera shops. **Foto Figueroa,** one block west of the *zócalo,* well stocked with Kodak film and accessories, offers quick develop-and-print, at Hidalgo 516, corner 20 de Noviembre, tel. (951) 637-66. Open Mon.-Sat. 0900-1330 and 1600-1930.

Express Kolor, half a block down 20 de Noviembre, is even better stocked, with scores of point-and-shoot cameras and many Minolta, Vivitar, and Olympus accessories. They also stock Konica, Fuji, Kodak, and Agfa films in color and black-and-white, both roll and sheet. Located on 20 de Noviembre 225; tel. (951) 614-92; open Mon.-Sat. 0900-1400 and 1600-2000.

SERVICES

Money Exchange

Several banks dot the downtown area. Two Banamex branches, corner Morelos and Díaz, tel. (951) 644-44, and Hidalgo at Cinco de Mayo, tel. (951) 659-00, money exchange Mon.-Fri. 0900-1200, usually give the best rates for U.S. cash and traveler's checks. If they're too crowded, try Bancomer, at Vigil and Morelos, tel. (951) 633-33. Otherwise, go to Banco Mexicano, one block from the zócalo at Independencia 605, tel. (951) 625-26; or its neighbor, Banco Serfin, tel. (951) 616-79, at the adjacent corner of Garcia Vigil, diagonally across from the zócalo cathedral.

After bank hours, go to Casa de Cambio Internacional de Divisas, tel. (951) 633-99, on the Alcalá street mall just north of the zócalo, behind the cathedral. Although they pay about two percent less than banks, they change many major currencies and traveler's checks. Open Mon.-Sat. 0800-2000, Sunday 0900-1700.

The local American Express agency operates an efficient, full-service office across the street, right at the zócalo's northeast corner. They cash American Express traveler's checks for about a dollar per hundred less than banks. On Viajes Mexico Istmo y Caribe, Valdiviesio 2, tel. (951) 627-00 or 629-19, fax 674-75; open Mon.-Fri. 0900-1400 and 1600-1800, Saturday 0900-1300; money service hours may be shorter.

Communication

The Oaxaca correo, tel. (951) 626-61, is across from the cathedral at the corner of the Alameda de León square and Independencia. Open Mon.-Fri. 0900-2000, Saturday 0900-1300.

Oaxaca area code is 951

Telégrafo, tel. (951) 649-02, at the next corner, Independencia and 20 Noviembre, offers money orders, telephone, and public fax. Hours are Mon.-Fri. 0900-2000 (money orders 0900-1800) and Saturday 0900-1300 (money orders 0900-1200).

After hours, you can take advantage of a pair of efficient Computel long-distance phone and public fax offices: on Independencia, by Banco Mexicano, across from the Plaza Alameda de León, tel. (951) 480-84, open 0700-2200; and at Trujano 204, just off the zócalo's southwest corner, tel. (951) 473-19, same hours.

Consulates

The U.S. Consul, tel. (951) 430-54, holds hours Mon.-Fri. 0900-1400 at Alcalá 201, three blocks north of the zócalo. The Canadian Consul does the same for Canadian citizens at Dr. Liceaga 119, no. 8, tel. (951) 337-77.

The Consular Corps of Oaxaca, which includes representatives from a number of countries, handles business at offices at Hidalgo 817, Suite 5, tel. (951) 656-00.

Language Courses

The Instituto de Comunicacion y Cultura, in offices at 307 Alcalá, second floor, offers Spanish courses for visitors. The minimum is one week for $75. Classes begin each Monday. They also arrange homestays with Mexican families. Contact director Yolanda Garcia, tel. (951) 634-43, fax 632-65, during regular office hours, or 627-52 Sunday.

The Universidad Autonoma de Benito Juárez also offers 80-hour courses every four weeks (class size four, around $280 per month) and homestays. Contact them through the director at Independencia and Alcalá, Oaxaca, Oaxaca 68000, tel. (951) 659-22. Be aware occasional strikes have sometimes interrupted the university class schedule.

Informal, minimal-fee Spanish instruction is available by appointment from volunteers at the Benedict Crowell Memorial Lending Library of Oaxaca, M. Alcalá 305, corner of Murguia; open Mon.-Fri. 1000-1300 and 1600-1900, Saturday 1000-1300.

INFORMATION

Tourist Information

Oaxaca Turismo runs an efficient, very helpful office at the corner of 5 de Mayo and Morelos two blocks north, one block east from the *zócalo*, tel. (951) 648-28, tel./fax 609-84. The friendly staff distributes a good state-city map. Open daily 0900-2000.

Medical, Police, and Emergencies

If you get sick, ask your hotel desk to recommend a doctor. Otherwise, go to Sanatorio Carmen, one of Oaxaca's best hospitals at Abasolo 215, tel. (951) 600-27.

For routine medicines and drugs, go to one of many pharmacies, such as the Farmacia Hidalgo, corner 20 Nov. and Hidalgo, one block west of the *zócalo*, tel. (951) 644-59; open Mon.-Sat. 0900-2200 and Sunday 0900-1400 and 1800-2100.

For police emergencies, call the Dirección de Seguridad, tel. (951) 627-26, at Aldama 108, just north of the *zócalo*. For fire, call the *bomberos*, tel. (951) 622-31.

Publications

One of Oaxaca's best sources of new English-language books about Mexico is the Corazón del Pueblo store on the second floor of Plaza Alcalá, Alcalá 307, tel. (951) 305-47; open Mon.-Sat. 1000-2000.

Another good source is Librería Universitaria at Guerrero 104, half a block east of the *zócalo*, tel. 642-43. They have English paperbacks, both used and new, a number of indigenous language dictionaries, and guides, cookbooks, art, and history books. Open Mon.-Sat. 0930-1400 and 1600-2000.

The daily English-language *News* of Mexico City is usually available late mornings at stands near the southwest corner of the *zócalo*. If not, try the small news shop near the same corner at Trujano 106A, open daily 0800-2130. Besides the *News*, they might also have *Time* and *Newsweek*.

Pick up a copy of the informative monthly, the *Oaxaca Times*, at your hotel or at the publisher, the Instituto de Comunicación y Cultura,

tel. (951) 634-43, at 307 Alcalá, second floor. The newspaper prints cultural and historical features, tourist hints, and a list of local events.

Libraries

The Biblioteca (public library), in a lovingly restored ex-convent, is worth a visit, if only for its graceful, cloistered Renaissance interiors and patios. At the corner of Morelos and Alcalá, two blocks north of the *zócalo*, tel. (951) 656-81. Open Mon.-Sat. 1000-1400 and 1600-2000.

Visitors starving for a good read will find satisfaction from at least one of the thousands of volumes at the Benedict Crowell Memorial Lending Library of Oaxaca, M. Alcalá 305, corner of Murguia; open Mon.-Fri. 1000-1300 and 1600-1900, Saturday 1000-1300.

GETTING THERE AND AWAY

By Air

The Oaxaca airport (code-designated OAX) has several daily flights that connect with Mexican destinations.

Mexicana Airlines flights connect four times daily with Mexico City. Three of these flights depart Mexico City early enough to allow same-day connections to Oaxaca from many U.S. destinations. For flight information and reservations, call (951) 684-14 or 472-48.

Aeroméxico flights connect twice daily with Mexico City and once with Guadalajara. For flight information and reservations, call (951) 637-65 or 610-66.

One Aerovias Oaxaqueñas flight connects daily with Puerto Escondido. For reservations, call their office at the airport, tel. (951) 152-00.

Aviacsa airlines connects once daily (except Sunday) with Chiapas, Tabasco, and Yucatán destinations of Tuxtla Gutiérrez, Villahermosa, Mérida, and Cancún. For information and reservations, call (951) 318-09 or 318-01.

PAL Aerolineas connects Oaxaca directly with Acapulco, Ixtapa-Zihuatanejo, Mexico City, Cancún, and Guadalajara. For information and reservations, call toll-free tel. 91-800 220-12 or 91-800 90-463.

The Oaxaca airport is not large, with few services other than a few shops and car rentals.

Since there is no money-exchange agency, arrive with enough pesos to last until you can get to a bank.

Arrival transportation for the six-mile trip into town is easy. Fixed-fare collective taxi tickets run about $3 per person ($6 to north-side Hotels Misión de los Angeles, Fortín Plaza, and Victoria). For the same trip, a *taxi especial* (private taxi) ticket runs about $10 for three persons. No public buses run between the airport and town.

Car rental agents operating at the Oaxaca Airport are Budget, tel. (951) 100-36 airport; Dollar, tel. (951) 150-31 airport (663-29 downtown); and Hertz, tel. (951) 624-34 downtown.

On **departure,** save enough dollars or pesos for your $12 international departure tax (which may instead be collected in Mexico City). If you lose your tourist card, best contact the helpful **Turismo** information office downtown, 5 de Mayo and Morelos, tel. (951) 648-28, open daily 0900-2000, for assistance *before* your planned day of departure.

By Car or RV

Paved (but long and winding) roads connect Oaxaca south with Puerto Ángel, southwest with Pinotepa Nacional, northwest with Mexico City, and southeast with Tehuantepec.

South to **Puerto Ángel,** narrow **National Hwy. 175** connects along 148 winding miles (238 km) over the Sierra Madre del Sur to its junction with Hwy. 200 at Pochutla (thence six miles to Puerto Ángel). The road climbs to 9,000 feet through winter-chilly pine forests and Chatino and Zapotec Indian villages. Fill up with Magna Sin at the last-chance Mihuatlán Pemex heading south and Pochutla heading north; carry water and blankets and be prepared for emergencies. Allow about five and a half driving hours south from Oaxaca to Puerto Ángel, about seven in the opposite direction.

The 229-mile (368-km) **Hwy. 190-Hwy. 125** route connects Oaxaca southwest with **Pinotepa Nacional.** Although winding most of the way, the generally uncongested road is smooth and safely driveable from Oaxaca in about six driving hours if you use the *cuota* (toll) Hwy. 190 *autopista* northwest of Oaxaca city. Add an hour for the 5,000-foot climb in the opposite direction.

The 350-mile (564-km) winding **Hwy. 190-160** Oaxaca-Cuernavaca-Mexico City route requires one very long day, or better two, for safety. Under the best of conditions, driving time runs 10 hours either way. Take it easy and stop over en route. (Make sure you arrive in Mexico City on a day when your car is permitted to drive. See special topic "Mexico City Driving Regulations.")

The relatively easy 157-mile (252-km) Oaxaca-Tehuantepec **Hwy. 190** route requires around five hours either way. From there, roads connect east to Chiapas, Yucatán, and Guatemala, or northwest along the coast with Bahías de Huatulco and Puerto Ángel.

By Bus

Autobuses de Oriente and Cristóbal Colón, Oaxaca's luxury- and first-class carriers, operate out of the big modern terminal on Hwy. 190, Calz. Héroes de Chapultepec 1036 at Carranza, on the north side of town.

Autobuses de Oriente, tel. (951) 517-03, offers many connections northwest along the Hwy. 190 corridor; dozens daily with Mexico City, four with Puebla, and two with Veracruz.

Cristóbal Colón (tel. 512-14), on the other hand, connects northeast with Villahermosa, southeast with Tehuantepec, Chiapas, and Guatemala, and south (via Highways. 190 and 200) with Bahías de Huatulco, Pochutla-Puerto Ángel, Puerto Escondido, and Pinotepa Nacional.

A swarm of second-class buses runs from the **Central Camionera Abastos** by the *periférico,* prolongation of Trujano, southeast side of town. **Autotransportes Oaxaca-Pacífico,** tel. (951) 691-03, and **Autobuses Estrella del Valle,** tel. (951) 457-00 or 657-29, travel the Hwy. 175 route north-south between Oaxaca and Pochutla-Puerto Ángel. Both lines connect along coastal Hwy. 200 with Bahías de Huatulco and Puerto Escondido.

For a backcountry adventure, ride **Estrella Roja del Sureste,** tel. (951) 606-94, whose first- and second-class buses connect along bone-jangling, partly paved Hwy. 131 north-south via Sola de Vega and Juquila directly with Puerto Escondido. From there, they make coastal connections with Pochutla-Puerto Ángel, Bahías de Huatulco, and Pinotepa Nacional.

By Train

Although they're sometimes painfully slow, trains connect Oaxaca (via Puebla) with Mexico City, and thence with most of Pacific Mexico. (See "By Rail to Pacific Mexico" map, in the On the Road chapter.)

One Mexico-City-bound train departs daily from the station on Calz. Madero about a mile and a half west of downtown. Service, very cheap, is by first- and second-class coach only and includes a restaurant car. Call the station, tel. (951) 622-53 or 625-64, for departure information and prices.

AROUND THE VALLEY OF OAXACA

Oaxaca offers much of interest—archaeological sites, crafts villages and weekly markets—outside the city. Valley market towns each have their market day, when local color is at a maximum and prices are at a minimum. Among the choices, starting on the east side (see "Valley of Oaxaca" map) are: Teotitlán del Valle, half an hour east, Saturday; Tlacolula, one hour east, Sunday; Ocotlán, half an hour south, Friday; Zaachila, half an hour southwest, Thursday; Zimatlán, one hour southwest, Wednesday; and San Pedro y San Pablo Etla, half an hour northeast, Wednesday.

These market visits are conveniently combined with stops at handicrafts villages, ruins (notably Mitla, on the east side, and Monte Albán, west), and other sights along the way.

Getting around the Valley of Oaxaca

Although droves of second-class buses from the Abastos terminal run everywhere in the Valley of Oaxaca, it would take you a month touring that way. It's better to rent a car—call Hertz, tel. (951) 624-34; Dollar, tel. (951) 663-29; or Automovilista Rojo, tel. (951) 664-22—or ride one of the reasonably priced tour buses leaving daily from the Hotel Señorial (on the *zócalo*, tel. 951-639-33) or the Hotel del Ángel (tel. 951-666-33 or 601-99) on the corner of Mier y Terán and Mina, six blocks southwest of the *zócalo*. Many other hotels also have such tour arrangements. See your desk clerk.

EAST SIDE:
EL TULE, TEOTITLÁN DEL VALLE, AND TLACOLULA

Enough attractions lie along this route for days of exploring. For example, you could visit El Tule and the Saturday Teotitlán market, continuing for an overnight at Mitla. Next morning, explore the Mitla ruins for a couple of hours, then return, spending the afternoon at the Sunday market at Tlacolula along the way.

El Tule is a gargantuan Mexican cedar *(ahuehuete)*, probably the largest tree in Latin America and maybe the world. Its gnarled, house-size trunk divides into a forest of elephantine limbs that rise to festoons of bushy branches reaching 15 stories overhead. The small town of Santa María del Tule, nine miles (14 km) east of the city on Hwy. 190, seems built around the tree. A crafts market, a church, and the town plaza, where residents celebrate their El Tule with a fiesta on 7 October, all surround the beloved 2,000-year-old living giant.

Teotitlán del Valle, nine miles farther, at the foot of the Sierra, means "Place of the Gods" in Nahuatl; before that it was known as Xa Quire, or "Foot of the Mountain," by the Zapotecs who settled it around A.D. 1000. Dominican missionaries introduced the first sheep, whose wool, combined with local skills, results in the fine serapes, carpets, and blankets that seem to fill every shop in town.

Nearly every house is a mini-factory where people card, spin, and dye wool, often using traditional hand-gathered cochineal, indigo, and moss dyes. Every step of wool preparation is laborious; pure water is even a chore—families typically spend two days a week collecting it from mountain springs. The weaving, on traditional hand looms, is the easy part.

The best day to visit Teotitlán is on market day Saturday, when your choices will be manifold. You can visit the shops of renowned masters such as Isaac Vasquez or other humbler but excellent shops, such as that of Reynaldo Sosa, who markets the work of the Mujeres Tejedoras ("Women Weavers") cooperative at Hidalgo 31, two blocks from the town plaza and market.

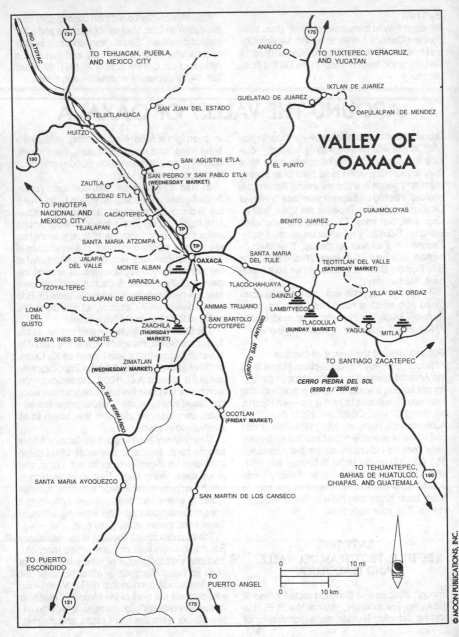

VALLEY OF OAXACA

Later, you can select from the the hosts of bright displays at the market itself, by the church, end of Hidalgo.

The best weaving is generally the densest, typically packing in about 20 strands per inch; ordinary weaving uses about half that. Please don't bargain too hard. Even the highest prices typically bring the weavers less than a dollar an hour for their labor.

While you're at the Teotitlán market, stop by the local museum, called, in Zapotec, the **Balaa Xtee Guech Gulal** ("House of the Old Town"), in the brick building at the plaza end of Hidalgo. Exhibits detail the Teotitlán weaving tradition, archaeological artifacts, and traditions surrounding the traditional Zapotec marriage ceremony.

The Zapotecs who founded **Tlacolula** (24 miles, 38 km, from Oaxaca) around A.D. 1250 called it Gulchibaa ("Town of Heaven"). Besides its Sunday market, its 1523 chapel, Señor de Tlacolula (with a headless St. Paul), and its adjacent 1531 church, Tlacolula is famous for mescal. Get a good free sample at friendly **La Favorita** shop, on main street Juárez no. 9, as you head toward the market. Besides a pet monkey and many hand-embroidered Amusgo *huipiles* and Teotitlán weavings, La Favorita offers mescal in 20 flavors, 10 for women and 10 for men.

MITLA

Mitla is but the last (although best known) of the famous series of ruins east of Oaxaca city. For energetic explorers, Dainzú (15 miles, 24 km), Lambityeco (18 miles, 28 km), and Yagul (28 miles, 45 km) are all worth a visit.

Mitla, however, about 31 miles (50 km) east of Oaxaca, is a "must" for Valley of Oaxaca sightseers. Mitla (Liobaa in Zapotec, the "Place of the Dead") flowered late, reaching a population of perhaps 10,000 during its apex around A.D. 1350. It remained occupied and in use for generations after the conquest.

During Mitla's heyday, several feudalistic, fortified city-states vied for power in the Valley of Oaxaca. Concurrently, Mixtec-speaking people arrived from the north, perhaps under pressure from Aztecs and others in central Mexico. Evidence suggests that these Mixtec groups, in interacting with the resident Zapotecs, created

the unique architectural styles of late cities such as Yagul and Mitla. Archaeologists believe, for example, that the striking *greca* (Greek-like) frets that honeycomb Mitla facades result from the Mixtec influence.

Exploring the Site

In a real sense, Mitla lives on. The ruins coincide with the present town of San Pablo Villa de Mitla, whose main church actually occupies the northernmost of five main groups of monumental ruins. Virtually anywhere archaeologists dig within the town they hit remains of the myriad ancient dwellings, plazas, and tombs that connected the still-visible landmarks.

Of the five ruins clusters, the best preserved is the fenced-in Columns Group. Its exploration requires about an hour. The others—the Arroyo and Adobe groups beyond an arroyo, and the South Group across the Mitla River—are rubbly, unreconstructed mounds. The North Group has

Weaving is but the climax of the laborious processes that include growing, shearing, washing, carding, spinning, and dyeing wool.

suffered due to past use by the local parish. Evidence indicates the Adobe and South groups were ceremonial compounds, while the Arroyo, North, and Columns groups were palaces.

The public entrance to the Columns Group leads from the parking lot, past a tourist market and through the gate (open daily 0900-1700, admission $3). Inside, two large patios, joined at one corner, are each surrounded on three sides by elaborate apartments. A shrine occupies the center of the first patio. Just north of this stands the **Palace of Columns,** the most important of Mitla's buildings. It sits atop a staircase, inaccurately reconstructed in 1901.

Inside, a file of six massive monolithic columns supported the roof. A narrow "escape" passage exits out the right rear side to a large patio enclosed by a continuous narrow room. The purely decorative *greca* facades, which required around 100,000 cut stones for the entire complex, embellish the walls. Remnants of the original red and white stucco that lustrously embellished the entire complex hide in niches and corners.

Walk south to the second patio, which has a similar layout. Here, the main palace occupies the east side, where a passage descends to a tomb beneath the front staircase. Both this and another tomb beneath the building at the north side of the patio are intact, preserving their original crucifix shapes. (The guard, although he is not supposed to, may try to collect a tip for letting you descend.) No one knows who and what were buried in these tombs, which were open and empty at the time of the conquest.

The second tomb is similar, except that it contains a stone pillar called the Column of Life; by embracing it, legend says, you will learn how many years you have left.

The Church Group (notice the church domes) on the far side of the Palace of Columns is worth a visit. Builders used the original temple stones to erect the church here. On its north side is a patio leading to another interior patio surrounded by another *greca* fret-embellished palace.

Museum, Accommodation, and Food

The University of the Americas (Mexico City) houses an exceptionally fine Oaxaca artifact collection at the **Frissell Museum,** tel. (951) 582-69, just west of (left as you enter) the Mitla town plaza. Displays include a host of finely preserved ceramic figurines, yet-to-be-deciphered Zapotec glyphs, and a Zapotec marriage certificate in stone. Open 0900-1700 daily. A good restaurant in the museum serves regional dishes from 0900 to about 1630.

Hotel La Zapoteca, 5 de Febrero 12, Mitla, Oaxaca 70430, tel. (951) 800-26, just south of the Mitla River bridge, has a good homey restaurant and clean, reasonably priced lodgings, okay for an overnight. The 20 rooms with bath rent for about $14 s, $18 d, $23 t with hot water and parking.

The Yagul archaeological zone, on a valley-view hilltop near Mitla, includes a restored ball court (foreground), ceremonial platforms, and a maze-like palace complex.

BRUCE WHIPPERMAN

hieroglyph of Mitla
("Place of the Dead")

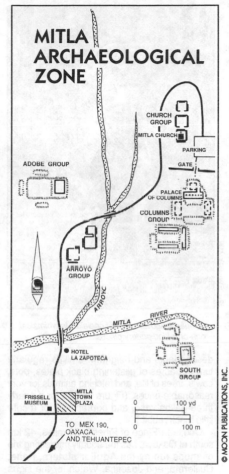

Breezy *palapa* **Restaurant Centeotl** on the Yagul archaeological zone entrance road (about three miles back toward Oaxaca from Mitla) is worth a stop all by itself. Here, you can quickly double your Mexican food vocabulary, by sampling such regional delights as *coloradito* (savory red *mole* chicken or beef stew), *verde de espinazo* (similar ingredients, but stewed in green mole), *sopa de guias* (corn and squash soup), and *estofado* (tasty chiletomato-pork soup).

Besides its gastronomical significance, Centeotl (sayn-tay-OH-tl) is an earnest cultural-ecological endeavor of the friendly elderly owner, who articulately explains his purpose in prose and verse. Ask for his pamphlet, *folleto* (foh-YAY-toh), about Centeotl.

As you leave, take a look at the pre-Columbian ball game ring mounted by the restaurant entrance. Although the ring is interesting all by itself, the cannonball-sized stone sphere perched atop the ring doubles the intrigue, since (if it's authentic as the owner claims) a stone ball is in variance with general archaeological opinion that the pre-Columbian ball game was played with a rubber, rather than a rock ball. (Pity the pre-Columbian ball players who had to bat such a hard, heavy missile around with their arms, shoulders, and torsos.)

SOUTH SIDE: SAN BARTOLO COYOTEPEC AND OCOTLÁN DE MORELOS

These crafts towns make a nice pair to visit on Ocotlán's Friday market day. Coyotepec ("Hill of the Coyote") on Hwy. 175, 14 miles (23 km) south of the city, is famous for its pottery

and its 24 August festival, when masked villagers, costumed half-man, half-woman in tiaras, blond wigs, tin crowns, and velvet cloaks dance in honor of their patron, San Bartolo.

Their pottery, the renowned black *barra* sold all over Mexico, is available at a number of cottage factory-shops (watch for signs) off the highway on (east side) Juárez Street. **Doña Rosa,** who passed away in 1980, pioneered the technique of crafting lovely big round jars without a potter's wheel. With their local clay, Doña Rosa's

BRUCE WHIPPERMAN

Ocotlán's Aguilar sisters specialize in whimsical, one-of-a-kind pottery pieces.

descendants and neighbor families regularly turn out acres of glistening black plates, pots, bowls, trees of life, and fetching animals for very reasonable prices. (Figure on $25 for a pearly three-gallon vase, and perhaps $2 for a cute little black rabbit.)

Ocotlán ("Place of Pines"), 26 miles, 42 km south of Oaxaca, has the equally interesting trio of shops run by the **Aguilar sisters,** Irene, Guillerma, and Josefina. Watch for the signs about a quarter mile on the Oaxaca side from the town plaza. Their creations include a host of fanciful figures in clay: vendors with big ripe strawberries, green and red cactus, goats in skirts, and bikini-clad blondes.

Your main Ocotlán attraction (unless you're lucky enough to arrive during the 18 May fiesta) will be the big Friday market. Hint: Since markets are best in the morning, make Ocotlán your *first* Friday stop.

SOUTHWEST SIDE: ARRAZOLA, CUILAPAN, AND ZAACHILA

This excursion is best on Thursday, when you can begin fresh in the morning at the big weekly market and ruins in Zaachila, then head back to the ex-Convent Santiago Aposto near Cuilapan, continuing toward town for a visit to see the animals being crafted in Arrazola village.

Get there by tour bus or by car heading toward Monte Albán (look for the big road sign) west over the Atoyac River from the *periférico* at the south edge of town. Just after crossing the bridge fork left (south) from the Monte Albán road on to the Zaachila road.

Your destination is the Zaachila town plaza-market about 10 miles south of Oaxaca. Like Mitla, **Zaachila** overlies the ruins of its ancient namesake city, which rose to prominence after the decline of Monte Albán. Although excavations have uncovered many Mixtec-style remains, historical records nevertheless list a number of Zapotec kings who ruled Zaachila as a virtual Zapotec capital. On the eve of the conquest, it was a Mixtec noble minority who dominated the Zapotec-speaking inhabitants, whose leaders the Mixtec warriors had sent fleeing for their lives to Tehuantepec.

The big forested hill that rises north of the plaza-market is topped by a large, mostly unexplored pyramid. Several unexcavated mounds and courtyards dot the hill's north and south flanks. The site parking lot and entrance gate are adjacent to the colonial church just north of the plaza.

In 1962, archaeologist Roberto Gallegos uncovered a pair of unopened tombs beneath the summit of the Zaachila pyramid. They yielded a trove of polychrome pottery, gold jewelry (including a ring still on a left hand), and jade fan handles. Tomb 1, which is open for public inspection, descends via a steep staircase to an entrance decorated with a pair of cat-motif heads. On the antechamber walls a few steps farther on are depictions of owls and a pair of personages (perhaps former occupants) inscribed respectively with (month-week) name-dates 5 Flower and 9 Flower. Do not miss the bas-reliefs on the tomb's back wall (take a flashlight), which depict a man whose torso is covered with a turtle shell and another whose head is emerging from a serpent body.

Hint: The narrow tomb staircase is negotiable by only a few persons at a time and often requires an hour for a tour bus crowd to inspect it. Rather than wasting your market time standing in line, go downhill, stroll around the market, and return when the line is smaller. If driving, arrive early, around nine on Thursday, to avoid tour bus crowds.

Cuilapan de Guerrero, a few miles north toward Oaxaca, is known for its elaborate unfinished ex-Convent of Saint Santiago (visible from the highway) where President Guerrero was executed in 1831. Although begun in 1535, the cost of the basilica and associated monastery began to balloon. In 1550, King Philip demanded humility and moderation of the builders, whose work was finally ended by a 1570 court ruling. The extravagances—soaring, roofless basilica, magnificent baptismal font, splendid Gothic cloister, and elaborate frescoes—remain as national treasures.

Arrazola is the source of the intricately painted fanciful wooden creatures that are increasingly turning up in shops all over Mexico and foreign countries. To get there turn west onto signed Hwy. 145 a few miles farther north, or about five miles south of the Atoyac River Bridge. Few, if any, signs direct visitors to the workshops. Turn right after a few miles at Calle Obregón (just past the basketball court) and start looking around near the top of the hill. Although every family along the street seems to craft its own variations, **Pepe Santiago** and his Santa's workshop of craftspersons seems to have the edge. Inside the Santiago compound (on the left just before the hilltop), men saw and carve away, while a cadre of young women painstakingly add riots of painted brocade to whimsical dragons, gargoyles, armadillos, giraffes, rabbits, and everything in between.

NORTHEAST OF TOWN: MONTE ALBÁN AND ETLA

Monte Albán is among Mesoamerica's most regal and spectacular ruined cities. The original name is lost in antiquity. "Monte Albán" was probably coined by a local Spaniard because of its resemblance to a similarly named Italian hill town.

Monte Albán's people cultivated corn, beans, squash, chiles, and fruits on the hillsides and adjacent valleys, occasionally feasting on meat from deer, small game, and perhaps (as did other ancient Mexicans) domesticated dogs. Tribute from surrounding communities directly enriched Monte Albán's ruling classes, and, by extension, its artisans and farmers.

Monte Albán reigned for at least 1,200 years, between 500 B.C. and A.D. 750, as the capital of the Zapotecs and the dominant force between Teotihuacán in the Valley of Mexico and the Maya empires of the south.

Archaeologists have organized the Valley of Oaxaca's history from 500 B.C. to the conquest in five periods, known as Monte Albán I through V. Over those centuries, the hilltop city was repeatedly reconstructed, with new walls, plazas, and staircases, which, like peels of an onion, now overlie earlier construction.

Remains from Monte Albán Period I (500 B.C.-A.D. 0) reveal an already advanced culture, with gods, permanent temples, a priesthood, writing, numerals, and a calendar. Sharply contrasting house styles indicate a differentiated, multilayered society. Monte Albán I ruins abound in graceful polychrome ceramics of uniquely Zapotec style.

Concurrent Olmec influences have also been found, notably in the buildings known as the **Danzantes** ("Dancers"), decorated with unique bas-reliefs, similar to those unearthed along the Veracruz and Tabasco coasts.

Monte Albán II people (A.D. 0-300), by contrast, came under heavy influence from Chiapas and Guatemala in the south. They built strange, ship-shaped buildings, such as Monte Albán's Building J, and left unique remains of their religion, such as the striking jade bat-god now on display in the Anthropology Museum in Mexico City.

Monte Albán reached its apex during Period III (A.D. 300-800), attaining a population of perhaps 40,000 in an urban zone of about three square miles, which spread along hilltops (including the El Gallo and Atzompa archaeological sites) west of the present city of Oaxaca.

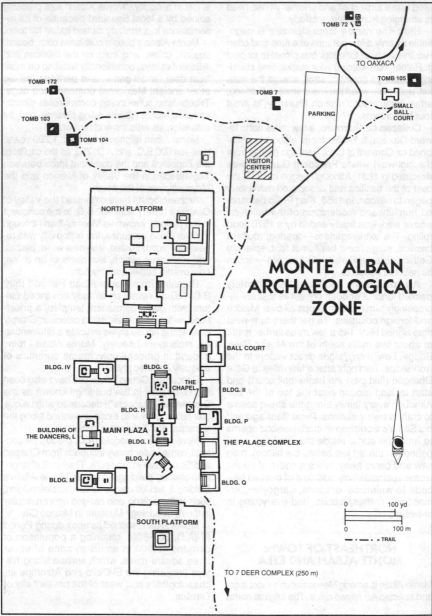

TOMB 72

TO OAXACA

TOMB 105

TOMB 172

TOMB 7

SMALL
BALL
COURT

TOMB 103

PARKING

TOMB 104

VISITOR
CENTER

NORTH PLATFORM

MONTE ALBAN
ARCHAEOLOGICAL
ZONE

BALL COURT

BLDG. IV

BLDG. G

THE
CHAPEL

BLDG. II

BLDG. H

BLDG. P

BUILDING OF
THE DANCERS, L

MAIN PLAZA

BLDG. I

THE PALACE COMPLEX

BLDG. J

BLDG. M

BLDG. Q

MOON

SOUTH PLATFORM

0   100 yd

0   100 m

— · — · — = TRAIL

TO 7 DEER COMPLEX (250 m)

© MOON PUBLICATIONS, INC.

Vigorous Period III leaders rebuilt the main hilltop complex as we see it today. Heavily influenced by the grand Teotihuacán styles, the buildings were finished with handsome sloping staircases, corniced walls, monumental carvings, ball courts, and hieroglyph-enscribed stelae depicting gods, kings, and heroic scenes of battle.

By A.D. 750 few foreign influences were continuing to enrich Monte Albán's uniquely Zapotec pottery styles. Quality declined until they seemed like mere factory copies. Concurrently, the Zapotec pantheon expanded to a horde of gods, as if mere numbers could protect the increasingly isolated Valley of Oaxaca from the outside world.

In A.D. 800, Monte Albán, mysteriously cut off from the rest of Mesoamerica, was declining in population and power. By A.D. 1000, the city was nearly abandoned. The reasons—whether drought, disease, or revolt—and the consequent loss of the necessarily imported water, wood, salt, and food supplies, remain an enigma.

During Periods IV and V, Mixtec peoples from the north invaded the Valley of Oaxaca. They warred with valley Zapotecs and, despite their relatively small numbers, became a ruling class in a number of Valley city-states. The blend of Mixtec and Zapotec art and architecture sometimes led to new forms, especially visible at the west-valley sites of Yagul and Mitla.

Monte Albán, meanwhile, although abandoned, was not forgotten. It became both a refuge and a venerated burial place. In times of siege, local people retreated within the walls of a fortress built around Monte Albán's South Platform. At other times, Mixtec nobles opened tombs and reused them as burial vaults right down until the eve of the conquest.

Exploring Monte Albán

Visitors to Monte Albán enjoy a panoramic view of green mountains rising above the checker-

carved wooden rabbit from Arrazola, in the Valley of Oaxaca

board of the Valley of Oaxaca. Monte Albán is fun for a picnic; or, alternatively, it is an auspicious place to perch atop a pyramid above the grand Main Plaza, etched by lengthening afternoon shadows, and contemplate the ages.

As you enter past the visitor center, north is on your right, marked by the grand **North Platform**, topped by clusters of temples. The **Ball Court** will soon appear below on your left. Twenty-foot-high walkways circumscribe the sunken "I"-shaped playing field. To ensure true bounces, builders spread smooth stucco over all surfaces, including the slopes on opposite sides (which, contrary to appearances, did not seat spectators). This, like all Oaxacan ball courts, had no stone ring (for supposed goals), but rather four mysterious niches at the court's opposite "I"-end corners.

The **Main Plaza,** 1,000 feet long and exactly two-thirds that wide, is aligned along a precise north-south axis. Probably serving as a market and civic-ceremonial ground, the monumentally harmonious Main Plaza was the Zapotec "navel" of the world.

Monte Albán's oldest construction, of the **Danzantes** (surmounted by newer Bldg. L, on the west side of the plaza between Buildings M and IV) dates from Period I. Its walls are graced with a host of personages, known commonly as the *danzantes* (dancers) from their oft-contorted postures—probably chiefs, vanquished by Monte Albán's armies. Their headdresses, earplugs, bracelets, and necklaces mark them among the nobility, while glyphs around their heads identify each individual.

Building J (circa A.D. 0), one of the most remarkable in Mesoamerica, stands nearby in mid-plaza at the foot of the South Platform. Speculation has raged since excavators unearthed its arrow-shaped base generations ago. It is not surprising that Alfonso Caso, Monte Albán's principal excavator, theorized it was an astronomical observatory. In the mind's eye, it seems like some fantastic ocean (or space?) vessel, being navigated to some mysteriously singular southwest destination by a ghostly

ERIN DWYER

crew oblivious of its worldly, earthbound brother monuments.

The **South Platform,** especially during the late afternoon, affords Monte Albán's best vantage point. Starting on the right-hand, Palace complex side, **Building II** has a peculiar tunnel on its near side, covertly used by priests for privacy or perhaps some kind of magical effect. To the south stands Building P, an undistinguished, albeit multi-room palace.

The South Platform itself is only marginally explored. Looters have riddled the mounds on its top side. Its bottom four corners were embellished by fine bas reliefs, two of which had their engraving *intentionally buried* from view. You can admire the fine sculpture and yet-undeciphered Zapotec hieroglyphs on one of them, along with others, at the South Platform's plaza-edge west side.

Still atop the South Platform, turn southward, where you can see the 7 Deer complex, a few hundred yards away, labeled for the name-date inscribed on its great lintel.

Turning northward again, look just beyond Building J to Buildings G, H, and I at plaza-center, erected mostly to cover a rocky mound impossible to remove without the then-unavailable dynamite. Between these buildings and the Palace complex on the right stands the small **chapel** where the remarkable bat-god jade sculpture was found.

On Monte Albán's northern periphery stand a number of tombs which, when excavated, yielded a trove of artifacts, now mostly housed in museums. Walking west from the Northern Platform's northeast base corner, you will pass Mound X on the right. A few hundred yards farther comes the **Tomb 104** mound, presided over by an elaborate ceramic urn representing Cojico, the Zapotec god of rain. Just north of this is **Tomb 172,** with the skeletons and offerings left intact.

Heading back along the northernmost of the two paths from Tomb 104, you will arrive at **Tomb 7** a few hundred feet behind the visitor center. Here, around 1450, Mixtec nobles removed the original 8th-century contents and reused the tomb, burying a deceased dignitary and two servants for the netherworld. Along

with the bodies they left a fabulous treasure in gold, silver, jade, alabaster, and turquoise, now visible at the regional Museo de Oaxaca. (See "City Sights" above.)

A few hundred feet toward town on the opposite side of the road from the parking lot is a trail, leading past a small ball court to the Cerro de Plumaje ("Hill of Plumage"), site of **Tomb 105.** A magnificent entrance door lintel, reminiscent of those at Mitla, welcomes you inside. Past the patio, descend to the mural-decorated tomb antechamber. Inside the cruciform tomb itself, four figures walk in pairs toward a great glyph, flanked by a god and goddess, identified by their name-dates.

Visitor Center and Getting There

The Monte Albán Visitor Center has a small museum, cafe, information counter, and good store, with many books—guides, histories, art, folklore—on Mesoamerica. One of the most useful archaeological guides is Ignacio Bernal's *Official Guide of the Oaxaca Valley,* which includes Monte Albán, Cuilapan, Zaachila, Dainzu, Lambityeco, Yagul, and Mitla. Also covering the same territory, but in more depth, is *Oaxaca, the Archeological Record* by archaeologist Marcus Winter.

Get to Monte Albán either by driving yourself (follow the big "Monte Albán" sign on the *periférico,* end of Cabrera) over the Río Atoyac bridge; bear right after the bridge, and continue about four miles (six km), bearing uphill, to the summit; or on a bus tour departing from your hotel or downtown Hotel Señorial (tel. 951-639-33) or Hotel del Ángel (tel. 951-666-33 or 601-99). Tours leave daily. Or take one of the very frequent Monte Albán buses from the Abastos terminal, on the *periférico,* end of Trujano.

Monte Albán is open daily from 1000, closing promptly at 1700.

Etla

The untouristed, very colorful Wednesday market at Etla (officially San Pedro y San Pablo Etla), northeast of Oaxaca, could be visited either separately or in coordination with a visit to Monte Albán. Although Etla's market invariably has stalls overflowing with its famous white vendors offer much other old-fashioned merchandise. (How would you like, for example, some fresh sheepskins, burro packframes, green Atzompa pottery, or red Oaxaca tamales?)

Preferably visit the market in the forenoon and Monte Albán in the midafternoon. Arrive at Monte Albán by 1430 to allow enough leisure to tour the ruins before closing at 1700.

Getting to Etla: By car, head north along Hwy. 190 about nine miles (15 km) from the city center, turn left just before the Pemex station. San Pablo y San Pedro Etla is about half a mile from the highway. By bus, ride one of the many "Etla" buses from the Abastos second-class terminal, or a tour bus.

mask with unusual
monkey mascot motif

BOOKLIST

Some of these books are informative, others are entertaining, and all of them will increase your understanding of Mexico. Some are easier to find in Mexico than at home, and vice versa. Take a few along on your trip. If you find others that are especially noteworthy, let us know. Happy reading.

HISTORY

Calderón de la Barca, Fanny. *Life in Mexico, with New Material from the Author's Journals.* New York: Doubleday, 1966. Edited by H.T. and M.H. Fisher. An update of the brilliant, humorous, and celebrated original 1913 book by the Scottish wife of the Spanish ambassador to Mexico.

Casasola, Gustavo. *Seis Siglos de Historia Gráfica de Mexico* (Six Centuries of Mexican Graphic History). Mexico City: Editorial Gustavo Casasola, 1978. Six fascinating volumes of Mexican history in pictures, from 1325 to the present.

Cortés, Hernán. *Letters From Mexico.* Translated by Anthony Pagden. New Haven: Yale University Press, 1986. Cortés's five long letters to his king, in which he describes contemporary Mexico in fascinating detail, including, notably, the remarkably sophisticated life of the Aztecs at the time of the conquest.

Díaz del Castillo, Bernal. *The True Story of the Conquest of Mexico.* Translated by Albert Idell. Garden City: Doubleday, 1956. A soldier's still-fresh tale of the conquest from the Spanish viewpoint.

Garfias, Luis. *The Mexican Revolution.* Mexico City: Panorama Editorial, 1985. A concise Mexican version of the 1910-1917 Mexican revolution, the crucible of present-day Mexico.

León-Portilla, Miguel. *The Broken Spears: The Aztec Account of the Conquest of Mexico.* New York: Beacon Press, 1962. Provides an interesting contrast to Díaz del Castillo's account.

Meyer, Michael, and William Sherman. *The Course of Mexican History.* New York: Oxford University Press, 1991. An insightful, 700-plus-page college textbook in paperback. A bargain, especially if you can get it used.

Novas, Himlice. *Everything You Need to Know About Latino History.* New York: Plume Books (Penguin Group), 1994. Chicanos, Latin rhythm, La Raza, the Treaty of Guadalupe Hidalgo, and much more, interpreted from an authoritative Latino point of view.

Reed, John. *Insurgent Mexico.* New York: International Publisher's Co., 1994. Re-publication of 1914 original. Fast-moving (but not unbiased) description of the 1910 Mexican revolution by the journalist famed for his reporting of the subsequent 1917 Russian revolution. Reed, memorialized by the Soviets, was resurrected in the 1981 film biography *Reds.*

Ruíz, Ramon Eduardo. *Triumphs and Tragedy: A History of the Mexican People.* New York: W.W. Norton, Inc., 1992. A pithy, anecdote-filled history of Mexico, from an authoritative Mexican-American perspective.

Simpson, Lesley Bird. *Many Mexicos.* Berkeley: The University of California Press, 1962. A much-reprinted, fascinating broad-brush version of Mexican history.

UNIQUE GUIDE AND TIP BOOKS

American Automobile Association. *Mexico Travelbook.* Heathrow, FL: 1995. Published by the American Automobile Association, offices at 1000 AAA Drive, Heathrow, FL 32746-5063. Short sweet summaries of major Mexican tourist destinations and sights. Also includes information on fiestas, accommodations, restaurants, and a wealth of information relevant to car travel in Mexico. Available in bookstores, or free to AAA members at affiliate offices.

Burton, Tony. *Western Mexico, A Traveller's Treasury*. Guadalajara: Editorial Agata (Juan Manuel 316, Guadalajara 44100). A well-researched and lovingly written and illustrated guide to dozens of fascinating places to visit, both well-known and out of the way, in Michoacán, Jalisco, and Nayarit.

Franz, Carl. *The People's Guide to Mexico.* Santa Fe: John Muir, 9th edition, 1993. An entertaining and insightful A to Z general guide to the joys and pitfalls of independent economy travel in Mexico.

Freedman, Jacqueline, and Susan Gerstein. *Traveling Like Everybody Else*. Adama Books. Your handicap needn't keep you at home.

Graham, Scott. *Handle With Care*. Chicago: The Noble Press, 1991. Should you accept a meal from a family who lives in a grass house? This insightful guide answers this and hundreds of other tough questions for persons who want to travel responsibly in the third world.

Howells, John, and Don Merwin. *Choose Mexico.* Oakland, CA: Gateway Books (distributed by Publishers Group West, Dept. M, 2023 Clemens Rd., Oakland, CA 94602). A pair of experienced Mexico residents provide a wealth of astute counsel about the important questions—health, finance, home ownership, work, driving, legalities—of long-term travel, residence, and retirement in Mexico. Includes specific sections on Puerto Vallarta, Guadalajara, and Lake Chapala.

Jeffries, Nan. *Adventuring With Children*. San Francisco: Foghorn Press/Avalon House, 1992. This unusually detailed book starts where most travel-with-children books end. It contains, besides a wealth of information and practical strategies for general travel with children, specific chapters on how you can adventure—trek, kayak, river-raft, camp, bicycle, and much more—successfully with the kids in tow.

Nelson, Mike. *Mexico From the Driver's Seat.* McAllen, TX: Scrivener Press, 2009 S. 10th St., McAllen, TX 78502. "Mexico" Mike's entertaining and informative compendium of anecdotal episodes from his yearly 20,000 miles of traveling Mexico's byways, from Baja to the Yucatán.

Rogers, Steve, and Tina Rosa. *The Shopper's Guide to Mexico.* Santa Fe: John Muir, 1989. A well-written guide to shopping in Mexico, with emphasis on handicrafts. Contains inventory details and locations of out-of-the-ordinary shops in towns and cities all over Mexico, including much on the Pacific centers, especially Puerto Vallarta, greater Guadalajara, Mazatlán, Pátzcuaro, and Oaxaca.

Weisbroth, Ericka, and Eric Ellman. *Bicycling Mexico.* New York: Hunter, 1990. These intrepid adventurers describe bike trips from Puerto Vallarta to Acapulco, coastal and highland Oaxaca, and highland Jalisco and Michoacán.

Werner, David. *Where There Is No Doctor.* Palo Alto: Hesperian Foundation (P.O. Box 1692, Palo Alto, CA 94302). How to keep well in the backcountry.

Whitman, John. *The Best Mexican and Central American Travel Tips.* New York: Harper and Row. Although travelers may not agree with some of the author's advice, many of his thousands of tips might save you money, time, and trouble in Mexico.

FICTION

Fuentes, Carlos. *Where the Air Is Clear.* New York: Farrar, Straus and Giroux, 1971. The seminal work of Mexico's celebrated novelist.

Jennings, Gary. *Aztec.* New York: Atheneum, 1980. Beautifully researched and written monumental tale of lust, compassion, love, and death in preconquest Mexico.

Peters, Daniel. *The Luck of Huemac.* New York: Random House, 1981. An Aztec noble family's tale—of war, famine, sorcery, heroism, treachery, love, and finally disaster and death—in the Valley of Mexico.

Porter, Katherine Ann. *The Collected Stories.* New York: Delacorte, 1970.

Rulfo, Juan. *The Burning Plain.* Austin: University of Texas Press, 1967. Stories of people torn between the old and new in Mexico.

Traven, B. *The Treasure of the Sierra Madre.* New York: Hill and Wang, 1967. *Campesinos, federales,* gringos, and *indígenas* all figure in this modern morality tale set in Mexico's rugged outback. The most famous of the mysterious author's many novels of oppression and justice set in Mexico's jungles.

Villaseñor, Victor. *Rain of Gold.* New York: Delta Books (Bantam, Doubleday, and Dell), 1991. The moving, best-selling epic of the author's family's gritty travails. From humble rural beginnings in the Copper Canyon, they flee revolution and certain death, struggling through parched northern deserts to sprawling border refugee camps. From there they migrate to relative safety and an eventual modicum of happiness in Southern California.

PEOPLE AND CULTURE

Berrin, Kathleen. *The Art of the Huichol Indians.* Lovely, large photographs and text by a symposium of experts provide a good interpretive introduction to Huichol art and culture.

Lewis, Oscar. *Children of Sanchez.* New York: Random House, 1961. Poverty and strength in the Mexican underclass, sympathetically described and interpreted by renowned sociologist Lewis.

Meyerhoff, Barbara. *Peyote Hunt: the Sacred Journey of the Huichol Indians.* Ithaca: Cornell University Press, 1974. A description and interpretation of the Huichol's religious use of mind-bending natural hallucinogens.

Riding, Alan. *Distant Neighbors: A Portrait of the Mexicans.* New York: Random House Vintage Books. Rare insights into Mexico and Mexicans.

Wauchope, Robert, ed. *Handbook of Middle American Indians.* Vols 7 and 8. Austin: University of Texas Press, 1969. Authoritative surveys of important Indian-speaking groups in northern and central (vol. 8) and southern (vol. 7) Mexico.

FLORA AND FAUNA

Goodson, Gar. *Fishes of the Pacific Coast.* Stanford, California: Stanford University Press, 1988. Over 500 beautifully detailed color drawings highlight this pocket version of all you ever wanted to know about the ocean's fishes (including common Spanish names) from Alaska to Peru.

Leopold, Starker. *Wildlife of Mexico.* Berkeley: University of California Press. Classic, illustrated layperson's survey of common Mexican mammals and birds.

Mason, Jr., Charles T., and Patricia B. Mason. *Handbook of Mexican Roadside Flora.* Tucson: University of Arizona Press, 1987. Authoritative identification guide, with line illustrations, of all the plants you're likely to see in Pacific Mexico.

Morris, Percy A. *A Field Guide to Pacific Coast Shells.* Boston: Houghton Mifflin. The compleat beachcomber's Pacific shell guide.

Novick, Rosalind, and Lan Sing Wu. *Where to Find Birds in San Blas, Nayarit.* Order through the authors at 178 Myrtle Court, Arcata, CA 95521, tel. (707) 822-0790.

Pesman, M. Walter. *Meet Flora Mexicana.* Delightful anecdotes and illustrations of hundreds of common Mexican plants. Published around 1960, now out of print.

Petersen, Roger Tory, and Edward L. Chalif. *Field Guide to Mexican Birds.* Boston: Houghton Mifflin. With hundreds of Petersen's crisp color drawings, this is a must for serious birders and vacationers interested in the life that teems in Pacific Mexico's beaches, jungles, lakes, and lagoons.

Wright, N. Pelham. *A Guide to Mexican Mammals and Reptiles.* Mexico City: Minutiae Mexicana, 1989. Pocket-edition lore, history, descriptions, and pictures of commonly seen Mexican animals.

ART, ARCHITECTURE, AND CRAFTS

Baird, Joseph. *The Churches of Mexico.* Berkeley: University of California Press. Mexican colonial architecture and art, illustrated and interpreted.

Cordrey, Donald, and Dorothy Cordrey. *Mexican Indian Costumes.* Austin: University of Texas Press, 1968. A lovingly photographed, written, and illustrated classic on Mexican Indians and their dress, emphasizing textiles.

Covarrubias, Miguel. *Indian Art of Mexico and Central America.* New York: Knopf, 1957. A timeless work by the renowned interpreter of *indígena* art and design.

Martínez Penaloza, Porfirio. *Popular Arts of Mexico.* Mexico City: Editorial Panorama, 1981. An excellent, authoritative, pocket-sized exposition of Mexican art.

GLOSSARY

Many of these words have a social-historical meaning; others you will not find in the usual English-Spanish dictionary.

abarrotería—grocery store

andando—walkway, or strolling path

alcalde—mayor or municipal judge

artesanías—handicrafts, as distinguished from *artesanio,* a person who makes handicrafts

audiencia—one of the royal executive-judicial panels sent to rule Mexico during the 16th century

ayuntamiento—either the town council or the building where it meets

birria—goat, pork, or lamb stew, in spiced tomato broth, especially typical of Jalisco

boleto—ticket, boarding pass

cabercera—head town of a municipal district, or headquarters in general

cabrón—literally a cuckold, but more commonly, bastard, rat, or S.O.B.; sometimes used affectionately

cacique—chief or boss

calandria—early 1800s-style horse-drawn carriage, common in Guadalajara

campesino—country person; farm worker

casa de huéspedes—guesthouse, usually operated in a family home

caudillo—dictator or political chief

charro—gentleman cowboy

chingar—literally, to "rape," but also the universal Spanish "f" word, the equivalent of "screw" in English

Churrigueresque—Spanish baroque architectural style incorporated into many Mexican colonial churches, named after José Churriguera (1665-1725)

científicos—President Porfirio Díaz's technocratic advisers

colectivo—collective taxi or minibus that picks up and deposits passengers along a designated route

colegio—preparatory school or junior college

colonia—suburban subdivision-satellite of a larger city

Conasupo—government store that sells basic foods at subsidized prices

correo—post office

criollo—person of all-Spanish descent born in the New World

cuadra—Huichol yarn painting, usually rectangular

curandero(a)—Indian medicine man or woman

damas—ladies, as in "ladies room"

de lujo—deluxe

encomienda—colonial award of tribute from a designated Indian district

ejido—traditional form of community, with shared land ownership and cooperative decision making

estación ferrocarril—railroad station

farmacia—pharmacy, or drugstore

finca—farm

fonda—foodstall or small restaurant, often in a traditional market complex

fraccionamiento—city sector or subdivision

fuero—the former right of clergy to be tried in separate ecclesiastical courts

gachupín—"one who wear spurs"; a derogatory term for a Spanish-born colonial

gasolinera—gasoline station

gente de razón—"people of reason"; whites and mestizos in colonial Mexico

gringo—once-derogatory but now commonly used term for North American whites

grito—impassioned cry, as in Hidalgo's Grito de Dolores

hacienda—large landed estate; also the government treasury

hidalgo—nobleman; called honorifically by "Don" or "Doña"

indígena—indigenous or aboriginal inhabitant of all-Indian descent who speaks his or her native tongue. Commonly, but incorrectly, an Indian (*indio*).

jejenes—"no-see-um" biting gnats, especially around San Blas, Nayarit

jugería—stall or small restaurant providing a large array of squeezed vegetable and fruit *jugos* (juices)

larga distancia—long-distance telephone service, or the *caseta* (office) where it's provided

licencado—academic degree (abbrev. Lic.) approximately equivalent to a bachelor's degree

líquido—liquid

machismo; macho—exaggerated sense of maleness; person who holds such a sense of himself

mestizo—person of mixed Indian-European descent

mescal—alcoholic beverage distilled from the fermented hearts of maguey (century plant)

milpa—Indian farm plot, usually of corn

mordida—slang for bribe; "little bite"

palapa—thatched-roof structure, often open and shading a restaurant

panga—outboard launch *(lancha)*

papier mâché—the craft of glued, multilayered paper sculpture, especially in Tonalá, Jalisco, where creations resemble fine pottery or lacquerware

Pemex—acronym for Petróleos Mexicanos, the national oil corporation

peninsulares—the Spanish-born ruling colonial elite

peones—poor wage-earners, usually country Indians

piñata—papier mâché decoration, usually in animal or human form, filled with treats and broken open during a fiesta

plan—political manifesto, usually by a leader or group consolidating or seeking power

Porfiriato—the 34-year (1876-1910) ruling period of president-dictator Porfirio Díaz

pozole—stew, usually of hominy in broth, topped by shredded pork and cabbage, and diced onion

presidencia municipal—the headquarters, like a U.S. city or county hall, of a Mexican *municipio,* county-like local governmental unit

pronunciamiento—declaration of rebellion by an insurgent leader

pueblo—town or people

puta—whore, bitch, or slut

quinta—a villa or country house

quinto—the royal "fifth" tax on treasure and precious metals

retorno—cul-de-sac

rurales—former federal country police force created to fight *bandidos*

Semana Santa—pre-Easter holy week

taxi especial—private taxi, as distinguished from *taxi colectivo,* or collective taxi

telégrafo—telegraph office, lately converting to high-tech *telcoomunicaciones,* or *telecoms,* offering telegraph, telephone, and public fax services

vaquero—cowboy

vecindad—neighborhood

yanqui—Yankee

zócalo—town plaza or central square

ENGLISH-SPANISH MINI-DICTIONARY

A profitable route to learning Spanish in Mexico is to refuse to speak English. Prepare yourself (instead of watching the in-flight movie) with a basic word list in a pocket notebook. Use it to speak Spanish wherever you go.

Basic and Courteous
Courtesy is very important to Mexican people. They will appreciate your use of basic expressions. (Note: The upside-down Spanish question mark merely warns the reader of the query in advance.)

hello—*hola*

How are you?—*¿Cómo está usted?*

Very well, thank you.—*Muy bien, gracias.*

okay, good—*bueno*

not okay, bad—*malo, feo*

and you?—*¿y usted?*

(Note: Pronounce *"y,"* the Spanish "and," like the English "ee," as in "keep.")

Thank you very much.—*Muchas gracias.*

please—*por favor*

You're welcome.—*De nada.*

Just a moment, please.—*Momentito, por favor.*

How do you say . . . in Spanish?—*¿Cómo se dice . . . en español?*

Excuse me, please (when you're trying to get attention).—*Excúseme, con permiso.*
Excuse me (when you've made a boo-boo).—*Lo siento*
good morning—*buenos días*
good afternoon—*buenas tardes*
good evening—*buenas noches*
Sir (Mr.), Ma'am (Mrs.), Miss—*Señor, Señora, Señorita*
What is your name?—*¿Cómo se llama usted?*
Pleased to meet you.—*Con mucho gusto.*
My name is . . .—*Me llamo . . .*
Would you like . . . ?—*¿Quisiera usted . . . ?*
Let's go to . . .—*Vámonos a . . .*
I would like to introduce my . . .—*Quisiera presentar mi . . .*
wife—*esposa*
husband—*esposo*
friend—*amigo* (male), *amiga* (female)
sweetheart—*novio* (male), *novia* (female)
son, daughter—*hijo, hija*
brother, sister—*hermano, hermana*
father, mother—*padre, madre*
See you later (again).—*Hasta luego (la vista).*
goodbye—*adiós*
yes, no—*sí, no*
I, you, he, she—*yo, usted, él, ella*
we, you (pl.), they—*nosotros, ustedes, ellos*
Do you speak English?—*¿Habla usted inglés?*

Getting Around

If I could use only two Spanish phrases, I would choose "Excúseme," followed by "¿Dónde está . . . ?"
Where is . . . ?—*¿Dónde está . . . ?*
the bus station—*la terminal autobús*
the bus stop—*la parada autobús*
the taxi stand—*el sitio taxi*
the train station—*la terminal ferrocarril*
the airport—*el aeropuerto*
the boat—*la barca*
the bathroom, toilet—*el baño, sanitorio*
men's, women's—*el baño de hombres, de mujeres*
the entrance, exit—*la entrada, la salida*
the pharmacy—*la farmacia*
the bank—*el banco*
the police, police officer—*la policía*
the supermarket—*el supermercado*
the grocery store—*la abarrotería*

the laundry—*la lavandería*
the stationery (book) store—*la papelería (librería)*
the hardware store—*la ferretería*
the (long distance) telephone—*el teléfono (larga distancia)*
the post office—*el correo*
the ticket office—*la oficina boletos*
a hotel—*un hotel*
a cafe, a restaurant—*una café, un restaurante*
Where (Which) is the way to . . . ?—*¿Dónde (Cuál) está el camino a . . . ?*
How far to . . . ?—*¿Qué tan lejos a . . . ?*
How many blocks?—*¿Cuántos cuadras?*
(very) near, far—*(muy) cerca, lejos*
to, toward—*a*
by, through—*por*
from—*de*
the right, the left—*la derecha, la izquierda*
straight ahead—*derecho, directo*
in front—*en frente*
beside—*a lado*
behind—*atrás*
the corner—*la esquina*
the stoplight—*la semáforo*
a turn—*una vuelta*
right here—*aquí*
right here—*allí*
somewhere around there—*allá*
street, boulevard, highway—*calle, bulevar, carretera*
bridge, toll—*puente, cuota*
address—*dirección*
north, south—*norte, sur*
east, west—*oriente, poniente (oeste)*

Doing Things

Verbs are the key to getting along in Spanish. They employ mostly predictable forms and come in three classes, which end in ar, er, and ir, respectively:

to buy—*comprar*
I buy, you (he, she, it) buys—*compro, compra*
we buy, you (they) buy—*compramos, compran*

to eat—*comer*
I eat, you (he, she, it) eats—*como, come*
we eat, you (they) eat—*comemos, comen*

to climb—*subir*
I climb, you (he, she, it) climbs—*subo, sube*
we climb, you (they) climb—*subimos, suben*

Got the idea? Here are more (with irregularities marked in bold).

to do or make—*hacer*
I do or make, you (he she, or it) does or makes—*hago, hace*
we do or make, you (they) do or make—*hacemos, hacen*

to go—*ir*
I go, you (he, she, or it) goes: *voy, va*
we go, you (they) go: *vamos, van*

to have—*tener* (regular except for *tengo,* I have)
to come—*venir* (regular except for *vengo,* I come)
to give—*dar* (regular except for *doy,* I give)
to love—*amar*
to swim—*nadar*
to walk—*andar*
to work—*trabajar*
to want—*desear*
to read—*leer*
to write—*escribir*
to repair—*reparar*
to arrive—*llegar*
to stay—*quedar*
to look at—*mirar*
to look for—*buscar*
Spanish has two forms of "to be." Use *estar* when speaking of location: "I am at home." *"Estoy en casa."* Use *ser* for state of being: "I am a doctor." *"Soy un doctor."* *Estar* is regular except for *estoy,* I am. *Ser* is very irregular:
to be—*ser*
I am, you (he, she, it) is—*soy, es*
we are, you (they) are—*somos, son*

At the Station and on the Bus
I'd like a ticket to . . .—*Quisiera un boleto a . . .*
first (second) class—*primera (segunda) clase*
roundtrip—*ida y vuelta*
how much?—*¿cúanto?*
reservation—*reservación*
reserved seat—*asiento reservado*
seat number . . .—*número asiento . . .*

baggage—*equipaje*
Where is this bus going?—*¿Dónde va este autobús?*
What's the name of this place?—*¿Cómo se llama este lugar?*
Stop here, please.—*Pare aquí, por favor.*

Eating Out
A *restaurante* (rays-tah-oo-RAHN-tay) generally implies a fairly fancy joint, with prices to match. The food and atmosphere, however, may be more to your liking at other types of eateries (in approximate order of price): *comedor, café, fonda, lonchería, jugería, taquería.*

I'm hungry (thirsty).—*Tengo hambre (sed).*
menu—*lista, menú*
order—*orden*
soft drink—*refresco*
coffee, cream—*café, crema*
tea—*té*
sugar—*azúcar*
drinking water—*agua pura, agua potable*
bottled carbonated water—*agua mineral*
bottled uncarbonated water—*agua sin gas*
glass—*vaso*
beer—*cerveza*
dark—*obscura*
draft—*de barril*
wine—*vino*
white, red—*blanco, tinto*
dry, sweet—*seco, dulce*
queso—*cheese*
snack—*antojo, botana*
daily lunch special—*comida corrida*
fried—*frito*
roasted—*asada*
barbecue, barbecued—*barbacoa, al carbón*
breakfast—*desayuno*
eggs—*huevos*
boiled—*tibios*
scrambled—*revueltos*
bread—*pan*
roll—*bolillo*
sweet roll—*pan dulce*
toast—*pan tostada*
oatmeal—*avena*
bacon, ham—*tocino, jamón*
salad—*ensalada*
lettuce—*lechuga*
carrot—*zanahoria*

tomato—*tomate*
oil—*aceite*
vinegar—*vinagre*
lime—*limón*
mayonnaise—*mayonesa*
fruit—*fruta*
mango—*mango*
watermelon—*sandía*
papaya—*papaya*
banana—*plátano*
apple—*manzana*
orange—*naranja*
fish—*pescado*
shrimp—*camarones*
oysters—*ostiones*
clams—*almejas*
octopus—*pulpo*
squid—*calamare*
meat (without)—*carne (sin)*
chicken—*pollo*
pork—*puerco*
beef, steak—*res, biftec*
the check—*la cuenta*

At the Hotel

In Puerto Vallarta region resorts, finding a reasonably priced hotel room presents no problem except during the high-occupancy weeks after Christmas and before Easter.

Is there . . . ?—*¿Hay . . . ?*
an (inexpensive) hotel—*un hotel (económico)*
an inn—*una posada*
a guesthouse—*una casa de huéspedes*
a single (double) room—*un cuarto sencillo (doble)*
with bath—*con baño*
shower—*ducha*
hot water—*agua caliente*
fan—*abanico, ventilador*
air-conditioned—*aire acondicionado*
double bed—*cama matrimonial*
twin beds—*camas gemelas*
How much for the room?—*¿Cuánto cuesta el cuarto?*
dining room—*comedor*
key—*llave*
towels—*toallas*
manager—*gerente*
soap—*jabón*
toilet paper—*papel higiénico*
swimming pool—*alberca, piscina*
the bill, please—*la cuenta, por favor*

At the Bank

El banco's often-long lines, short hours, and minuscule advantage in exchange rate make a nearby private *casa de cambio* a very handy alternative:

money—*dinero*
money-exchange bureau—*casa de cambio*
I would like to exchange traveler's checks.—
 Quisiera cambiar cheques de viajero.
What is the exchange rate?—*¿Cuál es el cambio?*
How much is the commission?—*¿Cuánto cuesta el comisión?*
Do you accept credit cards?—*¿Aceptan tarjetas de crédito?*
money order—*giro*
teller's window—*caja*
signature—*firma*

Shopping

Es la costumbre—it is the custom—in Mexico that the first price is never the last. Bargaining often transforms shopping from a perfunctory chore into an open-ended adventure. Bargain with humor, and be prepared to walk away if the price is not right.

How much does it cost?—*¿Cuánto cuesta?*
too much—*demasiado*
expensive, cheap—*caro, barato (económico)*
too expensive, too cheap—*demasiado caro, demasiado barato*
more, less—*más, menos*
small, big—*chico, grande*
good, bad—*bueno, malo*
smaller, smallest—*más chico, el más chico*
larger, largest—*más grande, el más grande*
cheaper, cheapest—*más barato, el más barato*
What is your final price?—*¿Cuál es su último precio?*
Just right!—*¡Perfecto!*

Telephone, Post Office

In smaller Mexican towns, long-distance connections must be made at a central long-distance office, where people sometimes can sit, have coffee or a *refresco,* and socialize while waiting for their *larga distancia* to come through.

long-distance telephone—*teléfono larga distancia*
I would like to call . . .—*Quisiera llamar a . . .*
station to station—*a quien contesta*
person to person—*persona a persona*
credit card—*tarjeta de crédito*
post office—*correo*
general delivery—*lista de correo*
letter—*carta*
stamp—*estampilla*
postcard—*tarjeta*
aerogram—*aerogramo*
air mail—*correo aero*
registered—*registrado*
money order—*giro*
package, box—*paquete, caja*
string, tape—*cuerda, cinta*

Formalities

Although crossing into Mexico is relatively easy, many experienced travelers find it among the most exotic of destinations—more so than either India or Japan.

border—*frontera*
customs—*aduana*
immigration—*migración*
tourist card—*tarjeta de turista*
inspection—*inspección, revisión*
passport—*pasaporte*
profession—*profession*
marital status—*estado civil*
single—*soltero*
married, divorced—*casado, divorciado*
widowed—*viudado*
insurance—*seguros*
title—*título*
driver's license—*licencia de manejar*
fishing, hunting, gun license—*licencia de pescar, cazar, armas*

At the Pharmacy, Doctor, Hospital

For a third-world country, Mexico provides good health care. Even small Pacific Mexico towns have a basic hospital or clinic.

Help me please.—*Ayúdeme por favor.*
I am ill.—*Estoy enfermo.*
Call a doctor.—*Llame un doctor.*
Take me to . . .—*Lleve me a . . .*
hospital—*hospital, sanatorio*

drugstore—*farmacia*
pain—*dolor*
fever—*fiebre*
headache—*dolor de cabeza*
stomache ache—*dolor de estómago*
burn—*quemadura*
cramp—*calambre*
nausea—*náusea*
vomiting—*vomitar*
medicine—*medicina*
antibiotic—*antibiótico*
pill, tablet—*pastilla*
aspirin—*aspirina*
ointment, cream—*pomada, crema*
bandage—*venda*
cotton—*algodón*
sanitary napkins (use brand name)
birth control pills—*pastillas contraceptivos*
contraceptive foam—*espuma contraceptiva*
diaphragm (best carry an extra)
condoms—*contraceptivas*
toothbrush—*cepilla dental*
dental floss (bring an extra supply)
toothpaste—*croma dontal*
dentist—*dentista*
toothache—*dolor demuelas*

At the Gas Station

Some Mexican gas station attendants are experts at shortchanging you in both money and gasoline. If you don't have a locking gas cap, either insist on pumping the gas yourself, or make certain the pump is zeroed before the attendant begins pumping. Furthermore, the kids who hang around gas stations are notoriously light fingered. Stow every loose item—cameras, purses, binoculars—out of sight *before* you pull into the *gasolinera.*

gas station—*gasolinera*
gasoline—*gasolina*
leaded, unleaded—*plomo, sin plomo*
full, please—*lleno, por favor*
gas cap—*tapón*
tire—*llanta*
tire repair shop—*vulcanizadora*
air—*aire*
water—*agua*
oil (change)—*aceite (cambio)*
grease—*grasa*
My . . . doesn't work.—*Mi . . . no sirve.*

battery—*batería*
radiator—*radiador*
alternator, generator—*alternador, generador*
tow truck—*grúa*
repair shop—*taller mecánico*
tune-up—*afinación*
auto parts store—*refraccionería*

Numbers and Time

zero—*cero*
one—*uno*
two—*dos*
three—*tres*
four—*cuatro*
five—*cinco*
six—*seis*
seven—*siete*
eight—*ocho*
nine—*nueve*
10—*diez*
11—*once*
12—*doce*
13—*trece*
14—*catorce*
15—*quince*
16—*dieciseis*
17—*diecisiete*
18—*dieciocho*
19—*diecinueve*
20—*veinte*
21—*veinte y uno,* or *veintiuno*
30—*treinta*
40—*cuarenta*
50—*cincuenta*
60—*sesenta*
70—*setenta*
80—*ochenta*
90—*noventa*
100—*ciento*
101—*ciento y uno,* or *cientiuno*
200—*doscientos*
500—*quinientos*
1,000—*mil*
10,000—*diez mil*
100,000—*cien mil*
1,000,000—*milión*

1995—*mil novecientos noventa y cinco*
one-half—*medio*
one-third—*un tercio*
one fourth—*un quarto*

What time is it?—*¿Qué hora es?*
It's one o'clock.—*Es la una.*
It's three in the afternoon.—*Son las tres de la tarde.*
It's 4 a.m.—*Son las cuatro de la mañana.*
six-thirty—*seis y media*
a quarter till eleven—*un quarto hasta once*
a quarter past five—*un quarto después cinco*

Monday—*lunes*
Tuesday—*martes*
Wednesday—*miércoles*
Thursday—*jueves*
Friday—*viernes*
Saturday—*sábado*
Sunday—*domingo*

January—*enero*
February—*febrero*
March—*marzo*
April—*abril*
May—*mayo*
June—*junio*
July—*julio*
August—*agosto*
September—*septiembre*
October—*octubre*
November—*noviembre*
December—*diciembre*

last Sunday—*domingo pasado*
next December—*diciembre próximo*
yesterday—*ayer*
tomorrow—*mañana*
an hour—*una hora*
a week—*una semana*
a month—*un mes*
a week ago—*hace una semana*
after—*después*
before—*antes*

A LITTLE SPANISH

Your Pacific Mexico adventure will be more fun if you use a little Spanish. Mexican folks, although they may smile at your funny accent, will appreciate your halting efforts to break the ice and transform yourself from a foreigner to a potential friend.

Spanish commonly uses 30 letters—the familiar English 26, plus four straightforward additions: ch, ll, ñ, and rr, which are explained in "Consonants," below.

Vowels

Once you learn them, Spanish pronunciation rules (in contrast to English) don't change. Spanish vowels generally sound softer than in English. (Note: The capitalized syllables below receive stronger accents.)

Pronounce *a* like ah, as in hah: *agua* AH-gooah (water), *pan* PAHN (bread), *casa* CAH-sah (house).

Pronounce *e* like ay, as in may: *mesa* MAY-sah (table), *tela* TAY-lah (cloth), and *de* DAY (of, from).

Pronounce *i* like ee, as in need: *diez* dee-AYZ (ten), *comida* ko MEE-dah (meal), and *fin* FEEN (end).

Pronounce *o* like oh, as in oh: *peso* PAY-soh (weight), *ocho* OH-choh (eight), and *poco* POH-koh (a bit).

Pronounce *u* like oo, as in cool: *uno* OO-noh (one), *cuarto* KOOAHR-toh (room), *usted* oos-TAYD (you).

Accent

The rule for accent, the relative stress given to syllables within a given word, is straightforward. If a word ends in a vowel, an n, or an s, accent the next-to-last syllable; if not, accent the last syllable.

Pronounce *gracias* GRAH-seeahs (thank you), *orden* OHR-dayn (order), and *carretera* kah-ray-TAY-rah (highway).

Otherwise, accent the last syllable: *venir* vay-NEER (to come), *ferrocarril* fay-roh-cah-REEL (railroad), and *edad* ay-DAHD (age).

For practice, apply the accent ("vowel, n, or s") rule for the vowel-pronunciation examples above. Try to accent the words correctly without looking at the "answers" to the right.

Exceptions to the accent rule are always marked with an accent sign: (á, é, í, ó, or ú), such as *teléfono* tay-LAY-foh-noh (telephone), *jabón* hah-BON (soap), *rápido* RAH-pee-doh (rapid).

Consonants

Seventeen Spanish consonants, *b, d, f, k, l, m, n, p, q, s, t, v, w, x, y, z* and *ch*, are pronounced almost as in English: *h* occurs, but is silent—not pronounced at all.

As for the remaining seven *(c, g, j, ll, ñ, r, and rr)* consonants, pronounce *c* "hard," like k as in keep: *cuarto* KOOAR-toh (room), Topio tay-PEEK (capital of Nayarit state). Exception: Before *e* or *i,* pronounce *c* "soft," like an English s, as in sit: *cerveza* sayr-VAY-sah (beer), *encima* ayn-SEE-mah (atop).

Before *a, o, u,* or a consonant, pronounce *g* "hard," as in gift: *gato* GAH-toh (cat), *hago* AH-goh (I do, make). Otherwise, pronounce *g* like h as in hat: *giro* HEE-roh (money order), *gente* HAYN-tay (people).

Pronounce *j* like an English h, as in has: *jueves* HOOAY-vays (Thursday), *mejor* may-HOR (better).

Pronounce *ll* like y, as in yes: *toalla* toh-AH-yah (towel), *ellos* AY-yohs (they, them).

Pronounce *ñ* like ny, as in canyon: *año* AH-nyo (year), *señor* SAY-nyor (Mr., sir).

The Spanish *r* is lightly trilled, with tongue at the roof of your mouth like the British r in very ("vehdy"). Pronounce *r* like a very light English d, as in ready: *pero* PAY-doh (but), *tres* TDAYS (three), *cuatro* KOOAH-tdoh (four).

Pronounce *rr* like a Spanish *r,* but with much more emphasis and trill. Let your tongue flap. Practice with *burro* (donkey), *carretera* (highway), and Carrillo (proper name), then really let go with *ferrocarril* (railroad).

ACCOMMODATIONS INDEX

Italicized page numbers indicate references in charts. Accommodations beginning with "Hotel" are indexed by the following word; e.g., Hotel Buenaventura can be found under Buenaventura, Hotel.

RESTAURANT INDEX

Establishments beginning with "Restaurant" or "Restaurante" are indexed by the following word; e.g., Restaurant Los Arcos can be found under Los Arcos, Restaurant.

GENERAL INDEX

Page numbers in *italics* indicate information found in captions,
charts, illustrations, maps, or special topics.

ABOUT THE AUTHOR

In the early 1980s, the lure of travel drew Bruce Whipperman away from a 20-year physics teaching career. The occasion was a trip to Kenya which included a total solar eclipse and a safari. He hasn't stopped traveling since.

With his family grown, he has been free to let the world's wild, beautiful corners draw him on: to the ice-clawed Karakoram, the Gobi Desert's trellised oases, the pink palaces of Rajastan, Japan's green wine country, Bali's emerald terraces, and now, Pacific Mexico's palm-shaded beaches, colorful towns, and pine-scented highland valleys.

Bruce has always pursued his travel career for the fun of it. He started with slide shows and photo gifts for friends. Others wanted his photos, so he began selling them. Once stranded in Ethiopia, he began to write. A dozen years later, after scores of magazine and newspaper feature stories, *Pacific Mexico Handbook* became his first book.

Travel, after all, is for returning home; and that coziest of journeys always brings a tired but happy Bruce back to his friends, son, daughter, and wife Linda in Berkeley, California.

For him, travel writing heightens his awareness and focuses his own travel experiences. He always remembers what a Nepali Sherpa once said: "Many people come, looking, looking; few people come, see."

Bruce invites *Pacific Mexico Handbook*'s readers likewise to "come see"—and discover and enjoy—Pacific Mexico's delights with a fresh eye and renewed compassion.

MOON TRAVEL HANDBOOKS
THE IDEAL TRAVELING COMPANIONS

Moon Travel Handbooks provide focused, comprehensive coverage of distinct destinations all over the world. Our goal is to give travelers all the background and practical information they'll need for an extraordinary, unexpected travel experience.

Every Handbook begins with an in-depth essay about the land, the people, their history, art, politics, and social concerns—an entire bookcase of cultural insight and introductory information in one portable volume. We also provide accurate, up-to-date coverage of all the practicalities: language, currency, transportation, accommodations, food, and entertainment. And Moon's maps are legendary, covering not only cities and highways, but parks and trails that are often difficult to find in other sources.

Below are highlights of Moon's Mexico Travel Handbook series. Our complete list of Handbooks covering North America and Hawaii, Mexico, Central America and the Caribbean, and Asia and the Pacific, are listed on the order form on the accompanying pages. To purchase Moon Travel Handbooks, please check your local bookstore or order by phone: (800) 345-5473 Monday-Friday 8 a.m.-5 p.m. PST.

MOON OVER MEXICO
MEXICO TRAVEL HANDBOOK SERIES

> "The finest are written with such care and insight they deserve listing as literature."
>
> —*American Geographical Society*

BAJA HANDBOOK   by Joe Cummings, 360 pages, $15.95
"Very thorough. Particularly useful are the additions of sidetrips for travelers eager to trek off the beaten path" —*Arizona Daily Star*

CABO HANDBOOK   by Joe Cummings, 275 pages, $14.95
The southern tip of Mexico's Baja peninsula features two of the country's most popular tourist destinations–Cabo San Lucas and La Paz. Author Joe Cummings chronicles the rich history and culture of this region in *Cabo Handbook*. Discover 19th-century stone-and-stucco architecture in La Paz, hike in the Sierra de La Laguna, or wander through the aisles of Mercado Mexicano. A master navigator of the road less traveled, Cummings guides visitors to rustic fruitstands and remote adobe villages, as well as the resorts of Los Cabos.

CANCUN HANDBOOK by Chicki Mallan, 260 pages, **\$13.95**
"Finally, there is a thorough, well-organized and clearly presented guidebook for the independent traveler venturing to Mexico's eastern shores to soak up more than sun and sand."
—Small Press Magazine

CENTRAL MEXICO HANDBOOK
by Chicki Mallan, 350 pages, **\$15.95**
"A most enjoyable read, even for the armchair traveler . . . Of particular interest are the discussions and descriptions of the lesser-known sites." *—Frankfurter Allegemaine Zeitung*

MEXICO HANDBOOK
by Joe Cummings and Chicki Mallan, 1000 pages, **\$21.95**
This is the definitive guide on Mexican travel from the preeminent publisher of regional Handbooks on Mexico. Veteran authors Joe Cummings and Chicki Mallan have teamed up to create a single-volume reference that combines practical travel information with the cultural insight that is standard in the Moon Handbook series. Organized by region, *Mexico Handbook* is more user-friendly and comprehensive than competing all-Mexico guidebooks. Suggestions for outdoor recreation are voluminous, and excursion travelers will appreciate the driving information, including tips on renting cars and hundreds of up-to-date maps.

NORTHERN MEXICO HANDBOOK
by Joe Cummings, 528 pages, **\$16.95**
"Fill in an important gap in Mexican travel information—and does it with great style." *—Adventures in Mexico*

PACIFIC MEXICO HANDBOOK by Bruce Whipperman,
504 pages, **\$16.95**
"An excellent overview of life along the Pacific coast."
—Small Press Magazine

PUERTO VALLARTA HANDBOOK
by Bruce Whipperman, 300 pages, **\$14.95**
Puerto Vallarta Handbook brings the insight of an award-winning travel writer to one of Mexico's most popular destinations. Join author Bruce Whipperman on a tour through the lush hundred-mile stretch between San Blas and Puerto Vallarta, the villages and quiet beaches areound the Bay of Banderas, and the historic city of Guadalajara. Discover the charm of Old Puerto Vallarta or the excitement of Fiesta de Mayo. With regional history and special features on Mexico's diverse population, this guidebook provides visitors with a cultural perspective to an increasingly popular destination.

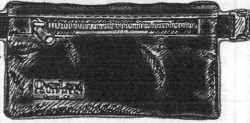

TRAVEL MATTERS

Travel Matters is Moon Publications' free quarterly newsletter, loaded with specially commissioned travel articles and essays that tell it like it is. Recent issues have been devoted to Asia, Mexico, and North America, and every issue includes:

Feature Stories: Travel writing unlike what you'll find in your local newspaper. Andrew Coe on Mexican professional wrestling, Michael Buckley on the craze for wartime souvenirs in Vietnam, Kim Weir on the Nixon Museum in Yorba Linda.

Transportation: Tips on how to get around. Rick Steves on a new type of Eurail pass, Victor Chan on hiking in Tibet, Joe Cummings on how to be a Baja road warrior.

Health Matters: Articles on the most recent findings by Dr. Dirk Schroeder, author of *Staying Healthy in Asia, Africa, and Latin America.* Japanese encephalitis, malaria, the southwest U.S. "mystery disease" . . . forewarned is forearmed.

Book Reviews: Informed assessments of the latest travel titles and series. The *Rough Guide* to *World Music,* Let's Go vs. Berkeley, Dorling Kindersley vs. Knopf.

The Internet: News from the cutting edge. The Great Burma Debate in rec.travel.asia, hotlists of the best WWW sites, updates on Moon's massive "Road Trip USA" exhibit.

There are also booklists, Letters to the Editor, and anything else we can find to interest our readers, as well as Moon's latest titles and ordering information for other travel products, including Periplus Travel Maps to Southeast Asia.

To receive a free subscription to *Travel Matters,* call (800) 345-5473, write to Moon Publications, P.O. Box 3040, Chico, CA 95927-3040, or e-mail travel@moon.com.

Please note: subscribers who live outside the United States will be charged $7.00 per year for shipping and handling.

MOON TRAVEL HANDBOOKS

MEXICO

Baja Handbook (0528). $15.95
Cabo Handbook (0285) $14.95
Cancún Handbook (0501). $13.95
Central Mexico Handbook (0234) $15.95
*Mexico Handbook (0315) $21.95
Northern Mexico Handbook (0226) $16.95
Pacific Mexico Handbook (0323) $16.95
Puerto Vallarta Handbook (0250) $14.95
Yucatán Peninsula Handbook (0242). $15.95

ASIA AND THE PACIFIC

Bali Handbook (3379) $12.95
Bangkok Handbook (0595). $13.95
Fiji Islands Handbook (0382). $13.95
Hong Kong Handbook (0560) $15.95
Indonesia Handbook (0625) $25.00
Japan Handbook (3700). $22.50
Micronesia Handbook (3808) $11.95
Nepal Handbook (3646). $12.95
New Zealand Handbook (3883) $18.95
Outback Australia Handbook (3794) $15.95
Philippines Handbook (0048) $17.95
Southeast Asia Handbook (0021) $21.95
South Pacific Handbook (3999) $19.95
Tahiti-Polynesia Handbook (0374) $13.95
Thailand Handbook (3824) $16.95
Tibet Handbook (3905) $30.00
*Vietnam, Cambodia & Laos Handbook (0293) $18.95

NORTH AMERICA AND HAWAII

Alaska-Yukon Handbook (0161). $14.95
Alberta and the Northwest Territories Handbook (0676) . . . $17.95
Arizona Traveler's Handbook (0536) $16.95
Atlantic Canada Handbook (0072) $17.95
Big Island of Hawaii Handbook (0064) $13.95
British Columbia Handbook (0145) $15.95
Catalina Island Handbook (3751) $10.95

Colorado Handbook (0137). $17.95
Georgia Handbook (0609) $16.95
Hawaii Handbook (0005) $19.95
Honolulu-Waikiki Handbook (0587). $14.95
Idaho Handbook (0617). $14.95
Kauai Handbook (0013). $13.95
Maui Handbook (0579) $14.95
Montana Handbook (0544). $15.95
Nevada Handbook (0641). $16.95
New Mexico Handbook (0153). $14.95
Northern California Handbook (3840) $19.95
Oregon Handbook (0102). $16.95
Texas Handbook (0633). $16.95
Utah Handbook (0684) $16.95
Washington Handbook (0552). $15.95
Wyoming Handbook (3980) $14.95

CENTRAL AMERICA AND THE CARIBBEAN
Belize Handbook (0370). $15.95
Caribbean Handbook (0277) $16.95
Costa Rica Handbook (0358). $18.95
Jamaica Handbook (0129) $14.95

INTERNATIONAL
Egypt Handbook (3891). $18.95
Moon Handbook (0668). $10.00
Moscow-St. Petersburg Handbook (3913). $13.95
Staying Healthy in Asia, Africa, and Latin America (0269) . . $11.95

* New title, please call for availability

PERIPLUS TRAVEL MAPS
All maps $7.95 each

Bali	Hong Kong	Singapore
Bandung/W. Java	Java	Vietnam
Bangkok/C. Thailand	Ko Samui/S. Thailand	Yogyakarta/C. Java
Batam/Bintan	Penang	
Cambodia	Phuket/S. Thailand	

WHERE TO BUY MOON TRAVEL HANDBOOKS

BOOKSTORES AND LIBRARIES: Moon Travel Handbooks are sold worldwide. Please write to our sales manager for a list of wholesalers and distributors in your area.

TRAVELERS: We would like to have Moon Travel Handbooks available throughout the world. Please ask your bookstore to write or call us for ordering information. If your bookstore will not order our guides for you, please contact us for a free title listing.

Moon Publications, Inc.
P.O. Box 3040
Chico, CA 95927-3040 U.S.A.
Tel: (800) 345-5473
Fax: (916) 345-6751
E-mail: travel@moon.com

IMPORTANT ORDERING INFORMATION

PRICES: All prices are subject to change. We always ship the most current edition. We will let you know if there is a price increase on the book you order.

SHIPPING AND HANDLING OPTIONS: Domestic UPS or USPS first class (allow 10 working days for delivery): $3.50 for the first item, 50 cents for each additional item.

EXCEPTIONS:

Tibet Handbook and *Indonesia Handbook* shipping $4.50; $1.00 for each additional *Tibet Handbook* or *Indonesia Handbook*.

Moonbelt shipping is $1.50 for one, 50 cents for each additional belt.

Add $2.00 for same-day handling.

UPS 2nd Day Air or Printed Airmail requires a special quote.

International Surface Bookrate 8-12 weeks delivery: $3.00 for the first item, $1.00 for each additional item. Note: Moon Publications cannot guarantee international surface bookrate shipping. Moon recommends sending international orders via air mail, which requires a special quote.

FOREIGN ORDERS: Orders that originate outside the U.S.A. must be paid for with either an international money order or a check in U.S. currency drawn on a major U.S. bank based in the U.S.A.

TELEPHONE ORDERS: We accept Visa or MasterCard payments. Minimum order is US$15.00. Call in your order: (800) 345-5473, 8 a.m.-5 p.m. Pacific Standard Time.

ORDER FORM

Be sure to call (800) 345-5473 for current prices and editions or for the name of the bookstore nearest you that carries Moon Travel Handbooks • 8 a.m.–5 p.m. PST.
(See important ordering information on preceding page.)

Name: _____ Date: _____

Street: _____

City: _____ Daytime Phone: _____

State or Country: _____ Zip Code: _____

QUANTITY	TITLE	PRICE

Taxable Total_____

Sales Tax (7.25%) for California Residents_____

Shipping & Handling_____

TOTAL_____

Ship: ☐ UPS (no P.O. Boxes)   ☐ 1st class   ☐ International surface mail

Ship to: ☐ address above   ☐ other _____

_____

Make checks payable to: **MOON PUBLICATIONS, INC.** P.O. Box 3040, Chico, CA 95927-3040 U.S.A. We accept Visa and MasterCard. **To Order:** Call in your Visa or MasterCard number, or send a written order with your Visa or MasterCard number and expiration date clearly written.

Card Number: ☐ **Visa**   ■ **MasterCard**

☐ ☐ ☐ ☐   ☐ ☐ ☐ ☐   ☐ ☐ ☐ ☐   ☐ ☐ ☐ ☐

Exact Name on Card: _____

Expiration date:_____

Signature:_____

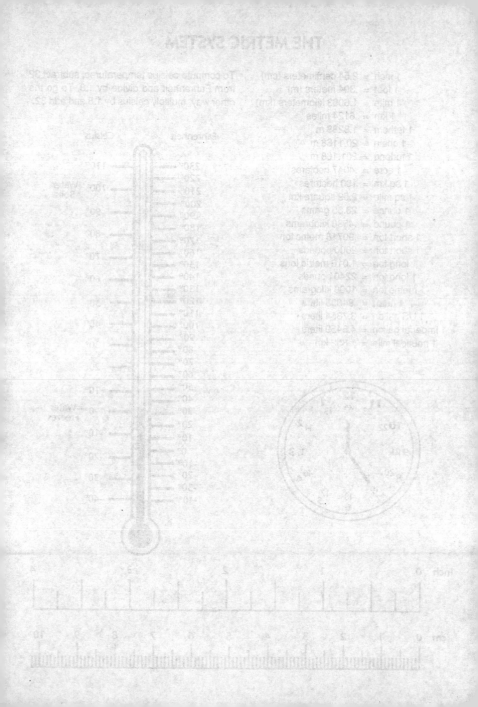

THE METRIC SYSTEM

1 inch = 2.54 centimeters (cm)
1 foot = .304 meters (m)
1 mile = 1.6093 kilometers (km)
1 km = .6124 miles
1 fathom = 1.8288 m
1 chain = 20.1168 m
1 furlong = 201.168 m
1 acre = .4047 hectares
1 sq km = 100 hectares
1 sq mile = 2.59 square km
1 ounce = 28.35 grams
1 pound = .4536 kilograms
1 short ton = .90718 metric ton
1 short ton = 2000 pounds
1 long ton = 1.016 metric tons
1 long ton = 2240 pounds
1 metric ton = 1000 kilograms
1 quart = .94635 liters
1 US gallon = 3.7854 liters
1 Imperial gallon = 4.5459 liters
1 nautical mile = 1.852 km

To compute celsius temperatures, subtract 32 from Fahrenheit and divide by 1.8. To go the other way, multiply celsius by 1.8 and add 32.

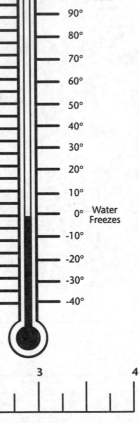

Fahrenheit	Celsius	
230°	110°	
220°		
210°	100°	Water Boils
200°		
190°	90°	
180°		
170°	80°	
160°		
150°	70°	
140°	60°	
130°		
120°	50°	
110°		
100°	40°	
90°		
80°	30°	
70°	20°	
60°		
50°	10°	
40°		
30°	0°	Water Freezes
20°		
10°	-10°	
0°	-20°	
-10°		
-20°	-30°	
-30°		
-40°	-40°	

inch 0   1   2   3   4

cm 0 1 2 3 4 5 6 7 8 9 10